Managerial Economics

First Canadian Edition

APPLICATIONS STRATEGY AND TACTICS

Managerial Economics

First Canadian Edition

APPLICATIONS STRATEGY AND TACTICS

James R. McGuigan
JRM Investments

William F. Rentz
*School of Management,
University of Ottawa*

Alfred L. Kahl
*School of Management,
University of Ottawa*

R. Charles Moyer
*Babcock Graduate School of Management,
Wake Forest University*

Frederick H. deB. Harris
*Babcock Graduate School of Management,
Wake Forest University*

THOMSON

NELSON

Australia   Canada   Mexico   Singapore   Spain   United Kingdom   United States

THOMSON

NELSON

Managerial Economics: Applications, Strategy, and Tactics, First Canadian Edition

by James R. McGuigan, William F. Rentz, Alfred L. Kahl, R. Charles Moyer, and Frederick H. deB. Harris

Associate Vice President, Editorial Director:
Evelyn Veitch

Executive Editor:
Anthony Rezek

Marketing Manager:
Charmaine Sherlock

Developmental Editor:
Elke Price

Photo Researcher:
Cynthia Howard

Permissions Coordinator:
Cynthia Howard

Senior Production Editor:
Natalia Denesiuk

Copy Editor and Proofreader:
June Trusty

Technical Editor: Richard Zind

Indexer: Andrew Little

Senior Production Coordinator:
Kathrine Pummell

Design Director: Ken Phipps

Interior Design Modifications:
Andrew Adams

Cover Design: Peter Papayanakis

Cover Image:
Peter Papayanakis/Thomson Nelson

Compositor:
Interactive Composition Corporation

Printer:
Transcontinental

**Library and Archives Canada Cataloguing
in Publication**

Managerial economics : applications,
strategy, and tactics / James R. McGuigan ..
[et al.].—1st Canadian ed.

Includes bibliographical references
and index.
ISBN 0-17-622428-9

1. Managerial economics—Textbooks.
2. Managerial economics—Problems,
exercises, etc. I. McGuigan, James R.

HD30.22.M35 2005   338.5′024′658
C2005-906859-0

Brief Contents

Contents

Preface

Managerial economics is concerned with resource-allocation, strategic, and tactical decisions that are made by managers, analysts, and consultants in the private, public, and not-for-profit sectors of the economy. Managerial economic techniques seek to achieve the objectives of the organization in the most efficient manner, while considering both explicit and implicit constraints.

This first Canadian edition of *Managerial Economics* is organized around the twin themes of product-line rivalry and shareholder wealth maximization, with major emphasis on analytical tools and managerial insights.

Pedagogical Approach: Theory in Context

Managerial economics is an applied branch of microeconomics. Along a continuum of pedagogical methods from abstract theory lecturing at one extreme to pure case teaching at the other, our theory-in-context approach fits squarely in the middle. Conceptual frameworks based on microeconomic theory provide the ever-present skeletal backbone of discipline-specific knowledge. But because of our emphasis on real-world business applications, new economic theory in *Managerial Economics* is always presented in a deep fact–situation context.

Teaching potential managers using this theory-in-context approach is far preferable to teaching either applications alone or theory alone. This approach not only stimulates student interest at the inception of the learning process, but also promotes mastery of challenging analytical tools and facilitates the acquisition of complex managerial insights. Perhaps most importantly, the theory-in-context approach empowers students to spot analogous real-world situations and apply appropriate tools and insights outside of the classroom and beyond the final exam.

Real-world management decision problems seldom have simple, uniquely correct answers that apply to all future contingencies. To convey some of this complexity, we have incorporated a feature entitled *What Went Right/What Went Wrong*, documenting situations at a variety of companies. Also, we continue to stimulate interest in the topics in each chapter with a *Managerial Challenge* taken from the business press or our own management consulting experience. The individual topics within chapters are then illustrated with many real-world applications, in-depth examples, or case exercises. We have deliberately increased the number of such applications, examples, and exercises relative to other books while retaining a focus on rigorous analytical tools. We believe this theory-in-context approach elicits the students' commitment to the lifelong learning required for best-practices management throughout their careers. An appreciation for best practices, the application of careful analysis, and a healthy dose of managerial insight provide the winning formula for students who can make a difference as employees and managers.

Course Content

Our surveys of adopters, conducted at a wide variety of universities and in degree programs, suggest great diversity of use for this book. The very broad topical coverage is intended to give instructors much flexibility in designing a course suited to the needs of their students.

Organization of This Book

Managerial Economics provides an introduction to both analytical tools and descriptive materials that are useful in managerial economics. Although the subject matter in this book is divided into distinct parts, in reality and practice, the various types of managerial economics decisions are interrelated.

Each chapter begins with a **preview** of the material to be covered and **learning objectives**. This is followed by a **managerial challenge** faced by a real organization that is related to the material in the chapter. This **challenge is revisited** at the end of the chapter. In addition, there is a **point-by-point summary** at the end of each chapter. The chapters end with some **self-test exercises,** as well as other **exercises** and **short cases** that provide opportunities to solve realistic decision problems. A **glossary** of key terms used in the book, as well as complete **solutions to the self-test exercises** and **check answers** to selected exercises all appear at the back of the book. Red boldfaced numbers or letters indicate the exercises for which answers are provided at the back of the book or, in the case of Web chapters and appendixes, on the website for this book at www.mcguigan.nelson.com.

Parts of This Book

Part 1: Introduction and Demand Analysis   Part 1 provides an introductory overview of managerial economics along with a review of some fundamental concepts that are used in later chapters. Chapter 1 provides an introduction to managerial economics and strategic decision making. Chapter 2 reviews some fundamental economic concepts, including marginal analysis and supply and demand analysis, while Web Appendix 2A provides a self-contained introduction to optimization and constrained optimization techniques, including applications of basic calculus. (*Note:* All appendixes and Chapters 13–19 can be accessed at www.mcguigan.nelson.com.) Chapter 3 develops the theory of demand and introduces the elasticity properties of the demand function. It also covers indifference curve analysis as well as income and substitution effects and attribute analysis.

Part 2: Production and Cost   Part 2 deals with production and cost analysis decisions. Chapter 4 develops the theory of production decisions using primarily graphical tools of analysis. Production decisions include the determination of the type and amount of resources that are used in the production of a desired amount of output. Web Appendix 4A looks at real-world process choice decisions in a linear programming framework. Chapter 5 develops the theory of cost analysis. Cost measures are combined with revenue estimates to determine optimal levels and mixes of output. Web Appendix 5A discusses break-even and contribution analyses. Web Appendix 5B discusses long-run costs with a Cobb–Douglas production function.

Part 3: Pricing and Output Decisions   Part 3 covers profit-maximizing price–output decisions as they relate to the firm's strategic choices. Asymmetric information conditions as well as ideal full information exchanges are discussed. Chapter 6 discusses price and output decisions in pure and monopolistically competitive markets. Game-theoretic applications are also introduced. Chapter 7 covers price and output decisions for monopolistic and dominant firms. Chapter 8 covers price and output decisions in oligopolistic markets and extends the game-theoretic approach to decision making. Chapter 9 examines value-based rather than cost-based differential pricing in theory and practice. Web Appendix 9A presents some fundamental revenue management concepts. Web Appendix 9B addresses specialized pricing problems, including those of a multiproduct firm, as well as pricing of joint products and transfer pricing.

Part 4: Special Topics   Part 4 addresses the most important special topics in managerial economics. Chapter 10 discusses the theory of business contracting, the principal–agent problem and corporate governance, vertical integration, and more generally, the choice of organizational form. This chapter further extends the game-theoretic framework to decision making. Chapter 11 addresses the economic regulation of business, including competition legislation, patenting, and licensing, as well as externalities. Chapter 12 introduces international managerial economics, including the determination of exchange rates, trade policy, and other factors that are crucial for effectively managing import–export trade.

Part 5: Web Chapters—Estimating and Forecasting   Part 5 deals with the topics of estimating and forecasting demand and costs. Web Chapter 13 examines the procedures that may be used in making empirical estimates of demand relationships. Web Appendix 13A discusses applications of the linear regression model. Web Appendix 13B provides some statistical tables to support both Web Chapter 13 and Web Appendix 13A. Web Chapter 14 discusses the applications of cost theory, including measurement of short- and long- run cost relationships. Web Appendix 14A discusses the learning curve concept as applied to manufacturing. Web Chapter 15 covers business and economic forecasting.

Part 6: Web Chapters—Game-Theory Extensions   Part 6 further extends the game-theory concepts introduced in Part 3. Chapter 16 presents a game-theoretic framework for analyzing rival firms' response tactics. Chapter 17 uses game theory to explore the optimal mechanism design in servicing queues, in designing auctions, and in incentive-compatible revelation mechanisms for joint ventures and partnerships.

Part 7: Web Chapters—Long-Term Investment Decisions and Risk Management   Part 7 deals with capital investment decisions. Investments in new, long-term assets have a major impact on a firm's future stream of cash flows and the riskiness of those cash flows. Web Chapter 18 discusses the net present value of a project, benefit–cost analysis, and cost-effectiveness analysis. Web Appendix 18A presents some fundamental time value of money concepts. Web Appendix 18B provides some time value of money tables to support both Web Chapter 18 and Web Appendix 18A. Web Chapter 19 examines decision making under risk and uncertainty. It also reviews the techniques for managing risk.

Student Preparation

This text is designed for use by undergraduate and graduate students in departments of economics, and in schools of business management, public administration, and information technology. Students are presumed to have a background in the basic principles of economics. Prior course work in statistics and quantitative methods is desirable but not essential. All statistical material is confined to Web Chapters 13–15. The book makes occasional use of elementary concepts of differential calculus. A review of these basic concepts is provided in Web Appendix 2A. In all cases where calculus is employed, one or more alternative approaches, such as graphical, algebraic, or tabular analysis, are also presented. Spreadsheet applications have become so prominent in the practice of managerial economics that we now explain many concepts of optimization in this context.

Pedagogical Features of the First Canadian Edition

The first Canadian edition of *Managerial Economics* makes extensive use of pedagogical learning aids to enhance student learning. The key features of the book are:

- **Part Openers:** Each major section of the book opens with a brief discussion of the material contained in the following chapters.
- **Chapter Preview:** Each chapter begins with a *Chapter Preview* that briefly summarizes the major issues that are covered in the chapter.
- **Learning Objectives:** Each chapter begins with a list of the main learning objectives of the chapter.
- **Managerial Challenge:** Each chapter opens with a *Managerial Challenge* illustrating a real-life economic analysis problem faced by Canadian managers that is related to the material to be covered in the chapter.
- **Key Terms:** In the margins of the text, new terms are defined as they are introduced. The placement of the glossary terms next to the location where the term is first used reinforces the importance of these new concepts and aids in later studying. These terms also appear in the *Glossary* at the back of the book.
- **Extensive Use of Examples:** Many real-world applications and examples derived from actual practice are provided and highlighted throughout the text. These examples help to bring the tools and concepts alive, thereby enhancing student learning. The Internet URL of each real firm is included the first time the firm is mentioned.
- **Diversity of Presentation Approaches:** Important analytical concepts are presented in several different ways, including tabular analysis, graphical analysis, and algebraic analysis. When elementary differential calculus is used, at least one alternative mode of analysis also is presented.

- **What Went Right | What Went Wrong:** Most chapters contain a *What Went Right | What Went Wrong* feature that allows students to relate real-world business decisions to what they have learned, and to show how management decisions can have positive and negative outcomes.

- **International Perspectives:** Throughout *Managerial Economics,* special *International Perspectives* sections are provided that illustrate the application of managerial economics concepts to problems faced by managers in an increasingly global economy.

- **Managerial Challenge Revisited:** At the end of the chapters, the *Managerial Challenge* mentioned at the beginning of the chapter is revisited, based on the knowledge gained in studying the chapter.

- **Point-by-Point Chapter Summaries:** Each chapter ends with a detailed, point-by-point summary of important concepts from the chapter.

- **Self-Test Exercises:** Each chapter in the book contains self-test exercises that students can use to test their learning. Detailed solutions are provided at the back of the book.

- **Exercises:** Each chapter contains a large set of exercises. Check answers to selected exercises, colour-coded in red boldfaced type, are provided at the end of the book.

- **Short Case Exercises:** Most chapters include short case exercises that extend the concepts and tools developed in the chapter.

- **Internet Margin Notes:** Internet URLs in the margins tie applications and examples to the websites of the real firms being discussed or to other relevant sites. Students gain not only the additional information and data found at the sites, but also the experience of using the Internet to find relevant information.

Ancillary Materials

A complete set of ancillary materials is available to adopters to supplement the text, including:

- The *Managerial Economics* support website is at www.mcguigan.nelson.com. Web appendixes and Chapters 13–19 are available at this site, along with instructor resources and student resources like online quizzing and Internet application links and updates.

- An *Instructor's Solutions Manual with Test Bank,* prepared by the authors, contains suggested answers to the end-of-chapter exercises and cases. The authors have taken great care to provide an error-free manual for instructors to use. The Test Bank contains a large collection of true–false, multiple-choice, and numerical problems.

- *ExamView* software for the test bank is available to simplify the preparation of quizzes and exams. *ExamView* contains all of the questions in the printed test bank and is an easy-to-use test-creation software compatible with Microsoft Windows. Instructors can add or edit questions, instructions, and answers, and select questions by previewing them on the screen; selecting them randomly, or selecting them by number. Instructors can also create and administer quizzes online.

- *Microsoft® PowerPoint®* presentation packages are available for students as study aids, and for the instructor as a lecture aid. These slides can be customized by instructors to meet their specific course needs.

- *Excel for Economics* is an interactive stand-alone spreadsheet package, created by Thomas Palm, Professor Emeritus, Portland State University. *Excel for Economics* lifts static, printed textbook models, equations, and graphs, and changes them into dynamic spreadsheets. Users can enter numerical values and change them at will in *what-if* entries that simulate managerial decision making. Multiple linked spreadsheets can be used simultaneously, and calculations and graphing are done automatically to allow the student to focus on the meanings, implications, and applicability of the decisions.

Acknowledgments

A number of reviewers, users, and colleagues have been particularly helpful in providing us with many worthwhile comments and suggestions at various stages in the development of this and earlier editions of the book. Included among these individuals are:

Swati Basu, McGill University
Dick Beason, University of Alberta
Byron Eastman, Laurentian University
Alan Hochstein, Concordia University
Joseph Kushner, Brock University
Alan Matadeen, Simon Fraser University
Richard Mueller, University of Lethbridge

People who were especially helpful in the preparation of the first Canadian edition include Lloyd Atkinson and Richard Zind, both of whom are independent economic consultants.

We wish to express our appreciation to the members of the Thomson Nelson staff—particularly Anthony Rezek, Natalia Denesiuk, and Charmaine Sherlock—for their help in the preparation and promotion of this book. Most of all we would like to thank our developmental editor, Elke Price, who is a constant source of excellent advice and encouragement. Her high standards of performance and her total knowledge of the publishing field have helped immensely with this project. We also want to thank June Trusty for her excellent copy-editing work.

We are grateful to the Literary Executor of the late Sir Ronald A. Fisher, FRS; to Dr. Frank Yates, FRS.; and to Longman Group, Ltd., London, for permission to reprint Table III from their book *Statistical Tables for Biological, Agricultural, and Medical Research* (6th ed., 1974).

James R. McGuigan
William F. Rentz
Alfred L. Kahl
R. Charles Moyer
Frederick H. deB. Harris

About the Authors

James R. McGuigan

James R. McGuigan owns and operates his own numismatic investment firm. Prior to this activity, he was Associate Professor of Finance and Business Economics in the School of Business Administration at Wayne State University. He also taught at the University of Pittsburgh.

McGuigan received his undergraduate degree from Carnegie-Mellon University. He earned an M.B.A. at the Graduate School of Business at the University of Chicago, and his Ph.D. from the University of Pittsburgh.

In addition to his interest in economics, he has co-authored books in financial management, including *Contemporary Financial Management*. His research articles on options have been published in the *Journal of Financial and Quantitative Analysis*.

William F. Rentz

William F. Rentz is Associate Professor of Finance and Business Economics at the School of Management of the University of Ottawa. Previously, he taught at Northwestern University and at the University of Texas at Austin.

He has been a visiting professor at the Universidad Internacional de las Americas in Costa Rica, and the University of Florida, the State University of New York at Binghamton, and Stanford University in the United States, as well as the University of Basel in Switzerland.

He earned his S.B. in electrical engineering from the Massachusetts Institute of Technology, and his A.M. and Ph.D. in economics from the University of Rochester.

Professor Rentz has been a productive scholar. In addition to coauthoring this text, he has also coauthored *Contemporary Financial Management*, First Canadian Edition (Thomson Nelson, 2004); *Canadian Financial Management*, Fourth Canadian Edition (Dryden, 1994); *Spreadsheet Applications in Engineering Economics* (West, 1992); and *Engineering Economics* (McGraw-Hill Ryerson, 1986).

Professor Rentz has published extensively in leading academic and professional journals, including the *Journal of Finance, Journal of Business Finance and Accounting, Journal of Risk and Insurance, Financial Review, American Economic Review, Management Science*, and many others.

Alfred L. Kahl

Alfred L. Kahl is Adjunct Professor of Finance and Strategic Management at the School of Management of the University of Ottawa. Previously, he taught at Minnesota State University–Mankato, the University of Georgia, Gannon University, and the University of Tunis.

He has been a visiting professor at the University of Lethbridge in Canada, the Universidad Internacional de las Americas in Costa Rica, the Sorbonne in France, the Riga Business School in Latvia, the Academy of Economic Studies in Romania, and at Xian-Jiaotong University in China. He has taught online for the University of Maryland and the Florida Institute of Technology.

He earned his B.A. at the University of Maryland, his M.B.A. at the University of Pittsburgh, and his Ph.D. in Economics and Finance from the University of Florida.

Professor Kahl is a chartered economist and certified professional consultant. He also has been a productive scholar. In addition to coauthoring this book, he has also coauthored *Contemporary Financial Management,* First Canadian Edition (Thomson Nelson, 2004); *Canadian Financial Management,* Fourth Canadian Edition (Dryden, 1994); *Introduction aux Affaires* (Morin, 1993); and *Spreadsheet Applications in Engineering Economics* (West, 1992); as well as *Engineering Economics* (McGraw-Hill Ryerson, 1986).

Professor Kahl has published extensively in leading academic and professional journals, including the *Journal of Finance, Journal of Business Finance and Accounting, Accounting and Business Research, International Journal of Accounting, Journal of Public and International Affairs, Financial Review, American Economic Review, Decision Science, Management Science, Management International Review,* and many others.

R. Charles Moyer

R. Charles Moyer is Dean Emeritus, and holds the GMAC Insurance Chair in Finance, at the Babcock Graduate School of Management, Wake Forest University. Previously, he was Professor of Finance and Chairman of the Department of Finance at Texas Tech University. Professor Moyer has also taught at the University of Houston, Lehigh University, and the University of New Mexico, and spent a year at the Federal Reserve Bank of Cleveland.

Moyer earned his B.A. in Economics from Howard University, and his M.B.A. and Ph.D. in Finance and Managerial Economics from the University of Pittsburgh.

In addition to this text, Moyer has also coauthored *Contemporary Financial Management,* and *Financial Management with Lotus 1-2-3.* He has been published in many leading journals, including *Financial Management, Journal of Financial and Quantitative Analysis, Journal of Finance, Financial Review, Journal of Financial Research, International Journal of Forecasting,* and many others.

Frederick H. deB. Harris

Frederick H. deB. Harris is the John B. McKinnon Professor of Managerial Economics and Finance at the Babcock Graduate School of Management, Wake Forest University. His specialties are pricing tactics and capacity planning. Professor Harris has taught managerial economics courses in three business schools in the United States and Europe. He holds a B.A. in Economics from Dartmouth College and a Ph.D. in Financial Economics from the University of Virginia.

Professor Harris has published widely in financial and economics journals, including the *Review of Economics and Statistics, Journal of Financial and Quantitative Analysis, Journal of Financial Markets,* and *Journal of Industrial Economics.* From 1988–1993, he served on the Board of Associate Editors of the *Journal of Industrial Economics.* In addition, Professor Harris often benchmarks the revenue management functions of large companies and writes about his findings in management practice journals such as *Marketing Management* and the *Journal of Operations Management.*

His awards and recognitions include several awards for Best Academic Publication of the Year, Babcock School Professor of the Year, and Most Popular Courses designations. Additionally, *Inc. Magazine* (2000) and *BusinessWeek's Guide to the Best Business Schools* (1997–2003) identify Professor Harris as among outstanding faculty members.

Part One

Introduction and Demand Analysis

Part 1 presents an overview of managerial economics analysis and introduces some key economic concepts and tools. In Chapter 1, (1) the goals of an organization (both for-profit and not-for-profit) are developed; (2) the decision-making process and the philosophy of optimization are introduced; (3) the role of profit is discussed; (4) strategic decisions are discussed; and (5) the relationships between managerial economics techniques and accounting, finance, marketing, operations management, and human resource management are highlighted.

Fundamental economic concepts, including marginal analysis, supply and demand analysis, and decision analysis are reviewed in Chapter 2. Web Appendix 2A provides a self-contained introduction to optimization and constrained optimization techniques, including applications of basic calculus. To access Web chapters and appendixes, go to the Nelson website for this book at www.mcguigan.nelson.com.

Chapter 3 develops the theory of demand and introduces the elasticity properties of the demand function. Chapter 3 also includes an introduction to indifference curve analysis as well as income and substitution effects.

The tools and concepts developed in Part 1 are central to the analyses used throughout the rest of the text.

Introduction and Goals of the Firm

Chapter Preview

Managerial economics is the application of microeconomic theory and methodology to decision-making problems faced by private, public, and not-for-profit organizations. Managerial economics assists decision makers (managers) to efficiently allocate scarce resources, plan strategy, and execute effective tactics. Economic profit is the difference between total revenue and total economic cost and plays a key role in allocating resources in a free enterprise system. Economic cost includes a "normal" return to capital providers. The normative goal of the firm is to maximize shareholder wealth, so managers should focus on how their decisions influence shareholder wealth.

In the modern firm, there are agency problems associated with the separation of ownership and control. Compensation plans that align managers' interests with shareholders' interests are an important step in minimizing agency problems. Every organization should have a vision of what it wants to be, a mission statement of what it is, and a strategy that links the two. Competitive strategy includes the organization's capabilities, its processes, and adaptive innovation to its changing environment. Porter's five forces (threat of substitutes, threat of entry, power of buyers, power of suppliers, and intensity of rivalrous tactics) comprise a framework for strategic analysis.

Obtaining sufficient market share to achieve economies of scale is an important step in maximizing shareholder wealth. However, additional market share solely for its own sake is not usually shareholder wealth maximizing, because the additional economic costs often outweigh the additional revenues. Managerial economics also provides normative goals to guide resource-allocation decisions in public sector and not-for-profit organizations.

Learning Objectives

After studying this chapter, you should be able to:

1. Explain how managerial economics draws on microeconomic theory and models to assist managers in decision making.

2. Define *economic profit* as the *difference between total revenues* and *total economic costs*.

3. Explain the importance of the *shareholder wealth-maximization model* as the overall objective of the firm.

4. Recognize that deviations from the shareholder wealth-maximization objective are often called *agency costs*.

5. Understand that *competitive strategy* entails analysis of the firm's capabilities, its production processes, and innovation based on the firm's vision and mission.

6. Understand how an organization's sustainable competitive advantage results from pursuing one of *three generic strategies*.

7. Describe a *relevant market* as a group of economic agents that interact with each other in a buyer–seller relationship.

8. Identify how the *five forces strategy model* determines sustainable incumbent profitability in a particular industry.

9. Understand that *not-for-profit enterprises* exist to supply a good or service desired by their constituencies.

10. Explain why both public and private organizations should seek to furnish their goods or services in the most *resource-efficient manner*.

Executive Compensation: Stuart Energy Corporation Bonus Plan*

Separation of ownership (shareholders) and control (management) in corporations permits managers to pursue goals—such as maximization of their own personal welfare—that are not always in the long-term interests of shareholders. To avoid this, many corporations seek to forge a closer alliance between the interests of shareholders and managers with compensation plans that have performance-based bonuses.

One Canadian plan, devised by Stuart Energy Corporation, provides an annual base salary to some of the top executives plus bonuses that are based on the performance of the firm's shares. During 2003, the firm's share price on the Toronto Stock Exchange rose by 35 percent over the prior year. The firm's chief executive officer (CEO) was paid a salary of $350,000 and a bonus of $275,000, and the firm's vice president for research and development (R&D) was paid a salary of $180,000 and a bonus of $130,500. The firm's chief operating officer (COO) was paid a salary of $146,667 and a bonus of $133,466, and the vice president of sales and marketing was paid a salary of $160,000 and a bonus of $103,200. Thus, the managers received very significant amounts of compensation related to the market value added during the year, which motivated them to manage the firm to achieve this good performance.

The objectives of the firm and how to motivate managers to pursue these objectives are some of the topics introduced in this chapter and covered in more detail in Chapter 10 and Web Chapter 17.

As you read each chapter, you should think about how to solve the chapter's managerial challenge, which is revisited at the chapter's end.

---

* Based on "Stuart Energy," *Financial Post*, January 21, 2004, p. FP2.

COURTESY OF STUART ENERGY CORPORATION

- For more information on Stuart Energy Corporation, go to **www.stuartenergy.com**.
- Subsequent to the development of this Managerial Challenge, Stuart Energy was acquired by Hydrogenics Corporation. For more on the acquisition, see **www.hydrogenics.com**.
- For annual reports and information about other Canadian companies, go to **www.sedar.com**.

What Is Managerial Economics?

Managerial Economics
Applies microeconomic reasoning to real-world decision-making problems.

Managerial economics deals with the application of microeconomic reasoning to real-world decision-making problems faced by private, public, and not-for-profit institutions. Managerial economics extracts from microeconomic theory those concepts and techniques that enable the decision maker to select strategic direction, to allocate efficiently the resources of the organization, and to respond effectively to tactical issues.

Managerial Economics and Economic Theory

Most decisions made by managers usually involve questions of resource allocation within the organization in both the short and the long run. In the short run, a manager may be interested in estimating demand and cost relationships to make decisions about the price to charge for a product and the quantity of output to produce. The areas of micro-economics dealing with demand theory and with the theory of cost and production are obviously useful in making decisions on such matters. Macroeconomic theory also enters into decision making when a manager attempts to forecast future demand based on forces influencing the overall economy.

In the long run, decisions must be made about expanding or contracting production and distribution facilities, developing and marketing new products, and possibly acquiring other firms. Basically, these decisions require the organization to make capital expenditures—that is, expenditures made in the current period that are expected to yield returns in future periods. Economists have developed a theory of capital budgeting that can be used in deciding whether to undertake specific capital expenditures.

The Decision-Making Model

The ability to make good decisions is the key to successful managerial performance. All decision making shares several common elements. First, the decision maker must establish or identify the objectives of the organization. Failure to identify organizational objectives correctly can result in the complete rejection of an otherwise well-conceived and well-implemented plan. Later sections of this chapter deal with the issue of organizational objectives.

Next, the decision maker must identify the problem requiring a solution. For example, the manager of a brewing plant in Halifax may note that the plant's profit margin on sales has been decreasing. This could be caused by pricing errors, labour force problems, or the use of outdated production equipment. Once the source or sources of the problem are identified, the manager can move to an examination of potential solutions. If the problem is the use of technologically inefficient equipment, two possible solutions are (1) updating and replacing the plant's equipment or (2) building a completely new plant. The choice between possible alternatives depends on the relative costs and benefits, as well as other organizational and societal constraints that may make one alternative preferable to another.

The final step in the process, after all alternatives have been identified and evaluated and the best alternative has been chosen, is the implementation of the decision. This phase often requires constant monitoring to ensure that results are as expected. If they are not, corrective action needs to be taken when possible. This five-step decision-making process is illustrated in Figure 1.1.

The Role of Profits

Economic Profit
The difference between total revenue and total economic cost. Economic cost includes a "normal" rate of return on the capital contributions of the firm's owners.

Economic profit is the difference between total revenue and total economic cost. Total revenue is measured as the sales receipts of a firm, that is, price times quantity sold. The *economic cost* of any activity may be thought of as the highest valued alternative opportunity that is foregone. To attract economic resources to some activity, the firm must pay a price for these factors (labour, capital, natural resources, and management) that is sufficient to convince the owners of these resources to sacrifice other alternatives and commit the resources to this use. Thus, economic costs may be thought of as opportunity costs, or the costs of attracting a resource from its next best alternative use. Accordingly, the term "economic cost" in this book refers to all economic costs, both explicit and implicit, and includes in it a normal return (profit) for the owners who have contributed their financial resources. In a general sense, economic profit may be defined as the *difference between total revenue and total economic cost*. When we refer to "profit maximization" in this book, we mean an objective of maximizing the economic profit of the firm.

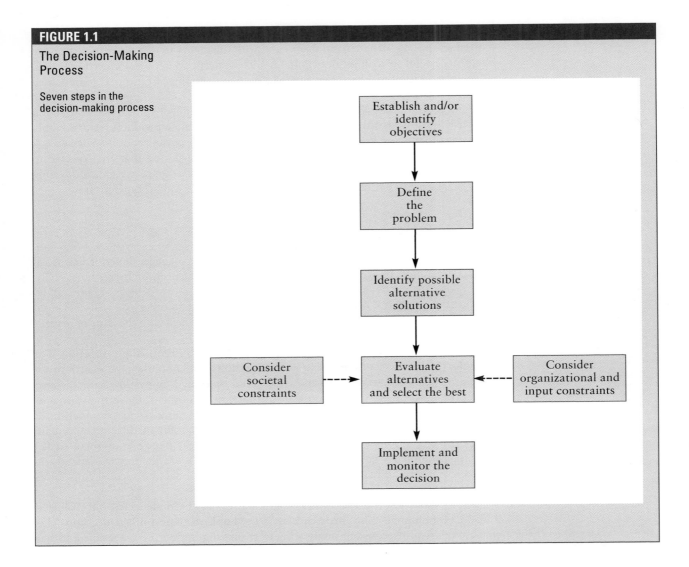

Why Are Profits Necessary?

In a free enterprise system, economic profits play an important role in guiding the decisions made by the thousands of competing, independent economic units. The existence of profits (resulting from the excess of revenues over costs) determines the type and quantity of goods and services that are produced and sold. It also determines the demand for various factors of production—labour, capital, natural resources, and management.

Return opportunities play a major role in determining the efficient allocation of resources in our economy. Without the market signals that economic profits give, it would be necessary to develop alternative schemes on which to base resource-allocation decisions. These alternatives are often highly bureaucratic and frequently lack the responsiveness to changing market conditions that a free enterprise system provides.

Objective of the Firm

One common model of the firm assumes that the objective of the owners of the firm is to maximize economic profits. This profit-maximization model of firm behaviour has been extremely rich in its decision-making implications. The marginal (and incremental) decision rules that have been derived from this theory provide very useful guidelines for making a wide range of resource-allocation decisions. For example, any business decision is profitable if one of these results occurs:

1. It increases revenue more than costs.

2. It decreases some costs more than it increases others (assuming revenues remain constant).

3. It increases some revenues more than it decreases others (assuming costs remain constant).

4. It reduces costs more than revenue.

The Shareholder Wealth-Maximization Model of the Firm

The simple profit-maximization model of the firm has provided decision makers with useful insights regarding efficient resource management and allocation. However, the profit-maximization model is limited because it *does not* incorporate the time dimension in the decision process and it *does not* consider risk. The **shareholder wealth** maximization model of the firm overcomes these limitations.

The shareholder wealth-maximization goal states that a firm's management should maximize the *present value* of the *expected future cash flows* to the equity owners (shareholders). This is equivalent to maximizing the market value added (*MVA*), where *MVA* is the difference between the market and book values of owners' equity. *MVA* is equal to the present value of all expected economic profits, discounted at the shareholders' required rate of return,[1] or

Shareholder Wealth
A measure of the value of a firm. Shareholder wealth is equal to the value of a firm's common shares. This, in turn, is equal to the present value of all future cash returns expected to be generated by the firm for the benefit of its owners.

(1.1)

$$MVA = \frac{\pi_1}{(1 + k_e)^1} + \frac{\pi_2}{(1 + k_e)^2} + \frac{\pi_3}{(1 + k_e)^3} + \cdots + \frac{\pi_\infty}{(1 + k_e)^\infty}$$

$$MVA = \sum_{t=1}^{\infty} \frac{\pi_t}{(1 + k_e)^t}$$

where *MVA* is the current (present) market value added, π_t represents the economic profits expected in each of the future periods (1 through ∞), and k_e equals the investors' required rate of return. Equation 1.1 assumes that the reader is familiar with the concept of discounting and present values. (A review of this concept is found in Web Appendix 18A.) For the purposes of analysis here, it is only necessary to recognize that $1 received one year from today is generally worth less than $1 received today. This is because $1 today can be invested at some rate of interest, for example, 15 percent, to yield $1.15 at the end of one year. Thus, an investor who requires (or has an opportunity to earn) a 15 percent annual rate of return on an investment would place a current value of $1 on $1.15 expected to be received in one year.

Equation 1.1 explicitly considers the timing of future profits. By discounting all future profits at the required rate of return, k_e, Equation 1.1 recognizes that a dollar received in the future is worth less than a dollar received immediately.

Equation 1.1 also provides a conceptual basis for evaluating differential levels of risk. For example, if a series of future profits is highly uncertain (i.e., likely to diverge substantially from their expected values), the discount rate, k_e, can be increased to account for this risk. Thus, the greater the risk associated with receiving a future benefit (profit), the lower the value placed by investors on that benefit. The shareholder wealth-maximization model of the firm is therefore capable of dealing with the two primary shortcomings of the static profit-maximization model.

---

[1] See Al Ehrbar, *EVA: The Real Key to Creating Wealth* (New York: Wiley, 1998).

SHAREHOLDER WEALTH MAXIMIZATION: BERKSHIRE HATHAWAY INC.

For shareholder reports and other information, go to **www. berkshirehathaway. com**.

Warren E. Buffett, who is widely considered to be the world's most successful investor, is the chairman and chief executive officer of Berkshire Hathaway Inc. He has described the long-term economic goal of Berkshire Hathaway as "to maximize the average annual rate of gain in intrinsic business value on a per-share basis."* The firm's book value per share has increased from US$19.46 in 1964, when Buffett acquired the firm, to US$46,727 at the end of 2002, a compound annual rate of growth of about 22 percent.

The growth rate in the market value of the firm's shares has been even greater, with the market value per share reaching US$95,700 on February 25, 2004. The firm's directors are all major shareholders. At least four of the directors have more than 50 percent of their family's net worth invested in Berkshire. Insiders own more than 47 percent of the firm's shares. Buffet's firm has placed a high premium on the goal of maximizing shareholder wealth; that is, maximizing the value of the owners' portion of the firm.

Annual Report, Berkshire Hathaway Inc., 2002.

Additional insight regarding the achievement of the shareholder wealth-maximization goal can be gained by decomposing the profit concept, π, into its important elements. Profit in period t, π_t, is equal to total revenue (TR_t) minus total costs (TC_t), or

$$(1.2) \qquad \pi_t = TR_t - TC_t$$

Similarly, total revenue in period t equals price per unit (P_t) times quantity sold (Q_t), or

$$(1.3) \qquad TR_t = P_t \times Q_t$$

Total cost in period t equals variable cost per unit (V_t) times the number of units of output (Q_t) plus fixed costs in period $t(F_t)$, or

$$(1.4) \qquad TC_t = V_t \times Q_t + F_t$$

By combining Equations 1.2, 1.3, and 1.4 with Equation 1.1, we get

$$(1.5) \qquad MVA = \sum_{t=1}^{\infty} \frac{P_t \times Q_t - V_t \times Q_t - F_t}{(1 + k_e)^t}$$

The term $P_t \times Q_t$ represents the total revenue generated by the firm. From a decision-making perspective, this value is dependent on the firm's demand function (discussed in Chapter 3) and the firm's pricing decisions (see Chapters 6–9).

The firm's costs, both fixed (F_t) and variable (V_t) are discussed in Chapters 4–5. In addition, the choice of investments made by the firm—the capital budgeting decisions—determines what proportion of total cost will be fixed and what proportion will be variable. A firm that chooses a capital-intensive production technology will tend to have a higher proportion of its total costs of operation represented as fixed costs than will a firm that chooses a more labour-intensive technology. Capital budgeting decisions are discussed in Web Chapter 18.

The discount rate, k_e, that investors use to value the stream of income generated by a firm is determined by the perceived risk of the firm and by conditions in the financial markets, including the level of expected inflation. Risk and its relationship to required rates of return are discussed in Web Chapter 19.

In summary, the value of an enterprise is determined by the amount, timing, and risk of the profits expected to be generated by the enterprise.

Economic Profits, Accounting Profits, and Cash Flows

The economic profit concept we are using is not the same as the accounting definition of earnings, or net income, for several reasons. First, accounting profits are subject to ambiguous interpretation because of the broad latitude provided by generally accepted accounting principles (GAAP). Also, the accounting profit concept does not consider some important economic costs, such as the opportunity cost of the capital invested by owners. Finally, accounting profit concepts may not be reflective of the actual *cash flows* collected and paid by a company over time, especially when one considers the different methods of computing depreciation and of inventory valuation that are allowed by GAAP.

In practice, managers who seek to maximize shareholder wealth focus on maximizing the present value of the cash flows available to the equity owners of the firm. The cash flow definition of benefits available to a firm's owners is unambiguous and consistent with the objective of maximizing the present value of expected future economic profits. Throughout the text, when the term "profit" is used, it means economic, not accounting-defined, profits. When used in this way, the profit concept is consistent with the cash flow concept and will lead to wealth-maximizing decisions by managers.

Managerial Actions to Influence Shareholder Wealth

A tangible measure of shareholder wealth is the market price of the firm's shares. Many factors ultimately influence the firm's share price. Some of these factors are related to the external economic environment and are largely outside the direct control of managers. Other factors can be directly manipulated by the managers. Figure 1.2 illustrates the factors affecting share prices. The top panel enumerates some of the factors in the economic environment that have an impact on the strategic decisions managers can make. The economic environment factors are largely outside the direct control of managers (e.g., anticombines policy or the yen/dollar exchange rate), but managers must be aware of how these factors affect the policy decisions under the control of management. Many of these economic environment factors act as constraints, or limitations, on the value-maximizing decisions available to managers.

The policy decision areas are enumerated in the next panel of Figure 1.2. Managers make choices regarding the products to be produced, the technology used to produce them, the marketing effort and distribution channels, and the selection of employees and their compensation. In addition, managers establish investment policies, the ownership structure of the firm, the capital structure (use of debt) of the firm, working capital management policies, and dividend policies. Managers also initiate restructuring events, such as mergers, spinoffs, and alliances in an attempt to increase capitalized value. The decisions made in these key policy decision areas determine the amount, timing, and risk of the firm's expected cash flows. Participants in the financial markets evaluate the profits expected by the firm in relation to alternative streams of profits expected from other firms and ultimately establish the price of the firm's shares. The firm's share price is influenced at any point in time by general conditions in the financial markets, including the level of interest rates, anticipated inflation rates, and the level of investor optimism regarding the future.

FIGURE 1.2

Factors Affecting Share Prices

Five major factors that affect sustainable industry profitability

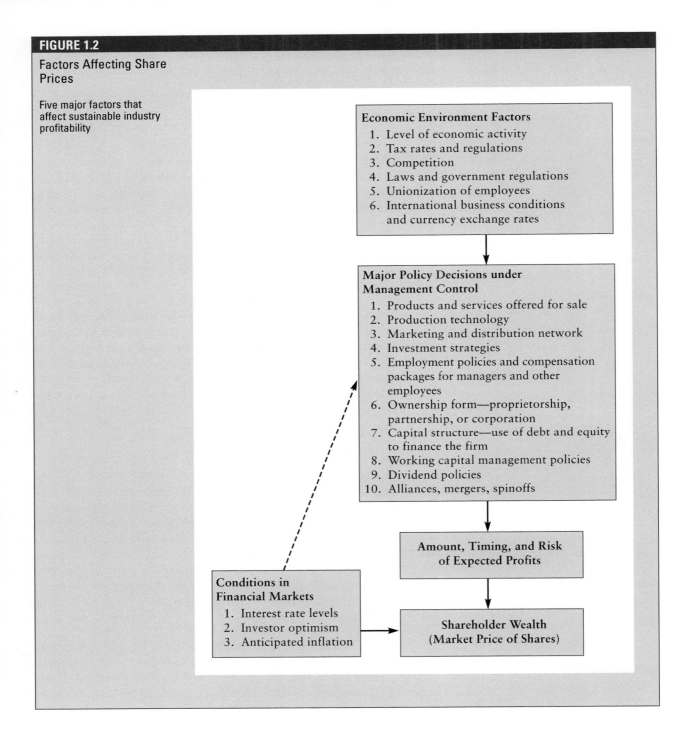

Separation of Ownership and Control:
The Agency Problem

The marginal (or incremental) decision criteria, derived from the static profit-maximization objectives and the dynamic shareholder wealth-maximization objectives, are useful in cases where alternative decisions are easily enumerated and outcomes (costs and revenues) associated with these alternatives can be estimated. These cases include scheduling for optimal production, determining an optimal inventory policy given some pattern of sales and available production facilities, and choosing from among alternative means of achieving some desirable end result (for example, buying or leasing a machine or refunding an outstanding bond issue). In other cases, however, where the alternatives are less clear or the incremental effects are debatable, economists have frequently found a divergence between theory and practice. What are the reasons for this divergence? As the small business enterprise grew and expanded into the modern corporation of today, the roles of ownership and management became increasingly separated,[2] permitting managers to pursue their own self-interests.

Divergent Objectives

Separation of ownership and control has permitted managers to pursue goals more consistent with their own self-interests, subject, of course, to the constraint that they satisfy shareholders sufficiently to maintain control of the corporation. Instead of seeking to maximize some objective (such as shareholder wealth), management is said to "satisfice" or seek acceptable levels of performance, while maximizing its own welfare.[3]

Maximization of their own personal welfare (or utility) may also lead managers to be concerned with long-run survival (job security). The concern for long-run survival may lead management to minimize (or limit) the amount of risk incurred by the firm, because unfavourable outcomes can lead to their dismissal or possible bankruptcy for the firm. Likewise, the desire for job security is cited as one reason management often opposes takeover offers (mergers) by other companies.

Agency Problems

The existence of divergent objectives between owners and managers is one example of a class of problems arising from agency relationships. **Agency relationships** occur when one or more individuals (the principals) employ another individual (the agent) to perform a service on behalf of the principals.[4] In an agency relationship, decision-making authority often is delegated to the agent from the principals. In the context of managerial economics, the most important agency relationship is the relationship between shareholders (owners) and managers.

Agency Relationship
A basis for delegating decision-making authority from principals to agents.

Shareholders and Managers Inefficiencies that arise because of agency relationships have been called agency problems. These problems occur because each party to a transaction is assumed to act in a manner consistent with maximizing personal utility (welfare). The concern of some managers for long-run survival (job security), rather than for shareholder wealth maximization, is an example of an agency problem. Another example is the consumption of on-the-job perquisites (such as the use of company airplanes, limousines, and luxurious offices) by managers who have no (or only partial) ownership interest in the firm. Shirking by managers is also an agency-related problem.

Two common factors that give rise to all principal–agent problems are the unobservability of some manager–agent action and the presence of random disturbances in team production. The job performance of parking gate attendants and piecework garment workers is easily monitored, but the work effort of salespeople and manufacturers' trade representatives may not be observable at less-than-prohibitive cost. Directly observing

---

[2] Adolph Berle and Gardiner C. Means, *The Modern Corporation and Private Property* (New York: Macmillan, 1932).

[3] Herbert Simon stated the case for satisficing behaviour in "Theories of Decision-Making in Economic and Behavioral Science," reprinted in E. Mansfield, *Microeconomics: Selected Readings,* 5th ed. (New York: Norton, 1985).

[4] See Amir Barnea, R. Haugen, and L. Senbet, *Agency Problems and Financial Contracting* (Englewood Cliffs, NJ: Prentice-Hall, 1985), for an overview of the agency problem issue. See also Michael Jensen and William Meckling, "Theory of the Firm: Managerial Behavior, Agency Costs, and Ownership Structure," *Journal of Financial Economics,* October 1976, pp. 305–360, and Eugene Fama, "Agency Problems and the Theory of the Firm," *Journal of Political Economy,* April 1980, pp. 288–307.

the managerial input is even more problematic because managers contribute an input one might call "creative ingenuity." Creative ingenuity in making the company's decisions is inherently unobservable. Owners know it when they see it, but do not recognize when it is missing. As a result, the managerial input is inseparable from good and bad luck in explaining fluctuations in company performance. Owners therefore find it difficult to know when to reward managers and when to blame them for poor performance.

Managerial motivations to act in the interest of shareholders include the structure of their compensation package, the threat of dismissal, and the threat of takeover by a new group of owners. Remaining agency problems reduce the value of the firm's shares in the marketplace and increase the likelihood of takeovers.

To mitigate these agency problems the firm incurs several **agency costs**. Examples of these agency costs include:

1. Expenditures to structure the organization in such a way as to minimize the incentives for management to take actions contrary to shareholder interests, such as providing a portion of management's compensation in the form of company shares.

2. Expenditures to monitor management's actions, such as paying for audits of managerial performance and internal audits of the firm's expenditures.

3. Bonding expenditures to protect the owners from managerial dishonesty.

4. The opportunity cost of lost profits arising from complex organizational structures that prevent management from making timely responses to opportunities.

Agency Costs
Costs associated with resolving conflicts of interest among shareholders, managers, and lenders. These include the cost of monitoring and bonding performance, the cost of constructing contracts designed to minimize agency conflicts, and the loss in efficiency resulting from unresolved agent–principal conflicts.

Implications of Shareholder Wealth Maximization

Critics of aligning management interests with equity owner interests often allege that shareholder wealth maximization focuses on short-term payoffs to the exclusion of long-term investment. The evidence suggests just the opposite. Near-term cash flows can explain only a small fraction of the capitalized market value reflected in a firm's share price. Shareholder wealth maximization is long term not short term in focus. Moreover, it is forward-looking, not merely extrapolative. Wealth-maximizing managers must anticipate change and proactively plan for all relevant contingencies.

Shareholder wealth maximization is an explicitly dynamic objective reflecting the currently available public information regarding a company's expected future cash flows and foreseeable risks. As such, it reflects the strategic investment opportunities a management team develops, not only the firm's preexisting positive net present value investments. Value-maximizing behaviour as the objective of management is also distinguishable from satisficing behaviour. In particular, any time the marginal benefits of an action exceed their marginal cost, just do it! In general, then, shareholder wealth maximization implies that management should seek to develop a forward-looking, dynamic, and long-term outlook; anticipate and manage change; acquire strategic investment opportunities; and maximize the present value of expected cash flows to owners, as allowed by legal and regulatory constraints.

Vision, Mission, and Strategy

Most organizations have a vision of what they want to become, an overriding idea of what the organization should be. Sometimes this vision is the founder's dream. Most organizations have a clear and concise vision statement that explains what the organization wishes to become, and everyone in the organization should understand the vision and buy into it with passion. Most organizations also have a clear and concise mission statement that describes the business (industry) context within which the organization now works.

The organization's strategy is what it is going to do to achieve its vision and mission. Strategies are plans that have specific objectives that are measurable, achievable, and can be realized within a stated time frame, such as three to five years. Tactics are specific

VISION AND STRATEGY AT MOLSON

For more information, go to **www.molson.com**, **www.coors.com**, and **www.molsoncoors. com**.

According to Molson's annual report*: "Molson's vision is to remain one of the top performing brewers in the world as measured by long-term shareholder value." The Molson strategy is focused on five key objectives for sustainable shareholder value: (1) grow operating profit by 14.5 percent annually, (2) grow market share annually, (3) grow volume by 4 to 5 percent annually, (4) organizational renewal, and (5) quality improvement. Molson's tactics include pursuing growth outside of Canada, mainly in Brazil and the United States. Brazil is the fourth-largest beer market in the world. The Molson subsidiary, Molson USA, markets the Molson brands in the United States, one of the fastest-growing import beer markets in the world.

The vision is, of course, a long-term goal. The first three key objectives may not be realized in each annual reporting period. For example, in the period ending September 30, 2004, Molson had a net loss of more than $49 million, compared with a net profit of more than $151 million a year earlier. The 2004 results were impacted by losses in Brazil and stronger competition from other brewers in both Canada and the United States, as well as in Brazil. This was one of the reasons for the merger with Coors—Molson Coors is now the fifth-largest brewer in the world.

* *Annual Report,* Molson Inc., 2003.

actions that will achieve the strategic plans. Managerial economics can help managers make effective decisions to develop and carry out their strategic plans.

Competitive Strategy

Competitive strategic analysis provides a framework for thinking proactively about threats to a firm's business model, about new business opportunities, and about the future reconfigurations of the firm's resources, capabilities, and core competencies.

Figure 1.3 displays the components of a business model in the context of a firm's prerequisite knowledge and strategic decisions. All successful business models begin by identifying *target markets*—i.e., what businesses one wants to enter and stay in. Physical assets, human resources, and intellectual property (such as patents and licences) sometimes limit the firm's capabilities, but business models are as unbounded as the ingenuity of entrepreneurial managers in finding ways to address new business opportunities. Next, all successful business models lay out a *value proposition* grounded in customer expectations of perceived value, and then identify what part of the *value chain* leading to end products the firm plans to create. Business models always must clarify *how and when revenue will be realized* and analyze the sensitivity of *gross and net margins* to various possible changes in the firm's cost structure. In specifying the *required investments,* business models also assess the potential for creating *value in network relationships* with complementary businesses and in joint ventures and alliances. Finally, all successful business models develop a competitive strategy.

The essence of competitive strategy is threefold: resource-based capabilities, production processes, and adaptive innovation.[5] First, competitive strategy analyzes how

---

[5] This section is based on H. Chesbrough, *Open Innovation* (Boston, MA: Harvard Business School Press, 2003), pp. 73–83.

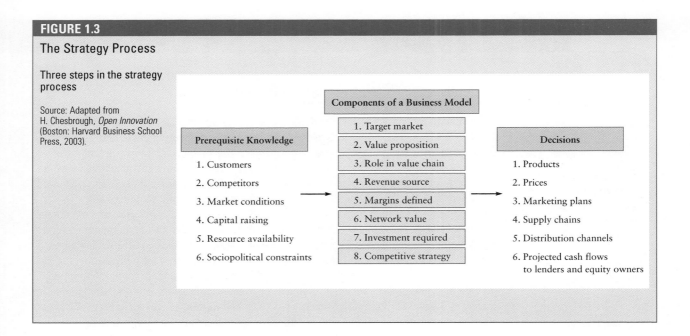

FIGURE 1.3

The Strategy Process

Three steps in the strategy process

Source: Adapted from H. Chesbrough, *Open Innovation* (Boston: Harvard Business School Press, 2003).

Components of a Business Model

Prerequisite Knowledge

1. Customers
2. Competitors
3. Market conditions
4. Capital raising
5. Resource availability
6. Sociopolitical constraints

1. Target market
2. Value proposition
3. Role in value chain
4. Revenue source
5. Margins defined
6. Network value
7. Investment required
8. Competitive strategy

Decisions

1. Products
2. Prices
3. Marketing plans
4. Supply chains
5. Distribution channels
6. Projected cash flows to lenders and equity owners

the firm can secure differential access to key resources such as patents or distribution channels. From humble beginnings as an Internet bookseller that contracted out its warehousing and book delivery service, Amazon managed to become the preferred fulfillment agent for many types of Internet sales. Similarly, Dell created a direct-to-the-customer sales process. It builds to order with subassembly components bought just in time from outside contractors, and it realizes cash from a sale within 48 hours. These value-creating business processes generated a high return on investment at Dell.

Finally, competitive strategy provides a road map for sustaining a firm's profitability through innovation. As industries emerge, evolve, and morph into other product spaces (e.g., think of calculators and mobile phones), firms must anticipate these changes and plan how they will sustain their positioning in the industry, and ultimately migrate their business to new industries. IBM, the dominant mainframe leasing company in the 1970s, reinvented itself twice—first in the 1980s as a PC manufacturer and a second time in the 1990s as a systems solution provider.

Generic Types of Strategy

Strategic thinking initially focuses on *industry analysis* and in which industries it would be attractive to do business. Michael Porter's five forces model (discussed below) illustrates this approach. Soon thereafter, however, managers want to conduct *competitor analysis* to learn more about how firms can sustain their relative profitability in a group of related firms. Efforts to answer these questions are often described as competitive *strategic positioning*. Finally, strategists try to isolate the *core competencies* that any particular firm possesses as a result of its *resource-based capabilities,* in order to identify *sustainable competitive advantages* vis-à-vis their competitors in a relevant market.

Profitability clearly depends on the ability to create sustainable competitive advantages. Any one of three generic types of strategies may suffice. A firm may establish a product differentiation strategy, a cost leadership strategy, or a niche strategy. *Product differentiation strategy* usually involves competing on the basis of capabilities, branding, or product endorsements. Coca-Cola is by far the world's most widely recognized brand, with almost 80 percent of sales outside the United States. However, it is followed closely by Marlboro, Gillette, Nestlé, and Kellogg, all with more than 50 percent of their

THINK SMALL TO GROW BIG: WESTJET AIRLINES

For more information, go to **www.westjet.com**; see also Paul Grescoe, *Flight Path* (Mississauga, ON: Wiley, 2004).

WestJet uses operations processes for ticket sales, boarding, plane turnaround, crew scheduling, flight frequency, maintenance, and jet fuel hedging that deliver exceptionally reduced operating costs to target customers in their price-sensitive market niche. Anything that works against this focus must be jettisoned from the business plan.

WestJet has clearly accomplished its goal. As air travel plummeted in the months following the September 11, 2001, attacks on the World Trade Center, only WestJet had a break-even point that was low enough to continue to make money— WestJet can cover all of its costs at 64 percent load factors (unit sales/seat capacity). Since September 11, the dominant Canadian airline, Air Canada, and the major U.S. airlines have been operating well below the break-even point.

sales outside their home markets. All of these branded products command a price premium worldwide simply because of the product image and lifestyle associated with their successful branding. Nike is also a widely recognized brand with its swoosh logo. However, it further differentiates its products based on endorsements. For example, Steve Nash, the National Basketball Association's 2005 Most Valuable Player, has a multiyear endorsement contract with Nike for his basketball shoes.[6]

Which of the three generic types of strategy will be most effective depends in part on a firm's choice of *competitive scope*—that is, the number and type of product lines and market segments, the number of geographic locations, and the network of horizontally and vertically integrated businesses in which the company decides to invest. Competitive scope decisions are especially pivotal for cost-based strategy. A firm like WestJet with a *cost leadership strategy* must limit its business plan to focus narrowly on point-to-point, medium-distance, and nonstop routes.

Finally, firms can seek their *sustainable competitive advantage* among relevant market rivals by pursuing a *niche strategy* such as information technology. Southland Corporation's 7-Eleven convenience stores across Japan provide a good example (see the International Perspectives feature "The E-Commerce of Sandwiches at 7-Elevens in Japan").

In conclusion, competitive strategy can secure higher profitability if a company configures its resource-based capabilities, business processes, and adaptive innovations in such a way as to obtain a sustainable competitive advantage. Whether differentiation, cost leadership, or niche strategy provides the most effective route to competitive advantage depends in large part on the firm's strategic focus.

The Relevant Market Concept

Relevant Market
A group of firms that interact with each other in a buyer–seller relationship.

A **relevant market** is a group of firms that interact with each other in a buyer–seller relationship. Relevant markets often have both spatial and product characteristics. For example, the market for Microsoft's Windows operating system is worldwide, whereas the market for Winnipeg-origin air travel is confined to suppliers in that area.

The *market structure* within these relevant markets varies tremendously. The four largest producers of breakfast cereals control 86 percent of the total industry output— a *concentrated* market. In contrast, the market for concrete block and brick is

---

[6] Based on information retrieved on June 1, 2005, from www.askmen.com.

The e-Commerce of Sandwiches at 7-Elevens in Japan*

Japanese office workers put in very long hours, often arriving at 8 A.M. and staying well into the evening. In the midst of this long day, most take a break to go out on the street and pick up lunch. Boxed lunches, rice balls, and sandwiches are the routine offerings, but the fashion-conscious Japanese want to be seen eating what's "in" this week. This situation makes an excellent opportunity for 7-Eleven, which became the biggest retailer in Japan in 2001. Half of sales revenue comes from these lunch items.

The key to 7-Eleven's success has been its use of information technology. 7-Eleven collects sales information by proprietary satellite communication networks from 8,500 locations three times a day. Like other retailers, it uses the data for merchandising studies to improve its product packaging and shelf placements with laboratory-like experiments in matched-pair stores throughout the country. But there is more, much more. The firm has built systems to analyze the entire data inflow in just 20 minutes. It is interested in what sells this morning and what sold yesterday evening (and the local weather) as a forecast of what sandwiches to prepare for the lunch crowd rush hour today. As customers become more fickle, product fashion cycles in sandwiches are shortening from 7 weeks to, in some cases, as little time as 10 days. 7-Eleven forecasts the demand item by item, store by store, on a daily basis.

Of course, such short-term demand forecasting would be useless if food preparation were a production-to-stock process with many weeks of lead-time required. Instead, supply chain management practices are closely monitored and adapted continuously with electronic commerce tools. Delivery trucks carry bar-code readers that upload instantaneously to headquarters databases. Orders for a particular sandwich at a particular store are placed before 10 A.M., processed through the supply chain to all component input companies in less than 7 minutes, and delivered by 4 P.M. for the next day's sales.

Most customers praise the extraordinary freshness, quality ingredients, and minimal incidence of out-of-stock items. All this competitive advantage over rival grocers and noodle shops has led to consistent price premiums for 7-Eleven's in-house brand.

* Based on "Over the Counter Commerce," *The Economist*, May 26, 2001, pp. 77–78.

fragmented—with the largest four firms accounting for only 8 percent of the total output. These differences in market structures and changes in market structure over time have important implications for the determination of price levels, price stability, and the likelihood of sustained profitability in these relevant markets.

Porter's Five Forces Strategic Framework

Michael Porter[7] has developed a conceptual framework for identifying the threats from competition in a relevant market. Incumbent firms attempt to secure competitive advantages through their choice of management strategy. Porter's five forces framework conceptualizes management strategy in terms of the likelihood of sustained profitability

[7] Michael Porter, *Competitive Strategy* (Cambridge, MA: The Free Press, 1998). See also Cynthia Porter and Michael Porter, eds., *Strategy: Seeking and Securing Competitive Advantage* (Cambridge, MA: Harvard Business School Press, 1992).

for a particular industry or line of business. Figure 1.4 displays Porter's five forces: the threat of substitutes, the threat of entry, the power of buyers, the power of suppliers, and the intensity of rivalry.

Threat of Substitutes

First, incumbent profitability is determined by the threat of substitutes. Is the product generic, like office supplies, or is it branded, like Coca-Cola? The more brand loyalty, the less the threat of substitutes and the higher the incumbent's profitability will be. Also, the more distant the substitutes outside the relevant market, the less price responsive will be demand, and the larger will be the optimal markups and profit margins.

The closeness or distance of substitutes often hinges not only on consumer perceptions created by advertising, but also on segmentation of the customers into separate distribution channels. Pantyhose distributed through convenience stores has many fewer substitutes at 9 P.M. the night before a business trip than does pantyhose sold through the department store distribution channels. Consequently, the threat of substitutes is reduced, and the profit margin on convenience store pantyhose is high.

Threat of Entry

A second force determining the likely profitability of an industry or product line is the threat of potential entrants. The higher the barriers to entry, the more profitable an incumbent will be. Barriers to entry can arise from several factors. First, consider high capital costs. Few potential entrants with the necessary capital implies a lesser threat of entry and higher incumbent profitability.

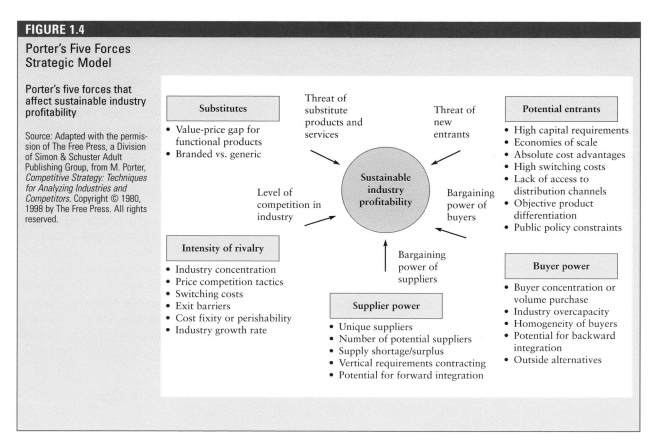

FIGURE 1.4

Porter's Five Forces Strategic Model

Porter's five forces that affect sustainable industry profitability

Source: Adapted with the permission of The Free Press, a Division of Simon & Schuster Adult Publishing Group, from M. Porter, *Competitive Strategy: Techniques for Analyzing Industries and Competitors.* Copyright © 1980, 1998 by The Free Press. All rights reserved.

Substitutes
- Value-price gap for functional products
- Branded vs. generic

Threat of substitute products and services

Threat of new entrants

Potential entrants
- High capital requirements
- Economies of scale
- Absolute cost advantages
- High switching costs
- Lack of access to distribution channels
- Objective product differentiation
- Public policy constraints

Level of competition in industry

Sustainable industry profitability

Bargaining power of buyers

Intensity of rivalry
- Industry concentration
- Price competition tactics
- Switching costs
- Exit barriers
- Cost fixity or perishability
- Industry growth rate

Bargaining power of suppliers

Supplier power
- Unique suppliers
- Number of potential suppliers
- Supply shortage/surplus
- Vertical requirements contracting
- Potential for forward integration

Buyer power
- Buyer concentration or volume purchase
- Industry overcapacity
- Homogeneity of buyers
- Potential for backward integration
- Outside alternatives

Second, economies of scale and absolute cost advantages can provide another barrier to entry. The first mover has a tremendous scale economy in spreading fixed cost across a large customer base. (Of course, new technology could lower this barrier.)

Third, if customers are brand-loyal, the costs of inducing a customer to switch to a new entrant's product may pose a substantial barrier to entry. A new entrant therefore has a very high cost associated with becoming an effective entry threat in these markets.

Access to distribution channels is another potential barrier that has implications for the profitability of incumbents. The shelf space in grocery stores is very limited. A new supplier might have to offer huge inducements to displace one of a firm's incumbent suppliers. Government regulatory agencies also can approve or deny access to distribution channels. For example, Health Canada approves prescription drugs for certain therapeutic uses but not for others.

Finally, a barrier to entry may be posed by product differentiation. If the differences between products are objective, the entrant can reverse-engineer the product. Perceived product differentiation is actually harder to imitate and therefore poses a more effective barrier.

Especially with the increasing globalization of commerce, objective product differentiation is always subject to reverse-engineering, violations of intellectual property, and offshore imitation even of patented products. In contrast, product differentiation based on customer perceptions of lifestyle images and product positioning (e.g., Coca-Cola) can erect barriers to entry that allow incumbent firms to better survive competitive attack. In sum, the higher any of these barriers to entry, the lower the threat of potential entrants and the higher the potential industry profitability.

Power of Buyers and Suppliers

The third and fourth forces are the bargaining power of buyers and suppliers. Buyers may be highly concentrated, like Boeing and Airbus in the purchase of large aircraft engines, or extremely fragmented, like the restaurants that are customers of wholesale grocery companies. If industry capacity approximately equals or exceeds demand, concentrated buyers can force price concessions that reduce incumbent profitability. On the other hand, fragmented buyers have little bargaining power unless excess capacity and inventory overhang persist.

Unique suppliers may also reduce industry profitability. The Coca-Cola Company establishes exclusive franchise arrangements with independent bottlers. No other supplier can provide the secret ingredients in the concentrate syrup. Bottler profitability is therefore rather low. In contrast, Coke's own suppliers are numerous. Many potential sugar and flavouring manufacturers would like to win the Coca-Cola account, and the syrup inputs are nonunique commodities. These factors raise the likely profitability of the concentrate manufacturers because of the lack of power among their suppliers.

Finally, buyers and suppliers will have more bargaining power and reduce firm profitability when they possess more outside alternatives and can credibly threaten to vertically integrate into the industry.

Intensity of Rivalrous Tactics

In the global economy, few companies can establish and maintain dominance in anything beyond niche markets. Reverse-engineering of products, imitation of advertising images, and offshore production at low cost imply that a firm cannot hope to rid itself of competitors. Instead, to sustain profitability in such a setting, companies must avoid intense rivalries and elicit passive, more cooperative responses from close competitors. The intensity of the rivalry in an industry depends on several factors: industry concentration, the degree of price competition, switching costs, the presence of exit barriers, the industry growth rate, and the ratio of fixed to total cost (termed the *cost fixity*) in the typical cost structure.

What firms and what products offer close substitutes for potential customers in the relevant market determines the degree of industry concentration. One measure of industry concentration is the sum of the market shares of the four largest or eight largest firms in an industry. The larger the market shares and the smaller the number of competitors, the more interdependence each firm will perceive, and the less intense the rivalry. For example, because Titleist and Spalding dominate the golf ball market, the rivalrous intensity is less than in the fragmented golf club business.

Sustainable profitability is increased by tactics that focus on nonprice rather than price competition. Airlines are more profitable when they can avoid price wars and focus their competition for passengers on service quality—e.g., delivery reliability, change order responsiveness, and schedule convenience. But airline flights between major cities provide generic transportation with nearly identical service quality and departure frequency. Consequently, fare wars are frequent, and the profitability of these routes is therefore low. In contrast, long-standing rivals Coca-Cola and Pepsi have never discounted their cola concentrates. This absence of "gainshare discounting" and a diminished focus on price competition tactics in general increases the profitability of the concentrate business.

Sometimes price versus nonprice competition simply reflects the lack of product differentiation available in commodity-like markets (e.g., in selling cement). However, the incidence of price competition is also determined in part by the cost structure prevalent in the industry. Where fixed costs as a percentage of total costs are high, margins will tend to be larger. If so, firms are tempted to fight tooth and nail for incremental

EXAMPLE

PRICE COMPETITION IN SOFT DRINKS*

For more information, go to **www.cott.com**.

Soft drinks are marketed through several distribution channels at different prices. Shelf slots in the store channels are full, and bottlers compete on stocking services and retailer rebates for prime shelf space and vending machine locations in an attempt to grow their brands. With 34 percent and 32 percent market shares in the stores, the Coca-Cola- and PepsiCo-owned bottlers attempt to avoid head-to-head price competition, which would simply lower profits for both firms, and instead seek predictable patterns of company-sponsored once-every-other-week discounts. Where independent beverage resellers have established a practice of persistent gainshare discounting, the Coca-Cola Company and PepsiCo have often attempted to purchase the franchises and replace them with company-owned bottlers. Vending operations are very high margin

businesses, and PepsiCo and Coca-Cola increasingly service vending machines directly from their company-owned bottlers. To date, little price competition has emerged in the vending channel, in part because independents must purchase from exclusive franchise bottlers in their areas.

Supermarket chains have discovered that their own discounted brands of carbonated soft drinks, such as President's Choice, can be quite profitable. Accordingly they have increased the allocation of shelf space to their own brands. Many of these supermarket chains in North America and the United Kingdom are supplied by the Cott Corporation. Cott is a Canadian firm that is the world's leading supplier of such private brand soft drinks. This trend has led to some erosion of the market shares for both Coke and Pepsi over the last decade.

* Based on *Cola Wars Continue*, Harvard Business School Case Publishing, 1994.

customers because every additional unit sale represents a substantial contribution to covering the fixed costs. Gainshare discounting will therefore tend to increase, the greater the fixed cost is.

Barriers to exit usually increase the intensity of rivalry. If remote plants specific to a particular line of products (e.g., aluminum smelting plants) are nonredeployable, tactics will be more aggressive because no competitor can fully recover its sunk cost should margins collapse. Trucking companies, on the other hand, own very redeployable assets. If a trucking company attacks its rivals, encounters aggressive retaliation, then fails and must liquidate its assets, the owners can hope to receive nearly the full value of the economic working life remaining in their trucks. As a result, competitive tactics in the trucking industry are not as effective in threatening rivals.

Finally, industry demand growth can influence the intensity of rivalry. When sales to established customers are increasing and new customers are appearing in the market, rival firms are often content to maintain market share and realize high profitability. When demand growth declines, competitive tactics sharpen in many industries, especially if capacity planning has failed to anticipate the decline. For example, furniture companies discount steeply when housing demand slows.

The Myth of Market Share

In summary, the key to profitability in many businesses is to design a strategy that reduces the threat of substitutes, the power of buyers and suppliers, and the threat of entry. Then, firms must adopt tactics and elicit tactical responses from their rivals that do not erode the profit potential in their effective business strategy. This often means forsaking gainshare discounting and other aggressive tactics that would spiral the industry into price wars.

More generally, discounting and excessive promotions designed to grab market share are seldom a source of long-term profitability and often result in lower capitalized value. 7-Up doubled and tripled its market share in the late 1970s largely because of discounting. Profits declined, and the company was eventually acquired by Cadbury Schweppes.

After the initial penetration of a new product or new technology into a relevant market, market share should never become an end in itself. Increasing market share is the means to achieve scale economies and learning curve-based cost advantages. But additional share points at any cost almost always mean a reduction in profits, not the reverse.

Goals in the Public Sector and the Not-for-Profit Enterprise

The value-maximization objective developed for private sector firms is not an appropriate objective in the public sector or in not-for-profit (NFP) organizations.[8] These organizations pursue a different set of objectives because of the nature of the good or service they supply and the manner in which they are funded.

Three characteristics of NFP organizations distinguish them from for-profit enterprises and influence decision making in the enterprise. First, no one possesses a right to receive profit or surpluses in an NFP enterprise. The absence of a profit motive can have a serious impact on the incentive to be efficient. Second, NFP enterprises are exempt from taxes on corporate income. Finally, many NFP enterprises benefit from the fact that donations to them are tax-deductible. These tax benefits give NFP enterprises an advantage when competing with for-profit enterprises.

---

[8] This section draws heavily on Burton A. Weisbrod, *The Nonprofit Economy* (Cambridge, MA: Harvard University Press, 1988).

THE BIG BLUE BOOBOO*

IBM is frequently called "Big Blue." IBM was the "smart" second mover to enter the personal computer market in 1981. Since it was competing with Apple, the first mover, IBM decided to adopt an innovative strategy of using off-the-shelf components to assemble the hardware as well as third-party software (Apple still follows its proprietary strategy). The operating systems for the IBM PC, MS DOS, and some of the application software were supplied by Microsoft.

Because of IBM's reputation, many businesses that had refused to consider Apple computers started to use personal computers instead of or in addition to the large mainframe computers that were IBM's principal product. The PC industry grew very rapidly. Apple's share of the market fell, and IBM initially had more than 50 percent of the market. By 2002, however, IBM had only 5 percent of the PC market. The largest market share, 31 percent, belonged to Dell, an innovative company that builds computers to customer order, while Hewlett Packard, a more traditional build-to-inventory company's share was 21 percent.

When IBM announced in late 2004 that it wanted to sell its PC business, some people assumed that it was due to off-shoring. However, since both Dell and HP build computers from components, it is obvious that IBM's problem is not that there are lower cost competitors—it is simply that IBM's competitors have been better innovators.

* Based on Paul Kedrosky, "Big Blue Booboo," *Financial Post*, December 4, 2004, p. FP 11.

Not-for-profit organizations include performing arts groups, museums, libraries, hospitals, churches, volunteer organizations, cooperatives, credit unions, labour unions, professional societies, foundations, and fraternal organizations. Some of these organizations offer services to a group of clients, such as the patients of a hospital. Others provide services primarily to members, such as the members of a country club or credit union. Finally, some NFP organizations produce public benefits, as in the case of a local symphony or theatre company.

Public sector (government) agencies tend to provide services with a significant public-good character. In contrast to private goods like bite-sized candy bars, **public goods** may be consumed by more than one person at the same time and entail high transaction costs in excluding those who do not pay. Examples of public goods include national defence and flood control. If a flood control levee is constructed, those behind it cannot be excluded from its protection even if they refuse to contribute to the cost.

Even if one could charge market prices, the indivisibility in consumption of a public good makes the incremental cost (and therefore the efficient price) of another participant quite low. Some goods, such as recreational facilities and the performing arts, have both private- and public-good characteristics. For example, concerts and parks may be shared (within limits) and are partially nonexcludable since quality performing arts and recreational facilities convey prestige and quality-of-life benefits to the entire community.[9] The more costly the exclusion, the more likely the good or service will be provided by the public sector rather than the private sector. Portrait artists and personal fitness trainers

Public Goods
Goods that may be consumed by more than one person at the same time with little or no extra cost, and for which it is expensive or impossible to exclude those who do not pay.

---

[9] William J. Baumol and W. G. Bowen, *Performing Arts: The Economic Dilemma* (Brookfield, VT: Ashgate Publishing Co., 1993).

Managing in a Global Competitive Economy

For more information on international trade and the balance of payments, go to **www.statcan.ca**.

North American manufacturers face serious economic challenges from firms located in Japan, Korea, and other countries in the Far East, as well as those in the European Community. As other economies have developed and trade barriers have been lowered, North American firms have found themselves facing increasingly intense competition from abroad. While the U.S. foreign trade deficit (i.e., the dollar value of exports minus imports) grew during the five years ending in 2004, Canada had a trade surplus during this same period.

The study of managerial economics is important for future managers who face the growing challenge of global competition. Often, Canadian managers can learn from the successful experiences of their foreign competitors. For example, the just-in-time inventory management techniques and quality management practices that have exploded in popularity over the past decade have been adapted from successful Japanese firms. Managers who face the challenge of global competition must pay even closer attention to the principles of efficient resource allocation that are at the core of managerial economics. Our global competitors understand these principles and, in many cases, have applied them effectively to enhance their competitive position.

Chapter 12 addresses international managerial economics in more detail. Throughout the text, we will highlight specific issues and opportunities that face managers in a global, competitive economy.

offer pay-as-you-go private fee arrangements. On the other hand, chamber music fans and tennis court users often organize consumption-sharing and cost-sharing clubs, and open-air symphony concerts and large parks usually necessitate some public financing.

Not-for-Profit Objectives

For NFP organizations that rely heavily on external contributions, the overriding objective is to satisfy current and prospective contributors. It is common to find an NFP organization that seeks to satisfy its contributors by (1) efficiently managing its resources, (2) increasing its capacity to supply high-quality goods or services, and (3) providing a rewarding work environment for its administrators. As reliance on outside contributors lessens, the other objectives gain importance to the organization.

Several organizational objectives have been suggested for the NFP enterprise. These include:

1. Maximization of the quantity and quality of output subject to a break-even budget constraint.
2. Utility maximization of the administrators.
3. Maximization of cash flows.
4. Maximization of the utility (satisfaction) of contributors.

The Efficiency Objective

Whatever set of objectives the organization decides to pursue, these objectives should be pursued in the most resource-efficient fashion possible. The model that has been developed to provide a framework for the allocation of public and NFP resources among competing uses primarily has been the benefit–cost analysis model. This model is the analogue to the capital budgeting model in the private sector. Benefits and costs

Executive Compensation and Shareholder Wealth Maximization

How should corporations structure the compensation (i.e., salary and incentives) of officers and directors to motivate these managers to make decisions that maximize shareholder wealth? One approach, such as the Stuart Energy example cited earlier in the Managerial Challenge, is to offer managers cash bonuses based on the overall performance of the firm or division in the firm. Another approach is to offer executives options to buy company shares at some predetermined price. If the firm prospers, then both the owners and managers reap the rewards of higher share prices. However, this approach does not always lead to a long-term wealth-maximization perspective on the part of managers. Instead of retaining their ownership interest in the firm, executives sometimes exercise the options and sell the shares relatively quickly.

Several corporations have tried an alternative approach to getting officers and directors to think of themselves as owners, rather than as hired help, by requiring (or strongly encouraging) them to own company shares. Another approach to encourage officers and directors to act in the interests of shareholders—which has not yet gained widespread use—is to compensate them with company shares. The growth of performance-based compensation plans is an attempt to realign the interests of managers with those of shareholders. This helps avoid costly inefficiencies that can arise because of a divergence of interests. Executive compensation is further discussed in Chapter 10 and Web Chapter 17.

associated with investments are estimated and discounted by an appropriate discount rate, and projects are evaluated on the basis of the magnitude of the discounted benefits in relation to the costs. Because government and NFP organization spending is normally constrained by a budget ceiling, the criterion actually used in evaluating expenditures for any public purpose may be one of the following:

1. Maximize benefits for given costs.
2. Minimize costs while achieving a fixed level of benefits.
3. Maximize net benefits (benefits minus costs).

Although **benefit–cost analysis** can serve as a guide to a more efficient allocation of resources by a public agency or an NFP organization, such analysis typically does not consider the effect of a proposed project on income distribution. Concern for these matters must be introduced at a later stage in the analysis, generally through the political process.

Benefit–Cost Analysis
A resource-allocation model that can be used by public sector and not-for-profit organizations to evaluate programs or investments on the basis of the magnitude of the discounted costs and benefits.

Summary

■ *Managerial economics* is the application of economic theory and analytical tools to decision-making problems faced by managers of private, not-for-profit, and public organizations. These decision-making problems are frequently international.

■ Managerial economics draws on microeconomic theory and macroeconomic models to assist managers in making optimal resource-allocation decisions.

- *Economic profit* is defined as the difference between *total revenues* and *total economic costs.* Economic costs include a normal rate of return on the capital contributed by the firm's owners.

- As an overall objective of the firm, the *shareholder wealth-maximization* model is very appealing. It is flexible enough to account for differential levels of risk and timing differences in the receipt of benefits and the incurring of future costs. Because shareholder wealth is defined in terms of the value of the common shares, this goal provides a precise measure of performance, which is free from the problems associated with using various accounting measures.

- Managers may not always behave in a manner consistent with the wealth-maximization objective. The costs associated with these deviations from the objective are often called *agency costs.*

- Shareholder wealth maximization implies forward-looking, long-run-oriented, dynamic strategies that anticipate change in a risky market environment. Managers can focus on maximizing the present value of the firm's cash flows.

- *Competitive strategy* entails an analysis of the firm's resource-based capabilities, the design of production processes that can secure sustainable competitive advantage, and the development of a road map for innovation.

- Types of strategic thinking include industry analysis, competitor analysis, strategic positioning, and identification of core competencies derived from resource-based capabilities.

- *Sustainable competitive advantage* arises from the pursuit of one of the three *generic strategies:* (1) *product differentiation,* (2) *cost leadership,* or (3) a *niche strategy.*

- A *relevant market* is a group of economic agents that interact with each other in a buyer–seller relationship. Relevant markets often have both spatial and product characteristics.

- The *five forces strategy model* identifies threat of substitutes, threat of entry, power of buyers, power of suppliers, and the intensity of rivalry as the determinants of sustainable incumbent profitability in a particular industry.

- The *threat of substitutes* depends on the number and closeness of substitutes as determined by the product development, advertising, brand-naming, and segmentation strategies of preexisting competitors.

- The *threat of entry* depends on the height of barriers to potential entrants, including capital requirements, economies of scale, absolute cost advantages, switching costs, access to distribution channels, and trade secrets and other difficult-to-imitate forms of product differentiation.

- The *bargaining power of buyers and suppliers* depends on their number, their size distribution, the relationship between industry capacity and industry demand, the uniqueness of the inputs, the potential for forward and backward integration, and the extent to which each party to the bargain has outside alternatives.

- The *intensity of rivalry* depends on the number and size distribution of sellers in the relevant market, the relative frequency of price versus nonprice competition, switching costs, the proportion of fixed to total cost, the barriers to exit, and the growth rate of industry demand.

- *Not-for-profit enterprises* exist to supply a good or service desired by their primary contributors. Public sector organizations often provide services having significant public-good characteristics. That is, they may be consumed by more than one person at a time with little additional cost, and the transaction cost of excluding those who do not pay exceeds the benefits that are derived by charging the efficient price.

- Regardless of their specific objectives, both public and private institutions should seek to furnish their goods or services in the most *resource-efficient manner.* The marginal decision rules from the profit-maximization model are often very valuable in this context.

Self-Test Exercise

Network television operating profit in 2000 at MTV was approximately triple that of the CBC or CTV. Provide a Porter five forces analysis of each type of network. Why is MTV so profitable relative to the others?

Exercises

1. Try to define, in as operational a manner as possible, the objectives that your university seeks to pursue.
   a. How may success in achieving these objectives be measured?
   b. To what extent do the objectives of various subunits of your university complement (or contradict) each other?
   c. Who are the major constituencies served by your university? What role do they play in the formation of these objectives?
   d. You may want to talk with some of your school's administrators and compare their views on the university's goals and objectives with your own.
2. In the context of the shareholder wealth-maximization model of the firm, what is the expected impact of each of the following events on the value of the firm?
   a. New foreign competitors enter the market.
   b. Strict pollution control requirements are implemented by the government.
   c. A previously nonunion workforce votes to unionize.
   d. The rate of inflation increases substantially.
   e. A major technological breakthrough is achieved by the firm, reducing its costs of production.
3. After the U.S. invasion of Iraq, the price of jet fuel used by airlines increased dramatically. As the CEO of Air Canada, you have been presented with the following options to deal with this problem:
   a. Raise airfares to offset cost increases.
   b. Reduce the number of flights per day in some markets.
   c. Make long-term contracts to buy jet fuel at a fixed price for the next two years and set airfares to a level that will cover these costs.

   Evaluate these options in the context of the text's decision-making model.
4. How would each of the following actions be expected to affect shareholder wealth?
   a. The Canadian firm Manulife takes over the U.S. firm John Hancock for $19.1 billion, making it the second-largest insurer in North America.
   b. General Motors offers large rebates to stimulate sales of its automobiles.
   c. Rising interest rates cause the required returns of shareholders to increase.
   d. Import restrictions are placed on Ford's Asian competitors.
   e. There is a sudden drop in the expected future rate of inflation.
   f. A new labour-saving machine is purchased by Maple Leaf Foods Inc. and results in the layoff of 300 employees.
5. The profitability of the leading cola syrup manufacturers, PepsiCo and Coca-Cola, and of the bottlers in the cola business is very different. PepsiCo and Coca-Cola enjoy an 81 percent operating profit as a percentage of sales. Bottlers experience only a 15 percent operating profit as a percentage of sales. Perform a Porter's five forces analysis that explains why one type of business is potentially so profitable relative to the other.

6. The costs of building a conventional hot-rolled steel mill have declined substantially as a result of the new mini-mill technology that requires only scrap metal, an electric furnace, and 300 workers rather than iron ore raw materials, enormous blast furnaces, rolling mills, reheating furnaces, and thousands of workers. What effect on the potential industry profitability would Porter's five forces framework suggest this new technology would have? Why?

CASE EXERCISES

REDUCING GREENHOUSE GASES

The U.N. Kyoto Protocol of December 1997 obligates Canada to reduce by approximately 25 percent the emission of carbon dioxide and other greenhouse gases between 2000 and 2010. Brazil, China, India, and Mexico were all exempted from the agreement. Explain the efficiency advantages of a tradable pollution permit alternative to Kyoto's regulatory quota system.[10]

REFORMING THE FORMER SOVIET ECONOMY

The failure of the state-controlled, centrally planned economies of the Eastern European countries and of the former Soviet Union to produce adequate quantities of high-quality products that are desired by consumers has led to major economic and political reform in these countries. East Germany ceased to exist as an independent nation–state in a little over one year and was merged into a united Germany in late 1990. Economic and political pressures have led to major changes in the organization of the economies (and governments) of Hungary, Poland, Rumania, and the Soviet Union itself.

The failure of state-controlled economies that did not permit the private ownership of property or capital and did not permit competition among profit-seeking enterprises can be viewed as a reflection of a major agency problem. Plant managers had little to gain from more efficient operations. There was neither the pressure from competitors nor from potential takeovers by a more efficient group of owner–managers, as is true in Western economies. Furthermore, as state-chartered monopolies, there was no risk of failure of the enterprise.

The Soviet Union finally collapsed under the pressure of a failed economic system and political reforms that permitted open criticism of the government. Boris Yeltsin, president of Russia at the time, quickly moved to reform the economic system. Price controls were lifted on most goods and services, state subsidies were eliminated, and steps were taken that should lead to the international convertibility of the Russian currency, the ruble. These steps were designed to increase the accountability of managers to the new owners, add an important element of competition to the former Soviet economy, and increase the efficiency of economic enterprises in the former Soviet Union. This ambitious plan to privatize the former Soviet economy raises a host of interesting challenges for managers.

Questions

1. When state-owned enterprises are sold, how should their value be established? Should the value be based on the cost of the assets in place, the past earning power of the enterprise, or the future earning potential in a competitive economy?

[10] Based on "Letting the Free Market Clear the Air," *BusinessWeek*, November 6, 2000, pp. 200–204.

2. How can the future earning capacity of privatized enterprises be estimated?

3. What long-term effect do you think the lifting of price controls will have on inflation in the former Soviet Union?

4. What effect do you think the privatization of currently state-run enterprises will have on the employment levels in these enterprises in the near term? In the longer term?

REFORMING HEALTH CARE: LESSONS FROM SWITZERLAND

Most people and their governments desire that necessary medical care be provided to all residents without regard to the individual's capacity to pay for the health care. There is no consensus, however, on how the economy should pay for health care. Canada has a universal, comprehensive, portable, accessible, and publicly administered health care system. The United States is one of the very few developed countries that does not have a universal health care system. The U.S. system is primarily privately financed by insurance companies that pay the private health care providers. Retirees and the indigent in the United States do benefit from publicly funded insurance plans, Medicare and Medicaid. In Mexico, health care is separated into public and private sectors. In the public sector, employed persons receive medical care similar to that in Canada, while unemployed people are confronted with a system that closely resembles that of the United States. The private sector health care in Mexico is for the elite who can afford the high fees charged for the excellent services they receive. Thus, the three NAFTA countries do not agree on how to pay for health care. Can we learn from the Swiss?

In Switzerland, *krankenkasse* (health insurance) is mandatory. Swiss residents can choose their own insurance from competing public and private sector plans. People with lower income receive an income supplement, not an insurance subsidy, so they can still choose the plan they prefer. Insurers set their own premiums based on actual health care costs. Monthly premiums range from $100 to $400 and are tax-deductible. Thus, the Swiss system makes the patient a source of profit for the private providers of the health care services. Waiting times for medical procedures are not a significant issue, but have been increasing.

Switzerland also offers better access to key technology. The Swiss have 12.9 MRI machines per million population, compared with only 3.5 in Canada. They have 3.5 physicians per thousand population, compared with only 2.1 in Canada. They also have 4.1 acute-care hospital beds per thousand population, compared with only 3.2 in Canada. Swiss life expectancy is also greater than that of Canadians—an average of 80 years, compared with only 79 years here. However, Swiss health care costs are higher: 11 percent there compared with only 10 percent here.[11] Is the extra year of life worth it?

Questions

1. Is it feasible for a country such as Canada to split health care purchase from health care provision? That is, could we have public insurance and privately provided health care? Discuss.

2. What effect do you think the privatization of currently provincially run hospitals would have on the employment levels in these enterprises in the near term?

3. Can you suggest any incentives that might improve the Canadian health care system?

[11] Based on George Koch and John Weissenberger, "A Swiss Lesson in Health Reform," *National Post*, July 22, 2004, p. A14.

CHAPTER 2

Review of Fundamental Economic Concepts

Chapter Preview

Among the most important fundamental economic concepts are marginal analysis, net present value, the meaning and measurement of risk, tradeoffs between risk and return, markets, demand and supply, and equilibrium.

Marginal analysis tools are central when a decision maker is seeking to optimize some objective, such as profits or shareholder wealth. The net present value concept provides the linkage between the long-term decisions made by a firm and the shareholder wealth-maximization objective. Because most economic decisions involve an element of risk, the meaning and measurement of risk is an important concept for managers. Risk-return analysis is important to an understanding of the many tradeoffs that managers must make as they plan new products, expand capacity, or change prices.

Markets make possible the exchange of goods and services. Demand is the amount of a good or service that consumers are willing and able to purchase. Supply is the amount of a good or service that producers are willing and able to offer for sale. In free markets, demand and supply interact to establish prices that allocate resources to their best uses. Equilibrium is achieved when the quantity demanded equals the quantity supplied.

Web Chapters 18 and 19 and Web Appendix 18A (all of which can be accessed on the Nelson website for this book at www.mcguigan.nelson.com) provide further discussion of long-term investment analysis, decision making under risk and uncertainty, and the time value of money for those who wish to go beyond the coverage of these topics in this chapter.

Learning Objectives

After studying this chapter, you should be able to:

1. Understand that *marginal analysis* compares the additional (marginal) costs and additional (marginal) benefits associated with a proposed action. If the marginal benefits exceed the marginal costs, the action should be taken.

2. Define the *net present value* (NPV) of an investment.

3. Identify *risk* and how it can be measured either by the *standard deviation* (absolute measure) or *coefficient of variation* (relative measure).

4. Understand that a positive relationship exists between *risk* and *required rates of return* on securities and physical asset investments.

5. Explain the importance of *markets, demand and supply*, and *market equilibrium* to effective managerial decision making.

 6. (Web Appendix 2A) Illustrate how decision analysis finds the action that optimizes (that is, maximizes or minimizes) the value of an objective function.

Airline Revenue Management*

Airlines face highly cyclical demand. Demand also fluctuates day to day. One of the ways that airlines cope with random demand is through revenue management techniques. Revenue or "yield" management is an integrated demand-management, order-booking, and capacity-planning process that focusses on marginal analysis.

To win orders in a service industry *without slashing prices* requires that companies create perceived value for segmented classes of differentiated customers. Business travellers on airlines, for example, want and will pay for last-minute responsiveness to their change orders. Other business travellers demand exceptional delivery reliability and on-time performance. In contrast, most vacation excursion travellers want commodity-like service at rock-bottom prices. Although only 15–20 percent of most airlines' seats are in the business segment, 65–75 percent of the profit contribution on a typical flight comes from this group. The problem is that airline capacity must be planned and allocated well in advance of customer arrivals—often before demand is fully known—yet unsold inventory perishes at the moment of departure. This same management challenge faces consulting firms, TV stations, and printing businesses, all of which must acquire and schedule capacity before the demands for next week's crisis management team, Thursday's network TV ads, or the afternoon press run are fully known.

One approach to minimizing unsold inventory and yet capturing all last-minute high-profit business is to auction off capacity to the highest bidder. In airlines (like many other service businesses), prices cannot be adjusted quickly as the moment of departure approaches. Instead, revenue managers employ large historical databases to predict segmented customer demand in light of current arrivals on the reservation system. They then compare the expected marginal profit from holding in reserve another seat in business class in anticipation of last-minute demand to the expected marginal profit from accepting another reservation request in a discount class.

Suppose on the 9 A.M. Toronto to Chicago flight next Monday, 63 of the 170 seats have been protected for first-class, business-class, and full coach fares, but only 50 have been sold. The remaining 107 seats have been authorized for sale at a discount. A new reservation request arrives in the discount class, which is presently full. Should the airline reallocate capacity and take on the new discount passenger? The answer is "maybe." It depends on the relative profit margins from each class and the predicted probability today, three days before departure, of excess demand (beyond 63 seats) next Monday in the business classes.[†]

---

* Based on Robert Cross, *Revenue Management* (New York: Broadway Books, 1995), and Frederick Harris and Peter Peacock, "Hold My Place Please: Yield Management Improves Capacity Allocation Guesswork," *Marketing Management,* Fall 1995, pp. 34–46.
[†] Web Appendix 9A explains how these demand assessments take into account the likely incidence of cancellations and no-shows—i.e., an optimal level of overbooking.

Talus Solutions specializes in revenue management. Visit its website at **www.talussolutions. com** for case studies and industry information.

If the $721 full coach fare has a $500 profit margin and the $155 discount fare has a $100 profit margin, the seat in question should not be reallocated from business to discount customers when the probability of "stocking out" in business is greater than 0.20. For example, if the probability is 0.25, the expected marginal profit from holding an empty seat for another potential business customer is $125, whereas the marginal profit from selling that seat to the discount customer is only $100. Even an advance-payment, no-refund seat request from the discount class should be refused. Every firm has some viable orders that should be refused. Excess capacity in business class is not "idle capacity" but rather a predictable revenue opportunity waiting to happen.

In this chapter, we introduce the methods of marginal analysis that can be used to solve an airline's seat allocation decision problem. Chapter 9 discusses the price discrimination analysis that underlies revenue management, and Web Appendix 9A applies the techniques of revenue management.

Marginal Analysis

Marginal Analysis
A basis for making various economic decisions that analyzes the additional (marginal) benefits derived from a particular decision and compares them with the additional (marginal) costs incurred.

Marginal analysis is one of the most useful concepts of economic decision making. Resource-allocation decisions typically are expressed in terms of the marginal conditions that must be satisfied to attain an optimal solution. The familiar profit-maximization rule for the firm of setting output at the point where "marginal cost equals marginal revenue" is one such example. Long-term investment decisions (capital expenditures) also are made using marginal analysis decision rules. If the expected return from an investment project (that is, the *marginal return* to the firm) exceeds the cost of funds that must be acquired to finance the project (the *marginal cost* of capital), then the project should be undertaken. Following this important marginal decision rule leads to the maximization of shareholder wealth.

In the marginal analysis framework, resource-allocation decisions are made by comparing the marginal (or incremental) benefits of a change in the level of an activity with the marginal (or incremental) costs of the change. *Marginal benefit* is defined as the change in total benefits that are derived from undertaking some economic activity, such as additional shipbuilding at Davie Shipyard. For example, marginal revenue (a benefit) is the additional revenue derived from producing and selling one more ship. Similarly, *marginal cost* is defined as the change in total costs that occurs from undertaking some economic activity, such as the production of an additional ship design. Recall from Chapter 1 that total (economic) costs include opportunity costs, and therefore may not necessarily always be equal to the cash outlays alone.[1]

A change in the level of an economic activity is desirable if the marginal benefits exceed the marginal costs. This is equivalent to saying that the increase in total revenues, for example, exceeds the increase in total costs. Therefore, in decisions involving the expansion of an economic activity, the optimal level occurs at the point where the marginal benefits are equal to the marginal costs. If we define *net marginal return* as the *difference* between marginal benefits and marginal costs, then an equivalent optimality condition is that the level of the activity should be increased to the point where the net marginal return is zero.

---

[1] The concept of economic cost is examined in more detail in Chapter 5.

MARGINAL ANALYSIS AND INVESTMENT DECISIONS: ATI CORPORATION

The investment (capital budgeting) decision problem facing a typical firm, such as ATI Corporation, can be used to illustrate the application of marginal analysis decision rules. The firm has the following schedule of potential investment projects, all assumed to be of equal risk, available to it.

Project	Investment Required ($ Million)	Expected Rate of Return	Cumulative Investment ($ Million)
A	$25.0	27.0	$25.0
B	15.0	24.0	40.0
C	40.0	21.0	80.0
D	35.0	18.0	115.0
E	12.0	15.0	127.0
F	20.0	14.0	147.0
G	18.0	13.0	165.0
H	13.0	11.0	178.0
I	7.0	8.0	185.0

ATI has estimated the cost of acquiring the funds needed to finance these investment projects as shown in the following table.

Block of Funds ($ Million)	Cost of Capital (%)	Cumulative Funds Raised ($ Million)
First $50.0	10.0	$50.0
Next $25.0	10.5	75.0
Next $40.0	11.0	115.0
Next $50.0	12.2	165.0
Next $20.0	14.5	185.0

The expected rate of return on the projects listed above can be thought of as the marginal (or incremental) return available to the firm as it undertakes each additional investment project. Similarly, the cost-of-capital schedule may be thought of as the marginal cost of acquiring the needed funds.

Following the marginal analysis rules means that ATI should invest in additional projects as long as the expected rate of return on the project exceeds the marginal cost of capital funds needed to finance the project. Project A, which offers an expected return of 27 percent and requires an outlay of $25 million, is acceptable because the marginal return exceeds the marginal cost of capital (10.0 percent for the first $50 million of funds raised by the firm). In fact, an examination of the tables indicates that projects A through G all meet the marginal analysis test because the marginal return from each of these projects exceeds the marginal cost of capital funds needed to finance these projects. In contrast, projects H and I should not be undertaken because they offer returns of 11 and 8 percent, respectively, compared with a marginal cost of capital of 14.5 percent for the $20 million in funds needed to finance these projects.

In summary, marginal analysis instructs decision makers to determine the additional (marginal) costs and additional (marginal) benefits associated with a proposed action. *Only if the marginal benefits exceed the marginal costs* (that is, if net marginal benefits are positive) should the action be taken.[2]

Total, Marginal, and Average Relationships

Economic relationships can be presented using tabular, graphic, and algebraic frameworks. Let us first use a tabular presentation. Suppose that the total profit, π_T, of a firm is a function of the number of units of output produced, Q, as shown in columns 1 and 2 of Table 2.1. Marginal profit, which represents the change in total profit resulting from a one-unit increase in output, is shown in column 3 of the table. (A Δ is used to represent a "change" in some variable.) The marginal profit $\Delta\pi(Q)$ of any level of output Q is calculated by taking the difference between the total profit at this level $\pi_T(Q)$ and at one unit below this level $\pi_T(Q - 1)$.[3] In comparing the marginal and total profit functions, we note that for increasing output levels, the marginal profit values remain positive as long as the total profit function is increasing. Only when the total profit function begins decreasing—that is, at $Q = 10$ units—does the marginal profit become negative.

The average profit function values $\pi_A(Q)$, shown in column 4 of Table 2.1, are obtained by dividing the total profit figure $\pi_T(Q)$ by the output level Q. In comparing the marginal and the average profit function values, we see that the average profit function $\pi_A(Q)$ is increasing as long as the marginal profit is greater than the average profit; that is, up to $Q = 7$ units. Beyond an output level of $Q = 7$ units, the marginal profit is less than the average profit and the average profit function values are decreasing.

By examining the total profit function $\pi_T(Q)$ in Table 2.1, we see that profit is maximized at an output level of $Q = 9$ units. Given that the objective is to maximize total profit, then the optimal output decision would be to produce and sell 9 units. If the

Table 2.1	Total, Marginal, and Average Profit Relationships		
(1) **Number of Units of** **Output Per Unit of Time** Q	**(2)** **Total Profit** $\pi_T(Q)$ **($)**	**(3)** **Marginal Profit** $\Delta\pi(Q) = \pi_T(Q) - \pi_T(Q-1)$ **($/Unit)**	**(4)** **Average Profit** $\pi_A(Q) = \pi_T(Q)/Q$ **($/Unit)**
0	−200	—	—
1	−150	50	−150.00
2	−25	125	−12.50
3	200	225	66.67
4	475	275	118.75
5	775	300	155.00
6	1,075	300	179.17
7	1,325	250	189.29
8	1,475	150	184.38
9	1,500	25	166.67
10	1,350	−150	135.00

[2] Strictly speaking, an action may also be undertaken if marginal benefits equal marginal costs. In this case, the firm's change in profit will be just equal to zero, and the manager will be indifferent to taking the action.

[3] Web Appendix 2A expands on the idea that the total profit function can be maximized by identifying the level of activity at which the marginal profit function goes to zero.

marginal analysis decision rule discussed earlier in this section is used, the same (optimal) decision is obtained. Applying the rule to this problem, the firm would expand production as long as the *net* marginal return—that is, marginal revenue minus marginal cost (marginal profit)—is positive. From column 3 of Table 2.1, we can see that the marginal profit is positive for output levels up to $Q = 9$. Therefore, the marginal profit decision rule would indicate that 9 units should be produced—the same decision that was obtained from the total profit function.

The relationships among the total, marginal, and average profit functions and the optimal output decision also can be represented graphically. A set of *continuous* profit functions, analogous to those presented in Table 2.1 for discrete integer values of output (Q), is shown in Figure 2.1. At the break-even output level Q_1, both total profits and average profits are zero. The marginal profit function, which equals the *slope* of the total profit function, takes on its maximum value at an output of Q_2 units. This point corresponds to the *inflection point*. Below the inflection point, total profits are increasing at an increasing rate, and hence marginal profits are increasing. Above the inflection point, up to an output level Q_4, total profits are increasing at a decreasing rate and consequently marginal profits are decreasing. The average profit function,

FIGURE 2.1

Total, Average, and Marginal Profit Functions

At output Q_1, break-even for total profit corresponds to zero average profit. At output Q_2, the inflection point for total profit corresponds to maximum marginal profit. At output Q_3, the tangency point A for total profit corresponds to identical marginal and average profits. At output Q_4, maximum total profit corresponds to zero marginal profit.

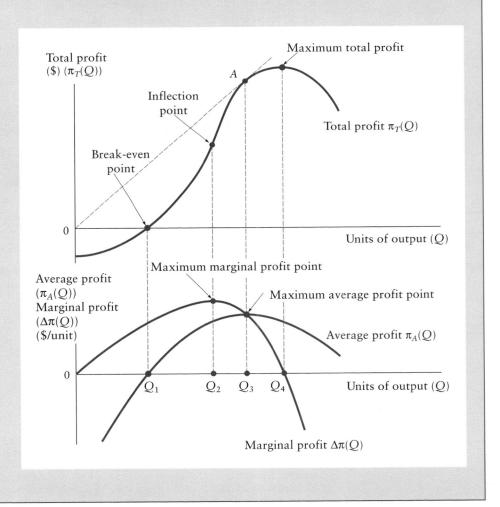

which represents the slope of a straight line drawn from the origin 0 to each point on the total profit function, takes on its maximum value at an output of Q_3 units. The average profit necessarily equals the marginal profit at this point. This follows because the slope of the $0A$ line, which defines the average profit, is also equal to the slope of the total profit function at point A, which defines the marginal profit. Finally, total profit is maximized at an output of Q_4 units, where marginal profit equals 0. Beyond Q_4, the total profit function is decreasing, and consequently the marginal profit function takes on negative values.

The Net Present Value Concept

To achieve the objective of shareholder wealth maximization, a set of appropriate decision rules must be specified. We just saw that the decision rule of setting *marginal revenue (benefit) equal to marginal cost ($MR = MC$)* provides a framework for making many important resource-allocation decisions. The $MR = MC$ rule is best suited for situations when the costs and benefits occur at approximately the same time. Many economic decisions require that costs be incurred immediately but result in a stream of benefits over several future time periods. In these cases, the *net present value (NPV) rule* provides appropriate guidance for decision makers.

Determining the Net Present Value of an Investment

To understand the NPV rule, consider the following situation. You have just inherited $1 million. Your financial advisor has suggested that you use these funds to purchase a piece of land near a proposed new highway interchange. Your advisor, who is also an advisor to several provincial politicians, is certain that the interchange will be built and that in one year the value of this land will increase to $1.2 million. Hence, you believe initially that this is a riskless investment. At the end of one year, you plan to sell the land. You are being asked to invest $1 million today in the anticipation of receiving $1.2 million a year from today, or a profit of $200,000. You wonder whether this profit represents a sufficient return on your investment.

You feel it is important to recognize that there is a one-year difference between the time you make your outlay of $1 million and the time you receive $1.2 million from the sale of the land. A return of $1.2 million received one year from today must be worth less than $1.2 million today, because you could invest your $1 million today to earn interest over the coming year. *A dollar received in the future is worth less than a dollar in hand today, because a dollar today can be invested to earn a return immediately.* Therefore, to compare a dollar received in the future with a dollar in hand today, it is necessary to multiply the future dollar by a *discount factor* that reflects the alternative investment opportunities that are available.

Instead of investing your $1 million in the land venture, you are aware that you could also invest in a one-year Canada bond that currently offers a return of 5 percent. The 5 percent return represents the return (the opportunity cost) foregone by investing in the land project. The 5 percent rate also can be thought of as the compensation to an investor who agrees to postpone receiving a cash return for one year. The appropriate discount factor, also called a *present value interest factor (PVIF)*, is equal to

$$PVIF = \frac{1}{(1 + i)}$$

where i is the compensation for postponing receipt of a cash return for one year. The **present value (PV_0)** of an amount received one year in the future (FV_1) is equal to that amount times the discount factor, or

(2.1)
$$PV_0 = FV_1 \times (PVIF)$$

For more details on calculating present values, see Web Appendix 18A.

Present Value
The value today of a future amount of money or a series of future payments evaluated at the appropriate discount rate.

In the case of the land project, the present value of the promised $1.2 million expected to be received in one year is equal to

$$PV_0 = \$1.2 \text{ million}\left(\frac{1}{1 + 0.05}\right) = \$1,142,857$$

If you invested $1,142,857 today to earn 5 percent for the coming year, you would have $1.2 million at the end of the year. You are clearly better off with the proposed land investment (assuming that it really is as riskless as the Canada bond investment). How much better off are you?

The answer to this question is at the heart of NPV calculations. The land investment project is worth $1,142,857 today to an investor who demands a 5 percent return on this type of investment. You, however, have been able to acquire this investment for only $1,000,000. Thus your present wealth by undertaking this investment has increased by $142,857 (the $1,142,857 present value of the projected investment opportunity payoffs minus the required initial investment of $1,000,000). The NPV of this investment is $142,857. In general, the **net present value** of an investment is equal to

$$(2.2) \qquad \text{NPV} = \text{Present value of future returns} - \text{Initial outlay}$$

This example was simplified by assuming that the returns from the investment were received exactly one year from the date of the initial outlay. The NPV rule can be generalized to cover returns received over any number of future time periods. See Web Chapter 18 for further development of the net present value concept.

Net Present Value and Shareholder Wealth Maximization

The NPV of an investment made by a firm represents the contribution of that investment to the value of the firm and, accordingly, to the wealth of shareholders. The net present value concept is used to evaluate the cash flows generated from the firm's activities. Hence, the NPV concept plays a central role in the achievement of shareholder wealth maximization. Recall from Chapter 1 that shareholder wealth maximization is the overall objective of the firm.

Market Efficiency A central theme of much of the financial economics thinking and research has been the *efficiency of the capital markets*. The more efficient capital markets are, the more likely it is that resources will find their highest value (risk-adjusted) uses.

In an efficient capital market, share prices provide an unbiased estimate of the true value of an enterprise. Share prices reflect a present value estimate of the firm's *expected cash flows*, evaluated at an appropriate *required rate of return*. The required rate of return is determined by conditions in the financial markets, including the supply of funds from savers, the investment demand for funds, and expectations regarding future inflation rates. The required rate of return on a security also depends on the seniority of the security, the maturity of that security, the business and financial risk of the firm issuing the security, the risk of default, and the marketability of the security. The *efficiency of the capital markets* is the important "glue" that connects the present value of a firm's net cash flows—discounted at the appropriate risk-adjusted required rate of return—to shareholder wealth as measured by the market value of a company's common shares.

Sources of Positive Net Present Value Projects

What causes some projects to have a positive NPV and others to have a negative NPV? When product and factor markets are other than perfectly competitive, it is possible for a firm to earn above-normal profits (economic rents) that result in positive net present value projects. The reasons why these above-normal profits may be available arise from conditions that define each type of product and factor market and distinguish it from a perfectly competitive market. These reasons include the following barriers to entry and other factors:

1. Buyer preferences for established brand names.
2. Ownership or control of favoured distribution systems (such as exclusive auto dealerships or airline hubs).
3. Patent control of superior product designs or production techniques.
4. Exclusive ownership of superior natural resource deposits.
5. Inability of new firms to acquire necessary factors of production (management, labour, equipment).
6. Superior access to financial resources at lower costs (economies of scale in attracting capital).
7. Economies of large-scale production and distribution due to:
   a. Capital-intensive production processes.
   b. High initial start-up costs.

These factors can permit a firm to identify positive net present value projects for internal investment. If the barriers to entry are sufficiently high (such as a patent on key technology) so as to prevent any new competition or if the start-up period for competitive ventures is sufficiently long, then it is possible that a project may have a positive net present value. However, in assessing the viability of such a project, the manager or analyst must consider the likely period of time when above-normal returns can be earned before new competitors emerge and force cash flows back to a more normal level. It is generally unrealistic to expect to be able to earn above-normal returns over the entire life of an investment project.

Risk and the NPV Rule

The previously discussed land investment assumed that the investment was riskless. Therefore, the rate of return used to compute the discount factor and the net present value was the riskless rate of return available on a Canada bond having a one-year maturity. What if you do not believe your investment advisor who says that the construction of the new interchange is a certainty, or you are not confident about your advisor's estimate of the value of the land in one year? To compensate for the perceived risk of this investment, you decide that you require a 15 percent rate of return on your investment. Using a 15 percent required rate of return in calculating the discount factor, the present value of the expected $1.2 million sales price of the land is $1,043,478 [$1.2 million times (1/1.15)]. Thus, the NPV of this investment declines to $43,478. The increase in the perceived risk of the investment results in a dramatic decline in its NPV.

Meaning and Measurement of Risk

A primary problem facing managers is the difficulty of evaluating the risk associated with investments and then translating that risk into a discount rate that reflects an adequate level of risk compensation. We begin the discussion of risk analysis by defining several key terms and concepts. Although the examples presented here deal primarily with investment decisions, the ideas are applicable to all other types of economic decisions, such as those of pricing and production.

The Meaning of Risk-Free and Risky Investments

Risk implies a chance for some unfavourable outcome to occur. From the perspective of security analysis or the analysis of an investment project, risk is the *possibility that actual*

Risk

Risk

A decision-making situation in which there is variability in the possible outcomes, and the probabilities of these outcomes can be specified by the decision maker.

cash flows (returns) will be less than forecasted cash flows (returns). More generally, **risk** refers to the chance that you will encounter an outcome that differs from the expected outcome. When a range of potential outcomes is associated with a decision and the decision maker is able to assign probabilities to each of these possible outcomes, risk is said to exist.

An investment decision is said to be *risk-free* if the outcome (dollar returns) from the initial investment is known with certainty. A good example of a risk-free investment is Canadian government Treasury bills. There is virtually no chance that the Treasury bills will not be redeemed at maturity.[4]

In contrast, Nortel bonds constitute a *risky* investment opportunity because it is possible that Nortel will lack sufficient funds at maturity to redeem its bonds at face value. Bonds also make periodic interest payments. Thus, it is also possible that Nortel might default on one or more interest payments.

In summary, *risk* refers to the potential variability of outcomes from a decision. The more variable these outcomes are, the greater the risk.

Probability Distributions

Probability

The percentage chance that a particular outcome will occur.

The **probability** that a particular outcome will occur is defined as the relative frequency or *percentage chance* of its occurrence. Probabilities may be either objectively or subjectively determined. An objective determination is based on past outcomes of similar events, whereas a subjective determination is merely an opinion made by an individual about the likelihood that a given event will occur. In the case of decisions that are frequently repeated, such as the drilling of developmental oil wells in an established oil field, reasonably good objective estimates can be made about the success of a new well. In contrast, for totally new decisions or one-of-a-kind investments, subjective estimates about the likelihood of various outcomes are necessary. The fact that many probability estimates in business are at least partially subjective does not diminish their usefulness.

EXAMPLE

PROBABILITY DISTRIBUTIONS AND RISK: NORTEL BONDS

Consider an investor who is contemplating the purchase of Nortel bonds. That investor might assign the probabilities associated with the three possible outcomes from this investment, as shown in the following table.

Possible Outcomes from Investing in Nortel Bonds

Outcome	Probability
No default, bonds redeemed at maturity	0.30
Default on interest for two or more periods	0.65
No interest default, but bonds not redeemed at maturity	0.05
	1.00

These probabilities are interpreted to mean that a 30 percent chance exists that the bonds will not be in default over their life and will be redeemed at maturity, a 65 percent chance of interest default during the life of the bonds, and a 5 percent chance that the bonds will not be redeemed at maturity. In this example, no other outcomes are deemed possible.

---

[4] Treasury bills are sold at a discount and redeemed at face value at maturity.

Using either objective or subjective methods, the decision maker can develop a probability distribution for the possible outcomes. Table 2.2 shows the probability distribution of net cash flows for two sample investments. The lowest estimated annual net cash flow (NCF) for each investment—$200 for Investment I and $100 for Investment II—represents pessimistic forecasts about the investments' performance; the middle values—$300 and $300—could be considered normal performance levels; and the highest values—$400 and $500—are optimistic estimates.

Expected Values

From this information, the expected value of each decision alternative can be calculated. The **expected value** is defined as the weighted average of the possible outcomes. It is the value that is expected to occur on average if the decision (such as an investment) were repeated a large number of times.

Algebraically, the expected value may be defined as

$$(2.3) \qquad \bar{r} = \sum_{j=1}^{n} r_j p_j$$

where $\bar{r}$ is the expected value; r_j is the outcome for the jth case, where there are n possible outcomes; and p_j is the probability that the jth outcome will occur. The expected cash flows for Investments I and II are calculated in Table 2.3 using Equation 2.3. In this example both investments have expected values of annual net cash flows equalling $300.

Standard Deviation: An Absolute Measure of Risk

The **standard deviation** is a statistical measure of the dispersion of a variable about its mean. It is defined as the square root of the weighted average squared deviations of individual outcomes from the mean:

$$(2.4) \qquad \sigma = \sqrt{\sum_{j=1}^{n} (r_j - \bar{r})^2 p_j}$$

where σ is the standard deviation.

Table 2.2	Probability Distributions of the Annual Net Cash Flows (NCF) from Two Investments		
Investment I		**Investment II**	
Possible NCF	**Probability**	**Possible NCF**	**Probability**
$200	0.2	$100	0.2
300	0.6	300	0.6
400	0.2	500	0.2
	1.0		1.0

Table 2.3	Computation of the Expected Returns from Two Investments				
Investment I			**Investment II**		
r_j	p_j	$r_j \times p_j$	r_j	p_j	$r_j \times p_j$
$200	0.2	$ 40	$100	0.2	$ 20
300	0.6	180	300	0.6	180
400	0.2	80	500	0.2	100
	Expected value: $\bar{r}_I = \$300$				$\bar{r}_{II} = \$300$

The standard deviation can be used to measure the variability of a decision alternative. As such, it gives an indication of the risk involved in the alternative. The larger the standard deviation, the more variable the possible outcomes and the riskier the decision alternative. A standard deviation of zero indicates no variability and thus no risk.

Table 2.4 shows the calculation of the standard deviations for Investments I and II. These calculations show that Investment II appears to be *riskier* than Investment I because the expected cash flows from Investment II are *more variable.*

This example dealt with a *discrete* probability distribution of outcomes (net cash flows) for each investment. That is, a *limited* number of possible outcomes were identified and probabilities were assigned to them. In reality, however, many different outcomes are possible for each investment decision, ranging from losses each year to annual net cash flows in excess of the optimistic estimates of $400 and $500. To indicate the probability of *all* possible outcomes, it is necessary to construct a *continuous* probability distribution. Conceptually, this involves assigning probabilities to each possible outcome such that the sum of the probabilities over possible outcomes totals 1.0 (see Figure 2.2). This figure shows that Investment I has a tighter probability distribution and smaller standard deviation, indicating a lower variability of returns, and Investment II has a flatter distribution and larger standard deviation, indicating higher variability and, by extension, more risk.

Normal Probability Distribution

The outcomes from many decisions can be estimated by assuming that they follow the *normal* probability distribution. This assumption is often correct or nearly correct, and it greatly simplifies the analysis. The normal probability distribution is characterized by a symmetrical, bell-like curve. If the expected continuous probability distribution for the possible outcomes is approximately normal, a table of the *standard normal probability function* can be used to compute the probability of occurrence of any particular outcome. From such a table (see Table 13B.1 in Web Appendix 13B), for example, it is apparent that the actual outcome should be between plus and minus 1 standard

Table 2.4	Computation of the Standard Deviations for Two Investments						
	j	r_j	$\bar{r}$	$r_j - \bar{r}$	$(r_j - \bar{r})^2$	p_j	$(r_j - \bar{r})^2 p_j$
Investment I	1	$200	$300	$-100	$10,000	0.2	$2,000
	2	300	300	0	0	0.6	0
	3	400	300	100	10,000	0.2	2,000

$$\sum_{j=1}^{3} (r_j - \bar{r})^2 p_j = \$4,000$$

$$\sigma = \sqrt{\sum_{j=1}^{n} (r_j - \bar{r})^2 p_j} = \sqrt{4,000} = \underline{\$63.25}$$

Investment II	1	$100	$300	$-200	$40,000	0.2	$8,000
	2	300	300	0	0	0.6	0
	3	500	300	200	40,000	0.2	8,000

$$\sum_{j=1}^{3} (r_j - \bar{r})^2 p_j = \$16,000$$

$$\sigma = \sqrt{\sum_{j=1}^{n} (r_j - \bar{r})^2 p_j} = \sqrt{16,000} = \underline{\$126.49}$$

FIGURE 2.2

Continuous Probability Distributions for Two Investments

Investments I and II have identical means of $300. Investment II is riskier than Investment I because its standard deviation is twice as large.

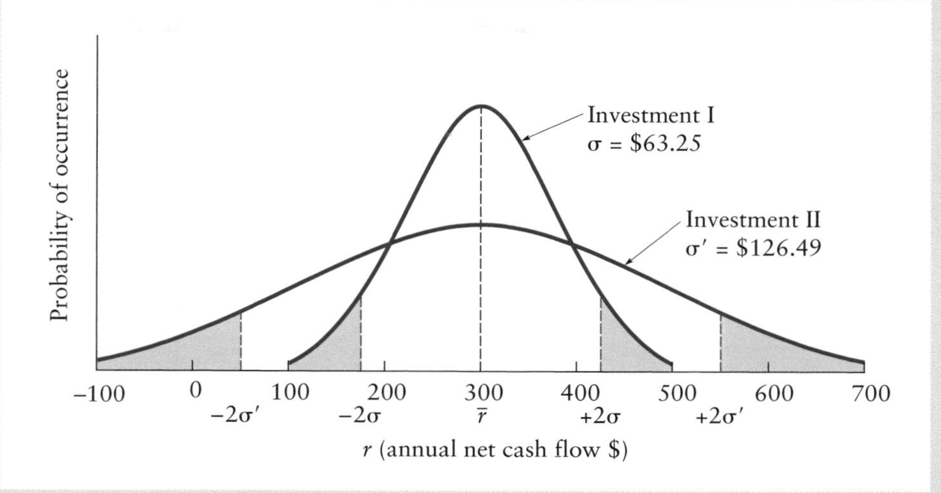

deviation from the expected value 68.26 percent of the time,[5] between plus and minus 2 standard deviations 95.44 percent of the time, and between plus and minus 3 standard deviations 99.74 percent of the time (see Figure 2.3). So a "3 sigma event" occurs less than 1 percent of the time, with a relative frequency 0.0026 (i.e., 1.0 − 0.9974), and a "9 sigma event" occurs almost never, with a relative frequency less than 0.0001. Nevertheless, extraordinary events can and do happen.

The number of standard deviations z that a particular value of r is from the mean $\bar{r}$ can be computed as

$$(2.5) \qquad z = \frac{r - \bar{r}}{\sigma}$$

Table 13B.1 in Web Appendix 13B and Equation 2.5 can be used to compute the probability of an annual net cash flow for Investment I being less than some value r—for example, $205. First, the number of standard deviations that $205 is from the mean must be calculated. Substituting the mean and the standard deviation from Tables 2.3 and 2.4 into Equation 2.5 yields

$$z = \frac{\$205 - \$300}{\$63.25}$$
$$= -1.50$$

In other words, the annual cash flow value of $205 is 1.5 standard deviations below the mean. Reading from the 1.5 row in Table 13B.1 gives a value of 0.0668 or 6.68 percent. Thus, a 6.68 percent probability exists that Investment I will have annual net cash flows less than $205. Conversely, there is a 93.32 percent probability (1 − 0.0668) that the investment will have a cash flow greater than $205.

---

[5] For example, Web Appendix Table 13B.1 indicates a probability of 0.1587 of a value occurring that is greater than $+1\sigma$ from the mean *and* a probability of 0.1587 of a value occurring that is less than -1σ from the mean. Hence the probability of a value *between* $+1\sigma$ and -1σ is 68.26 percent—that is, $1.00 - (2 \times 0.1587)$.

FIGURE 2.3

A Sample Illustration of Areas under the Normal Probability Distribution Curve

Note that over 68% of outcomes are within 1 standard deviation of the mean, over 95% are within 2 standard deviations, and over 99% are within 3 standard deviations.

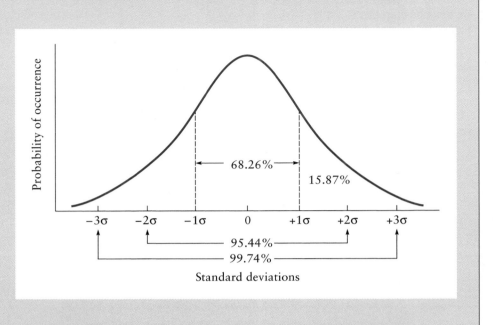

A Practical Approach for Estimating Standard Deviations

Most business decisions have outcomes best represented by a continuous probability distribution of possible outcomes, not the discrete distribution of outcomes, such as those shown in Table 2.2. Under these circumstances, a simple technique can be used to derive the standard deviation of possible outcomes. Assuming that the distribution of possible outcomes is approximately normally distributed, information can be developed in a form useful for making the necessary computations.

For example, the individual responsible for making estimates of the expected return and risk from a decision, such as an investment project or the pricing of a new product, could be asked to supply the following information:

1. Estimate the most optimistic outcome. The most optimistic outcome is defined to be an outcome that would not be exceeded more than 5 percent (or any other pre-specified percentage) of the time.

2. Estimate the most pessimistic outcome. The most pessimistic outcome is defined to be an outcome that you would not expect to do worse more than 5 percent of the time.

3. With a normal distribution, the expected value will be midway between the most optimistic and the most pessimistic estimate.

4. Calculate the value of one standard deviation from Table 13B.1 in Web Appendix 13B.

Coefficient of Variation: A Relative Measure of Risk

The standard deviation is an appropriate measure of risk when the decision alternatives being compared are approximately equal in size (that is, have similar expected values of the outcomes) and the outcomes are estimated to have symmetrical probability distributions. Because the standard deviation is an *absolute* measure of variability, however, it is generally not suitable for comparing alternatives of differing size. In these cases the **coefficient of variation** provides a better measure of risk.

The coefficient of variation (v) considers relative variation and thus is well suited for use when a comparison is being made between two unequally sized decision alternatives.

Coefficient of Variation
The ratio of the standard deviation to the expected value. A relative measure of risk.

ESTIMATION OF THE STANDARD DEVIATION: XARLINK

When pricing a new product, Xarlink's product manager estimates that the most optimistic (not expected to be exceeded more than 5 percent of the time) price the firm can charge is $5.00 per unit. The most pessimistic (not expected to be less than this amount more than 5 percent of the time) estimate of the price that can be charged is $3.50. Assuming normality, the expected price is $4.25. From Web Appendix Table 13B.1, the z-value that leaves 5 percent in either tail of the normal distribution is approximately 1.645 standard deviations (σ) to the right or left of the expected value. This z-value corresponds to the distance between the expected value and either the most optimistic or the most pessimistic estimate of price. Hence, the probability of a price of at least $5.00 is equal to the probability of a z-value *greater* than +1.645. To calculate the standard deviation (σ) of this distribution, use the most optimistic outcome ($5.00), the expected outcome ($4.25), and the z-value:

$$z = 1.645 = \frac{(\$5.00 - \$4.25)}{\sigma}$$

$$\sigma = \frac{\$0.75}{1.645}$$

$$= \$0.46$$

In this case, the expected value is $4.25, with a standard deviation of $0.46.

It is defined as the ratio of the standard deviation σ to the expected value $\bar{r}$, or

(2.6)
$$v = \frac{\sigma}{r}$$

In general, when comparing two equally sized decision alternatives, the standard deviation is an appropriate measure of risk. When comparing two unequally sized alternatives, the coefficient of variation is the more appropriate measure of risk.

The Relationship between Risk and Return

Understanding the tradeoff between risk and required (or expected) rates of return is integral to effective decision making. For example, investors who purchase common shares hope to receive returns that will exceed those that might be earned from alternative investments, such as a savings account, Canada bonds, or high-quality corporate bonds. Investors recognize that the expected return from common shares over the long run tends to be higher than the expected return from less risky investments. To receive higher returns, however, investors must be prepared to accept a higher level of risk.

Risk and Required Return

The relationship between risk and required return on an investment in either a physical asset or financial asset (security) can be defined as

(2.7)   Required return = Risk-free return + Risk premium

The *risk-free rate of return* is the return available on an investment with no risk of default. For debt securities, no default risk means that promised interest and principal payments are guaranteed to be made. The best example of risk-free securities are short-term Canadian government securities, such as Treasury bills. There is no risk of default on these securities because the government can always print more money. Of course, if the government recklessly prints money to pay its obligations, the purchasing power of

RELATIVE RISK MEASUREMENT: OUTIL TOOL COMPANY

Outil Tool Company is considering two investments, T and S. Investment T has expected annual net cash flows of $100,000 and a standard deviation of $20,000, whereas Investment S has expected annual net cash flows of $4,000 and a $2,000 standard deviation. Intuition tells us that Investment T is less risky because its *relative* variation is smaller. As the coefficient of variation increases, so does the relative risk of the decision alternative. The coefficients of variation for Investments T and S are computed as

Investment T:

$$v = \frac{\sigma}{r}$$

$$= \frac{\$20,000}{\$100,000}$$

$$= 0.20$$

Investment S:

$$v = \frac{\sigma}{r}$$

$$= \frac{\$2,000}{\$4,000}$$

$$= 0.50$$

Cash flows of Investment S have a larger coefficient of variation (0.50) than do cash flows of Investment T (0.20). Therefore, even though the standard deviation is smaller, Investment S is the *more* risky of the two alternatives.

the money will decline. So, risk-free returns equal the real rate of interest plus the expected rate of inflation. Nevertheless, the buyer of a Canadian government Treasury bill is always assured of receiving the promised *principal*. (Treasury bills pay no interest and sell at a discount from promised principal repayment at maturity.)

A *risk premium* is a potential "reward" that an investor can expect to receive from making a risky investment. The risk may arise for any number of reasons. The borrower firm may default on its contractual repayment obligations (a default risk premium). The investor may have little seniority in presenting claims against a bankrupt borrower (a seniority risk premium). The investor may be unable to sell his security interest (a liquidity risk premium), or debt repayment may occur early (a maturity risk premium). Finally, the return the investor receives may be highly volatile, exceeding expectations during one period and plummeting below expectations during the next period. Investors generally are considered to be *risk-averse*. That is, they expect, on average, to be compensated for any and all of these risks they assume when making an investment.

Markets, Demand and Supply, and Market Equilibrium

Understanding the important economic concepts of markets, demand and supply, and market equilibrium is essential to effective managerial decision making. *Markets* make possible the exchange of goods and services. *Demand* is the amount of a good or service that consumers are willing and able to purchase. *Supply* is the amount of a good or service that producers are willing and able to offer for sale. In free markets, supply and demand interact to establish prices that allocate resources to their best uses. *Equilibrium* is achieved when the quantity demanded equals the quantity supplied.

Markets

A **market** is a place where the orders of potential buyers can be matched with the offers of potential sellers. Thus, a market may be a single physical location, such as the Toronto Stock Exchange, or it may be virtual market, such as NASDAQ (where transactions take place through an electronic communications network). Buyers and sellers (or their representatives) can communicate with each other in the marketplace and make their transactions. The people who make these transactions must agree on the price at which the goods or services will be exchanged. These transactions may then be consummated with money or by barter. Barter requires the double coincidence of wants. For example,

WHAT WENT RIGHT
WHAT WENT WRONG

LONG-TERM CAPITAL MANAGEMENT MARKET EQUILIBRIUM?*

Long-Term Capital Management (LTCM) operated from June 1993–September 1998 as a hedge fund that invested highly leveraged private capital in arbitrage trading strategies on the financial derivative markets. LTCM's principal activity was examining interest rate derivative contracts throughout the world for evidence of very minor mispricing and then betting enormous sums on the subsequent convergence of those contracts to predictable equilibrium prices. Since the mispricing might be only several cents per thousand dollars invested, LTCM often risked millions or even billions on one bet. With sometimes as many as 100 independent bets spread across dozens of different government bond markets, LTCM appeared globally diversified. In a typical month, 60 such convergence strategies with positions in several thousand counterparty contracts would make money and another 40 strategies with a similar number of counterparties would lose money.

Steadily, the profits mounted. From approximately $1 billion of net asset value (equity) in February 1994, LTCM reached $7 billion of net asset value in January 1998. LTCM then paid out $2.4 billion in a one-time distribution to nonpartners. Shortly thereafter, in August 1998, the remaining $4.6 billion equity shrank by 45 percent, and then one month later, shrank by another 82 percent to less than $500 million. In September 1998, the hedge fund was taken over by 14 Wall Street banks that invested $3.6 billion to cover the firm's debts and assumed 90 percent of the ownership. What went wrong?

What appears to have gone wrong for LTCM was that the default of the Russian government debt in August 1998 set in motion a truly extraordinary sequence of events. Investors around the globe took a "flight to quality" and quickly bid up the price of U.S. Treasury securities, which set off general turmoil in the bond markets around the world. Within one month, interest rate volatility stood at a standard deviation of 36 percent per year, when 3 percent would have been typical. LTCM was caught on the wrong side of many interest rate derivative positions as the contract prices adjusted to this extraordinary volatility. LTCM was unable to sell off many of its money-losing positions at any positive price.

* Based on R. Lowenstein, *When Genius Failed* (New York: Random House, 2000), and "Case Study: LTCM," *eRisk*, 2000.

Demand

Amount of a good or service that consumers are willing and able to buy at every possible price.

Supply

Amount of a good or service that producers are willing and able to offer for sale at every possible price.

Law of Demand

Quantity demanded of a good or service increases (decreases) as its price decreases (increases).

Law of Supply

Quantity supplied of a good or service increases (decreases) as its price increases (decreases).

the buyer and seller must agree on how many apples to exchange for how many oranges. Hence, using money facilitates exchanges, because it is much easier to establish a monetarily equivalent price for any good or service.

Demand and Supply

Demand and supply determine the price of any good or service in a free market. **Demand** is the amount that consumers would be willing and able to buy at every possible price in a market. The *quantity demanded* is the amount of a good or service that people are willing to buy at a specific price at a particular time in a market. **Supply** is the amount that producers are willing and able to offer for sale at every possible price in a market. The *quantity supplied* is the amount of a good or service that producers are willing to offer for sale at a specific price at a particular time in a market.

The **law of demand** says that the quantity of a well-defined good or service that people are willing and able to buy during a particular period of time decreases as the price of the good or service rises and increases as the price falls, everything else held constant.

The **law of supply** says that the quantity of a well-defined good or service that producers are willing and able to offer for sale during a particular period of time increases as the price of the good or service increases and decreases as the price decreases, everything else held constant.

Market Equilibrium

The laws of supply and demand can be represented graphically, as shown in Figure 2.4. The supply curve SS' slopes upward and the demand curve DD' slopes downward. The intersection of the curves represents the market equilibrium price $P^* = \$2$ and market equilibrium quantity $Q^* = 2,000$. It indicates the price that clears the market by providing

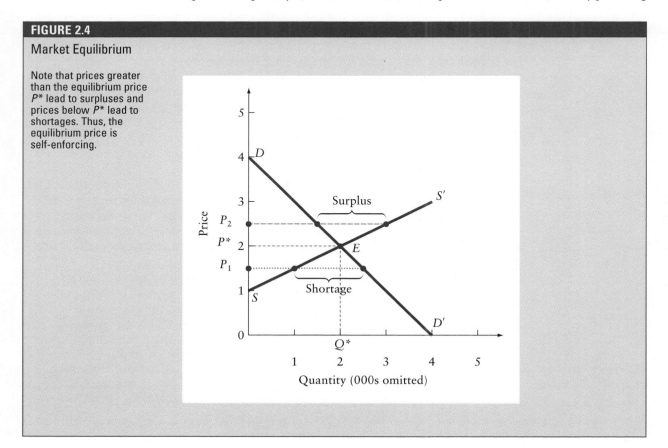

FIGURE 2.4

Market Equilibrium

Note that prices greater than the equilibrium price P^* lead to surpluses and prices below P^* lead to shortages. Thus, the equilibrium price is self-enforcing.

Airline Revenue Management

Revenue management is critical to the success of any airline. Airlines routinely turn away a customer who wants a discount fare if all discount seats are booked. It is logical for an airline to do this, as long as the expected revenue from the *last* seat held back for full-fare customers exceeds the discount fare. However, an empty seat generates no revenue whatsoever. Thus, it behooves an airline to dynamically adjust the number of seats held back as the time to flight departure diminishes. For more information on revenue management, first see the discussion of price discrimination in Chapter 9 and then see the application of revenue management techniques in Web Appendix 9A.

Market Equilibrium
Price at which quantity demanded equals quantity supplied.

all of the potential buyers with the goods or services they desire while also allowing the potential sellers to sell all that they desire. In other words, **market equilibrium** represents the price at which quantity demanded equals quantity supplied.

Suppose in Figure 2.4 that the price was initially below the equilibrium price P^*, say at $P_1 = \$1.50$. Then the quantity demanded would be 2,500 units and the quantity supplied would be 1,000 units. This represents a shortage of 1,500 units. Thus, many consumers would be unable to buy all that they want of the good or service at this price. This shortfall will induce some consumers to offer a higher price. This higher price will in turn induce more quantity to be supplied by producers and induce less quantity to be demanded by consumers. This action will continue until the price rises to P^* and quantity supplied once again equals quantity demanded.

Suppose in Figure 2.4 that the price was initially above the equilibrium price P^*, say at $P_2 = \$2.50$. Then the quantity supplied would be 3,000 units and the quantity demanded would be 1,500 units. This represents a surplus of 1,500 units. Thus, many producers would be unable to sell all that they want of the good or service at this price. This surplus will induce some producers to offer a lower price. This lower price in turn will induce more quantity to be demanded by consumers and induce less quantity to be supplied by producers. This action will continue until the price rises to P^* and again quantity demanded equals quantity supplied.

Thus, in competitive markets, the economic actions of market participants tend to restore market equilibrium.

Summary

- The *marginal analysis* concept requires that a decision maker determine the additional (marginal) costs and additional (marginal) benefits associated with a proposed action. If the marginal benefits exceed the marginal costs (that is, if the net marginal benefits are positive), the action should be taken.

- The *net present value* (NPV) of an investment is equal to the present value of expected future returns (cash flows) minus the initial outlay. NPV represents the contribution of an investment to the value of the firm and, accordingly, to the wealth of shareholders. NPV depends on the return required by investors, which, in turn, is a function of the perceived risk of the investment.

- *Risk* refers to the potential variability of outcomes from a decision alternative. It can be measured either by the *standard deviation* (an absolute measure of risk) or *coefficient of variation* (a relative measure of risk).
- A positive relationship exists between risk and required rates of return on securities and physical asset investments. *Investments involving greater risks must offer higher expected returns.*
- *Markets* make possible the exchange of goods and services.
- The *interaction of supply and demand* establishes the price of goods and services that are exchanged in markets.
- The *laws of supply and demand* state that more will be supplied at higher prices but that less will be demanded at higher prices.
- *Equilibrium* in a market is achieved when the quantity demanded equals the quantity supplied.

Self-Test Exercise

The manager of the aerospace division of Bombardier has estimated the price it can charge for providing satellite launch services to commercial firms. Her most optimistic estimate (a price not expected to be exceeded more than 10 percent of the time) is $2 million. Her most pessimistic estimate (a lower price than this one is not expected more than 10 percent of the time) is $1 million. The price distribution is believed to be approximately normal.

1. What is the expected price?
2. What is the standard deviation of the launch price?
3. What is the probability of receiving a price less than $1.2 million?

Exercises

1. The Ajax Company now has the set of projects shown below.

Project*	Investment Required ($ Million)	Expected Rate of Return (%)
A	$500	23.0
B	75	18.0
C	50	21.0
D	125	16.0
E	300	14.0
F	150	13.0
G	250	19.0

* Note: All projects have equal risk.

Ajax can raise funds with the following marginal costs:

First $250 million	14.0%
Next $250 million	15.5
Next $100 million	16.0
Next $250 million	16.5
Next $200 million	18.0
Next $200 million	21.0

Use the marginal cost and marginal revenue concepts developed in this chapter to derive an optimal capital budget for Ajax.

2. The demand for Quetek's products is related to the state of the economy. If the economy is expanding next year (an above-normal growth in GDP), the firm

expects sales to be $90 million. If there is a recession next year (a decline in GDP), sales are expected to be $75 million. If next year is normal (a moderate growth in GDP), sales are expected to be $85 million. Quetek's economists have estimated the chances that the economy will be either expanding, normal, or in a recession next year at 0.2, 0.5, and 0.3, respectively.

    a. Compute expected annual sales.

    b. Compute the standard deviation of annual sales.

    c. Compute the coefficient of variation of annual sales.

3. Two investments have the following expected returns (net present values) and standard deviation of returns:

Project	Expected Returns	Standard Deviation
A	$ 50,000	$ 40,000
B	$250,000	$125,000

Which one is riskier? Why?

4. An investment project has expected annual net cash flows of $100,000, with a standard deviation of $40,000. The distribution of annual net cash flows is approximately normal.

    a. Determine the probability that the annual net cash flows will be negative.

    b. Determine the probability that the annual net cash flows will be less than $20,000.

CASE EXERCISE

TORO SNOW BLOWERS AND THE PROBABILITY OF SNOW[6]

The maker of Toro snow blowers found that the big barrier to buying one of its machines was the fear that there wouldn't be enough snow to justify the cost of the machine to the purchaser, so the company designed a promotional campaign to overcome this problem. Toro agreed to refund the entire price of its machines purchased before December 10 if the snowfall during the ensuing winter was less than 20 percent of the 40-year average for the purchase location. In effect, then, the customer would get the snow blower free! If the snowfall was less than 50 percent of the 40-year average, Toro would refund part of the purchase price. This promotion led to significantly increased early season sales.

After the program ended, company management began to monitor closely reports from 172 weather stations. Toro also hedged its bets by purchasing weather insurance from Good Weather International. In the event of low snowfall amounts, Good Weather would reimburse Toro for its losses.

Questions

1. What factors might have led Toro management to consider purchasing weather insurance?

2. What factors would the managers at Good Weather have to consider in determining a price to charge Toro for this protection?

[6] Based on Bill Richards, "Executives at Toro Are Dreaming of White Winter—Very White," *The Wall Street Journal*, December 12, 1983.

CHAPTER 3

Demand Analysis

Chapter Preview

Demand analysis serves two major managerial objectives. First, it provides the insights necessary to effectively manipulate demand. Second, it helps forecast sales and revenues. This chapter develops the theory of demand and introduces the elasticity properties of the demand function. The chapter begins by examining only the relationship between price and unit sales, thereby assuming that the other factors that influence demand, such as income levels and advertising, remain unchanged or are held constant. Later, the effects of these other factors are added to the analysis.

One of the most important concepts from the theory of demand is the concept of elasticity. The price elasticity of demand is a measure of the responsiveness of quantity demanded to a change in one of the factors influencing demand, such as price, advertising, income levels, and the prices of substitute or complementary goods. In the latter part of the chapter, consumer indifference curves are used to develop the relationship between cost-of-living price indices and new product introductions.

A thorough understanding of demand theory and its applications is central to effective, wealth-maximizing decision making by a firm's managers, because demand relationships determine the revenue portion of a firm's cash flow stream.

Of course, before a demand analysis can be performed, the firm must estimate its demand function. For a discussion of demand function estimation, see Web Chapter 13 and Web Appendix 13A. Also relevant is Web Chapter 15, which discusses forecasting. To access these Web resources, go to the Nelson website for this book at www.mcguigan.nelson.com.

Learning Objectives

After studying this chapter, you should be able to:

1. Understand the different presentation methods to represent demand relationships.

2. Explain why the demand curve is typically downward sloping.

3. Identify the difference between *movement* along the demand curve and *shifts* of the entire demand curve.

4. Identify the factors that cause a shift in the entire demand curve.

5. Understand the meaning of *price elasticity of demand*.

6. Explain the effects of demand elasticity on total revenue.

7. Define *income elasticity of demand*.

8. Define *price elasticity of demand*.

9. Recognize how various elasticity measures for a product can be extremely helpful when forecasting demand and formulating plans.

10. Describe how *indifference curves* reveal the consumer's preference for various combinations of goods.

11. Understand how *budget lines* limit the choices available for consumption.

12. Identify the differences between *substitution effect* and *income effect*.

Health Care Reform and Cigarette Taxes*

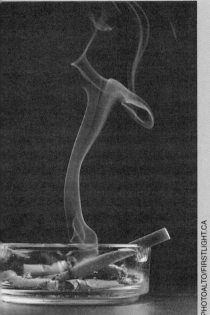

Between 1982 and 1992, Canadians experienced the dramatic effect that a substantial price increase could have on cigarette consumption. When the government raised the cigarette taxes enough to push the price per pack to over $4, adult smoking declined by 38 percent and teenage smoking declined even more (by 61 percent). In 1997, a similar U.S. excise tax increase funded the "Tobacco settlement"—cigarette manufacturers agreed to pay $368 billion over 25 years to achieve immunity from civil liability in class action suits. Under the settlement, the average price of a pack rose by 35 percent. Some critics of the proposal insisted at the time that the tobacco tax should be higher to deter young smokers from acquiring the habit.

One important element of the debate regarding the "optimal" cigarette tax increase depends on how sensitive consumption is to changes in price. A measure of this sensitivity is the price elasticity of demand. In general, the price elasticity of demand represents the percentage change in quantity demanded that occurs as a result of some percentage change in price. Economists have estimated the price elasticity of adult cigarette demand to be −0.4, indicating that for a 10 percent increase in price, quantity demanded can be expected to decline by 4 percent. For teenagers, however, the price elasticity is thought to be 50 percent higher—namely, −0.6—indicating that for a 10 percent increase in price, quantity demanded can be expected to decline by 6 percent.

In the ongoing debate over the amount of cigarette tax required for health care cost recovery, policy makers faced a difficult set of tradeoffs. On the one hand, if the primary objective is to generate income to fund health care costs, the tax should be set so that it will maximize tax revenue. On the other hand, if the primary objective is to discourage smoking, a much higher tax could be justified. In either case, however, knowledge of the true price elasticity of demand is an essential element of this important policy decision. In this chapter, we investigate how to analyze such demand relationships.

---

* Based in part on "Add $2 to the Cost of a Pack of Cigarettes" and "And Even Teen Smokers May Kick the Habit," *BusinessWeek*, March 15, 1993, p. 18; "Critics Question Tobacco Pact's Effect on Teen Smoking," *The Wall Street Journal*, August 19, 1997, p. A20; "Major Makers of Cigarettes Raise Prices," *The Wall Street Journal*, August 31, 1999, p. A3; and "Politicians Are Hooked on Cigarette Taxes," *The Wall Street Journal*, February 20, 2002, p. A2.

Demand Relationships: The Demand Schedule and the Demand Curve

Demand relationships can be represented in the form of a schedule (table), graph, or algebraic function. Each of these forms of presentation provides insights into demand relationships. This section focuses on schedules and graphs. The next section discusses algebraic functions.

The Demand Schedule Defined

The demand schedule is the simplest form of the demand relationship. It is merely a list of prices and corresponding quantities of a commodity that would be demanded by some individual or group of individuals at uniform prices.[1] Table 3.1 shows the demand schedule for regular-sized pizzas at a local Pizza Hut restaurant. This demand schedule indicates that if the price of pizzas was $9, consumers would purchase 60 pizzas. Note that the lower the price, the greater the quantity of pizzas that would be demanded. This inverse or negative relationship between price and quantity demanded is generally referred to as the "law of demand." At lower prices, people are able and willing to purchase more of a commodity than at a higher price.

Constrained Utility Maximization and Demand

The concept of demand is based on the theory of consumer choice. Each consumer faces a constrained optimization problem, where the objective is to choose among the combinations of goods that maximize personal satisfaction or utility, subject to a constraint on the amount of funds available (i.e., budget) to purchase these goods. Think of a food and entertainment budget allowance from your employer while you are travelling on an extended business trip or, alternatively, a set of friends who share these expenses while rooming together. In this constrained utility-maximizing framework, economists have identified two basic reasons for the increase in quantity demanded as the result of a price reduction. These factors are known as the *income effect* and the *substitution effect*.

Income Effect When the price of a good—for example, steak—declines, the effect of this decline is that the real income or purchasing power of the consumer has increased. This is known as the *income effect*. For example, if an individual normally purchases two kilograms of steak per week at $10 per kilogram, a price decline to $8 per kilogram would enable the consumer to purchase the same amount of steak for $4 less per week. This saving of $4 represents an increase in real income of $4, which may be used to purchase greater quantities of steak each week. Sometimes the income effect of a price reduction is miniscule because so little of the household's budget is expended on the

Table 3.1	Simplified Demand Schedule: Pizza Hut Restaurant
Price of Pizza ($/Unit)	**Quantity of Pizzas Sold (Units per Time Period)**
10	50
9	60
8	70
7	80
6	90
5	100

---

[1] The terms *commodity, good,* and *product* are used interchangeably throughout the text to describe both physical goods and services. Prices are assumed to be uniform across all buyers.

good (consider salt), but at other times the change in purchasing power is enormous. Consider a young family who spends 40 percent of its disposable income on apartment housing.

Substitution Effect When the price of a good—such as steak—declines, it becomes less expensive in relation to other goods—for example, chicken. As a result of the price decline, the rational consumer can increase personal satisfaction (or utility) by purchasing more of the good for which the price has declined and less of the other goods. This is known as the *substitution effect.*

For example, suppose that the prices of steak and chicken are $10 and $4 per kilogram, respectively. Furthermore, assume that an individual purchases two kilograms of steak and two kilograms of chicken per week, for a total expenditure of $28. Suppose that the price of steak declines to $8 per kilogram. As a result of this price decrease, an individual who has a preference for steak may decide to increase consumption of steak to three kilograms per week and decrease consumption of chicken to one kilogram per week—which requires the same total expenditure of $28 per week. Thus, we see that a decrease in the price of steak (relative to that of chicken) has led to an increase in the demand for steak.

In summary, because of the combined impact of the income and substitution effects, a decline in the price will always have an impact on the quantity demanded. For normal goods for which more is preferred to less as income rises (e.g., single-family housing), both the substitution and income effects dictate an increase in quantity demanded at lower prices. For inferior goods like efficiency apartments, mackerel, and subcompact cars,[2] the income and substitution effects have opposite and partially offsetting impacts on the quantity demanded. The net effect of both actions, even in the case of inferior goods, is that more will likely be demanded at lower prices.

Individual and Market Demand Curves

The expenditure decisions made by individuals determine personal demand curves. The market demand curve for a good is equal to the sum of the individual demands. As shown in Figure 3.1, for two individuals, the market demand curve is obtained through the horizontal summation of the quantities demanded at each price.[3] For example, at a price of $5 per unit, consumers 1 and 2 would purchase 20 and 15 units, respectively, yielding a market demand of 35 units. Other points on the market demand curve are obtained in a similar manner. Market demand is generally of more interest than individual demand relationships to a firm's managers, because the market demand curve serves as a basis for making many pricing and output decisions.

Demand Relationships: The Demand Function

The demand curve specifies the relationship between prices and the quantity of a good or service that will be demanded at those prices at some point in time, *holding constant the influence of all other factors.* A number of these other factors may effect a change in the shape as well as the position of the demand curve as time passes. Decision variables that management will often consider include the design and packaging of products, the amount and distribution of the firm's advertising budget, the size of the sales force,

---

[2] "Inferior goods" are those that are consumed less as income rises, and vice versa.
[3] For goods that can be shared, like pools, concerts, and flood control projects, market demand is the vertical summation of the willingness to pay of the individual demanders.

FIGURE 3.1

Individual and Market Demand Curves

The left and middle graphs represent the individual demand curves for consumers 1 and 2, respectively. The market demand curve for these two consumers is built by summing the quantity demanded by each consumer as the price is changed.

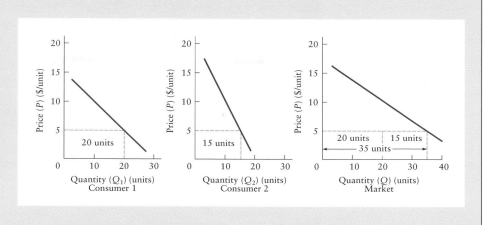

Demand Function

The relationship that exists during some period of time between the number of units of a good or service that consumers are willing to buy and a given set of conditions that influence the willingness to purchase, such as price, income level, and advertising.

Substitute Goods

Two goods are substitutes if the quantity demanded of one *increases* (decreases) when the price of the other *increases* (decreases), assuming all other factors affecting demand remain unchanged.

Complementary Goods

Two goods are complementary if the quantity demanded of one *decreases* (increases) when the price of the other *increases* (decreases), assuming all other factors affecting demand remain unchanged.

promotional expenditures, the time period of adjustment for any price changes, and taxes or subsidies. Algebraically, the **demand function** can be represented as

$$(3.1) \qquad Q_D = f(P, P^S, P^C, Y, A, A^C, N, C^P, P^E, T^A, T/S, \ldots)$$

where Q_D = quantity demanded of the good or service
  P = price of the good or service
  P^S = price of **substitute goods** or services
  P^C = price of **complementary goods** or services
  Y = income of consumers
  A = advertising expenditures (and other marketing expenditures)
  A^C = competitors' advertising expenditures on the good or service
  N = population (and other demographic factors)
  C^P = consumer tastes and preferences for the good or service
  P^E = expected (future) changes in price
  T^A = adjustment time period
  T/S = taxes or subsidies

This representation of the demand function indicates that quantity demanded is a function of a number of different factors (i.e., independent variables). Table 3.2 summarizes some of the factors that affect the shape and/or position of the demand curve. For export products, Chapter 12 shows how other variables, such as the foreign exchange rate, may be equally important in explaining demand.

The demand schedule or demand curve deals with merely the price–quantity relationship. Changes in the price (i.e., P) of the good or service will result only in movement along the demand curve, whereas changes in any of the other independent variables (i.e., $P^S, P^C, Y, A, A^C, N, C^P, P^E, \ldots$) in the demand function result in a shift of that curve.

This is illustrated graphically in Figure 3.2. The initial demand relationship is line DD'. If the original price were P_1, quantity Q_1 would be demanded. If the price declined to P_2, the quantity demanded would increase to Q_2. If, however, changes occurred in the other independent variables, we would expect to have a shift in the entire curve. If, for example, a tax reduction was approved and consumer disposable income increased, the

Table 3.2 Partial List of Factors Affecting Demand

Factor	Expected Effect
Increase (decrease) in price of substitute goods[a] (P^S)	Increase (decrease) in demand (Q_D)
Increase (decrease) in price of complementary goods[b] (P^C)	Decrease (increase) in Q_D
Increase (decrease) in consumer income levels[c] (Y)	Increase (decrease) in Q_D
Increase (decrease) in the amount of advertising and marketing expenditures (A)	Increase (decrease) in Q_D
Increase (decrease) in level of advertising and marketing by competitors (A^C)	Decrease (increase) in Q_D
Increase (decrease) in population (N)	Increase (decrease) in Q_D
Increase (decrease) in consumer preferences for the good or service (C^P)	Increase (decrease) in Q_D
Expected future price increases (decreases) for the good (P^E)	Increase (decrease) in Q_D
Time period of adjustment increases (decreases) (T^A)	Increase (decrease) in Q_D
Taxes (subsidies) on the good increase (decrease) (T/S)	Decrease (increase) in Q_D

[a] Two goods are substitutes if an increase (decrease) in the price of good 1 results in an increase (decrease) in the quantity demanded of good 2, holding other factors constant, such as the price of good 2, other prices, income, and so on, or vice versa. For example, margarine may be viewed as a rather good substitute for butter. As the price of butter increases, more people will decrease their consumption of butter and increase their consumption of margarine.

[b] Goods that are used in conjunction with each other, either in production or consumption, are called "complementary goods." For example, DVDs are used in conjunction with DVD players. An increase in the price of DVD players would have the effect of decreasing the demand for DVDs, all other things remaining unchanged. In other words, two goods are complementary if a decrease in the price of good 1 results in an increase in the quantity demanded of good 2, all other things remaining unchanged. Similarly, two goods are complements if an increase in the price of good 1 results in a decrease in the quantity demanded of good 2.

[c] The case of inferior goods—that is, those goods that are purchased in smaller total quantities as income levels rise—will be discussed below in a consideration of the concept of income elasticity.

new demand curve might become $D_1 D_1'$. At any price, P_1, along $D_1 D_1'$, a greater quantity, Q_3, will be demanded than at the same price on the original curve DD'. Similarly, if the prices of substitute products were to decline, the demand curve would shift downward and to the left. At any price, P_1, along the new curve $D_2' D_2$, a smaller quantity, Q_4, would be demanded than at the same price on either DD' or $D_1 D_1'$.

In summary, movement along a demand curve is often referred to as a change in the quantity demanded, while holding constant the effects of factors other than price that affect demand. A shift of the entire demand curve is often referred to as a change in demand and is always caused by some demand factor, other than price.

Other Factors Affecting Demand

Durable Goods Up to this point it has been implicitly assumed that we are considering the demand for consumer goods to be of a nondurable nature. These are goods purchased largely to meet current needs, and they generally provide service on a short-term basis.

FIGURE 3.2

Shifts in Demand

DD' represents the original demand curve. The demand curve $D_1 D_1'$ represents a positive shift in demand because demand increases for each price. Similarly, $D_2 D_2'$ represents a negative shift in demand.

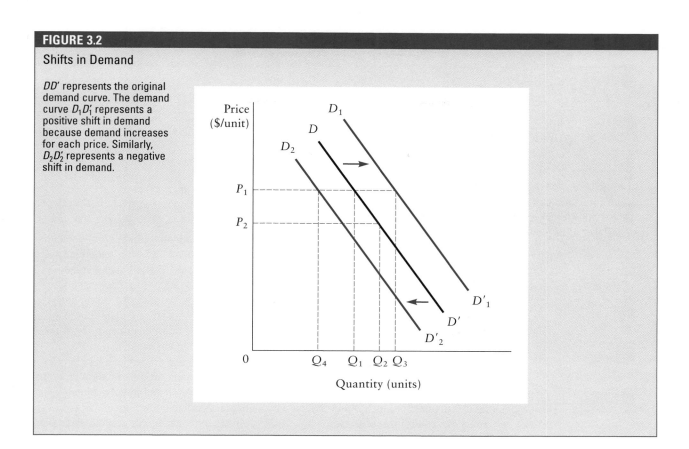

Durable Good

A good that yields benefits to the owner over a number of future time periods.

Food items, holiday decorations, and virtually all services fall in this category, but housing and DVD players are clearly different. One reason for this is that by their very nature, **durable goods** *may be stored*. Another is that the replacement of a durable item may be delayed from period to period by performing additional maintenance on existing items or by merely tolerating an old model. For example, an automobile may be repaired (or its out-of-date styling merely endured); an electric range may be fixed (at considerably less cost than buying a new range); or the discomforts of old furniture may be tolerated for "one more year."

Obsolescence in style, convenience, and prestige value play a larger role in affecting the replacement of durables than does physical deterioration. Also, consumer expectations regarding future levels of income, the availability of complements, and future product price play a major role in explaining the demand for durable goods. For example, a consumer may ask the following sorts of questions when embarking on a personal computer purchase:

■ Will new products soon make my computer obsolete?

■ Will my income be sufficient and steady enough to make the payments on the computer?

■ Are prices likely to rise or fall over the next year?

■ Will adequate software be available over the economic working life of my PC?

Because these expectational factors come into play in evaluating replacement demand, demand for durable goods is more volatile, and its analysis is more complex than a similar analysis for nondurables.

COMPLEMENT STRATEGY AT GENERAL MOTORS*

You can access information on General Motors at **www.gmcanada.com**.

Identifying, developing, and managing relationships with complement products in order to increase demand for one's own product has become a key element of corporate strategy. Porter's five forces of competitive strategy (threat of substitutes, intensity of rivalry, threat of entry, power of buyers, and power of suppliers) are much more difficult to influence.[†] To eliminate competition from substitute products requires a never-ending upstaging of new imitators and can seldom provide sustainable competitive advantage. To cooperate effectively with rivals often constitutes a violation of the Canadian *Competition Act*, the stronger U.S. antitrust laws, or the even tougher European Union competition laws. To erect permanent barriers to entry requires the best product differentiation ad campaigns and relationship marketing. Furthermore, after improving coordination with vertical integration and total quality management, the remaining power of buyers and suppliers is often beyond a firm's control. Consequently, many companies today seek to develop complementary products as a driver of demand for their existing products.

General Motors (GM) invests heavily in and thereby expands the capacity of high-end auto loans (GMAC). GM does so not only because these are particularly profitable assets on their own, but mainly because reduced time and convenience in arranging such loans are strong complements to the sale of profitable Suburbans, Cadillacs, and other luxury cars and trucks.

Other examples that illustrate a company's astute use of complements to increase demand for their primary products are Michelin tires and travel guides, Chapters–Indigo books and in-store coffee bars, inexpensive reading glasses displayed alongside Hallmark greeting cards, and convenience stores or fast-food outlets in gas stations.

---

* Adam Brandenberg and Barry Nalebuff explain this role of complementary products in *Co-Opetition* (New York: Bantam Books, 1996).
† Michael Porter's five forces model was described in Chapter 1 (see Figure 1.4).

Producer's Good
A good that is not produced for direct consumption, but rather is the raw material or capital equipment that is used to produce a consumer good (or some other producer's good).

Derived Demand for Producer's Goods **Producer's goods** differ from consumer goods in that they are not produced for direct consumption but rather are the raw materials, capital equipment, and parts that are combined to produce a consumer good (or some other producer's good). As such, the demand for producer's goods may be thought of as a *derived demand* because it is derived from some ultimate consumer desire. For example, the demand for aluminum, a raw material, is dependent on consumer desires and tastes for those products that are wholly or partially composed of aluminum, such as home siding and rain gutters, and for those services that are dependent on aluminum, such as plane travel.

Therefore, when analyzing derived demand for producer's goods, account must be taken of two new sets of factors. First, we must consider the criteria or specifications used by the purchasing agent of the producing company that guide the agent in selecting one material, machine, process, or product over competitive alternatives. Second, and perhaps more important, we must take account of the significant factors affecting the demand for the ultimate consumer goods for which the producer's goods are inputs.

Exchange Rate Considerations In addition to the above determinants of demand, the demand for goods traded in foreign markets is also influenced by external factors, such as exchange rate fluctuations. When ATI Technologies Inc. sells computer graphics cards overseas, it prefers to be paid in U.S. dollars. Although ATI is a Canadian firm, its functional currency is the U.S. dollar. To accept euros or Australian dollars in payment would introduce an exchange rate risk exposure for which ATI would want to be compensated in the form of higher prices. Consequently, the offshore exports of ATI are typically transacted in U.S. dollars. As the value of the U.S. dollar rises, offshore buyers must pay a larger amount of their own currency to obtain the U.S. dollars required to pay ATI, and this decreases the export demand. Similarly, a lower value of the U.S. dollar reduces the euro price of the product, raising the export demand for ATI's products. Canadian companies often find that export demand considerations are key determinants of their overall demand.

Price Elasticity of Demand

From a decision-making perspective, the firm needs to know the effect of changes in any of the independent variables in the demand function on the quantity demanded. Some of these variables are under the control of management, such as price, advertising, product quality, and customer service. For these variables, management must know the effects of changes on quantity to assess the desirability of instituting the change. Other variables, including income, prices of competitors' products, and expectations of consumers regarding future prices, are outside the direct control of the firm. Nevertheless, effective demand management requires that the firm be able to measure the impact of changes in these variables on the quantity demanded.

Price Elasticity Defined

The most commonly used measure of the responsiveness of quantity demanded to changes in any of the variables that influence the demand function is *elasticity*. In general, elasticity may be thought of as a ratio of the percentage change in one quantity (or variable) to the percentage change in another, *ceteris paribus* (all other things remaining unchanged). In other words, how responsive is some dependent variable to changes in a particular variable? With this in mind, we define the **price elasticity of demand** (E_D) as the ratio of the percentage change in quantity demanded to a percentage change in price:

$$(3.2) \qquad\qquad E_D = \frac{\%\Delta Q}{\%\Delta P}, \textit{ ceteris paribus}$$

where ΔQ = change in quantity demanded
$\qquad \Delta P$ = change in price

Because of the normal inverse relationship between price and quantity demanded, the sign of the price elasticity coefficient will be negative. Occasionally, price elasticities are referred to as "absolute values." In the passages that follow, the use of absolute values will be indicated where appropriate.

Arc Price Elasticity

The *arc* price elasticity of demand is a technique for calculating price elasticity between two prices.[4] It indicates the effect of a change in price, from P_1 to P_2, on the quantity

---

[4] As we will see in the following section, the price elasticity of a straight-line demand curve is different at each point on the demand curve. Hence an "arc price elasticity" computed between two prices may be thought of as an "average" of the various point elasticities between the two prices.

demanded. The following formula is used to compute this elasticity measure:

$$(3.3) \qquad E_D = \frac{\dfrac{Q_2 - Q_1}{\left(\dfrac{Q_2 + Q_1}{2}\right)}}{\dfrac{P_2 - P_1}{\left(\dfrac{P_2 + P_1}{2}\right)}} = \frac{Q_2 - Q_1}{P_2 - P_1} \cdot \frac{P_2 + P_1}{Q_2 + Q_1} = \frac{\Delta Q}{\Delta P} \cdot \frac{P_2 + P_1}{Q_2 + Q_1}$$

where Q_1 = quantity sold before a price change
Q_2 = quantity sold after a price change
P_1 = original price
P_2 = price after a price change

The fraction $(Q_2 + Q_1)/2$ represents average quantity demanded in the range over which the price elasticity is being calculated. $(P_2 + P_1)/2$ also represents the average price over this range.

Rearranging Equation 3.3 shows that the elasticity measurement depends on the inverse of the slope of the ordinary demand curve (i.e., the sensitivity of demand in the target market to price changes)

$$\frac{Q_2 - Q_1}{P_2 - P_1}$$

as well as the *position* on the curve (i.e., the price point positioning) where elasticity is calculated

$$\frac{P_2 + P_1}{Q_2 + Q_1}$$

Because the slope remains constant over the entire schedule (assuming linearity), but the value of $(P_2 + P_1)/(Q_2 + Q_1)$ changes, depending on where on the demand curve elasticity is being calculated, the value of the elasticity measure generally changes throughout the length of the demand curve. Price elasticity at higher prices and small volume is therefore larger (in absolute value) than price elasticity for the same product and same demanders at lower price points and large volume.

Point Price Elasticity

The preceding formulas measure the *arc elasticity* of demand. That is, elasticity is computed over a discrete range of the demand curve or schedule. Because elasticity is normally different at each point on the curve, arc elasticity is a measure of the average elasticity over that range.

By employing some elementary calculus, the elasticity of demand at any point along the curve may be calculated with the following expression:

$$(3.4) \qquad E_D = \frac{\partial Q_D}{\partial P} \cdot \frac{P}{Q_D}$$

where $\dfrac{\partial Q_D}{\partial P}$ = the partial derivative of quantity with respect to price (the inverse of the slope of the demand curve)
Q_D = the quantity demanded at price P
P = the price at some specific point on the demand curve

EXAMPLE

CALCULATING PRICE ELASTICITY OF DEMAND: MARK'S WORK WEARHOUSE

For more information about Mark's Work Wearhouse, go to **www.marks.ca**.

To illustrate, consider the demand schedule shown in Table 3.3 for Denver Hayes Jeanswear in a local Mark's Work Wearhouse store. Calculate the price elasticity between an original price of $38 (14 units are demanded) and a new price of $36. Substituting the relevant data from Table 3.3 into Equation 3.3 yields

$$E_D = \frac{\dfrac{16 - 14}{(16 + 14)/2}}{\dfrac{\$36 - \$38}{(\$36 + \$38)/2}} = -2.47$$

A price elasticity of demand coefficient of −2.47 means that a 10 percent increase (decrease) in price can be expected to

result in a 24.7 percent decrease (increase) in quantity demanded, *ceteris paribus*.

Now assume that the original price was $24, and a new price of $22 is set. Determine the price elasticity of demand. Using Equation 3.3 and the relevant data from Table 3.3 yields

$$E_D = \frac{\dfrac{30 - 28}{(30 + 28)/2}}{\dfrac{\$22 - \$24}{(\$22 + \$24)/2}} = -0.79$$

A price elasticity of demand of −0.79 means that a 10 percent increase (decrease) in price can be expected to result in a 7.9 percent decrease (increase) in quantity demanded, *ceteris paribus*.

Table 3.3	Demand Schedule: Denver Hayes Jeanswear
Price, P ($/Unit)	**Quantity Sold, Q_D (Units per Period)**
40	12
38	14
36	16
34	18
32	20
24	28
22	30

The partial derivative of quantity with respect to price, $\partial Q_D/\partial P$, is merely an indication of the rate of change in quantity demanded as the price changes. This incremental change ratio is analogous to the

$$\frac{Q_2 - Q_1}{P_2 - P_1} = \frac{\Delta Q}{\Delta P}$$

discrete change ratio in the arc elasticity measure.

The daily demand function for Christmas trees at sidewalk seasonal sales lots in mid-December can be used to illustrate the calculation of the point price elasticity.

Using Price Elasticity of Demand: Court Corporation

We can also use Equation 3.3 to compute a price that would have to be charged to achieve a particular level of sales. Consider the Court Corporation (CC), which had monthly basketball shoe sales of 10,000 pairs (at $100 per pair) before a price cut by its major competitor. After this competitor's price reduction, CC's sales declined to 8,000 pairs a month. From past experience, CC has estimated the price elasticity of demand to be about −2.0 in this price–quantity range. If CC wishes to restore its sales to 10,000 pairs per month, what price must be charged?

Letting $Q_2 = 10{,}000$, $Q_1 = 8{,}000$, $P_1 = \$100$, and $E_D = -2.0$, the required price, P_2, may be computed using Equation 3.3:

$$-2.0 = \frac{\dfrac{10{,}000 - 8{,}000}{(10{,}000 + 8{,}000)/2}}{\dfrac{P_2 - \$100}{(P_2 + \$100)/2}}$$

$$P_2 = \$89.50$$

A price cut to $89.50 would be required to restore sales to 10,000 pairs per month.

Suppose that demand can be written algebraically as quantity demanded per day:

$$(3.5) \qquad Q_D = 45{,}000 - 2{,}500P + 2.5Y$$

If one is interested in determining the point price elasticity when the price (P) is equal to $40 and per capita disposable personal income (Y) is equal to $30,000, taking the partial derivative of Equation 3.5 with respect to P yields

$$\frac{\partial Q_D}{\partial P} = -2{,}500 \text{ trees per dollar}$$

Substituting the relevant values of P and Y into Equation 3.5 gives

$$Q_D = 45{,}000 - 2{,}500(40) + 2.50(30{,}000) = 20{,}000$$

From Equation 3.4 one obtains

$$E_D = (-2{,}500 \text{ trees/\$})(\$40/20{,}000 \text{ trees}) = -10.0$$

Interpreting the Price Elasticity: Relationship between the Price Elasticity and Revenues

Once the price elasticity of demand has been calculated, it is necessary to interpret the meaning of the number obtained. The elasticity coefficient may take on *absolute values* over the range from 0 to ∞ (infinity). Values in the indicated ranges are described in Table 3.4.

When demand is unit elastic, a percentage change in price P is matched by an equal percentage change in quantity demanded, Q_D. When demand is elastic, a percentage change in P is exceeded by the percentage change in Q_D. For inelastic demand, a percentage change in P results in a smaller percentage change in Q_D. The theoretical

Table 3.4   Price Elasticity of Demand in Absolute Values

Range	Description
$E_D = 0$	Perfectly inelastic
$0 < |E_D| < 1$	Inelastic
$|E_D| = 1$	Unit elastic
$1 < |E_D| < \infty$	Elastic
$|E_D| = \infty$	Perfectly elastic

extremes of perfect elasticity and perfect inelasticity are illustrated in Figure 3.3. AAA-grade January wheat sells on the Winnipeg spot market with perfectly elastic demand facing any particular grain dealer. Panel (a) illustrates this case. Heroin addicts have almost perfectly inelastic demand. Their quantity demanded is fixed no matter what the price, as indicated in panel (b). However, these extremes are rarely encountered. Rather, they illustrate the limits of price elasticity.

The price elasticity of demand indicates the effect a change in price will have on the total revenue that is generated. Because total revenue, TR, is equal to price (average revenue), P, times the number of units sold, Q_D, from our knowledge of demand elasticity we can determine the effect on total revenue when price changes.

When demand elasticity is less than 1 in absolute value (i.e., inelastic), an increase (decrease) in price will result in an increase (decrease) in total consumer expenditures $(P \cdot Q_D)$. This occurs because an inelastic demand indicates that a given percentage increase in price results in a smaller percentage decrease in quantity sold, the net effect being an increase in the total expenditures, $P \cdot Q_D$. Table 3.5 illustrates this point. When

FIGURE 3.3

Perfectly Elastic and Inelastic Demand Curves

In panel (a), the horizontal demand curve is perfectly elastic. In panel (b), the vertical demand curve is perfectly inelastic.

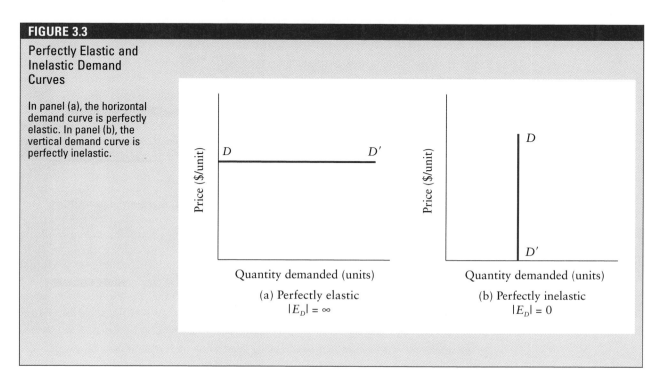

Table 3.5   Relationship between Elasticity and Marginal Revenue

Price, P ($/Unit)	Quantity, Q_D (Units)	Elasticity E_D	Total Revenue $P \cdot Q_D$ ($)	Marginal Revenue ($/Unit)
10	1		10	
9	2	−6.33	18	8
8	3	−3.40	24	6
7	4	−2.14	28	4
6	5	−1.44	30	2
5	6	−1.00	30	0
4	7	−0.69	28	−2
3	8	−0.46	24	−4
2	9	−0.29	18	−6
1	10	−0.15	10	−8

demand is inelastic—that is, $|E_D| < 1$—an increase in price from $2 to $3, for example, results in an increase in total revenue from $18 to $24.[5]

In contrast, when demand is elastic—that is, $|E_D| > 1$—a given percentage increase (decrease) in price is more than offset by a larger percentage decrease (increase) in quantity sold. An increase in price from $9 to $10 results in a reduction in total consumer expenditure from $18 to $10 (again, see Table 3.5).

When demand is unit elastic, a given percentage change in price is exactly offset by the same percentage change in quantity demanded, the net result being a constant total consumer expenditure. If the price is increased from $5 to $6, total revenue would remain constant at $30 because the decrease in quantity demanded at the new price just offsets the price increase (see Table 3.5). When the price elasticity of demand $|E_D|$ is equal to 1 (or is unit elastic), the total revenue function is maximized. In the example, total revenue equals $30 when price P equals either $5 or $6 and quantity demanded, Q_D, equals either 6 or 5.

The relationship among price, quantity, elasticity measures, marginal revenue, and total revenue is illustrated graphically in Figure 3.4. When total revenue is maximized, marginal revenue equals zero and demand is unit elastic. At any price higher than P_2, the demand function is elastic. Hence, successive equal percentage increases in price may be expected to generate higher and higher percentage decreases in quantity demanded because the demand function is becoming increasingly elastic. Alternatively, successive equal percentage reductions in price below P_2 may be expected to generate ever-lower percentage increases in quantity demanded because the demand function is more inelastic at lower prices.

The relationship between a product's price elasticity of demand and the marginal revenue at that price point is one of the most important in managerial economics. This relationship can be derived by analyzing the change in revenue resulting from a price change. To start, **marginal revenue** is defined as the change in total revenue resulting from lowering price to make an additional unit sale. Lowering price from P_1 to P_2 in Figure 3.4 to increase quantity demanded from Q_1 to Q_2 results in a change in the initial revenue, $P_1 A Q_1 0$ to $P_2 B Q_2 0$. The difference in these two areas is illustrated in Figure 3.4 as the two shaded rectangles. The horizontal shaded rectangle is the loss of revenue caused by the price reduction $(P_2 − P_1)$ over the previous units sold, Q_1. The vertical

Marginal Revenue
The change in total revenue that results from a one-unit change in quantity demanded.

---

[5] The symbol $|E_D| < 1$ indicates that we are talking about the absolute value of the elasticity coefficient, rather than its actual negative value.

FIGURE 3.4

Price Elasticity over Demand Analysis

Total revenue is maximized at output Q_2, where marginal revenue is zero and elasticity of demand is 1. Since marginal cost is typically positive, profit maximization occurs at the lower level of output, Q_1, where demand is elastic and positive marginal cost (not shown) equals positive marginal revenue.

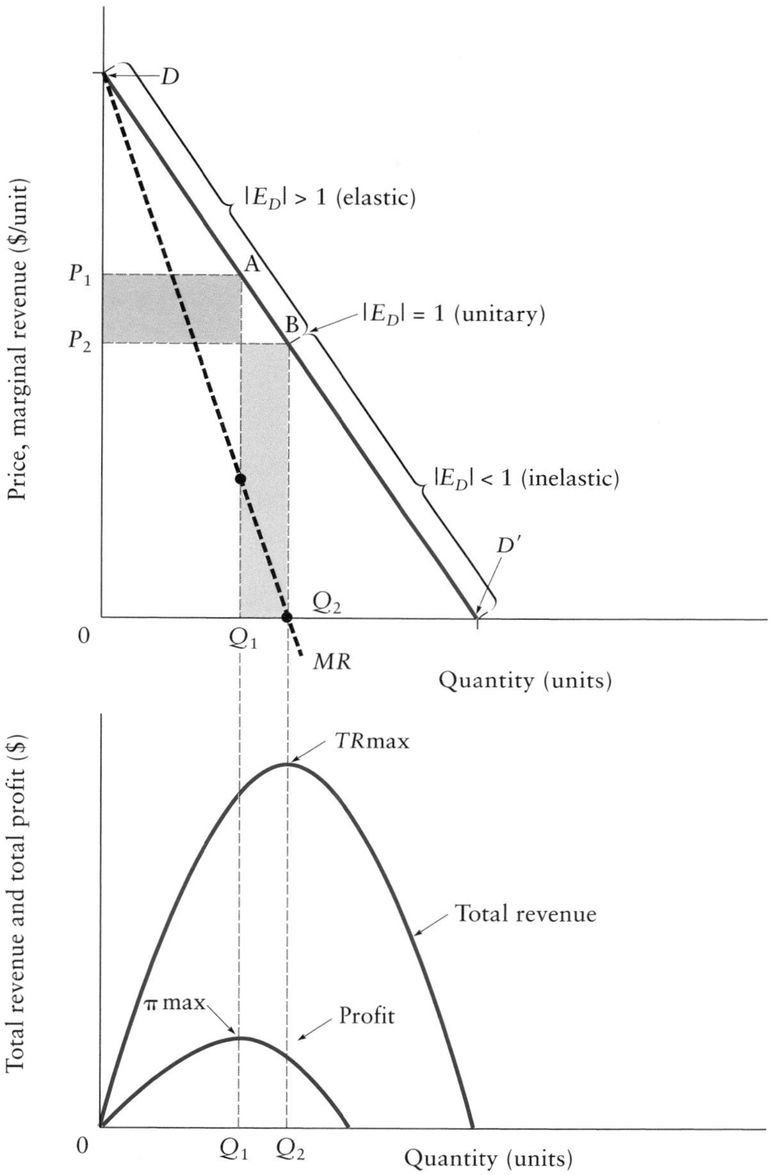

shaded rectangle is the gain in revenue from selling $(Q_2 - Q_1)$ additional units at the new price, P_2. That is, the change in total revenue from lowering the price to sell another unit can always be written as follows:

$$(3.6) \qquad MR = \frac{\Delta TR}{\Delta Q} = \frac{P_2(Q_2 - Q_1) + (P_2 - P_1)Q_1}{(Q_2 - Q_1)}$$

where $P_2(Q_2 - Q_1)$ is the vertical shaded rectangle and $(P_1 - P_2)Q_1$ is the horizontal shaded rectangle. Rearranging, we have

$$MR = P_2 + \frac{(P_2 - P_1)Q_1}{(Q_2 - Q_1)}$$

$$= P_2\left(1 + \frac{(P_2 - P_1)Q_1}{(Q_2 - Q_1)P_2}\right)$$

$$MR = P_2\left(1 + \frac{\Delta P Q_1}{\Delta Q P_2}\right)$$

The ratio term is the inverse of the price elasticity at the price point P_2, using the quantity Q_1. For small price and quantity changes, this number closely approximates the arc price elasticity in Equation 3.3 between P_1 and P_2. Therefore, the relationship between marginal revenue and price elasticity can be expressed algebraically as follows:[6]

(3.7) $$MR = P\left(1 + \frac{1}{E_D}\right)$$

Using this equation, one can demonstrate that when demand is unit elastic, marginal revenue is equal to zero. Substituting $E_D = -1$ into Equation 3.7 yields

$$MR = P\left(1 + \frac{1}{-1}\right)$$

$$= P(0)$$

$$= 0$$

---

[6] This equation also can be derived from the definitions of marginal revenue and price elasticity using calculus. Marginal revenue is equal to the first derivative of total revenue:

$$MR = \frac{d(TR)}{dQ_D} = \frac{d(P \cdot Q_D)}{dQ_D}$$

Using the rule for taking the derivative of a product (see Web Appendix 2A, Equation 2A.17) yields

$$MR = P \cdot \frac{dQ_D}{dQ_D} + Q_D\frac{dP}{dQ_D}$$

$$= P + Q_D\frac{dP}{dQ_D}$$

This equation may be rewritten as

$$MR = P\left(1 + \frac{Q_D}{P} \cdot \frac{dP}{dQ_D}\right)$$

Recalling that the point price elasticity of demand is

$$E_D = \frac{dQ_D}{dP} \cdot \frac{P}{Q_D}$$

it can be seen that the term $\frac{Q_D}{P} \cdot \frac{dP}{dQ_D}$ is the reciprocal of the point price elasticity measure.

Hence, substituting $\frac{1}{E_D}$ for $\frac{Q_D}{P} \cdot \frac{dP}{dQ_D}$ results in Equation 3.7:

$$MR = P\left(1 + \frac{1}{E_D}\right)$$

The fact that total revenue is maximized (and marginal revenue is equal to zero) when $|E_D| = 1$ can be shown with the Custom-Tees example on the next page.

Importance of Elasticity–Revenue Relationships

Elasticity is often the key to marketing plans. A product-line manager will attempt to maximize sales revenue by allocating a marketing expense budget among price promotions, advertising, retail displays, trade allowances, direct mail, and in-store couponing. Knowing whether and at what magnitude demand is responsive to each of these marketing initiatives depends on careful estimates of the various demand elasticities of price, advertising, displays, etc.

Firms should always seek to raise prices for any products in the inelastic range of their demand. To lower prices in such a range would both increase costs (of producing and distributing additional output) and decrease revenue. It is better to approach unit elasticity by raising prices, and thereby increase revenue and save the production and distribution costs. In fact, profit-maximizing firms will carry these price increases right on into the elastic range beyond the point of maximum revenue and unit elasticity (above and beyond point B at P_2 and Q_2 in Figure 3.4). Starting from the other direction at zero output, a profit-maximizing firm will lower price to increase revenue as long as the incremental change in total revenue (the *MR* in Figure 3.4) exceeds the change in total variable cost. That is, the profit-maximizing output will always occur in the elastic region of the firm's demand—for example, at a price above the unit elastic price point.

As we saw earlier, unit elasticity is also of special significance for commission-based employees or anyone whose paycheque rises as sales revenue increases. In general, composers, playwrights, patent holders, authors, and e-business content providers want to

EXAMPLE

AUTHORS PRESS PUBLISHING FIRMS TO INCREASE SALES REVENUE

Entertainment and publishing companies pay composers, playwrights, and authors a fixed percentage of realized sales revenue as a royalty. The two groups often differ as to the preferred price and unit sales. Referring to Figure 3.4, total revenue can be increased by lowering the price anytime the quantity sold is less than Q_2. That is, at any price above P_2 (where marginal revenue remains positive), the total revenue will continue to climb only if prices are lowered and additional units sold. Composers, playwrights, patent holders, and authors often therefore press their licensing agents and publishers to lower prices whenever marginal revenue remains positive—i.e., to the point where

demand is unit elastic. The publisher, on the other hand, will wish to charge higher prices and sell less quantity because operating profits arise from marginal revenue in excess of marginal cost. Unless marginal cost is zero, the publisher always wants a positive marginal revenue and therefore a price greater than P_2 (for example, P_1).

A commission-based sales force and senior management have this same conflict. Salespeople often develop ingenious hidden discounts to try to circumvent a company's list pricing policies. Lowering the price from P_1 to P_2 to set $|E_D| = 1$ will always maximize sales revenue (and therefore, maximize total commissions).

TOTAL REVENUE, MARGINAL REVENUE, AND ELASTICITY: CUSTOM-TEES

Custom-Tees operates a kiosk in Hanes Mall where it sells custom-printed T-shirts. The demand function for the shirts is

(3.8) $Q_D = 150 - 10P$

where P is the price in dollars per unit and Q_D is the quantity demanded in units per period.

The inverse demand curve can be rewritten in terms of P as a function of Q_D.

(3.9) $P = 15 - \dfrac{Q_D}{10}$

Total revenue (TR) is equal to price times quantity sold.

$$TR = P \cdot Q_D$$

$$= \left(15 - \frac{Q_D}{10}\right) Q_D$$

$$= \left(15 Q_D - \frac{Q_D^2}{10}\right)$$

Marginal revenue (MR) is equal to the first derivative of total revenue with respect to Q_D:

$$MR = \frac{d(TR)}{dQ_D}$$

$$= 15 - \frac{Q_D}{5}$$

To find the value of Q_D where total revenue is maximized, set marginal revenue equal to zero:[7]

$$MR = 0$$

$$15 - \frac{Q_D}{5} = 0$$

$$Q_D^* = 75 \text{ units}$$

Substituting this value into Equation 3.9 yields

$$P^* = 15 - \frac{75}{10} = \$7.50 \text{ per unit}$$

Thus, total revenue is maximized at $Q_D^* = 75$ and $P^* = \$7.50$. Checking:

$$E_D = \frac{\partial Q_D}{\partial P} \cdot \frac{P}{Q_D} = (-10)\frac{(7.5)}{75} = -1$$

$$|E_D| = 1$$

In addition to showing that $|E_D| = 1$ when the total revenue function is at its maximum, this example also demonstrates that marginal revenue MR is equal to zero when total revenue is maximized. This finding is not surprising when we remember that the definition of marginal revenue is the increase in total revenue resulting from the sale of one additional unit. Beyond the output level where total revenue is maximized, marginal revenue becomes negative and total revenue declines; that is, $|E_D| < 1$.[8]

maximize revenue. Because operating profits occur only when marginal revenue is in excess of marginal cost, managers want higher prices with somewhat reduced revenue, much reduced costs, and therefore higher profits. One solution to this incentives conflict is to involve the content providers in the company's profit-sharing plan.

---

[7] To be certain that one has found values for P and Q_D where total revenue is maximized rather than minimized, check the second derivative of TR to see that it is negative. In this case $d^2TR/dQ_D^2 = -1/5$, so the total revenue function is maximized.

[8] Additional applications of the relationship among price, marginal revenue, and elasticity (Equation 3.7) are examined in the discussions of pricing by monopolists (Chapter 7) and the practice of price discrimination (Chapter 9).

Factors Affecting the Price Elasticity of Demand

Price elasticities can vary greatly among different products and services. Some of the factors that account for the differing responsiveness of consumers to price changes are examined below.

Availability and Closeness of Substitutes The most important determinant of the price elasticity of demand is the availability and closeness of substitutes. The greater the number of substitute goods, the more price elastic is the demand for a product, because a customer can easily shift to a substitute good if the price of the product in question increases. The availability and closeness of substitutes relates not only to different products, such as beef and chicken, but also to the availability of the same product from different producers. For example, the demand for Chevrolets is likely to be very price elastic because of the ready availability of close substitutes such as Fords, Toyotas, and Hondas. Intravenous feeding solution has few (if any) substitutes for hospital patients in shock or otherwise unable to digest food, but the price elasticity of demand for Johnson & Johnson Band-Aids is high because numerous companies offer a nearly identical product.

Durable Goods The demand for durable goods tends to be more price elastic than the demand for nondurables. This is true because of the ready availability of a relatively inexpensive substitute in many cases—for instance, the repair of a used television, car, or refrigerator, rather than buying a new one. In addition, consumers of durable goods are often in a position to wait for a more favourable price, a sale, or a special deal when buying these items.

Percentage of Budget The demand for relatively high-priced goods tends to be more price elastic than the demand for inexpensive items, because expensive items account for a greater proportion of a person's expenditures than do low-priced items. Consequently, we would expect the demand for automobiles to be more price elastic than the demand for children's toys. The greater the percentage of the budget spent on a good, the larger the purchasing power released by any given price reduction or absorbed by any given price increase. And the larger this "income effect," the greater the price elasticity for normal goods. German households often spend as much as 20–30 percent of their disposable income on cars. French households do the same with food, but spend half as much as Germans on automobile transportation. Therefore, *ceteris paribus,* we would expect the price elasticity of demand for standard sedan autos to be higher in Germany than in France.

Time Frame of Analysis Over time, the demand for many products tends to become more elastic because of the increase in the number of effective substitutes that become available. For example, in the short run, the demand for gasoline may be relatively price inelastic because the only available alternatives are not taking a trip or using some form of public transportation. Over time, as consumers replace their cars, they find another excellent substitute for gasoline—namely, more fuel-efficient vehicles. Also, other product alternatives may become available, such as electric cars or cars powered by natural gas.

Another reason the time frame of analysis affects the elasticity involves transaction costs. Almost all purchases necessitate a certain transportation and time expense on the part of both buyer and seller. In addition, to respond to a price decrease, potential customers must first learn about the discount and then incur the cost of adjusting their own schedules to complete a purchase during the sale period. Because both search and adjustment costs for consumers are higher if sale prices last only a few minutes, the demand response to price changes is diminished the shorter the time period of adjustment. Predictable end-of-model-year promotions in the auto industry lasting throughout the month of August stimulate much more elastic demand than unannounced "Midnight Madness" sales that last only a few hours.

Recall that this reasoning assumes that all other factors influencing quantity demanded have remained unchanged. If this assumption (*ceteris paribus*) is not met, the elasticity measure may be quite different. This warning applies to all elasticity calculations and analysis.

Income Elasticity of Demand

Among the variables that affect demand, income is often one of the most important. One can also compute an income elasticity of demand, which is analogous to the price elasticity of demand.

Income Elasticity Defined

Income Elasticity
The ratio of the percentage change in quantity demanded to the percentage change in income, assuming that all other factors influencing demand remain unchanged.

Income elasticity of demand measures the responsiveness of a change in demand of some commodity to a change in income. It can be expressed as

$$(3.10) \qquad E_y = \frac{\% \Delta Q_D}{\% \Delta Y}, \textit{ceteris paribus}$$

where ΔQ_D = change in demand
ΔY = change in income

Various measures of income can be used in the analysis. One commonly used measure is consumer disposable income, calculated on an aggregate, household, or per capita basis.

Arc Income Elasticity

The *arc* income elasticity is a technique for calculating income elasticity between two income levels. It is computed as

$$(3.11) \qquad E_y = \frac{\dfrac{Q_2 - Q_1}{(Q_2 + Q_1)/2}}{\dfrac{Y_2 - Y_1}{(Y_2 + Y_1)/2}} = \frac{\Delta Q}{\Delta Y} \frac{(Y_1 + Y_2)}{(Q_1 + Q_2)}$$

where Q_2 = demand after an income change
Q_1 = demand before an income change
Y_2 = new level of income
Y_1 = original level of income

For example, assume that an increase in disposable personal income in Prince Edward Island from $1.0 billion to $1.1 billion is associated with an increase in boat sales in the province from 5,000 to 6,000 units. Determine the income elasticity over this range. Substituting the relevant data into Equation 3.11 yields

$$E_y = \frac{\dfrac{6,000 - 5,000}{(6,000 + 5,000)/2}}{\dfrac{\$1.10 - \$1.00}{(\$1.10 + \$1.00)/2}} = \frac{1,000}{\$0.10} \frac{(\$2.10)}{(11,000)} = 1.91$$

Free Trade and the Price Elasticity of Demand

The 1990s were characterized by an explosion of free trade agreements among important trading partners. The Europe 1992 plan virtually eliminated trade barriers, and goods now flow freely and without tariffs from one European country to another. Increasing standardization of products in these markets will further reduce trading barriers. On January 1, 1994, the North American Free Trade Agreement (NAFTA) was implemented in the United States, Canada, and Mexico. On January 1, 1995, the World Trade Organization came into existence, leading to a worldwide reduction in tariffs and other trade barriers.

What are the implications of these reduced trade barriers for estimates of price elasticity of demand? Free trade results in an effective increase in the number of substitute goods that are available to consumers and businesses in any country. Consequently, as barriers to free trade come down, the demand will become more price elastic for goods that historically have not been able to flow easily (without significant tariffs or quotas) between countries. Nestlé's yogurt and custard products now travel from manufacturing sites in the British Midlands to Milan in 17 hours, whereas the Customs processing and transportation bottlenecks once required 38 hours. Similarly, iron forging of crankshafts and engine blocks for North American autos now occurs primarily in Mexico. The winners in this globalization process should be consumers, who will have a wider variety of products to choose from at competitive prices. The losers will be those firms that cannot compete in a global market on the basis of cost, quality, and service.

Thus, a 1 percent increase in income would be expected to result in a 1.91 percent increase in demand, *ceteris paribus*.

Point Income Elasticity

The arc income elasticity measures the responsiveness of quantity demanded to changes in income levels over a range. In contrast, the *point* income elasticity provides a measure of this responsiveness at a specific point on the demand function. The point income elasticity is defined as

$$(3.12) \qquad E_y = \frac{\partial Q_D}{\partial Y} \cdot \frac{Y}{Q_D}$$

where Y = income

Q_D = demand for some commodity

$\dfrac{\partial Q_D}{\partial Y}$ = the partial derivative of quantity with respect to income

The algebraic demand function for Christmas trees (Equation 3.5) introduced earlier in the chapter can be used to illustrate the calculation of the point income elasticity. Suppose one is interested in determining the point income elasticity when the price is equal to $40 and per capita personal disposable income is equal to $30,000. Taking the partial derivative of Equation 3.5 with respect to Y yields

$$\frac{\partial Q_D}{\partial Y} = 2.5$$

Recall from the point price elasticity calculation described earlier in the chapter that substituting $P = \$40$ and $Y = \$30,000$ into Equation 3.5 gave Q_D equal to 20,000 units. Therefore, from Equation 3.12, one obtains

$$E_y = 2.50 \left(\frac{\$30,000}{20,000} \right) = 3.75$$

Thus, from an income level of $30,000, one could expect demand for Christmas trees to increase by 37.5 percent for each 10 percent increase in per capita disposable income, *ceteris paribus*.

Interpreting the Income Elasticity For most products, income elasticity is expected to be positive, that is, $E_y > 0$. Such goods are referred to as *normal goods*. Those goods having a calculated income elasticity that is negative are called *inferior goods*. Inferior goods are those that are purchased in smaller absolute quantities as the income of the consumer increases. Such food items as canned mackerel, dried beans, and subcompact autos are frequently cited as examples of inferior goods. They may compose a large part of a low-income diet or transportation budget, but may virtually disappear as income levels increase.

Income elasticity is typically defined as being low when it is between 0 and 1 and high if it is greater than 1. Goods that are usually considered luxury items generally have a high income elasticity, whereas goods that are necessities (or perceived as necessities) have low income elasticities. Normal goods with $E_y > 1$ are called *superior goods*.

Knowledge of the magnitude of the income elasticity of demand for a particular product is especially useful in relating forecasts of economic activity. In industries that produce goods having high income elasticities (such as new furniture), a major increase or decrease in economic activity will have a significant impact on demand. Knowledge of income elasticities is also useful in developing marketing strategies for products. For example, products having a high income elasticity can be promoted as being luxurious and stylish, whereas goods having a low income elasticity can be promoted as being economical.

Cross Price Elasticity of Demand

Another variable that often affects the demand for a product is the price of a related (substitute or complementary) product.

Cross Price Elasticity Defined

Cross Price Elasticity
The ratio of the percentage change in the quantity demanded of product A to the percentage change in the price of product B, assuming that all other factors influencing demand remain unchanged.

The **cross price elasticity** of demand, E_x, is a measure of the responsiveness of changes in the demand (Q_{DA}) for product A to price changes for product B (P_B).

(3.13)
$$E_x = \frac{\% \Delta Q_{DA}}{\% \Delta P_B}, \, ceteris \, paribus$$

where ΔQ_{DA} = change in demand for product A
ΔP_B = change in price of product B

Arc Cross Price Elasticity

The *arc* cross price elasticity is a technique for computing cross elasticity between two price levels. It is calculated as

$$(3.14) \qquad E_x = \frac{\dfrac{Q_{A2} - Q_{A1}}{(Q_{A2} + Q_{A1})/2}}{\dfrac{P_{B2} - P_{B1}}{(P_{B2} + P_{B1})/2}} = \frac{\Delta Q_A}{\Delta P_B} \frac{(P_{B2} + P_{B1})}{(Q_{A2} + Q_{A1})}$$

where Q_{A2} = demand for product A after a price change in product B
$\quad Q_{A1}$ = original demand for product A
$\quad P_{B2}$ = new price for product B
$\quad P_{B1}$ = original price for product B

For example, suppose the price of butter, P_B, increases from \$2 to \$3 per kilogram. As a result, the demand for margarine, Q_A, increases from 500 kilograms to 600 kilograms per month at a local grocery store. To compute the arc cross price elasticity of demand, substitute the relevant data into Equation 3.14:

$$E_x = \frac{\dfrac{600 - 500}{(600 + 500)/2}}{\dfrac{\$3 - \$2}{(\$3 + \$2)/2}} = \frac{100}{\$1} \frac{(\$5)}{(1,100)} = 0.45$$

This indicates that a 10 percent increase in the price of butter will lead to a 4.5 percent increase in the demand for margarine, which is, of course, a butter substitute.

Point Cross Price Elasticity

In a similar fashion, the *point* cross price elasticity between products A and B may be computed as

$$(3.15) \qquad E_x = \frac{\partial Q_A}{\partial P_B} \cdot \frac{P_B}{Q_A}$$

where P_B = price of product B
$\quad Q_A$ = demand for product A at price point P_B
$\quad \dfrac{\partial Q_A}{\partial P_B}$ = the partial derivative of Q_A with respect to P_B

Interpreting the Cross Price Elasticity

If the cross price elasticity measured between products A and B is *positive* (as might be expected in our butter/margarine example or between such products as plastic wrap and aluminum foil), the two products are referred to as *substitutes* for each other. The higher the cross price elasticity, the closer the substitute relationship. A *negative* cross price elasticity, on the other hand, indicates that two products are *complementary*. For example, a significant decrease in the price of DVD players would probably result in a substantial increase in the demand for DVDs.

Competition Regulation and Cross Price Elasticities

The number of close substitutes may be an important determinant of the degree of competition in a market. The fewer and poorer the number of close substitutes that exist for a product, the greater the amount of monopoly power that is possessed by the producing or selling firm. An important issue in competition cases involves the appropriate definition of the relevant product market to be used in computing statistics of market control (e.g., market share).

As Wal-Mart has demonstrated, shoppers will flock to a superstore despite numerous closer small retailers. So, despite the enormous preexisting supply of traditional rivals and the exceptional ease of entry (and exit) at small scale, competition for superstore retailers appears to come only from other superstore retailers. An appropriate application of the *Competition Act* probably should bar superstore mergers as a route to near-monopoly status.

Other Demand Elasticity Measures

Price, income, and cross-elasticity measures are the most common applications of the elasticity concept to demand analysis. However, elasticity is a general concept. We will discuss some less common elasticities.[9]

Advertising Elasticity

Advertising elasticity measures the responsiveness of sales to changes in advertising expenditures. It is measured by the ratio of the percentage change in sales to a percentage change in advertising expenditures. The higher the advertising elasticity coefficient, the more responsive sales are to changes in the advertising budget. An awareness of this elasticity measure may assist advertising or marketing managers in their determination of appropriate levels of advertising outlays relative to price promotions or display and packaging expenditures.

Elasticity of Price Expectations

In an inflationary environment or in projecting durable goods demand (houses, for example), the elasticity of price expectations may provide helpful insights. It is defined as the percentage change in *future* prices expected as a result of current percentage price changes. A coefficient that exceeds unity indicates that buyers expect future prices to rise (or fall) by a greater percentage amount than current prices. A positive coefficient that is less than unity indicates that buyers expect future prices to increase (or decrease) but by a lesser percentage amount than current price changes. A zero coefficient indicates that consumers feel that current price changes have no influence on future changes. Finally, a negative coefficient indicates that consumers believe an increase (decrease) in current prices will lead to a decrease (increase) in future prices.

A positive coefficient of price expectations (especially one greater than unity) suggests that current price increases may shift the demand function to the right. This may result in the same or greater sales at the higher prices, as consumers try to beat future price increases by stockpiling the commodity. The stockpiling that occurs when crops freeze (e.g., coffee beans in South America) or otherwise appear in short supply (e.g., crude oil during the Venezuelan general strike of 2002) can be explained, at least in part, by the effects of a high elasticity of price expectations.

---

[9] In addition to demand elasticities, one can also define a price elasticity of *supply*. The price elasticity of supply measures the responsiveness of quantity supplied by producers to changes in prices. An inelastic supply function is one whose price elasticity coefficient is less than unity. It indicates that a 1 percent change in price will lead to a less than 1 percent change in quantity supplied. An elastic supply function has an elasticity coefficient greater than unity, indicating that a 1 percent change in price will result in a greater than 1 percent change in quantity supplied. Because producers are normally willing to supply more at higher prices, the sign of the price elasticity coefficient of supply will normally be positive.

Combined Effect of Demand Elasticities

When two or more of the factors that affect demand change simultaneously, one is often interested in determining their combined impact on quantity demanded. For example, suppose that a firm plans to increase the price of its product next period and anticipates that consumers' incomes will also increase next period. Other factors affecting demand such as advertising expenditures and competitors' prices are expected to remain the same in the next period. From the formula for the price elasticity (Equation 3.2), the effect on quantity demanded of a price increase would be equal to

$$\%\Delta Q_D = E_D(\%\Delta P)$$

Similarly, from the formula for the income elasticity (Equation 3.10), the effect on quantity demanded of an increase in consumers' incomes would be equal to

$$\%\Delta Q_D = E_y(\%\Delta Y)$$

Each of these percentage changes (divided by 100 to put them into a decimal form) would be multiplied by current period demand (Q_1) to get the respective changes in quantity demanded caused by the price and income increases. Assuming that the price and income effects are independent and additive, the quantity demanded next period (Q_2) would be equal to current period demand (Q_1) plus the changes caused by the price and income increases:

$$Q_2 = Q_1 + Q_1\,[E_D(\%\Delta P)] + Q_1[E_y(\%\Delta Y)]$$

or

(3.16) $$Q_2 = Q_1\,[1 + E_D(\%\Delta P) + E_y(\%\Delta Y)]$$

The combined use of income and price elasticities, illustrated here for forecasting demand, can be generalized to include any of the elasticity concepts that were developed in the preceding sections of this chapter.

E X A M P L E

PRICE AND INCOME EFFECTS: THE SEIKO COMPANY

Seiko's Internet site is located at **www.seiko.co.jp**.

Suppose Seiko is planning to increase the price of its watches by 10 percent in the coming year. Economic forecasters expect real disposable personal income to increase by 6 percent during the same period. From past experience, the price elasticity of demand has been estimated to be approximately −1.3 and the income elasticity has been estimated at 2.0. These elasticities are assumed to remain constant over the range of price and income changes anticipated. Seiko currently sells 200,000 watches per year. Determine the forecasted demand for next year (assuming that the percentage price and income effects are independent and additive). Substituting the relevant data into Equation 2.16 yields

$$Q_2 = 200{,}000\,[1 + (-1.3)(0.10) + (2.0)(0.06)]$$
$$= 198{,}000 \text{ units}$$

The forecasted demand for next year is 198,000 watches, assuming that other factors that influence demand (e.g., advertising and competitors' prices) remain unchanged. In this case, the positive impact of the projected increase in household income is more than offset by the decline in quantity demanded associated with a price increase.

Indifference Curve Analysis

The derivation of a consumer's demand function is based on indifference curves and budget lines. **Indifference curves** reveal the consumer's consumption preferences, or utility, for various combinations of goods. **Budget lines** limit the choices available for consumption, based on the prices of various goods and on the consumer's income.

Consider the situation of a consumer who wishes to allocate an available subbudget of income between two commodities, restaurant food (F) and entertainment (E). The utility, U, or satisfaction the consumer receives from the two goods, can be expressed as

$$(3.17) \qquad U = f(Q_F, Q_E)$$

where Q_F and Q_E are the respective quantities of food and entertainment consumed. The utility received from consuming various combinations of goods F and E can be ranked in an ordinal fashion. That is, it is possible to indicate that a consumer prefers 8 restaurant meals and 3 movies per month to an alternative combination, such as 10 meals and 1 movie. This notion of ordinal utility can be depicted by *indifference curves*. An indifference curve is a plotting of points representing various combinations of two goods, for example F and E, such that the consumer is *indifferent* among any combinations along a specific indifference curve.

Figure 3.5 shows two indifference curves, U_1 and U_2. The consumer is indifferent among combinations 1, 2, and 3 on curve U_1, but prefers any combination of E and F, such as points 4 and 5 on curve U_2 to any combination available on curve U_1. The most important properties of indifference curves are:

1. Any combination of commodities lying on an indifference curve (U_2, for example) that is above and to the right of another indifference curve (such as U_1) is the preferred combination.

FIGURE 3.5

Indifference Curves

The indifference curve U_2U_2 represents tradeoffs of entertainment and food that provide the same level of individual satisfaction or utility. The indifference curve U_1U_1 also represents such tradeoffs, albeit at a lower level of satisfaction.

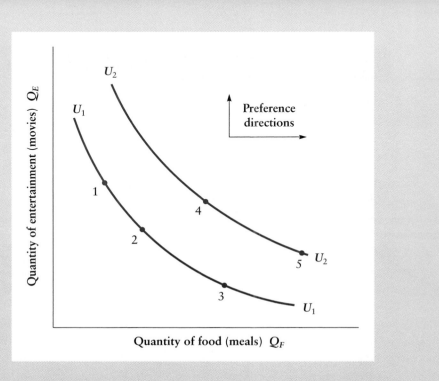

2. Indifference curves have a negative (downward) slope to the right, indicating that more of E can be obtained only by consuming less of F.

3. Indifference curves never intersect.

4. Indifference curves are convex to the origin. The absolute value of the slope of an indifference curve is the marginal rate of substitution of F for E. The convex shape of an indifference curve indicates that the slope diminishes as one moves to the right (i.e., the consumer is willing to give up fewer and fewer units of E to gain an increasing number of units of F). This is consistent with the law of diminishing marginal utility, which states that the additional satisfaction, or marginal utility, derived from successive units of a good is thought to decline.

EXAMPLE

ATTRIBUTE ANALYSIS: A MARKETING APPLICATION OF INDIFFERENCE CURVES

Why would one consumer prefer a Sony television set and another prefer a Hitachi? Modern consumer theory suggests that a consumer purchases a product (or service) based on the utility or satisfaction derived from its attributes. Consumer A may purchase a Sony because he perceives that the Sony has a better reputation and greater colour accuracy. Consumer B may purchase a Hitachi because she notes that it has a longer warranty and a brighter picture. *Attribute analysis* is important when designing and marketing a product. Firms often spend considerable sums for marketing research on desirable attributes and what consumers will pay for them.

Attribute analysis is multidimensional. To simplify the attribute analysis of purchasing a television set, however, assume that only colour accuracy and picture brightness matter to the consumer. Further

assume that each manufacturer has designed a TV for the same price point, and at this price, the consumer can afford and will buy only one TV. Table 3.6 shows these attributes for three TV brands.

In Figure 3.6, points for these three brands are denoted as H for Hitachi, P for Panasonic, and S for Sony. Suppose there are many other manufacturers that have targeted the same price point and that they have targeted market niches of attribute combinations that fill in the gaps between Hitachi and Panasonic and between Panasonic and Sony. The consumer would face a tradeoff curve of feasible choices denoted by SPH in Figure 3.6. The figure shows an indifference curve AA' for consumer A, and an indifference curve BB' for consumer B that reflect the differences in their preferences. Thus, Figure 3.6 shows that consumer A prefers the Sony and consumer B prefers the Hitachi.

Table 3.6   Attributes of Three TV Brands

TV Brand	Attribute Rating	
	Colour Accuracy	**Picture Brightness**
Hitachi	6	9
Panasonic	8	8
Sony	9	6

FIGURE 3.6

Attribute Analysis

Consumers A and B face the same tradeoff curve, SPH, of feasible attribute choices of colour TV sets at the same price. However, consumers A and B choose different TVs because their individual indifference curves *AA'* and *BB'*, respectively, differ.

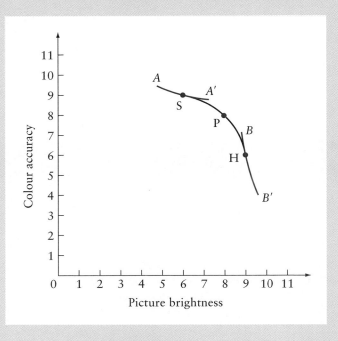

Budget Lines

In choosing the amount of goods *F* and *E* that maximizes personal utility, the consumer is limited by the amount of income available to purchase these goods. The consumer faces an $(F + E)$ subbudget of the household budget constraint, of the form

(3.18) $$M = P_F Q_F + P_E Q_E$$

where *M* represents the amount of income available to the consumer to be spent on goods *F* and *E*. P_F and P_E represent the price of a unit of *F* and *E*, respectively. The amount spent on *F*—$P_F Q_F$—plus the amount spent on *E*—$P_E Q_E$—equals the total amount of income available, *M*. This budget line is shown in Figure 3.7. It intersects the *y*-axis (vertical) at M/P_E—the number of movies consumed if the entire subbudget is spent on *E*. The budget line intersects the *x*-axis (horizontal) at M/P_F—the number of meals consumed if the entire subbudget is spent on *F*. Any combination of meals and movies lying on or below the budget line is available to the consumer. Any household that prefers more meals and movies to less will select for consumption some combination of *F* and *E* that lies on the subbudget constraint—i.e., a consumption bundle that exhausts the subbudget.

Graphical Determination of the Optimal Combination

Given the indifference curves and budget constraint, the consumer's problem is to choose the combination of *F* and *E* that *maximizes* the utility derived without overspending the budget. Because a consumer's satisfaction increases with combinations

FIGURE 3.7

Optimal Combination

The line $(M/P_E)(M/P_F)$ represents the consumer's budget constraint. The consumer attains the highest feasible level of utility at point D, where the budget constraint is tangent to the indifference curve U_2U_2.

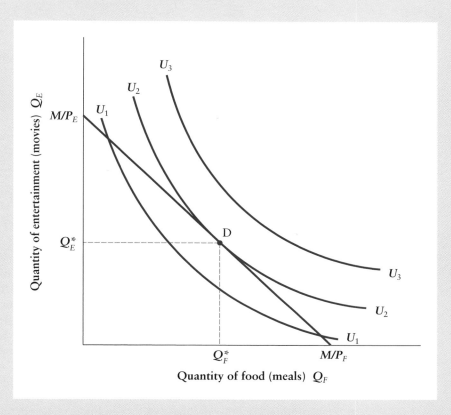

moving upward and/or to the right, utility is maximized at the point of *tangency* between the budget constraint and the highest consumer indifference curve, as illustrated in Figure 3.7. Given three possible indifference curves and a budget constraint, the optimal combination of goods F and E for this consumer is given at point D. At this point the consumer can achieve a U_2 level of satisfaction by consuming Q_F^* units of F and Q_E^* units of E. These levels provide the highest utility without violating the budget constraint.

At the point of tangency of the indifference curve (U_2) and the budget line in Figure 3.7, the slope[10] of the indifference curve is equal to the slope of the budget line. The slope ($\Delta Q_E/\Delta Q_F$) of the budget line is equal to the ratio of the price of commodity $F(P_F)$ to the price of commodity $E(P_E)$; that is

(3.19)
$$\frac{\Delta Q_E}{\Delta Q_F} = \frac{(M/P_E - 0)}{(M/P_F - 0)} = \frac{P_F}{P_E}$$

The slope of the indifference curve ($\Delta Q_E/\Delta Q_F$) at any point measures the consumer's *marginal rate of substitution* (*MRS*) of commodity E for commodity F (holding utility

---

[10] Note that the slopes of the indifference curves and budget line are both negative. In the remainder of this section, slope will be taken to mean *absolute value*.

constant). This slope is equal to the ratio of the marginal utility of F ($MU_F = \partial U/\partial Q_F$) to the marginal utility of E($MU_E = \partial U/\partial Q_E$), that is

(3.20)
$$\frac{\Delta Q_E}{\Delta Q_F} = MRS = \frac{MU_F}{MU_E}$$

At the optimum (tangency) point, setting Equation 3.19 equal to Equation 3.20 yields[11]

(3.21)
$$\frac{MU_F}{MU_E} = \frac{P_F}{P_E}$$

or

(3.22)
$$\frac{MU_F}{P_F} = \frac{MU_E}{P_E}$$

Graphical Derivation of the Demand Function

A consumer's demand function for a good can be derived graphically based on the consumer's indifference curves and budget line.

Consider a consumer whose indifference curves and budget line are shown in Figure 3.8. Assume that the consumer has \$350 to spend on products F and E. The initial price of E is \$5 per movie and the initial price of F is \$10 per restaurant meal. Under these conditions, the consumer could acquire 70 movies or 35 meals or any other combination thereof (illustrated by the lower budget line). Three indifference curves are plotted, U_1, U_2, and U_3. Given the income constraint of \$350 and the initial prices of F (\$10) and E (\$5), the consumer would choose combination X on curve U_1. At this point, the consumer would acquire 16 units of F. Hence, at a price of \$10 per unit, the consumer would demand 16 meals. This point is now plotted on the lower panel of Figure 3.8 as point X'.

If the price of F declines to \$5, a new budget line is defined that intersects the Q_F axis at 70 units. The new optimum occurs at point Y, with 35 units of F being demanded at a price of \$5. This point is plotted on the lower panel at Y'.

Finally, at a price of \$3.50 for a unit of F, a new optimum point occurs at Z, with 64 units of F being demanded. By plotting in the lower panel of Figure 3.8 the three prices and associated quantities demanded, the familiar demand curve, D_F, for food is derived. This is illustrated by the curve that connects points X', Y', and Z'.

Income and Substitution Effects

Indifference curve analysis can also be used to illustrate the income and substitution effects of a price decline. Consider the case of a consumer who consumes food and entertainment with an initial budget constraint given in Figure 3.9 as XV. The consumer will buy Q_1 units of F and Q_4 units of E, as indicated at point 1.

If the price of food declines such that the new budget line becomes XV', point 2 represents the new optimum for the consumer. This point falls on the higher of the two

---

[11] A more rigorous approach to the determination of the optimal combination of goods F and E can be obtained by using the Lagrangian multiplier technique. Maximizing a consumer's utility subject to a budget constraint can be represented by

$$U_\lambda = f(Q_F, Q_E) - \lambda(P_F Q_F + P_E Q_E - M)$$

Differentiating this function with respect to Q_F, Q_E, and λ, and setting the derivatives equal to zero yields

$$MU_F = \lambda P_F, MU_E = \lambda P_E, M = P_F Q_F + P_E Q_E$$

Clearly, the ratio of the marginal utilities equals the price ratio given by Equation 3.21.

FIGURE 3.8

Derivation of a Demand Function

The points X, Y, and Z in the top panel illustrate how an individual's consumption of entertainment and food changes. The points X′, Y′, and Z′ in the bottom panel illustrate how an individual consumer's demand curve for food is derived from the analysis of the indifference curves and budget constraints in the top panel.

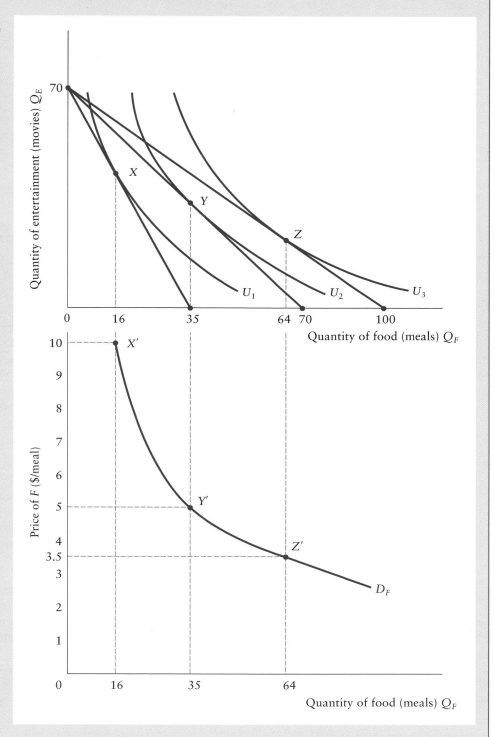

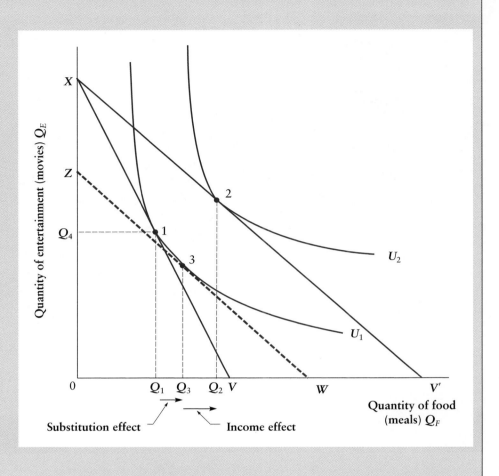

FIGURE 3.9

Income and Substitution Effects for Normal Goods

Lowering the price of food allows the consumer to move from point 1 to point 2. This movement can be decomposed into two effects. The first is the substitution effect that is the movement along the original indifference curve from point 1 to point 3. The second is the income effect that is the movement from point 3 on the budget line *ZW* to point 2 on the parallel but higher budget line *XV'*.

Substitution Effect

Movement along an indifference curve due to a price change while holding "real" income constant.

Income Effect

Movement from one indifference curve to another due to the change in "real" income caused by a price change.

indifference curves, U_2, plotted on the figure. Given the new lower price for food, the consumer demands Q_2 units of F.

Next, we construct a new, artificial budget line, *ZW*, which is parallel to *XV'* and tangent to the original indifference curve U_1. From the original optimal combination of food and entertainment, point 1, to the artificial optimum, point 3, the "real" income of the consumer has remained the same in the sense that the consumer experiences the same utility at point 1 and point 3. The change in demand for F from Q_1 to Q_3 may be thought of as representing the "pure" substitution effect of food for entertainment resulting from the price reduction for food. That is, the **substitution effect** is the movement along an indifference curve due to a price change while holding "real" income constant.

In contrast, the increased consumption of food measured from points Q_3 to Q_2 may be thought of as the "pure" income effect. This is so because the only difference between *ZW* and *XV'* is the level of income that each reflects. That is, the **income effect** is the movement from one indifference curve to another due to the change in "real" income caused by a price change.

In summary, a decline in price for food results in the consumer demanding $Q_3 - Q_1$ more units of food because of the substitution effect, and $Q_2 - Q_3$ more units of food because of the income effect for a superior good.

CONDITIONAL VERSUS UNCONDITIONAL GRANTS: A NONPROFIT APPLICATION OF INDIFFERENCE CURVES

The federal government and provincial governments are often at odds over whether a federal grant to the provinces should be conditional or unconditional. The federal government prefers conditional grants to ensure that the grant money is spent for the intended purposes. Provinces, however, prefer no strings to be attached. Consider a province that currently has a budget of $10 billion. Point A in Figure 3.10 represents the highest attainable level of social utility for this provincial budget of $10 billion with $4 billion in health care expenditures and $6 billion in other expenditures.

Suppose the federal government provides the province with a conditional grant of $0.50 for additional health care services for every $1 that the province spends on health care. For simplicity, assume that this grant is capped at $5 billion. That is, if the province spends its entire budget of $10 billion on health care, it would receive a federal grant of $5 billion that also must be spent on health care. Thus, the province's initial budget line GH in Figure 3.10 rotates around point G to become the conditional grant budget line GI. From the provincial viewpoint, the conditional federal grant has

FIGURE 3.10

Health Care Grants: Conditional vs. Unconditional

Point A represents the province's initial equilibrium. Point B represents the province's equilibrium if the federal government simply subsidizes one-third of health care cost. Point D represents the province's equilibrium if it is constrained by the federal government to increase health care expenditures by 50%. Point E represents the province's equilibrium if the federal government gives it $2 billion with no constraints on its use.

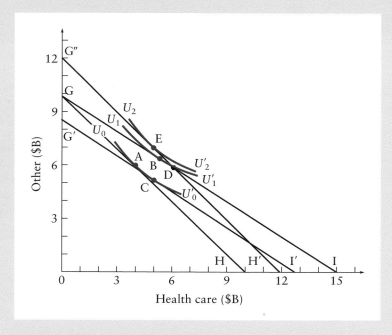

the same effect as a price reduction for the unit cost of health care. For example, suppose the unit cost of health care is $10 per procedure. Initially, the province could purchase at most $10 billion/ ($10 per procedure) = 1 billion procedures. Now from the provincial viewpoint, the cost to the province is $6.67 for each procedure because the federal government pays the other $3.33. Thus, the province can now provide at most $10 billion/($6.67 per procedure) = 1.5 billion procedures.

With this new budget line GI, the highest attainable level of social utility is point B, with $5.4 billion in health care expenditures. The movement from point A to point B in Figure 3.10 can be decomposed into a substitution effect and an income effect. The movement from point A to point C represents the substitution effect. "Real" income is held constant because the province remains on the initial social indifference curve $U_0 U_0'$. The budget line $G'I'$ has the same relative prices at the budget line GI, but is tangent to $U_0 U_0'$. The movement from point C to point B represents the income effect as the province moves from budget line $G'I'$ to the parallel budget line GI that represents higher income.

Since the province is now spending $5.4 billion on health care, the federal government's share of the cost is $1.8 billion. Even though the federal grant of $1.8 billion is conditional, the provincial government has increased health care expenditures by only $1.4 billion and has "diverted" $0.4 billion away from health care to other provincial expenditures. Of course, the federal government may wish that the province increase its expenditures on health care by the full amount of any funds that the federal government conditionally grants. If the province were to comply with this request, then the federal government must actually provide a $2 billion conditional grant. This is because the province is currently operating at point A in Figure 3.10, with $6 billion in other expenditures and $4 billion in health care expenditures.

From the province's viewpoint, compliance is costly in a social utility sense. A $2 billion federal grant that must be spent on health care in addition to the $4 billion that the province currently spends means the province operates at point D in Figure 3.10. Note, though, that the province prefers point B to point D, even though point B represents a grant of only $1.8 billion, because the province attains a higher level of social utility at point B.

Suppose the federal government does not have an effective enforcement mechanism for how the supposedly conditional grant is spent. The province would then argue for a $2 billion grant based on its current health care spending of $4 billion, with the vague promise to appropriately spend the additional $2 billion. The province prefers to treat the $2 billion as an unconditional grant and proceeds to operate along the budget line $G''H'$ that represents provincial expenditures of $12 billion. The new optimal combination is point E on the social indifference curve $U_2 U_2'$. Point E represents $7.2 billion in other expenditures and $4.8 billion in health care expenditures, maintaining the 60/40 percent split in expenditures that it had at point A.

Health Care Reform and Cigarette Taxes

Cigarette smoking increases health care costs not only for smokers but also, because of second-hand smoke risk factors, for non-smokers. Thus, maximizing tax revenue from cigarettes is an inappropriate objective. Such a tax rate would be too low to discourage much smoking, and health care costs would be high.

A more appropriate objective would be for the government to set the tax rate high enough to discourage smoking but not so high that consumers would widely switch to contraband (stolen or smuggled) cigarettes. For example, in Ontario, "Tobacco-related diseases cost the health care system $1.7 billion annually and result in $2.6 billion in productivity losses."[*] Furthermore, "Smoking is the leading cause of preventable [premature] death, killing an estimated 16,000 people every year."[†]

[*]"Ontario's Latest Bid to Crush Smoking," *Ottawa Citizen*, December 15, 2004, p. A3. For the latest information, see the Smoke-Free Ontario site at www.health.gov.on.ca.
[†]Ibid.

Summary

- Demand relationships can be represented in the form of a schedule (table), graph, or algebraic function. Each of these methods of presentation provides insights into the demand concept.

- The demand curve is typically downward sloping, indicating that consumers are willing to purchase more units of a good or service at lower prices.

- Changes in price result in *movement* along the demand curve, whereas changes in any of the other variables in the demand function result in *shifts* of the entire demand curve. Thus "changes in quantity demanded along" a particular demand curve result from price changes. In contrast, when one speaks of "changes in demand," one is referring to shifts in the entire demand curve.

- Some of the factors that cause a shift in the entire demand curve are changes in the income level of consumers, the price of substitute and complementary goods, the level of advertising, competitors' advertising expenditures, population, consumer preferences, time period of adjustment, taxes or subsidies, and price expectations.

- *Elasticity* refers to the responsiveness of one economic variable to changes in another, related variable. Thus, *price elasticity of demand* refers to the percentage change in quantity demanded associated with a percentage change in price, holding constant the effects of other factors thought to influence demand. Demand is said to be relatively price *elastic* if a given percentage change in price results in a greater percentage change in quantity demanded. Demand is said to be relatively price *inelastic* if a given percentage change in price results in a lesser percentage change in quantity demanded.

■ When demand is unit elastic, marginal revenue equals zero and total revenue is maximized. When demand is elastic, an increase (decrease) in price will result in a decrease (increase) in total revenue. When demand is inelastic, an increase (decrease) in price will result in an increase (decrease) in total revenue.

■ *Income elasticity* of demand refers to the percentage change in quantity demanded associated with a percentage change in income, holding constant the effects of other factors thought to influence demand.

■ *Cross elasticity* of demand refers to the percentage change in quantity demanded of good A associated with a percentage change in the price of good B.

■ An understanding of the magnitude of various elasticity measures for a product can be extremely helpful when forecasting demand and formulating marketing or operations plans.

■ *Indifference curves* reveal the consumer's preference for various combinations of goods.

■ *Budget lines* limit the choices available for consumption based on the prices of various goods and the consumer's income.

■ *Substitution effect* is the movement along an indifference curve due to a price change while holding "real" income constant.

■ *Income effect* is the movement from one indifference curve to another due to the change in "real income" caused by a price change.

Self-Test Exercises

1. A number of empirical studies of automobile demand have been made, yielding the following estimates of income and price elasticities:

Study	Income Elasticity	Price Elasticity
Chow	+3.0	−1.2
Alkinson	+2.5	−1.4
Roos and Von Szeliski	+2.5	−1.5
Suits	+3.9	−1.2

Assume that income and price effects on automobile sales are *independent* and *additive*. Assume also that the auto companies intend to increase the average price of an automobile by about 6 percent in the next year, and that next year's disposable personal income is expected to be 4 percent higher than this year's. If this year's automobile sales in North America were 11 million units, how many would you expect to be sold under each pair of price and income demand elasticity estimates?

2. The following table gives hypothetical data for the weekly purchase of sirloin steak by a college fraternity house. Compute all meaningful arc elasticity coefficients (price, cross, and income). Remember that the effects of the other factors must be held constant when computing any of these elasticities.

Week	Price per Kg of Steak	Quantity of Steak Purchased (Kg)	Income (Member Dues)	Price per Kg of Hamburger
1	$5.00	100	$1,000	$1.80
2	5.20	95	1,000	1.80
3	5.20	100	1,100	1.80
4	5.20	105	1,100	1.90
5	5.00	115	1,100	1.90
6	5.00	105	1,100	1.80
7	5.00	100	1,000	1.80
8	5.30	90	1,000	1.80
9	5.30	110	1,000	2.00
10	5.30	90	800	2.00

3. If the price of DVD players declines by 20 percent and the total revenue from the sale of DVD players rises, what can you say about the price elasticity of demand for DVD players? Will this price reduction necessarily lead to an increase in profits for DVD player manufacturers?

Exercises

1. Jenkins Photo Company manufactures an automatic camera that currently sells for $90. Sales volume is about 2,000 cameras per month. A close competitor, the ABC Photo Company, has cut the price of a similar camera it makes from $100 to $80. Jenkins' economist has estimated the cross elasticity of demand between the two firms' products at about 0.4, given current income and price levels.

   What impact, if any, will the action by ABC have on total revenue generated by Jenkins, if Jenkins leaves its current price unchanged?

2. The Potomac Range Corporation manufactures a line of microwave ovens costing $500 each. Its sales have averaged about 6,000 units per month during the past year. In August, Potomac's closest competitor, Spring City Stove Works, cut its price for a closely competitive model from $600 to $450. Potomac noticed that its sales volume declined to 4,500 units per month after Spring City announced its price cut.

   a. What is the arc cross elasticity of demand between Potomac's oven and the competitive Spring City model?

   b. Would you say that these two firms are very close competitors? What other factors could have influenced the observed relationship?

   c. If Potomac knows that the arc price elasticity of demand for its ovens is −3.0, what price would Potomac have to charge to sell the same number of units it did before the Spring City price cut?

3. The price elasticity of demand for personal computers is estimated to be −2.2. If the price of personal computers declines by 20 percent, what will be the expected percentage increase in the quantity of computers sold?

4. The Olde Yogurt Factory has reduced the price of its popular Mmmm Sundae from $2.25 to $1.75. As a result, the firm's daily sales of these sundaes have increased from 1,500/day to 1,800/day. Compute the arc price elasticity of demand over this price and consumption quantity range.

5. The subway fare in your community has just been increased from a current level of 50 cents to $1.00 per ride. As a result, the transit authority notes a decline in ridership of 30 percent.

   a. Compute the price elasticity of demand for subway rides.

   b. If the transit authority reduces the fare back to 50 cents, what impact would you expect on the ridership? Why?

6. The demand for mobile homes in Azerpajama, a small, oil-rich sheikdom, has been estimated to be $Q_D = 250{,}000 - 35P$. If this relationship remains approximately valid in the future:

   a. How many mobile homes would be demanded at a price of $2,000? $4,000? $6,000?

   b. What is the *arc* price elasticity of demand between $2,000 and $4,000? Between $4,000 and $6,000?

   c. What is the *point* price elasticity of demand at $2,000, $4,000, and $6,000?

   d. If 25,000 mobile homes were sold last year, what would you expect the average price to have been?

   e. In a move to increase his popularity (and in the face of rapidly accumulating oil royalties), Sheik Ahmed has decided to subsidize the price of mobile homes and offer them to all who want them at a price of only $1,000. As the sheik's chief advisor, how many homes would you expect to be bought at this bargain-basement price? At this price, how confident are you of the estimated demand equation?

   f. Without subsidy, what is the highest theoretical price that anyone would pay for a mobile home in the sheikdom?

7. A typical consumer behaved in the following manner with respect to purchases of butter over the past eight years:

Year	Price of Butter ($/Kg)	Quantity of Butter Purchased (Kg)	Real Income (Dollars)	Price of Margarine ($/Kg)
1	$1.90	200	$11,000	$0.65
2	2.20	180	11,000	0.65
3	2.20	190	11,500	0.65
4	2.20	200	11,500	0.90
5	2.30	170	11,500	0.90
6	1.98	190	11,500	0.90
7	1.98	175	10,500	0.90
8	1.98	150	10,500	0.65

   Compute all meaningful price, income, and cross-elasticity coefficients. (Remember that the effects of other factors need to be held constant when computing any one of these coefficients.)

8. If the marginal revenue from a product is $15 and the price elasticity of demand is -1.2, what is the price of the product?

9. Excess inventory overhang in some markets like autos and clothing results in price adjustment to clear the market. In other markets, however, such as restaurant food and milk, inventory overhang leads to a slashing of production orders with little or no price change. Why do some markets adopt the one adjustment mechanism while others adopt just the opposite?

10. The demand function for bicycles in Holland has been estimated to be

$$Q = 2,000 + 15Y - 5.5P$$

where Y is income in *thousands* of euros, Q is the quantity demanded in units, and P is the price per unit. When $P = 150$ euros and $Y = 15(000)$ euros, determine the following:

a. Price elasticity of demand.

b. Income elasticity of demand.

11. Two goods have a cross price elasticity of $+1.2$.

a. Would you describe these goods as substitutes or complements?

b. If the price of one of the goods increases by 5 percent, what will happen to the demand for the other product, holding constant the effects of all other factors?

12. In an attempt to increase revenues and profits, a firm is considering a 4 percent increase in price and an 11 percent increase in advertising. If the price elasticity of demand is -1.5 and the advertising elasticity of demand is $+0.6$, would you expect an increase or decrease in total revenues?

13. During 2004, the demand for a firm's product has been estimated to be

$$Q = 1,000 - 200P$$

During 2005, the demand for that same firm's product has been estimated to be

$$Q = 1,150 - 225P$$

If the price was \$2 during 2004 and \$3 during 2005, has the price elasticity of demand for this product been increasing or decreasing?

14. Between 2003 and 2004, the quantity of automobiles produced and sold declined by 20 percent. During this period the real price of cars increased by 5 percent, real income levels declined by 2 percent, and the real cost of gasoline increased by 20 percent. Knowing that the income elasticity of demand is $+1.5$ and the cross price elasticity of gasoline and cars is -0.3, compute:

a. The impact of the decline in real income levels on the demand for cars.

b. The impact of the gasoline price increase on the demand for cars.

c. The price elasticity of the demand for cars during this period.

15. Compute the price elasticity of demand and the income elasticity of demand at the prices and income specified in the following demand function:

$$Q = 25 - 4P + 6I$$

a. When $I = 10$ and $P = 4$

b. When $I = 4$ and $P = 6$

16. Over the past six months, Heads-Up Hair Care, Inc., has normally had sales of 500 bottles of A-6 Hair Conditioner per week. On the weeks when Heads-Up ran sales on its B-8 Hair Conditioner, cutting the price of B-8 from \$10 to \$8, sales of A-6 declined to 300 bottles.

a. What is the arc cross elasticity of demand between A-6 and B-8?

b. If the price of B-8 was increased to \$12, what effect would you expect this to have on the quantity demanded of A-6?

c. What does the evidence indicate about the relationship between B-8 and A-6?

17. The income elasticity of demand for residential use of electricity has been estimated as 0.3. If the price of electricity is expected to remain constant and the price of substitute goods is expected to remain constant, what would you expect to happen to the demand for electricity by residential customers if disposable personal income was expected to decline by 10 percent over the next year?

18. A study of the long-term income elasticity of demand for housing by renters is in the range of 0.8 to 1.0, whereas the income elasticity for owner–occupants is from 0.7 to 1.15.

   a. If income levels are expected to increase at a compound annual rate of 4 percent per year for the next five years, forecast the impact of this increase in income levels on the quantity of housing demanded in the two markets (rental and owner–occupant) in five years (assume that the price of housing does not change over this period).

   b. What would be the impact of price increases during this period on the levels of demand forecasted in part (a)?

19. Given the following demand function:

Price P ($)	Quantity Q_D (Units)	Arc Elasticity E_D	Total Revenue ($)	Marginal Revenue ($/Unit)
$12	30	n.a.	_____	n.a.
11	40	_____	_____	_____
10	50	_____	_____	_____
9	60	_____	_____	_____
8	70	_____	_____	_____
7	80	_____	_____	_____
6	90	_____	_____	_____
5	100	_____	_____	_____
4	110	_____	_____	_____

   a. Compute the associated arc elasticity, total revenue, and marginal revenue values.

   b. On separate graphs, plot the demand function, total revenue function, and marginal revenue function.

20. The Stopdecay Company sells an electric toothbrush for $25. Its sales have averaged 8,000 units per month over the last year. Recently, its closest competitor, Decayfighter, reduced the price of its electric toothbrush from $35 to $30. As a result, Stopdecay's sales declined by 1,500 units per month.

   a. What is the arc cross elasticity of demand between Stopdecay's toothbrush and Decayfighter's toothbrush? What does this indicate about the relationship between the two products?

   b. If Stopdecay knows that the arc price elasticity of demand for its toothbrush is −1.5, what price would the firm have to charge to sell the same number of units as it did before the Decayfighter price cut? Assume that Decayfighter holds the price of its toothbrush constant at $30.

   c. What is Stopdecay's average monthly total revenue from the sale of electric toothbrushes before and after the price change determined in part (b)?

   d. Is the result in part (c) necessarily desirable? What other factors would have to be taken into consideration?

21. The demand for renting motorboats in a resort town has been estimated to be $Q_D = 5{,}000 - 50P$, where Q_D is the quantity of boats demanded (boat-hours) and P is the average price per hour to rent a motorboat. If this relationship holds true in the future:

   a. How many boat-hours will be demanded at rental prices of $10, $20, and $30 per hour?

   b. What is the *arc* price elasticity of demand between $10 and $20? Between $20 and $30?

   c. What is the *point* price elasticity of demand at $10, $20, and $30?

   d. If the number of boat rental hours was 4,250 last year, what would you expect the average rental rate per hour to have been?

Table 1		
Average Daily Transit Riders (2002)	**Round-Trip Fare**	**Average Downtown Parking Rate**
5,000	$1.00	$5.50

Table 2		
Year	**Round-Trip Fare**	**Average Parking Rates**
2003	$1.00	$6.50
2004	$1.25	$6.50

22. The Highlands Transportation Company operates an urban bus system. Economic analysis performed by the firm indicates that two major factors influence the demand for its services: fare levels and downtown parking rates. Table 1 above presents information available from 2002 operations. Forecasts of future fares and daily parking rates are presented in Table 2 above.

    The firm's economists supplied the following information so that the firm can estimate ridership in 2003 and 2004. Based on past experience, the coefficient of cross elasticity between bus ridership and downtown parking rates is estimated at 0.2, given a fare of $1.00 per round trip. This is not expected to change for a fare increase to $1.25. The price elasticity of demand is currently estimated at -1.1, given daily parking rates of $5.50. It is estimated, however, that the price elasticity will change to -1.2 when parking rates increase to $6.50. Using these data, estimate the average daily ridership for 2003 and 2004.

23. The Reliable Aircraft Company manufactures small, pleasure-use aircraft. Based on past experience, sales volume appears to be affected by changes in the price of the planes and by the state of the economy as measured by consumers' disposable personal income. The following data pertaining to Reliable's aircraft sales, selling prices, and consumers' personal income were collected:

Year	Aircraft Sales	Average Price	Disposable Personal Income (in Constant 2003 Dollars—Billions)
2003	525	$7,200	$61
2004	450	8,000	61
2005	400	8,000	59

  a. Estimate the arc price elasticity of demand using the 2003 and 2004 data.

  b. Estimate the arc income elasticity of demand using the 2004 and 2005 data.

  c. Assume that these estimates are expected to remain stable during 2006. Forecast 2006 sales for Reliable assuming that its aircraft prices remain constant at 2005 levels and that disposable personal income will increase by $4 billion. Also assume that arc income elasticity computed in (b) above is the best available estimate of income elasticity.

  d. Forecast 2006 sales for Reliable given that its aircraft prices will increase by $500 from 2005 levels and that disposable personal income will increase by $4 billion. Assume that the price and income effects are *independent* and *additive* and that the arc income and price elasticities computed in parts (a) and (b) are the best available estimates of these elasticities to be used in making the forecast.

24. Celia Jones consumes three products, A, B, and C. She has decided that her last purchase of A gave her 8 units of satisfaction, her last purchase of B gave her 10 units of satisfaction, and her last purchase of C gave her 5 units of satisfaction. The prices of A, B, and C are $4, $5, and $3 per unit, respectively.

As a rational consumer, what should Jones purchase?

CASE EXERCISE

POLO GOLF SHIRT PRICING

Complete the following demand and total revenue spreadsheet for daily sales of a golf shirt in each of Ralph Lauren's discount stores. What price maximizes sales revenue? What price maximizes operating profit? Why? Who would pursue the first objective? How could Ralph Lauren's managers provide an incentive for profit-maximizing behaviour?

Quantity Sold	Uniform Price	Total Revenue	Marginal Revenue	Variable Cost
0	$50.00	$ 0	$ 0	$28
1	$48.00	$ 48	$48	$28
2	$46.00	$ 92	$44	$28
3	$45.00	$135	$43	$28
4	$44.00	$176	$41	$28
5	$42.00	$210	$34	$28
6	$40.00	$240	$30	$28
7	$38.31	$268	$28	$28
8	$36.50	$292	$24	$28
9	$34.50	$311	$19	$28
10	_____	_____	$16	$28
11	_____	_____	$13	$28
12	_____	_____	$10	$28
13	_____	_____	$ 7	$28
14	_____	_____	$ 4	$28
15	_____	_____	$ 0	$28
16	_____	_____	($ 1)	$28
17	_____	_____	($ 4)	$28
18	_____	_____	($ 7)	$28

Production and Cost

Part 2 deals with the production and cost analysis decisions facing managers of an economic enterprise. In Chapter 4, the theoretical basis of production decisions is developed using primarily graphical tools of analysis. Production decisions include the determination of the type and amount of resources—such as land, labour, materials, capital equipment, and managerial skills—that are used in the production of a desired amount of output. The objective is to combine these inputs in the most efficient manner to produce the desired output. Web Appendix 4A looks at real-world process choice decisions in a linear programming framework. To access Web chapters and appendixes, go to the Nelson website for this book at www.mcguigan.nelson.com.

In Chapter 5, the theoretical basis of cost analysis is developed. Cost measures are combined with revenue estimates to determine optimal (wealth-maximizing) levels and mixes of output. Web Appendix 5A discusses break-even analysis versus contribution analysis. Web Appendix 5B discusses long-run costs with a Cobb–Douglas production function.

Production Economics

Chapter Preview

Managers are required to make resource-allocation decisions about production operations, marketing, financing, and personnel. Although these decisions are interrelated, it is useful to discuss each of them separately. Production decisions determine the type and amount of inputs—such as land, labour, raw and processed materials, factories, machinery, equipment, and managerial talent—to be used in the production of a desired quantity of output. The production manager's objective is to minimize cost for a given output or, in other circumstances, to maximize output for a given input budget. First, we analyze the choice of a single variable input with fixed input prices. Later, we analyze the optimal multi-input combination with changing input prices and introduce the concept of returns to scale. Web Appendix 4A discusses production decisions and linear programming.

Learning Objectives

After studying this chapter, you should be able to:

1. Define a *production function.*

2. Define *marginal product* and *average product* functions.

3. Define the *law of diminishing marginal returns.*

4. Explain the relationship between total product, marginal product, and average product, and identify the three stages of production.

5. Understand that in the short run, the *optimal output level* occurs where marginal revenue product equals marginal factor cost.

6. Describe a *production isoquant* as either a geometric curve or an algebraic function.

7. Define the *marginal rate of technical substitution.*

8. Understand that in the long run, minimizing cost subject to an output constraint requires that the production process be operated at the point where the marginal product per dollar input cost of each factor is equal.

9. Identify the differences between *technical efficiency, allocative efficiency, overall production efficiency,* and *scale efficiency.*

10. Define physical *returns to scale.*

11. Describe the *Cobb–Douglas production function* and how its properties allow managers to draw conclusions, based on parameter estimates, about returns to scale.

12. (Web Appendix 4A) Describe how linear programming analysis is more appropriate for production decisions requiring discrete choices of machinery involved in a fixed-proportions production process.

Deregulation of Ontario Electricity?*

CP/KEVIN FRAYER

In Canada, electricity is provided by provincially owned Crown corporations except in Alberta, which has several privately owned companies. Deregulating the electrical energy industry was a key part of Ontario's "Common Sense Revolution." Ontario passed legislation in 1998 to open wholesale and retail electricity markets to competition, starting in 2000. This date was then changed to December 2002 because Ontario hoped to avoid California's energy deregulation problems, which resulted in a crucial shortage of electrical power, rolling blackouts, and the reported tripling of customers' electric bills, billions of dollars in economic loss, and layoffs, followed by the necessity for emergency legislation.

Large-scale electric power plants entail huge capital investments, with the costs of pollution abatement technology in coal-fired plants and redundant safety devices in nuclear plants running into the hundreds of millions of dollars. A Candu nuclear power plant might cost as much $6 billion. But larger scale coal- and nuclear-powered plants have a 30 to 40 percent advantage in variable input costs over smaller scale natural gas- and fuel oil-powered plants. In addition, the smaller plants require that a utility regularly buy electricity in the spot market to meet unexpected peak demand.

The tradeoff between investing in low-fixed-cost natural gas- and fuel oil-powered plants with higher and much more volatile variable costs versus high-fixed-cost coal- and nuclear-powered plants with lower and stable variable costs came into focus during the electricity deregulation crisis in California.

In 1998, California implemented legislation to decouple electricity generation and distribution, allowing large retail and industrial customers to purchase electricity from alternative providers. As a result, two California utilities scaled back their generating plant expansion plans and began to purchase 25 percent of their power in wholesale spot markets from bottlenecked long-distance transmission line suppliers and from numerous small-scale fuel oil and natural gas independent generating plants. It has been estimated that as much as 55 percent of the variation in peak-hour daily wholesale prices is attributable to extraordinary transmission line fees and old inefficient plants fired up to meet the last 5 percent of peak demand. Unfortunately, between 2000 and 2001, natural gas prices quadrupled, and the monthly average wholesale price of electricity in California shot up from $25–$50 to $198–$231 per megawatt-hour (mWh). California Edison and PG&E were restrained by a $54/mWh price cap from passing through to their retail customers more than $11 billion in higher wholesale costs. Not surprisingly, therefore, only ½ of 1 percent of Californians elected to switch away

---

* Based on "The Lessons Learned" and "Think Small," *The Wall Street Journal,* September 17, 2001, pp. R4, R13, R15 and R17; "Are Californians Starved for Energy?" *The Wall Street Journal,* September 16, 2002, p. A1; and "How to Do Deregulation Right," *BusinessWeek,* March 26, 2001, p. 112.

from their traditional utility providers, whereas 30 percent of British citizens, for example, did so within two years after electricity market deregulation in the United Kingdom.

In March 2001, the independent transmission line operator for the power grid in California announced rolling blackouts across the state to balance deficient supply against peak period demand. Only then did the California Public Utility Commission approve a 46 percent increase in retail electricity rates. California was forced to arrange a very expensive long-term bailout. In light of this California "energy nightmare," other U.S. states, as well as some Canadian provinces, decided to revise or delay their electricity deregulation initiatives. Other states and provinces have either rejected electricity deregulation altogether, or are continuing to study the issues.

One new approach is to charge customers a variable rate per megawatt-hour to reflect differential cost at different hours of the day, days of the week, and seasons of the year. We discuss such real-time differential pricing in Chapter 9. Another new approach is *distributed generation* by extremely small-scale diesel generators or natural gas-fired microturbine generators in factories and photo-voltaic cells (solar panels) in households. Operating costs of the microturbines are $70–$120/mWh, whereas solar panels cost $220–$400/mWh, both much higher than utility-supplied electricity. Yet, the capital cost that must be recovered is less than 1/1000 of traditional power plants. Like cogeneration of steam for heat and electricity for lighting, these distributed generation systems offer the added advantage of increased reliability, reducing projected brownout and blackout periods from hours to seconds per year.

In this chapter, we will study the dilemma of whether to substitute higher cost variable inputs for fixed inputs.

The Production Function

The economic theory of production consists of a formal framework to assist the manager in deciding how to combine most efficiently the various inputs[1] needed to produce the desired output (product or service), given the existing technology. This technology consists of available production processes, equipment, labour and management skills, and information-processing capabilities. Production analysis is often applied by managers in assigning costs to the various feasible output levels and in communicating with plant engineers about the operations plans of the company.

The theory of production is centred on the concept of a production function. A **production function** relates the maximum quantity of output that can be produced from given amounts of various inputs for a given technology. It can be expressed in the form of a mathematical model, schedule (table), or graph. A change in technology, such as the introduction of more automated equipment or the substitution of skilled for unskilled workers, results in a new production function. The production of most outputs (goods and services) requires the use of large numbers of **inputs**. The production of a house, for

Production Function
A mathematical model, schedule (table), or graph that relates the maximum feasible quantity of output that can be produced from given amounts of various inputs.

Input
A resource or factor of production (such as a raw material, labour skill, or piece of equipment) employed in a production process.

---

[1] The terms *input, factor,* and *resource* are used interchangeably throughout the chapter. They all have the same meaning in production theory.

example, requires the use of many different labour skills (carpenters, plumbers, and electricians), raw materials (lumber, cement, bricks, and insulating materials), and types of equipment (bulldozers, saws, and cement mixers). Also, many production processes result in more than one output. For example, in the meat-processing industry, the slaughtering of a steer results in the joint output of various cuts of meat, hide, and fertilizer. To simplify the analysis and to illustrate the basic theory, the following discussion is limited to a two-input, one-output production function.

Letting L and K represent the quantities of two inputs (labour L and capital K) used in producing a quantity Q of output, a production function can be represented in the form of a mathematical model, such as

$$(4.1) \qquad\qquad Q = f(L, K)$$

Production functions also can be expressed in the form of a *schedule* (or table), as illustrated in the following Deep Creek ore-mining example.

E X A M P L E

AN ILLUSTRATIVE PRODUCTION FUNCTION: DEEP CREEK MINING COMPANY

The Deep Creek Mining Company uses capital (mining equipment) and labour (workers) to mine uranium ore. Various sizes of ore-mining equipment, as measured by its brake horsepower (bhp) rating, are available to the firm. The amount of ore mined during a given period is a function only of the number of workers assigned to the crew operating a given piece of equipment. The data in

Table 4.1 show the amount of ore produced (measured in tonnes) when various sizes of crews are used to operate the equipment. In this example, the two inputs are labour, *L*—that is, number of workers—and capital, *K*—that is, size of drilling equipment—and the output, *Q*, is the number of tonnes of ore produced with the given combination of inputs.

Table 4.1   Total Output Table—Deep Creek Mining Company

Labour Input *L* (Number of Workers)	Capital Input *K* (Brake Horsepower: bhp)							
	250	500	750	1,000	1,250	1,500	1,750	2,000
1	1	3	6	10	16	16	16	13
2	2	6	16	24	29	29	44	44
3	4	16	29	44	55	55	55	50
4	6	29	44	55	58	60	60	55
5	16	43	55	60	61	62	62	60
6	29	55	60	62	63	63	63	62
7	44	58	62	63	64	64	64	64
8	50	60	62	63	64	65	65	65
9	55	59	61	63	64	65	66	66
10	52	56	59	62	64	65	66	67

A two-input, one-output production function at Deep Creek Mining can also be represented *graphically* as a three-dimensional production surface, where the height of the square column associated with each input combination in Figure 4.1 indicates the amount of iron ore output produced.

Production Function— Deep Creek Mining Company

This 3-D graph of the production function represents total output for various combinations of inputs.

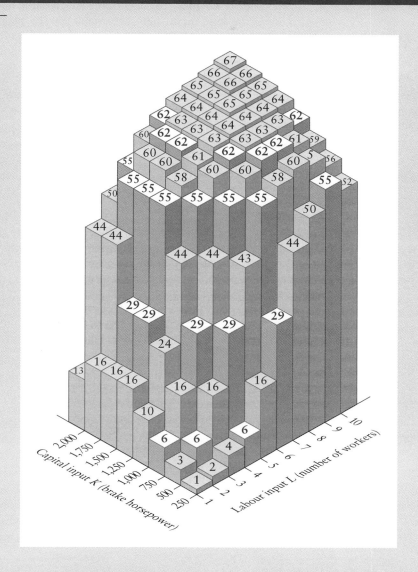

Fixed and Variable Inputs

In deciding how to combine the various inputs (L and K) to produce the desired output, inputs are usually classified as being either fixed or variable. A *fixed input* is defined as one required in the production process but whose quantity employed in the process is constant over a given period of time regardless of the quantity of output produced. The costs of a fixed input must be incurred regardless of whether the production process is operated at a high or a low rate of output. A *variable input* is defined as one whose quantity employed in the process changes, depending on the desired quantity of output to be produced.

The **short run** corresponds to the period of time in which one (or more) of the inputs is fixed. This means that to increase output, the firm must employ more of the variable input(s) with the given quantity of fixed input(s). Thus, for example, with an auto assembly plant of fixed size and capacity, the firm can increase output only by employing more labour, such as by paying workers overtime or by scheduling additional shifts.

As the time period under consideration (the planning horizon) is lengthened, however, more of the fixed inputs become variable. Over a planning horizon of about six months, most firms could acquire or build additional plant capacity and order more manufacturing equipment. Production facilities would no longer be a fixed factor. In lengthening the planning horizon, a point is eventually reached where all inputs are variable. This period of time is called the **long run.**

In the short run, because some of the inputs are fixed, only a subset of the total possible input combinations is available to the firm. By contrast, in the long run, all possible input combinations are available to the firm. Consequently, in the long run, the firm can choose between increasing production through the use of more labour (overtime or hiring more workers) or through plant expansion, depending on which combination of labour and plant size is most efficient at producing the desired output.

In developing some of the concepts of production theory, a production function with one fixed and one variable input is examined first. The objective of the analysis is to determine how to combine different quantities of the variable input with a given amount of the fixed input to produce various quantities of output most efficiently. The total, average, and marginal products are defined and illustrated, and the law of diminishing returns and marginal revenue product are discussed. Then a slightly more complex situation is considered: A production function with two variable inputs is used to illustrate the pivotal multi-input concepts of isoquants and returns to scale.

Production Functions with One Variable Input

Suppose, in the Deep Creek Mining Company example in the previous section, that the amount of capital input K—that is, the size of mining equipment—employed in the production process is a fixed factor. Specifically, suppose that the firm owns or leases a piece of mining equipment having a 750-bhp rating. Depending on the amount of labour input, L, used to operate the 750-bhp equipment, varying quantities of output will be obtained, as shown in the "750" column of Table 4.1 and again in the second column of Table 4.2.

Marginal and Average Product Functions

Once the total product function is given (in tabular, graphic, or algebraic form), the marginal and average product functions can be derived. The **marginal product** is defined as the incremental change in total output ΔQ that can be produced by the use of one more unit of the variable input ΔL, while K remains fixed. The marginal product is defined as[2]

$$(4.2) \qquad\qquad MP_L = \frac{\Delta Q}{\Delta L} \quad \text{or} \quad \frac{\partial Q}{\partial L}$$

for discrete and continuous changes, respectively.

The marginal product of labour in the ore-mining example is shown in the third column of Table 4.2 and as MP_L in Figure 4.2.

---

[2] Strictly speaking, the ratio $\Delta Q/\Delta L$ represents the *incremental* product rather than the *marginal* product. For simplicity, we continue to use the term *marginal* throughout the text, even though this and similar ratios are calculated on an incremental basis.

Short Run
The period of time in which one (or more) of the resources employed in a production process is fixed or incapable of being varied.

Long Run
The period of time in which *all* of the resources employed in a production process can be varied.

Marginal Product
The incremental change in total output that can be obtained from the use of one more unit of an input in the production process (while holding constant all other inputs).

Table 4.2	Total Product, Marginal Product, Average Product, and Elasticity—Deep Creek Mining Company (Capital input, brake horsepower = 750)			
Labour Input, L (Number of Workers)	Total Product $TP_L (= Q)$ (Tonnes of Ore)	Marginal Product of Labour, MP_L ($\Delta Q \div \Delta L$)	Average Product of Labour, AP_L ($Q \div L$)	Production Elasticity, E_L ($MP_L \div AP_L$)
0	0	—	—	—
1	6	+6	6	1.00
2	16	+10	8	1.25
3	29	+13	9.67	1.34
4	44	+15	11	1.36
5	55	+11	11	1.00
6	60	+5	10	0.50
7	62	+2	8.86	0.23
8	62	0	7.75	0.00
9	61	−1	6.78	−0.15
10	59	−2	5.90	−0.34

FIGURE 4.2

Total Product, Marginal Product of Labour, and Average Product of Labour—Deep Creek Mining Co.

This graph shows the relationships among marginal, average, and total products for Deep Creek. AP_L peaks when $AP_L = MP_L$. TP peaks when $MP_L = 0$.

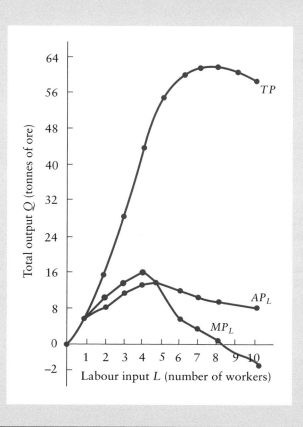

Average Product
The ratio of total output to the amount of the variable input used in producing the output.

The **average product** is defined as the ratio of total output to the amount of the variable input used in producing the output. The average product of labour is

$$(4.3) \qquad AP_L = \frac{Q}{L}$$

The average product of labour for the Deep Creek ore-mining example is shown in the fourth column of Table 4.2.

The discussion of the theory of demand in Chapter 3 introduced the concept of price elasticity of demand. Similarly in production analysis, it is useful to define the **elasticity of production** as the percentage change in output Q resulting from a given percentage change in the amount of the variable input L, with K remaining constant. This responsiveness of output to changes in the given input is equal to

Elasticity of Production
A measure of proportionality between changes in the variable input(s) and the resulting change in output.

$$E_L = \frac{\% \Delta Q}{\% \Delta L}$$

$$(4.4) \qquad = \frac{\dfrac{\Delta Q}{Q}}{\dfrac{\Delta L}{L}}$$

Rearranging terms yields

$$E_L = \frac{\dfrac{\Delta Q}{\Delta L}}{\dfrac{Q}{L}} = \frac{\Delta Q}{\Delta L} \times \frac{L}{Q}$$

or, because $MP_L = \Delta Q / \Delta L$ and $AP_L = Q/L$:

$$(4.5) \qquad E_L = \frac{MP_L}{AP_L}$$

which shows that the elasticity of production is equal to the ratio of the marginal product to the average product of input L.

The elasticity of production for the Deep Creek ore-mining example is shown in the fifth column of Table 4.2. A production elasticity greater than (less than) 1.0 indicates that output increases more than (less than) proportionately with a given percentage increase in the variable input.

Law of Diminishing Marginal Returns

The tabular production function just discussed illustrates the production law of diminishing marginal returns. Initially, the assignment of more workers to the crew operating the mining equipment (the fixed factor) allows greater labour specialization in the use of the equipment. As a result, the marginal output of each worker added to the crew at first increases, and total output increases at an increasing rate. Thus, as listed in Table 4.2 and graphed in Figure 4.2, adding a second worker to the crew results in 10 additional tonnes of output, adding a third worker results in 13 additional tonnes of output, and adding a fourth worker yields 15 additional tonnes. However, in adding more workers to the crew, a point is eventually reached where the marginal increase in output for each worker added to the crew begins to decline. This occurs because only a limited number of ways exist to achieve greater labour specialization and because each additional worker introduces crowding effects. Thus, adding a fifth worker to the crew yields a marginal increase in output of 11 additional tonnes, compared with the marginal increase of 15 additional tonnes for the fourth worker. Similarly, the additions of the sixth and seventh workers to the crew yield successively smaller increases of 5 and 2 tonnes, respectively.

With enough additional workers, the marginal product of labour becomes zero or even negative. Note that the eighth, ninth, and tenth workers listed in Table 4.2 have marginal products of 0, −1, and −2 tonnes, respectively. Some work is just more difficult to accomplish when superfluous personnel are present. Such crowding effects can overwhelm the small additional output from the extra worker or other variable inputs.

Increasing Returns with Network Effects

The law of diminishing marginal returns is *not* a mathematical theorem, but an empirical assertion that has been observed in almost every economic production process as the amount of the variable input increases. An interesting exception occurs, however, with selling effort after the adoption of a new industry standard (e.g., high-definition television—HDTV) and with *network effects*. The greater the installed base of a network product, like Microsoft Windows XP, the larger the number of compatible network connections and therefore the more possible value added for a new customer. Consequently, as the Windows XP installed base increases, selling efforts become increasingly more productive.

A similar reason for increasing returns at Microsoft is that the more adoptions Microsoft Windows XP secures, the more Windows-compatible applications will be introduced by independent software developers. And the more applications introduced, the greater the chance will be for further adoptions. The higher the market share goes, the lower the promotional costs required to trigger another adoption. The only limiting

EXAMPLE

INCREASING RETURNS AT SONY

For more information on Sony, visit the world headquarters website at **www.sony.net** or the Canadian website at **www.sony.ca**.

A manufacturer's product-line costs usually now include marketing and distribution activities as well as the labour and material direct costs of standard production and assembly. The reason is that, like service firms, many manufacturers today compete on customer inquiry systems, change order responsiveness, delivery schedule conformance, product reliability, and technological updates, not just on product delivery and warranty repairs. Qualifying for and actually winning a customer order often require quality characteristics and support services beyond the physical unit of production. For example, Ford wants all of its manufacturing suppliers to meet the ISO 9000 manufacturing quality standards for continuous improvement processes. Wal-Mart requires that its fashion clothing

suppliers deliver shipments just in time (JIT) for planned departure from Wal-Mart distribution centres.

At times, these additional marketing and distribution activities can exhibit increasing returns and declining cost. For example, securing the adoption of an industry standard favourable to one's own product (e.g., digital HDTV) involves promotional and other selling efforts that grow *more productive* the larger the product's market share. The greater the installed base of Sony digital TV receivers, the more programs that are produced to be transmitted with this technology, and the more programs that are available, the easier and cheaper it is to secure the next household's adoption of the innovation.

factor in the adoption of such innovations is the appearance of still newer technologies. Normal sales penetration or saturation curves (like the MP_L curve in Figure 4.2) exhibit initially increasing marginal returns to promotional expenses, followed by eventually diminishing marginal returns. However, with the adoption of new industry standards or a network technology, increasing returns can persist.

When Microsoft managed to achieve a critical level of adoption for the Windows graphical user interface (GUI), the amount of marketing and promotional expenditure required to secure the next adoption actually began to fall.[3] Selling efforts are generally subject to diminishing returns, but when the number of other users of a network-based device reaches a 30–40 percent share, the next 40–50 percent share points are cheaper and cheaper to promote. Then, beyond a market share of 80–90 percent, diminishing returns again set in, and securing the final adopters becomes increasingly expensive. These relationships are depicted in Figure 4.3.

From 0 percent to 30 percent market share, the selling efforts required to achieve each additional share point have a diminishing effect on the probability of adoption by the next potential user (note the reduced slope of the sales penetration curve in Figure 4.3). Consequently, additional share points become more and more expensive over this range. Beyond the 30 percent *inflection point,* however, each additional share point of users connected to Windows leads to an increasing probability of adoption by another user and, therefore, a decrease in the marketing expense required to secure another unit sale (note the increased slope of the sales penetration curve in this middle

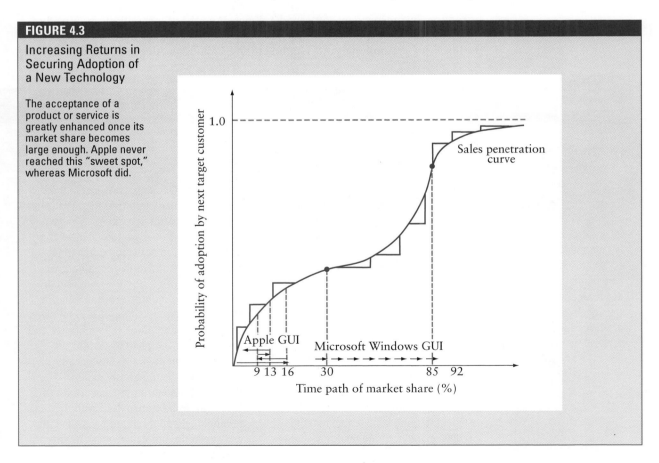

FIGURE 4.3

Increasing Returns in Securing Adoption of a New Technology

The acceptance of a product or service is greatly enhanced once its market share becomes large enough. Apple never reached this "sweet spot," whereas Microsoft did.

---

[3] Based on "The Theory That Made Microsoft: Increasing Returns," *Fortune,* April 29, 1996, pp. 65–68.

range). These network-based effects of compatibility with other users reflect increased value to the potential adopter. The same thing occurs when an ever-increasing number of independent software vendors (ISVs) write applications for an operating system like Windows that has achieved more than 30 percent acceptance in the marketplace and has therefore effectively become an industry standard.

Eventually, at 85 percent, share points again become increasingly more expensive because selling efforts have again become subject to diminishing returns. That is, at 85 percent, Microsoft encountered a second inflection point. Over the middle 30–85 percent range of the sales penetration curve, Microsoft's increasing returns made an 85 percent monopoly control of the operating system market highly likely. Whatever customer relationships preexisted, once Microsoft achieved a 30 percent share, increasing returns in marketing its product offering introduced a disruptive technology that displaced other competitors. Inexorably, Microsoft's share grew to 92 percent, and other products collapsed. Netscape's Internet browser experienced exactly this same sort of displacement by Microsoft's Internet Explorer when Microsoft achieved 30 percent-plus penetration by bundling Internet Explorer with Windows, effectively giving away the browser for free to reach the middle sales penetration range of increasing returns.

Producing Information Services in the "New Economy"

It is insightful to compare the production economics of old-economy companies that produce *things* to new-economy companies that produce *information*. Things, when sold, the seller ceases to own. Information, when sold, the seller can sell again (at least until the information spillovers from earlier sales and the difficulty in excluding those who do not pay overwhelm the target market). Things must be replicated through expensive manufacturing processes. Information is replicable at almost zero incremental cost. Things exist in one location. Information can exist simultaneously in many locations. The production and marketing of things are subject to eventually diminishing returns. The marketing (and maybe the production) of information is subject to increasing returns—that is, the more people who use my information, the more likely it is that another person will want to acquire it (for any given marketing cost) or, said another way, the cheaper it is to secure another sale.

Things often involve economies of scale in production. Information is producible by small companies at comparably low costs. Things focus a business on supply-side thinking and the high costs of distribution. Information products focus a business on demand-side thinking and have almost no costs of distribution. By getting the next customer to adopt, one can set in motion a "virtuous circle" of higher customer value, lower overhead costs, and lower prices and costs for the next customer. Hence, Microsoft evolved to dominate an information-oriented business like computer network software. Chapter 7 discusses increasing returns as a source of dominant firm market power.

Relationship between Total, Marginal, and Average Product

In contrast to Figure 4.2, which illustrates discrete choices for the single variable input (labour), Figure 4.4 illustrates a production function (*TP*) with a continuous single variable input. Several relationships among the *TP*, *AP*, and *MP* curves can be seen in the graph. In the first region, labelled "Increasing returns," the *TP* function (total output) is increasing at an *increasing rate*. Because the *MP* curve measures the slope of the *TP* curve ($MP = \partial Q / \partial L$), the *MP* curve is increasing up to L_1. In the region labelled "Decreasing returns," the *TP* function is increasing at a *decreasing rate,* and the *MP* curve is decreasing up to L_3. In the region labelled "Negative returns," the *TP* function is *decreasing* and the *MP* curve continues decreasing, becoming negative beyond L_3. An inflection point occurs at L_1. Next, if a line is drawn from the origin, 0, to any point on the *TP* curve, it can be seen that the slope of this line, Q/L, is at a maximum when the line touches the *TP* curve at an input value of L_2. The slope of this line, Q/L, measures

FIGURE 4.4

Relationships among Total, Average, and Marginal Product Curves

This graph shows the three stages of production: Stage I represents the range of labour input where $MP_L > AP_L$. Stage II represents the range of labour input where $AP_L > MP_L > 0$. Stage III represents the range of labour input where $MP_L < 0$.

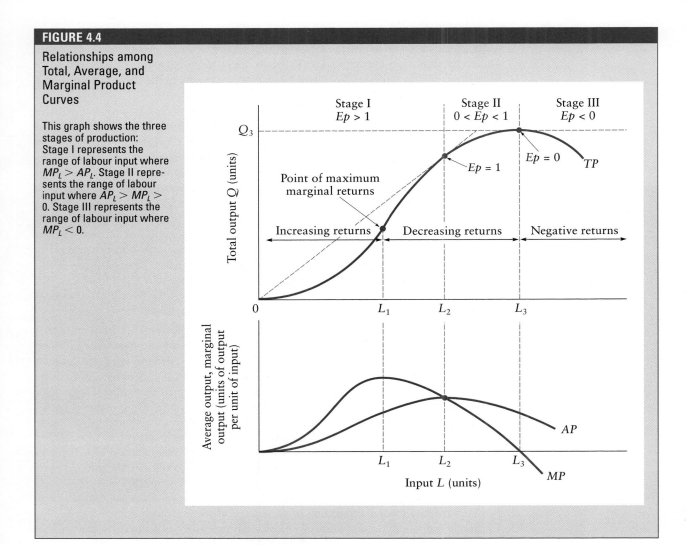

the average product AP. Hence, we see that the AP curve reaches a maximum at this point.[4]

Three Stages of Production

In analyzing the production function, economists have identified three different stages of production based on the relationships among the TP, AP, and MP functions. Stage I is defined as the *range of L over which the average product is increasing*. This occurs from

---

[4] Note also that the marginal product MP equals the average product AP at L_2. This follows because the marginal product MP is equal to the slope of the TP curve ($MP = \partial Q/\partial L$), and at L_2 the average product AP is also equal to the slope of the TP curve.

Consider, for example, the following analogy: A baseball player's batting *average* for the season is 0.250. If that player has an excellent night at bat (his *marginal* performance) and goes 4 for 4 (1.000), then his season average will be pulled up. On the other hand, if he goes hitless, this poor *marginal* performance will pull down his season average. If he goes 1 for 4, this marginal performance will have no impact on his season average (marginal performance equals average performance). Hence the MP curve will always intersect with the AP curve when it is at a maximum. As we will see in the next chapter, a firm's marginal cost curve always intersects the average cost curve at its minimum point, for the same reason.

the origin (0) up to L_2 and represents the region of net gains from specialization. Stage II corresponds to the *range of L from the point at which the average product is at a maximum* (L_2) *to the point where the marginal product* (MP) *declines to zero* (L_3). The endpoint of Stage II thus corresponds to the point of maximum output on the *TP* curve. Stage III encompasses the *range of L over which the total product is declining* or, equivalently, *the marginal product is negative*. Stage III thus corresponds to all values of L greater than (i.e., to the right of) L_3, where crowding effects overwhelm any output attributable to additional workers.

The determination of the optimal quantity of labour input L to be used in producing a given amount of output Q is described in the next section. However, one can eliminate several values of L from consideration at this point. First, the rational producer would not operate the production process over the range of values of input L contained in Stage III. In Stage III, an excessive amount of the variable input, relative to the fixed input K, is being used to produce the desired output. In other words, because the marginal product of input L is negative beyond L_3, using more than L_3 units would cause a *reduction* in total output. Any desired output (up to the maximum obtainable with the given amount of the fixed input, that is, Q_3) could be produced by using less than L_3 units of the variable input. No manager would ever knowingly increase labour expenses to hire additional workers whose presence reduces output (e.g., Stage III). Even if the variable input were free, the rational producer would not wish to proceed into Stage III. By the same token, no manager whose productivity per worker is rising due to the gains from specialization (i.e., AP increasing in Stage I) should stop adding workers as long as the incremental cost for additional workers remains constant.

In general, then, how much of the variable input should be employed over the remaining range of potentially optimal input choice (Stage II) depends on variable input costs. If labour costs are high, as in a unionized assembly plant, production may proceed just a short distance into Stage II in hiring labour. If labour costs are lower, in a nonunionized plant, for example, labour hiring may proceed well across Stage II to include relatively low-level productivity workers, such as apprentices.

Determining the Optimal Use of the Variable Input

With one of the inputs (K) fixed in the short run, the producer must determine the optimal quantity of the variable input (L) to employ in the production process. Such a determination requires the introduction into the analysis of product (output) prices and factor costs. Therefore, the analysis begins by defining *marginal revenue product* and *marginal factor cost*.

Marginal Revenue Product

Marginal Revenue Product (*MRP*)

The amount that an additional unit of the variable production input adds to total revenue. Also known as "marginal value added."

Marginal revenue product (*MRP*) is defined as the amount that an additional unit of the variable input adds to total revenue, or

$$(4.6) \qquad MRP_L = \frac{\Delta TR}{\Delta L}$$

where ΔTR is the change in total revenue associated with the given change (ΔL) in the variable input, and MRP_L is equal to the marginal product of $L(MP_L)$ times the marginal revenue (MR_Q) resulting from the increase in output obtained:

$$(4.7) \qquad MRP_L = MP_L \cdot MR_Q$$

Consider again the Deep Creek Mining Company example (Table 4.2) in the previous section, where K (capital) is fixed at 750 bhp. Suppose that the firm can sell all the ore it can produce at a price of $10 per tonne (that is, in a *perfectly competitive market*). The marginal revenue product of labour (MRP_L) is computed using Equation 4.7 and is shown in Table 4.3.[5] Note that in a perfectly competitive market, marginal revenue is equal to the selling price.

Marginal Factor Cost

Marginal Factor Cost (*MFC*)
The amount that an additional unit of the variable input adds to total cost.

Marginal factor cost (*MFC*) is defined as the amount that an additional unit of the variable input adds to total cost, or

$$(4.8) \qquad MFC_L = \frac{\Delta TC}{\Delta L}$$

where ΔTC is the change in cost associated with the given change (ΔL) in the variable input.

In the ore-mining example, suppose that the firm can employ as much labour (L) as it needs by paying the workers $50 per period ($C_L$). In other words, the labour market is assumed to be *perfectly competitive*. Under these conditions, the marginal factor cost (MFC_L) is equal to C_L, or $50 per worker. It is constant regardless of the level of operation of the mine (see the last column of Table 4.3).

Optimal Input Level

Given the marginal revenue product and marginal factor cost, we can compute the optimal amount of the variable input to use in the production process. Recall from the discussion of marginal analysis in Chapter 2 that an economic activity (for example, production) should be expanded as long as the marginal benefits (revenues) exceed the marginal costs. The optimal level occurs at the point where the marginal benefits are equal to the marginal costs. For the short-run production decision, the optimal level of the variable input occurs where

$$(4.9) \qquad MRP_L = MFC_L$$

As can be seen in Table 4.3, the optimal input is $L = 6$ workers, because $MRP_L = MFC_L = \$50$ at this point. At less than six workers, $MRP_L > MFC_L$ and the addition of more labour (workers) to the production process will increase revenues more than it

Table 4.3   Marginal Revenue Product and Marginal Factor Cost—Deep Creek Mining Company

Labour Input L (Number of Workers)	Total Product $Q = (TP_L)$ (Tonnes of Ore)	Marginal Product of Labour MP_L (Tonnes/Worker)	Total Revenue $TR = P \cdot Q$ ($)	Marginal Revenue $MR_Q = \dfrac{\Delta TR}{\Delta Q}$ ($/Tonne)	Marginal Revenue Product $MRP_L = MP_L \cdot MR_Q$ ($/Worker)	Marginal Factor Cost MFC_L ($/Worker)
0	0	—	0	—	—	—
1	6	6	60	10	60	50
2	16	10	160	10	100	50
3	29	13	290	10	130	50
4	44	15	440	10	150	50
5	55	11	550	10	110	50
6*	60	5	600	10	50	50
7	62	2	620	10	20	50
8	62	0	620	10	0	50

* Indicates the optimal input level.

[5] Input levels in Stage III ($MP_L < 0$) have been eliminated from consideration.

will increase costs. Beyond six workers, the opposite is true—costs will increase more than revenues.

Production Functions with Two Variable Inputs

Using the Deep Creek Mining Company example, suppose now that both capital—as measured by the maximum brake horsepower rating of the equipment—and labour—as measured by the number of workers—are variable inputs to the ore-mining process. The firm can choose to operate the production process using any of the capital–labour combinations shown previously in Table 4.1.

Production Isoquants

Production Isoquant
An algebraic function or a geometric curve representing all the various combinations of two inputs that can be used in producing a given level of output.

A production function with two variable inputs can be represented graphically by a set of two-dimensional production isoquants. A **production isoquant** is either a geometric curve or an algebraic function representing all of the various combinations of the two inputs that can be used in producing a given level of output. In the Deep Creek example, a production isoquant shows all of the alternative ways in which the number of workers and various sizes of mining equipment can be combined to produce any desired level of output (tonnes of ore). Several of the production isoquants for the ore-mining example are shown in Figure 4.5. For example, an output of 6 tonnes can be produced using any of three different labour–capital combinations—1 worker and 750-bhp equipment, 2 workers and 500-bhp equipment, or 4 workers and 250-bhp equipment. Similarly, as seen in the graph, an output of 62 tonnes can be produced using any one of five different labour–capital combinations.

FIGURE 4.5

Production Isoquants— Deep Creek Mining Company

The combinations of inputs that yield the production isoquants $Q = 6, 29, 55$ and 62, respectively, were previously shown in a contrasting colour in Figure 4.1.

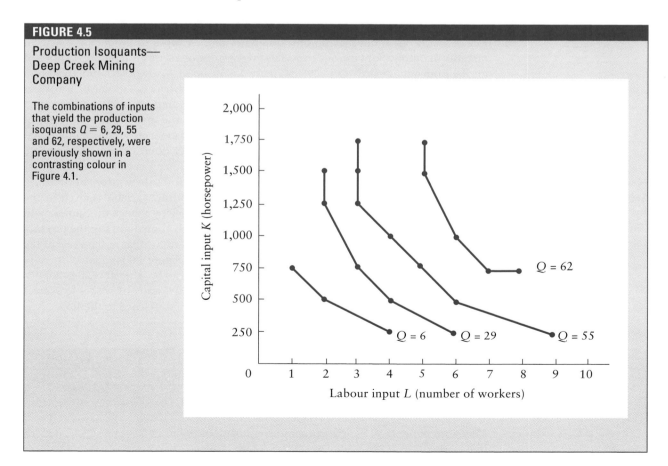

Although each isoquant indicates how quantities of the two inputs may be *substituted* for one another, these choices are normally limited for two reasons. First, some input combinations in Figure 4.5 employ an excessive quantity of one input. Just as more than eight workers result in negative marginal returns in choosing a single variable input for Deep Creek Mining (see Figure 4.2), the same is true here—with 750-bhp machinery, the eighth worker contributes no additional output along the isoquant $Q = 62$ in Figure 4.5. The presence of a ninth worker would necessitate additional capital equipment simply to maintain output at 62 tonnes. That is, in the absence of additional capital equipment, the crowding effects introduced by the ninth worker would actually reduce output. Similarly, more than 1,750-bhp machinery would result in negative marginal returns with only five workers. Another 250 horsepower (from 1,750 to 2,000 bhp) would require an additional (sixth) worker just to maintain output at 62 tonnes. Because all such inefficient mixes of capital and labour increase the input requirements (and therefore costs) without increasing output, they should be excluded from consideration in making input substitution choices.

Second, input substitution choices are also limited by the technology of production, which often involves machinery that is not divisible. Although one can find smaller and larger mining equipment, not every brake horsepower machine listed on the K-axis of Figure 4.5 will be available. The industrial engineering of mining operations often requires that we select from three or four possible fixed-proportions production processes involving a particular size of mining drill and a particular size of labour force to run it. We discuss the concept of a fixed-proportions production process in the next section.

Marginal Rate of Technical Substitution

In addition to indicating the quantity of output that can be produced with any of the various input combinations that lie on the isoquant curve, the isoquant also indicates the *rate* at which one input may be substituted for another input in producing the given quantity of output. Suppose one considers the meaning of a shift from point A to point B on the isoquant labelled "$Q = 29$" in Figure 4.6. At point A, 3 workers and a 750-bhp machine are being used to produce 29 tonnes of output, whereas at point B, 4 workers and a 500-bhp machine are being used to produce the same amount of output. In moving from point A to point B, one has substituted 1 additional unit of labour for 250 units of capital. The rate at which capital has been replaced with labour in producing the given output is equal to 250/1 or 250 units of capital per unit of labour. The rate at which one input may be substituted for another input in the production process, while total output remains constant, is known as the **marginal rate of technical substitution,** or *MRTS*.

The rate of change of one variable with respect to another variable is given by the slope of the curve relating the two variables. Thus, the rate of change of input K with respect to input L—that is, the rate at which K may be substituted for L in the production process—is given by the slope of the curve relating K to L—that is, the slope of the isoquant. The slope of the AB segment of the isoquant in Figure 4.6 is equal to the ratio of AC to CB. Algebraically, $AC = K_1 - K_2$ and $CB = L_1 - L_2$. Therefore, the slope is equal to $(K_1 - K_2) \div (L_1 - L_2)$. Because the slope is negative and one wishes to express the substitution rate as a positive quantity, a negative sign is attached to the slope:

$$(4.10) \qquad MRTS = -\frac{K_1 - K_2}{L_1 - L_2} = -\frac{\Delta K}{\Delta L}$$

In the Deep Creek Mining Company example, $\Delta L = 3 - 4 = -1$, $\Delta K = 750 - 500 = 250$. Substituting these values into Equation 4.10 yields

$$MRTS = -\frac{250}{-1} = 250$$

Therefore, along $Q = 29$ between input combinations A and B, 250 bhp substituted for one worker.

Marginal Rate of Technical Substitution

The *rate* at which one input may be substituted for another input in producing a given quantity of output.

FIGURE 4.6

Production Isoquant Curve—Deep Creek Mining Company

This graph illustrates the marginal rate of technical substitution between points A and B on the production isoquant $Q = 29$.

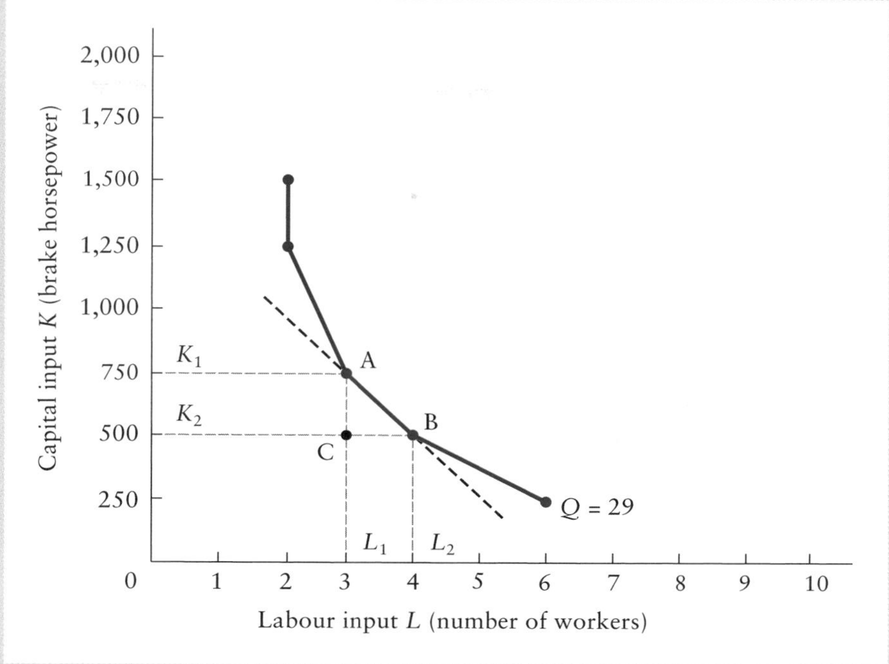

It can be shown that the *MRTS* is equal to the ratio of the marginal products of *L* and *K* by using the definition of the marginal product (Equation 4.2). This definition yields $\Delta L = \Delta Q / MP_L$ and $\Delta K = \Delta Q / MP_K$. Substituting these expressions into Equation 4.10 (and dropping the minus sign) yields

(4.11)

$$MRTS = \frac{\Delta Q / MP_K}{\Delta Q / MP_L}$$

$$MRTS = \frac{MP_L}{MP_K}$$

For the Deep Creek Mining Company example, $MP_L = \Delta Q / \Delta L = (29 - 16)/(4 - 3) = 13$, $MP_K = \Delta Q / \Delta K = (29 - 16)/(750 - 500) = 13/250$. Substituting these values into Equation 4.11 yields $MRTS = 250$, the same result as the above direct calculation:

$$MRTS = \frac{13}{13/250} = 250$$

Perfect Substitute and Complementary Inputs

Production inputs vary in the degree to which they can be substituted for one another in a given process. The extreme cases are *perfect substitutes* and *perfect complements*. Isoquants for these two cases are shown in Figure 4.7. The isoquants for inputs that are

FIGURE 4.7

Production Isoquants:
Perfect Substitute and
Complementary Inputs

Panel (a) illustrates two
inputs that are perfect
substitutes (i.e., constant
MRTS). Panel (b) illustrates
two inputs that are perfect
complements. The corner
point of each isoquant
represents no idle or
wasted input.

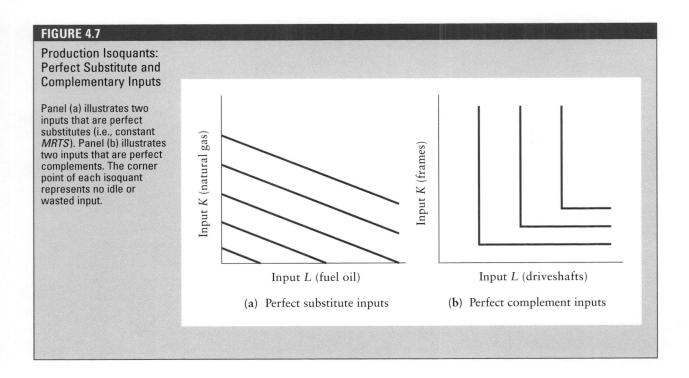

(a) Perfect substitute inputs   **(b)** Perfect complement inputs

perfect substitutes for one another consist of a series of parallel lines, as shown in panel (a). Examples of perfect substitutes are the use of alternative fuels (inputs), such as fuel oil or natural gas in the production of electricity, or the use of soybeans or oats in the production of nutrients in animal feeds. The isoquants for inputs that are *perfect complements* for one another consist of a series of right angles, as shown in panel (b). Such inputs are said to have zero substitutability. Examples of perfect complements include component parts that must be combined in fixed proportions, such as driveshafts and frames for automobiles or foundations and roofs for houses.

Most production inputs fall somewhere between the extreme cases of perfect complements and perfect substitutes. For most production functions, isoquants are convex to the origin, as shown earlier in Figure 4.6. This shape implies that the production inputs are imperfectly substitutable and that the rate of substitution declines as one input is substituted for another.

Determining the Optimal Combination of Inputs

As shown in the previous section, a given level of output can be produced using any of a large number of possible combinations of two inputs. The firm needs to determine which combination will minimize the total costs for producing the desired output.

Isocost Lines

The total cost of each possible input combination is a function of the market prices of these inputs. Assuming that the inputs are supplied in perfectly elastic input markets, the per-unit price of each input will be constant, regardless of the amount of the input that is purchased. Letting C_L and C_K be the per-unit prices of inputs L and K, respectively, the total cost (C) of any given input combination is

(4.12) $$C = C_L L + C_K K$$

Isocost Determination: Deep Creek Mining Company (continued)

In the Deep Creek Mining Company example discussed earlier, suppose that the cost per worker is $50 per period ($C_L$) and that mining equipment can be leased at a price of $0.20 per brake horsepower per period (C_K). The total cost per period of using L workers and equipment having K brake horsepower to produce a given amount of output is

(4.13) $C = 50L + 0.20K$

From this relationship, it can be seen that the mining of 55 tonnes of ore per period using 5 workers and equipment having 750 bhp would cost $50(5) + 0.20(750) = 400. However, this is not the only combi-

nation of workers and equipment costing $400. Any combination of inputs satisfying the equation

$$\$400 = 50L + 0.20K$$

would cost $400. Solving this equation for K yields

$$K = \frac{\$400}{0.20} - \frac{50}{0.20}L = 2{,}000 - 250\,L$$

Thus, the combinations $L = 1$ and $K = 1{,}750$; $L = 2$ and $K = 1{,}500$; $L = 3$ and $K = 1{,}250$ (plus many other combinations) all cost $400.

The combinations of inputs costing $400 can be represented as the line in Figure 4.8 labelled "$C = \$400$." This line is

---

FIGURE 4.8

Isocost Lines—Deep Creek Mining Company

The lines $C = \$200, \$300, \$400,$ and $\$500,$ respectively, are combinations of inputs that have the same cost.

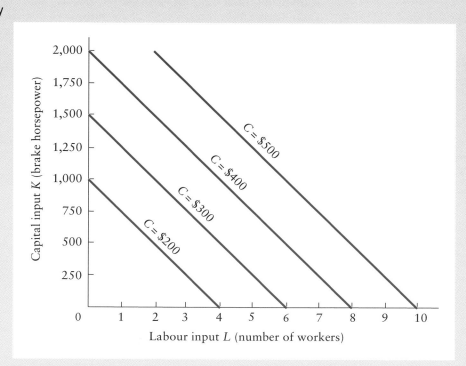

called an *isocost* line, because it shows all the combinations of inputs having *equal* total costs. An isocost line exists for every possible total cost C. Solving Equation 4.13 for K gives the equation of each isocost line in Figure 4.8. Note that only the *y*-intercept C/0.20 changes as one moves from one isocost line to another. That is, all the isocost lines are parallel, each one having a slope of −250.

$$(4.14) \qquad K = \frac{C}{0.20} - 250\,L$$

In general, the set of isocost lines consists of the set of equations given by the solution of Equation 4.12 for various values of C:

$$(4.15) \qquad K = \frac{C}{C_K} - \frac{C_L}{C_K}L$$

Once the isoquants and isocosts are specified, it is possible to solve for the optimum combination of inputs. The production decision problem can be formulated in two different ways, depending on the manner in which the production objective or goal is stated. One can solve for the combination of inputs that either

1. Minimizes total cost subject to a given constraint on output, or
2. Maximizes output subject to a given total cost constraint.

Constrained cost minimization in option 1 is the dual problem to the constrained output maximization problem in option 2.

Minimizing Cost Subject to an Output Constraint

Consider first the problem in which the director of operations desires to release to production a number of orders for at least $Q^{(2)}$ units of output. As shown in Figure 4.9, this

---

FIGURE 4.9

Cost Minimization Subject to an Output Constraint

The feasible region represents combinations of inputs that produce at the least the desired output $Q^{(2)}$. The point D (where the isocost line $C^{(2)}$ is tangent to the boundary of the feasible region) represents the least-cost combination of inputs that achieve the target output $Q^{(2)}$.

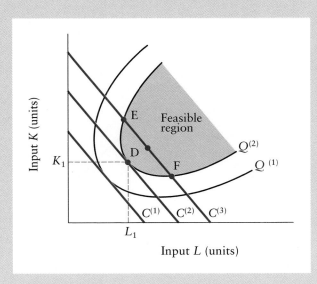

constraint requires that the solution be in the feasible region containing the input combinations that lie either on the $Q^{(2)}$ isoquant or on isoquants that fall above and to the right having larger output values (the shaded area). The total cost of producing the required output is minimized by finding the input combinations within this region that lie on the lowest cost isocost line. Combination D on the $C^{(2)}$ isocost line satisfies this condition. Combinations E and F, which also lie on the $Q^{(2)}$ isoquant, yield higher total costs because they fall on the $C^{(3)}$ isocost line. Thus, the use of L_1 units of input L and K_1 units of input K will yield a (constrained) minimum cost solution of $C^{(2)}$ dollars.

At the optimal input combination, the slope of the given isoquant must equal the slope of the $C^{(2)}$ lowest isocost line. As in the previous section, the slope of an isoquant is equal to dK/dL and

$$(4.16) \qquad -\frac{dK}{dL} = MRTS = \frac{MP_L}{MP_K}$$

Taking the derivative of the isocost equation (Equation 4.15), the slope of the isocost line is given by

$$(4.17) \qquad \frac{dK}{dL} = -\frac{C_L}{C_K}$$

Multiplying Equation 4.17 by (-1) and setting the result equal to Equation 4.16 yields

$$-\frac{dK}{dL} = -\left(-\frac{C_L}{C_K}\right)$$
$$= \frac{MP_L}{MP_K}$$

Thus, the following equilibrium condition, the "equimarginal criterion"

$$\frac{MP_L}{MP_K} = \frac{C_L}{C_K}$$

or, equivalently,

$$(4.18) \qquad \frac{MP_L}{C_L} = \frac{MP_K}{C_K}$$

must be satisfied in order for an input combination to be an optimal solution to the problem of minimizing cost subject to an output constraint. Equation 4.18 indicates that the marginal product per dollar input cost of one factor must be equal to the marginal product per dollar input cost of the other factor.

Note in Figure 4.10 that maximizing output subject to a feasible region demarcated by the $Q^{(2)}$ cost constraint yields exactly the same (L_1, K_1) optimal input combination that satisfies the equimarginal criterion. The logic of this optimality condition is equivalent to that developed in Chapter 3 for consumer demand choices that maximize utility subject to a household budget constraint.[6]

---

[6] Maximizing output subject to a cost constraint can be represented by the Lagrangian function:

$$Q_\lambda = f(L, K) - \lambda(C_L L + C_K K - C)$$

Differentiating this function with respect to L, K, and λ and setting the derivatives equal to zero yields

$$MP_L = \lambda C_L, MP_K = \lambda C_K, C = C_L L + C_K K$$

Clearly, the ratio of the marginal products equals the price ratio, which is equivalent to Equation 4.18 that was derived by minimizing cost subject to an output constraint.

Furthermore, compare the approach here with the approach used in footnote 11 of Chapter 3 to maximize utility subject to a budget constraint. Note the similarities.

FIGURE 4.10

Output Maximization
Subject to a Cost
Constraint

The feasible region represents combinations of
inputs that cost no more
than $C^{(2)}$. The point A
(where the production isoquant $Q^{(2)}$ is tangent to the
boundary of the feasible
region) represents the
maximum output combina-
tion of inputs that achieve
the target cost $C^{(2)}$. Note
that the maximum output
combination (L_1, K_1) is the
same as the least-cost
combination in Figure 4.9.

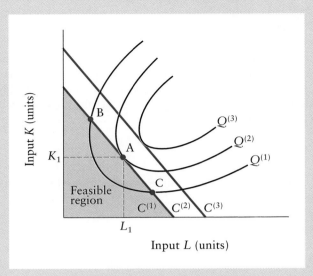

Determining the Cost-Minimizing Production Process

The previous section analyzed the least-cost combination of divisible inputs in variable proportions production, where one input substituted continuously for another. However, Deep Creek Mining's production choices involve indivisible capital equipment, such as one small or one large mining drill and a predetermined number of workers to run it. Similarly, an auto fender-stamping machine in an assembly plant must be used in fixed proportion to a certain quantity of labour and sheet metal supplies. And 3 hours of setup, maintenance, and cleaning may be required to support a 5-hour printing press run. Three additional hours of work by maintenance personnel would be required for a second press run, and a third shift of maintenance workers would be required for 24-hour printing operations. Although a higher output rate can be achieved by scaling up all of the inputs, each of these production processes is one of fixed, not variable, proportions.

Linear programming techniques are available to determine the least-cost process for fixed-proportions production. The Deep Creek Mining Company example can be used to illustrate the graphic approach to finding such a solution.

Production Processes and Process Rays

Production Process
A fixed-proportions production
relationship.

A **production process** can be defined as one in which the inputs are combined in fixed proportion to obtain the output. By this definition, a production process can be represented graphically as a ray through the origin having a slope equal to the ratio of the number of units of the respective resources required to produce one unit of output. Three production process rays for Deep Creek Mining are shown in Figure 4.11. Along process ray M_1, the inputs are combined in the ratio of two workers to a 1,250-bhp drilling machine. Hence, ray M_1 has a slope of 625 bhp per mine worker.

Cost Minimization: Deep Creek Mining Company (Continued)

Suppose one is interested in finding the combination of labour input and capital equipment that minimizes the cost of producing at least 29 tonnes of ore. Assume that the isocost lines are the ones defined by Equation 4.13 and graphed in Figure 4.8 earlier in this section. Figure 4.11 combines several isoquants and isocost lines for the ore-mining problem. The shaded area in the graph represents the set of feasible input combinations, that is, those labour and capital production processes that yield at least $Q = 29$ tonnes of output. Processes M_2 and M_3 minimize the cost of producing 29 tonnes at $300. M_1 imposes higher costs of $350.

FIGURE 4.11

A Fixed-Proportions Production Decision—Deep Creek Mining Company

This graph illustrates that the production rays M_1, M_2, and M_3 represent three different production processes. Ray M_2 is the least-cost process.

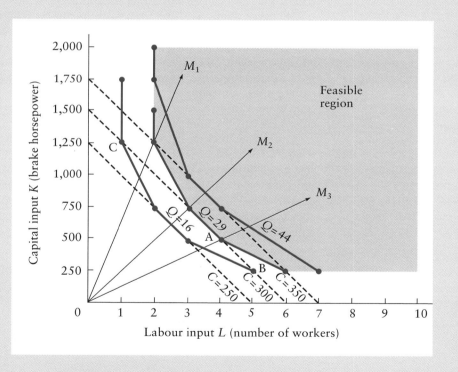

Operating multiple production processes like M_1, M_2, and M_3 can offer a firm flexibility in dealing with unusual orders, interruptions in the availability of resources, or binding resource constraints. However, not all fixed-proportions production processes are equally efficient. The firm will prefer to use one or two production processes exclusively if they offer the advantage of substantial cost savings. Mine 1 employs process M_1 to produce

29 tonnes with 2 workers and a 1,250-bhp drilling machine at a total cost of $50(2) + 0.20(1,250) = \$350$ or $\$350/29 = \$12.07$ per tonne. Mine 2 uses a more labour-intensive process (M_2) with 3 workers and a smaller 750-bhp machine and incurs a lower total cost of $300. Mine 2 is the benchmark operation for Deep Creek in that this M_2 process produces 29 tonnes at minimum cost—specifically, $\$300/29 = \$10.34$ per tonne.

Measuring the Efficiency of a Production Process

Mine 1 with production process M_1 is said to be allocatively inefficient because it has chosen the wrong input mix. The mine has allocated its input budget incorrectly. Its 1,250-bhp machine is too large for the number of workers hired and the output desired. By producing 29 tonnes of output for $350 relative to the lowest cost benchmark at $300, process M_1 exhibits only $\$300/\$350 = 85.7$ percent **allocative efficiency.**

In addition to allocative inefficiency involving the incorrect input mix, a production operation can also exhibit technical inefficiency. For example, the industrial engineering indicated by the production isoquants in Figure 4.11 suggests that the process M_3 also should be capable of producing 29 tonnes. The "$C = \$300$" isocost line is tangent to the boundary of the feasible region (i.e., the "$Q = 29$" isoquant) at not only 3 workers and a 750-bhp machine (M_2), but also at 4 workers and a 500-bhp machine (M_3). In principle, both production processes yield the desired 29 tonnes of ore at a minimum total cost of $300 and will thereby satisfy the condition in Equation 4.18.

However, suppose Mine 2 has been unable to achieve more than 27 tonnes of output. Although it has adopted a least-cost process, Mine 2 would then be characterized as *technically inefficient.* In particular, Mine 2 exhibits only 27 tonnes/29 tonnes = 93 percent **technical efficiency** despite its least-cost process. However, 93 percent technical efficiency may be inadequate. Benchmark plants often do substantially better, with many processes meeting 98 percent and 99 percent of their production goals. In addition, as technically inefficient plants approach the current standard of excellence, continuous quality improvement initiatives may raise the standards.

Overall production efficiency is defined as the product of allocative, technical, and scale efficiencies. **Scale efficiency** is the ratio of the lowest possible minimum average cost for all production processes to the potential average cost of a particular production process for a given level of output. The topic of scale efficiency is further discussed in Chapter 5 and in Web Chapter 14. If a 100 percent scale-efficient plant has 85.7 percent allocative efficiency and 93 percent technical efficiency, then its overall production efficiency is $0.857 \times 0.93 \times 1.0 = 0.797$, or 79.7 percent. Your job as an operations

Allocative Efficiency
A measure of how closely production achieves the least-cost input mix or process, given the desired level of output.

Technical Efficiency
A measure of how closely production achieves maximum potential output given the input mix or process.

Overall Production Efficiency
The product of allocative, technical, and scale efficiency.

Scale Efficiency
A measure of how close the potential average cost of production is to the lowest possible minimum average cost.

EXAMPLE

GM's A-Frame Supplier Achieves 99.998 Percent Technical Efficiency

For more information on General Motors, go to **www.gm.com**.

Just-in-time delivery systems have accentuated the need for very high reliability and technical efficiency to produce on time as promised with near-zero defects. One A-frame supplier to General Motors assembly plants has reduced defective parts to five per million (i.e., 0.002 of 1 percent) and has

agreed to pay a $4,000 *per minute* "charge back" for any late deliveries resulting in assembly line delays. Such a company must constantly monitor and proactively solve production problems before they arise in order to ensure near-100 percent technical efficiency.

How Exactly Have Computerization and Information Technology Lowered Costs at Merck?*

For more information on Merck, go to **www.merck.com**.

In processing insurance claims or typesetting newspapers and magazines, it is clear how computerization has made output per worker higher and therefore lowered unit labour cost. Personal computers have decreased dramatically the time and talent required to perform routine work done previously with paper forms and time-consuming repetitive human tasks. However, not every business uses large numbers of PCs. How have computerization and information technology raised productivity and lowered cost so widely across other industries?

One key seems to be the enhanced analytical and research and development capability provided by computers and information technology systems. Pharmaceutical research and development has experienced a benefit from computerization. Drug industry basic research always starts with biochemical or biogenetic modelling of the disease mechanism. In the past, once a mechanism for Hodgkin's disease, for example, became well understood, researchers at Merck and other drug companies experimented on known active compounds one by one in time-consuming chemical trials. Today, machines controlled and automated by microchips perform thousands of reactions at once and tally the results. The total time to discovery has been cut by more than two-thirds, and all attendant costs have declined sharply.

* Based on "The Innovators: The Rocket Under the High Tech Boom," *The Wall Street Journal*, March 30, 1999.

manager might be to decide which least-cost process Mine 1 in Figure 4.11 should now adopt. Because M_2 and M_3 are both allocatively efficient for 29 tonnes of output, but process M_2 has experienced technical inefficiency problems resulting in an inability to realize its maximum potential output, process M_3 would be preferred.

Effect of a Change in Input Prices

As shown above, the optimal combination of inputs in both the cost-minimization and output-maximization problems is a function of the relative prices of the inputs, that is, C_L and C_K. As the price of input L rises, one would expect the firm to use less of this input and more of the other input, K, in the production process, all other things being equal. This shift is demonstrated in Figure 4.12. The firm is interested in minimizing the cost of producing a given quantity of output $Q = 29$. Initially, the prices of inputs are $C_L = \$50$ and $C_K = \$0.20$, resulting in the isocost line $C = 300$. Given these conditions, the firm would operate at tangency point A—using 4 units of labour input and 500 units of the capital input. Now suppose that the price of labour itself is increased to $300. This has the effect of increasing the slope of the isocost lines, as shown in the graph. A $300 input budget, before the labour price increase, purchased 1,500-bhp machinery or 6 workers. Now $300 purchases the same 1,500-bhp machine or just 1 worker. To produce $Q = 29$ units of output at minimum cost, the firm would operate at input combination D, using a 1,250-bhp machine and 2 workers. Cost for 29 tonnes of ore has risen from $300 to $580 (1,250 × $0.2 + 2 × $300 = $850), but the cost is far less than if the original process at A had been continued. In that case, cost for 29 tonnes would have risen from $300 to $1,300 (i.e., 500 × $0.2 + 4 × $300 = $1,300). Often,

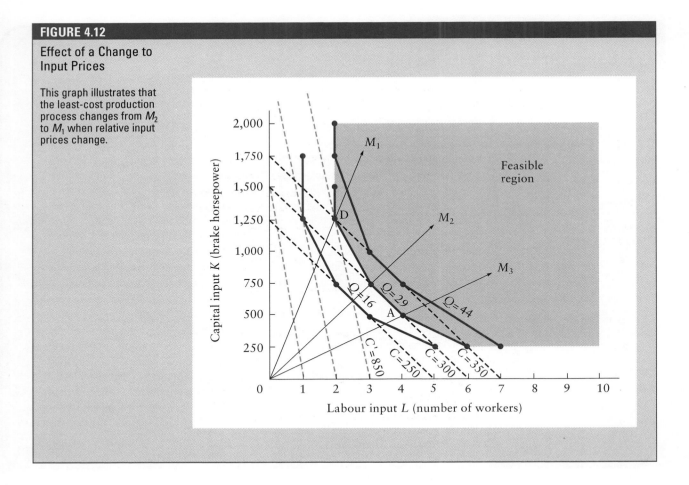

FIGURE 4.12

Effect of a Change to Input Prices

This graph illustrates that the least-cost production process changes from M_2 to M_1 when relative input prices change.

these *input substitution effects* are reinforced by a negative *output effect*—that is, higher input costs are passed through (as higher prices) to consumers who respond by cutting back their consumption. As less output than $Q = 29$ is ordered, the amount of sixfold-more-expensive labour hired may fall below 2 workers.

From this analysis, one can see that as the price of one input increases, the firm will substitute away from this input and use more of the relatively less expensive input. Since the Industrial Revolution, this phenomenon has been observed in the shift toward more capital-intensive production processes (that is, greater use of labour-saving equipment) because the price of labour has increased relative to the price of capital. In 1984, Chrysler Corporation decided to assemble its most successful product, the minivan, in an automated Canadian factory, in part because of rising union wages and restrictive workplace rules in its Detroit assembly plants.

This and the previous sections have been concerned with the effect on production output of arbitrary changes in either or both of the two inputs and in finding the optimal combination of inputs. The following section examines the effects on output of proportional changes in both inputs simultaneously, in other words, an investigation of the effects of a change in the overall scale of production.

Returns to Scale

This section begins with a definition of *returns to scale*, followed by discussions of measurement of returns to scale, homogeneous production functions, and the economic rationale for increasing and decreasing returns to scale.

Definition of Returns to Scale

Returns to Scale

The proportionate increase in output that results from a given proportionate increase in *all* of the inputs employed in the production process.

An increase in the scale of production consists of a simultaneous proportionate increase in *all* of the inputs used in the production process. The proportionate increase in output that results from the given proportionate increase in all of the inputs is defined as the physical **returns to scale.** Suppose, in the Deep Creek Mining Company example, one is interested in determining the effect on the number of tonnes of ore produced (output) of a 1.50-factor increase in the scale of production from a given labour–capital combination of 4 workers and 500-bhp equipment. A 1.50-factor increase in the scale of production would constitute a labour–capital combination of $4 \times 1.5 = 6$ workers and equipment having $500 \times 1.5 = 750$ bhp. From Table 4.1, note that the labour–capital combination of 4 workers and 500 bhp yields 29 tonnes of output, whereas the combination of 6 workers and 750 bhp yields 60 tonnes of output. Output has increased by the ratio of $60/29 = 2.07$. Thus, a 1.50-factor increase in input use has resulted in more than a 1.50-factor output increase (specifically, 2.07) in the quantity of output produced. Clearly, this relationship between the proportionate increases in inputs and outputs is not required to be the same for all increases in the scale of production. Another 1.50-factor increase in the scale of production from 6 workers and 750 bhp to 9 workers and 1,125 bhp results in an increase in output from 60 to approximately 63.5 tonnes—an increase by a factor of only 1.06.

Measurement of Returns to Scale

An increase in the scale of production can be represented graphically in a two-dimensional isoquant map, as is shown in Figure 4.13. Increasing the scale of production by a factor of $\lambda = 2$ from the combination of 10 units of input L and 100 units of input K to 20 units of input L and 200 units of K results in an increase in the quantity of output from $Q^{(1)}$ to $Q^{(2)}$. Three possible relationships that can exist between the increase in inputs and the increase in outputs are as follows:

1. *Increasing* returns to scale: Output increases by *more than* λ; that is, $Q^{(2)} > \lambda Q^{(1)}$.

2. *Decreasing* returns to scale: Output increases by *less than* λ; that is, $Q^{(2)} < \lambda Q^{(1)}$.

3. *Constant* returns to scale: Output increases by *exactly* λ; that is, $Q^{(2)} = \lambda Q^{(1)}$.

Figure 4.13 illustrates three different production functions that exhibit these three types of returns to scale. In panel (a), showing increasing returns to scale, doubling

---

FIGURE 4.13

Production Isoquants Exhibiting Increasing, Decreasing, and Constant Returns to Scale

Panel (a) illustrates increasing returns to scale, where doubling both inputs more than doubles output. Panel (b) illustrates decreasing returns to scale, where doubling both inputs results in output that is less than double. Panel (c) illustrates constant returns to scale, where doubling both inputs exactly doubles output.

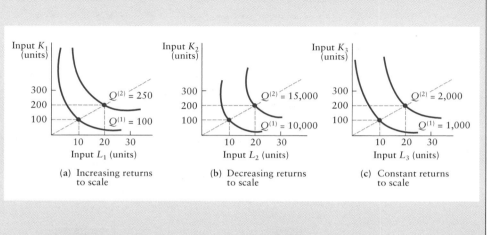

(a) Increasing returns to scale

(b) Decreasing returns to scale

(c) Constant returns to scale

INCREASING RETURNS TO SCALE AT THE WELLINGTON COMPANY

Suppose one is interested in determining the returns to scale for the following production function of the Wellington Company:

(4.19) $Q = 10LK - 2L^2 - K^2$

First, increase each of the inputs by a factor of λ; that is $L' = \lambda L$ and $K' = \lambda K$. Next, substitute these values into the production function as follows:

$$Q_0 = 10(\lambda L)(\lambda K) - 2(\lambda L)^2 - (\lambda K)^2$$
$$= 10\lambda^2 LK - 2\lambda^2 L^2 - \lambda^2 K^2$$
$$= \lambda^2(10LK - 2L^2 - K^2)$$
$$= \lambda^2 Q$$

Because output increases by *more than* λ—by a factor of λ^2—Wellington's production function exhibits *increasing* returns to scale.

input L from 10 to 20 units and input K from 100 to 200 units yields more than double the amount of output—an increase from 100 to 250 units. In panel (b), showing decreasing returns to scale, a similar doubling of two inputs, L and K, yields less than double the amount of output—an increase from 10,000 to 15,000 units. Finally, in panel (c), showing constant returns to scale, a similar doubling of inputs L and K yields exactly double the amount of output—an increase from 1,000 to 2,000 units.

Homogeneous Production Functions and Returns to Scale

Many of the algebraic production functions used in analyzing production processes are said to be *homogeneous*. Homogeneous functions have certain mathematical properties that make them desirable in modelling production processes. If each input in the production function is multiplied by an arbitrary constant λ and if this constant can be factored out of the function, then the production function is defined as *homogeneous*.

One can also measure the degree of homogeneity of a production function. A production function $Q = f(L, K)$ is said to be *homogeneous of degree n* if

(4.20) $f(\lambda L, \lambda K) = \lambda^n f(L, K)$ for $\lambda \neq 0$

where λ is some constant. The following production function

(4.21) $f(L, K) = 0.6L + 0.2K$

is homogeneous of degree 1.0 because

$$f(\lambda L, \lambda K) = 0.6(\lambda L) + 0.2(\lambda K)$$
$$= \lambda^1(0.6L + 0.2K)$$
$$= \lambda^1 f(L, K)$$

If the degree of homogeneity (n) is equal to 1.0, then the production function is said to be *linearly homogeneous*. In this linear homogeneous case, when one doubles the inputs, output doubles.

The degree of homogeneity (n) indicates the type of returns to scale (i.e., increasing, decreasing, or constant) that characterizes a homogeneous production function.

If $n = 1$, as with the case in Equation 4.21, the production function exhibits constant returns to scale. If $n > 1$, the production function exhibits increasing returns to scale. If $n < 1$, the production function exhibits decreasing returns to scale. The nonlinear production function of the Wellington Company represented by Equation 4.19, which has a degree of homogeneity (n) equal to 2.0, exhibits increasing returns to scale. Here, when one doubles the inputs ($\lambda = 2$), output increases by a factor of 4 (λ^2).

Increasing and Decreasing Returns to Scale

In addition to satisfying the law of diminishing marginal returns discussed earlier, a firm's production function is often characterized by first increasing and then decreasing physical returns to scale. A number of industrial engineering arguments have been presented to justify this characteristic of the production function. The major argument given for initial increasing returns, as the scale of production is first increased, is the opportunity for *specialization in the use of capital and labour.* As the scale of production is increased, equipment that is more efficient in performing a limited set of tasks can be substituted for less efficient all-purpose equipment. Similarly, the efficiency of workers in performing a small number of related tasks is greater than that of less highly skilled, but more versatile, workers. Practical limits on the degree of specialization, however, may prevent increasing returns from being realized in producing ever-larger quantities of output.

A principal argument given for the existence of decreasing returns to scale is the increasingly complex *problems of coordination and control* faced by management as the scale of production is increased. Limitations on the ability of management to transmit and receive information (such as decisions and reports on performance) may diminish the effectiveness of management in exercising control and coordination of increasingly larger scales of production. As a result, proportionate increases in all of the inputs of the production process, including the input labelled "management," may eventually yield less than proportionate increases in total output.

The Cobb–Douglas Production Function

Cobb–Douglas Production Function

A particular type of mathematical model, known as a "multiplicative exponential function," which is used to represent the relationship between inputs and output.

The **Cobb–Douglas production function** is a homogeneous function with a degree of homogeneity (n) equal to ($\beta_1 + \beta_2$):

$$(4.22) \qquad Q = \alpha L^{\beta_1} K^{\beta_2}$$

This can be shown as follows. Multiplying L and K by a constant λ yields

$$
\begin{aligned}
f = (\lambda L, \lambda K) &= \alpha(\lambda L)^{\beta_1}(\lambda K)^{\beta_2} \\
&= \alpha(\lambda^{\beta_1} L^{\beta_1})(\lambda^{\beta_2} K^{\beta_2}) \\
&= \lambda^{\beta_1 + \beta_2}(\alpha L^{\beta_1} K^{\beta_2}) \\
&= \lambda^{\beta_1 + \beta_2} f(L, K)
\end{aligned}
$$

Because the exponent of λ is equal to ($\beta_1 + \beta_2$), the degree of homogeneity is equal to ($\beta_1 + \beta_2$). Depending on whether $n = \beta_1 + \beta_2$ is less than, equal to, or greater than 1, the Cobb–Douglas production function will exhibit decreasing, constant, or increasing returns, respectively.

The multiplicative exponential Cobb–Douglas function can be estimated as a linear regression relation by taking the logarithm of Equation 4.22 to obtain

$$(4.23) \qquad \log Q = \log \alpha + \beta_1 \log L + \beta_2 \log K$$

Thus, once the parameters of the Cobb–Douglas model are estimated, the sum of the exponents of the labour (β_1) and capital (β_2) variables can be used to test for the presence of increasing, constant, or decreasing returns to scale.

Deregulation of Ontario Electricity?

If electricity is regulated and the price is set too low, most users are unlikely to seriously attempt conservation measures. This can lead to brownouts or even blackouts, as was the situation in Ontario and parts of the United States in August 2003. Furthermore, the private sector, even if permitted to do so, is unlikely to provide additional capacity because investors probably are unable to earn a normal return when the price of electricity is low. Thus, the argument for deregulation is to let the marketplace find an equilibrium price for electricity that will reduce consumption and increase capacity.

Unfortunately, since it takes a long time to add capacity, there is the danger of substantial price spikes under deregulation before additional capacity comes on line. Users are voters, and they consider electricity an essential commodity. Thus, it presents quite a challenge to politicians to find a way to move to a deregulated system without incurring the wrath of voters.

Empirical Studies of the Cobb–Douglas Production Function

Since the original production function studies of Cobb–Douglas, literally dozens of similar studies have been undertaken.[7] Using time-series data, production functions have been developed for entire economies (e.g., the United States, Norway, Finland, and New Zealand), geographical regions (Massachusetts, and Victoria and New South Wales in Australia), and major sectors of the economy (manufacturing, mining, and agriculture). Also, Cobb–Douglas functions have been estimated for various sectors of an economy using cross-sectional industry data (Canada, the United States, and Australia) and for various industries using cross-sectional data on firms within an industry (railways, coal, clothing, chemicals, electricity, milk, and rice).

Summary

- A *production function* is a schedule (table), graph, or mathematical model relating the maximum quantity of output that can be produced from various quantities of inputs.

- For a production function with one variable input, the *marginal product* is defined as the incremental change in total output that can be produced by the use of one more unit of the variable input in the production process.

- For a production function with one variable input, the *average product* is defined as the ratio of total output to the amount of the variable input used in producing the output.

- The *law of diminishing marginal returns* states that, with all other productive factors held constant, the use of increasing amounts of the variable factor in the production process beyond some point will result in diminishing marginal increases in total output. *Increasing returns* can arise with *network effects*.

- In the short run, with one of the productive factors fixed, the optimal output level (and optimal level of the variable input) occurs where marginal revenue product equals marginal factor cost. *Marginal revenue product* is defined as the amount that

[7] See R.G. Chambers, *Applied Production Analysis* (New York: Cambridge University Press, 1988).

an additional unit of the variable input adds to total revenue. *Marginal factor cost* is defined as the amount that an additional unit of the variable input adds to total cost.

■ A *production isoquant* is either a geometric curve or algebraic function representing all the various combinations of inputs that can be used in producing a given level of output.

■ The *marginal rate of technical substitution* is the rate at which one input may be substituted for another input in the production process, while total output remains constant. It is equal to the ratio of the marginal products of the two inputs.

■ In the long run, with both inputs being variable, minimizing cost subject to an output constraint (or maximizing output subject to a cost constraint) requires that the production process be operated at the point where the marginal product per dollar input cost of each factor is equal.

■ *Technical efficiency* of a production process is the ratio of observed output to the maximum potentially feasible output for that process, given the same inputs.

■ *Allocative efficiency* of a production process is the ratio of total cost for producing a given output level with the least-cost process to the observed total cost of producing that output.

■ *Scale efficiency* is the ratio of the lowest possible minimum average cost for all production processes to the potential average cost of a particular production process for a given level of output.

■ *Overall production efficiency* is the product of allocative, technical, and scale efficiencies.

■ Physical *returns to scale* is defined as the proportionate increase in the output of a production process that results from a given proportionate increase in all the inputs.

■ The *Cobb–Douglas production function,* which is used extensively in empirical studies, is a multiplicative exponential function in which output is a (nonlinear) monotonically increasing function of each of the inputs.

■ The Cobb–Douglas production function has various properties that allow one to draw conclusions, based on parameter estimates, about returns to scale.

Self-Test Exercises

1. The amount of fish caught per week on a trawler is a function of the crew size assigned to operate the boat. Based on past data, the following production schedule was developed.

Crew Size (Number of Persons)	Amount of Fish Caught per Week (Kg)
2	3
3	6
4	11
5	19
6	24
7	28
8	31
9	33
10	34
11	34
12	33

a. Over what ranges of workers are there (i) increasing, (ii) constant, (iii) decreasing, and (iv) negative returns?

b. How large a crew should be used if the trawler owner is interested in maximizing the total amount of fish caught?

c. How large a crew should be used if the trawler owner is interested in maximizing the average amount of fish caught per person?

2. Consider the previous exercise again. Suppose the trawler owner can sell all of the fish that the crew can catch for $75 per 100 kilograms and can hire as many crew members as needed by paying them $150 per week. Assuming that the trawler owner is interested in maximizing profits, determine the optimal crew size.

3. Consider the following short-run production function (where L = variable input, Q = output): $Q = 10L - 0.5L^2$. Suppose that output can be sold for $10 per unit. Also assume that the firm can obtain as much of the variable input (L) as it needs at $20 per unit.

a. Determine the marginal revenue product function.

b. Determine the marginal factor cost function.

c. Determine the optimal value of L, given that the objective is to maximize profits.

4. Consider the following Cobb–Douglas production function for the bus transportation system in a particular city:

$$Q = \alpha L^{\beta_1} F^{\beta_2} K^{\beta_3}$$

where L = labour input in worker hours

F = fuel input in litres

K = capital input in number of buses

Q = output measured in millions of bus kilometres

Suppose that the parameters (α, β_1, β_2, and β_3) of this model were estimated using annual data for the past 25 years. The following results were obtained:

$$\alpha = 0.0012 \qquad \beta_1 = 0.45 \qquad \beta_2 = 0.20 \qquad \beta_3 = 0.30$$

a. Determine the (i) labour, (ii) fuel, and (iii) capital-input production elasticities.

b. Suppose that labour input (worker hours) is increased by 2 percent next year (with the other inputs held constant). Determine the approximate percentage change in output.

c. Suppose that capital input (number of buses) is decreased by 3 percent next year (that is, certain older buses are taken out of service). Assuming that the other inputs are held constant, determine the approximate percentage change in output.

d. What type of returns to scale appears to characterize this bus transportation system (ignore the issue of statistical significance)?

5. Determine whether each of the following production functions exhibits increasing, constant, or decreasing returns to scale:

a. $Q = 1.5L^{0.70}K^{0.30}$

b. $Q = 0.4L + 0.5K$

c. $Q = 2.0LK$

d. $Q = 1.0L^{0.6}K^{0.5}$

Exercises

1. In the Deep Creek Mining Company example described in this chapter (Table 4.1), suppose again that labour is the variable input and capital is the fixed input. Specifically, assume that the firm owns a piece of equipment having a 500-bhp rating.
   a. Complete the following table.

Labour Input L (No. of Workers)	Total Product $TP_L\,(= Q)$	Marginal Product MP_L	Average Product AP_L	Elasticity of Production, E_L
1	_____	_____	_____	_____
2	_____	_____	_____	_____
3	_____	_____	_____	_____
4	_____	_____	_____	_____
5	_____	_____	_____	_____
6	_____	_____	_____	_____
7	_____	_____	_____	_____
8	_____	_____	_____	_____
9	_____	_____	_____	_____
10	_____	_____	_____	_____

   b. Plot the (i) total product, (ii) marginal product, and (iii) average product functions.
   c. Determine the boundaries of the three stages of production.

2. From your knowledge of the relationships among the various production functions, complete the following table.

Variable Input L	Total Product $TP_L\,(= Q)$	Average Product AP_L	Marginal Product MP_L
0	0	_____	_____
1	_____	_____	8
2	28	_____	_____
3	_____	18	_____
4	_____	_____	26
5	_____	20	_____
6	108	_____	_____
7	_____	_____	-10

3. Suppose the short-run total product curve (TP_L) is a linear function of the variable input over some range of values. Determine the shape of the corresponding marginal product (MP_L) and average product (AP_L) functions.

4. Consider the following short-run production function (where L = variable input, Q = output):

$$Q = 6L^2 - 0.4L^3$$

   a. Determine the marginal product function (MP_L).
   b. Determine the average product function (AP_L).
   c. Find the value of L that maximizes Q.
   d. Find the value of L at which the marginal product function takes on its maximum value.

e. Find the value of L at which the average product function takes on its maximum value.

f. Plot the (i) total, (ii) marginal, and (iii) average product functions for values of $L = 0, 1, 2, 3, \ldots, 12$.

5. In the Deep Creek Mining Company example described in this chapter (Table 4.1), suppose one is interested in maximizing output subject to a cost constraint. Assume that the per-unit prices of labour and capital are $45 and $0.24, respectively. Total costs (the sum of labour and capital costs) are constrained to $360 or less.

a. Using graphical isoquant–isocost analysis, determine the optimal combination of labour and capital to employ in the ore-mining process and the optimal output level.

b. Determine the optimal combination of labour and capital and optimal output level if the per-unit prices of labour and capital are $60 and $0.18, respectively.

6. Suppose that as the result of recent labour negotiations, wage rates are *reduced* by 10 percent in a production process employing only capital and labour. Assuming that other conditions (for example, productivity) remain constant, determine what effect this decrease will have on the desired proportions of capital and labour used in producing the given level of output at minimum total cost. Illustrate your answer with an isoquant–isocost diagram.

7. The production schedule below was developed for a production process (where the entries represent output measured in units).

Labour Input L (Worker Hours)	Capital Input K (Machine Hours)							
	1	2	3	4	5	6	7	8
1	39	55	69	81	91	99	105	109
2	57	72	86	96	105	112	117	120
3	73	88	99	109	117	123	127	129
4	87	100	111	120	127	132	135	136
5	99	111	121	129	135	139	141	141
6	109	120	129	136	141	144	145	144
7	117	127	135	141	145	147	147	145
8	123	132	139	144	147	148	147	144
9	127	135	141	145	147	147	145	141
10	129	136	141	144	145	144	141	136

a. Plot isoquants for 99, 109, 117, 129, 136, 141, 145, and 147 units of output.

b. Assume that labour costs are $10 per worker hour and machine costs are $15 per machine hour. Determine the maximum output that can be obtained given a cost constraint of $120.

8. A firm uses two variable inputs, labour (L) and raw materials (M), in producing its output. At its current level of output:

$$C_L = \$10/\text{unit} \qquad MP_L = 25 \qquad C_M = \$2/\text{unit} \qquad MP_M = 4$$

a. Determine whether the firm is operating efficiently, given that its objective is to minimize the cost of producing the given level of output.

b. Determine what changes (if any) in the relative proportions of labour and raw materials need to be made to operate efficiently.

9. Suppose that a firm's production function is given by the following relationship:

$$Q = 2.5\sqrt{LK} \qquad (\text{i.e., } Q = 2.5L^{0.5}K^{0.5})$$

where Q = output

L = labour input

K = capital input

a. Determine the percentage increase in output if labour input is increased by 10 percent (assuming that capital input is held constant).

b. Determine the percentage increase in output if capital input is increased by 25 percent (assuming that labour input is held constant).

c. Determine the percentage increase in output if *both* labour and capital are increased by 20 percent.

10. Given the following production function

$$Q = 1.40L^{0.70}K^{0.35}$$

a. Determine the elasticity of production with respect to
   (i) Labour (L)
   (ii) Capital (K)

b. Give an economic interpretation of each value determined in part (a).

11. Determine if the following production functions are homogeneous and, if so, the degree of homogeneity:

a. $Q = 2L^{0.7} + 3K^{0.7}$

b. $Q = 2L^{0.5}K^{0.5}$

c. $Q = \dfrac{2L^3 + 3K^3}{6L^2 - 2K^2}$

d. $Q = 3L^2K^2 - 0.1L^3K^3$

e. $Q = 2L^{0.8} + 3K^{0.7}$

12. Show that elasticity of production for capital input is constant and equal to β_2 for the Cobb–Douglas production function (Equation 4.22).

13. *Extension of the Cobb–Douglas Production Function:* The Cobb–Douglas production function (Equation 4.22) can be shown to be a special case of a larger class of constant elasticity of substitution (*CES*) production functions having the following mathematical form:

$$Q = \gamma[\alpha K^{-\rho} + (1 - \alpha)L^{-\rho}]^{-\nu/\rho}$$

γ is an efficiency parameter that shows the output that results from given quantities of inputs. α is a distribution parameter ($0 \le \alpha \le 1$) that indicates the division of factor income between capital and labour. ρ is a substitution parameter that is a measure of substitutability of capital for labour (or vice versa) in the production process. ν is a scale parameter ($\nu > 0$) that indicates the type of returns to scale (increasing, constant, or decreasing). Show that when $\nu = 1$, this function exhibits constant returns to scale. (*Hint:* Increase capital K and labour L each by a factor of λ—$K^* = \lambda K$ and $L^* = \lambda L$—and show that output Q also increases by a factor of λ—$Q^* = \lambda Q$.)

14. Lobo Lighting Ltd. currently employs 100 unskilled labourers, 80 factory technicians, 30 skilled machinists, and 40 skilled electricians. Lobo feels that the marginal product of the last unskilled labourer is 400 lights per week, the marginal product of the last factory technician is 450 lights per week, the marginal product of the last skilled machinist is 550 lights per week, and the marginal product of the last skilled electrician is 600 lights per week. Unskilled labourers

earn $400 per week, factory technicians earn $500 per week, machinists earn $700 per week, and electricians earn $750 per week.

Is Lobo using the lowest cost combination of workers to produce its targeted output? If not, what recommendations can you make to assist the company?

15. Consider the following short-run cubic production functions, holding constant the firm's capital inputs:

$$Q = -0.005L^3 + 0.30L^2$$

where: Q = units of output
L = units of labour input

a. What output is produced when $L = 0$?
b. What is the average product of labour?
c. What is the marginal product of labour?
d. At what level of labour input is the marginal product of labour maximized?
e. At what level of labour input is the marginal product of labour equal to the average product of labour? What happens to total product of labour at this point?

CASE EXERCISE

PRODUCTION FUNCTION: BELANGER COMPANY

Economists at the Belanger Company are interested in developing a production function for fertilizer plants. They have collected data on 15 different plants that produce fertilizer (see data table below).

Plant	Output (000 Tonnes)	Capital ($000)	Labour (000 Worker Hours)
1	605.3	18,891	700.2
2	566.1	19,201	651.8
3	647.1	20,655	822.9
4	523.7	15,082	650.3
5	712.3	20,300	859.0
6	487.5	16,079	613.0
7	761.6	24,194	851.3
8	442.5	11,504	655.4
9	821.1	25,970	900.6
10	397.8	10,127	550.4
11	896.7	25,622	842.2
12	359.3	12,477	540.5
13	979.1	24,002	949.4
14	331.7	8,042	575.7
15	1,064.9	23,972	925.8

Questions

1. Estimate the Cobb–Douglas production function $Q = \alpha L^{\beta_1} K^{\beta_2}$, where Q = output; L = labour input; K = capital input; and α, β_1, and β_2 are the parameters to be estimated. (*Note:* If the regression program on your computer does not have a natural logarithmic transformation, manually transform the preceding data into the logarithms before entering the data into the computer.) For information on regression analysis, see Web Chapters 13 and 14.

2. Test whether the coefficients of capital and labour are statistically significant.

3. Determine the percentage of the variation in output that is "explained" by the regression equation.

4. Determine the labour and capital production elasticities and give an economic interpretation of each value.

5. Determine whether this production function exhibits increasing, decreasing, or constant returns to scale (ignore the issue of statistical significance).

CHAPTER 5

Cost Analysis

Chapter Preview

"Economic cost" refers to the cost of attracting a resource from its next best alternative use (the opportunity cost concept). Managers seeking to make the most efficient use of resources to maximize value must be concerned with both short-run and long-run opportunity costs. Short-run cost–output relationships help managers to plan for the most profitable level of output, given the capital resources that are immediately available. Long-run cost–output relationships involve attracting additional capital to expand or contract the plant size and the scale of operations.

Of course, before a cost analysis can be performed, the firm must estimate its cost function. For a discussion of cost function estimation, see Web Chapter 14. Also relevant is Web Chapter 15, which discusses forecasting. To access Web chapters and appendixes, go to the Nelson website for this book at www.mcguigan.nelson.com.

Learning Objectives

After studying this chapter, you should be able to:

1. Define *cost* and the different approaches used in measuring costs.

2. Understand that a *cost function* is a schedule (table), graph, or mathematical relationship showing the minimum achievable cost of producing various quantities of output.

3. Understand that short-run *total costs* equal the sum of *fixed* and *variable costs*.

4. Define *marginal cost*.

5. Explain why short-run average variable and marginal cost functions are hypothesized to be U-shaped.

6. Understand that the theoretical long-run average cost function is often L-shaped due to the presence of scale economies and absence of scale diseconomies.

7. Explain how volume discounts in purchasing inputs and learning curve effects can be distinguished from scale effects.

8. Describe how to achieve *minimum efficient scale*.

9. (Web Appendix 5A) Illustrate *linear break-even analysis* using both the graphical and algebraic methods.

10. (Web Appendix 5A) Identify the differences and limitations of *break-even analysis versus contribution analysis*.

11. (Web Appendix 5A) Define the *degree of operating* leverage (DOL) as the multiplier effect resulting from the use of fixed operating costs and business risk as the inherent variability or uncertainty of a firm's earnings before interest and taxes (EBIT).

Air Canada's Cost Structure*

CP/ANDREW VAUGHAN

Air Canada is Canada's "national" airline and the dominant firm in the domestic airline industry, with many international flights as well. The airline uses a diverse fleet of aircraft produced by Airbus, Boeing, and Bombardier, unlike the more successful WestJet Airlines, which flies only one type of plane, the Boeing 737. This diversity results in higher costs of maintenance and crew training, and much more complex crew scheduling. Air Canada's cost per available seat mile (CASM) is almost the highest in the North American airline industry—US¢10.5 per available seat mile. This compares to a cost of slightly over US¢9.5 for American Airlines, a comparable large U.S. airline, and only US¢7.5 for WestJet.

The combination of high fares and very high costs per available seat mile invited competition, which WestJet is attempting to provide, especially in the core business area of flights connecting Toronto with Montreal and Ottawa. In addition, other low-cost Canadian airlines, such as CanJet, are also entering Air Canada's traditional markets, including even some flights to U.S. destinations.

As a result of massive losses due to the downturn in travel after September 11, 2001, and to its high cost structure, Air Canada entered bankruptcy protection in 2003. Cost control is a difficult problem in any corporation. It is, however, especially difficult in a heavily unionized, capital-intensive industry such as airlines.

In this chapter we consider many of the important cost relationships that are essential to a firm's long-term competitive success.

---

* Based on Paul Vieira, "For Airlines, CASM Is Everything," *Financial Post*, April 30, 2004, page IN1.

The Meaning and Measurement of Cost

In its most elementary form, *cost* refers simply to the sacrifice incurred whenever an exchange or transformation of resources takes place. This association between foregone opportunities and economic cost applies in all circumstances. However, the appropriate manner to measure costs is a function of the purpose for which the information is to be used.

Accounting versus Economic Costs

Accountants have primarily been concerned with measuring costs for *financial reporting purposes.* As a result, they define and measure cost by the *historical outlay of funds* that takes place in the exchange or transformation of a resource. Thus, whenever A sells a product or commodity to B, the *price* paid by B, expressed in dollars, measures the accounting cost of the product to B. When A exchanges labour services for money or other items of value, the *wages* that A receives represent the accounting cost of A's services to the employer. Similarly, the *interest* paid to the bondholder or lending institution is used to measure the accounting cost of funds to the borrower.

Economists have mainly been concerned with measuring costs for *decision-making purposes*. The objective is to determine the present and future costs of resources associated with various alternative courses of action. Such an objective requires a consideration of the opportunities foregone (or sacrificed) whenever a resource is used in a given course of action. So, although both the accounting cost and the economic cost of a product will include such *explicit* costs as labour, raw materials, supplies, rent, interest, and utilities, economists will also include the **opportunity costs** of time and capital that the owner–manager has invested in the enterprise. The opportunity cost of the owner's time is measured by the most attractive salary or other form of compensation that the owner could have received by applying personal talents, skills, and experience in the management of a similar (but second-best) business owned by someone else. Similarly, the opportunity cost of the capital is measured by the profit or return that could have been received if the owner had chosen to employ capital in the second-best (alternative) investment of comparable risk.

When one recognizes that such first-best and second-best uses change over time, it becomes clear that the historical outlay of funds to obtain a resource at an earlier date

Opportunity Costs
The value of a resource in its next best alternative use. Opportunity cost represents the return or compensation that must be foregone as a result of the decision to employ the resource in a given economic activity.

EXAMPLE

OPPORTUNITY COSTS AT BENTLEY CLOTHING STORE

Robert Bentley owns and operates the Bentley Clothing Store. A traditional income statement for the business is shown in panel (a) of Table 5.1. The mortgage on the store has been paid, so no interest expenses are shown on the income statement. Also, the building has been fully depreciated, so no depreciation charges are shown. From an *accounting* standpoint, Bentley is earning a *positive accounting profit* of $190,000 (before taxes).

However, consider the store's profitability from an *economic* standpoint. Economic profit is defined as the difference between total revenues and total economic costs. Algebraically, economic profit is given by

(5.1)

$$\text{Economic} \atop \text{profit} = \text{Total} \atop \text{revenues} - \text{Explicit} \atop \text{costs} - \text{Implicit} \atop \text{costs}$$

As indicated earlier in the chapter, implicit costs include the opportunity costs of time and capital that the entrepreneur has invested in the firm. Suppose that Bentley could go to work as a clothing department manager for a large department or specialty store chain and receive a salary of $130,000 per year. Also assume that Bentley could rent his building to another merchant for $88,000 (net) per year. Under these conditions, as shown in panel (b) of Table 5.1, Bentley is earning a *negative economic profit* (−$28,000 before taxes). By renting his store to another merchant and going to work as a manager in a different store, he could make $28,000 more than he is currently earning from his clothing store business. Thus, accounting profits, which do not include opportunity costs, are not always a valid indication of the economic profitability (or loss) of an enterprise.

Table 5.1 Profitability of Bentley Clothing Store

(a) Accounting Income Statement

Net sales		$650,000
Less: Cost of goods sold		250,000
Gross profit		400,000
Less: Expenses		
Employee compensation*	150,000	
Advertising	30,000	
Utilities and maintenance	20,000	
Miscellaneous	10,000	
Total		210,000
Net profit before taxes		$190,000

(b) Economic Profit Statement

Total revenues		$650,000
Less: Explicit costs		
Cost of goods sold	250,000	
Employee compensation*	150,000	
Advertising	30,000	
Utilities and maintenance	20,000	
Miscellaneous	10,000	
Total		460,000
Accounting profit before taxes		*190,000*
Less: Implicit costs		
Salary (manager)	130,000	
Rent on building	88,000	
Total		218,000
Economic profit (or loss) before taxes		($ 28,000)

*Employee compensation does not include any salary paid to Robert Bentley.

(the accounting cost basis) may not be the appropriate measure of opportunity cost in a decision problem today. For example, consider the following three cases of a substantive distinction between economic cost and accounting cost: depreciation cost measurement, inventory valuation, and sunk cost of underutilized facilities.

Depreciation Cost Measurement The production of a good or service typically requires the use of licences and plant and equipment. As these **capital assets** are used, their service life is expended. Eventually, the assets wear out or become obsolete. Depreciation is the cost of using these assets in producing the given output. If a firm owns a machine that has a current market value of $8,000 and is expected to have a value of $6,800 after one more year of use, then the opportunity cost of using the machine for one year (the economist's measure of depreciation cost) is $8,000 − $6,800 = $1,200. Assuming that

Capital Asset
A durable input that depreciates with use, time, and obsolescence.

2,000 units of output were produced during the year, the depreciation cost would be $1,200 ÷ 2,000 units = $0.60 per unit.

Unfortunately, it is often very difficult, if not impossible, to determine the service life of a capital asset and the future changes in its market value.[1] Some assets are unique (patents). Others are not traded in liquid resale markets (plants). Still others are rendered obsolete with little predictability (computers). Accountants have adopted procedures for allocating a portion of the acquisition cost of an asset to each accounting time period (and, in turn, to each unit of output that is produced within that time period). This is typically done by estimating the service life of the asset and then arbitrarily assigning a portion of the historical cost of the asset against income during each year of the service life. If the machine is purchased by the firm for $10,000 and is expected to have a 10-year life and no salvage value, the straight-line method of depreciation[2] ($10,000 ÷ 10 = $1,000) would calculate the depreciation cost of this asset each year. Assuming that 2,000 units of output are produced in a given year, then $1,000 ÷ 2,000 = $0.50 would be allocated to the cost of each unit produced by the firm.

Note that the straight-line method for allocating depreciation costs is arbitrary. The calculated accounting depreciation cost does not equal the economic depreciation cost incurred, if in fact the market value of the machine drops to $6,800 after one year.

Inventory Valuation Whenever materials are stored in inventory for a period of time before being used in the production process, the accounting and economic costs may differ if the market price of these materials has changed from the original purchase price. The accounting cost is equal to the actual *acquisition* cost, whereas the economic cost is equal to the current *replacement* cost. As the Westside Plumbing and Heating example on the next page illustrates, the use of the acquisition cost can lead to incorrect production decisions.

Sunk Cost of Underutilized Facilities A manufacturing firm recently discontinued a product line and was left with 50,000 square metres of unneeded warehouse space. The firm leases the entire warehouse (200,000 square metres) from the owner for $10,000,000 per year (i.e., $50 per square metre) under a long-term (10-year) lease agreement. A nearby company that is expanding its operations offered to rent the 50,000 square metres of unneeded space for one year for $1,250,000 (i.e., $25 per square metre). Should the firm accept the offer to rent the unused space, assuming that no higher offers for the warehouse space are expected?

One could argue that the firm should reject the offer because the additional rent (revenue) of $25 per square metre is less than the lease payment (cost) of $50 per square metre. Such reasoning, however, will lead to an incorrect decision. The lease payment ($50 per square metre) represents a **sunk cost** that must be paid regardless of whether or not the other company rents the unneeded warehouse space. Renting the unneeded warehouse space *reduces* the net cost of the warehouse from $10,000,000 to $8,750,000, a savings of $1,250,000 per year. The relevant comparison is between the incremental revenue ($1,250,000) and the incremental costs ($0 in this case). Thus, sunk costs (such as the lease payment of $50 per square metre in this example) should not be considered relevant costs because such costs are unavoidable, independent of the course of action chosen.

Sunk Cost
A cost incurred regardless of the alternative action chosen in a decision-making problem.

---

[1] This concept of the future cost of the partially consumed asset is termed the *replacement cost* of the asset.
[2] The *straight-line* depreciation method allocates an equal amount of the cost of the asset to each period during the life of the asset. Other *accelerated* depreciation methods are also used. For more information see D. Cyr et al., *Contemporary Financial Management,* 1st Canadian ed. (Toronto: Thomson Nelson Canada, 2004), Chapter 9.

INVENTORY VALUATION AT WESTSIDE PLUMBING AND HEATING

Westside Plumbing and Heating Company is offered a contract for $100,000 to provide the plumbing for a new building. The labour and equipment costs are calculated to be $60,000 for fulfilling the contract. Westside has the materials in inventory to complete the job. The materials originally cost the firm $50,000. However, prices have since declined and the materials could now be purchased for $37,500. Material prices are not expected to increase in the near future and hence no gains can be anticipated from holding the materials in inventory. The question is: Should the firm accept the contract? An analysis of the contract under both methods for measuring the cost of the materials is shown in Table 5.2. Assuming that the materials are valued at the acquisition cost, the firm should not accept the contract because an apparent loss of $10,000 would result. By using the replacement cost as the value of the materials,

however, the contract should be accepted, because a profit of $2,500 would result.

To see which method is correct, examine the firm's income statement at the end of the accounting period. If the contract *is not* accepted, then the firm will have to reduce the cost of its inventory by $12,500 ($50,000 − $37,500) to reflect the lower market value of this unused inventory. The firm will thus incur a loss of $12,500. If the contract *is* accepted, then the company will make a profit of $2,500 on the contract, but will also incur a loss of $12,500 on the materials used in completing the contract. The firm will thus incur a *net* loss of only $10,000. Hence, acceptance of the contract results in a smaller overall loss than does rejection of the contract. For decision-making purposes, replacement cost is the appropriate measure of the cost of materials in inventory, and the firm should accept the contract.

Table 5.2	Effect of Inventory Valuation Methods on Measured Profit—Westside Plumbing and Heating Company	
	Acquisition Cost	**Replacement Cost**
Value of contract	$100,000	$100,000
Costs		
Labour, equipment, etc.	$60,000	$60,000
Materials	50,000	37,500
	110,000	97,500
Profit (or loss)	($10,000)	$ 2,500

Conclusions Several conclusions can be drawn from this discussion of the concept of cost:

1. Costs can be measured in different ways, depending on the purpose for which the cost figures are to be used.

2. The costs appropriate for financial reporting purposes are not always appropriate for decision-making purposes. Typically, changes and modifications have to be made to

reflect the opportunity costs of the various alternative actions that can be chosen in a given decision problem. The *relevant cost* in economic decision making is the opportunity cost of the resources rather than the historical outlay of funds required to obtain the resources.

3. Sunk costs, which are incurred regardless of the alternative action chosen, should not be considered in making decisions.

4. The opportunity costs of a given action in a decision problem are sometimes highly subjective, but often the more objective accounting cost estimates may be arbitrary.

Short-Run Cost Functions

Cost Function
A mathematical model, schedule (table), or graph that shows the cost (such as total, average, or marginal cost) of producing various quantities of output.

In addition to measuring the costs of producing a given quantity of output, economists are also concerned with determining the behaviour of costs as output is varied over a range of possible values. The relationship between cost and output is expressed in terms of a **cost function**—a schedule (table), graph, or mathematical relationship showing the minimum achievable cost of producing various quantities of output.

The discussion in Chapter 4 concerning the inputs used in the production process distinguished between fixed and variable inputs. A fixed input was defined as an input that is required in the production process, but whose quantity used in the process is constant over a given period of time regardless of the level of output produced. Short-run questions relate to a situation in which one or more of the inputs to the production process is fixed. Long-run questions relate to a situation in which *all* inputs are variable. That is, no restrictions are imposed on the amount of a resource that can be employed in the production process.

Capital-Intensive
A characteristic of costs associated with a high proportion of fixed to variable inputs, usually due to extensive investment in plant and equipment.

The actual period of time corresponding to the long run for a given production process will depend on the nature of the inputs employed in the production process. Generally, the more capital equipment used relative to labour and other inputs (that is, the more **capital-intensive** the process), the longer will be the period of time required to increase significantly all the factors of production and the scale of operations. A period of five or more years may be required for a new or expanded electric utility-generating facility, steel mill, or oil refinery to be constructed and put into operation. Before the expansion is completed (i.e., in the short run), increases in production output can be achieved only by operating existing production facilities at higher rates of use through the utilization of greater amounts of labour and other variable inputs. In comparison, a service-oriented production process (such as an employment agency, trucking company, consulting firm, or government agency), which uses a relatively small amount of capital equipment, may have a long-run planning horizon of only a few months. This is especially true if the company rents or short-term leases much of its equipment. Such a company can abruptly change the scale of operations as business conditions dictate.

Associated with the short-run and long-run planning periods are short-run and long-run cost functions. This section discusses the development and interpretation of short-run costs and cost functions. The next section contains a similar discussion of cost functions associated with long-run decisions.

Total Cost Function

Fixed Costs
The costs of inputs to the production process that are constant over the short run.

The total cost of producing a given quantity of output is equal to the sum of the costs of each of the inputs used in the production process. In discussing short-run cost functions, it is useful to classify costs as either *fixed* or *variable costs*. **Fixed costs** represent the costs of all of the inputs to the production process that are fixed or constant over the short run. These costs will be incurred regardless of whether a small or large quantity of

SHORT-RUN COST FUNCTIONS: DEEP CREEK MINING COMPANY

To illustrate the nature of short-run costs and show how the short-run cost function can be derived from the production function for the firm, consider again the Deep Creek Mining Company example that was discussed in Chapter 4. It was assumed that two inputs, capital and labour, are required to produce or mine ore. Various-sized pieces of capital equipment, as measured by their brake horsepower (bhp) rating, K, are available to mine the ore. Each of these pieces of equipment can be operated with various-sized labour crews, L. The amount of output (tonnes of ore) that can be produced in a given period with each capital–labour input combination is shown again in Table 5.3. It was also assumed that the rental cost of using the mining equipment per period is $0.20 per brake horsepower and that the cost of each worker employed (labour) per period is $50. This yielded the following total cost equation for any given combination of labour L and capital K (Equation 4.12):

$$C = 50L + 0.20K$$

Suppose that Deep Creek has signed a lease agreeing to rent, for the next year, a 750-bhp piece of mining equipment (capital). During the ensuing year (the short run), the amount of capital that the company can employ in the ore-mining process is fixed at 750 bhp. Therefore, for each period, a fixed cost of $0.20 × 750 = $150 will be incurred, regardless of the quantity of ore that is produced. The firm must operate the production process at one of the capital–labour combinations shown in the third column of Table 5.3. Output can be increased (decreased) by employing more (less) labour in combination with the given 750-bhp capital equipment. Labour is thus a variable input to the production process.

The short-run cost functions for Deep Creek are shown in Table 5.4.[3] The various possible output levels Q and the associated capital–labour input combinations L and K are obtained from Table 5.3. The short-run variable cost, VC, is equal to $50 times the number of workers (L) employed in the mining process. The short-run fixed cost, FC, is equal to the rental cost of the 750-bhp equipment ($150). The total cost in the short run is the sum of the fixed and variable costs:

(5.2) $$TC = FC + VC$$

In Figure 5.1 on page 142, the three curves from the data given in Table 5.4 are plotted. Note that the TC curve has an identical shape to that of VC, being shifted upward by the FC of $150.

Variable Costs
The costs of the variable inputs to the production process.

output is produced during the period. **Variable costs** consist of the costs of all of the variable inputs to the production process. Whereas variable costs may not change in direct proportion to the quantity of output produced, they will increase (or decrease) in some manner as output is increased (or decreased).[4]

---

[3] The rational producer would not employ more than seven workers in the short run because the use of additional workers will not result in any increase in the quantity of ore that is produced. That is, labour has first a zero and then a negative marginal value added beyond seven workers.

[4] A third category, *semivariable costs*, can also be considered. Semivariable costs are constant when output varies within a given range. They increase or decrease only when output moves outside this range.

Table 5.3 Production Function—Deep Creek Mining Company

Labour Input, L (Number of Workers)	Capital Input K (Brake Horsepower)							
	250	500	750	1,000	1,250	1,500	1,750	2,000
1	1	3	6	10	16	16	16	13
2	2	6	16	24	29	29	44	44
3	4	16	29	44	55	55	55	50
4	6	29	44	55	58	60	60	55
5	16	43	55	60	61	62	62	60
6	29	55	60	62	63	63	63	62
7	44	58	62	63	64	64	64	64
8	50	60	62	63	64	65	65	65
9	55	59	61	63	64	65	66	66
10	52	56	59	62	64	65	66	67

Table 5.4 Short-Run Cost Functions—Deep Creek Mining Company

Output	Variable Cost		Fixed Cost		Total Cost	Average Fixed Cost	Average Variable Cost	Average Total Cost	Marginal Cost
Q	Labour Input L	$VC = \$50 \cdot L$	Capital Input K	$FC = \$150$	$TC = FC + VC$	$AFC = \dfrac{FC}{Q}$	$AVC = \dfrac{VC}{Q}$	$ATC = \dfrac{TC}{Q}$	$MC = \dfrac{\Delta TC}{\Delta Q}$
0	0	$ 0	750	$150	$150	—	—	—	—
6	1	50	750	150	200	$25.00	$8.33	$33.33	$\dfrac{50}{6} = \$8.33$
16	2	100	750	150	250	9.38	6.25	15.63	$\dfrac{50}{10} = \$5.00$
29	3	150	750	150	300	5.17	5.17	10.34	$\dfrac{50}{13} = \$3.85$
44	4	200	750	150	350	3.41	4.55	7.95	$\dfrac{50}{15} = \$3.33$
55	5	250	750	150	400	2.73	4.55	7.27	$\dfrac{50}{11} = \$4.55$
60	6	300	750	150	450	2.50	5.00	7.50	$\dfrac{50}{5} = \$10.00$
62	7	350	750	150	500	2.42	5.65	8.06	$\dfrac{50}{2} = \$25.00$

Average and Marginal Cost Functions

Once the total cost function is determined, one can then derive the average and marginal cost functions. The average fixed cost, *AFC*, average variable cost, *AVC*, and average total cost, *ATC*, are equal to the respective fixed, variable, and total costs divided by the quantity of output produced:

(5.3)
$$AFC = \frac{FC}{Q}$$

FIGURE 5.1

Short-Run Variable, Fixed, and Total Cost Functions—Deep Creek Mining Company

For each level of output, Q, the total cost function is $150 more than the variable cost function. The $150 is the fixed cost.

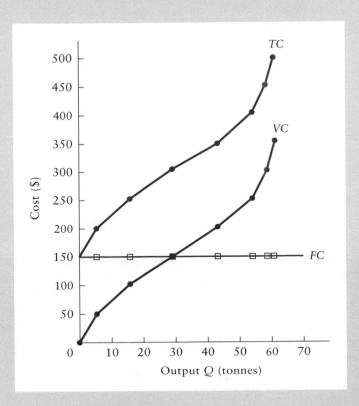

$$(5.4) \qquad AVC = \frac{VC}{Q}$$

$$(5.5) \qquad ATC = \frac{TC}{Q}$$

Also,

$$(5.6) \qquad ATC = AFC + AVC$$

Marginal Cost

The incremental increase in total cost that results from a one-unit increase in output.

Marginal cost is defined as the incremental increase in total cost that results from a one-unit increase in output, and is calculated as[5]

$$MC = \frac{\Delta TC}{\Delta Q}$$

$$(5.7)$$

$$= \frac{\Delta VC}{\Delta Q}$$

---

[5] Technically, the ratio $\Delta TC/\Delta Q$ represents the *incremental* cost associated with a discrete change in output by more than one unit rather than the *marginal* cost associated with *one* additional unit of output.

or, in the case of a continuous *TC* function, as

$$(5.8) \qquad MC = \frac{d(TC)}{dQ}$$

$$(5.9) \qquad = \frac{d(VC)}{dQ}$$

The average and marginal costs for Deep Creek that were calculated in Table 5.4 are plotted in the graph shown in Figure 5.2. Except for the *AFC* curve, which is continually declining, note that all other average and marginal cost curves are U-shaped.

Relationships among the Various Cost and Production Curves

To investigate further the properties of and relationships among the various cost and production curves, assume now that the cost and production curves can be represented by smooth continuous functions, as shown in Figure 5.3. Also assume that input *L* is the variable factor, with an associated variable cost *VC*; that the per-unit price of each of the factors of production (i.e., C_L and C_K) is *constant* over all usage levels; and that input *K* is the fixed factor, with an associated fixed cost *FC*. First, note that variable costs (and total costs) initially increase at a decreasing rate as output *Q* is increased up to Q_1. Correspondingly, the marginal cost function *MC* is declining. Over this range of output, the marginal

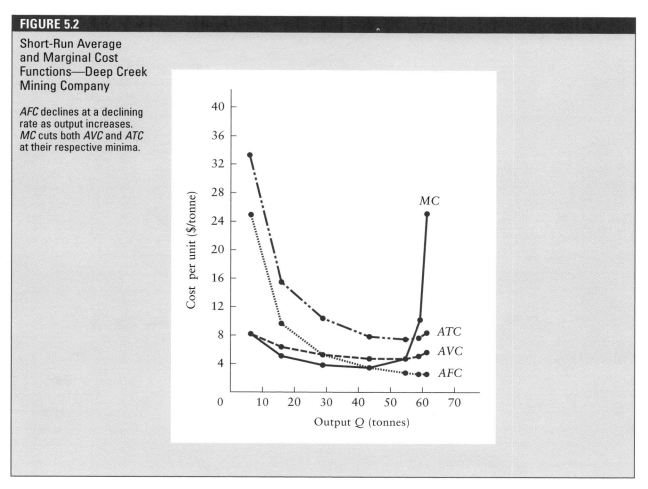

FIGURE 5.2

Short-Run Average and Marginal Cost Functions—Deep Creek Mining Company

AFC declines at a declining rate as output increases. *MC* cuts both *AVC* and *ATC* at their respective minima.

FIGURE 5.3

Short-Run Cost and Production Functions

Maximum MP_L in the top graph corresponds to minimum MC in the middle graph and the inflection points for VC and TC in the bottom graph. Maximum AP_L (where $MP_L = AP_L$) in the top graph corresponds to minimum AVC in the middle graph. Minimum ATC in the middle graph occurs when $ATC = MC$.

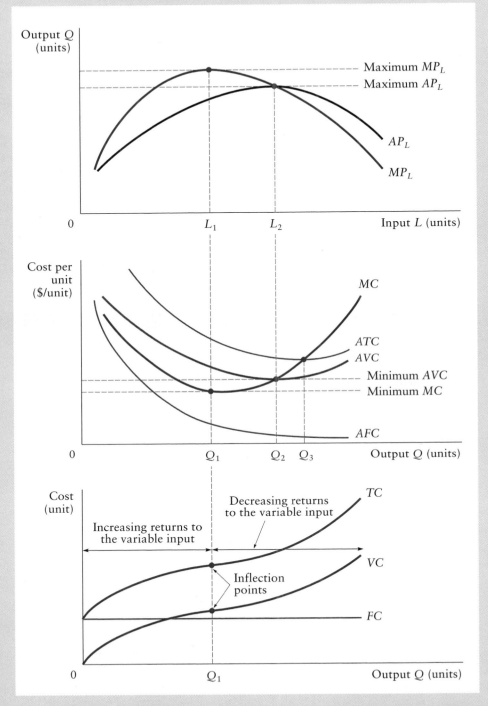

EXAMPLE

COST FUNCTIONS FOR HUDON LIMITÉE

Cost data are sometimes given in functional form. Suppose that fixed costs for Hudon Limitée are equal to $100, and the company's variable costs are given by the following relationship (where Q = output):

(5.10) $\quad VC = 60Q - 3Q^2 + 0.10Q^3$

Given this information, one can derive the total cost function using Equation 5.2:

$$TC = 100 + 60Q - 3Q^2 + 0.10Q^3$$

Next, AFC, AVC, and ATC can be found using Equations 5.3, 5.4, and 5.5,

respectively, as follows:

$$AFC = \frac{100}{Q}$$

$$AVC = 60 - 3Q + 0.10Q^2$$

$$ATC = \frac{100}{Q} + 60 - 3Q + 0.10Q^2$$

Finally, the firm's marginal cost function can be obtained by differentiating the variable cost function (Equation 5.10) with respect to Q:

$$MC = \frac{d(VC)}{dQ} = 60 - 6Q + 0.30Q^2$$

product of the variable input L is increasing. Because it has been assumed that the unit cost of L is constant, an increasing marginal product for input L necessarily implies that the marginal cost function must be declining.[6] The minimum point on the MC curve at Q_1 corresponds to the maximum point on the MP_L curve at L_1. Beyond Q_1, variable (and total) costs increase at an increasing rate and, correspondingly, the marginal cost curve is increasing. Over this range of output, the marginal product of L is decreasing and, for reasons analogous to those just noted, marginal cost must necessarily be rising.

Examining the average variable cost curve, AVC, in Figure 5.3, note that it is declining over output levels to Q_2 and is increasing thereafter. The shape of the average variable cost function, like the shape of the marginal cost function, is closely related to the production function defined in Chapter 4. *Given that the unit cost of the variable input is constant,* an increasing (and then decreasing) average product for input L necessarily implies that the average variable cost will be decreasing (and then increasing).[7] The minimum point on the AVC curve at Q_2 corresponds to the maximum point on the AP_L curve at L_2. Note also in Figure 5.3 that the marginal cost curve intersects the average variable cost function at its minimum value. This necessarily follows because the marginal product curve intersects the average product curve at its maximum value.

The average total cost curve, which is equal to the sum of the vertical heights of the average fixed cost and average variable cost curves, likewise initially declines and subsequently begins rising beyond some level of output. At a level of output of Q_3, the average total cost curve is at its minimum value.

---

[6] The relationship can be shown algebraically. MC is defined as $\Delta TC/\Delta Q$, which is also equal to $\Delta VC/\Delta Q$. ΔVC is equal to $C_L\Delta L$, where C_L is the unit cost of the variable input L. Thus, $MC = C_L(\Delta L/\Delta Q)$. However, the marginal product of input L, MP, was defined in Equation 4.2 as $\Delta Q/\Delta L$, or, in reciprocal form, $1/MP = \Delta L/\Delta Q$. Substituting $1/MP$ in the relationship for MC, we obtain $MC = C_L(1/MP)$. Because the marginal productivity of L is increasing, the marginal cost must be decreasing.

[7] This relationship can be shown analogously to that of the preceding footnote. So, we obtain $AVC = C_L(1/AP)$. Thus, if the average product is increasing, the average variable cost must be decreasing, and vice versa.

As discussed in the previous chapter, more intensive use of the variable inputs (specialization) in combination with fixed inputs to the production process is believed to yield initially more than proportionate increases in output. Subsequently, due to the law of diminishing returns, more intensive use yields less than proportionate increases. This reasoning is used to explain the U-shaped pattern of the *ATC*, *AVC*, and *MC* curves. Initially, specialization in the use of the variable resources results in increasing returns and declining average and marginal costs. Eventually, however, the gains from specialization are overwhelmed by crowding effects, and then marginal and average costs begin increasing.

Long-Run Cost Functions

Over the long-run planning horizon, using the available production methods and technology, the firm can choose the plant size, types and sizes of equipment, labour skills, and raw materials that, when combined, yield the lowest cost of producing the desired amount of output. Once the optimal capacity combination of inputs is chosen to produce the desired level of output at least cost, some of these inputs (plant and equipment) become fixed in the short run. If demand increases unexpectedly and the firm wishes to produce not Q_1, as planned, but rather Q_2 as shown in Figure 5.4, it may have little choice but to lay on additional variable inputs, such as overtime labour, and expedite the rush-order delivery of supplies to meet its production goals. Of course, such arrangements are expensive, and short-run average cost will temporarily rise to C'_2. Should this demand persist, a larger fixed input investment in plant and equipment is warranted. Then, unit cost can be reduced to C_2.

Another short-run average cost function like SAC_2 exists for this new set of inputs. In theory, an optimal combination of inputs and a minimum total cost exists for each level of output. Associated with the fixed inputs in each of these optimal combinations is a short-run average cost function. Several of these other short-run average cost

---

FIGURE 5.4

Long-Run and Short-Run Average Cost Functions

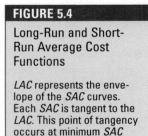

LAC represents the envelope of the *SAC* curves. Each *SAC* is tangent to the *LAC*. This point of tangency occurs at minimum *SAC* only for the *SAC* curve that is tangent to the *LAC* at minimum *LAC*.

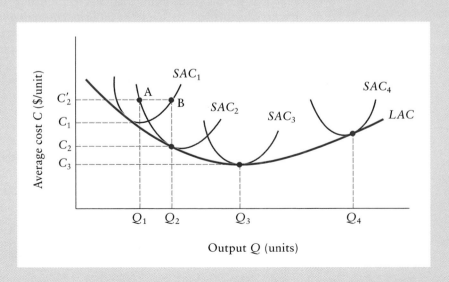

functions (SAC_3, SAC_4) are shown in Figure 5.4. The long-run average cost function consists of the *lower boundary* or *envelope* of all of these (infinitely many) short-run curves. No other combination of inputs exists for producing each level of output Q at an average cost below the cost that is indicated by the *LAC* curve.[8]

Optimal Capacity Utilization: Three Concepts

The relationship between the short-run and long-run average cost functions can be further illustrated by examining in more detail the effect on costs of an expansion in output from Q_1 to Q_2 in Figure 5.4. Assume that the firm has been producing Q_1 units of output using a plant of size "1," having a short-run average cost curve of SAC_1. The average cost of producing Q_1 units is therefore C_1, and Q_1 is the optimal output for the plant size represented by SAC_1. **Optimal output for a given plant size** is a short-run concept of capacity utilization. Suppose that the firm wishes to expand output to Q_2. What will the average cost be of producing this higher volume of output?

In the short run, as we saw earlier, the average cost would be C_2'. However, in the long run, it would be possible for the firm to build a plant of size "2," having a short-run average cost curve of SAC_2. With this larger plant, the average cost of producing Q_2 units of output would be only C_2. Thus, because the firm has more options available to it in the long run, average total cost of any given output generally can be reduced. SAC_2 represents the **optimal plant size for the output rate** Q_2. However, even these inputs and costs of production that are fixed in the short run can be altered in the long run to obtain a still more efficient allocation of resources. Only when optimal output increases to Q_3, where the firm will build the universally least-cost **optimal plant size** represented by SAC_3, will further opportunities for cost reduction cease. This is a long-run concept of optimal capacity utilization, given the technology in place at this plant.

Short-run average total cost (SAC) with underutilization of capacity at point A or SAC with overutilization of capacity at point B in Figure 5.4 is always higher than the minimum average total cost in the long run (LAC) when the production manager can vary plant and equipment, matching capacity to desired output requirements. The LAC can be obtained using the **expansion path** of input combinations that satisfy the condition:

$$(5.11) \qquad \frac{MP_L}{C_L} = \frac{MP_K}{C_K}$$

Recall from the previous chapter that this equimarginal condition must be satisfied in order for a given input combination to be an optimal solution to either the output-maximization or cost-minimization problem.

As shown in Figure 5.5, the expansion path can be represented by a line that connects these various tangency points between the isoquants and isocost lines,[9] and the long-run total cost function can be obtained from the corresponding cost and output values. Thus, for example, from point 1 in Figure 5.5 one obtains the cost–output combination (C_1, $Q^{(1)}$), which is then plotted in Figure 5.6. The cost–output combinations (C_2, $Q^{(2)}$) and (C_3, $Q^{(3)}$) are obtained in a similar manner. Connecting these points yields the long-run total cost (LTC) curve shown in Figure 5.6. The long-run average

---

Optimal Output for a Given Plant Size
Output rate that results in lowest average total cost for a given plant size.

Optimal Plant Size for a Given Output Rate
Plant size that results in lowest average total cost for a given output.

Optimal Plant Size
Plant size that achieves minimum long-run average total cost.

Expansion Path
The input combinations that minimize cost for each level of output.

---

[8] From the graph one can see that the long-run average cost of producing any given level of output, in general, does *not* occur at the point where short-run average costs are minimized. Only at the output level Q_3, corresponding to the minimum cost point on the *LAC* curve, does the long-run average cost equal the minimum short-run average cost.

[9] As in the development of the short-run cost functions in the previous section, it is assumed that the per-unit price of each input is constant, regardless of the quantity used in the production process. We comment further on this assumption in the next section.

FIGURE 5.5

Expansion Path

The expansion path is the collection of least-cost combinations of inputs for different output levels. Alternatively, it can be viewed as the collection of maximum output combinations of inputs for different cost levels.

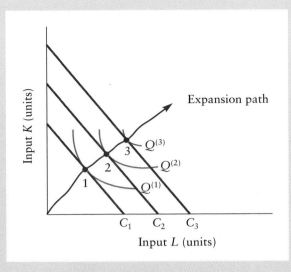

FIGURE 5.6

Long-Run Total Cost Function

The long-run total cost function represents the least cost for different output levels when all inputs can be varied.

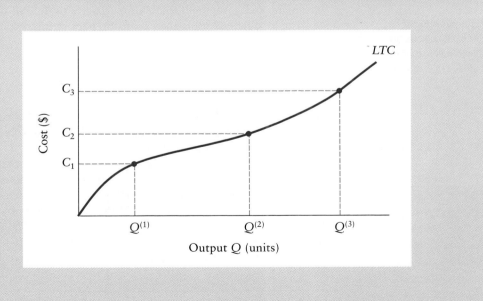

cost (*LAC*) and long-run marginal cost (*LMC*) curves are defined and calculated in a manner similar to their short-run counterparts:[10]

$$(5.12) \qquad LAC = \frac{LTC}{Q}$$

$$(5.13) \qquad LMC = \frac{\Delta LTC}{\Delta Q}$$

Economies and Diseconomies of Scale

The long-run average cost function is hypothesized to decline over lower ranges of capacity (scale economies) and rise over higher ranges of capacity (scale diseconomies).

Internal Economies of Scale

Declining long-run average costs are usually attributed to three possible sources of **internal economies of scale:**

- Product-level economies—internal economies of scale related to the output of one product.

- Plant-level economies—internal economies of scale related to the total output (of multiple products) of one plant.

- Firm-level economies—internal economies of scale related to the total output of a firm's operations.

Internal Economies of Scale
Declining long-run average costs as the rate of output for a product, plant, or firm is increased.

Product-Level Economies A number of different sources of scale economies are associated with producing larger volumes of a single product. As discussed in the previous chapter, increasing physical returns to scale can be realized from *greater specialization in the use of capital and labour.* As the scale of production is increased, special-purpose equipment, which is more efficient in performing a limited set of operations, can be substituted for less efficient general-purpose equipment. Likewise, as the scale of production is increased, the production process can be broken down into a series of smaller tasks, and workers can be assigned to the tasks for which they are most qualified. Workers are then able to acquire additional proficiency through more frequent repetition of the tasks to which they are assigned.

Learning Curve Effect
Declining unit cost attributable to greater cumulative volume.

In manufacturing, a related phenomenon called the **learning curve effect** is often observed. That is, the amount of labour input and the associated fringe benefit costs required to produce each unit of output decreases for successive increases in the cumulative volume of output. The learning curve concept is discussed further in Web Appendix 14A. In general, internal economies of scale can be distinguished from learning curve effects or volume discounts (so-called **external economies of scale**) because the latter always result from increases in cumulative volume of output, no matter how small the output rate per unit time period.

External Economy of Scale
Volume discounts in purchasing inputs.

Plant-Level Economies Sources of scale economies at the plant level include capital investment, overhead, and required reserves of maintenance parts and personnel. With respect to *capital investment,* capital costs tend to increase less than proportionately with the productive capacity of a plant, particularly in such process-type industries as petroleum refining and chemicals. For example, a pipeline with twice the radius of another

---

[10] Alternatively, the long-run cost function can be derived algebraically from the production function. Such a derivation for the Cobb–Douglas production function is examined in Web Appendix 5B.

pipeline can be constructed for perhaps as little as twice the cost, yet have four times the capacity (i.e., $\pi(2r)^2 = 4\pi r^2$ versus πr^2) of the smaller one. Another source of scale economies is overhead costs, which include such items as administrative costs (e.g., management salaries) and other indirect expenditures (e.g., heating and lighting expenses). Overhead costs can be spread over a higher volume of output in a larger plant, thus reducing average costs per unit. Finally, scale economies can be realized in equipment maintenance. *Reserves of replacement parts and maintenance personnel needed to deal with randomly occurring equipment breakdowns normally increase less than proportionately with increases in the size of the plant.*

The cost of a particular product can be affected by the interactions between product-level and plant-level economies. **Economies of scope** are present whenever the cost of producing two (or more) products jointly by one plant or firm is less than the cost of producing these products separately by different plants or firms.[11] Economies of scope occur whenever inputs can be shared in the production of different products. For example, in the airline industry, the cost of transporting both passengers and freight on a single airplane is less than the cost of using two airplanes to transport passengers and freight separately.

Economies of scope
Economies that exist whenever the cost of producing two (or more) products jointly by one plant or firm is less than the cost of producing these products separately by different plants or firms.

Firm-Level Economies In addition to product-level and plant-level economies of scale, there are other scale economies associated with the overall size of the firm. Often, these other scale economies can be realized only by the large, multiproduct, multiplant firm. One possible source of firm-level scale economies is in *distribution*. For example, multiplant operations may permit a larger firm to maintain geographically dispersed plants. Delivery costs are often lower for a geographically dispersed multiplant operation compared with one (larger) plant.

Another possible source of scale economies for the firm is in the *raising of capital funds*. Because flotation costs increase less than proportionately with the size of the security (share or bond) issue, average flotation costs per dollar of funds raised is smaller for larger firms.[12] Similar scale economies also exist in *marketing and sales promotion*. These scale economies can take such forms as (1) quantity discounts in securing advertising media space and time, or (2) the ability of the large firm to spread the fixed costs of advertising preparation over greater output. In addition, the large firm may be able to achieve a relatively greater degree of brand recognition and brand loyalty from its higher level of sales promotion expenditures over an extended period of time.

A final source of firm-level scale economies is in *technological innovation*. Unlike smaller firms, large firms can afford sizable research and development (R&D) laboratories and costly specialized equipment and research personnel. Also, the large firm is better able to undertake a diversified portfolio of R&D projects and can thus reduce the risk associated with the failure of any one (or small number) of the projects. The smaller firm, in contrast, may be unwilling to undertake a large R&D project, because failure of the project could result in bankruptcy.

Diseconomies of Scale

Diseconomies of Scale
Rising long-run average costs as the level of output is increased.

Rising long-run average costs at higher rates of output are attributed to **diseconomies of scale**. A primary source of diseconomies of scale associated with an individual production plant is *transportation costs*. Another possible source of plant diseconomies is

---

[11] See William J. Baumol, John C. Panzer, and Robert D. Willig, *Contestable Markets and the Theory of Industry Structure* (New York: Harcourt Brace Jovanovich, 1982), Chapter 4.
[12] *Flotation costs* are the costs paid to the investment underwriter or securities dealer who arranges the sale of the securities issue to investors.

How Japanese Companies Deal with the Problems of Size*

Many large North American firms are attempting to deal with the problems of size by decentralizing their operations. These companies are setting up independent business units, each with its own profit-and-loss responsibility, thereby giving managers more flexibility and freedom in decision making.

Japanese corporations are often collections of hundreds of individual companies. For example, Matsushita Electric Industrial Co., Ltd., consists of 161 consolidated units. Another example is Hitachi, Ltd., which is composed of 660 companies, with the stock of 27 of these companies being publicly traded.

James Abegglen, an expert on Japanese management, has observed that "As something new comes along . . . it gets moved out to a subsidiary so the elephant does not roll over and smother it. If all goes well, it becomes a successful company on its own. If not, it gets pulled back in."

* Based on "Is Your Company Too Big?" *BusinessWeek,* March 17, 1989, pp. 84–94.

labour requirements. Higher wage rates or costly worker recruiting and relocation programs may be required to attract the necessary personnel, particularly if the plant is located in a sparsely populated area. Finally, large-scale plants are often inflexible operations designed for long production runs of one product.

Diseconomies of scale at the firm level result from *problems of coordination and control encountered by management* as the scale of operations is increased. First, the size of management staffs and their associated salary costs may rise more than proportionately as the scale of the firm is increased. Also, less direct and observable costs may occur, such as the losses arising from delayed or faulty decisions and weakened or distorted managerial incentives.

Overall Effects of Scale Economies and Diseconomies

For some industries, such as textile and furniture manufacturing, long-run average costs for the firm remain constant over a wide range of output once scale economies are exhausted. Many plant sizes are consistent with least-cost production. In other industries, such as steel ingot production and engine block casting, long-run average costs rise at very large scale. The possible presence of both economies and diseconomies of scale leads to the hypothesized long-run average cost function for a typical manufacturing firm being U-shaped with a flat middle area, as shown in Figure 5.7. Up to some **minimum efficient scale (MES),** that is, the smallest scale at which minimum long-run average total costs are attained, economies of scale are present. In most industries, it is possible to increase the size of the firm significantly beyond the MES without incurring diseconomies of scale, as shown in Figure 5.7. Over this range, average costs per unit are relatively constant. However, expansion beyond the maximum efficient scale eventually will result in problems of inflexibility, lack of managerial coordination, and rising long-run average costs.

Minimum Efficient Scale (MES)

The smallest scale at which minimum costs per unit are attained.

FIGURE 5.7

Long-Run Average Cost
Function and Scale
Economics

LAC typically exhibits
economies of scale initially,
followed by neither
economies nor dis-
economies for some range.
Thereafter, diseconomies
occur.

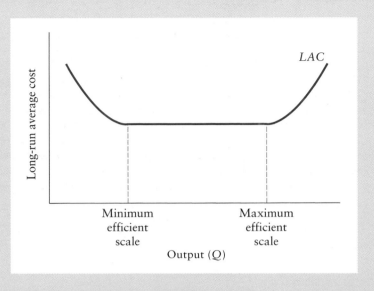

EXAMPLE

*ALUMINUM-INTENSIVE VEHICLE LOWERS THE MINIMUM EFFICIENT SCALE AT FORD**

For more information
on Ford, go to
www.ford.com.

The aluminum space-frame automobile that Ford has designed is less than half as heavy as today's conventional steel and sheet metal cars. These lighter cars increase gas kilometrage and markedly reduce CO_2 emissions. Aluminum-intensive vehicles also will change the scale economies of auto assembly dramatically. Aluminum space-frame components are cast, forged, and extruded into different thicknesses, depending on where strength is needed. Aluminum does not require the massive body-stamping machines employed to bend sheet metal. Consequently, the tens of millions of dollars of fixed asset investment for this largest piece of capital equipment will no longer be needed.

Since a body-stamping machine has a physical working life of 600,000 vehicles, this single piece of equipment has been the source of substantial scale economies in the production of most auto models. Only 19 of the 197 models sold in 1999 in North

---

* Based on "Aluminum Cars," *The Economist,* April 15, 2000, p. 89; *Consumer Reports,* April 1997, p. 26; "The Global Gambles of GM," *The Economist,* June 24, 2000, p. 67; and "Daimler-Chrysler Merger," *The Wall Street Journal,* May 8, 1998, p. A10.

America and Western Europe had sufficient sales volume to fully depreciate a body-stamping machine within two model years. Most moderately successful models sell less than 100,000 units per year. Therefore, a six-year period is required to "wear out" a body-stamping machine making repetitive presses on a typical model's platform.

One common approach to this problem of achieving minimum efficient scale has been to export the product beyond limited domestic markets and sell the same model under different names in different countries. Another approach has been to consolidate companies across several continents to get access for domestic models into foreign markets. The Jeep Grand Cherokee, for example, was projected to do quite well in European Mercedes-Benz showrooms.

Nevertheless, most managers of model-specific product planning have continued to face a tough dilemma. Should they change body shapes and structural components every three to five years to keep their model "current"? Or should they forego the body style changes and fully depreciate their model's body-stamping machines over a six-year period or longer? The former decision necessitates scrapping a machine with substantial physical working life remaining and recovering the capital equipment investment with a much higher unit cost per vehicle.

This classic economy of scale issue is avoided with aluminum space-frame production. While 10 percent more costly on average than the typical steel and sheet metal vehicle, the minimum efficient scale of an aluminum-intensive auto assembly process is only 50,000 cars. As illustrated in Figure 5.8, a marketing plan for smaller volume niche products like the Chevrolet Corvette, Ford Mustang, and Jeep Wrangler can achieve minimum efficient scale at point A with these new aluminum production techniques. Previously with sheet metal and steel automobiles, production runs at this reduced scale resulted in unit costs at point B that were more than twice as large as those at point C.

FIGURE 5.8

Minimum Efficient Scale in Autos

Minimum *LAC* for steel autos is less than minimum *LAC* for aluminum autos. Nevertheless, for specialty cars with small production runs, aluminum cars could be cheaper to produce because minimum *LAC* for aluminum autos occurs at far lower production levels.

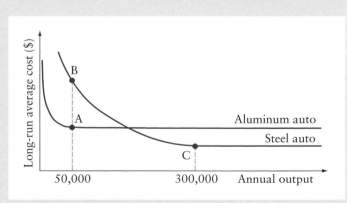

Air Canada's Cost Structure*

For more information, visit
www.aircanada.com.

The restructured Air Canada came out of bankruptcy in September 2004. It is now owned and operated by ACE Aviation Holdings Inc. Comparing third-quarter 2004 results to those for the third quarter of 2003, ACE stated that Air Canada's cost per available seat mile (CASM) declined by 3 percent. Given that fuel costs rose considerably from third quarter 2003 to third quarter 2004, this decline in CASM is significant. Nevertheless, it still appears that Air Canada's costs are higher than its competitors'.

* ACE Aviation Holdings Inc., "Management Discussion and Analysis," *Third-Quarter 2004 Report*, p. 2.

Summary

- *Cost* is defined as the sacrifice incurred whenever an exchange or transformation of resources takes place.

- Different approaches are used in measuring costs, depending on the purposes for which the information is to be used. For financial reporting purposes, the historical outlay of funds is usually the appropriate measure of cost, whereas for decision-making purposes, it is often appropriate to measure cost in terms of the opportunities foregone or sacrificed.

- A *cost function* is a schedule (table), graph, or mathematical relationship showing the minimum achievable cost (such as total, average, or marginal cost) of producing various quantities of output.

- Short-run *total costs* are equal to the sum of *fixed* and *variable costs*.

- *Marginal cost* is defined as the incremental increase in total cost that results from a one-unit increase in output.

- The short-run average variable and marginal cost functions of economic theory are hypothesized to be U-shaped, first falling and then rising as output is increased. Falling short-run unit costs are attributed to the gains available from specialization in the use of capital and labour. Rising short-run unit costs are attributed to diminishing returns in production.

- The theoretical long-run average cost function is often found to be L-shaped. This is due to the frequent presence of scale economies and frequent absence of scale diseconomies. *Economies of scale* are attributed primarily to the nature of the production process or the factor markets, whereas *diseconomies of scale* are attributed primarily to problems of coordination and inflexibility in large-scale organizations.

- Volume discounts in purchasing inputs and learning curve effects, both of which result from a larger cumulative volume of output, can be distinguished from scale effects, which depend on the firm's rate of output per unit time period. Learning curve advantages often, therefore, arise in small-scale plants able to make long production runs.

- *Minimum efficient scale* is achieved by a rate of output sufficient to reduce long-run average total cost to the minimum possible level. Smaller rates of output imply smaller plant sizes to reduce unit cost, albeit to higher levels than would be possible if a firm's business plan could support minimum efficient scale production.

Self-Test Exercises

1. Howard Bowen is a large-scale grain farmer. His land and machinery have a current market value of $4,000,000. Bowen owes his bank $3,000,000. Last year, Bowen sold $5,000,000 worth of grain. His variable operating costs were $4,500,000; accounting depreciation was $40,000, although the actual decline in value of Bowen's machinery was $60,000 last year. Bowen paid himself a salary of $50,000, which is not considered part of his variable operating costs. Interest on his bank loan was $400,000. If Bowen worked for another farmer or a local manufacturer, his annual income would be about $30,000. If the farm was sold, Bowen could invest any funds that would be derived, to earn 10 percent annually. (Ignore taxes.)

   a. Compute Bowen's accounting profits.

   b. Compute Bowen's economic profits.

2. Suppose a firm's variable cost function is given by the relationship

$$VC = 150Q - 10Q^2 + 0.5Q^3$$

   where Q is the quantity of output produced.

   a. Determine the output level Q at the point at which the *average* variable cost function takes on its minimum value.

   b. What are the values of the variable cost and average variable cost functions at the output level in part (a)?

   c. Determine the output level Q at the point at which the *marginal* cost function takes on its minimum value.

   d. What are the values of the variable cost and marginal cost functions at the output level in part (c)?

3. The Blair Company has three assembly plants, located in British Columbia, New Brunswick, and Quebec. Currently, the firm purchases a major subassembly, which becomes part of the final product, from an outside firm. Blair has decided to manufacture the subassemblies itself and must now consider whether to rent one centrally located facility (for example, in Manitoba, where all the subassemblies would be manufactured) or to rent three separate facilities, each located near one of the assembly plants, where each facility would manufacture only the subassemblies needed for the nearby assembly plant. A single, centrally located facility, with a production capacity of 18,000 units per year, would have fixed costs of $900,000 per year and a variable cost of $250 per unit. Three separate decentralized facilities, with production capacities of 8,000, 6,000, and 4,000 units per year, would have fixed costs of $475,000, $425,000, and $400,000, respectively, and variable costs per unit of only $225 per unit, owing primarily to the reduction in shipping costs. The current production rates at the three assembly plants are 6,000, 4,500, and 3,000 units, respectively.

   a. Assuming that the current production rates are maintained at the three assembly plants, which alternative should management select?

   b. If demand for the final product were to increase to production capacity, which alternative would be more attractive?

   c. What additional information would be useful before making a decision?

Exercises

1. Kay Evans has just completed her B.A. degree and is considering pursuing doctoral (Ph.D.) studies in economics. If Kay takes a job immediately after graduation with a B.A., she can earn $50,000 during the first year, with an anticipated raise

of $4,000 per year over the next five years. If Kay pursues the doctorate, five more years of school are required. Kay has been offered an assistantship paying $15,500 per year plus tuition. Books and computer purchases needed for her studies will cost an average of $1,500 per year. These costs will not be incurred if Kay takes a job immediately. On graduation with a doctorate, Kay expects an annual income level of $70,000 during her first year of teaching. The growth rate in Kay's teaching salary is expected to equal the growth rate of the income she would make if she did not pursue the Ph.D. How should Kay evaluate her decision to pursue a Ph.D.? What other information do you need? What factors other than salary should be considered?

2. Air Canada owns a plot of land near the Ottawa International Airport. The land originally cost $375,000. The airline is considering building a new training centre on this land. Air Canada has determined that the proposal to build the new facility is acceptable if the original cost of the land is used in the analysis, but the proposal does not meet the airline's project acceptance criteria if the land cost is more than $850,000. A developer has recently offered $2.5 million for the land. Should the training facility be built at this location? (Ignore taxes.)

3. Indira Pannu has worked as a RE/MAX real estate agent for 15 years. Her annual income is approximately $100,000 per year. Indira is considering establishing her own real estate agency. She expects to generate revenues during the first year of $2,000,000. Salaries paid to her employees are expected to total $1,500,000. Operating expenses (i.e., rent, supplies, utility services) are expected to total $250,000. To begin the business, Indira must borrow $500,000 from her bank at an interest rate of 15 percent. Equipment will cost Indira $50,000. At the end of one year, the value of this equipment will be $30,000, even though the depreciation expense for tax purposes is only $5,000 during the first year.

   a. Determine the (pretax) accounting profit for this venture.
   b. Determine the (pretax) economic profit for this venture.
   c. Which of the costs for this firm are explicit and which are implicit?

4. In the ore-mining example described earlier in the chapter (Table 5.3), suppose again that labour (L) is a variable input and capital (K) is a fixed input. Specifically, assume that the firm has a 500-bhp-rated machine.

   a. Complete the table shown below.
   b. Plot the variable, fixed, and total cost functions on one graph.
   c. Plot the marginal, average variable, average fixed, and average total cost functions on another graph.

Output Q	Input X	Variable Cost VC	Input Y	Fixed Cost FC	Total Cost TC	Avg. Variable Cost AVC	Avg. Fixed Cost AFC	Avg. Total Cost ATC	Marginal Cost MC
____	0	____	____	____	____	____	____	____	____
____	1	____	____	____	____	____	____	____	____
____	2	____	____	____	____	____	____	____	____
____	3	____	____	____	____	____	____	____	____
____	4	____	____	____	____	____	____	____	____
____	5	____	____	____	____	____	____	____	____
____	6	____	____	____	____	____	____	____	____
____	7	____	____	____	____	____	____	____	____
____	8	____	____	____	____	____	____	____	____

5. From your knowledge of the relationships among the various cost functions, complete the following table.

Q	TC	FC	VC	ATC	AFC	AVC	MC
0	125	___	___	___	___	___	
10	___	___	___	___	___	___	5
20	___	___	___	10.50	___	___	___
30	___	___	110	___	___	___	___
40	255	___	___	___	___	___	___
50	___	___	___	___	___	3	___
60	___	___	___	___	___	___	3
70	___	___	___	5	___	___	___
80	___	___	295	___	___	___	___

6. Economists at General Industries have been examining operating costs at one of its parts manufacturing plants in an effort to determine if the plant is being operated efficiently. From weekly cost records, the economists developed the following cost–output information concerning the operation of the plant:

a. *AVC* (average variable cost) at an output of 2,000 units per week is $7.50.

b. At an output level of 5,000 units per week, *AFC* (average fixed cost) is $3.

c. *TC* (total cost) increases by $5,000 when output is increased from 2,000 to 3,000 units per week.

d. *TVC* (total variable cost) at an output level of 4,000 units per week is $23,000.

e. *AVC* (average variable cost) decreases by $0.75 per unit when output is increased from 4,000 to 5,000 units per week.

f. *AFC* plus *AVC* for 8,000 units per week is $7.50 per unit.

g. *ATC* (average total cost) decreases by $0.50 per unit when output is decreased from 8,000 to 7,000 units per week.

h. *TVC* increases by $3,000 when output is increased from 5,000 to 6,000 units per week.

i. *TC* decreases by $7,000 when output is decreased from 2,000 to 1,000 units per week.

j. *MC* (marginal cost) is $16 per unit when output is increased from 8,000 to 9,000 units per week.

Given the preceding information, complete the following cost schedule for the plant. (*Hint:* Proceed sequentially through the list, *filling in all the related entries before proceeding to the next item of information in the list.*)

Output (Units Per Week)	TFC	TVC	TC	AFC	AVC	ATC	MC
0	___	___	___	X	X	X	X
1,000	___	___	___	___	___	___	___
2,000	___	___	___	___	___	___	___
3,000	___	___	___	___	___	___	___
4,000	___	___	___	___	___	___	___
5,000	___	___	___	___	___	___	___
6,000	___	___	___	___	___	___	___
7,000	___	___	___	___	___	___	___
8,000	___	___	___	___	___	___	___
9,000	___	___	___	___	___	___	___

7. Consider the following variable cost function (Q = output):

$$VC = 200Q - 9Q^2 + 0.25Q^3$$

Fixed costs are equal to $150.

a. Determine the total cost function.

b. Determine the (i) average fixed, (ii) average variable, (iii) average total, and (iv) marginal cost functions.

c. Determine the value of Q at the point at which the average variable cost function takes on its minimum value. (*Hint:* Take the first derivative of the *AVC* function, set the derivative equal to 0, and solve for Q. Also, use the second derivative to check for a maximum or minimum.)

d. Determine the value of Q at the point at which the marginal cost function takes on its minimum value.

8. Consider Exercise 7 again.

a. Plot the (i) *AVC* and (ii) *MC* functions on a single graph for the values of $Q = 2, 4, 6, \ldots, 24$.

b. Based on the cost functions graphed in part (a), determine the value of Q that minimizes (i) *AVC* and (ii) *MC*.

c. Compare your answers in part (b) with those obtained earlier in 7(c) and 7(d).

9. A manufacturing plant has a potential production capacity of 1,000 units per month (capacity can be increased by 10 percent if subcontractors are employed). The plant is normally operated at about 80 percent of capacity. Operating the plant above this level significantly increases variable costs per unit because of the need to pay the skilled workers higher overtime wage rates. For output levels up to 80 percent of capacity, variable cost per unit is $100. Above 80 percent and up to 90 percent, variable costs on this *additional* output *increase* by 10 percent. When output is above 90 percent and up to 100 percent of capacity, the *additional* units cost an *additional* 25 percent over the unit variable costs for outputs up to 80 percent of capacity. For production above 100 percent and up to 110 percent of capacity, extensive subcontracting work is used and the unit variable costs of these *additional* units are 50 percent above those at output levels up to 80 percent of capacity. At 80 percent of capacity, the plant's fixed costs per unit are $50. Total fixed costs are not expected to change within the production range under consideration. Based on the preceding information, complete the following table.

Q	TC	FC	VC	ATC	AFC	AVC	MC
500	___	___	___	___	___	___	___
600	___	___	___	___	___	___	___
700	___	___	___	___	___	___	___
800	___	___	___	___	___	___	___
900	___	___	___	___	___	___	___
1,000	___	___	___	___	___	___	___
1,100	___	___	___	___	___	___	___

10. Kitchen Helper Company has decided to produce and sell food blenders and is considering three different types of production facilities (plants). Plant A is a labour-intensive facility, employing relatively little specialized capital equipment. Plant B is a semiautomated facility that would employ less labour than plant A but would also have higher capital equipment costs. Plant C is a completely automated facility using much more high-cost, high-technology capital equipment

and even less labour than plant B. Information about the operating costs and production capacities of these three different types of plants is shown in the following table.

	Plant Type		
	A	B	C
Unit variable costs			
Materials	$3.50	$3.25	$3.00
Labour	4.50	3.25	2.00
Overhead	1.00	1.50	2.00
Total	$9.00	$8.00	$7.00
Annual fixed costs			
Depreciation	$ 60,000	$100,000	$200,000
Capital	30,000	50,000	100,000
Overhead	60,000	100,000	150,000
Total	$150,000	$250,000	$450,000
Annual capacity	75,000	150,000	350,000

a. Determine the average total cost schedules for each plant type for annual outputs of 25,000, 50,000, 75,000, . . . , 350,000. For output levels beyond the capacity of a given plant, assume that multiple plants of the same type are built. For example, to produce 200,000 units with plant A, three of these plants would be built.

b. Based on the cost schedules calculated in part (a), construct the long-run average total cost schedule for the production of blenders.

CASE EXERCISE

COST ANALYSIS

The Leisure Products (LP) Company produces lawn and patio furniture. Most of its output is sold to do-it-yourself warehouse stores and to retail hardware and department store chains, which then distribute the products under their respective brand names. LP is not involved in direct retail sales. Last year, the firm had sales of $35 million.

One of LP's divisions manufactures folding (aluminum and vinyl) chairs. Sales of the chairs are highly seasonal, with 80 percent of the sales volume concentrated in the January–June period. Production is normally concentrated in the September–May period. Approximately 75 percent of the hourly workforce (unskilled and semiskilled workers) is laid off (or takes paid vacation time) during the June–August period of reduced output. The remainder of the workforce, consisting of salaried plant management (line managers and supervisors), maintenance, and clerical staff, is retained during this slow period. Maintenance personnel, for example, perform major overhauls of the machinery during the slow summer period.

LP planned to produce and sell 500,000 of these chairs during the coming year at a projected selling price of $7.15 per chair. The cost per unit was estimated as follows:

Direct labour	$2.25
Materials	2.30
Plant overhead*	1.15
Administrative and selling expense*	0.80
Total	$6.50

*These costs are allocated to each unit of output based on the projected annual production of 500,000 chairs.

A 10 percent markup ($0.65) was added to the cost per unit in arriving at the firm's selling price of $7.15 (plus shipping).

In May, LP received an inquiry from Southam Department Stores concerning the possible purchase of folding chairs for delivery in August. Southam indicated that it would place an order for 30,000 chairs if the price did not exceed $5.50 each (plus shipping). The chairs could be produced during the slow period using the firm's existing equipment and workforce. No overtime wages would have to be paid to the workforce in filling the order. Adequate materials were on hand (or could be purchased at prevailing market prices) to complete the order.

LP management was considering whether to accept the order. The firm's chief accountant felt that the firm should *not* accept the order because the price per chair was less than the total cost and contributed nothing to the firm's profits. The firm's chief economist argued that the firm should accept the order *if* the incremental revenue would exceed the incremental cost.

The following cost accounting definitions may be helpful in making this decision:

- Direct labour—labour costs incurred in converting the raw materials into the finished product.
- Materials—raw materials that enter into and become part of the final product.
- Plant overhead—all costs other than direct labour and materials that are associated with the product, including wages and salaries paid to employees who do not work directly on the product but whose services are related to the production process (such as line managers, maintenance, and janitorial personnel); heat; light; power; supplies; depreciation; taxes; and insurance on the assets used in the production process.
- Selling and distribution costs—costs incurred in making sales (for example, billing and salespeople's compensation), storing the product, and shipping the product to the customer. (In this case, the customer pays all shipping costs.)
- Administrative costs—items not listed in the preceding categories, including general and executive office costs, research, development, engineering costs, and miscellaneous items.

Questions

1. Calculate the incremental (that is, marginal) cost per chair to LP of accepting the order from Southam.
2. What assumptions did you make in calculating the incremental cost in Question 1? What additional information would be helpful in making these calculations?
3. Based on your answers to Questions 1 and 2, should LP accept the Southam order?
4. What additional considerations might lead LP to reject the order?

Part Three

Pricing and Output Decisions

In the previous chapters, we discussed the analysis of demand, production, and cost relationships in a firm. In this part, we consider the profit-maximizing price–output decisions, especially as they relate to the firm's strategic choices in competitive markets. Asymmetric information conditions as well as ideal full information exchanges are discussed.

Game theory examples are used wherever appropriate, especially in Chapters 6 and 8. (Web Chapter 16 is completely dedicated to game-theoretic decision making.) All Web chapters and appendixes can be accessed on the Nelson website at www.mcguigan.nelson.com.

Chapters 6, 7, and 8 consider price and output determination in competitive, monopolistic and oligopolistic markets. Chapter 9 examines value-based (not cost-based) differential pricing in theory and practice and transfer pricing with no external markets.

Web Appendix 9A discusses revenue management. Web Appendix 9B addresses specialized pricing problems, including pricing for the multiproduct firm, pricing of joint products, and transfer pricing with external markets.

CHAPTER 6

Price and Output Determination: Pure and Monopolistic Competition

Chapter Preview

Shareholder wealth-maximizing managers seek a pricing and output strategy that will maximize the present value of the future profit stream to the firm. The determination of the wealth-maximizing strategy depends on the production capacity, cost levels, demand characteristics, and the potential for immediate and longer-term competition. In this chapter, we provide an introduction to competitive pricing and output determination in markets where pure and monopolistic conditions exist. The implications of asymmetric information and the resulting problem of adverse selection in competitive markets are also discussed.

Learning Objectives

After studying this chapter, you should be able to:

1. Explain why a profit-maximizing firm generally operates at the output level where marginal cost equals marginal revenue.

2. Explain the characteristics of purely competitive, monopoly, and oligopoly market structures.

3. Understand that in a monopolistically competitive industry, many firms sell a differentiated product.

4. Explain why selling and promotional (advertising) expenses are one of the most important tools of nonprice competition.

5. Explain how exchanges under incomplete information and under asymmetric information differ.

6. Explain why asymmetric information in *experience-good markets* leads to *adverse selection* and how managers may solve this problem.

Resurrecting Apple Computer?*

Despite superior products, Apple Computer has discovered that competitive advantages may not be sustainable when products are imitated successfully. In the 1980s, Apple's Macintosh revolutionized personal computing by introducing the graphical user interface. However, by 1997, Apple had been surpassed by competitors. Microsoft had come to dominate the PC operating system business, with Microsoft Windows enjoying a 92 percent market share. IBM, and then Hewlett Packard and Dell, had come to dominate the PC assembly business. Apple remained the market leader in only the education, graphics design, and publishing submarkets. Since 55 percent of all PC and operating systems sales are in industry, 33 percent are in the home, 7 percent in government, and only 5 percent are in education, Apple's market share slipped from 9.6 percent in 1993 to 5.2 percent in 1996 to 2.6 percent in 1997.

One problem was pricing, and another was distribution. Personal computer assembly of outsourced components is now a small minimum efficient scale business, necessitating perhaps only 200,000 unit sales. For example, Dell Computers assembles whatever components the buyer wants and delivers them by direct mail order. With little inventory and just-in-time manufacturing from a masterfully managed supply chain of component suppliers, Dell became the most profitable company in the personal computer industry. In 1998, Dell's market share of 9 percent surpassed IBM's. By 2000, Dell had 20 percent. Soon other component assemblers like Gateway entered this direct-to-the-consumer channel, and sales in the direct channel grew at twice the industry growth rate.

With few outsourced components and relatively high in-house manufacturing costs, large overhead, and extensive R&D, Apple's least expensive product offering was $1,700, while "comparable" IBM machines were $1,100 and Dell's PCs were as low as $800. Apple also continued to sell primarily through retail outlets, even though the emergence of mass merchandisers like Best Buy and the direct-to-customer channel had radically changed the nature of PC distribution.

In addition, Apple had stale product design and closed architecture. Connectivity to IBM and the Windows operating systems had been resisted by Apple. This closed architecture strategy proved disastrous for exploiting the numerous complementary relationships available with the huge installed base of initially DOS-based IBM and later Windows- and Intel-based Microsoft customers. An installed base of customers attracts independent software vendors to write applications programs. Without compatibility to this Wintel installed base, Apple's software stagnated.

In 1999, Steve Jobs regained leadership of the company, intent on restoring the brand image of the once highly innovative Apple machines. The spiffy iMac PC made a good start, allowing market share to climb back to 5 percent. What other products to offer, prices to charge, distribution channels (direct, retail, etc.) to use, and alliances to form had to be decided.

For more information on Apple Computer, go to **www.apple.com** and **www.apple.ca**.

CP/PAUL SAKUMA

---

* Based on *Apple Computer 1992, 1995 (A), 1996, and 1997,* Harvard Business School Publishing, and "The Road Ahead," *The Wall Street Journal,* November 18, 2000, p. A3.

Pricing and Output Decision-Making Models

Pricing and output decisions are based on a framework for thinking proactively about present and future reconfigurations of the firm's resources, capabilities, and core competencies.

All successful decision-making models begin by identifying *target markets*—i.e., what businesses one wants to enter and stay in. Physical assets, human resources, and intellectual property (like patents and licences) sometimes limit the firm's capabilities, but business managers must still attempt to maximize profits or minimize costs while choosing the optimal price to charge for the firm's goods or services. The decision-making models must always clarify *how and when revenue will be realized* and analyze the sensitivity of *gross and net margins* to various possible changes in the firm's cost structure. Finally, all successful business managers must develop a strategy to accomplish their objectives.

We begin by considering the continuum of market structures from pure competition through to pure monopoly within which a business firm must operate. Then, we discuss some pricing and output decision situations.

A Continuum of Market Structures

The relationship between individual firms and the relevant market as a whole is referred to as the industry's *market structure* and depends on:

1. The number and relative size of firms in the industry.

2. The similarity of the products sold by the firms in the industry (that is, the degree of product differentiation).

3. The degree to which decision making by individual firms is independent, not interdependent or collusive.

4. The conditions of entry and exit.

Four specific market structures are often distinguished: pure competition, monopoly, monopolistic competition, and oligopoly.

Pure (Perfect) Competition

The **pure competition** industry model has the following characteristics:

1. A large number of buyers and sellers, each of which is so small that its actions cannot have a perceptible impact on the market price.

2. A homogeneous product produced by each firm (that is, no product differentiation, as with Winnipeg Commodity Exchange-grade wheat).

3. Complete knowledge of all relevant market information by all firms, each of which acts totally independently.

4. Free entry and exit from the market (that is, minimal barriers to entry and exit).

The single firm in a perfectly competitive industry is, in essence, a price taker—because the products of each producer are perfect substitutes for the products of every other producer, the single firm in pure competition can do nothing but offer its entire output at the going market price. As a result, the individual firm's demand curve approaches perfect elasticity at the market price. It can sell nothing at a higher price because all buyers will rationally shift to other sellers. If the firm sells at a price slightly below the long-run market price, it will lose money.

For example, Figure 6.1 indicates the nature of the industry and firm demand curves under pure competition in tract home building. Line *DD'* represents the total industry or market demand curve for tract houses and *S'S* is the market supply curve. At price

FIGURE 6.1

Pure Competition in Tract Home Building

The left panel shows the demand and supply curves for a perfectly competitive industry. The right panel shows the perfectly elastic demand curve for an individual firm at the market equilibrium price. The firm will earn zero economic profit because it will operate at minimum *ATC*, which will equal the equilibrium price.

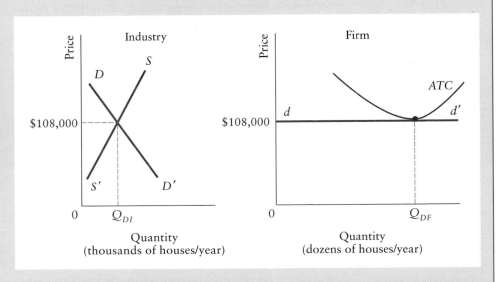

$108,000, the market price, a total of Q_{DI} houses will be demanded by the sum of all firms in the industry. Line dd' represents the demand curve facing each individual firm. The individual firm sells its entire output, Q_{DF}, at the market price $108,000. By definition, the quantity Q_{DF} represents only a small fraction of the total industry demand of Q_{DI}.

Why get involved in industries where revenues per sale ($108,000 in Figure 6.1) are just sufficient to cover fully allocated unit costs of $108,000 when the going market price is $108,000? The reason is that these "hairline margins" are the ticket to the occasional windfalls when demand increases and price rises enough to generate excess profits (for a few months in the tract home business, a few days in wildcat oil wells, or a few minutes in Winnipeg Commodity Exchange contracts). Note that the timing and magnitude of these windfalls are not predictable. Otherwise the respective real estate development land, oil leases, and grain silos would rise in value, and the expected excess profit would again reduce to hairline break-even. Also, remember that, at competitive equilibrium, the business owner–manager is receiving a salary or other return as great as could be received from the next best activity. In short, this is not the business environment where venture capital and entrepreneurial returns of 40 percent on invested capital occur when things go right, but it does provide perhaps a steady 12 percent with good managerial skills and cost controls. Occasionally, in such a competitive setting, windfall profits erupt for a short time.

Monopoly

Monopoly
A market structure characterized by one firm producing a highly differentiated product in a market with significant barriers to entry.

The **monopoly** model at the other extreme of the market structure spectrum from pure competition is characterized as follows:

1. Only one firm producing some specific product line in a specified market area (like an exclusive cable TV franchise).

2. Low cross-price elasticity of demand between the monopolist's product and any other product (that is, no close substitute products).

3. No interdependence with other competitors because the firm is a monopolist in its relevant market.

4. Substantial barriers to entry prevent competitors from entering the industry. These barriers may include any of the following:

   a. Absolute cost advantages of the established firm, resulting from economies in securing inputs or from patented production techniques.

   b. Product differentiation advantages, resulting from consumer loyalty to established products.

   c. Scale economies, which increase the difficulty for new firms in financing an efficient-sized plant or building up a sufficient sales volume to achieve lowest unit costs in such a plant. The need to build a large plant to compete effectively is also likely to lead to excess capacity in the industry, depressed prices, and reduced profits for all firms. These prices may not be high enough to permit the new entrant to survive and generate profits, and its prospect may deter many potential entrants from actually entering a market where scale economies are substantial.

   d. Large capital requirements, exceeding the financial resources of potential entrants.

   e. Legal exclusion of potential competitors, as is the case for public utilities and for those companies with patents and exclusive licensing arrangements.

   f. Trade secrets not available to potential competitors.

   By definition, the demand curve of the individual monopoly firm is identical with the industry demand curve, because the firm is the industry. Hence, the identity between the firm and industry demand curves allows decision making for the monopolist to be a relatively simple matter, compared to the complexity of rivalrous tactics with few close competitors in tight oligopoly groups.

Monopolistic Competition

Monopolistic Competition
A market structure very much like pure competition, with the major distinction being the existence of a differentiated product.

Edward Chamberlin and Joan Robinson coined the term **monopolistic competition** to describe industries with characteristics both of competitive markets (i.e., many firms) and of monopoly (i.e., product differentiation).[1] The market structure of monopolistic competition is characterized as follows:

1. A few dominant firms and a large number of competitive fringe firms.

2. Dominant firms selling products that are differentiated in some manner: real, perceived, or just imagined.

3. Independent decision making by individual firms.

4. Ease of entry and exit from the market as a whole but very substantial barriers to effective entry among the leading brands.

   By far the most important distinguishing characteristic of monopolistic competition is that the outputs of each firm are differentiated in some way from those of every other firm. In other words, the cross-price elasticity of demand between the products of individual firms is lower than among tract home builders, oil wildcatters, WCE wheat suppliers, or T-bill resellers in purely competitive markets. Product differentiation may be based on exclusive features (Disney World), trademarks (Nike's swoosh logo), trade names (Bass Weejuns), packaging (L'eggs hosiery), quality (Coach handbags), design (Sony Walkman), colour and style (Swatch watches), or the conditions of sale. These

---

[1] E. H. Chamberlin, *The Theory of Monopolistic Competition* (Cambridge, MA: Harvard University Press, 1933), p. 56. See also Joan Robinson, *The Economics of Imperfect Competition* (New York: Macmillan, 1933).

conditions may include such factors as credit terms, location of the seller, congeniality of sales personnel, after-sale service, warranties, and so on.

Because each firm produces a differentiated product, it is difficult to define an industry demand curve in monopolistic competition. Thus, rather than well-defined industries, one tends to get something of a continuum of products. Generally, it is rather easy to identify groups of differentiated products that fall into the same industry, like light beers, after-shave colognes, or perfumes.

Oligopoly

Oligopoly
A market structure in which the number of firms is so small that the actions of any one firm are likely to have noticeable impacts on the performance of other firms in the industry.

The **oligopoly** market structure of an industry describes a market having a few closely related firms. The number of firms is so small that actions by an individual firm in the industry with respect to price, output, product style or quality, terms of sale, and so on, have a perceptible impact on the sales of other firms in the industry. In other words, oligopoly is distinguished by a noticeable degree of *interdependence* among firms in the industry. The products or services that are produced by oligopolists may be homogeneous—as in the cases of air travel, 12-metre steel I-beams, aluminum, and cement—or they may be differentiated—as in the cases of automobiles, cigarettes, home appliances, cruise ships, colas, and cereals.

Although the degree of product differentiation is an important factor in shaping the single oligopolist's demand curve, the degree of interdependence of firms in the industry is of even greater significance. Primarily because of this interdependence, defining a single firm's demand curve is complicated. The relationship between price and output for a single firm is determined not only by consumer preferences, product substitutability, and level of advertising, *but also by the responses that other competitors may make to a price change by the firm.* A full discussion of rival response expectations will be deferred until Chapter 8.

Price–Output Determination under Pure Competition

As discussed above, the individual firm in a purely competitive industry is effectively a price taker because the products of every producer are perfect substitutes for the products of every other producer. This leads to the familiar horizontal or perfectly elastic demand curve of the purely competitive firm. Although we rarely find instances where all of the conditions for pure competition are met, securities exchanges and the commodity markets approach these conditions. For instance, the individual wheat farmer or T-bill reseller has little choice but to accept the going price for wheat.

Short Run

A firm in a purely competitive industry may either make transitory profits (in excess of normal returns to capital and entrepreneurial labour) or operate at a loss in the short run.

In pure competition, the firm must sell at the market price (p_1 or p_2), and its demand curve is represented by a horizontal line (D_1 or D_2) at the market price, as shown in Figure 6.2. In the purely competitive case, marginal revenue (MR) is equal to price (P), because the sale of each additional unit increases total revenue by the price of that unit (which remains constant at all levels of output). For instance, if

$$P = \$8/\text{unit}$$

then

$$\text{Total revenue} = TR = P \cdot Q$$
$$= 8Q$$

FIGURE 6.2

**Firm in Pure
Competition: Short Run**

In the short run, the supply
curve of the perfectly competitive firm corresponds to
the part JI of the *MC* curve
that lies above minimum
AVC.

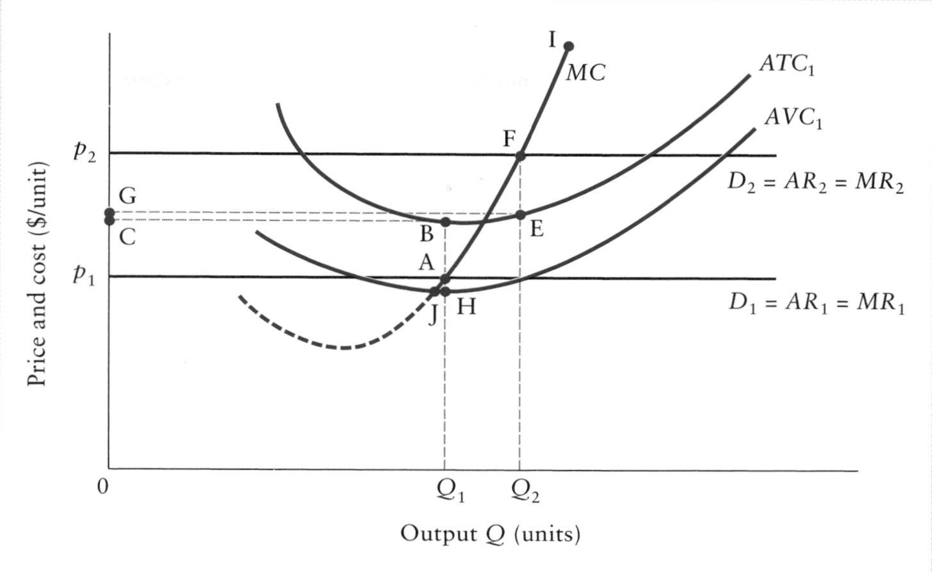

Marginal revenue is defined as the change in total revenue resulting from the sale of one additional unit, or the derivative of total revenue with respect to Q:

$$MR = \frac{dTR}{dQ} = \$8/\text{unit}$$

and marginal revenue equals price.

The profit-maximizing firm will produce at that level of output where marginal revenue equals marginal cost. Beyond that point, the production and sale of one additional unit would add more to total cost than to total revenue ($MC > MR$), and hence total profit ($TR - TC$) would decline. Up to the point where $MC = MR$, the production and sale of one more unit would increase total revenue more than total cost ($MR > MC$), and total profit would increase as an additional unit is produced and sold. *Producing at the point where marginal revenue MR equals marginal cost MC is equivalent to maximizing the total profit function.*[2]

The individual firm's supply function in Figure 6.2 is equal to that portion of the MC curve from point J to point I. At any price level below point J, the firm would shut down because it would not even be covering its variable costs (i.e., $P < AVC$). Temporary shutdown would result in limiting the losses to fixed costs alone.

---

[2] This can be proven as follows:

$$\pi = TR - TC$$

$$\frac{d\pi}{dQ} = \frac{dTR}{dQ} - \frac{dTC}{dQ} = MR - MC = 0$$

or, $MR = MC$ when profits are maximized.

Check for profit maximization by taking the second derivative of π with respect to Q, or d^2p/dQ^2. If it is less than zero, then π is maximized.

PROFIT MAXIMIZATION IN PURE COMPETITION (SHORT RUN): ABENECKI CORPORATION

This example illustrates the profit-maximization conditions for a firm operating in a purely competitive market environment in the short run. Assume Abenecki Corporation faces the following total revenue and total cost functions:

$$\text{Total revenue } TR = 8Q$$
$$\text{Total cost } TC = Q^2 + 4Q + 2$$

Marginal revenue and marginal cost are defined as the first derivative of total revenue and total cost, or

$$\text{Marginal revenue } MR = \frac{dTR}{dQ} = \$8/\text{unit}$$

$$\text{Marginal cost } MC = \frac{dTC}{dQ} = 2Q + 4$$

Similarly, total profit equals total revenue minus total cost:

$$\text{Total profit } (\pi) = TR - TC$$
$$= 8Q - (Q^2 + 4Q + 2)$$
$$= -Q^2 + 4Q - 2$$

To maximize total profit, we take the derivative of π with respect to quantity, set it equal to zero, and solve for the profit-maximizing level of Q. (It is also necessary to check the second derivative to be certain we have found a maximum, not a minimum!)[3]

$$\frac{d\pi}{dQ} = -2Q + 4 = 0$$

$$Q^* = 2 \text{ units}$$

But because $MR = \$8/\text{unit}$ and $MC = 2Q + 4 = [2(2) + 4] = \$8/\text{unit}$, when total profit is maximized, we are merely setting $MC = MR$.

Returning to Figure 6.2, if price $P = p_1$, the firm would produce the level of output Q_1 where $MC = MR$ (profits are maximized or losses minimized). In this case, the firm would incur a loss per unit equal to the difference between average total cost ATC and average revenue or price. This is represented by the height BA in Figure 6.2. The total loss incurred by the firm at Q_1 level of output and price p_1 equals the rectangle p_1CBA. This may be conceptually thought of as the loss per unit (BA) times the number of units produced and sold (Q_1). At price p_1, losses are minimized, because average variable costs AVC have been covered and a contribution remains to cover part of the fixed costs (AH per unit times Q_1 units). If the firm did not produce, it would incur losses equal to the entire amount of fixed costs (BH per unit times Q_1 units). Hence, we may conclude that, in the short run, a firm will produce and sell at that level of output where $MR = MC$, as long as the variable costs of production are being covered ($P > AVC$).

If price were p_2, the firm would produce Q_2 units and make a profit per unit of EF, or a total profit represented by the rectangle FEGp_2. The supply curve of the competitive

---

[3] The check for profit maximization goes as follows:

$$\frac{d^2\pi}{dQ^2} = -2$$

Because the second derivative is negative, we know we have found a maximum value for the profit function.

NORTH SEA AND WEST TEXAS OIL FIELDS CONTINUED TO PRODUCE DESPITE PRICES BELOW ATC*

Throughout 1998, the Organization of the Petroleum Exporting Countries (OPEC) attempted to cut production by 3.1 million barrels per day (roughly 10 percent of OPEC total production), and crude prices rose immediately from $13 per barrel to $17 per barrel (all prices are in U.S. dollars). However, numerous quota violations by OPEC members and lower demand for energy from slumping Asian economies resulted in a price collapse to $9.96 per barrel. This lowest price range is typical of historical crude oil prices, which hovered around an inflation-adjusted price of $10 for most of the 20th century—see Figure 6.3, panel (a).

Oil in the Persian Gulf region is cheapest to find, develop, and extract at an average *total* cost of $2 per barrel. In contrast, Venezuelan oil breaks even at $7 per

---

FIGURE 6.3

Crude Oil Prices and Costs

Panel (a) shows the price of oil per barrel in constant 1997 dollars. Panel (b) shows the cost per barrel, again in 1997 dollars, of producing oil from various regions of the world.

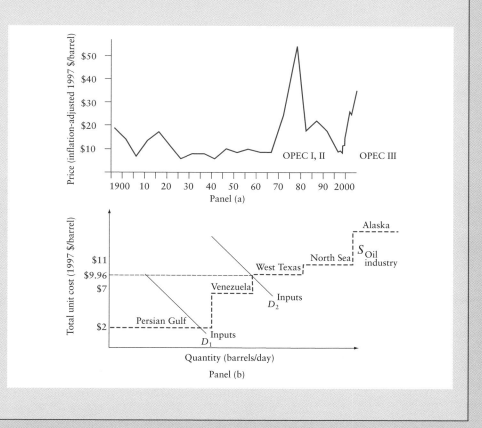

---

* "OPEC Talks Tough Again," *Time,* March 22, 1999, p. 62; "Cheap Oil: The Next Shock?" *The Economist,* March 6, 1999, pp. 23–25; and "Poised to Strike," *The Economist,* September 9, 2000, pp. 17–18.

barrel, West Texas oil at $10 per barrel, and the North Sea fields necessitate offshore oil rigs and expensive extraction technology that generate $11-per-barrel average total cost. These producers and their associated output trace out a traditional upward-sloping, long-run supply curve (here a step function) for the crude oil industry—see Figure 6.3, panel (b). At $9.96 world market oil prices, North Sea and West Texas fields may have ceased exploration and development for new oil but did not shut down operations in known fields.

Temporary shutdown is contemplated only when the market price falls below the average *variable* cost for these higher-cost fields, equal to about $4 per barrel. At $9.96 per barrel, both West Texas and North Sea wells lose less by operating (i.e., $10 − $9.96 = $0.04 and $11 − $9.96 = $1.04, respectively) than by shutting down, which would incur a loss of $6 and $7 average fixed cost, respectively. The decision to not shut down, not interrupt deliveries, and not threaten distribution relationships paid handsome dividends in 2000 as crude oil prices tripled to $34 per barrel—again see Figure 6.3, panel (a). Even if the market price had remained as low as $9.96, West Texas and North Sea producers (as well as all the less expensive producing areas) would have been better off operating than shutting down.

firm is therefore often identified as the marginal cost schedule above minimum *AVC* (i.e., the *MC* schedule from J to I). Industry supply is the horizontal summation of these firm supply curves.

Long Run

In the long run, all inputs are free to vary. Hence, no differentiation exists between fixed and variable costs. Under long-run conditions, average cost will tend to be just equal to price and all excessive profits will be eliminated (in Figure 6.4, see point A where $p_1 = AC_1$). If not, and if, for example, a price above p_1 exceeds average total costs, more firms will enter, the industry supply will increase (as illustrated by the parallel shift outward to the right of the $\Sigma_{SR} S_{FIRM}$ along market demand D^2_{MKT} in Figure 6.4), and market price will again be driven down toward the equilibrium, zero-profit level p_1.

In addition, as more firms bid for available factors of production (skilled labour, managerial talent), in some cases the cost of these factors will tend to rise. In that event, the entire cost structure of MC_1 and AC_1 will rise to reflect the higher input costs. This shift up in the firm's cost structure to AC_2 (see Figure 6.4) results in a two-way squeeze on excess profit and is referred to as an **external diseconomy of scale.** External scale diseconomies are distinguished from internal scale economies and diseconomies in that the latter reflect unit cost changes as the rate of output increases, *assuming no change in input prices*, whereas the former reflect exactly the bidding up of input prices as the industry expands in response to an increase in market demand. Under a constant input price assumption, the long-run industry supply curve $_{LR}S_{IND}$ in Figure 6.4 would be flat, a so-called *constant-cost industry* like coal-fired electricity. However, with the rising input prices for crude oil depicted in Figure 6.3, panel (b), the long-run supply curve $_{LR}S_{IND}$ for the downstream final product gasoline rises to the right, signifying an *increasing-cost industry*, as depicted in Figure 6.4. (It is quite possible to have downward-sloping long-run supply curves. A decreasing-cost industry occurred in the 1980s in calculators and again in the 1990s in PCs. Computer chip inputs became less expensive as the personal computer market expanded.)

External Diseconomy of Scale

An increase in unit costs reflecting higher input prices.

FIGURE 6.4

Long-Run Equilibrium under Pure Competition (Increasing-Cost Industry)

Panel (a) illustrates what is happening at the firm level in a perfectly competitive industry that is facing increasing costs. Panel (b) shows the long-run supply curve and market equilibriums over time as the market demand curve shifts.

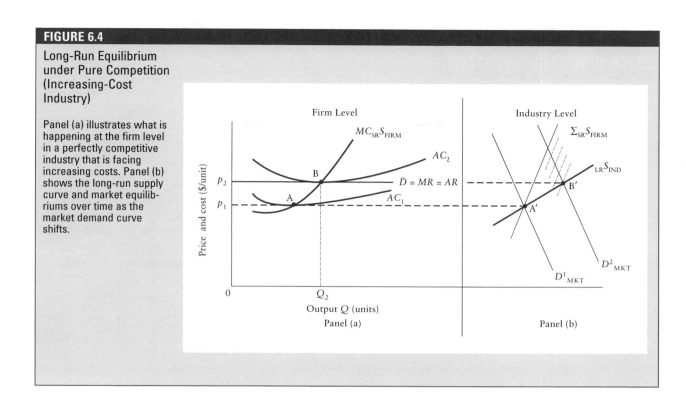

The net result is that in the long-run equilibrium, all purely competitive firms will tend to have identical costs, and prices will tend to equal average total costs (i.e., the average total cost curve AC will be tangent to the horizontal price line p_2). Thus, we may say that at the long-run profit-maximizing level of output under pure competition, equilibrium will be achieved at a point where $P = MR = MC = AC$. In long-run equilibrium, each competitive firm is producing at its most efficient (that is, its lowest unit cost) level of output.

Price–Output Determination under Monopolistic Competition

Monopolistic competition is a market structure with a relatively large number of firms, each selling a product that is differentiated in some manner from the products of its fringe competitors, and with substantial barriers to entry into the group of leading firms.

Product differentiation may be based on special product characteristics, trademarks, packaging, quality perceptions, distinctive product design, or conditions surrounding the sale, such as location of the seller, warranties, and credit terms. The demand curve for any one firm is expected to have a negative slope and be extremely elastic because of the large number of close substitutes. The firm in monopolistic competition has limited discretion over price (as distinguished from the firm in pure competition) because of customer loyalties arising from real or perceived product differences. Profit maximization (or loss minimization) again occurs when the firm produces at that level of output and charges that price at which marginal revenue equals marginal cost.

THE DYNAMICS OF COMPETITION AT AMAZON.COM*

Visit Amazon's websites at **www.amazon.com** and **www.amazon.ca**.

Online retailing started very slowly in clothing and other search goods that buyers want to "touch and feel," but it has excelled in one experience good—namely, books. One dollar of every $27 spent on the Internet in 1996 went to Amazon Books, the first online retailer in this industry. Amazon stocks fewer than 1,000 bestsellers but displays and provides reviews on 2.5 million popular titles. Using Ingram Book Group, the world's largest book wholesaler, Amazon is able to ship most selections in one to three days. Sales have doubled each half-year and in 1999 topped $1.6 billion. The potential growth for electronic booksellers is enormous. Nevertheless, Amazon.com shares declined 41 percent in value from September 1999 to September 2000.

One difficulty for Amazon.com is that Internet retailing is a classic example of a business with low barriers to entry and exit. As soon as Amazon's business systems for display, order taking, shipping, and payments stabilized, since profits were present, one expected substantial entry activity. For example, Barnes and Noble entered into an exclusive contract with America Online to pitch electronic book sales to AOL's 8.5 million subscribers.

Borders then quickly announced plans to enter electronic retailing. And many specialist booksellers of jet plane books, history books, auto books, and so forth, have flooded onto the Internet search engines. Even Amazon's wholesale supplier Ingram Book Group has entered the fray. For $2,500, Ingram support services will set up a website on behalf of any new book retailer.

Amazon.com responded by offering customized notification and book discussion services to add value for readers with special interests. The information revolution has made relationship marketing to established customers a pivotal element in securing repeat purchases. Nevertheless, the numerous open opportunities for fast, easy, and cheap entry likely will erode the profits in electronic book retailing down to the competitive rates of return on time, talent, and investment, perhaps only 7 percent.

The imperfect consumer information, limited time for comparison shopping, and brand loyalty that retailers have depended on are disappearing with Internet search engines, and retailing's traditionally slim profit margins are quickly becoming hairline-thin or nonexistent.

* Based on "Web Browsing," *The Economist,* March 29, 1997, p. 71; "In Search of the Perfect Market: A Survey of Electronic Commerce," *The Economist,* May 10, 1997; "The Net: A Market Too Perfect for Profits," *BusinessWeek,* May 11, 1998, p. 20; and "Comparison Shopping Is the Web's Virtue—Unless You're a Seller," *The Wall Street Journal,* July 23, 1998, p. A1.

Short Run

Just as in the case of pure competition, a monopolistically competitive firm may or may not generate a profit in the short run. For example, consider a demand curve such as $D'D'$ in Figure 6.5, with marginal revenue equal to MR'. Such a firm will set its prices where $MR' = MC$, resulting in price P_3 and output Q_3. The firm will earn a profit of EC dollars per unit of output. However, the low barriers to entry in a monopolistically competitive industry will not permit these short-run profits to be earned for long. As new firms enter the industry, industry supply will increase, causing the equilibrium price to fall. This is reflected in a downward movement in the demand curve facing any individual firm.

FIGURE 6.5

Long-Run Equilibrium in Monopolistic Competition

Just as under perfect competition, economic profit is zero in the long run under monopolistic competition. However, unlike perfect competition, the individual firm's demand curve is downward-sloping because of product differentiation.

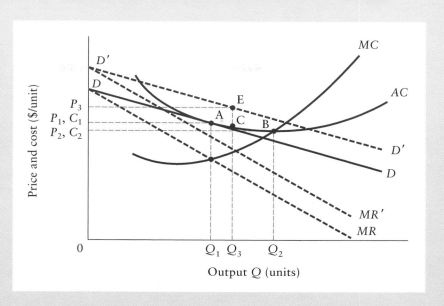

Long Run

With relatively free entry and exit into the competitive fringe, average costs and a firm's demand function will be driven *toward* tangency at a point such as A in Figure 6.5. At this price, P_1, and output, Q_1, marginal cost is equal to marginal revenue. Hence a firm such as an airline is producing at its optimal level of output. Any price lower or higher than P_1 will result in a loss to the firm because average costs will exceed price.

Because the monopolistic competitor produces at a level of output where average costs are still declining (between points A and B in Figure 6.5), monopolistically competitive firms produce with "excess" capacity. Of course, this argument overlooks the extent to which idle capacity may be a source of product differentiation. Idle capacity means a firm such as an airline can operate with high delivery reliability and change order responsiveness, which can be very important to business travellers on congested planes, and that warrants a price premium relative to competitive fringe airlines.

Selling and Promotional Expenses

In addition to varying price and quality characteristics of their products, firms may also vary the amount of their advertising and other promotional expenses in their search for profits. This kind of promotional activity generates two distinct types of benefits. First, demand for the general product group may be shifted upward to the right as a result of the individual firm and industry advertising activities. The greater the number of firms in an industry, the more diffused will be the effects of a general demand-increasing advertising campaign by any one firm. In contrast, a monopolist such as an electric utility or a highly concentrated oligopoly such as computer operating systems will be more inclined to undertake an advertising campaign.

The second, more widespread incentive for advertising is the desire to shift the demand function of a particular firm at the expense of other firms offering similar products. This strategy will be pursued both by oligopolists like Rothmans and Molson and by firms in more monopolistically competitive industries like cellular phones.

LONG-RUN PRICE AND OUTPUT DETERMINATION: VIDEO MAGIC RENTALS, LTD.

The market for video rentals in Calgary can best be described as monopolistically competitive. The demand for video rentals is estimated to be

$$P = 10 - 0.004Q$$

where Q is the number of weekly video rentals. The long-run average cost function for Video Magic is estimated to be

$$LRAC = 8 - 0.006Q + 0.000002Q^2$$

Video Magic's managers want to know the profit-maximizing price and output levels, and the level of expected total profits at these price and output levels.

First, compute total revenue (TR) as

$$TR = P \cdot Q = 10Q - 0.004Q^2$$

Next, compute marginal revenue (MR) by taking the first derivative of TR:

$$MR = \frac{dTR}{dQ} = 10 - 0.008Q$$

Compute total cost (TC) by multiplying $LRAC$ by Q:

$$TC = LRAC \cdot Q = 8Q - 0.006Q^2 + 0.000002Q^3$$

Compute marginal cost (MC) by taking the first derivative of TC:

$$MC = \frac{dTC}{dQ} = 8 - 0.012Q + 0.000006Q^2$$

Next, set $MR = MC$:

$$10 - 0.008Q = 8 - 0.012Q + 0.000006Q^2$$
$$0.000006Q^2 - 0.004Q - 2 = 0$$

Use the quadratic formula to solve for Q. Q^* is equal to 1,000.* At this quantity, price is equal to

$$P^* = 10 - 0.004(1,000)$$
$$= 10 - 4$$
$$= \$6$$

Total profit is equal to the difference between TR and TC, or

$$\pi = TR - TC$$
$$= 10Q - 0.004Q^2 - [8Q - 0.006Q^2 + 0.000002Q^3]$$
$$= 10(1,000) - 0.004(1,000)^2 - [8(1,000) - 0.006(1,000)^2 + 0.000002(1,000)^3]$$
$$= \$2,000$$

The MR and MC at these price and output levels are $2.

The fact that Video Magic expects to earn a profit of $2,000 suggests that the firm can anticipate additional competition, resulting in price cutting that will ultimately eliminate this profit amount.[†]

---

* The solution of the quadratic formula, $aQ^2 + bQ + c = 0$, is

$$Q = \frac{-b \pm \sqrt{b^2 - 4ac}}{2a} = \frac{-(-0.004) \pm [(-0.004)^2 - 4(0.000006)(-2)]^{0.5}}{2(0.000006)}$$
$$= 1,000; -333.33$$

Only the positive solution is feasible.
[†] Recall that the TC function includes a "normal" level of profit. Hence this $2,000 represents an economic *rent* above a normal profit level.

Determining the Optimal Level of Selling and Promotional Outlays

Selling and promotional expenses, often collectively referred to as "advertising," are one of the most important tools of nonprice competition.

To illustrate the effects of advertising expenditures and to determine the optimal selling expenses of a firm, consider the case where price and product characteristics already have been determined, and all retailers are selling at the manufacturer's suggested retail price.

The determination of the optimal advertising outlay is a straightforward application of the marginal decision-making rules followed by profit-maximizing firms. Define MR to be the change in total revenue received from a one-unit increase in output (and the sale of that output). For fixed-price settings, MR just equals the price, P. Define MC to be the change in total costs of producing and distributing (but not of advertising) an additional unit of output. The marginal profit or contribution margin from an additional unit of output is

$$(6.1) \qquad \text{Contribution margin } (pCM) = P - MC$$

The marginal cost of advertising (MCA) associated with the sale of an additional unit of output is defined as the change in advertising expenditures (ΔAk), where k is the unit cost of an advertising message, A, or

$$(6.2) \qquad MCA = \frac{\Delta Ak}{\Delta Q}$$

The optimal level of advertising outlays is the level of advertising where the marginal profit contribution (pCM) is equal to the marginal cost of advertising, or

$$(6.3) \qquad pCM = MCA$$

As long as a firm receives a greater contribution margin than the MCA it incurs to sell an additional unit of output, the advertising outlay should be made. If pCM is less than MCA, the advertising outlay should not be made and the level of advertising should be reduced until $pCM = MCA$. This marginal analysis also applies to other types of nonprice competition like after-sale service and product replacement guarantees.

EXAMPLE

OPTIMAL ADVERTISING: FLIN FLON FORD

Suppose that the marginal profit contribution from selling Ford automobiles at Flin Flon Ford (FFF) averages $1,000 across the various models it sells. The firm estimates that it will have to incur $550 of additional promotional expenses to increase its sales by one unit over the current level. Should the outlay for promotion be made?

Because $pCM > MCA$ (i.e., $1,000 > $550), FFF's profit will be increased by $450 if it incurs an additional $550 of promotional expenses. FFF should continue to make additional promotional outlays (which are likely to be less and less effective at triggering additional sales) up to the point where the marginal cost of advertising equals the expected marginal profit contribution.

If FFF were to find that MCA was greater than pCM, FFF should cut back on its promotional outlays until $pCM = MCA$.

Ford and P&G Tie Ad Agency Pay to Sales

For more information on these companies, visit **www.ford.com** and **www.pg.com**.

Historically, ad agencies have earned more income each time their clients buy another expensive 30-second slot on network TV (or other media), whatever the performance of the ad in generating incremental sales. In 1997, Ford and Procter & Gamble, two of the world's biggest advertisers, announced that henceforth all agency billings would need to be performance-based. These incentive payment plans will include a fixed fee for designing ad campaigns plus incentive pay based on the incremental sales traceable to the ad. Ford and P&G believe this system will encourage agencies to search for database marketing, Internet, and event sponsorships that far exceed the marginal media buy in advertising productivity, $\Delta Q/\Delta A$.

Optimal Advertising Intensity

Optimal expenditure on demand-increasing costs like promotions, couponing, direct mail, and media advertising can be compared across firms. For example, the total contributions from incremental sales relative to the advertising cost of beer ads can be compared to the total contributions relative to the advertising cost of cereal ads. Advertising is often placed in five media (network TV, local TV, radio, newspapers, and magazines). The "reach" of a TV ad is measured as audience thousands per minute of advertising message. Reach is directly related to the advertising message's cost (k). A manager should fully fund in the marketing budget any ad campaign for which

$$(6.4) \qquad (P - MC)(\Delta Q/\Delta A) > k$$

where $(P - MC)$ is the contribution margin and $(\Delta Q/\Delta A)$ is the increase in demand (i.e., a shift outward in demand) attributable to the increase in message units of advertising.[4]

Expanding Equation 6.4 identifies the two determinants of the optimal advertising expenditure per dollar sales or "advertising intensity." Ak/PQ is determined by the gross margin $(P - MC)/P$ and by the advertising elasticity of demand E_a:

$$(6.5) \qquad \frac{Ak}{PQ} = \frac{(P - MC)}{P} \frac{A}{Q}(\Delta Q/\Delta A)$$

$$(6.6) \qquad \frac{Ak}{PQ} = \frac{(P - MC)}{P} E_a$$

Both factors are important. With high margins (near 70 percent) and very effective ads, Kellogg spends 30 percent of every dollar of sales revenue on cereal advertising. In contrast, the jewellery industry has 92 percent margins, but Peoples Jewellers advertising inserts in the weekend paper simply do not trigger many jewellery sales. The advertising elasticity of jewellery is low. Consequently, a company like Peoples spends less than 10 percent of sales revenue on advertising. Campbell Soup has relatively high advertising elasticity of demand given its strong brand name, but the margins on canned goods are very low (less than 5 percent). Consequently, Campbell Soup spends just one-tenth of what Kellogg spends on advertising as a percentage of sales revenue—just 3 percent of sales revenue.

---

[4] Sometimes, the price points at which the product can be sold change after a successful ad campaign. If so, the appropriate valuation of the incremental sales in Equation 6.4 is the new contribution margin.

OPTIMAL ADVERTISING INTENSITY AT KELLOGG AND GENERAL MILLS*

For more information on food marketing, go to **www.fmi.org**.

Visit the Kellogg and General Mills websites at **www.kelloggs.com** and **www.generalmills.com**.

The ready-to-eat (RTE) cereal industry spends 55 percent of its sales revenue on marketing and promotion—30 percent on advertising alone. In part, this resource-allocation decision reflects the fact that cereal demand is very sensitive to successful ad campaigns like General Mills' Wheaties, The Breakfast of Champions. In addition, however, RTE cereal margins are among the highest of any industry. For example, Kellogg's Raisin Bran sells for a 70 percent gross margin. This margin reflects brand loyalty built up over many years of advertising investments as well as Kellogg's 37 percent market share. In the highly concentrated RTE cereal industry, Quaker Oats (8 percent), Post (15 percent), General Mills (25 percent), and Kellogg control 85 percent of the market.

Until recently, advertising and retail displays were the predominant form of competition in cereals. Like Coca-Cola and PepsiCo, the dominant RTE cereal companies had concluded that price discounting would be mutually ruinous and ultimately ineffective. Therefore, each company decided independently to refrain from discounting prices to attempt to gain market share. However, in June 1996, 20 percent price cuts swept through the industry, in part in response to the growth of private-label cereals (e.g., President's Choice), which had collectively grabbed close to 10 percent of the market. Margins on some leading brand-name products fell to 50 percent with ingredients (15 percent), packaging (10 percent), wages (10 percent), and distribution (15 percent) accounting for the rest of the selling price. By late 1997, the price war had ended, and traditional advertising competition resumed.

*Based on "Cereals," *Winston-Salem Journal,* March 8, 1995, p. A1, and "Denial in Battle Creek," *Forbes,* October 7, 1996, pp. 44–46.

The Net Value of Advertising

Traditional economic analysis has tended to conclude that the primary impacts of advertising are to raise prices to consumers and to lead to the creation and maintenance of monopoly power.[5]

George Stigler and Phil Nelson[6] used the theory of the economics of information to argue that by giving consumers price information, advertising is expected to reduce the price paid. The discovery of price information may be costly and time-consuming in the absence of price advertising. If, for example, it costs a consumer $10 in time costs to discover the store that will offer a saving of $8 on the price of an item, the search for price information is not worthwhile. But if price advertising makes all consumers aware of the lowest price supplier of an item at an additional cost of only $1, then the great majority of consumers will be better off as a result of this advertising.

[5] Evidence in support of this view is presented in William Comaner and Thomas Wilson, *Advertising and Market Power* (Cambridge, MA: Harvard University Press, 1974).
[6] George J. Stigler, "The Economics of Information," *Journal of Political Economy* (June 1961), pp. 213–225, and Philip Nelson, "The Economic Consequences of Advertising," *Journal of Business* (April 1975), pp. 213–241.

In addition, Nelson found that advertisers of all products have substantial incentives to provide useful and truthful information to customers. High-quality information can reduce the search cost for consumers as they seek to make a choice between alternative goods. Because consumers can assess the truthfulness of the information contained in an advertisement and because advertising creates brand awareness (both for good and inferior brands), advertisers who misrepresent their products will not be successful in generating future (and repeat) business.

Competitive Markets under Asymmetric Information

Lemons Market
Asymmetric information exchange leads to the low-quality products and services driving out the higher quality products and services.

Adverse Selection
A limited choice of lower quality alternatives attributable to asymmetric information.

Incomplete Information
Uncertain knowledge of payoffs, choices, etc.

Asymmetric Information
Unequal, dissimilar knowledge.

In competitive markets for newsprint, crude oil, auto rentals, and delivered pizza, both buyers and sellers have full knowledge of the capabilities and after-sale performance of the standard products. Equilibrium price just covers the supplier's cost of production for a product of known reliable quality. If suppliers were to charge more, rival offers and entry would quickly erode their sales. If suppliers were to charge less, they could not afford to stay in business. This has been the message of this chapter so far. In competitive markets under ideal information conditions, you get what you pay for. These markets differ enormously from competitive markets under asymmetric information, which are sometimes called **lemons markets.** One prominent example of asymmetric information in a lemons market is used automobiles, in which the true quality of tires, mechanical repairs, or other features often is known only to the seller. Other such goods include house paint, mail-order computer components, and common cold remedies.

In a lemons market, the buyers discount all unverifiable claims by the sellers, who market only lower quality products because of the reduced prices buyers are willing to pay. This disappearance of higher quality products from the marketplace illustrates the concept of **adverse selection**—i.e., the lower quality products are selected in and the higher quality products are adversely selected out. To resolve the marketing problems posed by adverse selection requires credible commitment mechanisms such as warranties, brand-name reputations, collateral, or price premiums for reliable repeat-purchase transactions.

Incomplete versus Asymmetric Information

One distinction that can sharpen our understanding of these complicating factors in competitive exchange is that between asymmetric information and **incomplete information.** Incomplete information is associated with uncertainty, and uncertainty is pervasive. Practically all exchanges, whether for products, financial claims, or labour services, are conducted under conditions of uncertainty. On the one hand, decision makers often face uncertainty as to the effect of random disturbances on the outcome of their actions. This uncertainty typically leads to insurance markets. On the other hand, decision makers are sometimes uncertain as to the payoffs or even types of choices they face. This condition typically leads to intentionally incomplete contracting. Chapter 10 addresses incomplete contracting.

Asymmetric information exchange, in contrast, refers to situations in which either the buyer or the seller possesses information that the other party cannot verify or to which the other party does not have access. For example, mail-order suppliers of computer components or personal sellers of used cars often have an informationally advantaged position relative to the buyers. The sellers know the machine's capabilities, deficiencies, and most probable failure rate, but these are difficult matters for the buyer to assess. And the typical 90-day warranty does nothing to alter this information asymmetry. Both buyer and seller face uncertainty against which they may choose to insure, but one has more information or better information than the other. Asymmetric information can occur in any type of market structure.

Search Goods versus Experience Goods

In services, retailing, and many manufacturing industries, buyers generally search the market to identify low-price suppliers. Sometimes this search is accomplished by asking for recommendations from recent purchasers, by scouring catalogues and ads, or by visiting showrooms and sales floors. In selecting a supplier, many customers are also intensely interested in multiple dimensions of product and service quality, including product design, durability, image, conformance to specifications, order delay, delivery reliability, change order responsiveness, and after-sale service. Customers often spend as much time and effort searching the market for the desired quality mix as they do searching for lowest price. Retailers and service providers understand this and often offer many quality combinations at various prices to trigger a purchase of these **search goods.** Consider, for example, the many price–quality alternatives available from your favourite clothing, sporting goods, or furniture store.

On the other hand, some products and services have important quality dimensions that *cannot* be observed at the point of purchase. Consider used cars and other resale machinery, nonprescription remedies for the common cold, house paint, and mail-order computer components. The quality of these items can be detected only through experience in using the products. Hence, products and services of this type are termed **experience goods** and are distinguished from search goods.

Ultimately, the problem with experience goods in competitive market exchange is the unverifiability of asymmetric information. The seller knows how to detect the difference between high- and low-quality products (e.g., between lemons and cream puffs in the used car market), but cannot credibly relay this information to buyers, at least not in chance encounters between strangers. Fraudulent sellers will claim high quality when it is absent, and realizing this, buyers rationally discount all such information. Because of the private, impacted nature of the product quality information, the seller's claims and omissions can never be verified without experiencing the reliability of the auto, the efficacy of the common cold remedy, the durability of the house paint, or the capability of the computer component.

All of this is not to say that the buyers of experience goods are without recourse or that the sellers are without ingenuity as to how to market their products. Warranties and investments in reputations provide mechanisms whereby the sellers of house paint and computer components can credibly commit to delivering a high-quality product. The essential point is that in the absence of these bonding or hostage mechanisms, the experience-good buyer will rationally disbelieve the seller's claims. Consequently, the honest seller of truly high-quality experience goods will find little market for its higher cost, higher priced product. The "bad apples drive out the good" in many experience-good markets.

Adverse Selection and the Notorious Firm: A Game-Theoretic Approach

Suppose customers recognize that unverifiable private information about experience-good quality is present, yet knowledge of any fraudulent high-price sale of low-quality products spreads almost instantaneously throughout the marketplace. Is this extreme reputational effect sufficient to restore the exchange of high-quality/high-price experience goods? Or, can the notorious firm continue to defraud customers here and elsewhere? The answer depends on the conditions of entry and exit discussed earlier in this chapter, but not in the way you might expect.

Consider the cost structure and profits of such a notorious firm, depicted in Figure 6.6. If offered the low price P_l, the firm operates in competitive equilibrium at Q_1, where the price just covers the marginal cost and average total cost ($SAC_{low\ quality}$) for Q_1 units of the low-quality product. Alternatively, if offered the high price P_h, the firm can either competitively supply Q_1 of the high-quality experience good and again just break

Search Goods
Products and services whose quality can be detected through market search.

Experience Goods
Products and services whose quality is undetectable when purchased.

Read about U.S. economist and Nobel Prize winner George Akerlof's seminal paper on asymmetric information and the market for used cars at **http://nobelprize.org/ economics/articles/ akerlof**.

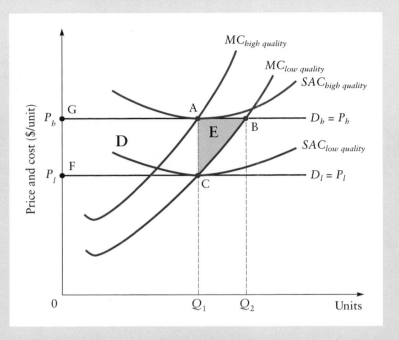

FIGURE 6.6

Low-Quality Experience Goods Emerge from Competitive Markets

If consumers cannot distinguish between goods of low quality and high quality, then consumers will offer only the price for goods of low quality. Producers of goods of high quality will be driven from the market, and markets will be incomplete.

even against the higher costs of $SAC_{high\ quality}$,[7] or the firm can deliver a low-quality experience good at Q_1 and continue to incur the lower costs $SAC_{low\ quality}$. The third alternative entails an expansion of output along $MC_{low\ quality}$ in response to the price rise and generates profits. That is, the incremental output $(Q_2 - Q_1)$ earns incremental profit equal to the difference between P_h and $MC_{low\ quality}$—namely, the shaded area ABC (labelled bold **E**)—and in addition, the original output Q_1 earns a fraudulent rent of area GACF (labelled bold **D**). Although the supplier observes his own cost directly and therefore detects the availability of **D** + **E**, the problem for the experience-good buyer is that in terms of point-of-sale information, high-price transactions at point B on $MC_{low\ quality}$ and at point A on $MC_{high\ quality}$ are indistinguishable. Both types of products have an asking price of P_h, and only the seller observes the output rate Q_1 versus Q_2.

Of course, the supplier is not indifferent between the two alternatives. The high-quality transaction offers a cash flow from operations just sufficient to cover capital costs and break even at point A, whereas the fraudulent transaction (a low-quality product at a high price at point B) offers a net profit for at least one period. Table 6.1 depicts this interaction between experience-good buyers and a potentially fraudulent firm as a payoff matrix. The seller can produce either low or high quality, and the buyer can offer either low or high prices. The row player (the seller) gets the below-diagonal payoffs in each cell, and the column player (the buyer) gets the above-diagonal payoffs in each cell. The buyer prefers to cover the high cost of high-quality products (in the

---

[7] The minimum cost output for the plant configuration and cost structure associated with high quality could shift right or left, but to simplify, assume that the SAC just increases vertically from point C to point A.

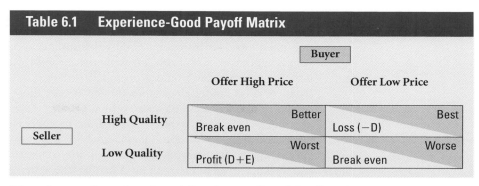

Table 6.1   Experience-Good Payoff Matrix

		Buyer	
		Offer High Price	**Offer Low Price**
Seller	**High Quality**	Break even / Better	Loss (−D) / Best
	Low Quality	Profit (D+E) / Worst	Break even / Worse

Column-player payoffs are above diagonal. Row-player payoffs are below diagonal.

northwest cell) rather than pay less and cover only the lower cost of low-quality products (in the southeast cell). However, the buyer is worst off when the seller fails to deliver a high-quality product for which the buyer has paid a high price (in the southwest cell). The buyer also recognizes that getting more than she pays for (in the northeast cell) would impose losses on the seller, who would prefer to break even with a low-price/low-quality transaction in the southeast cell.

Each player in this business game attempts to predict the other's behaviour and respond accordingly. Knowing that the seller prefers profits to breaking even at high prices and that the seller prefers breaking even to losses at low prices, the buyer predicts that low-quality product will be forthcoming irrespective of the price offered. Therefore, the buyer makes only low-price offers. Only those who wish to be repeatedly defrauded offer to pay high prices for one-shot transactions with strangers offering experience goods. This game-theoretic reasoning will be discussed in more detail in Chapter 8.

This reasoning motivates adverse selection by the rational seller in an experience-good market. Because sellers can anticipate only low-price offers from buyers, the sellers never produce high-quality products. That is, the market for experience goods will be incomplete in that not all product qualities will be available for sale. Anticipating that buyers will radically discount their unverifiable high-quality "cream puffs," individual sellers of used cars choose to place only low-quality "lemons" on the market. The "cream puffs" often are given away to relatives. Similarly, jewellers in vacation locations, anticipating that out-of-town buyers will radically discount high-grade, uncertified gemstones, choose to sell only lower quality gemstones. And unbranded mail-order computer components are inevitably of lower quality. Adverse selection always causes competitive markets with asymmetric information to be incomplete. Again, the bad apples drive out the good.

Insuring and Lending under Asymmetric Information: Another Lemons Market

This same adverse selection reasoning applies beyond experience-good product markets whenever asymmetric information is prominent. Consider the transaction between a bank loan officer and a new commercial borrower, or between an insurance company and a new auto insurance policyholder. Through an application and interview process and with access to various databases and credit references, the lender or insurer attempts to uncover the private, impacted information about the applicant's credit or driving history. Nevertheless, just as in the case of claims made by the itinerant seller of an experience good, verification remains a problem. The applicant has an incentive to omit facts that would tend to result in loan or insurance denial (e.g., prior business failures or unreported accidents), and knowing this, the lender may offer only higher rate loans and the insurer higher rate policies.

The problem is that higher rate loans and expensive insurance policies tend to affect the composition of the applicant pool, resulting in adverse selection. Some honest, well-intentioned borrowers and good-risk insurance applicants will now drop out of the applicant pool because of concern about their inability to pay principal and interest and insurance premiums on time as promised. But other applicants who never intended to repay (or drive carefully), or more problematically, those who will try less hard to avoid default or accidents, are undeterred by the higher rates. The asymmetric information and higher rates have adversely selected out precisely those borrowers and drivers the lender and auto insurance company wanted to attract to their loan portfolio and insurance risk pool. Recognizing this problem, the creditors and insurers offer a restricted and incomplete set of loan and insurance contracts. Credit rationing that excludes large segments of the population of potential borrowers and government-mandated protection against uninsured motorists are reflections of the adverse selection problem resulting from asymmetric information in these commercial lending and auto insurance markets.

Solutions to the Adverse Selection Problem

In both theory and practice, there are two approaches to eliciting the exchange of high-quality experience goods, commercial loans to new borrowers, or auto insurance policies to new residents. The first involves regulatory agencies. These agencies can attempt to set quotas (e.g., on minimum product durability, on minimum lending in "red-lined" underprivileged communities, or on minimum auto liability insurance coverage). They may also impose restrictions (e.g., on the sale of untested pharmaceuticals), enforce product safety standards (e.g., on the flammability of children's sleepwear), and monitor truth in advertising laws. We discuss public regulation at greater length in Chapter 11.

Mutual Reliance: Hostage Mechanisms Support Asymmetric Information Exchange

Reliance Relationship
Long-term, mutually beneficial agreements, often informal.

Hostage or Bonding Mechanism
A procedure for establishing trust by assigning valuable property contingent on nonperformance of an agreement.

A second, quite different approach involves self-enforcing private solution mechanisms where each party relies on the other. Such **reliance relationships** often involve the exchange of some sort of hostage, such as a reputational asset, an escrow account, or a surety bond. In general, **hostage or bonding mechanisms** are necessary to induce unregulated asymmetric information exchange. For this second approach to the adverse selection problem to succeed, buyers must be convinced that fraud is more costly to the seller than the cost of delivering the promised product quality. Then and only then will the customers pay for the seller's additional expected costs attributable to the higher-quality products. In other words, hostage mechanisms affect the game-theoretic reasoning of market participants.

One simple illustration of the use of a hostage mechanism to support asymmetric information exchange is a product warranty, perhaps for an auto tire. Tires are an experience good in that blowout protection and tread wear life are product qualities not detectable at the point of purchase. Only by driving many thousands of kilometers and randomly encountering many road hazards can the buyer ascertain these tire qualities directly. However, if a tread wear replacement warranty and a tire blowout warranty make the sellers conspicuously worse off should they fail to deliver high-quality tires, then buyers can rely on that manufacturer's product claims. As a consequence, buyers will be willing to offer higher prices for the unverifiably higher-quality product.

Hostage mechanisms can be either self-enforcing or enforced by third parties. In Chapter 8, we shall discuss the role of self-enforcing (third-party enforcing) hostage mechanisms in noncooperative (cooperative) games. Like warranties, a seller's representations about after-sale service and product replacement guarantees are ultimately contractual agreements that will be enforced by the courts. However, other hostage

CREDIBLE PRODUCT REPLACEMENT CLAIMS: DOONEY & BOURKE

For more information on this company, go to **www.dooney.com**.

The women's handbag market has a wide selection of brand names, prices, and qualities. Leather products have several search-good characteristics in that one can touch and feel the material in order to assess the fineness or coarseness of the grain, the evenness of the tanning process, and the suppleness of the leather, etc. In these respects, one can search for just that quality for which one is willing to pay. However, the susceptibility to discolouring with age or exposure to the elements and the quality of the stitching is much harder to detect at the point of purchase. As a result, some aspects of handbag purchase are an experience-good exchange. Therefore, one wonders how the wide variety of prices and qualities can be sustained. Dooney & Bourke resolved this question by offering an almost preposterous replacement guarantee. Dooney & Bourke offered to replace any handbag for the life of the customer. Because governments will assist customers in enforcing this promise, the commitment was credible, and the replacement guarantee provides a hostage that supports high-price, high-quality exchanges. In particular, customers can easily discern that Dooney & Bourke is better off producing an exceptionally high-quality handbag to deliver at the first transaction rather than an unlimited series of replacements.

mechanisms require no third-party enforcement. Suppose DuPont's industrial chemicals division reveals to potential new customers the names and addresses of several satisfied current customers. This practice of providing references is not only to assist potential buyers in gauging the quality of the product or service for sale but also to deliver an irretrievable hostage. Once new customers have the easy ability to contact regular customers and blow the whistle on product malfunctions or misrepresentations, the seller has an enhanced incentive to deliver high quality to both sets of buyers. Connecting all suppliers and customers in a real-time information system is a natural extension of this familiar practice of providing references. The total quality movement (TQM) ISO 9000 standards recommend that companies insist on just such information links to their suppliers.

Brand-Name Reputations as Hostages

A marketing mechanism that supports asymmetric information exchange is a brand-name reputation such as Sony colour televisions, Apple computers, and Lexus automobiles. Branding requires a substantial investment over extended periods of time. Moreover, brand names are capital assets that provide future net cash flows from repeat-purchase customers as long as the brand reputation holds up. To defraud customers by delivering less quality than the brand reputation promised would destroy the capitalized market value of the brand name. Buyers anticipate that value-maximizing managers will not intentionally destroy brand-name capital. Brand names therefore deliver a hostage, providing assurances to buyers that the seller will not misrepresent the quality of an experience good.

Ultimately, brand-name capital provides such a hostage because the disreputation effects on the brand name that result from delivering fraudulent product quality cannot be separated from the salable brand asset. Successful brands can be extended to sell other products. Nestlé's original hot chocolate brand can be extended to sell cereal-based candy bars, and Oreo cookies can be extended to sell ice cream. But the product failure of Texas Instruments (TI) personal computers means that now the TI brand name cannot be easily extended to other consumer electronic products. All the potential buyers have to figure out is whether the seller would be worse off sacrificing the value of the brand name by economizing on production expenses rather than simply incurring the extra expense to produce a high-quality product while retaining the brand value. A brand-name asset such as Denver Hayes Jeanswear may suggest one answer, whereas Joe's Garage suggests another.

If brand-name assets could be sold independent of their reputations (or disreputations), then this hostage mechanism would cease to support experience-good exchange. Assets that can be redeployed at the grantor's wish are not hostages in this reliance contracting sense. The implication is that easy entry and exit, which worked to ensure break-even prices just sufficient to cover costs in the normal competitive markets, may have undesirable consequences here in asymmetric information experience-good markets.

Price Premiums with Nonredeployable Assets[8]

Recall that if sellers are offered prices that just cover high-quality cost, sellers of experience goods prefer the profit from defrauding customers by delivering low-quality products. But suppose buyers offered reliable sellers a continuing price premium above the cost of high-quality products. At P_{hh} in Figure 6.7, the nonnotorious firm produces Q_1'

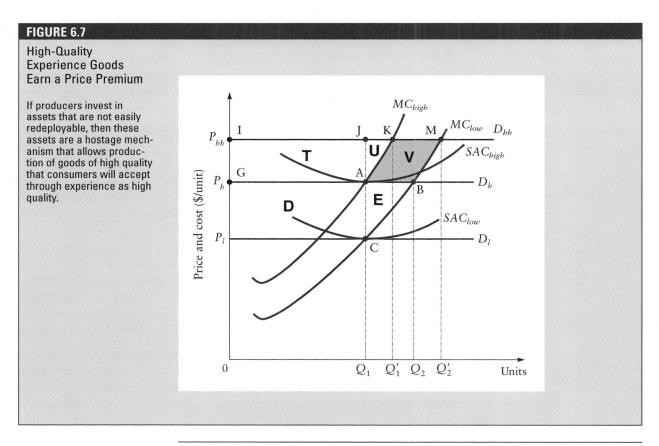

FIGURE 6.7

High-Quality Experience Goods Earn a Price Premium

If producers invest in assets that are not easily redeployable, then these assets are a hostage mechanism that allows production of goods of high quality that consumers will accept through experience as high quality.

---

[8] See B. Klein and K. Leffler, "The Role of Market Forces in Assuring Contractual Performance," *Journal of Political Economy*, Vol. 89, Number 4, 1981, pp. 615–641.

high-quality product and earns a continuous stream of profits (IJAG + JKA), labelled T + U. This perpetuity may now exceed (in present value) the notorious firm's one-time-only fraudulent rent from production at Q'_2—namely, D + T, plus incremental profit E + U + V. That is,

$$(6.7) \qquad (T + U)/d > [(D + T) + (E + U + V)]/(1 + d)$$

where d is an appropriate discount rate (e.g., the firm's weighted average cost of capital, perhaps 12 percent). By Equation 6.7, lower discount rates or faster rising marginal cost (i.e., a smaller incremental profit from the expansion of output, shaded area V in Figure 6.7) decreases the likelihood of fraudulent behaviour. If reliable delivery of a high-quality product does in fact earn long-term net profit in excess of the one-time-only profit from fraud, sellers will offer both low- and high-quality products at P_l and P_{hh}, respectively, and some buyers will purchase in each market.

However, transitory profits alone do not allow an escape from adverse selection. Because profits attract entry into competitive markets, the price premiums will erode, and notorious firm behaviour will then return. What is missing is a mechanism to dissipate the rent from the price premiums. If the sellers invest the high-quality price premiums in firm-specific assets, such as L'eggs retail displays for convenience stores or Ethan Allen interiors for their showrooms, then new entrants will encounter a higher entry barrier than previously. Such barriers cause potential entrants to perceive much lower potential net profit and therefore deter entry. L'eggs or Ethan Allen operating

EXAMPLE

EFFICIENT UNCUT DIAMOND SORTING: DE BEERS*

For more information on De Beers, go to **www.debeersgroup. com**.

Another illustration of experience-good exchange is block booking by the De Beers diamond cartel, which controls over 80 percent of the uncut wholesale diamond business. De Beers offers groupings of diamonds of various grades to approved wholesale buyers. Because buyers are not allowed to cull the less valuable stones, the quality of the diamonds in any given grouping is unverifiable at the point of purchase—hence, the term *sights*. If these arrangements were one time only, no buyer would purchase high-price sights or agree to the culling restrictions. But because block booking economizes on the duplicatory assessments of rejected stones that would otherwise result, De Beers can consistently offer its sights at net costs below the value at which the diamonds grade out.

Buyers therefore have a reason for purchasing high-quality experience goods from De Beers. If a competitor offered no culling restrictions and lower prices, diamond merchants would carefully weigh the additional cost of sorting the diamonds themselves against the price premiums at De Beers and might well decide to continue doing business with De Beers. Knowing this, very few potential competitors ever enter the uncut diamond wholesale business to challenge De Beers, despite its high markups and margins. De Beers' reputation for passing on its cost savings in diamond sorting to buyers is the hostage that brings buyers back time and time again.

* Based on R. Kenney and B. Klein, "The Economics of Block Booking," *The Journal of Law and Economics*, 26 (1983), pp. 497–540.

profits in excess of the production cost can then persist, and high-quality, high-price experience goods can survive in the marketplace.

The rent-dissipating investments must not be in generic retail sites easily redeployable to the next tenant or capital equipment easily redeployable to the next manufacturer (e.g., corporate jet aircraft). If that were the case, hit-and-run entry would recur each time high-quality prices rose above cost. New entrants would just move in on the business for a short time period and then sell off their assets in thick resale markets when profits eroded. Then, competitive equilibrium would again induce adverse selection in experience-good markets. Instead, the investment that dissipates the operating profit from high-quality products must be sunk cost investment in nonredeployable assets.

Nonredeployable Assets
Assets whose value in second-best use is near zero.

Asset Specificity
The difference in value between first-best and second-best use.

Nonredeployable assets are assets whose liquidation value in second-best use is low. Usually this occurs when the assets depend on a firm-specific input such as a L'eggs or Ethan Allen brand name. Without the brand name, no firm has a use for the egg-shaped retail racks designed for L'eggs original packaging or the lavish Ethan Allen showrooms. Many such nonredeployable assets have high value in their first-best use. The difference between value in first-best use and liquidation value is a measure of the **specificity of the asset.** Highly specific assets make the best hostages to convince customers that asymmetric information transactions will be nonfraudulent.

In summary, asymmetric information causes competitive markets for experience goods to differ rather markedly from the competitive markets for search goods. Long-run equilibrium for high-quality experience goods requires revenues in excess of total unit cost. These profits are invested by reliable sellers of experience goods in highly specific assets. Potentially notorious firms with redeployable assets attract only customers seeking low-price/low-quality experience goods. In experience-good markets, you get what you pay for when reputations matter or other hostage mechanisms establish the seller's credibility.

Managerial Challenge Revisited

Resurrecting Apple Computer?

Recall that the managerial challenge ended with questions about decisions to make with respect to what products to offer, prices to charge, distribution channels to use, and alliances to form. Since returning to head Apple as its interim CEO (or iCEO in Mac-speak), Steve Jobs has reenergized the firm. In addition to the iMac, other new products have been introduced, such as the iPod for downloading music at 99 cents per tune from the online Apple iTunes Music Store. The iPod and iTunes sales have done extremely well, leading to a 33 percent increase in Apple's revenues in 2004. Apple is estimated to have about 70 percent market share in this new market. Some industry insiders now joke that the iMac has become an iPod accessory. Other firms are also producing iPod accessories. Bose has a Sound Dock speaker that connects an iPod to a home stereo. New BMW cars have a connection device that lets drivers play music from their iPods through the auto's stereo system.

Summary

- In general, a profit-maximizing firm will desire to operate at that level of output where marginal cost equals marginal revenue.

- In a purely competitive market structure, the firm will operate in the short run as long as price is greater than average variable cost.

- In a purely competitive market structure, the tendency is toward a long-run equilibrium condition in which firms earn just normal returns, price is equal to marginal cost and average total cost, and average total cost is minimized.

- In a monopolistically competitive industry, a large number of firms sell a differentiated product. In practice, few market structures can be best analyzed in the context of the monopolistic competition model. Most actual market structures have greater similarities to the purely competitive market model or the oligopolistic market model.

- Advertising expenditures are optimal from a profit-maximization perspective if they are carried to the point where the marginal profit contribution from an additional unit of output is equal to the marginal cost of advertising. The optimal level of advertising intensity (the advertising expenditure per sales dollar) varies across products and industries. It is determined by the marginal profit contribution from incremental sales and by the advertising elasticity of demand.

- Exchange under incomplete information and under asymmetric information differ. *Incomplete information* refers to the uncertainty that is pervasive in practically all transactions and motivates insurance markets. *Asymmetric information,* on the other hand, refers to private information one party possesses that the other party cannot independently verify.

- Asymmetric information in *experience-good* markets leads to *adverse selection,* whereby high-price/high-quality products are driven from the market by low-quality products whose low quality is indistinguishable at the point of sale. Buyers in such *lemons markets* refuse to offer prices high enough to cover the cost of high quality because under competitive conditions, suppliers will predictably commit fraud and then perhaps move on to conduct business with unsuspecting customers under other product or company names.

- To escape adverse selection and elicit high-quality experience goods necessitates either intrusive and expensive regulation or some sort of bonding mechanism to induce *self-enforcing reliance relationships* between buyers and sellers. Warranties, independent appraisals, leases with a high residual, collateral, irrevocable money-back guarantees, contingent payments, and brand names all provide assurance to buyers that the seller will not misrepresent the product quality. Hostage mechanisms support asymmetric information exchange.

- Another way to escape adverse selection is for buyers to offer price premiums and repeat-purchase transactions to firms that resist fraudulently selling low-quality experience goods for high prices. These profits are invested by reliable sellers in *nonredeployable, highly specific assets.* Potentially *notorious firms* with redeployable assets continue to attract only customers seeking low-price/low-quality products. Under asymmetric information, at best you get what you pay for, never more than that.

Self-Test Exercises

1. The Jenkins Company has estimated the following demand equation for its product:

$$Q_D = 12{,}000 - 4{,}000P$$

where

$$P = \text{price/unit}$$
$$Q_D = \text{quantity demanded/year}$$

The firm's total costs are $4,000 when nothing is being produced. These costs increase by 50 cents for each unit produced.

a. Write an equation for the total cost function.

b. Specify the marginal cost function.

c. Write an equation for total revenue in terms of Q.

d. Specify the marginal revenue function.

e. Write an equation for total profits, π, in terms of Q. At what level of output are total profits maximized (that is, find the maximum of the total profit function)? What price will be charged? What will total profit be?

f. Check your answers in part (e) by equating marginal cost and marginal revenue and solving for Q.

g. What model of market pricing behaviour has been assumed in this problem?

2. Assume that a firm sells its product in a perfectly competitive market. The firm's fixed costs (including a "normal" return on the funds the entrepreneur has invested in the firm) are equal to $100 and its variable cost schedule is as follows:

Output (Units)	Variable Cost Per Unit
50	$5.00
100	4.50
150	4.00
200	3.50
250	3.00
300	2.75
350	3.00
400	3.50

a. Find the marginal cost and average total cost schedules for the firm.

b. If the prevailing market price is $4.50, how many units will be produced and sold?

c. What are total profits and profit per unit at the output level determined in part (b)?

d. Is the industry in long-run equilibrium at this price? Explain.

3. Wyandotte Company sells various chemicals to the automobile industry. The firm currently sells 30,000 litres of polyol per year at an average price of $15 per litre. Fixed costs of manufacturing polyol are $90,000 per year and total variable costs equal $180,000. The operations research department has estimated that a 15 percent increase in output would not affect fixed costs but would reduce average variable costs by 60 cents per litre. The marketing department has estimated the arc elasticity of demand for polyol to be −2.0.

a. How much would the firm have to reduce the price of polyol to achieve a 15 percent increase in the quantity sold?

b. Evaluate the impact of such a price cut on (i) total revenue, (ii) total costs, and (iii) total profits.

Exercises

1. What effect do you think a law requiring gasoline stations to post their prices prominently will have on the average price of gasoline charged? How can consumers benefit from such a law requiring the posting of gasoline prices?

2. At one point during the energy crisis of the 1970s, gasohol was viewed as one part of a solution to the problem of shortages of petroleum products. Gasohol was made from a blend of gasoline and alcohol derived from corn. What would you expect the impact of this program to be on the price of corn, soybeans, and wheat?

3. If the government sets a price floor for milk, would you expect that a need would arise for restrictions on the number of cows that farmers can milk? In the absence of these restrictions, what outcome would you expect?

4. The demand function for propane is

$$Q_D = 212 - 20P$$

The supply function for propane is

$$Q_S = 20 + 4P$$

a. What is the equilibrium price and quantity?
b. If the government establishes a price ceiling of $6, what quantity will be demanded and supplied?
c. If the government establishes a price floor (minimum price) of $9, what quantity will be demanded and supplied?
d. If supply increases to

$$Q'_S = 20 + 6P$$

what is the new equilibrium price and quantity?
e. If demand increases to

$$Q'_D = 250 - 19P$$

and the supply is as given in part (d), what is the new equilibrium price and quantity?

5. Assume that a firm in a perfectly competitive industry has the following total cost schedule:

Output (Units)	Total Cost ($)
10	$110
15	150
20	180
25	225
30	300
35	385
40	480

a. Calculate a marginal cost and an average cost schedule for the firm.
b. If the prevailing market price is $17 per unit, how many units will be produced and sold? What are profits per unit? What are total profits?
c. Is the industry in long-run equilibrium at this price?

6. During past wars, and more recently under programs designed to curb inflation, the government has imposed price ceilings on certain commodities. This is done

to keep prices from rising to the natural level that would prevail under supply–demand equilibrium. The result is that the quantity that sellers are willing to supply at the ceiling price often falls short of the quantity demanded at that price. To bring supply and demand more into equilibrium, ration coupons are sometimes issued.

   a. Show graphically, using both supply and demand curves, the effects of a ceiling price.
   b. On the black market, how much would you be willing to pay for a ration coupon good for the purchase of one unit of the rationed commodity?
   c. If the aggregate demand curve for commodity X is $P = 100 - 5Q$, and the industry supply curve for that product is $P = 10 + 10Q$, calculate the following:
      (i) The equilibrium price and quantity for commodity X.
      (ii) The quantity that will be sold if a ceiling price of $60 is established.
      (iii) The black market price of a ration coupon good for the purchase of one unit of X.

7. Royersford Ltd. sells women's knit underwear. The firm now sells about 20,000 pairs a year at an average price of $10 each. Fixed costs amount to $60,000, and total variable costs equal $120,000. The production department has estimated that a 10 percent increase in output would not affect fixed costs but would reduce average variable cost by 40 cents.

   The marketing department advocates a price reduction of 5 percent to increase sales, total revenues, and profits. The arc elasticity of demand with respect to prices is estimated at -2.

   a. Evaluate the impact of the proposal to cut prices on (i) total revenue, (ii) total cost, and (iii) total profits.
   b. If average variable costs are assumed to remain constant over a 10 percent increase in output, evaluate the effects of the proposed price cut on total profits.

8. A firm operating in a purely competitive environment is faced with a market price of $250. The firm's total cost function (short run) is

$$TC = 6,000 + 400Q - 20Q^2 + Q^3$$

   a. Should the firm produce at this price in the short run?
   b. If the market price is $300, what will total profits (losses) be if the firm produces 10 units of output? Should the firm produce at this price?
   c. If the market price is greater than $300, should the firm produce in the short run?

9. The Poster Bed Company believes that its industry can best be classified as monopolistically competitive. An analysis of the demand for its canopy bed has resulted in the following estimated demand function for the bed:

$$P = 1,760 - 12Q$$

The cost analysis department has estimated the total cost function for the poster bed as

$$TC = \frac{1}{3}Q^3 - 15Q^2 + 5Q + 24,000$$

   a. Calculate the level of output that should be produced to maximize short-run profits.

b. What price should be charged?

c. Compute total profits at this price–output level.

d. Compute the point price elasticity of demand at the profit-maximizing level of output.

e. What level of fixed costs is the firm experiencing on its bed production?

f. What is the impact of a $5,000 increase in the level of fixed costs on the price charged, output produced, and profit generated?

10. Exotic Metals, Inc., a leading manufacturer of zirilium, which is used in many electronic products, estimates the following demand schedule for its product:

Price ($/Kg)	Quantity (Kg/Period)
$25	0
18	1,000
16	2,000
14	3,000
12	4,000
10	5,000
8	6,000
6	7,000
4	8,000
2	9,000

Fixed costs of manufacturing zirilium are $14,000 per period. The firm's variable cost schedule is as follows:

Output (Kg/Period)	Variable Cost (Per Kg)
0	$ 0
1,000	10.00
2,000	8.50
3,000	7.33
4,000	6.25
5,000	5.40
6,000	5.00
7,000	5.14
8,000	5.88
9,000	7.00

a. Find the total revenue and marginal revenue schedules for the firm.

b. Determine the average total cost and marginal cost schedules for the firm.

c. What are Exotic Metals' profit-maximizing price and output levels for the production and sale of zirilium?

d. What is Exotic's profit (or loss) at the solution determined in part (c)?

e. Suppose that the federal government announces it will sell zirilium from its stockpile to anyone who wants it, at $6 per kilogram. How does this affect the solution determined in part (c)? What is Exotic Metals' profit (or loss) under these conditions?

11. Tennis Products, Inc., produces three models of high-quality tennis rackets. The following table contains recent information on the sales, costs, and profitability of the three models:

Model	Average Quantity Sold (Units/ Month)	Current Price	Total Revenue	Variable Cost per Unit	Contribution Margin per Unit	Contribution Margin*
A	15,000	$30	$ 450,000	$15.00	$15	$225,000
B	5,000	35	175,000	18.00	17	85,000
C	10,000	45	450,000	20.00	25	250,000
Total			$1,075,000			$560,000

*Contribution to fixed costs and profits.

The firm is considering lowering the price of Model A to $27 in an effort to increase the number of units sold. Based on the results of price changes that have been made in the past, the firm's chief economist estimated the arc price elasticity of demand to be −2.5. Furthermore, she has estimated the arc cross elasticity of demand between Model A and Model B to be approximately 0.5 and between Model A and Model C to be approximately 0.2. Variable costs per unit are not expected to change over the anticipated changes in volume.

a. Evaluate the impact of the price cut on the (i) total revenue and (ii) contribution margin of Model A. Based on this analysis, should the firm lower the price of Model A?

b. Evaluate the impact of the price cut on the (i) total revenue and (ii) contribution margin for the entire line of tennis rackets. Based on this analysis, should the firm lower the price of Model A?

12. Jordan Enterprises has estimated the gross margin $(P − MC)/P$ for its Air Express model of basketball shoes to be 40 percent. Based on market research and past experience, Jordan estimates the following relationship between the sales for Air Express and advertising/promotional outlays:

Advertising/Promotional Outlays	Sales Revenue
$500,000	$4,000,000
600,000	4,500,000
700,000	4,900,000
800,000	5,200,000
900,000	5,450,000
1,000,000	5,600,000

a. What is the marginal revenue from an additional dollar spent on advertising if the firm is currently spending $1,000,000 on advertising?

b. What level of advertising would you recommend to Jordan's management?

13. Which of the following products and services are likely to encounter adverse selection problems: golf shirts at travelling pro tournaments, certified gemstones from Birlas, graduation gift travel packages, or mail-order auto parts? Why or why not?

14. Without employing a tread wear warranty contract, how could the sellers of tires credibly commit to the delivery of high-quality products with long tread wear life?

15. If a particular supplier in Table 6.1 succeeds in reducing the cost of low-quality products and now earns a profit on the low-price transactions, is the likelihood of fraud by that firm greater or less?

16. If notorious firm behaviour (i.e., defrauding a buyer of high-priced experience goods by delivering low-quality goods) becomes known throughout the marketplace only with a lag of three periods, profits on high-quality transactions remain the same, and interest rates rise slightly, are customers more likely or less likely to offer high prices for an experience good? Explain.

CASE EXERCISE

Visit Apple's website at **www.apple.com**.

See also the website **www.economy.com/ dismal**, where Economy.com, Inc., provides a wide array of economic, financial, country, and industry research information.

APPLE COMPUTER

Investigate recent developments at Apple's website. Then, answer the following questions.

Questions

1. Does easy access to distribution channels or small minimum efficient scale indicate high or low barriers to entry in the PC business? Why?

2. Do suppliers appropriate little or most of the value in the PC value chain? Why?

3. What factors determine the intensity of rivalry in an industry? Is the intensity of rivalry in the PC industry high or low? Why?

Price and Output Determination: Monopoly and Dominant Firms

Chapter Preview

In this chapter, we analyze the optimal price and output decision for dominant firms operating in monopoly or near-monopoly markets. The most important implication of such markets is that the dominant firm does not have to accept the market price as a given. Rather, dominant firms have substantial latitude in establishing price–cost markups. In addition to considering price and output determination for "unregulated" monopolies and near-monopolies, we also look at these decisions for regulated industries—electric power, natural gas distribution and transmission, and broadcast communications. With public debate focused on deregulation, it is imperative that reform be consistent with microeconomic principles to avoid some of the problems inherent in the current system of utility regulation.

Learning Objectives

After studying this chapter, you should be able to:

1. Define a *monopoly market structure* and list the primary sources of monopoly power.

2. Understand the limitations of increasing returns from network effects.

3. Understand that monopolists will produce at that level of output where marginal cost equals marginal revenue if their goal is to maximize short-run profits.

4. Define *contribution margins* and explain how contribution margins and *markups* are inversely related to the price elasticity of demand.

5. Define *gross margins*.

6. Explain *limit pricing* strategy and how some monopolists use it to discourage rivals from entering an industry.

7. Define *public utilities* and explain the rationales for public utility regulation, including the natural monopoly argument.

8. Explain *peak-load pricing*.

Dominant Microprocessor Company Lagging Behind Next Trend*

With continuous innovation, ever-faster, more powerful chip designs, and a business plan riveted on supplying the PC industry, Intel Corporation has dominated the high-end market in microprocessors. After being forced out of the dynamic random access memory (DRAM) chip business by Japanese rivals in 1986, Intel reinvented itself as the lead supplier of microprocessors. Intel has an 85 percent market share in the microprocessor chips that control most personal computer functions and process software instructions. In addition, Intel sells 90 percent of the chip sets that control the flow of data from the microprocessor to the display screens, modems, and graphical user interface. With market dominance have come enormous economies of scale in production and increasing returns to marketing expenditures that allowed Intel to beat out its smaller rivals. High markups and margins (for mass-produced electronics products) resulted. For example, the Pentium series as well as the 486 microprocessors earned 25 percent net profit margins.

Using tight nondisclosure agreements with its customers, Intel has managed to protect its proprietary trade secrets about chip design and manufacture. Intellectual property is the company's most important asset, and some buyers of Intel chips have found that the dominant firm withholds vital information about technical specifications required to fully integrate the chips into new products unless it gets access to its customers' new technologies. Intergraph, a maker of high-end workstations for media applications, alleged recently that Intel withheld information about subtle bugs in some Intel chips until Intergraph agreed to license its graphical user interface technology to the chip supplier.

Although the worldwide PC market is expected to continue to grow at 15 percent per year, the penetration of PCs into North American households has stalled at 45 percent (versus TVs at 98 percent). Digital telephones, hand-held computers, video game players, and set-top control boxes for digital televisions may prove to be a market even bigger than the PC market. Such devices require inexpensive computer chips that process data very quickly, not high-end Intel chips designed to run Microsoft's complex software. Advanced Micro Devices, Inc. (AMD) is a likely leader in this new chip segment.

Intel may have missed one of the "strategic inflection points" that Intel president Andy Grove says is so important to the success of any high technology company. Grove knows Intel must get prepared for streamlined lower end chip products that sell for under $40, despite the fact that Intel's chips have sold for $87 to $200.

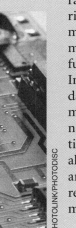

For more information on Intel Corporation and AMD, go to **www.intel.com** and **www.amd.com**.

---

* Based on "Hand-Held Combat," *The Wall Street Journal,* February 12, 1998, p. A1; "Showdown Looms Over Chip Giant's Power," *The Wall Street Journal,* June 8, 1998, p. B1; and "Intel Lags Behind in Cheap Chips," *The Wall Street Journal,* March 1, 1999, p. C15.

Monopoly Defined

Monopoly is defined as a market structure characterized by one firm producing a highly differentiated product in a market with significant barriers to entry. Because there are no close substitutes for the product of a monopolist, the demand curve facing a monopolist will have a significant negative slope and be less price elastic than comparable demands where there are more substitutes. A monopoly market structure may be thought of as the opposite extreme from pure competition in terms of the range of market structures.

Just as purely competitive market structures (e.g., for Winnipeg Commodity Exchange wheat) are rare, so too pure monopoly markets are also rare. All goods and services have some substitutes available for them. The more distant the substitutes that are available, the closer a market is to being a pure monopoly.

Sources of Market Power for a Monopolist

An amicus brief on the economics of intellectual property, prepared for the U.S. Supreme Court case of *Lotus Development Corporation v. Borland International,* can be found at **www.panix.com/~jesse/amicus/cover.html**.

Several sources of market power can be enjoyed by monopolists or near-monopoly dominant firms. First, a firm may possess a *patent* or *copyright* that prevents other firms from producing the same product. For example, Pharmacia & Upjohn, Inc. (now merged with Pfizer Inc.) originally had a patent on Rogaine, the hair growth stimulator for balding men. The long and expensive governmental approval process for competing products creates a significant barrier to entry for potential competitors.

Second, a firm may *control critical resources.* De Beers Consolidated Mines Limited owns or controls the vast majority of diamond production in South Africa and until recently had marketing agreements with other major diamond-producing countries, including the former Soviet Union. This control of raw materials enabled De Beers to maintain high world prices for cut diamonds for 65 years.

A third source of monopoly power may be a *government-authorized franchise.* In most cities, one firm is chosen to provide cable TV services to the community. The same type of monopoly power occurs when a government agency adopts an industry standard that heavily favours one industry or one company over all others. The adoption of Motorola's proposed HDTV standards has often been criticized on this basis. The alternative standard is one proposed by Sony, a Japanese firm.

Monopoly power may also arise because there are significant *economies of scale* over a wide range of output. Thus, the first entrant firm will enjoy declining long-run average

EXAMPLE

THE MICKEY MOUSE MONOPOLY: DISNEY

For more information on Disney, visit **www.disney.com**.

When it began, Disneyland in Anaheim, California, was unique. Other theme parks like Six Flags have since reduced Disney's monopoly power. Disney World in Orlando, Florida, was an attempt to resecure Disney's near-monopoly position in the market, but Universal Studios, SeaWorld, and other attractions throughout the Orlando area quickly offered additional theme park experiences. Were they a complement or a substitute for Disney World? Negative cross price elasticity of demand evidence suggests complementary relationships. Seventy percent of Disney World's business is repeat business. More variety inside or outside the park means more frequent returns for longer vacations. Anticipating these developments, Disney long ago became a major property owner throughout the Orlando area.

costs. Under these circumstances, it is natural for there to be only one supplier of the good or service, because that one supplier can produce the output more cheaply than can a group of smaller competitors. These so-called natural monopolies are usually closely regulated by government agencies to restrict the profits of the monopolist.

Increasing Returns from Network Effects

Finally, *increasing returns in network-based businesses* can be a source of monopoly market power. When Microsoft managed to achieve a critical level of adoption for its Windows graphical user interface (GUI), the amount of marketing and promotional expenditure required to secure the next adoption actually began to fall.

Marketing and promotions are generally subject to diminishing returns, as depicted in the 0 to 30 percent section of Figure 7.1. From 0 to 30 percent market share, the marketing required to achieve each additional share point has a diminishing effect on the probability of adoption by the next potential user (note the reduced slope of the sales penetration curve). Consequently, additional share points become more and more expensive over this range. But when the number of other users of a network-based device reaches a 30 percent share, the next 50 or so share points are cheaper to promote. That is, beyond the 30 percent inflection point, each additional share point of users connected to Windows leads to an increasing probability of adoption by another user; hence, there is a decrease in the marketing expense required to secure another unit sale (note the increased slope of the sales penetration curve in the 30 to 85 percent section of Figure 7.1). Then, beyond 85 percent, as shown in the figure, diminishing returns again set in.

These network-based effects of compatibility with other users reflect increased value to the potential adopter. The same thing occurs when an ever-increasing number of

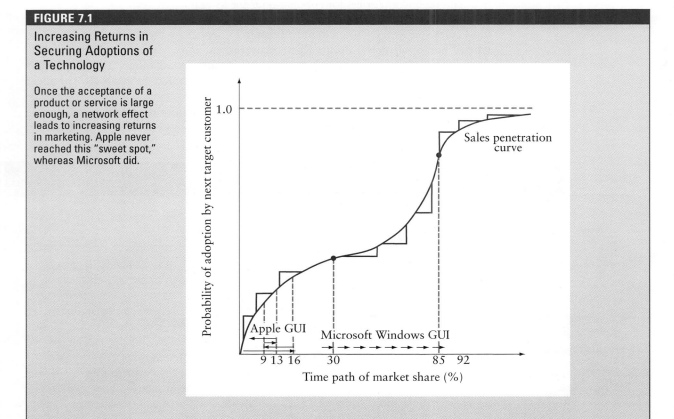

FIGURE 7.1

Increasing Returns in Securing Adoptions of a Technology

Once the acceptance of a product or service is large enough, a network effect leads to increasing returns in marketing. Apple never reached this "sweet spot," whereas Microsoft did.

200   *Part 3   Pricing and Output Decisions*

NEL

WHAT WENT RIGHT
WHAT WENT WRONG

WHAT WENT RIGHT AT MICROSOFT BUT WRONG AT APPLE COMPUTER?*

For more information on Apple, Microsoft, and Netscape, go to **www.microsoft.com**, **www.apple.com** and **www.netscape.com**.

Throughout much of its history, Apple Computer, discussed in the Managerial Challenge at the beginning of Chapter 6, has had less than a 10 percent market share in the North American personal computer market. Twice in its early history, Apple reached double-digit share points (16 percent in 1986 and 13 percent in 1993). At no time could Apple come close to achieving the inflection point (depicted at 30 percent in Figure 7.1). Apple therefore pursued increasing returns by attempting to become an industry standard in several personal computer submarkets like the desktop publishing, journalism, media-based advertising, and entertainment industries. In addition, despite fiercely defending its graphical user interface (GUI) code for almost two decades with patent applications and trade secret infringement suits, in 1998–1999, Apple reversed course and began discussing broad licensing and alliance agreements with both Microsoft and IBM.

Compatibility with other operating systems had been easy to achieve, but widespread adoption of Mac programming code by independent software vendors had not. Consequently, to obtain a critical mass of adoptions that would trigger independent software vendors to begin writing software applications for the Mac, Apple reversed its policy on the closed architecture of its GUI. The GUI code at Apple was clearly technically superior to the early-generation Windows products. However, as with the adoption race between VHS and Betamax videos, the technically superior product lost out to the product that first reached increasing returns—namely, Microsoft Windows GUI running on IBM-clone PCs.

Netscape once controlled 80 percent of the Internet browser market, but lost market share rapidly once Microsoft's Internet Explorer reached increasing returns. When Internet Explorer achieved 55 percent of the market share, Netscape made its browser services compatible and instead began positioning itself as a portal for Wintel machines to use in accessing the Net. Netscape was trying to avoid Apple's mistake of refusing to recognize an evolving industry standard and then finding itself buried by Microsoft's increasing returns.

* Based on "Netscape to Woo Microsoft's Customers, *Reuters,* October 1, 1998; W. Brian Arthur, "Increasing Returns and the New World of Business," *Harvard Business Review,* July–August 1996; and "Sorting Out the Deal," *U.S. News and World Report,* August 18, 1997, p. 20.

Network Effect
A source of unit cost reduction based on network value rather than scale of operations or volume purchase discounts.

independent software vendors (ISVs) write applications for an operating system like Windows, which has achieved more than 30 percent acceptance in the marketplace and has therefore effectively become an industry standard. Because of the inflection points in the sales penetration curve, Microsoft's increasing returns make an 85 percent monopoly control of the operating system market highly likely. Whatever customer relationships preexisted, once Microsoft achieved a 30 percent share, increasing returns in marketing its product offering introduced a disruptive technology **network effect** that displaced other competitors. Inexorably, Microsoft's share then grew and grew and grew to 92 percent. Netscape's Internet browser experienced exactly this same sort of displacement by Microsoft's Internet Explorer when Microsoft achieved a 30 percent-plus penetration by bundling Internet Explorer with Windows, effectively giving away the browser for free to reach the middle sales penetration range of increasing returns.

Even with increasing returns set off by network effects, monopoly is far from inevitable. The reasons are threefold. First, innovative new products can easily offset the cost savings from increasing returns to promotion spending. Second, network effects tend to occur in technology-based industries that are also experiencing external economies of scale—i.e., falling input prices. Figure 7.2 shows that between 1997 and 2002, the cost per megahertz for silicon computer chips fell from $2.00 to $0.10, and between 1998 and 2002, hard drive storage device cost per megabyte fell from $0.40 to $0.05, cost per month for a T1 high-speed data transmission line fell from $475 to $420, and even copper fell from $0.90 to $0.70 per pound.[1]

During the same period, Corning fibre-optic cable became essentially free to anyone who would carry it off. In short, as these input suppliers grew to serve the expanding product markets in computer equipment and telecom devices, they encountered new productivity from learning curves and innovative design breakthroughs that drove down their costs. And since the computer chip, memory device, and telecom equipment markets tend to be highly competitive, the cost savings of input suppliers like AMD and Corning get passed along to the final product producers like Sun Microsystems, PC-assembler Dell, cell-phone manufacturer Nokia, and router manufacturer Cisco. Consequently, generally lower costs for all inputs have offset in large part the advantage from increasing returns in promotion and selling expenses for companies like Microsoft, Dell, and Palm.

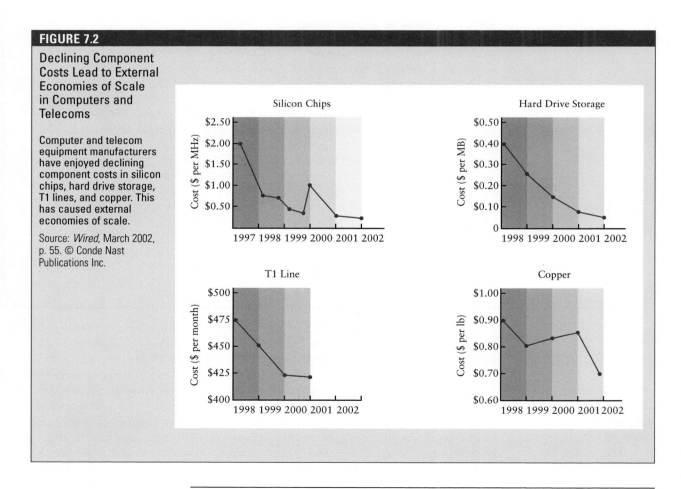

FIGURE 7.2

Declining Component Costs Lead to External Economies of Scale in Computers and Telecoms

Computer and telecom equipment manufacturers have enjoyed declining component costs in silicon chips, hard drive storage, T1 lines, and copper. This has caused external economies of scale.

Source: *Wired*, March 2002, p. 55. © Conde Nast Publications Inc.

---

[1] This commodity is traded internationally in U.S. cents per pound.

PILOT ERROR AT PALM*

For more information on these companies see **www.palm.com** and **www.blackberry.com**.

Palm Pilot, the once-dominant product in hand-held computers, demonstrates how fragile is the position of even an industry leader with increasing returns to promotional spending in a technology business. Despite having 80 percent of the hand-held operating system market and despite producing 60 percent of the hand-held hardware at its peak in 2000, Palm Inc. has lost market share to rivals, especially to the BlackBerry by Canadian producer Research in Motion.

Palm experienced growth so fast (165 percent year-over-year sales increases) that it gave little attention to operational issues such as managing the supply of inputs and forecasting demand. When in 2001 it mistimed the announcement of its m500-series product upgrades, which were delayed by supply chain bottlenecks, the customers stopped buying older models. Handspring, Sony, Hewlett-Packard, Microsoft's Pocket PC, and the popular BlackBerry drove prices lower and offered newer product features. Almost overnight, excess Palm IV and V inventory piled up on shelves, and inquiries about Microsoft's Pocket PC shot way up. Customers were awaiting the new model, and Palm was forced to take a $300 million write-down on its inventory losses. The share price fell from $25 to $2.

* Based on "How Palm Tumbled," *The Wall Street Journal*, September 7, 2001, p. A1.

Third, technology products whose primary value lies in their intellectual property—products like computer software, pharmaceuticals, and telecom networks—have revenue sources that are dependent on renewals of governmental licensures and product standards. Unlike autos or steel, once R&D costs have been recouped, the marginal cost of additional copies of the software, additional doses of the medicine, or additional users on the wireless system are close to zero. Every single unit sold thereafter is close to pure profit. Consequently, competitor firms who have incurred the up-front fixed costs but not succeeded in reaching the inflection point of increasing returns rationally spend enormous sums seeking to obtain these rents through the political process and in the courts. For example, Netscape and Sun succeeded during Microsoft's long antitrust trial of 1997–2002 in placing conduct restrictions on their competitor—e.g., restrictions on Microsoft's installation agreements for Windows, and prohibition of Microsoft's refusal to deal with Windows licensees who install Netscape's competing Web browser software.

How can firms get around the inflection point of Figure 7.1 and achieve increasing returns? Free trials for a limited period of use are one approach. Another is giving the technology away if it can be bundled with other revenue-generating product offerings. Microsoft was able to give Internet Explorer (IE) away for free without running the danger of a predatory pricing indictment because IE's variable cost was $0.004. That is, it rounded to zero. Another approach is to undertake consolidation mergers and acquisitions. This strategy underlaid IBM's acquisition of Lotus in 1995 and Oracle's hostile takeover of PeopleSoft in 2003. Some companies like Sun Microsystems also employ Java programming subsidies to independent software vendors whose applications will provide network effects as complements to Sun's Java-based operating system. Finally, securing the mandatory adoption of an industry standard favourable to your own product is a path to increasing returns. Motorola continues to work toward this end with its HDTV standard for the North American market.

Price and Output Determination for a Monopolist

Recall that the demand curve facing a pure monopolist is the same as the industry demand curve because one firm constitutes the entire industry. The price–output decision for a profit-maximizing monopolist is illustrated in Figure 7.3.

Just as in pure competition, profit is maximized at the price and output combination where $MC = MR$. This corresponds to a price of P_1, output of Q_1, and total profits equal to BC profit per unit times Q_1 units. For a negative-sloping demand curve, the MR function is not the same as the demand function. In fact, for any linear negatively sloping demand function, the marginal revenue function will have the same intercept on the P-axis as the demand function and a slope that is twice as great as that of the demand function. If, for example, the demand function was of the form

$$P = a - bQ$$

then

$$\text{Total revenue} = TR = P \cdot Q$$
$$= aQ - bQ^2$$

and

$$MR = \frac{dTR}{dQ} = a - 2bQ$$

The slope of the demand function is $-b$, and the slope of the MR function is $-2b$.

FIGURE 7.3

Price and Output Determination: Pure Monopoly

The monopolist sets $MR = MC$, which determines the output level Q_1. From the demand curve, this output level determines the price P_1. The monopolist earns a unit profit given by the length of the line segment BC. Note that the monopolist can earn this economic profit even in the long run if the monopolist can sustain the monopoly.

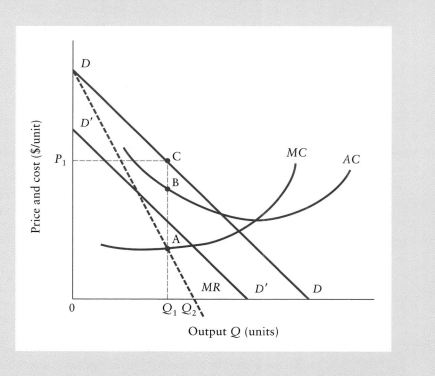

PROFIT MAXIMIZATION: MONOPOLY

Assume a monopolist is faced with the following demand function:

$$Q = 400 - 20P$$

and total cost function:

$$TC = 100 + 5Q + \frac{Q^2}{50}$$

To maximize profits, it would produce and sell that output where $MC = MR$, and charge the corresponding price:

$$MC = \frac{dTC}{dQ} = 5 + \frac{Q}{25}$$

MR may be found by rewriting the demand function in terms of Q:

$$P = \frac{-Q}{20} + 20$$

and then multiplying by Q to find TR:

$$TR = P \cdot Q$$

$$= -\frac{Q^2}{20} + 20Q$$

$$MR = \frac{dTR}{dQ} = -\frac{Q}{10} + 20$$

Setting $MR = MC$ yields

$$-\frac{Q^*}{10} + 20 = 5 + \frac{Q^*}{25}$$

$$Q^* = 107 \text{ units}$$

Substituting Q^* back into the demand equation, we may solve for P^*:

$$P^* = \frac{-107}{20} + 20$$

$$= \$14.65/\text{unit}$$

Hence, the profit-maximizing monopolist would produce 107 units and charge a price of \$14.65 each. This yields a profit of

$$\pi^* = TR - TC$$

$$= (P^* \cdot Q^*) - \left(100 + 5Q^* + \frac{Q^{*2}}{50}\right)$$

$$= 14.65(107) - \left(100 + 5(107) + \frac{(107)^2}{50}\right)$$

$$= \$703.57$$

The Importance of Price Elasticity of Demand

Recall from Chapter 3 that marginal revenue (MR), the incremental change in total revenue arising from one more unit sale, can be expressed in terms of price (P) and the price elasticity (E_D), or

(7.1)
$$MR = P\left(1 + \frac{1}{E_D}\right)$$

Equating MR with MC (as shown in Figure 7.3) yields the profit-maximizing relationship in terms of price and price elasticity, or

(7.2)
$$MC = P\left(1 + \frac{1}{E_D}\right)$$

For the monopoly case, price will be greater than marginal cost. For example, if price elasticity $E_D = -2.0$, price will equal

$$MC = P\left(1 + \frac{1}{-2}\right)$$

$$MC = 0.5P$$

$$P = 2MC$$

Note from Equation 7.2 that a monopolist should never operate in the area of the demand curve where demand is price inelastic (i.e., $|E_D| < 1$). If the absolute value of price elasticity is less than 1 ($|E_D| < 1$), then the reciprocal of price elasticity ($1/E_D$) will be less than minus 1 and marginal revenue [$P(1 + \frac{1}{E_D})$] will be negative. In Figure 7.3, the inelastic range of output is output beyond level Q_2. A negative marginal revenue means that total revenue can be increased by reducing output (through an increase in price). But we know that reducing output must also reduce total costs, thus resulting in an increase in profit. Hence a firm would continue to raise prices (and reduce output) as long as the price elasticity of demand is in the inelastic range. Therefore, for a monopolist, the price–output combination that maximizes profits must occur where $|E_D| \geq 1$.

Equation 7.2 also can be used to show that the more elastic the demand (suggesting the existence of better substitutes), the lower the price (relative to marginal cost) any given firm can charge. This relationship can be illustrated with the "Price Elasticity and Price Levels for Monopolists" example below.

Optimal Markup, Contribution Margin, and the Contribution Margin Percentage

Sometimes it proves useful and convenient to express these relationships among optimal price, price elasticity, and marginal cost as a cost markup percentage and as a contribution margin percentage. Rearranging Equation 7.2 to solve for optimal price yields

(7.3)
$$P = \frac{E_D}{(E_D + 1)}MC$$

where the multiplier term ahead of MC is 1.0 plus the cost markup percentage.[2] For example, the case of $E_D = -3$ is a product with a $-3/(-3 + 1) = 1.5$ multiplier—that is, a 50 percent cost markup. The optimal profit-maximizing price recovers the marginal cost and then marks up MC another 50 percent. If $MC = \$6$, this item would sell for $1.5 \times \$6 = \$9$ and the profit-maximizing cost markup is \$3, or 50 percent more than the marginal cost.

EXAMPLE

PRICE ELASTICITY AND PRICE LEVELS FOR MONOPOLISTS

Consider a monopolist with the following total cost function:

$$TC = 10 + 5Q$$

The marginal cost (MC) function is

$$MC = dTC/dQ = 5$$

The price elasticity of demand has been estimated to be -2.0. Setting $MC = MR$ (where MR is expressed as in Equation 7.1)

results in the following price rule for a profit-maximizing monopolist:

$$MC = \$5 = P(1 + 1/-2.0) = MR$$
$$P = 5/(0.5) = \$10/\text{unit}$$

If, however, demand is more price elastic, such as $E_D = -4.0$, the profit-maximizing monopolist would set the price at

$$P = \$5/(0.75) = \$6.67/\text{unit}$$

---

[2] The symbol MC may be understood to refer to the accountant's narrow definition of *variable costs*, operating costs that vary with the least aggregated unit sale in the business plan.

The difference between price and marginal cost (i.e., the absolute dollar size of the markup) is often referred to as the "contribution margin." That is, since incremental variable costs are already covered, these additional dollars are available to contribute to covering fixed cost and earning a profit. They are often expressed as a percentage of the total price (**contribution margin percentage**). In the previous example, the $3 cost markup above and beyond the $6 marginal cost represents a 33 percent contribution to fixed cost and profit. That is, a 33 percent contribution margin on the $9 item. To summarize, an elasticity of -3.0 implies that the profit-maximizing cost markup is 50 percent, and that 50 percent cost markup implies a 33 percent contribution margin. Using Equation 7.3 and $E_D = -3$,

Contribution Margin Percentage

The difference between the profit-maximizing price and marginal cost, often expressed as a percentage of the price. When more than one unit sale is involved, contribution margin is the difference between revenue and incremental variable cost.

$$\frac{(P - MC)}{P} = \frac{1.5MC - 1.0MC}{1.5MC}$$

$$\text{Contribution Margin \%} = \frac{0.5}{1.5} = 33\%$$

Price elasticity information therefore conveys implications for the marketing plan. Combining the contribution margin percentage (33 percent) with incremental variable cost information indicates what dollar cost markups and product prices to announce.

Thus, the more elastic the demand function for a monopolist's output, the lower the price that will be charged, *ceteris paribus*. At the limit, consider the case of a firm in pure competition with a perfectly elastic (horizontal) demand curve. In this case, the price elasticity of demand approaches $-\infty$. Hence, 1 divided by the price elasticity approaches 0 and marginal revenue in Equation 7.1 becomes equal to price. Thus, the profit-maximizing rule in Equation 7.2 becomes "Set price equal to marginal cost" and the profit-maximizing markup in Equation 7.3 is zero—i.e., the marginal cost multiplier is 1.0. Of course, this is the same price–cost solution developed in Chapter 6 in the discussion of price determination under pure competition.

Components of the Gross Profit Margin

Gross profit margin (or just "gross margin") is a term often used in manufacturing to refer to the contribution margin further reduced by *direct* fixed costs. For example, in a carpet plant, the gross margin on each product line would be the plant's wholesale revenue minus the sum of variable costs plus machinery setup costs for the production runs involving that type of carpet. A manufacturer's income statement identifies variable costs plus direct fixed manufacturing cost as the "direct cost of goods sold" (DCGS). Thus, the gross margin is revenue minus direct cost of goods sold.[3]

Gross Profit Margin

Revenue minus the sum of variable cost plus direct fixed cost, also known as "direct costs of goods sold" in manufacturing.

Gross profit margins differ across industries and across firms within the same industry for a variety of reasons. First, some industries are more capital-intensive than others. Airlines have 70 to 80 percent gross profit margins, not because they are particularly profitable relative to other industries, but because airlines have high indirect fixed costs. The capital asset cost of the aircraft is a large proportion of the total cost structure. An essential distinction arises, therefore, between operating profits (net income on an income statement) and net cash flow available to owners after interest and other fixed costs for capital assets have been paid. The first component of the gross profit margin percentage, then, is capital costs per sales dollar.

Second, differences in gross margins reflect differences in advertising, promotion, and selling costs. Leading brands in the ready-to-eat cereal industry have 70 percent

---

[3] The gross margin definition can be applied to retail firms but not to service firms whose direct cost of goods sold is undefined by accountants. In services, the contribution margin definition of unit profit is prevalent, and activity-based costing (ABC) determines what costs are variable to a product line or an account.

COMPONENTS OF THE GROSS MARGIN AT KELLOGG CO.*

For more information on the Kellogg Company, go to **www.kelloggs.com**.

The largest box of Kellogg's Raisin Bran sells at a 70 percent gross margin. The margin on Frosted Flakes is 72 percent; on Fruit Loops, 68 percent; and across all Kellogg's brands, 55 percent. These high margins reflect brand loyalties built up over many years by massive and continuous advertising investments. On the leading brands, Kellogg spends 30 percent of each sales dollar on advertising and adds another 5 percent on couponing, slot-in shelf space allowances, rebates, and other promotional expenses. Capital costs entail approximately 22 percent per sales dollar. Expenditures on headquarters, general administrative, R&D, and all other over-

heads total 8 percent. That leaves a net profit margin of about 5 percent.

Successful restaurants have almost twice the gross margin of convenience stores on food items sold (60 percent versus 32 percent), and much of that differential (perhaps 25 percent) reflects net profit. Not so in Kellogg's business where, as we have seen, most of its 70 percent gross margin goes to recover advertising, capital equipment, and other fixed costs. The much higher net profit margin in a successful restaurant is a reward for bearing high-failure risk. Long term, the incidence of success in restaurants is really quite low. Three out of five lose money.

* Based on "Cereals," *Winston-Salem Journal,* March 8, 1995, p. A1, and "Denial in Battle Creek," *Forbes,* October 7, 1996, pp. 44–46.

gross margins but half of that price–cost differential (fully 35 percent of every sales dollar) is spent on advertising and promotion. The automobile industry also spends hundreds of millions of dollars on advertising but only 9 percent per sales dollar. The second component of the gross profit margin percentage is advertising and selling expenses per sales dollar.

Third, differences in gross margins arise because of differential overhead in some businesses. The pharmaceutical industry has very high gross margins, in large part because of the enormous expenditures on research and development to find new drugs. To conduct business in that product line, other pharmaceutical firms then incur patent fees and licensing costs, which raise their overhead costs and set the industry-level prices. Overhead costs also may differ if headquarters salaries and other general administrative expenses are high in certain firms but not others.

Finally, after accounting for any differences in capital costs, selling expenses, or overheads, the remaining differences in gross margins do reflect differential profitability.

Monopoly and Capacity Investment

Because monopolists do not face the discipline of strong competition, they install excess capacity or, alternatively, fail to install enough capacity. Indeed, a monopolist seeking to restrain entry of new competitors into the industry may install excess capacity that can be used to credibly threaten to flood the market with supply and lower prices, thus making entry less attractive to potential competitors. Even in regulated monopolies such as electric utility companies, considerable evidence shows that regulation often provides incentives for a firm to overinvest or underinvest in generating capacity.

Because utilities are regulated so that they have an opportunity to earn a "fair" rate of return on their assets, if the allowed return is greater (less) than the firm's true cost of capital, there is an incentive to overinvest (underinvest) in new plant and equipment.

Limit Pricing

Maximizing *short-run* profits by setting marginal revenue equal to marginal cost in order to yield an optimal output of Q_1 and an optimal price of P_1 may not necessarily maximize the *long-run* profits (or shareholder wealth) of the firm. By keeping prices high and earning monopoly profits, the dominant firm encourages potential competitors to commit R&D or advertising resources in an effort to obtain a share of these profits. Instead of charging the short-run profit-maximizing price, the monopolist firm may decide to engage in *limit pricing*, where it charges a lower price, such as P_L in Figure 7.4, in order to discourage entry into the industry by potential rivals. With a limit-pricing strategy, the firm foregoes some of its short-run monopoly profits in order to maintain its monopoly position in the long run. The limit price, such as P_L in Figure 7.4, was set below the minimum point on a potential competitor's average total cost curve, (AC_{pc}). The appropriate limit price is a function of many different factors.[4]

The effect of the two different pricing strategies on the dominant firm's profit stream is illustrated in Figure 7.5. By charging the (higher) short-run profit-maximizing price, the firm's profits are likely to decline over time at a faster rate (panel a) than by charging

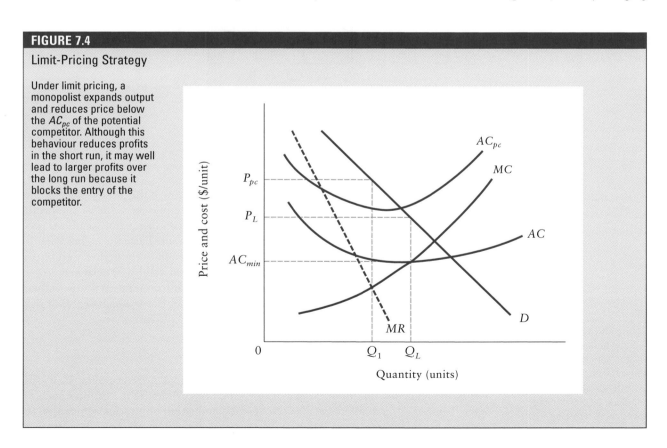

FIGURE 7.4

Limit-Pricing Strategy

Under limit pricing, a monopolist expands output and reduces price below the AC_{pc} of the potential competitor. Although this behaviour reduces profits in the short run, it may well lead to larger profits over the long run because it blocks the entry of the competitor.

---

[4] The limit-pricing model illustrates the importance of *potential* competition as a control device on existing firms. See D. Carlton and J. Perloff, *Modern Industrial Organization*, 3rd ed. (New York: HarperCollins, 1999), Chapter 10, for an expanded discussion of the limit-pricing concept.

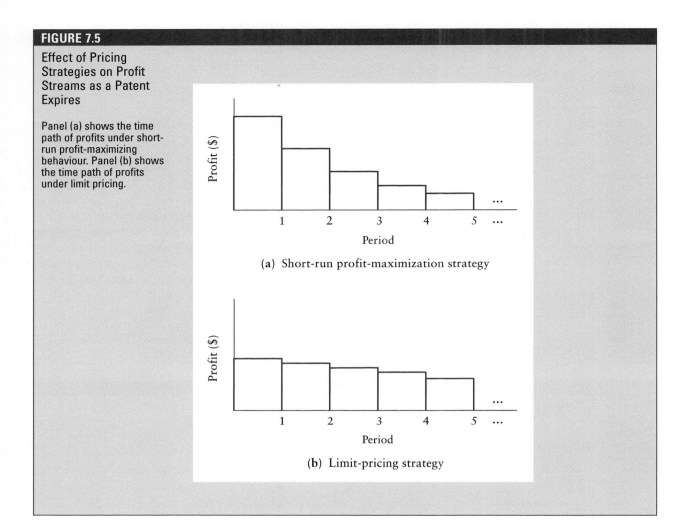

FIGURE 7.5

Effect of Pricing Strategies on Profit Streams as a Patent Expires

Panel (a) shows the time path of profits under short-run profit-maximizing behaviour. Panel (b) shows the time path of profits under limit pricing.

(a) Short-run profit-maximization strategy

(b) Limit-pricing strategy

a limit price (panel b). The firm should engage in limit pricing if the present value of the profit stream from the limit-pricing strategy exceeds the present value of the profit stream associated with the short-run profit-maximization rule of equating marginal revenue and marginal cost. Short-run profit maximization is more likely the higher the discount rate is. Choosing a high discount rate will place relatively higher weight on near-term profits in the calculation of present discounted value and relatively lower weight on profits that occur further into the future. A high discount rate is justified when the firm's long-term pricing policy and, hence, profits are subject to a high degree of risk or uncertainty. The higher the risk, the higher the appropriate discount rate.

Regulated Monopolies[5]

Several important industries in Canada operate as regulated monopolies. In broad terms, the regulated monopoly sector of the economy includes **public utilities** such as electric power companies, natural gas companies, and communications companies. In the past, much of the transportation industry (especially airlines and trucking) also was regulated closely, but these industries have been substantially deregulated over the past 10 to 25 years.

Public Utilities
A group of firms, mostly in the electric power, natural gas, and communications industries, that are closely regulated by one or more government agencies. The agencies control entry into the business, set prices, establish product quality standards, and influence the total profits that may be earned by the firms.

---

[5] Government regulation is covered in more detail in Chapter 11.

LIMIT PRICING TO DISCOURAGE GENERIC DRUGS: BRISTOL-MYERS SQUIBB*

Current financial information on Bristol-Myers Squibb is available at **www.bms.com/ investors/data**.

For more information on generic drug companies, go to **www.cdma-acfpp.org** (Canadian Generic Pharmaceutical Association), **www.apotex.com** (Apotex Inc.), and **www.cangene.com** (Cangene).

Patent protection is the key to financial success in the pharmaceutical industry. The typical patented drug emerges from tests on 250 chemical compounds, requires 15 years of research and governmental approval processes, and accumulates total costs of entry averaging $350 million.

Capoten is a Bristol-Myers Squibb (BMS) hypertension drug for use in reducing heart attack risk. Rather than limit pricing, BMS maintained Capoten's 57-cents-per-pill price right to the end of its 20-year patent protection in February 1996. Competition from generic drug companies, such as Apotex and Cangene, was swift and disastrously effective. BMS introduced its own generic product, which cannibalized sales of the branded product still further. By the fourth quarter of 1996, Capoten sales had collapsed to $25 million from $146 million the year before. BMS and other leading pharmaceutical companies are merging to realize economies of scale in R&D in the hope that a full pipeline of follow-on drugs with improved efficacy or reduced side effects can restore their profitability.

In contrast, Eli Lilly and Schering-Plough chose limit pricing and advertising for their leading medications, the antidepressant Prozac and the allergy treatment Claritin. Prozac lost patent protection in 2001, and Claritin in 2003. One reason Schering-Plough chose a different (limit) pricing strategy is that Claritin has no improved follow-on drug available. Furthermore, the government has demoted the prescription-only product to over-the-counter status at an identical dosage. As a consequence $100-per-month-per-patient revenue was projected to decline to $9 if short-run profit maximization continued. At a gross profit margin of 79 percent, Schering-Plough was facing a monumental loss of $2.1 billion in operating profits on $2.7 billion in Claritin sales.

In general, new biotechnologies have allowed imitation pharmaceuticals to appear much faster in the 1990s than in earlier decades. Indeed, the first hypertension drug, Inderal, enjoyed almost a decade (from 1968–1977) of pure monopoly sales before Capoten was introduced. Prozac, on the other hand, met competition from imitators within four years of its 1988 introduction. And Recombinate, a breakthrough drug for hemophiliacs patented in 1992, encountered copycat products by 1994. Tactics like limit pricing become all the more important in the presence of such quick and relatively easy imitation by fast-second competitors.

---

* Based on "Too Clever by Half," *The Economist,* September 20, 1997, p. 68; "Time's Up," *The Wall Street Journal,* August 12, 1997, p. A1; "Industry Merger Wave Heads to Europe," *The Wall Street Journal,* November 12, 1999, p. A15; "Wearing Off: Schering-Plough Faces A Future Without Claritin," *The Wall Street Journal,* March 22, 2002, p. A1.

Electric Power Companies

Investor-owned electric power companies, such as ATCO Electric, make up one large industry subject to economic regulation. Electric power is made available to the consumer through a production process characterized by three distinct stages. First, the power is generated in generating plants. Next, in the transmission stage, the power is transmitted at high voltage from the generating site to the locality where it is used. Finally, in the distribution stage, the power is distributed to the individual users. The complete process may take place as part of the operations of a single firm, or the producing firm may sell power at wholesale rates to a second enterprise that carries out the distribution function. In the latter case, the distribution firm often is a Crown corporation within the municipal government, serving the locality or a consumers' cooperative.

Firms producing electric power are subject to regulation at several levels. Integrated firms carrying out all three stages of production are usually regulated by public utility commissions.[6] These commissions set the rates to be charged to the final consumers. The firms normally receive exclusive rights to serve individual localities through franchises granted by local governing bodies. As a consequence of their franchises, electric power companies have well-defined markets within which they are the sole providers of output.

Natural Gas Companies

A second energy industry with extensive regulation is the natural gas industry. The furnishing of natural gas to users also includes a three-stage process. The first stage is the production of the gas in the field. Transportation to the consuming locality through pipelines is the second stage. Distribution to the final user makes up the third stage. The distribution function may be carried out by a private firm or by a government agency. In either event, the rates charged to final users also are controlled because the distribution firm often has a monopoly in its service area.

Communications Companies

In the communications industry, the most important activities are the provision of radio, cable, television, and telephone service regulated by the Canadian Radio-television and Telecommunications Commission (CRTC).

The Economic Rationale for Regulation

The preceding brief survey of the regulated sector reveals the crucial nature of the regulated industries: They furnish services that are critical to the functioning of the economy. Apart from this factor, do the regulated industries share any other common characteristics that account for the regulation imposed on them? This question can be answered by considering the major reasons cited as justifications for instituting economic regulation.

Natural Monopoly Argument

Natural Monopoly
An industry in which maximum economic efficiency is obtained when the firm produces, distributes, and transmits all of the commodity or service produced in that industry. The production of natural monopolists is typically characterized by increasing returns to scale throughout the range of output demanded by the market.

It is frequently asserted that firms operating in the regulated sector are **natural monopolies,** indicating that a tendency exists for a single supplier to emerge because of a production process characterized by increasing returns to scale. Increasing returns to scale imply that as all inputs are increased by a given percentage, the average total cost of a unit of output decreases. Consequently, the long-run unit cost of output declines throughout the range of output levels that is relevant. This situation is illustrated in Figure 7.6 for a firm in long-run stable equilibrium.

Suppose that the market demand curve for output is represented by the curve D in Figure 7.6. The socially optimal level of output would then be Q^*. At that level of output, price would be well below the average total cost per unit AC^* but equal to long-run marginal cost. A single producer is able to realize economies of scale that are unavailable to firms in the presence of competition. From a social perspective, competition would result

---

[6] "Public Utility Commission" is the generic term for the governmental regulatory agency; however, the exact nomenclature varies. The regulatory body in Alberta is the Alberta Energy and Utilities Board (EUB). In Ontario, it is the Ontario Energy Board (OEB).

FIGURE 7.6

Natural Monopoly: Price–Output Determination

If the regulator sets the regulated price equal to marginal cost, then the monopolist would be operating at an economic loss of $(AC^* - P^*)Q^*$. Eventually, the monopolist would exit the industry. To sustain the monopolist, the regulator must provide a subsidy or require users to pay a lump sum access fee that offsets this loss.

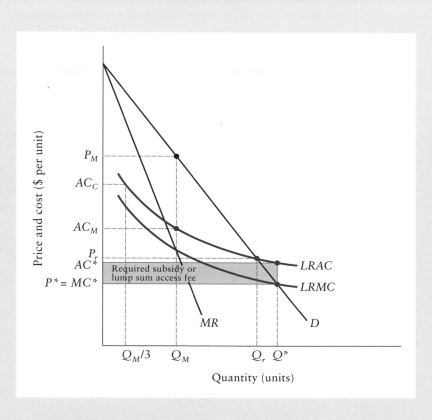

in inefficiency in the form of higher costs. For example, unit cost AC_C in Figure 7.6 is much higher than the monopoly unit cost AC_M. It often is argued that if there are production relations like those shown in Figure 7.6, a single supplier will eventually emerge. Competing firms will realize that their costs decrease as output expands. As a consequence, they will have an incentive to cut prices as long as MR exceeds $LRMC$. The weaker firms gradually leave the industry, until only a single producer remains. Thus, competitive forces contribute to the emergence of the natural monopoly.

If a monopolistic position were to exist in the absence of regulation, the monopolist would maximize profit by equating marginal revenue and marginal cost at an output like Q_M, leading to a higher price, P_M, and lower output. Thus, intervention through regulation is required to achieve the benefits of the most efficient organization of production. In its simplest form, this is the explanation of regulation based on the existence of natural monopolies.

Figure 7.6 illustrates one ever-present problem that arises in the presence of a genuine natural monopoly. Suppose that a regulatory agency succeeds in establishing the socially optimal price for output, P^*. As the cost curves indicate, this price would lead to losses for the producing firm, because price would be below the average total cost AC^*. This is obviously an unsustainable result. In this situation, the regulating agency normally sets the price at P_r, which equals $LRAC$ at the output Q_r. (In equilibrium, this will also equal $SRAC$, albeit for a smaller scale of plant than the socially optimal plant that produces the output Q^* at price P^*.) *This ensures revenues sufficient to cover all costs.* The most efficient way to realize said revenue, however, is to charge a per-unit price equal to *LRMC* (*P**) and collect the shaded deficit area in Figure 7.6 as a *lump sum access fee,* perhaps divided equally among the utilities customers. Alternatively, with time-of-day metering, the lump sum access fees can depend on when the customer uses power—higher lump sum access fees at peak periods like 4 P.M. to 8 P.M.

Peak-Load Utility Rates

When output cannot be stored in inventory and the power utility ordinarily stands ready to satisfy whatever level of demand is imposed by users, the cost of producing a unit of output varies according to a time dimension. For simplicity, suppose that there are only two levels of demand: an afternoon peak period when the demand is high and the rest of the day (an off-peak period) when the demand is below the level of afternoon demand. Because of the way in which electricity is produced, the generating capacity required to produce power for the afternoon period stands idle for the remainder of the firm's operating cycle. That is, there is excess generating capacity except during the period when demand is at its peak. The firm can produce additional output during the morning, for instance, at a relatively low marginal cost associated with the cost of the additional fuel used. In contrast, to produce an additional unit of output during the afternoon period, the firm would have to install an additional unit of generating capacity, implying that the marginal cost of that unit of output would be quite high. Because expanding output in the peak period requires the expansion of productive capacity, the basic principle of equating prices to marginal costs suggests that peak and off-peak output be priced differently to reflect the differences in marginal cost.

To analyze what type of pricing policy is appropriate in the presence of peak loads, consider the situation shown in Figure 7.7, where two independent demand periods are assumed. In the peak period (late afternoon), demand is represented by curve D_1, whereas in the off-peak period, demand is shown by D_2. All units of output require the use of fuel at a constant rate, assumed to be *b* per unit. In addition, capital or generating

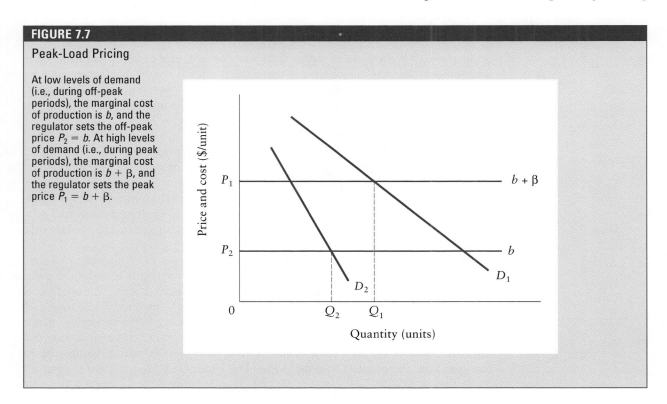

FIGURE 7.7

Peak-Load Pricing

At low levels of demand (i.e., during off-peak periods), the marginal cost of production is *b*, and the regulator sets the off-peak price $P_2 = b$. At high levels of demand (i.e., during peak periods), the marginal cost of production is $b + \beta$, and the regulator sets the peak price $P_1 = b + \beta$.

Dominant Microprocessor Company Lagging Behind Next Trend

Intel's biggest competitor in computer microprocessor chips is AMD. In 2004, AMD's share of the market increased at Intel's expense. AMD not only continued attacking Intel at the lower end but is now also pushing high-end 64-bit microprocessor chips that are hardware-compatible with previous generation 32-bit X86 chips. Initially, Intel wanted to switch to its Itanium 64-bit microprocessor, which is not hardware-compatible with X86 chips. Software for X86 32-bit chips must be run on the Itanium in emulation mode. This is a software solution that runs slowly compared with AMD 64-bit chips that run X86 32-bit software in native mode (i.e., hardware-compatible.)

capacity, which costs β per unit, is also required to produce all output. However, the capacity is not fully used except in the peak period.

The supply curve relevant for determining price and output during the late afternoon is the curve $b + \beta$, which reflects the marginal (and average) cost of supplying an additional unit of output during the peak period. At price $P_1 = b + \beta$, day users are just willing to pay the cost of producing a unit of output, so this is the appropriate price for peak service. At this price, Q_1 units of output are produced, implying that Q_1 is the level of capacity installed. At what price should off-peak output be sold? Given the existence of capacity Q_1, the appropriate price of off-peak output is P_2, equal to the marginal cost of fuel alone. Providing off-peak service imposes no other costs. As a result, the price should be no higher than b per unit at which Q_2 units of output are sold.[7]

This simplified example illustrates the basic principles of **peak-load pricing.** This policy encourages the most efficient use of existing capacity. Notice that in the usual case, users would be expected to purchase both peak and off-peak output, since air-conditioner use between 4 P.M. and 8 P.M. has very price inelastic demand. Peak-load pricing is an example of a two-part tariff. Two-part tariffs are further discussed in Chapter 9, along with other types of price discrimination.

This chapter provides only a brief introduction to government regulation. For a deeper discussion of government regulation, see Chapter 11.

Peak-Load Pricing
The process of charging a higher price during those periods of time when demand is heaviest and lower prices when demand is light.

Summary

- *Monopoly* is a market structure with one firm producing a differentiated product in a market with significant barriers to entry.

- In a *pure monopoly* market structure, firms will generally produce a lower level of output and charge a higher price than would exist in a more competitive market

---

[7] If base-load generation has high capital costs (i.e., if $\beta > b$), peak-load pricing can induce many consumers to shift their clothes drying and some cooking to off-peak times, for example, through the use of interruptible service or highly efficient water heaters that allow customers to heat water at night, rather than on demand. If this occurs, the peak period may be shifted to the current off-peak period. Of course, under these circumstances, the original peak-load prices will be incorrect. The solution is to charge a fraction of the capital cost during each period.

structure. This conclusion assumes no significant economies of scale that might make a monopolist more efficient than a large group of smaller firms.

- The primary sources of monopoly power include patents and copyrights, control of critical resources, government "franchise" grants, economies of scale, and increasing returns in networks of users of compatible complementary products.

- Increasing returns from network effects are limited by input cost reductions among competitors, by innovative new product introductions, and by lobbying efforts.

- Monopolists will produce at that level of output where marginal cost equals marginal revenue if their goal is to maximize short-run profits.

- The price charged by a profit-maximizing monopolist will be in that portion of the demand function where demand is elastic (or unit elastic). The greater the elasticity of demand facing a monopolist, the lower will be its price relative to marginal cost, *ceteris paribus.*

- *Contribution margins* are defined as revenue minus incremental variable cost, or revenue minus marginal cost when only one unit is sold.

- *Contribution margins* and *markups* are inversely related to the price elasticity of demand.

- *Gross margins* are defined as revenue minus direct costs of goods sold (incremental variable cost plus direct fixed cost) and serve to recover capital costs, selling costs, and overhead, as well as earn profits.

- *Limit pricing* is a strategy followed by some monopolists to discourage rivals from entering an industry. The monopolist prices its product below the short-run profit-maximizing level to forestall new entry in the long run.

- *Public utilities* are a group of firms, mostly in the electric power, natural gas distribution, natural gas pipeline, and communications industries that are closely regulated with respect to entry into the business, prices, service quality, and total profits.

- The rationales for public utility regulation are many. The *natural monopoly* argument is applied in cases where a product is characterized by increasing returns to scale. The one large firm can theoretically furnish the good or service at a lower cost than a group of smaller competitive firms. Regulators then set utility rates to prevent monopoly price gouging, ideally allowing the regulated firm to earn a return on investment just equal to its cost of capital.

- *Price discrimination* by utilities is often economically desirable on the basis of cost justifications and demand justifications.

- *Peak-load pricing* is designed to charge customers a greater amount for the services they use during periods of greater demand. Long-distance telephone services typically have been priced on a peak-load basis.

Self-Test Exercises

1. You have been retained as an analyst to evaluate a proposal by a privately owned municipal water company to increase its rates by 100 percent. The firm has argued that at the present rate level, it is earning only a 2 percent rate of return on invested equity capital. The firm believes a 16 percent rate of return is required in today's capital markets. Assume that you agree with the 16 percent rate of return proposed by the company.

   a. What factors need to be considered when setting rates designed to achieve this objective?

  b. Would your analysis differ if you knew that individuals were prohibited by law from drilling their own wells? What impact would this have on the price elasticity of demand?

  c. Water companies have a large proportion of fixed costs as compared with variable costs. How does this fact influence your analysis?

2. A monopolist faces the following demand function for its product:

$$Q = 45 - 5P$$

The fixed costs of the monopolist are $12 and the monopolist incurs variable costs of $5.00 per unit.

  a. What is the profit-maximizing level of price and quantity for this monopolist? What will profits be at this price and output level?

  b. If the government imposes a franchise tax on the firm of $10, what will be the profit-maximizing level of price, output, and profits?

  c. If the government imposes an excise tax of 50 cents per unit of output sold, what is the impact on the profit-maximizing level of price, output, and profits?

  d. If the government imposes a ceiling of $6 on the price of the firm's product, what output will the firm produce and what will be its total profits?

Exercises

1. If the regulatory process is working effectively, the aggregate of all projects undertaken by a nondiversified electric utility firm should have a net present value that equals zero. Why is this true?

2. Calgary Electric has a cost of equity capital of 16 percent. The firm has consistently been authorized a return on equity capital below this cost. Also, the effects of regulatory lag and attrition have further reduced the realized return to the 13 percent range. If the utility expects this problem to continue, what actions would you expect Calgary Electric to take or not take as a result?

3. Ajax Cleaning Products is a medium-sized firm operating in an industry dominated by one very large firm—Tile King. Ajax produces a multiheaded tunnel wall scrubber that is very similar to a model produced by Tile King. Ajax has decided to charge the same price as Tile King to avoid the possibility of a price war. The price charged by Tile King is $20,000.

  Ajax has the following short-run cost curve:

$$TC = 800{,}000 - 5{,}000Q + 100Q^2$$

  a. Compute the marginal cost curve for Ajax.

  b. Given Ajax's pricing strategy, what is the marginal revenue function for Ajax?

  c. Compute the profit-maximizing level of output for Ajax.

  d. Compute Ajax's total dollar profits.

4. One and Only, Inc., is a monopolist. The demand function for its product is estimated to be

$$Q = 60 - 0.4P + 6Y + 2A$$

where Q = quantity of units sold

   P = price per unit

   Y = per capita disposable personal income (thousands of dollars)

   A = hundreds of dollars of advertising expenditures

The firm's average variable cost function is

$$AVC = Q^2 - 10Q + 60$$

Y is equal to 3 (thousand) and A is equal to 3 (hundred) for the period being analyzed.

a. If fixed costs are equal to $1,000, derive the firm's total cost function and marginal cost function.

b. Derive a total revenue function and marginal revenue function for the firm.

c. Calculate the profit-maximizing level of price and output for One and Only.

d. What profit or loss will One and Only earn?

e. If fixed costs were $1,200, how would your answers change for parts (a) through (d)?

5. The Lumins Lamp Company, a producer of old-style oil lamps, has estimated the following demand function for its product:

$$Q = 120,000 - 10,000P$$

where Q is the quantity demanded per year and P is the price per lamp. The firm's fixed costs are $12,000 and variable costs are $1.50 per lamp.

a. Write an equation for the total revenue (TR) function in terms of Q.

b. Specify the marginal revenue function.

c. Write an equation for the total cost (TC) function in terms of Q.

d. Specify the marginal cost function.

e. Write an equation for total profits (π) in terms of Q. At what level of output (Q) are total profits maximized? What price will be charged? What are total profits at this output level?

f. Check your answers in part (e) by equating the marginal revenue and marginal cost functions, determined in parts (b) and (d), and solving for Q.

g. What model of market pricing behaviour has been assumed in this problem?

6. Unique Creations has a monopoly position in the production and sale of magnometers. The cost function facing Unique has been estimated to be

$$TC = \$100,000 + 20Q$$

a. What is the marginal cost for Unique?

b. If the price elasticity of demand for Unique is currently -1.5, what price should Unique charge?

c. What is the marginal revenue at the price computed in part (b)?

d. If a competitor develops a substitute for the magnometer and the price elasticity increases to -3.0, what price should Unique charge?

7. What motivation does a monopolist have to overinvest in plants and equipment? What factors might restrain the monopolist from such overinvesting?

8. A firm faces a demand function per day of

$$P = 29 - 2Q$$

and a total cost function of

$$TC = 20 + 7Q$$

a. Calculate the profit-maximizing price, output, and profit levels for this firm if it is not regulated.

b. If regulators set the maximum price the firm may charge equal to the firm's marginal cost, what output level will be produced and what will be the level of profits?

    c. If regulators seek to equate total costs (including a fair return to invested capital) with total revenues, what output level will be produced and what price will be charged?

9. The Oshawa Independent Phone Company (OIPC) is currently engaged in a rate case that will set rates for its area customer base. OIPC has total assets of $20 million. The Public Utility Commission has determined that an 11 percent return on its assets is fair. OIPC has estimated its annual demand function as follows:

$$P = 3,514 - 0.08Q$$

Its total cost function (not including the cost of capital) is

$$TC = 2,300,000 + 130Q$$

    a. OIPC has proposed a rate of $250 per year for each customer. If this rate is approved, what return on assets will OIPC earn?

    b. What rate can OIPC charge if the commission wants to limit the return on assets to 11 percent?

    c. What problem of utility regulation does this exercise illustrate?

CASE EXERCISE

DIFFERENTIAL PRICING OF PHARMACEUTICALS: THE HIV/AIDS CRISIS[8]

The HIV/AIDS crisis has been called the worst pandemic since the fourteenth-century Black Plague. The first incident of HIV/AIDS was discovered in 1981. Over the next two decades, 60 million people would become infected, and 22 million would die. Most HIV/AIDS cases are reported in the developing world, where 95 percent of those with HIV live today. Beyond social welfare and humanitarian concerns, as a result of globalization and the fastest growing international business opportunities in China and India, AIDS is now everybody's business. Because the pharmaceutical industry in particular relies on governmental authority to approve formularies for reimbursement, to protect its monopoly patent rights, and to prevent importation of unauthorized, unlicensed imitation medicines, the question of how to price AIDS drugs is a very public issue.

    Although no one has yet developed a cure for HIV, a number of companies have developed patented drugs that inhibit either the virus's ability to replicate or its ability to enter host cells. Without further drug discovery, however, the best that can be done at present once a person contracts HIV is to partially and temporarily suppress the virus, thus delaying progression of the infection. The drugs that suppress HIV are called antiretrovirals, and the first, known as Retrovir (also known by its generic name zidovudine or AZT), was introduced in 1987 by Burroughs Wellcome (now GlaxoSmithKline) and was the only approved therapy available to treat HIV until 1991. Since then, several

---

[8] E. Berndt, "Pharmaceuticals in U.S. Health Care: Determinants of Quality and Price," and M. Kremer, "Pharmaceuticals and the Developing World," *Journal of Economic Perspectives*, Fall 2002, pp. 45–90.

new antiretrovirals have been developed by large pharmaceutical companies such as Abbott Labs, Bristol-Myers Squibb, Merck, Roche, and smaller biotech companies such as Agouron (now part of Pfizer Inc.), Gilead Sciences, Triangle Pharmaceuticals, and Trimeris. Largely as a result of these drugs, the rate of increase of AIDS-related diseases (e.g., opportunistic infections) dramatically slowed in the United States from 1992–1995 and actually decreased in 1996 for the first time.

Yet, even in the early days of antiretroviral drug development, HIV/AIDS drug pricing was a serious and contentious issue. Burroughs Wellcome faced an enormous wave of protest in the late 1980s in the United States and Europe over its pricing of AZT and subsequently reduced the drug's price by 20 percent in 1987 and by a further 20 percent in 1989. The core problem is the fact that the vast majority of HIV/AIDS cases are outside what the United Nations classifies as "rich countries," such as the United States. North America registered about 980,000 cases of individuals living with HIV/AIDS and fewer than 10,000 deaths due to AIDS in 2002, but the comparative numbers for sub-Saharan Africa were nearly 30 million cases and more than two million deaths in 2002. Similarly, the U.S. adult infection rate was estimated at slightly more than one-half of a percent in 2002 versus almost 9 percent in sub-Saharan Africa, with a high of 38.8 percent in Botswana.

If the affordability of HIV/AIDS drugs in the United States (with a GDP per capita in excess of $30,000) is a serious issue, the problem is even more acute in the hardest-hit countries, where GDP per capita often is less than one-tenth of the U.S. GDP, in many cases even less than $1,000. Compounding the problem is the fact that many new AIDS drugs, especially those designed to attack the growth in drug-resistant HIV, become increasingly expensive. Trimeris and Roche introduced Fuzeon in early 2003, for example, at a wholesale price of €20,245 per annum, at least three times the price of any existing HIV/AIDS drug. The pricing decision sparked immediate protests in the United States and abroad. Even many providers of Medicaid, the state-based health assistance program for the indigent in the United States (and now the buyer of more than 50 percent of HIV/AIDS drugs in the United States), immediately suggested that they could not contemplate how they would possibly pay for such an expensive therapy.

GlaxoSmithKline and Roche, the leading HIV/AIDS drug manufacturers, and their cohorts now find they must balance the fiscal realities of their expensive R&D-intensive business model against enlarged, global, corporate social responsibilities. A nation–state specific pricing policy across global markets has resulted in a tenfold differential between the highest priced market, the United States, and the price charged in the poorest countries. Glaxo and Roche management teams face many serious business-ethics issues in this highly charged environment. Is such a tenfold price differential sustainable? How does one manage the resulting problem of parallel importing and secure trade protection from unauthorized reimportation of export drugs? What should they do if even 90 percent price reductions still leave the therapies too expensive for the majority of patients in less developed countries? Will abrogation of intellectual property in the developing world threaten intellectual property protection at home? Will a public affairs backlash in high-priced markets force drug price discounts? If so, how can the massive R&D investment required for ongoing drug discovery and development be recovered? Are these companies facing such a public relations disaster that their corporate brand equity could be radically affected? What are the corporate responsibilities of big pharmaceutical companies in a public health crisis? Should Glaxo (or Roche) go it alone, or instead pursue collaborative strategies with other big pharmaceutical rivals?

Questions

1. Is the monopoly on patented pharmaceuticals secure? What barrier to entry prevents the reimportation into the United States of pharmaceuticals sold at lower prices in Canada?

2. Analyze the contribution margin percentage on pharmaceuticals relative to ready-to-eat cereals. Identify three reasons why pharmaceutical margins are higher.

3. Suggest an approach to the big pharmaceutical company problem of differential pricing in the United States, Western Europe, and Japan versus the less developed world.

CHAPTER 8

Price and Output Determination: Oligopoly

Chapter Preview

The previous two chapters analyzed price and output decisions of firms that competed in relevant markets where there were either a large number of sellers (i.e., pure competition and monopolistic competition) or essentially no other sellers (i.e., monopoly). In pure competition, the firm made its price and output decisions independently of the decisions of other firms. The monopoly firm did not need to consider the pricing actions of rival firms, because it did not have any competitors.

This chapter examines price and output decisions by firms in oligopoly market structures where there are a small number of competitors, and each firm's decisions are likely to evoke a response from one (or more) of these rival firms. To maximize shareholder wealth, each oligopoly firm must take into account these rival responses in its own decision making. Game-theoretic analysis is introduced to assist in the analysis and prediction of rival responses.

Learning Objectives

After studying this chapter, you should be able to:

1. Define an *oligopoly*.

2. Explain the nature of interdependencies in oligopolistic industries.

3. Explain the importance of the *Cournot, Stackelberg*, and *Bertrand* oligopoly models.

4. Define a *cartel*.

5. Explain the *price leadership* strategy for an oligopolistic industry.

6. Explain the results in the *kinked demand curve* model if an oligopolistic firm reduces its prices.

7. Explain why the firm in a *game-theoretic* analysis of oligopolistic decision making chooses its own best strategy assuming that its competitor(s) will choose its (their) optimal decision-making strategy.

8. Explain how business strategy games may be classified as simultaneous play or sequential play, one-shot or repeated, zero-sum or nonzero-sum, two player or *n* player, and cooperative or noncooperative.

Are Nokia's Margins on Cellphones Collapsing?*

From a stodgy Finnish industrial conglomerate selling everything from rubber boots and wire cable to toilet paper and televisions, Nokia transformed itself into a relentlessly focused technology company. When Sweden's telecommunications equipment giant Ericsson developed a cellular network across Scandinavia in the 1980s, Nokia provided the wireless but bulky radio telephones. Recognizing the strategic opportunity presented by mobile telephony, Nokia spun off other business in the 1990s to rivet its attention on the enormous market potential of a digital (not analog) cellphone. Nokia grew from 22 percent market share in 1985 (about half of Motorola's 45 percent) to overtake the market leader in 1998 and sell 37 percent of the $58 billion in cellphones worldwide by 2002, relative to Motorola's 17 percent. With huge scale economies and a snazzy branded product, Nokia's cellphone margins at 19 percent outstripped Motorola's 5 percent. Ericsson, with margins at −30 percent, decided to join a venture with Sony cellphones and instead focus its efforts on cell transmission towers and equipment. From 1997 to 2000, the share prices of Alcatel, Siemens, and Motorola all doubled, but Nokia's share price grew elevenfold from $5 to $55.

In 2001, however, a disruptive new technology appeared. 3rd Generation Partnership Project (3GPP), a high-speed worldwide mobile phone network, rewrote the telecommunications landscape. European telephone company partners of Nokia went deeply into debt to pay $125 billion for 3GPP licences and spent another $100 billion for 3GPP network equipment. Nokia's share price collapsed from $55 to $15 amid concerns about cellphone margins.

First, the high-speed, data-intensive 3GPP technology allows the introduction of new wireless Web products into the handset marketplace—i.e., hand-held computers by Dell, pocket audio-visual terminals by Palm and Motorola, and game consoles from Sony-Ericsson. Nokia, NEC, and Panasonic have introduced an innovative cellphone with a built-in digital camera. Second, it's not about voice messaging anymore. These enhanced mobile phones will create value principally through their software applications provided by third-party independent software vendors (ISVs). And the ISVs will want their share of the gross margins that have made Nokia so profitable. In contrast, the power of these ISVs was virtually nonexistent in the voice-only mobile phone business.

Third, the developed world is nearly saturated with wireless services, which are achieving 60 percent penetration in some North American and European markets, and demand will consequently be growing at only 10 percent over the next few years, despite Nokia's projections of 25 percent. Furthermore, the next growth spurt in sales will likely come from China and Latin America, where Nokia will have to compete against or ally itself with well-connected or even nationalized telephone companies. This increased power of buyers will also reduce gross margins relative to the situation in the fragmented markets of North America and Western Europe. Fourth, the threat of entry is very real. Two Japanese consumer electronics manufacturers, NEC and Panasonic, have adapted

---

* Based on "Nokia: A Finish Tale," *The Economist,* October 14, 2000, pp. 83–85; "Is Nokia's Star Dimming?" *BusinessWeek,* January 22, 2001, pp. 66–72; and "Nokia Widens Gap," *The Wall Street Journal,* August 20, 2002, p. B6.

For more information on Nokia, go to **www.nokia.com**.

the same 3GPP technology into the first wireless Internet devices. Finally, Nokia's very substantial brand equity is likely to pose a low barrier to entry with these new devices that will likely involve unobtrusive headsets and otherwise remain hidden in pockets.

Should Nokia invest heavily in 3GPP infrastructure and product design? If not, what should the company do?

Oligopolistic Market Structures

An oligopoly is characterized by a relatively small number of firms offering a product or service. The product or service may be differentiated, as in soft drinks, cereals, and athletic shoes, or relatively undifferentiated, as in airlines, crude oil, aluminum, and cement. The distinguishing characteristic of oligopoly is that the number of firms is small enough that actions by any individual firm in the industry on price, output, product style or quality, introduction of new models, and terms of sale have a perceptible impact on the sales of other firms in the industry. Thus, the distinctive feature of oligopoly is the easily recognizable interdependence among the firms in the industry. Each firm is aware in its decision making that any new move, such as introducing a price cut or launching a large promotional campaign, is likely to evoke a countermove from its rivals.

In all oligopoly markets, rival response expectations are therefore the key to firm-level analysis. If rival firms are expected to match price increases and price cuts as in airlines, a share-of-the-market demand curve may characterize adequately the sales response to the pricing initiatives of one of the firms; for example, WestJet in Figure 8.1, panel (a). On the other hand, if rival firms are slow to match price increases and cuts, oligopolists can discount to gain share and will lose share in response to price hikes. In some markets like cellphone service, rivals match price cuts but ignore price increases. Consequently, Telus faces a much more price elastic demand above the going

FIGURE 8.1

Rival Response Expectations Determine Firm Demand

Panel (a) illustrates WestJet's share-of-the-market demand curve in the airline industry where rivals are likely to match any change in fares. Panel (b) illustrates Telus's kinked demand curve where rivals are likely to match any price cut but ignore any price increase in the cellphone industry. Panel (c) is an industry demand curve.

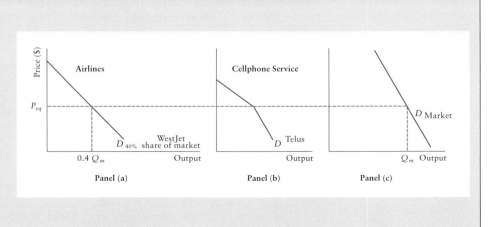

Chapter 8   Price and Output Determination: Oligopoly   **225**

HEWLETT-PACKARD DOMINANCE IN PRINTERS*

For more information on Hewlett Packard, go to **www.hp.com**.

The computer industry has spawned three very evenly distributed share distributions in personal computers, computer storage devices, and database software but in printers, Hewlett-Packard leads a pack of distant followers. At about 49 percent market share, sales of HP printers are five times larger than those of the closest rivals Xerox and Lexmark, which have 10 percent and 8 percent of the market, respectively. The HP business plan for printers calls for a razor-and-blades approach of relatively inexpensive machines followed by a long period of selling lucrative ink and toner replacement cartridges. In 2001, HP printers and supplies made $410 million in operating profits on $5 billion in sales revenue. This represents two-thirds of

HP's $647 million overall profit on only one-tenth of the $49 billion in sales. Despite vicious price wars for market share in the sub-$100 and sub-$200 segments, the printer business has clearly been a cash cow for HP.

On the horizon for high-end products, HP plans to launch a digital printing press to replace the plates and film required today for commercial offset printing. In the mass market targeted by Lexmark, Canon, and Epson, penetration of PCs into North American households and businesses has reached a plateau, but printing volume (and therefore demand for HP supplies) may continue to grow because of the printing of digital photographs and Web pages.

* Based on "HP Sees Room for Growth in Printer Market," *The Wall Street Journal*, June 28, 2001, p. B10.

equilibrium price than the share-of-the-market demand below that price. These asymmetric rival response expectations lead to kinked oligopoly firm demand schedules examined at length later in the chapter and illustrated in Figure 8.1, panel (b).

Oligopoly in Canada

Much of Canadian industry is best classified as oligopolistic in structure with a wide range of industry configurations. In beer, for example, the Molson and Labatt brands together have about 80 percent of the market. In banking, the six largest banks also have about 90 percent of the market. In both industries there are some other smaller competitors. Many Canadian companies compete not only in the domestic market, but in North America and the rest of the world as well. Canadian banks, for example, are among the largest in the Caribbean area.

In soft drinks, however, not one but two firms (Coke and Pepsi) dominate. Duopoly pairs of dominant firms often study complex tactical scenarios of moves and probable countermoves. In still other cases, three firms circle warily, planning their tactical activities. For example, in the tire industry, the market shares of the three largest rivals are Goodyear, 28 percent; Michelin, 23 percent; and Bridgestone/Firestone, 21 percent.

Interdependencies in Oligopolistic Industries

The nature of interdependencies in oligopolistic industries can be illustrated using the airline pricing example on the facing page.

These recognizable interdependencies can lead to varying degrees of competition and cooperation among the oligopolistic firms. At one extreme is the case of intense

AIRLINE PRICING: THE OTTAWA MARKET

Consider the case of the airline route between Ottawa and Vancouver. One can fly this route on Air Canada or WestJet, but on Wednesdays in 2004, only WestJet offered nonstop service between these cities. Air Canada flights, although more numerous during the day, required a stop and change of planes in either Toronto or Montreal, or a stop in Winnipeg en route. Many travellers prefer to avoid these stops and/or a change of planes, if possible. Although WestJet is the discount airline, in this case WestJet's fare was $17 higher than Air Canada's fare, which customers who could travel at the time WestJet departed Ottawa (8 A.M.) were more than happy to pay.

rivalry (i.e., no cooperation), where a firm may seek to drive its competitor(s) out of business. Air Canada did succeed in driving its former competitor, Canadian Airlines, out of business, finally taking it over in January 2000. Canadian Airlines attempted to compete head to head on the major routes with Air Canada. However, there were just not enough passengers to support all the flights that the two airlines scheduled. Thus, many flights flew less than half full. Air Canada's greater financial resources allowed it to win this particular battle.

Alternatively, some form of informal, or tacit, cooperation may take place among the oligopolistic firms—"conscious parallelism of action"—with respect to pricing and other decisions.[1] At the other extreme is a formal collusive agreement among the firms to act as a monopoly cartel (like the OPEC oil cartel) by setting prices to maximize total industry profits. Because of the wide scope of industry configurations that fall under the oligopoly classification, several normative models can be used to describe oligopolists' competitive behaviour regarding price, output, and other conditions surrounding the sale of their products.

Oligopoly Models

The simplistic approach to the interdependency problem among oligopolists is merely to ignore it. That is, for a firm to act as if the problem does not exist at all and assume that competitors will do likewise.

Cournot Model

One oligopoly model, proposed by the French economist Augustin Cournot, asserts that each firm determines its profit-maximizing output level *assuming that the other firm's output will not change.*

For example, suppose that two duopolists (Firms A and B) produce identical products. If Firm A observes Firm B producing Q_B units of output in the current period, then Firm A will seek to maximize its own profits, assuming that Firm B will continue producing the same Q_B units in the next period. Firm B acts in a similar manner: It attempts to maximize its own profits under the assumption that Firm A will continue producing the same amount of output in the next period as Firm A did in the current period. In the Cournot model, this pattern continues until long-run equilibrium is reached—a

---

[1] See F. M. Scherer and David Ross, *Industrial Market Structure and Economic Performance*, 3rd ed. (Chicago, IL: Rand McNally, 1990), pp. 339–346, for a discussion of the conscious parallelism doctrine.

COURNOT OLIGOPOLY SOLUTION: SIEMENS AND THALES

Suppose that two European electronics companies, Siemens (Firm S) and Thales (Firm T), jointly hold a patent on a component used in airport radar systems. Demand for the component is given by the following function:

$$(8.1) \qquad P = 1,000 - Q_S - Q_T$$

where Q_S and Q_T are the quantities sold by the respective firms and P is the (market) selling price. The total cost functions of manufacturing and selling the component for the respective firms are

$$(8.2) \quad TC_S = 70,000 + 5Q_S + 0.25Q_S^2$$
$$(8.3) \quad TC_T = 110,000 + 5Q_T + 0.15Q_T^2$$

Suppose that the two firms act independently, with each firm seeking to maximize its own total profit from the sale of the component.

Siemens' total profit is equal to

$$
\begin{aligned}
\pi_S &= PQ_S - TC_S \\
&= (1,000 - Q_S - Q_T)Q_S - (70,000 \\
&\quad + 5Q_S + 0.25Q_S^2) \\
&= -70,000 + 995Q_S - Q_TQ_S \\
&\quad - 1.25Q_S^2
\end{aligned}
$$

(8.4)

Note that Siemens' total profit depends on the amount of output produced and sold by Thales (Q_T). Taking the partial derivative of Equation 8.4 with respect to Q_S yields

$$(8.5) \qquad \frac{\partial \pi_S}{\partial Q_S} = 995 - Q_T - 2.5Q_S$$

Similarly, Thales' total profit is equal to

$$
\begin{aligned}
\pi_T &= PQ_T - TC_T \\
&= (1,000 - Q_S - Q_T)Q_T - (110,000 \\
&\quad + 5Q_T + 0.15Q_T^2) \\
&= -110,000 + 995Q_T - Q_SQ_T \\
&\quad - 1.15Q_T^2
\end{aligned}
$$

(8.6)

Note also that Thales' total profit is a function of Siemens' output level (Q_S). Taking the partial derivative of Equation 8.6 with respect to Q_T yields

$$(8.7) \qquad \frac{\partial \pi_T}{\partial Q_T} = 995 - Q_S - 2.3Q_T$$

Setting Equations 8.5 and 8.7 equal to zero yields

$$(8.8) \qquad 2.5Q_S + Q_T = 995$$
$$(8.9) \qquad Q_S + 2.3Q_T = 995$$

Solving Equations 8.8 and 8.9 simultaneously gives the optimal levels of output for the two firms—$Q_S^* = 272.32$ units and $Q_T^* = 314.21$ units. Substituting these values into Equation 8.1 yields an optimal (equilibrium) selling price of $P^* = \$413.47$ per unit. The respective profits for the two firms are obtained by substituting Q_S^* and Q_T^* into Equations 8.4 and 8.6 to obtain $\pi_S^* = \$22,695.00$ and $\pi_T^* = \$3,536.17$.

point where output and price are stable and neither firm can increase its profits by raising or lowering output. The example above illustrates the determination of the long-run Cournot equilibrium.

Stackelberg Model

In an oligopoly model proposed by the German economist Heinrich von Stackelberg, the first mover anticipates the reactions of the second mover to the original output level that the first mover selects. (The Stackelberg model is sometimes called the "Leader–Follower" model.) The first mover selects an output that maximizes its profits given the anticipated reaction of the second mover.

STACKELBERG OLIGOPOLY SOLUTION: SIEMENS AND THALES

Suppose that Thales has first-mover advantage and anticipates that Siemens will react to Thales' output level using Siemens' profit-maximizing reaction function (Equation 8.8). Solving this equation for Siemens' level of output as a function of Thales' output level yields

$$(8.10) \qquad Q_S = 398 - 0.4Q_T$$

Now Thales uses Siemens' reaction function (Equation 8.10) to substitute for Siemens' output level in Thales' profit function (Equation 8.6), which yields

$$(8.11) \quad \begin{aligned} \pi_T &= -110,000 + 995Q_T - (398 \\ &\quad - 0.4Q_T)Q_T - 1.15Q_T^2 \\ &= -110,000 + 597Q_T - 0.75Q_T^2 \end{aligned}$$

Taking the total derivative of Equation 8.11 with respect to Q_T yields

$$(8.12) \qquad \frac{d\pi_T}{dQ_T} = 597 - 1.50Q_T$$

Setting Equation 8.12 equal to zero and solving for Q_T gives the optimal output level $Q_T^* = 398$ for Thales. The optimal output level for Siemens is $Q_S^* = 238.80$, obtained by substituting Thales' optimal output level of 398 into Siemens' profit-maximizing reaction function (Equation 8.10). Substituting these values into Equation 8.1 yields an optimal (equilibrium) selling price $P^* = \$363.20$ per unit. The respective profits for the two firms are obtained by substituting Q_S^* and Q_T^* into Equations 8.4 and 8.11 (or alternatively, 8.6) to obtain $\pi_S^* = \$1,281.80$ and $\pi_T^* = \$8,803.00$. Clearly, if Siemens reacts according to Equation 8.10 and Thales correctly anticipates this before setting its initial output level, Thales will increase both its market share and level of profits compared to the Cournot solution. Siemens' market share and level of profits both fall compared to the Cournot solution. Accordingly, Siemens may not be such a willing follower.

What types of markets are better described by the Cournot model and what types are better described by the Stackelberg model? The Stackelberg model might better describe the printer market dominated by Hewlett-Packard, whose share is approximately 49 percent and whose closest competitors are Xerox and Lexmark with shares of 10 percent and 8 percent, respectively. The Cournot model might better describe the markets for personal computers and computer storage devices, where the three top firms in these markets have roughly equal market shares.

Bertrand Model

The French economist Joseph Bertrand also developed an oligopoly model. The following assumptions are not only consistent with his model but also with the Cournot and Stackelberg models discussed previously.

1. There are only two firms (i.e., a duopoly) and many consumers.
2. The firms sell identical products.
3. The consumers have perfect information and no transaction costs.
4. There are barriers to entry for new firms.
5. The market demand function is linear.

In addition, Bertrand assumes the firms have no fixed costs and identical constant marginal costs. Although this is a rather simplified cost assumption, both Cournot and Stackelberg also make simplifying cost assumptions. Thus, the cost functions given by Equations 8.2 and 8.3 represent generalizations of the Cournot and Stackelberg models. Later we will generalize Bertrand's model by also using these cost functions. (The generalized Bertrand model is also called the "Bertrand–Edgeworth model.")

Cournot and Stackelberg both assumed that the duopolists adjust output quantities and that the sum of these quantities determines the market price. Cournot assumes that neither rival anticipates the other's quantity adjustments, while Stackelberg assumes a leader that anticipates its rival's adjustments and a follower that does not.

Bertrand differs from Cournot and Stackelberg by assuming that each firm attempts to maximize its profits by setting a price for its product. In each period, the firm with the lower price provides all of the quantity demanded at that price and the other firm sells nothing. If the two firms set identical prices in a period, Bertrand assumes that the quantity demanded is equally divided. Under his cost assumptions, Bertrand argues that the two firms engage in cutthroat price competition until the following market equilibrium conditions occur:

1. Market price equals marginal cost.
2. Each firm has zero economic profits.

These are precisely the same equilibrium conditions obtained under perfect competition!

Under perfect competition, these two equilibrium conditions still hold even when firms have fixed costs and nonconstant marginal costs. Will this still be true for Bertrand's generalized model? The example below examines this issue using the nonidentical total

EXAMPLE

BERTRAND OLIGOPOLY SOLUTION: SIEMENS AND THALES

With constant and identical marginal costs, Bertrand assumed that demand was equally split when firms charged the same price. In the case of the asymmetric cost functions 8.2 and 8.3 for Siemens and Thales, respectively, a more reasonable assumption when firms set the same price is that demand is split in proportion to capacity. For each price, the capacity of a firm represents its profit-maximizing output under perfect competition; in other words, the level of output is such that marginal cost equals price.[2]

Based on the total cost functions 8.2 and 8.3, the marginal cost functions for the respective firms are

(8.13) $MC_S = 5 + 0.5Q_S$

(8.14) $MC_T = 5 + 0.3Q_T$

Using the demand function 8.1, the respective equilibrium conditions of price equals marginal cost for each firm are

(8.15) $1{,}000 - Q_S - Q_T = 5 + 0.5Q_S$

(8.16) $1{,}000 - Q_S - Q_T = 5 + 0.3Q_T$

Solving these two simultaneous equations yields the respective optimal output levels $Q_S^* = 314.21$ and $Q_T^* = 523.68$. Substituting these optimal output levels into Equation 8.1 yields an optimal (equilibrium) selling price of $P^* = \$162.11$ per unit. Substituting these optimal output levels into the profit functions 8.4 and 8.6 yields $\pi_S^* = -\$45{,}316.45$ and $\pi_T^* = -\$68{,}860.75$.

---

[2] This interpretation of demand splitting is consistent with Xavier Vives, *Oligopoly Pricing* (Cambridge, MA: MIT Press, 1999), especially pp. 122–123. Strictly speaking, the generalized Bertrand equilibrium solution used in this section represents the lowest price and highest total output among a range of feasible equilibriums.

cost functions 8.2 and 8.3 that were previously used in the generalized versions of the Cournot and Stackelberg models.

Note that when nonidentical cost functions such as Equations 8.2 and 8.3 are introduced into the Bertrand model, the quantity demanded at the market equilibrium price usually is no longer equally divided between the two firms. With these particular cost functions, Siemens' market share is $314.21/(314.21 + 523.68) = 37.5$ percent and Thales' market share is $523.68/(314.21 + 523.68) = 62.5$ percent. Further note that the Bertrand economic profits may no longer be zero when more general cost functions are used. In fact, in the Bertrand example both firms have negative economic profits. Thus, in the long run one or both of these firms will exit the industry because negative profits are not sustainable.

Of course, a Bertrand example could easily be constructed where both firms have positive economic profits. For example, if the fixed costs of Siemens and Thales were only \$20,000 and \$40,000, respectively, then the Bertrand optimal outputs and price level would remain unchanged. However, profits would improve by \$50,000 and \$70,000, respectively, because fixed costs were reduced by these amounts. Thus, the Bertrand optimal profits would now be $\pi_S^* = \$4,683.55$ and $\pi_T^* = \$1,139.25$, respectively. If barriers to entry can be successfully maintained, then these profits are sustainable in the long run.

How do the two firms avoid the cutthroat and potentially ruinous price competition indicated by the Bertrand model? One way is to somehow introduce a cost of switching for the consumer, such as the airline frequent flyer loyalty programs. Another way is to introduce product differentiation so that some consumers will still buy a firm's product even if its price is higher. Product differentiation was discussed in the monopolistic competition section of Chapter 6. A third approach is for the two firms to collude. We discuss the collusive approach next.

Cartels and Other Forms of Collusion

Cartel
A formal or informal agreement among firms in an oligopolistic industry. Cartel members may agree on such issues as prices, total industry output, market shares, and the division of profits.

Oligopolists may seek to reduce the inherent risk that exists because of the interdependencies of the industry structure by either formally or informally agreeing to cooperate or collude in decision making. Formal agreements of oligopolists are called **cartels**. In general, collusive agreements of any sort are illegal in the European Union and North America. However, some important exceptions exist. For example, prices and quotas of various agricultural products (e.g., milk, oranges) are set by growers in many countries with the approval of their governments. The International Air Transport Association (IATA), composed of airlines flying transatlantic routes, sets uniform prices for these flights. And ocean shipping rates are set by hundreds of collusive "conferences" on each major transoceanic route.

Illegal collusive arrangements, however, have also arisen from time to time. For example, General Electric was accused of conspiring with De Beers Centenary AG to fix industrial diamond prices.[3] In the largest criminal price-fixing case ever, the grain-processing giant Archer–Daniels–Midland (ADM) pleaded guilty in 1996 to organizing an explicit quota and pricing system among five firms in the lysine market (see Figure 8.2). Lysine is an amino acid food supplement that speeds the growth of livestock. ADM paid \$100 million in antitrust penalties, and ADM executives went to jail.[4] Roche and BASF, large Swiss and German industrial conglomerates in pharmaceuticals, chemicals, fragrances, and vitamins, agreed to pay \$500 million and \$225 million fines,

---

[3] Based on "GE Price-Fixing Case Won't Be Easy for Government," *The Wall Street Journal,* October 20, 1994, p. B3.
[4] "In ADM Saga, Executives Now on Trial," *The Wall Street Journal,* July 9, 1998, p. B10.

FIGURE 8.2

Lysine Manufacturers
Who Pleaded Guilty to
Price Fixing

The graph shows that the
lysine industry contains a
small number of competi-
tors with roughly compa-
rable market share. Under
these conditions, price
fixing is perhaps more likely
to occur.

Source: *The Wall Street Journal*, July 9, 1998.

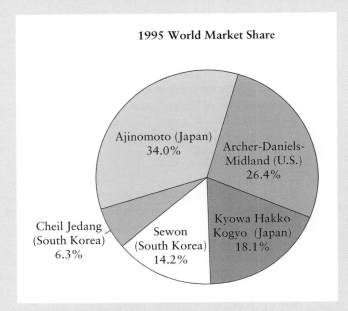

1995 World Market Share

Ajinomoto (Japan) 34.0%

Archer-Daniels-Midland (U.S.) 26.4%

Kyowa Hakko Kogyo (Japan) 18.1%

Sewon (South Korea) 14.2%

Cheil Jedang (South Korea) 6.3%

EXAMPLE

OCEAN SHIPPING CONFERENCES*

Since the U.S. *Shipping Act* of 1916, ocean freight companies have been exempted from the U.S. antitrust laws. Shipping rates on a transoceanic route are set jointly by 10 to 50 competitors acting as a "shipping conference." Two studies in 1993 and 1995 by U.S. government agencies found that rates were 18 or 19 percent lower when ocean shipping companies broke out of these conference arrangements and nego-tiated as independents. Nevertheless, the conferences maintain their market power by signing exclusive-dealing contracts with large-volume customers. The enormous capacity of the shipping conferences allows more schedule frequency and greater reliability than the independents can offer. And liquidated-damages penalty clauses in these exclusive contracts remove much of the incentive for even price-sensitive cargo to seek out inde-pendent shippers. Instead, circuitous trans-portation plans avoid the highest rates. Polaroid, for example, shipped film to Europe by first trucking about 480 kilome-tres to the port of Montreal, despite the fact that the product was manufactured 32 kilo-metres from the port of Boston.

* Based on "Making Waves," *The Wall Street Journal*, October 7, 1997, p. A1; J. Yong, "Excluding Capacity-Constrained Entrants through Exclusive Dealing: Theory and Applications to Ocean Shipping," *Journal of Industrial Economics*, Vol. 46, No. 2, June 1996; and "Shipmates," *The Wall Street Journal*, February 20, 2003, p. A1.

respectively, for their leadership of a price-fixing conspiracy in vitamin supplements. This 1999 antitrust settlement reduced Roche's profitability by 30 percent.[5] These severe penalties suggest that the inefficiencies arising from cartelization of an industry are indeed serious. Businesses that ignore the prohibition against price fixing do so at great peril.

Factors Affecting the Likelihood of Successful Collusion

The ability of oligopolistic firms to engage successfully in collusion depends on a number of factors, as examined below.

Number and Size Distribution of Sellers Effective collusion generally is more difficult as the number of oligopolistic firms involved increases. In the 1990s, the De Beers diamond cartel in Switzerland and South Africa was effective in part because Russia agreed in 1995 to sell 95 percent of its total wholesale supply through De Beers. De Beers' central selling organization and Russia alone accounted for over 75 percent of world supply at that time.[6]

Product Heterogeneity Products that are alike in all significant physical and subjective characteristics are said to be *homogeneous,* and price is the only characteristic that matters. When products are *heterogeneous* (or differentiated), cooperation is more difficult because competition is occurring over a broad array of product characteristics, such as durability, fashion timing, warranty, and after-sale policies.

Cost Structures The more cost functions differ among competing firms, the more difficult it will be for firms to collude on pricing and output decisions. Also, successful collusion is more difficult in industries where fixed costs are a high percentage of total costs. Of course, a higher percentage of fixed costs implies higher contribution margins to recover those fixed costs. Higher margins imply a lower break-even sales change required to make discounting attractive. Therefore, breakdowns in collusively high prices are most notable in industries that employ highly capital-intensive production processes, such as petroleum refining, steel making, and airlines.

Size and Frequency of Orders Successful oligopolistic cooperation also depends on the size distribution over time of customer orders. Effective collusion is more likely to occur when orders are small, frequent, and received regularly. When large orders are received infrequently at irregular intervals, as in the purchase of aircraft engines, it is more difficult for firms to collude on pricing and output decisions. Hence, Pratt & Whitney, Rolls-Royce, and General Electric, the major producers of aircraft jet engines, have never colluded, despite the fact that GE did collude with other manufacturers in hydroelectric power plant equipment.

Secrecy and Retaliation An oligopolistic firm will be less tempted to grant secret price concessions to selected customers if it feels that these price reductions will be detected, thereby provoking retaliation from other cartel members.

---

[5] "Scandal Costs Roche," *The Wall Street Journal,* May 25, 1999, p. A20.
[6] See "Disputes Are Forever," *The Economist,* September 17, 1994.

Percentage of External Output[7] Most cartels contain the seeds of their own destruction. With increased prices and profits, cartels attract outside entry. Increased supply, external to the cartel, means larger restrictions on output for cartel members in order to sustain any given market price. At one point in 1999, De Beers had to purchase for its own inventory $3.96 billion in diamonds (in only an $8 billion market) in order to stabilize prices because so many Canadian, Australian, and Russian diamonds (external to the De Beers cartel) had entered the market.

Finally, in 2000, with 37 percent of total diamond supply outside the cartel, De Beers declared its 65-year cartel ended. Similarly, the ocean shipping prices are breaking down because the rate-setting "conferences" now control less than 70 percent of the $85-billion North Atlantic market and less than 50 percent of the $262-billion trans-Pacific market. External suppliers reduce the likelihood of successful collusion to stabilize prices above their competitive level.

Cartel Profit Maximization and the Allocation of Restricted Output

Under both legal cartels and secret collusive agreements, an attempt is made to increase prices and profits above the level that would prevail in the absence of collusion. The profit-maximization solution for a two-firm cartel, Firms E and F, is shown graphically in Figure 8.3. The *industry* demand, D_{mkt}, marginal revenue, MR, and marginal cost, ΣMC, curves are shown in the right-hand panel. The industry marginal cost curve is obtained by *summing horizontally across outputs* the marginal cost curves of the individual firms in the centre and left-hand panels—that is, $\Sigma MC = MC_E + MC_F$. Total industry profits are maximized by setting total industry output (and consequently price) at the point where industry marginal revenue equals industry marginal cost—i.e., Q^*_{Total} units of output at a price of P^* per unit.

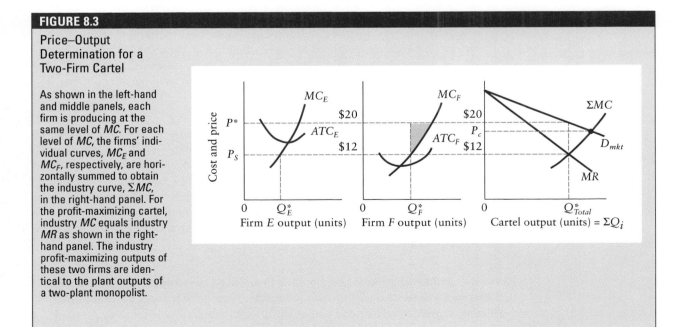

FIGURE 8.3

Price–Output Determination for a Two-Firm Cartel

As shown in the left-hand and middle panels, each firm is producing at the same level of *MC*. For each level of *MC*, the firms' individual curves, MC_E and MC_F, respectively, are horizontally summed to obtain the industry curve, ΣMC, in the right-hand panel. For the profit-maximizing cartel, industry *MC* equals industry *MR* as shown in the right-hand panel. The industry profit-maximizing outputs of these two firms are identical to the plant outputs of a two-plant monopolist.

[7] Based on "De Beers to Abandon Monopoly," *The Wall Street Journal*, July 13, 2000, p. A20, and "Atlantic Ocean Shipping Cartel Makes Concessions," *The Wall Street Journal*, February 7, 1997, p. A2.

If the cartel seeks to maximize its profits, the market share (or quota) for each firm should be set at a level such that the marginal cost of all firms is identical and at the level of the industry (summed) MC that just equates to MR. The optimal output allocation is for Firm E to produce a quota of Q_E^* units and for Firm F to produce a quota of Q_F^* units. If Firm E was producing at a level where its marginal costs exceeded Firm F's, cartel profits could be increased by shifting output from Firm E to Firm F until marginal costs were equal.[8]

Cartel pricing agreements are hard to reach, but the central problem for a cartel lies in monitoring these output shares or quotas. Detecting quota violations and effectively enforcing punishment schemes are nearly impossible. Consequently, most cartels are very unstable. Let's return to Figure 8.3 and see why.

Suppose you are Firm F facing a cartel-determined price (P^*) for crude oil of $20 per barrel. Your marginal costs are presently running $12 per barrel at your assigned quota of Q_F/Q_{Total}. The Aramco pipelines, which once consolidated all your throughput from the production wells to shipping terminals, have now been superseded by numerous independent shipping terminals, many within your own nation. In addition, your crude oil is relatively undifferentiated from that of many other OPEC members. Should you abide by your quota commitment? Is it in your best interest to do so? The answer depends on whether your additional sales beyond quota are detectable and whether your additional output will increase total supply enough to place downward pressure on the cartel price. If the answer to both questions is no, then because a 40 percent profit margin ($8) awaits your selling another barrel, a profit maximizer will be tempted to expand output and capture the shaded area of incremental profit in the middle panel of Figure 8.3.

Of course, the problem is that other cartel members may think exactly the same way. If everyone takes the cartel price as given and independently profit-maximizes, then cartel supply increases to ΣMC, and the black market price must fall to the competitive level (P_c) of perhaps $17 just to clear the market. Enforcement of the ideal quotas Q_F and Q_E is the Achilles' heel of every cartel.

The cartel solution presented in the example on page 236 is the same solution that a two-plant monopolist would use, with Siemens and Thales representing the respective plants. Cartels, however, often employ arrangements that may be less optimal from the viewpoint of maximizing industry profits. For example, firms may be allocated different geographical sales regions. When there are more than two firms in a cartel, cheating (i.e., producing more than one's quota) can easily become a serious problem in maintaining the cartel. Exclusive marketing regions may be easier to enforce than quotas.

Comparison of Cournot, Stackelberg, Bertrand, and Cartel Results: Siemens–Thales Example

Table 8.1 summarizes the results of the Siemens and Thales example for the Cournot, Stackelberg, Bertrand, and cartel cases discussed above. Several conclusions can be drawn from this comparison. First, total industry output (Q_{Total}^*) is lowest and selling price (P^*) is highest when the firms collude than when there is no collusion. Also, total industry profits (π_{Total}^*) are highest when the firms set prices and output jointly than when they act independently. Although this may not be true in all collusive agreements, one firm's profits (i.e., Siemens') are actually lower under the cartel solution than under Cournot competition. Therefore, to get Siemens to participate in the cartel, Thales probably would have to agree to share a significant part of the cartel's additional profits with Siemens if previously the two firms were Cournot competitors. Finally, under

---

[8] Note that the average total costs of the two firms are not necessarily equal at the optimal (profit-maximizing) output level. Note also that Firm E is given a sizable share of the total output even though its average total costs are higher than Firm F's.

EXAMPLE

Cartel Pricing and Output Decisions: Siemens and Thales

The determination of the profit-maximizing price and output levels for a two-firm cartel can also be determined algebraically when the demand and cost functions are given. Consider again the Siemens (Firm S) and Thales (Firm T) example discussed in the previous section. The demand function was given by Equation 8.1 and the cost functions for the two firms were given by Equations 8.2 and 8.3. Suppose that Siemens and Thales decide to form a cartel and act as a monopolist to maximize total profits from the production and sale of the components.

Total industry profits (π_{Total}) are equal to the sum of Siemens' and Thales' profits and are given by the following expression:

$$\begin{aligned}\pi_{Total} &= \pi_S + \pi_T \\ &= PQ_S - TC_S + PQ_T - TC_T \qquad (8.17)\end{aligned}$$

Substituting Equations 8.1, 8.2, and 8.3 into this expression yields

$$\begin{aligned}\pi_{Total} &= (1{,}000 - Q_S - Q_T)Q_S \\ &\quad - (70{,}000 + 5Q_S + 0.25Q_S^2) \\ &\quad + (1{,}000 - Q_S - Q_T)Q_T \\ &\quad - (110{,}000 + 5Q_T + 0.15Q_T^2) \\ &= 1{,}000Q_S - Q_S^2 - Q_SQ_T \qquad (8.18) \\ &\quad - 70{,}000 - 5Q_S - 0.25Q_S^2 \\ &\quad + 1{,}000Q_T - Q_SQ_T - Q_T^2 \\ &\quad - 110{,}000 - 5Q_T - 0.15Q_T^2 \\ &= -180{,}000 + 995Q_S - 1.25Q_S^2 \\ &\quad + 995Q_T - 1.15Q_T^2 - 2Q_SQ_T\end{aligned}$$

To maximize π_{Total} take the *partial* derivatives of Equation 8.18 with respect to Q_S and Q_T:

$$\frac{\partial \pi_{Total}}{\partial Q_S} = 995 - 2.50Q_S - 2Q_T$$

$$\frac{\partial \pi_{Total}}{\partial Q_T} = 995 - 2.30Q_T - 2Q_S$$

Setting these expressions equal to zero yields

$$(8.19) \qquad 2.5Q_S + 2Q_T - 995 = 0$$

$$(8.20) \qquad 2Q_S + 2.3Q_T - 995 = 0$$

Solving Equations 8.19 and 8.20 simultaneously gives these optimal output levels: $Q_S^* = 170.57$ units and $Q_T^* = 284.29$ units.

Substituting these values into Equations 8.1 and 8.18 gives an optimal selling price and total profit for the cartel of $P^* = \$545.14$ per unit and $\pi_{Total}^* = \$46{,}291.43$, respectively. Unless the cartel has a profit-sharing agreement, the respective firm profits of $\pi_S^* = \$14{,}858.15$ and $\pi_T^* = \$31{,}433.28$ are once again obtained from substituting the optimal output levels in Equations 8.4 and 8.6. The marginal costs of the two firms at the optimal output level are equal to

$$\begin{aligned}MC_S^* &= \frac{d(TC_S)}{dQ_S} = 5 + 0.50Q_S \\ &= 5 + 0.50(170.57) = \$90.29\end{aligned}$$

$$\begin{aligned}MC_T^* &= \frac{d(TC_T)}{dQ_T} = 5 + 0.30Q_T \\ &= 5 + 0.30(284.29) = \$90.29\end{aligned}$$

As in the graphical solution illustrated earlier in Figure 8.3, the optimal output (or market share) for each firm in the cartel occurs where the marginal costs of the two firms are equal.

Table 8.1	Comparison of Cournot, Stackelberg, Bertrand, and Cartel Results for Siemens and Thales			
	Cournot	**Stackelberg**	**Bertrand**	**Cartel**
Q_S^*	272.32	238.80	314.21	170.57
Q_T^*	314.21	398.00	523.68	284.29
Q_{Total}^*	586.53	636.80	837.89	454.86
P^*	$413.47	$363.20	$162.11	$545.14
π_S^*	$22,695.00	$1,281.80	−$45,316.45	$14,858.15
π_T^*	$3,536.17	$8,803.00	−$68,860.75	$31,433.28
π_{Total}	$26,231.17	$10,084.80	−$114,177.20	$46,291.43

Bertrand competition, total industry output (Q_{Total}^*) is highest, selling price (P^*) is lowest, and total industry profits (π_{Total}^*) are lowest. Of the three forms of competition, Bertrand most closely approximates the results of perfect competition.

Price Leadership

Another model of price–output determination in some oligopolistic industries is **price leadership.** Many industries exhibit a pattern where one or a few firms normally set a price and others tend to follow, frequently with a time lag of a few days. In the case of basic steel products, for example, the price that prevails within a week is generally uniform from one producer to another.

Effective price leadership exists when price movements initiated by the leader have a high probability of sticking and no maverick or nonconforming firms exist. The fewer the number of firms in the industry (that is, the greater the interdependencies of decision outcomes among firms), the more effective price leadership is likely to be. Two major price leadership patterns have been observed in various industries from time to time—*barometric* and *dominant price leadership.*

Barometric Price Leadership

In barometric price leadership, one firm announces a change in price that it hopes will be accepted by others. The leader need not be the largest firm in the industry. In fact, this leader may actually change from time to time. The leader must, however, be reasonably correct in its interpretation of changing demand and cost conditions so that suggested price changes will be accepted and stick. In essence, the barometric price leader merely initiates a reaction to changing market conditions that other firms find in their best interest to follow. These conditions might include such things as cost increases (or decreases) and sluggish (or brisk) sales accompanied by inventory buildups (or shortages) in the industry.

For example, General Motors has long been a price leader in the auto industry. During the auto sales slumps of 1981–1982, 1985–1986, 1990–1991, and 2000–2002, a cash-rebate or zero-percent financing program initiated by GM was promptly matched by the other firms within just a few days. In the banking industry, it is common for one bank to increase or decrease the prime rate before the others follow.

Dominant Firm Price Leadership

In dominant firm price leadership, one firm establishes itself as the leader because of its larger size, customer loyalty, or lower cost structure in relation to competing firms. The leader may then act as if it were a monopolist in its segment of the market. What is the incentive for followers to accept the established price? In some cases, it may be a fear of cutthroat retaliation from a low-cost dominant firm that keeps smaller firms from attempting to undercut the prevailing price. In other cases, following a price leader may be viewed as simply a convenience.

The price–output solution for the dominant firm model is shown in Figure 8.4. D_T shows total market demand for the product, MC_L represents the marginal cost curve for the dominant (leader) firm, and ΣMC_F constitutes the *horizontal summation* of the marginal cost curves for the follower firms, each of which may well have costs higher than MC_L. In the following analysis, *assume that the dominant firm sets the price knowing that follower firms will sell as much output as they wish at this price. The dominant firm then supplies the remainder of the market demand, that is, the residual demand in the dominant firm's segment of the market.*

Given that the follower firms can sell as much output as they wish at the price P_L established by the dominant firm, they are faced with a horizontal demand curve and a perfectly competitive market situation. The follower firms view the dominant firm's price, P_L, as their marginal revenue and maximize profits, producing that level of output where their marginal cost equals the established price. The ΣMC_F curve therefore shows the total output that will be *supplied* at various prices by the follower firms. The dominant firm's residual demand curve, D_L, is obtained by subtracting the amount supplied by the follower firms' ΣMC_F from the total market demand, D_T, at each price. For example, at a price of P_L, point G on the D_L curve is obtained by subtracting EC from ED. Other points on the D_L curve are obtained in a similar manner. At a price of P_1, the quantity supplied by the follower firms, Q_1, is equal to total market demand (point A), and the dominant firm's residual demand is therefore zero (point F). The dominant firm's marginal revenue curve, MR_L, is then obtained from its residual demand curve, D_L.

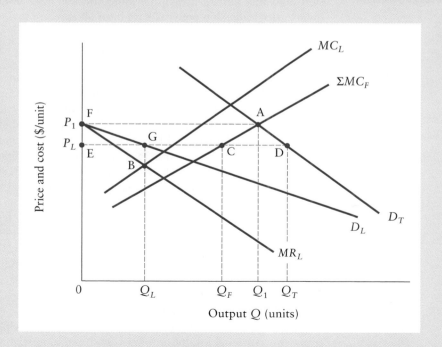

The dominant firm maximizes its profits by setting price and output where marginal cost equals marginal revenue. As shown in Figure 8.4, $MR_L = MC_L$ at point B. Therefore, the dominant firm should sell Q_L units of output at a price of P_L per unit. At a price of P_L, total demand is Q_T units, and the follower firms supply $Q_T - Q_L = Q_F$ units of output. The following example illustrates the application of these concepts.

EXAMPLE

PRICE LEADERSHIP: AEROTEK

Aerotek and six other smaller companies produce an electronic component used in small planes. Aerotek (L) is the price leader. The follower firms (F) sell the component at the same price as Aerotek. Aerotek permits the follower firms to sell as many units of the component as they wish at the established price. The company supplies the remainder of the demand itself. Total demand for the component is given by the following function:

$$(8.21) \qquad P = 10,000 - 10Q_T$$

where

$$(8.22) \qquad Q_T = Q_L + Q_F$$

That is, total output (Q_T) is the sum of the leader's (Q_L) and followers' (Q_F) outputs. Aerotek's marginal cost function is

$$(8.23) \qquad MC_L = 100 + 3Q_L$$

The aggregate marginal cost function for the other six producers of the component is

$$(8.24) \qquad \Sigma MC_F = 50 + 2Q_F$$

We are interested in determining the output for Aerotek and the follower firms and the selling price for the component given that the firms are interested in maximizing profits.

Aerotek's profit-maximizing output is found at the point where

$$(8.25) \qquad MR_L = MC_L$$

Its marginal revenue function (MR_L) is obtained by differentiating the firm's total revenue function (TR_L) with respect to Q_L. Total revenue (TR_L) is given by the following expression:

$$(8.26) \qquad TR_L = P \cdot Q_L$$

Q_L is obtained from Equation 8.22:

$$(8.27) \qquad Q_L = Q_T - Q_F$$

Using Equation 8.21, one can solve for Q_T:

$$(8.28) \qquad Q_T = 1,000 - 0.10P$$

To find Q_F, we note that Aerotek lets the follower firms sell as much output (i.e., components) as they wish at the given price (P). Therefore, the follower firms are faced with a horizontal demand function. Hence

$$(8.29) \qquad MR_F = P$$

To maximize profits, the follower firms will operate where

$$(8.30) \qquad MR_F = \Sigma MC_F$$

Substituting Equations 8.29 and 8.24 into Equation 8.30 gives

$$(8.31) \qquad P = 50 + 2Q_F$$

Solving this equation for Q_F yields

$$(8.32) \qquad Q_F = 0.50P - 25$$

Substituting Equation 8.28 for Q_T and Equation 8.32 for Q_F in Equation 8.27 gives

$$Q_L = (1,000 - 0.10P) - (0.50P - 25)$$
$$(8.33) \qquad = 1,025 - 0.60P$$

Solving Equation 8.33 for P, one obtains

$$(8.34) \qquad P = 1,708.3333 - 1.6667Q_L$$

Substituting this expression for P in defining total revenue yields

$$TR_L = (1,708.3333 - 1.6667Q_L)Q_L$$
$$(8.35) \qquad = 1,708.3333Q_L - 1.6667Q_L^2$$

Differentiating this expression with respect to Q_L, one obtains Aerotek's marginal revenue function:

$$MR_L = \frac{d(TR_L)}{dQ_L}$$

(8.36)
$$= 1{,}708.3333 - 3.3334Q_L$$

Substituting Equation 8.36 for MR_L and Equation 8.23 for MC_L and equating the two gives the following optimality condition:

(8.37)
$$1{,}708.3333 - 3.3334Q_L = 100 + 3Q_L$$

Solving this equation for Q_L^* yields

$$Q_L^* = 253.945 \text{ units}$$

or an optimal output for Aerotek of 254 units of the component. Substituting this value of Q_L into Equation 8.34 gives

$$P^* = 1{,}708.3333 - 1.6667(253.945)$$
$$= \$1{,}285.083$$

or an optimal selling price of $1,285.08. The optimal output for the follower firms is found by substituting this value of P into Equation 8.32:

$$Q_F^* = 0.50(1{,}285.083) - 25$$
$$= 617.542 \text{ units}$$

or an optimal output of 618 units.

The Kinked Demand Curve Model

Sometimes when an oligopolist cuts its prices, competitors quickly feel the decline in their sales and are forced to match the price reduction. Alternatively, if one firm raises its prices, competitors rapidly gain customers by maintaining their original prices and hence have little or no motivation to match a price increase. In a situation such as this, the demand curve facing an individual oligopolist would be far more elastic for price increases than for price decreases. If an oligopolist *raises* its price and others do not follow, the increase in price will lead to a declining share of the market. This is illustrated in Figure 8.5. Demand segment KD' is the *share-of-the-market demand curve* where all rivals match price and this firm's market share remains unchanged, perhaps at 21 percent. For price increases above P, however, if rival firms do not match price, the demand segment facing this firm is more elastic. For price increases, its market share declines, perhaps to 15 percent.

The oligopolist's demand curve is therefore represented by DKD', with the prevailing price as P and output as Q. The marginal revenue curve is discontinuous because of the kink in the demand curve at K. Hence, marginal revenue is represented by the two line segments MRX and YMR'. If the marginal cost curve MC passes through the gap XY in the marginal revenue curve, the most profitable alternative is to maintain the current price–output policy.[9] The profit-maximizing level of price and output remains constant for the firm, which perceives itself to be faced with a fixed unit price, even though costs may change over a rather wide range (for example, MC_2 and MC_1). Similarly, shifts in the demand curve either to the right (an increase in demand) or to the left (a decrease in demand) may not change the price decisions of the firm. Because the kink is determined at the *prevailing price,* a shift in demand shifts the gap XY in the marginal revenue curve to the right or left. If MC still passes through the gap, the prevailing price is maintained, although output will either increase or decrease.

---

[9] Profit may not be increased by increasing price (and decreasing output) because $MR > MC$, and this difference would increase with a price increase. Similarly, profit may not be increased by decreasing price (and increasing output) because $MR < MC$, and this difference would also increase with a price decrease.

FIGURE 8.5

Kinked Demand Curve Model

The upper demand segment (*DK*) represents the relatively elastic demand that the firm faces if it tries to increase its price because competitors do not match this price increase. The marginal revenue segment (*MRX*) is associated with this demand segment *DK*. The lower demand segment (*KD′*) represents the relatively inelastic demand that the firm faces if it tries to cut its price, because competitors will match this price decrease. The marginal revenue segment (*YMR′*) is associated with this demand segment *KD′*. The kinked demand curve (*DKD′*) creates a vertical gap (*XY*) in the marginal revenue curve associated with output (*Q*) and price (*P*). Shifts in the marginal cost curve from *MC* to either *MC₂* or to *MC₁* will leave the profit-maximizing output *Q* and price *P* unchanged, as long as the new marginal cost curve cuts the vertical *XY* gap in the marginal revenue curve.

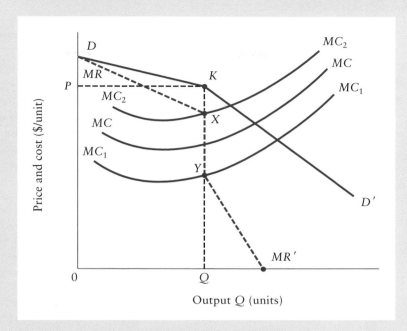

A number of criticisms have been made of the kinked demand curve model as a general model of oligopoly behaviour. Although the model does provide a theoretical explanation for why stable prices have been observed to exist in some oligopolistic industries, it takes the prevailing price as given and offers no justification for why that price level rather than some other is the prevailing price. For this reason alone, the kinked demand model of oligopolistic pricing must be viewed as incomplete.

Avoiding Price Wars

Knowing how to avoid a price war has become a critical success factor for many high-margin businesses in tight oligopolistic groups. Because each additional sale imposes few additional costs, high margins encourage price discounting to gain market share. So building a business plan or adopting a strategy that reduces the power of substitutes, entrants, buyers, and suppliers and thereby generates high profit margins is no guarantee of success. To sustain profitability, oligopoly firms also must avoid the gainshare discounting that would otherwise permeate the tactics in a high-margin business.

GOOD–BETTER–BEST PRODUCT STRATEGY AT KODAK*

For more information on Kodak, go to **www.kodak.com**.

Marriott Corporation and Kodak have responded to the fierce price competition in their respective industries by introducing upscale, high-quality mid-range, and down-market product lines to their respective target customers. Ritz–Carlton, Courtyards by Marriott, and Fairfield Inns all operate as subsidiary hotel chains under the parent Marriott Corporation, but as very distinct offerings.

Similarly, in the early 1990s, in response to declining perceived quality differentials, collapsing market share, and price pressure from private-label film, Kodak introduced a new lineup that included Royal Gold, Kodak Gold Plus, and Funtime film. Successful segmentation is the key to such a product strategy for avoiding ruinous price discounting. Funtime film (as well as the Kodak disposable cameras that followed) is positioned for everyday use to capture the hundreds of events, posed people, and scenery that highly accessible cheap film sold through convenience store distribution channels make possible. These are, however, photo shots that customers will later find "lost" in great stacks in file cabinets, desk drawers, and old shoeboxes. These films are not generally used to memorialize anything of significance. Instead, the snapshot accentuates the experiential event, as it happens.

"Kodak moments," however, pursue a very different set of value-drivers. Kodak Royal Gold provided exceptional picture resolution in many different light conditions. Although slower, Gold Plus is also able to memorialize subtleties of expressions of surprise, exaltation, pride in fulfilling challenging tasks, etc. Kodak's marketing research had found that many of its customers would pay a price premium to memorialize a personal emotion (such as when a woman demonstrably triumphs amid the worst rapids in the front-right corner hazard seat of a whitewater raft filled with men). Heavy advertising and event marketing further established this product image.

* Based on "Film-War Spoils: A Buck a Roll?" *The Wall Street Journal*, November 11, 1998, p. B1; "Eastman Kodak Company: Funtime Film," Harvard Business School Publishing, 1998; and "Kodak Is Rolling Out Digital Photo Processing," *The Wall Street Journal*, February 9, 1999, p. A4.

The ready-to-eat (RTE) cereal, beer, and film industries have all recently experienced price wars. In each case, the catalyst for the price war was the fast-rising market share of private labels in what had previously been a heavily branded category. Between 1989 and 1999, the price of Kodak Gold film for 35-mm cameras declined by 50 percent after a blistering series of attacks by discounted private-label films, many supplied by Fuji. Kodak responded with a good–better–best product strategy involving its own "fighting brand" of film, Funtime film, for everyday use and heavily defended its brand equity with "Kodak moment" ads. However, in the end, Kodak cut prices to preserve its 70 percent market share. Similarly in RTE cereals, Ralston supplies many grocery store chains with private-label cereals that sell at price points 30 percent less than the premium brands. The market share of these private-label store brands had grown rapidly, capturing 8.7 percent of the North American market in 1994 relative to only 5.6 percent in 1993, a 50 percent increase in one year!

One key to avoiding price wars in tight oligopolies is to recognize the ongoing nature of the pricing rivalry and attempt to mitigate the intensity of the price competition by growing the market. Kodak foresees a perpetual rivalry with Fuji Film. Pepsi is stuck with Coke. Consequently, each rival must anticipate retaliation for aggressive discounting designed to attract away the other company's regular customers. Far better to maintain high prices and expect your rivals to do the same. Then, each company can focus on opening new markets and selling more volume to established customers. Coke Classic now sells an average of six servings per day to heavy Coke drinkers. In recent years, Coke has introduced dozens of new soft drinks to countries throughout the world. As a result, the Coca-Cola concentrate syrup has never been discounted in 80 years.

Customer segmentation with differential pricing is another way to avoid price wars. If low-cost new entrants attack a major airline, one effective response that avoids initiating a price war with other major carriers involves matching prices to a very targeted customer segment and then carefully controlling how much capacity is released for sale to that segment. "Fencing" restrictions like 10-day advance-purchase requirements and Saturday night stay-overs prove crucial in segmenting the price-sensitive discretionary traveller from the regular business expense-account customer. The incumbent carriers can "meet the competition" in these restricted fare classes while reserving sufficient capacity for those who desire to pay for the reliability, convenience, and change order responsiveness of business-class and full-coach seats. And most importantly, the incumbent's established competitors can maintain high prices on unaffected departures, segments, and routes. In Web Appendix 9A, we discuss how revenue management techniques can help accomplish these goals. To access Web chapters and appendixes, go to the Nelson website for this book at www.mcguigan.nelson.com.

In addition to segmenting the target customers into more and less price-sensitive submarkets, product line extensions can also aid in avoiding gainshare price discounting by providing reference prices and framing effects that serve to help sell the mid-range product at full (undiscounted) price. Consumers of unbranded products tend to remember the last price they encountered on the shelf in deciding whether to purchase at the quoted price today. Branded products, however, trigger very long reference pricing. Discounting with a major branded item like Tide detergent or Kodak film tends to etch in the customer's mind a new lowball price that can be expected thereafter for many months.

EXAMPLE

WHAT WENT RIGHT AT INTERLINK SURGICAL STEEL?*

Until the early 1990s, Interlink sold replacement hypodermic syringes by the thousands to hospitals for 10 cents per syringe. Each time a catheter was changed, a new hypodermic syringe would be inserted into the patient's vein. A Japanese company entered the market with an identical product for 3 cents each. Interlink promptly introduced a replacement device that needs insertion only one time. That is, any new saline or pharmaceutical drip lines can be hooked directly to an Interlink syringe device that need not be removed and replaced. This new process reduces the risk of patient infection and the inherent hazard to the nursing staff of exposure to patient blood. Interlink again dominates the market, and prices have stabilized at higher levels.

* Based on "How to Fight a Price War," *Harvard Business Review,* March/April 2000, pp. 107–116, and "How to Escape a Price War," *Fortune,* June 13, 1994, pp. 82–90.

In the face of private-label discount competition, therefore, what one really might like to do is introduce a super-premium product offered at price points well above your traditional product. These highest reference prices too will be remembered by the regular brand-loyal customers. And since opportunity losses in descending from mid-range to bargain-basement products (while saving $2, for example) tend to weigh more heavily on consumers than the perceived satisfaction from moving upscale to super-premiums (at an equal $2 cost), one can expect the mid-range products to sell even better in the presence of the framing provided by super-premium products. In the late 1990s, Kodak introduced super-premium digital photography with a product line called Picture CD. Max and Advantrix film were also introduced by Kodak at price points 15 percent above Gold film, now sold in discounted multipacks through Wal-Mart. Max and Advantrix soon provided 38 percent of Kodak's sales with relatively little discounting.

Another way to avoid or at least mitigate the effects of price wars is to differentiate through innovation. Rather than matching price cuts, a higher-priced brand can call attention to the risks of disloyalty by highlighting conspicuous product innovations that the discounters have missed. Sony's digital cameras, for example, can record the eye's images on a mini-CD as well as the more familiar memory stick. The CD or memory stick can then be inserted into any PC that has the appropriate reading device (most computers now have a CD-ROM, while only a few Sony computers have built-in memory stick readers) for easy and immediate viewing and/or printing.

The digital camera market segment has grown for several years at an annual rate of 50 percent. While digital camera competitors were fixated on improving picture resolution to justify complicated expensive peripherals, Sony continued to innovate with smaller and easier-to-use cameras that markedly increased customer value. As a result, Sony continues to earn premium prices with its products. Sony's innovation objective is to establish full connectivity between digital cameras, cellphones, and TVs.

Figure 8.6 illustrates how an oligopolistic market with extreme brand loyalty attributable to innovation, customer risk avoidance, or effective brand-name advertising can

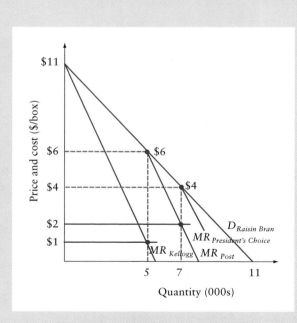

FIGURE 8.6

Segmented Oligopoly with Extreme Brand Loyalty

The graph shows extreme brand loyalty first to Kellogg, which sells a profit-maximizing output of 5,000 boxes of its Raisin Bran and charges $6 per box. For customers who want to pay less than $6, extreme brand loyalty switches to Post. Its profit-maximizing output is 2,000 boxes at a price per box of $4. Customers wanting to pay less than $4 per box must buy President's Choice.

NONPRICE TACTICS IN A PRICE WAR: KELLOGG*

Kellogg has the strongest brands in the cereal industry, with 12 of the 15 top-selling cereals. Rather than match Post's price cuts in 1995, Kellogg might have poured not two but three scoops of raisins into every box of Kellogg's Raisin Bran. In the first two months after the price cuts by Post and General Mills, Kellogg lost three share points (from 35 percent to 32 percent) and Post gained four (from 16 percent to 20 percent). At $80 million per share point and 55 percent gross margins (on average across the affected brands), Kellogg's contributions on the lost sales totalled $132 million ($-3 \times$ $80 million $\times$ 0.55). To retrieve that $132 million-per-year operating profit, Kellogg slashed prices 19 percent on two-thirds of its brands, sacrificing over $300 million ($-0.19 \times$ $2.4 billion sales $\times$ 0.66). Market share continued to decline to 29 percent in 1999, and the capitalized value of Kellogg fell by $7 billion. Many observers have wondered whether expending over $300 million (or half that much) on product innovation or on advertising would have accomplished more.

* Based on "Cereal Thriller," *The Economist,* June 15, 1996.

be analyzed. Kellogg's Raisin Bran faces an inverse demand segment, ($11 $-$ Q^d) $=$ Price, that includes the highest willingness to pay customers. Setting MR in this segment, $11 $-$ 2Q^d$, equal to a marginal cost of $1, Kellogg's Raisin Bran maximizes operating profit at $Q^* = 5(000)$ and a price per box of ($11 $-$ 5$) $=$ $6. Without as established a brand image, Post Raisin Bran must sell under $6 and accordingly faces a different segment, whose inverse demand may be written as ($6 $-$ Q^d) $=$ Price—i.e., the line segment from $6 downward to the right along D in Figure 8.6. Setting MR at Post, $6 $-$ 2Q$, equal to a higher $2 marginal cost per box yields a profit-maximizing output for Post of $2(000)$ at a profit-maximizing price of ($6 $-$ $2) $=$ $4 per box. These ($5/11 = 45\%$) and ($2/11 = 19\%$) market shares for Kellogg and Post, respectively, approximate their actual market shares in the ready-to-eat cereal market for raisin bran products. Additional firms with still less brand loyalty, like President's Choice, would supply the remaining segments illustrated still farther downward to the right.

Perhaps the best way to avoid a price war in a small oligopolistic rivalry group is to not start one in the first place. If someone else does start a price war, often the best response is simply to match the competition and then accentuate nonprice elements of the marketing mix by increasing services or advertising brands. Kellogg matched the Post price cut on only two-thirds of its premium brands. Two years later, cereal prices in the all-important grocery store distribution channel began to return to their 1995 pre-price-war levels.

A final key to avoiding price wars is to recognize the insights often available from game-theoretic analysis of various actions. With effective competitor surveillance to identify a rival's payoffs, the response of a competitor to one's own price cuts is often predictable, based on unilateral self-interest. In other circumstances, cooperative high-price outcomes may emerge from a convergence of mutual interest. In addition, simply recognizing the detailed structure of the pricing "game" can be a first step toward modifying the competitive environment to increase profitability. In the next section and in Web Chapter 16, we present game-theoretic techniques that have proven very useful for generating managerial insights into effective decision making.

Oligopolistic Rivalry and Game Theory

Most oligopolistic competition takes place today in product-line submarkets between a few rival incumbents, each with some market power over price. Consider Pepsi and Coke in colas, Canada's Wonderland and Disney in theme parks, and many airlines in air travel to Florida. Smaller competitors selling generic products are often present in fringe markets, but what distinguishes these oligopolists is the presence of some brand name or other barrier to effective entry. A small number of well-established, profitable, and highly interdependent incumbents is often the result. This oligopolistic market structure leads to some quite different forms of competition than we have previously encountered.

Recall that in a competitive industry, such as tract home building, each competitor can and must act independently. Each atomistic competitor takes price as "given," that is, determined externally in the open market, because any decision to expand or embargo its own supply has no appreciable effect on the industry supply. Even if one firm were to purchase all of the video rental outlets in a community, the barriers to entry are so low that any price above cost would surely attract enough new competitors to restore the competitive price-taking equilibrium.

In contrast, each firm in an oligopolistic market must pay very close attention to the moves and countermoves of its rivals, and often fiercely defends its market share. Ultimately, competitor surveillance is important in all market structures because quickly adaptive behaviour is preferable to reactive behaviour. But the intense interdependence of oligopolistic rivalry makes proactive behaviour best of all. Each oligopolist must try to predict well in advance the actions, responses, and counterresponses of its rivals and then choose optimal strategies accordingly. Modern **game theory** was invented for precisely this purpose.[10]

A Conceptual Framework for Game-Theoretic Analysis

A general definition of a **strategy game** is any consciously interdependent choice behaviour by purposeful individuals or hierarchical groups who share a common goal (e.g., tribes, sports teams, or value-maximizing companies). As such, strategy games have always been a part of human endeavours from the very beginning of prehistory. Some of the earliest formal analyses of strategy games involve voting games, bargaining games, and games of defence. Pliny the Younger, a first-century historian, records the pivotal role of strategic voting in the trial of a Roman senator, whose suicide was assisted by several freedmen. The accused preferred death to banishment and almost won acquittal despite a majority in favour of the conviction. Only by strategically voting a second-choice punishment of banishment did those senators in favour of execution prevent a minority control of the agenda from obtaining the acquittal.

Another example suggests that private property rights for one's personal effects evolved from a strategy game in which prehistoric tribes of hunter–gatherers had to decide between guarding consolidated property or marauding against targets of opportunity. The private property consolidators won out. Let's see why. In Table 8.2, two competing players (Randle and Kahn) compete for resources by selecting between two actions:

1. Maraude, which occasionally yields unguarded windfall treasures, but leaves one's own possessions vulnerable to counterattack.

2. Guard, which frees time between defensive struggles for consolidating and multiplying the fruits of one's labours.

Game Theory

A mathematical theory of decision making by the participants in a conflict-of-interest situation.

Strategy Game

A decision-making situation with consciously interdependent behaviour between two or more of the participants.

Learn more about game theory at **www. economics.harvard. edu/~aroth/alroth.html**.

---

[10] Three useful volumes on game theory are: R. McCain, *Game Theory* (Mason, OH: Thomson South-Western, 2004); A. Dixit and S. Skeath, *Games of Strategy* (New York: Norton, 1999); and Eric Rasmussen, *Games and Information*, 2nd ed. (Cambridge, MA: Basil Blackwell, 1993).

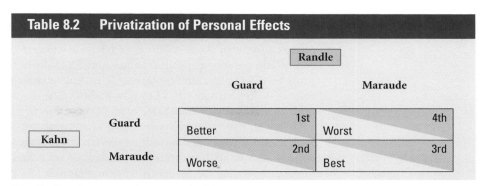

Table 8.2   Privatization of Personal Effects

		Randle	
		Guard	**Maraude**
Kahn	**Guard**	Better / 1st	Worst / 4th
	Maraude	Worse / 2nd	Best / 3rd

Note: Randle ranks outcomes from 1st to 4th; Kahn ranks outcomes from best to worst.

Dominant Strategy
An action rule that maximizes the decision maker's welfare independent of the actions of other players.

Kahn has an advantage against anything except strongly guarded positions, but knows too little about defence to be effective in guarding against attack. However, no matter what action Kahn decides to take, an examination of the payoff matrix in Table 8.2 reveals Randle is always better off selecting Guard. Guard is a **dominant strategy** for Randle in that Randle's outcomes from Guard exceed the outcomes from any alternative strategy, independent of the opponent's behaviour. Knowing this or discovering it through trial and error, Kahn predicts his rival Randle will continue to Guard. On that condition, Kahn then prefers Guard himself. {Guard, Guard} therefore emerges as the strategic equilibrium—i.e., a *dominant strategy equilibrium.*

Components of a Game

Normal Form of the Game
A representation of payoffs in a simultaneous-play game.

The essential elements of all strategy games are present in the Randle/Kahn example and include the following: players, actions, information sets, payoffs, an order of play, focal outcomes of interest, strategies, and equilibrium strategies. Let's illustrate with another example, taken this time from service quality competition. Suppose two *players,* Xerox and Sharp, must choose whether to discontinue copier repair service that is seven territories removed from their respective regional headquarters located in two different cities 320 kilometres apart. Six or seven territories of full-service repair are the *actions.* The *payoffs* from the decisions, which must be announced simultaneously at next week's industrial trade show, are shown in Table 8.3. This payoff matrix is the **normal form of the game,** which is an appropriate way of representing any simultaneous-play (versus sequential-play) game.

Sharp finds that full-service repair on demand in the more distant seventh territory is very expensive. Cutting back to six territories reduces cost by $15 per week per

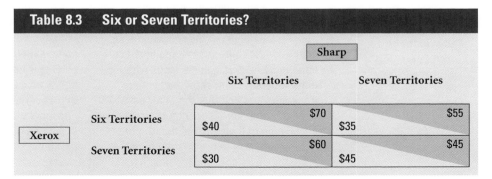

Table 8.3   Six or Seven Territories?

		Sharp	
		Six Territories	**Seven Territories**
Xerox	**Six Territories**	$40 / $70	$35 / $55
	Seven Territories	$30 / $60	$45 / $45

Note: Payoffs are profits. Sharp payoffs are above the diagonal; Xerox payoffs are below the diagonal.

customer and raises Sharp's profit from \$55 to \$70 per week when Xerox also cuts back, and from \$45 to \$60 per week when Xerox does not. The improved effectiveness of Sharp's service in the remaining six territories lowers the prices that rival Xerox can charge and reduces its profit from an initial \$45 down to only \$30 should Xerox continue servicing all seven territories. By cutting back to six territories itself, Xerox can restrict its losses to just \$5 (\$45 now to \$40). The common *information set* known to both players includes knowledge of all of these effects.

What strategy should Xerox adopt? First, using the concept of *dominant strategy,* it is clear that Sharp will discontinue service in the seventh territory. Sharp is better off cutting back to six territories independent of what Xerox does. For Sharp, the seven-territories strategy is *dominated* (unambiguously less preferred than six territories). Xerox wishes it were not so, because its most successful operation entails head-to-head, seven-territory competition against Sharp. Nevertheless, predictable reality lies elsewhere, and Xerox must predict six-territory behaviour on the part of its rival and proceed to reexamine its remaining options. Having eliminated Sharp's dominated strategy in the second column, Xerox now has an unambiguously preferred *strategy* of providing full-service repairs in only six territories itself. {Six, Six} is therefore the *equilibrium strategy* pair. That is, by applying the concept of a dominant strategy equilibrium to the prediction of its rival's behaviour, Xerox can iterate back to analyze its own best action. {Six, Six} is therefore referred to as an **iterated dominant strategy** equilibrium.

Iterated Dominant Strategy
An action rule that maximizes self-interest in light of the predictable dominant-strategy behaviour of other players.

The strategic equilibrium concept of eliminating dominated strategies in simultaneous games first appeared in *The Theory of Games and Economic Behaviour* (1944) by John von Neumann and Oskar Morgenstern. Von Neumann and Morgenstern confined their analysis primarily to cooperative games, in which players can form coalitions, arrange side payments, and enter into binding agreements. John Nash, Reinhard Selten, and John Harsanyi won the 1994 Nobel Prize in economic sciences for their extension of strategic equilibrium concepts to noncooperative games, sequential games, and games of imperfect information.

EXAMPLE

NOBEL GOES TO THREE GAME THEORISTS

Read more about Nash, Selten, and Harsanyi at the Nobel Prize website: **http://nobelprize. org/economics/ laureates/1994**.

Nash, Selten, and Harsanyi won the 1994 Nobel Prize for their work on equilibrium strategies in sequential games ranging from chess and poker to central bank interventions, limit pricing to deter entry, research and development competitions, and the auctioning of the radio magnetic spectrum. Not infrequently, multiple equilibria arise in such games—e.g., when either duopoly competitor may initiate price cuts and find that the other party will neither match nor discount further. Another implication of their work is that the order of play can have determinate effects on strategic decisions. Moving first in a preemptive product development can often foreclose a later competitor's threatened entry. In other circumstances, making the last response in the endgame, as dynamic technology changes to a new direction, can secure a strategic advantage. In addition, under incomplete information about opponent types, behaving like a "crazy" firm, which predatorily prices below cost when there is no later chance of recovering the losses, may deter an opponent's entry. Distinguishing between these and other complex paths to the most profitable strategy is the role of equilibrium strategies.

Cooperative and Noncooperative Games

Cooperative Game
Game structure that allows coalition formation, side payments, and binding third-party enforceable agreements.

In a **cooperative game,** players can form coalitions, make side payments, and communicate to one another their private information about their own prices, profit margins, or variable costs. This has limited the usefulness of cooperative game theory in business settings. An illustration of a side payment in cooperative games is the mandatory compensation scheme a manufacturer might impose when one sales representative violates another's exclusive territory. Also in cooperative games, a cartel might decide to enter into binding (i.e., third-party enforceable) contracts to segment the demander nations involved in a global diamond, coal, or coffee market. Most such cooperative game agreements between arms-length competitors to exchange price information or arrange side payments are illegal. Thus, business strategists paid relatively little attention to game theory until *noncooperative* strategic equilibrium concepts were developed.

Noncooperative Game
Game structure that prohibits collusion, side payments, and binding agreements enforced by third parties.

Noncooperative games prohibit collusive communication, side payment schemes, and third-party enforceable binding agreements. Instead, such games focus on self-enforcing reliance relationships to characterize strategic equilibrium and predict rival response. One example we have already encountered in Chapter 6 is the mutual reliance between sellers with nonredeployable assets and buyers of high-priced experience goods. Other examples include computer companies who build operating systems to a common standard that can communicate across PC platforms or competing airlines that announce high fares day after day despite the quick but short-lived attraction of breaking out as a renegade discounter. Clearly, these noncooperative games differ from cooperative games in important ways that make them more applicable to business strategy. Web Chapter 16 is devoted to an analysis of noncooperative games, with particular attention given to sequential equilibrium concepts such as first-mover/second-mover advantages and credible threats/credible commitments.

Other Types of Games

Games are also classified according to the number of players involved, the compatibility of their interests, and the number of replays of the game. We analyzed both of the above games as *single-period* (*"one-shot"*) *games.* Clearly, however, the ongoing rivalry between the players in "Guard–Maraude" and in "Six or Seven Territories?" is highly pertinent to the strategic situation. In Web Chapter 16, we turn our attention to the distinct and somewhat paradoxical implications of so-called *repeated games.* In a *two-person game,* each player attempts to obtain as much as possible from the other player through whatever methods of cooperation, bargaining, or threatening are available. *N-person games* are more difficult to analyze because subsets of players can form coalitions to impose solutions on the rest of the players. Coalitions can be of any size and can break up and re-form as the game proceeds. Parliamentary government is the classic example of *n*-person games. Although the possibility of coalitions adds greatly to the richness of the types of situations that can be considered by game theory, coalition-proofness is an equilibrium concept that adds substantial complexity to the theory required to analyze such games.

Two-Person Zero-Sum Game
Game in which net gains for one player necessarily imply equal net losses for the other player.

In a **two-person zero-sum game,** the players have exactly opposite interests. One player's gain is the other player's loss, and vice versa. Although a number of parlour games and some military applications can be analyzed with zero-sum games, the great preponderance of real-life conflict-of-interest situations do not fit within this model. In contrast, in a *two-person non-zero-sum game,* both players may gain or lose, depending on the actions each chooses to take. "Six or Seven Territories?" is a non-zero-sum game. Limiting competition to six territories raises the total profit from the interaction to $110 rather than $90. In all such games, at least one outcome is jointly preferred and, consequently, the players may be able to increase their payoffs through some form of cooperation. Perhaps the most famous generic structure for non-zero-sum games is the Prisoner's Dilemma. Many real-world conflict-of-interest situations, such as duopoly pricing between Pepsi and Coke, experience-good transactions, urban renewal decisions among adjacent landowners, and bargaining policy with terrorists, can be represented as Prisoner's Dilemma games.

In a Prisoner's Dilemma, two suspects are accused of jointly committing a crime.[11] To convict the suspects, however, a confession is needed from one or both of them. They are separated and no information can pass between them, so this is a noncooperative game. If neither suspect confesses, the prosecutor will be unable to convict them of the crime, and each suspect will receive only a short-term (1-year) prison sentence. If one suspect confesses and the other does not, then the one confessing will receive a suspended sentence and the other will receive a long-term (15-year) prison sentence. If both suspects confess, then each will receive an intermediate-term (6-year) prison sentence. Each suspect must decide, under these conditions, whether or not to confess. This conflict-of-interest situation can be represented in a game matrix like the one shown in Table 8.4.

This game can be examined by using the concept of a security level, or minimum payoff. For Suspect 1, the minimum payoff of the two alternative actions "Not Confess" and "Confess" are a 15-year and a 6-year prison sentence, respectively. The maximization of his security level would therefore motivate Suspect 1 to choose the second alternative action by confessing. Similar reasoning holds true for Suspect 2, and she also would be motivated to choose the alternative of confessing her guilt. Thus, the second alternative for each player (that is, "Confess") dominates the other strategy (that is, "Not Confess") and constitutes an equilibrium strategy pair and, in this sense, represents the solution of the game. A dominant strategy is one that provides a player with a larger payoff, regardless of what strategy the other player chooses. In this game, both suspects would clearly receive a larger payoff (that is, a shorter sentence) if they both decided to choose their first alternatives ("Not Confess"). However, in seeking to maximize their predictable payoffs (or, more accurately, to maximize their security levels), the first alternative is not a rational choice for either suspect.

As discussed above, in cooperative games the players have complete freedom of communication, with the opportunity to make threats and enter into binding and third-party enforceable agreements. Examining the Prisoner's Dilemma game again,

Table 8.4	Prisoner's Dilemma Payoff Matrix		
		Suspect 2	
		Not Confess	Confess
Suspect 1	**Not Confess**	1-year prison term / 1-year prison term	Suspended sentence / 15-year prison term
	Confess	15-year prison term / Suspended sentence	6-year prison term / 6-year prison term

---

[11] This example is discussed in more detail in R. D. Luce and H. Raiffa, *Games and Decisions* (New York: John Wiley & Sons, 1957), Section 5.4.

Coffee Cartel Dissolves*

In October 1991, the 17 top Colombian and Brazilian coffee producers announced an agreement to set up a coffee cartel. Each country and several African and Central American smaller producers agreed in principle to take millions of tonnes of coffee beans off the market in an effort to drive up wholesale prices. Brazilian producers would hold back 2 million bags of a projected 18-million-bag crop. Colombian producers would hold back 1.3 million bags. However, both countries opposed a formal quota system with assigned production ceilings, monitoring mechanisms, and penalization of violators. In July 1989, the previous International Coffee Agreement had collapsed over the refusal to accept assigned quotas.

When the 1992 harvest proved more plentiful than expected, coffee bean prices plummeted. Prisoner's Dilemma is less a "game" than a paradox about cooperation. If all major coffee bean producers could rely on one another to withhold production, all would have higher profitability. However, each cartel member maximizes self-interest by releasing excess supplies to the world market at just below the cartel official price. Because numerous other members think the same way, equilibrium market price will decline. Only dupes then continue to restrain output when world market prices collapse, signalling that other members are violating the agreement.

Coffee bean producers observed market price dropping precipitously in 1992 and concluded correctly that the cartel agreements to restrain output had dissolved.

* Based on "Non-Zero-Sum Strategic Game," *Financial Times*, July 2, 1995.

assume that the two players (that is, suspects) are able to communicate with each other and are able to enter into a binding agreement on which strategy each player will choose. In this case, because the cooperative outcome associated with both suspects not confessing is preferred to the noncooperative solution, the suspects would have an incentive to enter into a binding agreement for each to choose the strategy of not confessing. Without strong legal or moral sanctions to force the suspects to adhere to the agreement, however, each suspect would be tempted to double-cross the other suspect by confessing. The suspect who breaks the agreement has the possibility of reducing his or her sentence from a six-year prison term to a suspended sentence, as can be seen in Table 8.4. In a cooperative game, however, all such agreements are binding and enforceable.

The analogy to pricing and output decisions among firms in oligopolistic industries is striking. In some instances, cooperation may take the form of price leadership, where one firm takes on the role of price leader and the other firms act as followers. In other instances, the firms may enter into illegal price-fixing agreements and form a cartel. However, just as each of the suspects in the Prisoner's Dilemma game has an incentive to double-cross the other suspect, firms in oligopolistic industries have an incentive to depart from agreed-on prices or output quotas in any price-fixing agreement. As a

Are Nokia's Margins on Cellphones Collapsing?

For more information, go to **www.nokia.com**.

Recall that the managerial challenge ended with the question: Should Nokia invest heavily in 3GPP infrastructure and product design? The company's answer is yes. Nokia increased research and development expenditures in 2003 by 23 percent over those of 2002, which were higher than those of 2001. Therefore, Nokia was able to introduce many new cellphone models during 2004 as well as in early 2005.

result, these price-fixing agreements often break down quickly as one (or more) of the firms attempt(s) to increase its (their) profits through secret price reductions to customer(s). The Prisoner's Dilemma structure of many such pricing games predicts that the representative cartel member will have a dominant strategy to cheat on the cartel agreements.

We will see in Web Chapter 16 that raising the stakes from noncooperation or entering into a long-term, continuing relationship with opponents/cooperators can diminish this incentive to cheat. Nevertheless, most cartels are like the frequent price-fixing agreements that evolve several times a year among the manufacturers' sales representatives for cardboard packaging. Within two or three weeks, the collusive uniform pricing across alternative regional suppliers breaks down, often before the ink on legal indictments can dry.

Summary

- An *oligopoly* is an industry structure characterized by a relatively small number of firms in which recognizable *interdependencies* exist among the actions of the firms. Each firm is aware that its actions are likely to evoke countermoves from its rivals.

- In the *Cournot* oligopoly model, each of the firms determines its profit-maximizing output level assuming that the other firm's output will remain constant.

- In the *Stackelberg* oligopoly model, the leader determines its profit-maximizing output level by anticipating its rival's reaction to the leader' output level. The rival (follower) determines its profit-maximizing output level by assuming that the leader's output will remain constant.

- In the *Bertrand* oligopoly model, each firm attempts to maximize its profits by setting a price for its product. Bertrand equilibrium closely approximates the perfectly competitive result in the sense that price equals marginal cost.

- A *cartel* is a formal or informal agreement among oligopolists to cooperate or collude in determining outputs, prices, and profits. If the cartel members can enforce agreements and prevent cheating, they can act as a monopolist and maximize industry profits.

- A number of factors affect the ability of oligopolistic firms to engage successfully in some form of formal (or informal) cooperation. These include the number and size distribution of sellers, product heterogeneity, cost structures, size and frequency of orders, secrecy and retaliation, and the percentage of industry output external to the cartel.

- *Price leadership* is a pricing strategy in an oligopolistic industry in which one firm sets the price, and either by explicit or implicit agreement, the other firms tend to follow the decision. Effective price leadership exists when price movements initiated by the leader have a high probability of sticking and there are no maverick or non-conforming firms.

- In the *kinked demand curve* model, it is assumed that if an oligopoly firm reduces its prices, its competitors will quickly feel the decline in their sales and will be forced to match the reduction. Alternatively, if the oligopolist raises its prices, competitors will rapidly gain customers by maintaining their original prices and will have little or no motivation to match a price increase. Hence, the demand curve facing individual oligopolists is much more elastic for price increases than for price decreases and may lead oligopolists to maintain stable prices.

- In a *game-theoretic* analysis of oligopolistic decision making, the firm assumes that its competitor(s) will choose its (their) optimal decision-making strategy. Based on this assumption about its competitor(s), the firm chooses its own best counter-strategy.

- Business strategy games may be classified as simultaneous-play or sequential-play, one-shot or repeated, zero-sum or non-zero-sum, two-player or *n*-player, and cooperative or noncooperative.

- *Cooperative games* allow communication, coalition formation, binding side payment agreements, and third-party enforceable contracts.

Self-Test Exercises

1. Assume that two firms (C and D) are duopolists that produce identical products. Demand for the products is given by the following linear demand function:

$$P = 600 - Q_C - Q_D$$

where Q_C and Q_D are the quantities sold by the respective firms and P is the selling price. Total cost functions for the two firms are

$$TC_C = 25,000 + 100Q_C$$

$$TC_D = 20,000 + 125Q_D$$

Assuming that the firms act *independently* as in the Cournot model (that is, each firm assumes that the other firm's output will not change):

a. Determine the long-run equilibrium output and selling price for each firm.

b. Determine the total profits for each firm at the equilibrium output found in part (a).

2. Consider the previous exercise again. Assume that Firm D is a Stackelberg leader and Firm C is a Stackelberg follower. Recalculate your answers to parts (a) and (b).

3. Suppose that two Japanese companies, Hitachi and Toshiba, are the sole producers (i.e., duopolists) of a microprocessor chip used in a number of different brands of personal computers. Assume that total demand for the chips is fixed and that each firm charges the same price for the chips. Each firm's market share and profits are a function of the magnitude of the promotional campaign used to promote its version of the chip. Also assume that only two strategies are available to each firm—a limited promotional campaign (budget) and an extensive promotional campaign (budget). If the two firms engage in a limited promotional campaign, each firm will earn a quarterly profit of $7.5 million. If the two firms undertake an extensive promotional campaign, each firm will earn a quarterly profit of $5.0 million.

With this strategy combination, market share and total sales will be the same as for a limited promotional campaign, but promotional costs will be higher and hence profits will be lower. If either firm engages in a limited promotional campaign and the other firm undertakes an extensive promotional campaign, then the firm that adopts the extensive campaign will increase its market share and earn a profit of $9.0 million, whereas the firm that chooses the limited campaign will earn a profit of only $4.0 million.

a. Develop a payoff matrix for this decision-making problem.

b. In the absence of a binding and enforceable agreement, determine the dominant advertising strategy and minimum payoff for Hitachi.

c. Determine the dominant advertising strategy and minimum payoff for Toshiba.

d. Explain why the firms may choose not to play their dominant strategies whenever this game is repeated over multiple decision-making periods.

Exercises

1. Assume that two firms (A and B) are duopolists that produce identical products. Demand for the products is given by the following linear demand function:

$$P = 200 - Q_A - Q_B$$

where Q_A and Q_B are the quantities sold by the respective firms and P is the selling price. Total cost functions for the two companies are

$$TC_A = 1,500 + 55Q_A + Q_A^2$$
$$TC_B = 1,200 + 20Q_B + 2Q_B^2$$

Assume that the firms act *independently* as in the Cournot model (that is, each firm assumes that the other firm's output will not change).

a. Determine the long-run equilibrium output and selling price for each firm.

b. Determine Firm A, Firm B, and total industry profits at the equilibrium solution found in part (a).

2. Consider Exercise 1 again. Assume that Firm A is a Stackelberg leader and Firm B is a Stackelberg follower. Recalculate your answers to parts (a) and (b).

3. Consider Exercise 1 again. Assume that the firms act independently as in the Bertrand model (that is, each firm sets its price). Recalculate your answers to parts (a) and (b).

4. Consider Exercise 1 again. Assume that the firms form a *cartel* to act as a monopolist and maximize total industry profits (sum of Firm A and Firm B profits).

   a. Determine the optimum output and selling price for each firm.

   b. Determine Firm A, Firm B, and total industry profits at the optimal solution found in part (a).

   c. Show that the marginal costs of the two firms are equal at the optimal solution found in part (a).

5. Compare the optimal solutions obtained in Exercises 1 through 4. Specifically:

   a. How much higher (lower) is the optimal selling price when the two firms form a cartel to maximize industry profits, compared to the Cournot, Stackelberg, and Bertrand cases?

   b. How much higher (lower) is total industry output?

   c. How much higher (lower) are total industry profits?

6. Alchem (L) is the price leader in the polyglue market. All 10 other manufacturers (follower [F] firms) sell polyglue at the same price as Alchem. Alchem allows the other firms to sell as much as they wish at the established price and supplies the remainder of the demand itself. Total demand for polyglue is given by the following function ($Q_T = Q_L + Q_F$):

$$P = 20{,}000 - 4Q_T$$

   Alchem's marginal cost function for manufacturing and selling polyglue is

$$MC_L = 5{,}000 + 5Q_L$$

   The aggregate marginal cost function for the other manufacturers of polyglue is

$$\Sigma MC_F = 2{,}000 + 4Q_F$$

   a. To maximize profits, how much polyglue should Alchem produce and what price should it charge?

   b. What is the total market demand for polyglue at the price established by Alchem in part (a)? How much of total demand do the follower firms supply?

7. Chillman Motors believes it faces the following segmented demand function:

$$P = \begin{cases} 150 - 0.5Q & \text{when } 0 \le Q \le 50 \\ 200 - 1.5Q & \text{for } Q > 50 \end{cases}$$

   a. Indicate both verbally and graphically why such a segmented demand function is likely to exist. What type of industry structure is indicated by this relationship?

   b. Calculate the marginal revenue functions facing Chillman. Add these to your graph from part (a).

   c. Chillman's total cost function is

$$TC_1 = 500 + 15Q + 0.5Q^2$$

   Calculate the marginal cost function. What is Chillman's profit-maximizing price and output combination?

   d. What is Chillman's profit-maximizing price–output combination if total costs increase to the following?

$$TC_2 = 500 + 45Q + 0.5Q^2$$

e. If Chillman's total cost function changes to either

$$TC_3 = 500 + 15Q + 1.0Q^2$$

or

$$TC_4 = 500 + 5Q + 0.25Q^2$$

what price–output solution do you expect to prevail? Would your answer change if you knew that all firms in the industry witnessed similar changes in their cost functions?

8. Consider the following payoff matrix:

Exercise 8			

		Player B Strategy	
		1	2
Player A Strategy	1	$2,000 / $1,000	−$1,000 / −$2,000
	2	−$2,000 / −$1,000	$1,000 / $2,000

a. Does Player A have a dominant strategy? Explain why or why not.

b. Does Player B have a dominant strategy? Explain why or why not.

9. Suppose that two mining companies, Australian Minerals Company (AMC) and South African Mines, Inc. (SAMI), control the only sources of a rare mineral used in making certain electronic components. The firms have agreed to form a cartel to set the (profit-maximizing) price of the mineral. Each company must decide whether to *abide* by the agreement (i.e., not offer secret price cuts to customers) or *not abide* (i.e., offer secret price cuts to customers). If both firms abide by the agreement, AMC will earn an annual profit of $30 million and SAMI will earn an annual profit of $20 million from sales of the mineral. If AMC does not abide and SAMI abides by the agreement, then AMC earns $40 million and SAMI earns $5 million. If SAMI does not abide and AMC abides by the agreement, then AMC earns $10 million and SAMI earns $30 million. If both firms do not abide by the agreement, then AMC earns $15 million and SAMI earns $10 million.

a. Develop a payoff matrix for this decision-making problem.

b. In the absence of a binding and enforceable agreement, determine the dominant strategy for AMC.

c. Determine the dominant strategy for SAMI.

d. If the two firms can enter into a binding and enforceable agreement, determine the strategy that each firm should choose.

CELLPHONES DISPLACE MOBILE PHONE SATELLITE NETWORKS

Motorola's Iridium, a go-anywhere mobile phone system that beamed signals down from 66 satellites, was called "the eighth wonder of the world" by Motorola CEO Chris Galvin. However, at $1,500 for a handset the size of a brick, consumers balked, and few business customers needed the security and reliability offered in remote corners of the globe like Katmandu. As a result, Motorola's 25 percent market share in cellphones declined steadily to 13 percent in 2001, and Motorola shares fell 16 percent from 1997–2001, during a period when the S&P 500 Index was up 76 percent.

Questions

1. What trends did Nokia pursue as it designed mobile phone products in the late 1990s? Refer to this chapter's Managerial Challenge and Managerial Challenge Revisited.

2. What might a more proactive Motorola have done differently had it correctly perceived the steps its rival Nokia would take?

CHAPTER 9

Pricing Strategies

Chapter Preview

This chapter builds on the price and output determination models developed in Chapters 6 through 8, as it considers more complex pricing issues. The first two sections examine a value-based pricing conceptual framework. Then we characterize differential pricing in directly segmented markets, where different target customers are charged nonuniform prices for identical products or services at different times or places. Differential pricing in less segmented or indirectly segmented markets is accomplished with bundled pricing and nonlinear pricing using two-part tariffs (an access or entry fee combined with a user fee). Next, we discuss the concept of pricing throughout the product life cycle, including penetration pricing, target pricing, limit pricing, price skimming, and prestige pricing. Finally, we discuss transfer pricing for the situation of no external market for the intermediate product. Together, the pricing practices presented in this chapter provide an extensive overview of the way managers actually apply pricing techniques to maximize shareholder wealth.

Web Appendix 9A develops the powerful revenue management systems that have revolutionized pricing and capacity allocation for multiproduct firms with perishable products or services like airline seats, hotel rooms, rental cars, and satellite transmission. To access Web chapters and appendixes, go to the Nelson website for this book at www.mcguigan.nelson.com.

Web Appendix 9B discusses the pricing of joint products. It also extends this chapter's discussion of transfer pricing to the situations of competitive or imperfectly competitive external markets for the intermediate product. Web Chapter 16 provides additional insights on pricing strategies from a game-theoretic approach.

Learning Objectives

After studying this chapter, you should be able to:

1. Explain why all pricing decisions should be *proactive, systematic, and value-based*.

2. Describe *price discrimination* and explain the two conditions required for effective price discrimination, how to maximize profits using it, and how to implement it through two-part pricing.

3. Explain why *bundling* is a highly effective pricing mechanism.

4. Explain how firms that sell multiple products with interdependent demands make decisions to add or delete products in existing product lines considering the (positive or negative) impacts on sales of the firm's current outputs.

5. Understand that pricing strategy varies throughout the product or service life cycle.

6. Explain how *full-cost pricing* and *target pricing* can be consistent with the marginal pricing rules of economic theory and describe how *incrementalism* helps managers achieve more efficient and profitable operations.

7. Describe other pricing methods such as *penetration pricing, value-based pricing, limit pricing, niche pricing, skimming strategy, prestige pricing* and *Web-based pricing*.

8. Explain optimal transfer pricing methods.

9. (Web Appendix 9A) Explain the importance of revenue or yield management (YM) as a technique to deal with pricing and capacity-allocation problems under fixed capacity and random demand.

10. (Web Appendix 9B) Explain the pricing of joint products and transfer pricing.

Pricing of Apple Computers: Market Share vs. Current Profitability*

Apple manufactures and sells Macintosh, PowerBook, and iMac personal computers (PCs). Apple PCs compete against IBM-type PCs made by many companies, such as IBM, Toshiba, Dell, and Hewlett-Packard. Apple often uses microprocessor chips designed by Motorola as the "brains" of its PCs, whereas most of the other PC makers use Intel (or Intel clone) microprocessor chips in their machines.

Historically, Apple has priced its personal computers higher than similar models of other PC makers. For example, despite price cuts in early 1995 by both Apple and other PC companies, Macintosh systems were still priced $500 to $1,000 higher. Consequently, Apple's market share fell from 9.4 percent in 1993 to 8 percent in 1994. While industry shipments skyrocketed, Apple's margins increased (from 24 percent to 29 percent) on essentially flat unit sales.

By emphasizing current profit over market share, Apple discouraged independent software developers. Some observers believe that the firm must increase its market share to about 20 percent to motivate software firms to write application programs for Apple PCs.

Ian Diery, Apple's sales vice president, defended the firm's high prices, saying that Apple had to improve its balance sheet so that it could continue research and marketing efforts. This chapter focuses on a variety of different pricing strategies like Apple's decision to charge premium prices for its products.

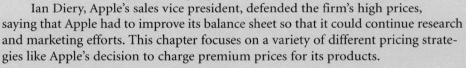

Access financial information about Apple Computer at **www.apple.com/investor**.

*Jim Carlton, "Apple's Choice: Preserve Profits or Cut Prices," *The Wall Street Journal*, February 22, 1995, p. B1.

Conceptual Framework for Proactive, Systematic-Analytical, Value-Based Pricing

In the past, pricing decisions were often treated as an afterthought and made in ad hoc fashion as a reaction to competitor initiatives. When pricing rivalry was more stable, many firms would simply routinely mark up cost. Today, pricing proactively with systematic analysis of which orders to accept (and which to refuse) at many different value-based prices has become a critical success factor for many businesses.

Proactive pricing is tactically astute and internally consistent with operations strategy. A high-cost airline cannot slash prices dramatically even if 10 or 20 percent increases in market share in a high-margin segment are thereby achievable. It must instead anticipate a matching price reaction by its lower-cost rivals, perhaps followed by still further price cuts below its own cost. Knowing all this in advance renders gainshare discounting much less attractive, despite the temptation of additional incremental sales in a high-margin business.

To take another example, in the men's aftershave industry, an incumbent recently encountered a new entrant whose product, Vibrance, was introduced with a penetration price 40 percent below the leading brand. The incumbent increased advertising but maintained its original price point and was astounded to observe a 50 percent decline in market share through its grocery store distribution channel. Only afterward was systematic analysis completed. Estimations showed that demand was very price elastic and advertising inelastic. Pricing decisions must be systematic and analytical, based on hard facts instead of ad hoc hunches.

Finally, the appropriate conceptual framework for setting prices is an analysis of the determinants of customer value. What triggers a customer's purchase is value in excess of asking price or a ratio of value to price greater than a competitor's ratio. Firms must begin their pricing decisions by identifying the value-drivers in each customer segment. Business air travellers value delivery reliability, the ability to change itineraries on short notice (i.e., change order responsiveness), and schedule convenience more than the service characteristics of attentive flight attendants, wide seats, or quiet flights. Because such process-based value-drivers are harder to imitate, sustainable price premiums are often associated with these operational processes rather than the product or service characteristics themselves.

On the other hand, Prestone and Zerex have leading anticorrosive radiator fluids whose product characteristics warrant a price premium. Under apparent price pressure, Zerex often simply meets the competition as long as competing prices on generic radiator fluid cover costs. A thorough value analysis reveals, however, that this reactive cost-based pricing fails to realize about one-third of Zerex's sustainable profit margin. Cost-based pricing has been called one of the "five deadly business sins" by management consultant and author Peter Drucker. What firms should do instead is "price-based costing." That is, firms should segment customers, perform extensive value analysis, and then develop products whose costs allow substantial profitability in each product line the firm chooses to enter. Each firm's marketing and operations capabilities are the key to then sustaining that profitability.

Costs are not irrelevant. Indeed, a key to effective revenue management is knowing precisely what activity-based costs are associated with each type of order from each customer segment. Knowledge of differential costs supports the adoption of differential pricing and, even more importantly, allows value-based pricing managers to discern *which orders to refuse*. Costs should be the result of a value-based pricing and product development strategy.

In sum, pricing decisions should be proactive and systematic-analytical, not reactive and ad hoc. And, most importantly, pricing should be value-based, not cost-based. This value-based conceptual framework leads naturally to a differential pricing environment in which mass-produced products or services are customized to the requirements of target customer classes and nonuniform pricing then ensues.

Read an article by Kevin M. Guthrie on value-based pricing at **www.arl.org/scomm/ scat/guthries.html**.

Intertemporal Pricing in Target Market Segments

Value-based differential pricing implies identifying the different value-drivers for various segments of the target market. Direct segmentation of target customers and the prevention of resale arbitrage between them can be accomplished with a variety of "fences." Two of the most frequent involve intertemporal pricing and pricing by delivery location.

Congestion Pricing
Charging a fee that reflects the true marginal cost imposed by demand in excess of capacity.

An example of intertemporal pricing, **congestion pricing** at peak demand periods on roadways, bridges, and subway systems, is illustrated in Figure 9.1. Peak-period drivers place demands on a toll road between 6 A.M. and 9 A.M. far in excess of its carrying capacity (Q_C). Charging peak-period commuters a toll equal to just the minuscule cost of wear-and-tear maintenance—i.e., an off-peak marginal cost—(MC_{OP}) induces many more cars to enter the highway (Q_{PEAK}) than can be accommodated (i.e., $Q_P > Q_C$). The result is slowdowns, stoppages, and a markedly increased travel time for each commuter. Beyond Q_C, the traffic volume at which this congestion begins, MC_P

FIGURE 9.1

Congestion Tolls with Peak–Off-Peak Demand

The price P_{OP} and traffic volume Q_{OP} are the socially optimal price and traffic volume for the off-peak period. If price remains at P_{OP} during the peak period, traffic volume rises to Q_{PEAK}. The resultant congestion on the road imposes incremental fuel and time costs on existing drivers whenever an additional driver enters. The marginal costs of these externalities are represented by the rising curve MC_P. The appropriate toll is set at P_P, where MC_P cuts the peak period demand curve D_{PEAK}. The increase in the toll from $P_{OP} = MC_{OP}$ to P_P is called the "congestion toll" $(P_P - MC_{OP})$. It induces the discretionary peak-period traveller to switch either to other travel times or to alternative modes of transportation.

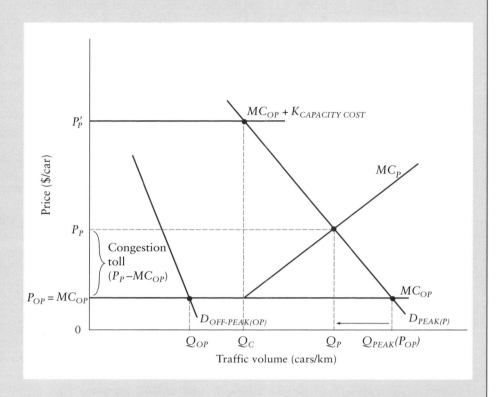

represents the incremental fuel and time costs imposed (by one additional car) on all of the other drivers along a 16-kilometre stretch of toll road. A congestion toll of $(P_P - MC_{OP})$ induces discretionary peak period travellers to switch to other travel times and alternative modes of transportation. If a toll road authority set peak-period prices just sufficient to cover this congestion cost, traffic volume would decline from $Q_{PEAK}(P_{OP})$ to Q_P, and the equilibrium differential prices P_P and P_{OP} would emerge. Congestion pricing accomplishes the goal of placing a true resource cost on the scarce transportation system capacity at peak travel times.

Like peak–off-peak roadway pricing, many other examples of differential pricing entail charging differential prices for the same capacity at different times. Intertemporal pricing at matinee and evening movie theatres, for example, involves segmented demanders not in rivalry for the same theatre seats. First-run movies and subsequent movie videos, hardback and later paperback editions of books, seasonal discounts in the resort and cruise ship businesses, and weekend discounts on airlines all represent effective intertemporal segmentation of different target customer classes. However, if two customer classes are in rivalry for the same capacity (e.g., the seats in economy class on a particular airplane flight), then differential pricing involves price discrimination, which is discussed below.

Direct segmentation of target customer classes can also be accomplished by geographic locations. Customers who arrive at the neighbourhood rental counters of Hertz and Avis have flexibly timed convenience-based uses for rental cars. Consequently, the neighbourhood-location demand is much more price sensitive than the airport-location demand by business travellers. In fact, there are firms such as Rent-A-Wreck that specialize in renting to the budget-conscious consumer. Since round-trip taxi fares from airports to the neighbourhood locations would typically far exceed the price difference, Avis and Hertz customers are effectively segmented.

Other examples of location-based segmentation would be electronic debits for driving in inner-city congestion zones (e.g., London, England, has recently imposed a £5/day charge in and around Westminster), and fashion clothing from France's Arche or Ralph Lauren sold less expensively in discount outlets in outlying locations or in vacation resort complexes.

Outlet shoppers almost never overlap with the customers these companies find in their trendy downtown boutiques. Hence, geographic segmentation works. Outlet shoppers will also buy a less costly, less durable version of the product (e.g., a lighter weight chemise cloth in Polo golf shirts), so in differential pricing, Ralph Lauren accomplishes more than just inventory clearance without any danger of cannibalizing full-price sales. Instead, such companies are "versioning" their products. Hal Varian and Carl Shapiro have argued that versioning is an especially good way to sell information economy items like software.[1] A voice recognition package sells for three different prices, depending on the version. All three versions derive from the same code, but the more enabled and comprehensive version generates one hundred times as much value to particular target customers. In contrast, when Amazon sells the *same* book or DVD at different prices to customers with different click streams, that's a different pricing practice. That's price discrimination.

Price Discrimination

Price Discrimination
Selling the same good or service, produced by a single firm, at different prices to different buyers, during the same time period.

Price discrimination is defined as the act of selling the same product (a good or service), produced under single control (that is, by one firm), at different prices to different buyers during the same period of time. Examples of price discrimination include the following:

- Lawyers and tax preparers who charge the rich more than the poor for the same quality of service.

- Dell selling its ultralight laptop at $2,307 to small business customers; at $2,228 to health care companies; and at $2,072 to governments.

- Firms that sell the exact same product under two different labels at widely varying prices (Whirlpool and Kenmore appliances, Michelin and Sears Roadhandler radial tires).

- Athletic teams that sponsor family nights and ladies' nights at discount prices, while other customers pay the full price.

- Hotels, restaurants, and other businesses that offer discounts to senior citizens.

- Airlines that offer discounted fares based on the length of stay (e.g., over Saturday night).

- Korean TV manufacturers who sell products direct to the customer at a lower price in North America than in Japan.

Most differential pricing to a firm's retail customers is perfectly legal and it unambiguously raises profits. This happens because the satisfaction or utility gained from the purchase of the product exceeds that which is lost from paying a uniform price, and a *consumer surplus* results. If a coffee aficionado was willing to pay $6 for a morning cup of java but found that Tim Hortons charged only $2, the consumer surplus would be $4. Price discrimination transfers some of this consumer surplus from the consumer to the seller.

---

[1] C. Shapiro and H. Varian, "Versioning," *Harvard Business Review*, November/December 1998, pp. 106–114.

E-BUSINESS CLICK STREAMS ALLOW PRICE DISCRIMINATION: PERSONIFY*

Personify, an Internet service company, has created software that allows Web businesses to categorize buyers based on their clickstream patterns. Relating these segments to their price sensitivity in past purchases, Virtual Vineyards and Amazon.com have begun charging different prices for the same wine or book. If it costs $200 to produce and stock a case of 20 bottles of wine, and if five customers will pay $24 a bottle (for one bottle each) while another fifteen customers will pay $8 a bottle, uniform pricing will result in a loss, and the vineyard will stop producing this wine. At an $8 uniform price, all twenty customers buy, and the winery loses $40. At a $24 price, five customers buy, and the winery loses $80.

But suppose the five customers pay $20 per bottle, while the fifteen are asked to pay $7. Each group paid less than their willingness to pay and less than their proposed uniform price, yet the winery makes a $5 profit.

* Based on "I Got It Cheaper Than You," *Forbes,* November 2, 1998, pp. 83–84.

In the limiting case of perfect price discrimination, the seller discovers the maximum each individual is willing to pay for each unit purchased, sometimes called the **reservation price.** The monopolist then charges all purchasers their own reservation prices and manages to capture the entire consumer surplus. For example, in the discriminatory descending price (Dutch) auction market for T-bills (discussed in Web Chapter 17), bidders each submit an entire demand schedule of bids at various quantities.

Reservation Price
The maximum price a customer will pay to reserve a product or service.

PRICELINE IMPLEMENTS PERFECT PRICE DISCRIMINATION*

Priceline.ca has taken price discrimination one step further by inducing potential buyers to post their differential offer prices on a website. Buyers of airline tickets on Priceline.ca, for example, don't get to specify their carrier, their departure time, or their number of stops. This "reverse auction" process imposes advance planning time costs, inconvenient trip itineraries, and the uncertainty as to whether any seller will accept the offer. However, for a deep enough discount, some customers purchase seats that would otherwise go empty. Other customers see the time, inconvenience, and unreliability as justification for paying the airline's own much higher posted prices. In effect, each customer in the Priceline distribution channel pays a different markup and has no opportunity to resell to those with higher willingness to pay. In principle, Priceline's system allows perfect price discrimination.

* Based on "Priceline Depends on Ignorance," *Pittsburgh Post-Gazette,* May 24, 2000, p. C-2.

Because the information required for such pricing is extremely rare, perfect price discrimination almost never occurs. Instead, firms usually attempt to price-discriminate among classes of customers using intertemporal and geographic segmentation. Even that degree of differential pricing may, however, lead to adverse customer reactions. As a result, sellers have adopted *indirect segmentation* techniques: two-part tariffs and bundling.

Two-Part Tariff

One effective method of implementing price discrimination is to charge both a lump sum entry fee and a user fee. Amusement parks, nightclubs, golf and tennis clubs, cellphone service providers, Internet access providers, and rental car companies often employ such pricing. Their revenue per unit sale is a nonlinear function of two parts: a lump sum monthly or daily fee that provides access to the facility, phone, computer, or rental car independent of use, and a per-hour or per-minute or per-kilometre fee that varies with usage. Although the magnitude of user fees should be and often is reflective of marginal costs, heavy demanders pay more through higher user fees. Companies differ on whether to set uniformly high or low entry fees and whether to charge high or low user fees. For example, Gillette practically gives away its razors but then charges steep prices for the blades. Golf and tennis clubs, in contrast, charge substantial membership fees and annual dues, but often adopt trivial user fees (e.g., $5 per court hour).

Consider the two-part pricing depicted in Figure 9.2 for separate customer segments with relatively elastic and relatively inelastic demand for rental autos. These might be young couples who are renting cars for vacationing (D_1) and manufacturers' trade representatives renting cars for making sales calls (D_2). The challenge is to find a uniform daily rate (the lump sum access fee) and a kilometrage charge that maximize profit and

EXAMPLE

TWO-PART TARIFFS FOR ELECTRICITY*

In principle, as experience has shown in Australia, Britain, and New Zealand, deregulation of electricity can work well if peak-load customers are asked to pay a price that reflects the marginal cost of the current. It has been estimated that as much as 55 percent of the variation in intraday cost is attributable to extraordinary transmission line fees and old inefficient plants fired up to meet the last 5 percent of peak demand. However, North American consumers are averse to advanced metering systems and time-of-day pricing. One alternative is to charge uniform prices per kilowatt-hour but add on access fees for interruptible (brownout) service far below those that hospital and computer system operators would pay for uninterruptible service. Industrial customers expect that such two-part pricing will lower their overall power costs by as much as 30 percent.

The real success or failure of the deregulatory initiative in electricity will hinge on whether residential customers will conserve energy when the marginal cost is high or, alternatively, will pressure their politicians to cap the price of electricity and then overburden the scarce capacity of underfunded electric companies.

---

* Based on "How to Do Deregulation Right," *BusinessWeek*, March 26, 2001, p. 112; "PG&E Gropes for a Way Out," *The Wall Street Journal*, January 4, 2001, p. A1; and A. Faruqui and K. Eakin, eds., *Pricing in Competitive Electricity Markets* (New York: Kluwer, 2000).

Chapter 9   Pricing Strategies

FIGURE 9.2

Optimal Two-Part Tariffs for Auto Rentals

This graph illustrates two different pricing alternatives for the two-part tariff (lump sum access fee and kilometrage fee) for auto rentals.

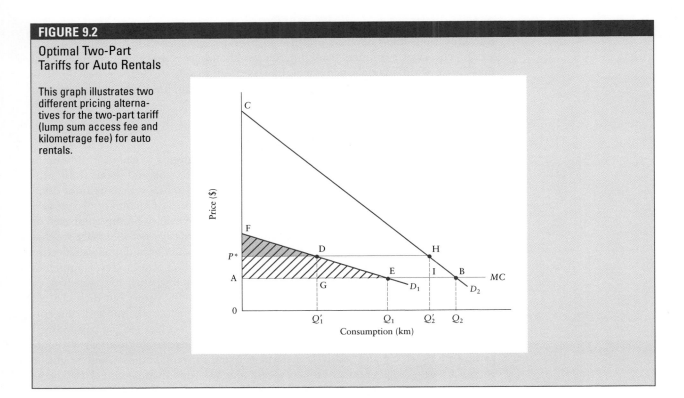

keep both segments in the market. One alternative would be to price the kilometrage at its marginal cost $(MC) = OA$ and elicit Q_1 and Q_2 usage while realizing from both customer segments the maximum daily rate (a lump sum access fee) that the price-sensitive D_1 demanders will pay (namely, hatched area AEF). Perhaps, however, a better alternative is available. Suppose the car rental agency raises the price to P^* and reduces the daily access fee to the hatched and shaded area P^*DF in Figure 9.2. Kilometrage will decline in both segments, and area P^*DEA will be net revenue lost by virtue of the reduced daily access fee in both segments. However, the additional net revenue from kilometrage charges (P^*DGA in one segment and P^*HIA in the other segment) will more than offset the lost access fees. Consequently, in addition to charging positive lump sum access fees, a price-discriminating monopolist will adopt two-part tariffs that price usage above its marginal cost. The more similar the demands of target customer segments, the closer the optimal user fee should be to marginal cost. The more dissimilar the segment demands are, the higher the optimal unit price above MC should be.

Where capacity is insufficient to absorb peak demand, two-part pricing is an efficient way to recover capacity cost and provide for additional capital equipment investment. Using such mechanisms, CompuServe delivered Internet connection on the customers' first try 97 percent of the time. AOL then decided to offer a "light usage" plan for $4.95 per month for the first three hours of Internet use, plus $2.50 for each additional hour. Without at least a small user fee to discourage trivial use, excess demand would have continued to plague their business.

Bundling

Another highly effective pricing mechanism that sellers use to capture consumer surplus is bundling. Have you ever wondered why cable TV firms offer the Movie Network only in a bundled package that includes the History Channel, which you usually ignore? One insight is that this particular bundle of product offerings occurs because someone else is a history buff who is wondering why the History Channel comes with a cable package that includes largely unwatched movies. That is, if sellers are restricted from quoting perfect price-discriminating differential prices to every customer, the operating profit to a seller from bundling negatively correlated demands may be larger than the operating profit from selling equally costly products separately. Let's see why.

Suppose that two sets of customers have the following reservation prices for two cable channels, each of which incurs variable licensing fees of $1 for a single showing to a single household. Movie buffs would pay $9 for access to first-run movies and $2 for access to historical documentaries. History buffs would pay $8 for access to the History Channel and $3 for access to movies. If the channels are priced uniformly to both customer segments as separate products, CableCo can realize at most $8 (or $9 − $1) on the Movie Network and $7 (or $8 − $1) on the History Channel for a total of $15 operating profit.[2] However, note that both types of customers would pay up to $11 for the combined pair of channels rather than do without. If CableCo made them available only as a bundled package, sales revenue would be $22 minus $4 licensing fees, for a total of $18 operating profit. The $18 profit exceeds $15 by quite a lot, and it turns out that this result is entirely general. As long as one customer is willing to pay more for an item that another customer wants less than some alternative item, the seller who is restricted to charging the two customers the same uniform price will always be better off bundling the two items, assuming all reservation prices exceed variable cost.

Now suppose the variable costs are higher at, say, $3. The History Channel valued at $2 by the movie buff is no longer a profitable sale. Pure bundling includes this unprofitable sale and generates the same $22 revenue but now incurs $12 of total variable cost, yielding a profit of only $10. Foregoing the sale of the History Channel to the movie buff by selling each product separately at a $9 price for the Movie Network and an $8 price for the History Channel generates $6 (or $9 − $3) on the Movie Network and $5 (or $8 − $3) on the History Channel, yielding a total of $11 operating profit. Quite intuitively, pure bundling will be less attractive than pricing separately when some of the bundled sales are unprofitable.

It is also easy to see why positively correlated demand across customers works against bundling. Figure 9.3 displays reservation prices along a "budget" line that our customers mentioned above are willing to spend on the two products.[3] The y-intercept is the total willingness-to-pay constraint for the two products—namely, $P_h + P_m = \$11$. With movie channel reservation prices on the vertical axis and History Channel reservation prices on the horizontal axis, each customer's mix of reservation prices lies along the line

$$(9.1) \qquad\qquad P_m = \$11 - 1\,(P_h)$$

The −1 in Equation 9.1 signifies the perfect negative correlation between the reservation prices (demand) of our movie buff and those of our history buff. But suppose CableCo has a third type of customer, whose reservation prices are positively correlated with those of the movie buffs—that is, a third type of customer who values the Movie Network at $8 and the History Channel at $5. These reservation prices are high when

---

[2] In this example, selling both products separately to both customer segments does not pay, because of the much lower prices required. Specifically, the Movie Network priced separately into both segments would have to sell for as little as $3, thereby earning operating profits of $4 (or $6 − $2), and the History Channel would have to sell for as little as $2, earning $2 (or $4 − $2). Thus, the total profit of $6 from selling all products to all customers at a uniform price would substantially diminish the potential profit ($15) from selling each product to its target market alone. If the asymmetric demands in the two segments were not so different, this result could reverse, as long as all the reservation prices were greater than variable cost.

[3] This budget line is analogous to the budget line of a household making consumption decisions, except in this case it is the firm that is constrained by the maximum expenditure the customer is willing to make on the two goods.

FIGURE 9.3

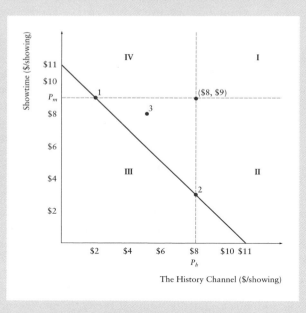

Reservation Prices for Three Customer Segments

Suppose that licence fees were $3 per channel. Then offering the bundle for $13 and the individual products at P_h = $8 and P_m = $9 (i.e., mixed bundling) would maximize profits at $18. Fees from customers 1, 2, and 3 would be $9, $8, and $13, respectively, and total $30. Licence fees would total $12.

the movie buff's reservation price is high and low when the movie buff's reservation price is low. Such positively correlated demand lies above the budget constraint in Figure 9.3 because the total willingness to pay on the left-hand side of Equation 9.1 is no longer $11 but rather is now $13, as shown for point 3 in the figure.

With positively correlated demands across two of the three customer types, CableCo could sell the Movie Network–History Channel bundle to all three for $11 and earn $15 (= 3 × [$11 − $6]).[4] However, a better alternative is available. **Mixed bundling** sells the products both separately and as a bundle with the bundled price discounted below the sum of the two separate prices. In our three-customer-type example, CableCo could sell the Movie Network for $9 and sell the History Channel for $8, while making the Movie Network–History Channel bundle available for the package price of $13. The third type of customer would opt for the bundle, whereas each of the other types of customers would buy one product only. Revenue for this mixed bundling approach totals $30, but only four licence fees are required, therefore earning $18 in profit. In general, pure bundling generates less profit than mixed bundling when positively correlated demands are involved.

Figure 9.3 can be used to characterize the attractiveness of pure bundling for the seller. If all customers have perfectly negatively correlated demands, their reservation prices lie, as we have seen, along the $11 budget constraint. If customers have positively correlated demands, their reservation prices will lie above or below this reservation budget constraint. With separate product prices of P_m = $9 and P_h = $8, customers with reservation prices in quadrant I in the figure will always buy both products rather than one of the separate products alone (quadrants II and IV), while those in quadrant III will never buy either product sold separately. In addition, however, we know that customers with reservation prices above the reservation budget constraint will buy the bundled package and those below will not. Optimally, customer 3 will therefore purchase the bundle, customer 1 will purchase the Movie Network alone, and customer 2 will purchase the History Channel alone. Only mixed bundling can achieve this result.

Mixed Bundling
Selling multiple products both separately and together for less than the sum of the separate prices.

---

[4] Here, we are again assuming that variable costs are at the higher level, $3 per showing.

We now investigate the optimal level at which price-discriminating prices should be set, returning to the simplest case of differential prices in directly segmented distribution channels.

Optimal Discriminating Price Levels

For more information on the Dairy Farmers of Ontario, visit its website at **www.milk.org**.

To maximize profits, *discriminating monopolists,* such as the Dairy Farmers of Ontario (DFO) Cooperative, must allocate their capacity shown in Figure 9.4 to produce output in such a way as to make identical the marginal revenue in all their segmented markets. If marginal revenue derived from the grocery store milk market exceeded marginal revenue derived from the school contract market, profits could be increased by transferring output from the school market to the store market. When the price rise in the school market (resulting from the output reduction) and the price decline in the store market (resulting from the output expansion) settle to such a level that MR is equal in both markets, the monopolist is at a profit-maximizing equilibrium allocation of capacity.

The total capacity to be allocated among the two or more market segments is determined by setting the combined marginal revenue of all markets equal to marginal cost. This is illustrated in Figure 9.4. The marginal revenue curves for store milk sales (MR_1) and school contract sales (MR_2) are added together horizontally to yield the total marginal revenue curve $MR_1 + MR_2$. Total capacity is set at the point where total marginal revenue equals marginal cost (that is, point A). Total capacity at this point is Q_T litres of milk. Because marginal revenue must be equal in each market to achieve profit maximization, one can determine the price and output combination that will prevail in each market at the profit-maximizing level of marginal revenue. In the store milk market, output will be Q_1 litres at a price of P_1, because this is the price–output combination that corresponds to the profit-maximizing level of marginal revenue required to cover the marginal cost of the last litre sold. Similarly, in the school market, output equals Q_2 litres at a price of P_2 (determined from the demand curve D_2D_2). The sum of the outputs in these two markets equals total output ($Q_1 + Q_2 = Q_T$). Not surprisingly, one finds that the price is higher in the less competitive store milk market, where the price elasticity of demand is less, than in the more competitive school market. As a general rule, one would expect to find an inverse relationship between the price elasticity of demand and price in markets served by discriminating monopolists.

FIGURE 9.4

Price Discrimination: DFO Cooperative

The price-discriminating monopolist maximizes profits by setting its marginal cost equal to marginal revenue in each market. The left-hand graph shows demand and marginal revenue for grocery store milk. The middle graph shows demand and marginal revenue for school contract milk. The right-hand graph shows the horizontal summation of the two individual marginal revenue curves and the DFO Cooperative's marginal cost curve.

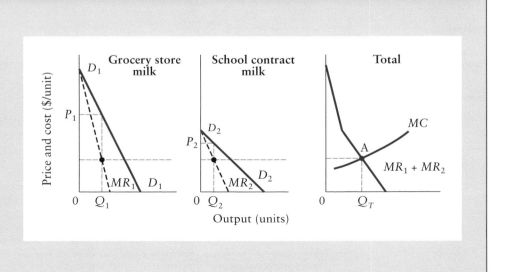

First-, Second-, and Third-Degree Price Discrimination

In the limiting case of perfect *or first-degree price discrimination,* the monopolist presumably knows not only the market demand curve but also the maximum each individual is willing to pay for any quantity.[5] The monopolist then charges each customer the highest price that purchaser is willing to pay for each unit purchased (providing this price exceeds the marginal cost of production). In this manner, the entire consumer surplus is captured by the producer. Because conditions such as these are extremely rare, consider next the more realistic cases of second- and third-degree price discrimination.

Second-degree price discrimination, or "block rate-setting" as it is sometimes called, is practised regularly by public utilities such as gas and electricity companies. Figure 9.5 illustrates second-degree price discrimination as practised by the TS Gas Company. Let DD_1 represent the household demand for natural gas in a community. If the firm charged P_1, Q_1 cubic metres of natural gas would be demanded. If, however, the firm wished to sell Q_3 cubic metres of gas, a price of P_3 would have to be charged. In second-degree discrimination, consumers would be charged a set of prices rather than a single price. For instance, the first Q_1 cubic metres used would be priced at P_1. The next block of usage, $Q_2 - Q_1$, would be priced at P_2, and the last block, $Q_3 - Q_2$, at P_3. If only one price was charged—for example, P_3—total revenue received by the firm would equal the price P_3 times Q_3 units sold. Consumer surplus in this case is given by the triangle DP_3C. By charging three separate prices, total revenue is now represented by rectangles P_1P_2EA plus P_2P_3FB, in addition to the original amount $P_3 0Q_3C$. The remaining consumer surplus, which the utility was unable to appropriate, is represented by the small triangles DP_1A, AEB, and BFC.

Second-degree discrimination is imperfect (in the eyes of the monopolist) because only part of the consumer surplus may be captured. Its use is somewhat limited because

[5] In the discussion, assume that the price-discriminating firm is a monopolist, although the practice has been frequently observed in other imperfectly competitive market structures as well. Only in highly competitive markets, where new sellers may move rapidly into higher-priced market segments thereby undermining price differentials charged, is discrimination unlikely.

FIGURE 9.5

Second-Degree Price Discrimination: TS Gas Company

Second-degree price discrimination is also called "block rate-setting." The first block of Q_1 cubic metres of natural gas is priced at P_1. The second block of $Q_2 - Q_1$ cubic metres of natural gas is priced at P_2. The third block of $Q_3 - Q_2$ cubic metres of natural gas is priced at P_3.

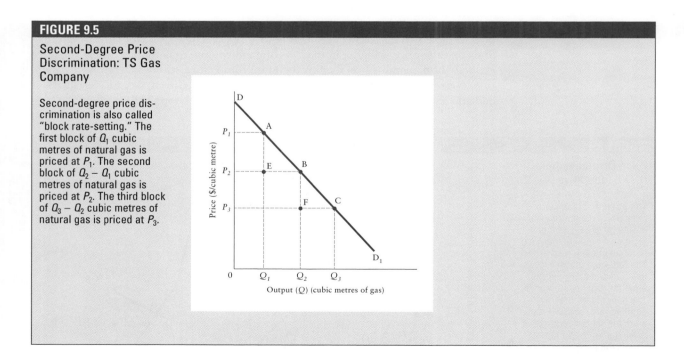

it is effective only in the case of services or products that are sold in easily metered units, such as cubic metres of gas and kilowatt-hours of electricity. Segmentation between limited users, who are charged only the higher price, and volume users, who get the benefit of lower rates as volume increases, is enforced by laws that prohibit customers from reselling gas and electricity.

Third-degree price discrimination is probably the most common form of price discrimination. It was discussed above in the example of the DFO Cooperative that charged different prices for milk, depending on whether the milk is to be sold in the grocery store market or in the more competitive surplus market, where it is sold to schools during the school year or used to make cheese, ice cream, powdered milk, and butter. The price of the monopoly-marketed milk invariably exceeds the price in the more competitive surplus market. This was illustrated in Figure 9.4.

Mathematics of Price Discrimination

This section develops the mathematics of price discrimination using some numerical examples.

Price Discrimination and the Price Elasticity of Demand

An inverse relationship must exist between price and price elasticity in the separate markets served by a discriminating monopolist. Recall that marginal revenue must be equal in each market served by the monopolist and must equal total marginal cost for profits to be maximized. If the marginal revenues are not equal, total revenue could be increased (with no impact on total cost) by shifting sales from the low marginal revenue market to the high one. In Chapter 3, the relationship between marginal revenue (MR) and price (P) was shown to be the following (Equation 3.7):

$$(9.2) \qquad MR = P\left(1 + \frac{1}{E_D}\right)$$

where E_D is the price elasticity of demand. If there are two markets such that P_1, P_2, E_1, and E_2 represent the prices and price elasticities in the two markets, we may equate marginal revenue in each market:

$$(9.3) \qquad MR_1 = MR_2$$

However, it must be the case that

$$MR_1 = P_1\left(1 + \frac{1}{E_1}\right) \quad \text{and} \quad MR_2 = P_2\left(1 + \frac{1}{E_2}\right)$$

Hence,

$$P_1\left(1 + \frac{1}{E_1}\right) = P_2\left(1 + \frac{1}{E_2}\right)$$

$$(9.4) \qquad \frac{P_1}{P_2} = \frac{\left(1 + \frac{1}{E_2}\right)}{\left(1 + \frac{1}{E_1}\right)}$$

Price Discrimination and Profitability of the Firm

The advantages to a monopolist of engaging in price discrimination can be illustrated with the Taiwan Instrument Company example on the next page. Two cases are considered—Case I, where the firm charges different prices for the same product in the two different markets, and Case II, where the firm charges the same price in the two different markets (i.e., does not engage in price discrimination).

PRICE DISCRIMINATION AND THE PRICE ELASTICITY OF DEMAND: AIR CANADA

Suppose that Air Canada has determined that the price elasticity of demand for Montreal–Vancouver unrestricted coach and Super Saver (stay-over Saturday night required) coach services are -1.25 and -2.50, respectively. Determine the relative prices (P_1/P_2) that Air Canada should charge if it is interested in maximizing profits on this route. Substituting $E_1 = -1.25$ and $E_2 = -2.50$ into Equation 9.4 yields

$$\frac{P_1}{P_2} = \frac{\left(1 + \frac{1}{-2.50}\right)}{\left(1 + \frac{1}{-1.25}\right)}$$

$$= 3.0$$

or

$$P_1 = 3.0 P_2$$

Thus, the price of an unrestricted coach seat (P_1) should be 3.0 times the price of a Super Saver coach seat (P_2). We see that when the elasticity in market 1 (unrestricted coach) is less (in absolute value) than that in market 2 (Super Saver coach), the price in market 1 will exceed the price in market 2.

PRICE DISCRIMINATION AND PROFITABILITY: TAIWAN INSTRUMENT COMPANY

Taiwan Instrument Company (TIC) makes computer memory chips in Taiwan, which it ships to computer manufacturers in Japan (market 1) and North America (market 2). Demand for the chips in the two markets is given by the following functions:

(9.5)   Japan: $P_1 = 12 - Q_1$

(9.6)   North America: $P_2 = 8 - Q_2$

where Q_1 and Q_2 are the respective quantities sold (in *millions* of units) and P_1 and P_2 are the respective prices (in dollars per unit) in the two markets. TIC's total cost function (in millions of dollars) for these memory chips is

(9.7) $C = 5 + 2(Q_1 + Q_2)$

Case I: Price Discrimination   TIC's total combined profit in the two markets equals

(9.8) $\pi = P_1 Q_1 + P_2 Q_2 - C$

$\quad = (12 - Q_1)Q_1 + (8 - Q_2)Q_2$
$\quad\quad - [5 + 2(Q_1 + Q_2)]$

(9.9) $= 12Q_1 - Q_1^2 + 8Q_2 - Q_2^2 - 5$
$\quad\quad - 2Q_1 - 2Q_2$

$\quad = 10Q_1 - Q_1^2 + 6Q_2 - Q_2^2 - 5$

To maximize π with respect to Q_1 and Q_2, find the partial derivatives of Equation 9.9 with respect to Q_1 and Q_2, set them equal to zero, and solve for Q_1^* and Q_2^*:

$$\frac{\partial \pi}{\partial Q_1} = 10 - 2Q_1 = 0$$

$$Q_1^* = 5 \text{ (million) units}$$

$$\frac{\partial \pi}{\partial Q_2} = 6 - 2Q_2 = 0$$

$$Q_2^* = 3 \text{ (million) units}$$

Substituting Q_1^* and Q_2^* into the appropriate demand and profit equations yields

$$P_1^* = \$7 \text{ per unit}$$
$$P_2^* = \$5 \text{ per unit}$$
$$\pi^* = \$29 \text{ (million)}$$

Maximizing π with respect to Q_1 and Q_2 is equivalent to setting $MR_1 = MR_2$. The equivalence of MR_1 and MR_2 may be proved by taking the partial derivatives of the TR function with respect to Q_1 and Q_2:

$$TR = P_1 \cdot Q_1 + P_2 \cdot Q_2$$

(9.10)
$$= (12 - Q_1)Q_1 + (8 - Q_2)Q_2$$
$$= 12Q_1 - Q_1^2 + 8Q_2 - Q_2^2$$

and substituting the solution values, $Q_1^* = 5$ and $Q_2^* = 3$:

$$MR_1 = \frac{\partial TR}{\partial Q_1} = 12 - 2Q_1$$

$$MR_1^* = 12 - 2(5) = \$2 \text{ per unit}$$

$$MR_2 = \frac{\partial TR}{\partial Q_2} = 8 - 2Q_2$$

$$MR_2^* = 8 - 2(3) = \$2 \text{ per unit}$$

which equals the total marginal cost, that is, the derivative of Equation 9.7 with respect to $(Q_1 + Q_2)$.

The respective elasticities in the Japanese and North American markets at the optimal solution are

$$E_1 = \frac{dQ_1}{dP_1} \cdot \frac{P_1}{Q_1}$$

$$= -1\left(\frac{7}{5}\right) = -1.40$$

and

$$E_2 = \frac{dQ_2}{dP_2} \cdot \frac{P_2}{Q_2}$$

$$= -1\left(\frac{5}{3}\right) = -1.67$$

Hence, we see that, as in the Air Canada example, when the elasticity of demand is less in Japan (market 1) than in the North America (market 2), the price in Japan is greater than in the North America.

Case II: No Price Discrimination Suppose that protectionist trade laws within NAFTA prohibit foreign computer chip manufacturers from selling these products for less than the prices charged in Japan. In other words, assume that TIC is not permitted to engage in price discrimination.

To determine the profits TIC will earn if it does not discriminate between the two markets, solve the two demand equations for Q_1 and Q_2 and add them to get a total demand function:

$$Q_1 = 12 - P_1$$
$$Q_2 = 8 - P_2$$
$$Q_T = Q_1 + Q_2$$
$$= 12 - P_1 + 8 - P_2$$

Because price discrimination is no longer possible, P_1 must equal P_2, and

$$Q_T = 20 - 2P$$

or

$$P = 10 - \frac{Q_T}{2}$$

Total profit is now

$$\pi = PQ_T - C$$

(9.11)
$$= 10Q_T - \frac{Q_T^2}{2} - 5 - 2Q_T$$

$$= 8Q_T - \frac{Q_T^2}{2} - 5$$

To find the profit-maximizing level of Q_T, differentiate Equation 9.11 with respect to Q_T, set it equal to zero, and solve for Q_T^*:

$$\frac{\partial \pi}{dQ_T} = 8 - Q_T = 0$$

$$Q_T^* = 8 \text{ (million) units}$$

Substituting Q_T^* into the appropriate equations yields

$$P^* = 10 - \frac{Q_T}{2} = \$6 \text{ per unit}$$

$$\pi^* = 8Q_T - \frac{Q_T^2}{2} - 5 = \$27 \text{ (million)}$$

$$Q_1^* = 12 - 6 = 6 \text{ (million) units}$$
$$Q_2^* = 8 - 6 = 2 \text{ (million) units}$$
$$MR_1^* = 12 - 2(6) = \$0 \text{ per unit}$$
$$MR_2^* = 8 - 2(2) = \$4 \text{ per unit}$$

The two cases are summarized in Table 9.1. Note that TIC's profits are higher when it engages in price discrimination ($29 million) than when it does not engage in price discrimination ($27 million).

Table 9.1   Taiwan Instrument Company: Effects of Price Discrimination

Market	Case I Price Discrimination		Case II No Price Discrimination	
	1 (Japan)	2 (NA)	1 (Japan)	2 (NA)
Price P^* ($/unit)	7	5	6	6
Quantity Q^* (million units)	5	3	6	2
Marginal Revenue MR^* ($/unit)	2	2	0	4
Profit π^* ($ million)		29		27

The example developed above shows that by charging different prices to different groups of customers, monopolists will always increase their profits above the level achieved if no market segmentation is attempted, as long as the groups of customers have differing demand elasticities.

Pricing of Multiple Products

Most firms produce or sell more than one product. Therefore, we must reexamine the basic model of a one-product firm, which maximizes profits by setting the marginal cost of production for the item equal to the marginal revenue derived from its sale alone. This model breaks down if firms have the opportunity to produce completely new products, new models of existing products, or new and different styles and sizes, by reallocating their productive capacity. As long as the new product (or modification of an existing product) can be sold at a price that exceeds the true marginal cost of producing and selling it, the profitability of the firm will be enhanced by its adoption.

Of course, the decision to add new or different products or drop some existing lines may have an impact on the sales of a firm's remaining outputs. Most new products may well compete with existing ones, lowering the net marginal revenue of the new product. Let us examine the nature of these demand interdependencies in more detail.

Products with Interdependent Demands

Consider the case of a firm that produces only two products (A and B). Total revenue (sales) for the firm can be represented as

$$(9.12) \qquad TR = TR_A + TR_B$$

where TR_A and TR_B are the respective revenues for the two products. Marginal revenue for product A is given by

$$(9.13) \qquad MR_A = \frac{\partial TR}{\partial Q_A} = \frac{\partial TR_A}{\partial Q_A} + \frac{\partial TR_B}{\partial Q_A}$$

The MR_A formula (Equation 9.13) shows that the marginal revenue associated with a change in the quantity sold of product A is composed of two parts. The first term, $\partial TR_A/\partial Q_A$, measures the change in total revenue for product A associated with a marginal increase (or decrease) in the quantity sold of product A. The second term, $\partial TR_B/\partial Q_A$, represents the demand interdependency between the two products—that is, the change in total revenue for product B associated with a marginal increase (or decrease) in the quantity sold of product A.

The interdependency second term, $\partial TR_B/\partial Q_A$ can be positive, negative, or zero. If the two products under consideration are *complements,* then this term will be *positive.* That is, an increase in the quantity sold of one product will result in an *increase* in total revenue for the other product—e.g., razors and blades. If the products are *substitutes,* then this second term will be *negative,* meaning that an increase in the quantity sold of one product will result in a *decrease* in total revenue for the other product. This phenomenon is often referred to as "cannibalization"—e.g., Mach3 razor sales may cannibalize Sensor razor sales. Finally, if there are no demand interdependencies between the two products, then the second term will be equal to zero.

Interdependent Products with Separate Production[6]

In this section, we develop a model that can be used in allocating resources when a firm produces multiple products that are produced separately. This analysis assumes that the productive resources of the firm can be transformed rather easily from one product to another, facilitating adaptation to changing market and product demands. *The market conditions that the firm faces for each of its products may range from pure competition to a near monopoly.* When the firm has excess personnel, organizational resources, and capacity, it may increase output with only a small additional cost. Instead of reducing prices and increasing output for an existing product, it may decide to penetrate new product markets where price is greater than marginal cost. New product markets are assumed to be invaded in order of their profitability.

Starting from a point where the firm is producing one product, marginal revenue equals marginal cost, and 20 to 30 percent of capacity is being used, we may now examine the decision to add products. Figure 9.6 illustrates a situation of a firm with five products, although that number might well be greater or less. D_1 represents the demand for product 1, D_2 for product 2, and so on. The number of units of product 1 that are sold equals Q_1, of product 2, $Q_2 - Q_1$, and so on. Profits are maximized when the firm produces and sells quantities of the five products such that marginal revenue is equal in all markets and equal to marginal cost. The line EMR represents *equal marginal revenue,* the firm's marginal revenue—i.e., the opportunity in other product lines. Because it is assumed that new product markets were entered in order of their profitability, the prices charged for the five products are arranged in declining order, from P_1 to P_5, and the elasticity of demand increases from D_1 to D_5. The EMR line is determined by the intersection of the firm's marginal cost curve MC and the marginal revenue curve for the last product market that may be profitably served. Theoretically, this would be the one with the most elastic demand, D_5.

The equilibrium condition where there is virtually an equivalence between P, MR, and MC in the marginal market illustrates the well-known fact that nearly all firms produce some products that generate little or no profit and are on the verge of being dropped or replaced. In some cases, such as the railway and utility industries, zero-profit products may be produced to keep the organization intact.

---

[6] For more on the real options involved in flexible manufacturing see D. Cyr et al., *Contemporary Financial Management,* 1st Canadian ed. (Toronto: Thomson Nelson Canada, 2004), pp. 380–383.

INTERDEPENDENT DEMANDS: THE GILLETTE COMPANY

Table 9.2 lists many of the products sold by the Gillette Company. Although most of Gillette's products have independent demands, several demand interdependencies are likely to exist. For example, the interdependency terms between Waterman pens and Braun electric shavers would likely be equal to zero, indicating that changes in demand for one product would have no effect on the demand for the other. However, one would expect the interdependency terms between the Mach3 and Sensor razors to be negative, because these products are substitutes for one another. Indeed, this is the case for these products. When Gillette introduced the Mach3, sales (total revenues) of the Sensor razor declined below the level of the previous year. Conversely, one would expect the interdependency terms between Foamy shaving cream and Gillette razors (and/or razor blades) to be positive, because these products are complements to one another.

Table 9.2 Gillette Company Products	
Razors and Blades	**Braun Personal Care Appliance Products**
Sensor	Electric shavers
Atra	Electric hair epilators
Trac II	Hair dryers
Good News	Electric curling wands
Daisy Plus	Electric toothbrushes
	Oral irrigators
Toiletries and Cosmetics	
Deodorants/Antiperspirants	
Right Guard	
Dry Idea	**Braun Household Appliances**
Shaving Cream	Steam irons
Foamy	Travel/alarm clocks
Hair Care	Toasters
White Rain	Coffee makers
Skin Care	Food processors
Jafra	Hand blenders
	Juicers
Stationery Products	
Writing Instruments	
Waterman	**Oral-B Preventive Dentistry Products**
Paper Mate	Toothbrushes
Flair	Dental floss
Correction Fluid	Interdental brushes
Liquid Paper	Professional dental supplies

As this example illustrates, managers must be aware of and take into account demand interdependencies when making price and output decisions. Failure to recognize these interdependencies may lead to decisions that do not maximize shareholder wealth.

FIGURE 9.6

Multiple-Product Pricing

Starting with the product with highest price, marginal revenue in each product line is equated to marginal cost.

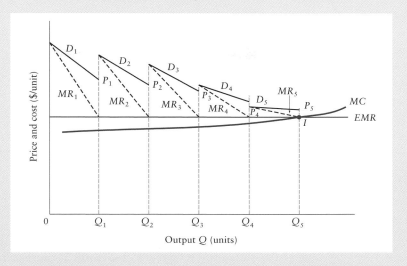

EXAMPLE

MULTIPLE-PRODUCT PRICING: SUPERMARKET PRICING

Supermarkets provide an illustration of this multiple-product pricing model. One of the primary productive resources of a supermarket is shelf space, which can be allocated among a wide variety of product categories—such as meat, dairy products, canned goods, frozen foods, and produce. Canned goods have only a 1 to 2 percent profit margin. Generally the markups and profit margins on staple items, such as bread, milk, and soap, are lower than on nonstaple items, such as imported foods and specialty items. In an effort to increase their overall profitability, many supermarkets have added higher profit-margin categories, such as delicatessens, in-store bakeries, fresh fish, and floral departments, to the mix of products they sell.[7] This can be accomplished either by reallocating existing shelf space through the reduction of the amount of shelf space assigned to lower profit-margin items or by expanding the overall size of the store. Expanding the size of the store may increase marginal costs whereas reallocating shelf space will unambiguously raise profitability if the newly added delicatessen demand is independent of preexisting fresh meat and cheese demand. If not, a careful analysis of the tradeoffs is warranted. Marginal revenue of the preexisting products lost should be subtracted from the projected marginal revenue of the new product.

---

[7] Allocation of shelf space within each product category also involves a consideration of profit margins when making decisions about stocking private-label versus national-brand canned goods, prepackaged versus fresh-cut meat, and so on.

Sometimes products are independent on the demand side but interdependent in production. For example, the demand for beef products may be independent of the demand for hides. Such joint products are discussed in Web Appendix 9B.

Pricing in Practice

To this point, this pricing chapter has been concerned with firms that seek to maximize (short-run) profits. However, pricing is one of the areas where a longer-run life cycle view of the firm's decision making proves very helpful.

Product Life Cycle Framework[8]

Life Cycle Pricing
Pricing that varies throughout the product life cycle.

In the early stages of **life cycle pricing** *in oligopolistic and monopolistically competitive markets,* the marketing, operations, and financial managers decide what the customer will value, how the firm can manage the supply chain to consistently deliver those characteristics, and how much it will cost, including the financing costs. If the value-based prices can cover this long-run full cost, the product becomes a prototype. Each proposed product or service then proceeds to marketing research, where the demand at various price points in several distribution channels usually is explored. Marketing research will identify a *target price* that the cross-functional product manager or the general managers will know is required on average over the product life cycle in order for the new product to provide sufficient revenue to cover fully allocated cost.

Once a product or service rollout takes place (usually at target price levels), the marketing plan often authorizes promotional discounts. In this stage of the life cycle, the firm is interested in penetrating the market. To do so requires coupons, free samples, name-recognition advertising, and slot-in allowances on retail shelves. **Penetration pricing** therefore characterizes an early stage of the product life cycle at which net prices to the manufacturer fall below the firm's target price, as shown in Figure 9.7.

Penetration Pricing
Setting entry price below target price to gain market share.

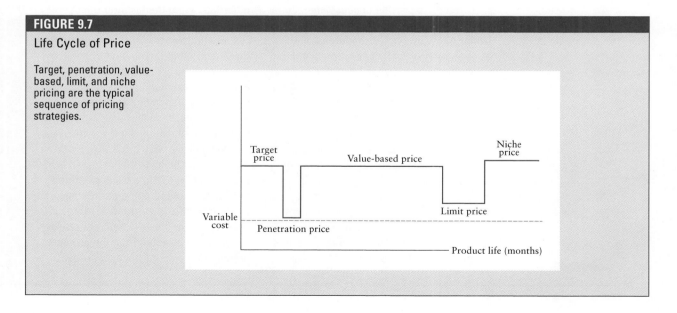

FIGURE 9.7

Life Cycle of Price

Target, penetration, value-based, limit, and niche pricing are the typical sequence of pricing strategies.

---

[8] On the conceptual framework of value-based pricing over a product's life cycle, see T. Nagle and R. Holden, *The Strategy and Tactics of Pricing,* 3rd ed. (Englewood Cliffs, NJ: Prentice-Hall, 2002), Chapter 7.

Value-Based Pricing
Adding value to maintain price.

Limit Pricing
Setting a low price to deter entry.

Niche Pricing
Setting a high price to stay in a market niche.

Full-Cost (or Cost-Plus) Pricing
A method of determining prices in which a charge to cover overhead, plus a percentage markup or margin, is added to variable production and marketing costs to arrive at a selling price.

In the mature stage of the product or service life cycle, the product managers focus on adding value in both product refinements and order management processes. These initiatives might include warranty service, brand-name advertising, product updates, or increased flexibility in accepting change orders from regular customers. Each decision at this mature stage is motivated by a desire to realize the highest **value-based pricing** allowed by the competitive conditions and potential entry threats. Although at times this view of pricing as a component of the product life cycle investment decision can be overwhelmed by short-term tactical firefighting, the product life cycle remains a planning framework to which the pricing manager often returns.

At a late mature stage of the product or service life cycle, product managers may decide to limit price, reducing it well below the value-based pricing level in order to deter entry. **Limit pricing** appears to be inconsistent with profit maximization but in fact is motivated by a long-term profitability objective.

Since competitors are constantly devising lower-cost ways of imitating leading products, limit pricing often has only temporary success. If the entry threat materializes into a real, live, new entrant, many incumbent firms then decide to accommodate by raising prices in a particular high-price, high-margin market niche. This pricing practice is often referred to as **niche pricing.** Concluding that declining market share from entry into the mass market is inevitable, the incumbent moves upmarket and sells its experience and expertise at high prices in the top-end segments of the market, much as it did at the start of the product life cycle.

Full-Cost Pricing Techniques

Full-cost pricing requires that estimates be made of the variable costs of production and marketing. A charge to cover overhead, plus a percentage markup or margin, is then added to variable costs to arrive at a final price. Overhead or indirect costs may be allocated among a firm's several products in a number of ways. One typical method is to estimate total indirect fixed costs assuming the firm operates at a standard level of output, such as 70 to 80 percent of capacity. These standard overhead costs are then allocated among the various products on some basis, such as unit sales as a percentage of

EXAMPLE

LOSS OF PATENT PROTECTION LIMITS PRICE OF PROZAC: ELI LILLY

When brand-name pharmaceuticals reach the end of their 20-year patent protection, sales may plummet unless prices are radically reduced. Some formerly patented drugs have lost as much as 80 percent of their sales in the *first year* after generic substitutes have been introduced. The ulcer relief medicine Zantac, Glaxo Wellcome's biggest seller, plummeted 51 percent in the first half year after loss of patent protection in July 1996. By yearend, 10 rival products were on the shelves. Zovinax, an antiherpes medication, lost 39 percent in the first six months after generics costing only 20 percent of Zovinax's price appeared in the marketplace. And sales of Bristol-Myers Squibb's Capoten, at 57 cents per pill, declined 83 percent the year that a 3-cents-per-pill substitute generic was introduced.

In light of these disastrous experiences throughout the pharmaceutical industry, Eli Lilly limited the price of the depression treatment Prozac to variable plus direct fixed costs in order to arrest or at least slow the onslaught of imitators into its antidepressants market.

FULL-COST PRICING LOSES A BIG CONTRACT FOR BRITISH TELEPHONE

This vicious circle of full costing can be disastrous for a company facing stiff competition. British Telephone once found that its bid to provide secure long-distance microwave business communication for the firm J.P. Morgan ended up $4 million higher than a rival's bid of $9 million. When BT executives did a follow-up study to see why they had been so undercut by Sprint, they discovered that the vice president of the BT subsidiary had attempted to recover the entire annual overhead for the subsidiary headquarters from this one account. Needless to say, BT lost J.P. Morgan's business with a full-cost bid of $13 million when Sprint had offered to do essentially the same thing for $9 million. Full-cost pricing always runs the risk of such undercutting by rivals.

total volume. For example, Wang Laboratories' average variable cost of producing and selling an early word processor was $500. The company added a charge of $600 to cover indirect or overhead charges. To this full average cost of $1,100, a markup of 20 percent was added, yielding a final price of $1,320. As IBM PCs took unit sales away from the Wang word processor, indirect charges rose. Rather than $600, first $800 and then $1,000 were allocated to the word processor. Of course, steeper prices meant faster and faster declines in sales volume, implying still higher indirect charges.

It is immediately apparent that full-cost pricing violates the marginal pricing rules of traditional theory, because fixed costs enter explicitly into the price determination formula. It has been argued, however, that when average (unit) costs remain nearly constant over the relevant output range, and when historical costs are adjusted to reflect costs actually incurred at the time prices are set, the use of cost-plus pricing may lead to nearly optimal decisions. These conditions are frequently encountered in the retail trades.

In addition, congestion-based pricing, which applies allocated costs for new capacity to wireless telephone customers who unexpectedly demand peak-period service, is another example of appropriate full-cost pricing techniques. One way to implement this pricing policy is with a target return on investment.

Under **target return-on-investment pricing,** or simply target pricing, the firm selects an acceptable profit rate on investment. This is usually defined as earnings before interest and depreciation divided by total gross operating assets. This return is then prorated over the number of units expected to be produced over the planning horizon. Target pricing rules may be expressed in equation form as

Target Return-on-Investment Pricing
A method of pricing in which a target profit, defined as the *desired profit rate on investment times total gross operating assets,* is allocated to each unit of output to arrive at a selling price.

$$(9.14) \qquad P = VC_1 + VC_m + VC_{mk} + \frac{F}{Q} + \frac{\pi K}{Q}$$

where
P = price per unit
VC_1 = unit labour cost
VC_m = unit material cost
VC_{mk} = unit marketing cost
F = total fixed or indirect costs
Q = number of units to be produced during the planning horizon
K = total gross operating assets
π = desired profit rate on investment

Full-Cost Pricing versus Incremental Contribution Analysis

Advocates of full-cost and target pricing argue that it is important to allocate all fixed costs among the various products produced by the firm and that each product should be forced to bear its fair share of the fixed-cost burden. In contrast, advocates of incremental pricing say that each product should instead be viewed in the light of its incremental contributions to covering fixed costs. The contribution analysis provides a sounder basis for considering whether the manufacture and sale of a product should be expanded, maintained, or discontinued in favour of some alternative that may make a greater contribution to covering company overhead and making a profit.

Every firm should have an effective control system in which a general manager continually monitors the overall contribution of the firm's complete product line. This person can then ensure that value-based prices are set sufficiently high in relation to both the variable cost of each product and the total fixed costs of the firm. Remember that target pricing must be met only on certain portions of the product's entire life cycle (see Figure 9.7).

Incremental Analysis
The real-world counterpart to marginal analysis. Incremental analysis requires that an estimate be made of the changes in total cost and revenue that will result from a price change or from a decision to add or delete a product, accept or reject a new order, or undertake a new investment.

The concept of **incremental analysis** is simple, but its application requires care. For instance, the decision to drop an item from the firm's product line requires that the loss in revenue from this action should be evaluated in the light of the total *actual* cost savings that may occur. The following questions must be addressed:

1. How much, if any, will sales of other items in the firm's product line increase because this item is dropped?

2. To what extent will some overhead or fixed costs be reduced?

3. Are there more profitable alternative uses for the firm's productive capacity?

4. What is the long-run sales and profit outlook for this item versus the alternatives being considered?

EXAMPLE

FULL-COST PRICING VERSUS INCREMENTAL ANALYSIS: PHONEMATE COMPANY

If PhoneMate's Model 7200 telephone answering machine accounts for 40 percent of sales but only 10 percent of the contribution to fixed costs and profits, the firm should seek ways to increase its contribution or replace it with a more profitable alternative. In this example, the full-cost pricing criteria might indicate that the product should be quickly discontinued because it is not covering its volume-weighted share of fixed costs. However,

any contribution to fixed costs is more consistent with profit maximization in the short run than dropping the product and merely shifting the burden of covering fixed costs to the remaining products of the firm. A longer-run analysis *might* indicate that dropping the 7200 model will result in actual fixed-cost savings that are greater than the maximum fixed-cost contribution that the 7200 model may be expected to generate.

INCREMENTALISM AT CONTINENTAL AIRLINES: NEWARK–OTTAWA

At one point, Continental Airlines was filling only about 50 percent of its available seats or about 15 percent less than the industry average. Eliminating only 5 percent of its flights would have resulted in a substantial increase in this load factor, but would have reduced profits as well. The airline industry is characterized by extremely high fixed costs, which are incurred whether a plane flies or not. There are depreciation costs, interest charges, and the cost of maintaining ground crews, not to mention headquarters staff overhead. Consequently, Continental has found it profitable to operate a flight as long as it covers variable or out-of-pocket costs plus a small contribution to fixed costs.

The analysis of whether to operate a flight proceeds as follows: First, management examines the majority of scheduled flights to be certain that depreciation, overhead, and insurance expenses are met for this basic schedule. Then the possibility of scheduling additional flights is considered, based on their impact on corporate net profit. If revenues on a flight exceed *actual variable costs* plus direct fixed costs, the flight should be added. These relevant costs are determined by soliciting inputs from every operating department that specify exactly what extra expenses are incurred as a result of the additional flight's operation. For instance, if a ground crew

that can service the additional flight is already on duty, none of the costs of this service are included in actual operating costs. If, on the other hand, overtime must be paid to service this flight, then that direct fixed cost varies with the decision to operate this flight and should be included among its costs.

Another example of such incremental analysis is the case of a late-night Continental flight from Newark to Ottawa and a very early morning return flight. Even though the flights often go with only a few passengers and very little freight, the cost of operating them is less than an overnight hangar rental in Newark. Hence, the flights are maintained.

In performing this type of incremental analysis, two important points must be stressed. First, someone in management must have coordinating authority to ensure that overall objectives are met before facing decisions based solely on incremental analysis. In the case of Continental, the vice president of flight planning assumed this task. Second, every reasonable attempt must be made to identify *actual* incremental costs and revenues that are associated with a particular decision. Once this has been accomplished, incremental analysis becomes a useful and powerful tool in considering a wide range of decision problems facing the firm.

Other Pricing Strategies

In addition to incremental and full-cost pricing strategies, several other pricing methods are used under particular circumstances addressed below. *Skimming* is often used in pricing new products. Also, some goods are deliberately priced very high to increase their prestige demand, especially in niche markets (see Figure 9.7). Finally, Web-based pricing of goods and services sold over the Internet is considered.

Skimming

When a new product is introduced by a firm, pricing for that product is a difficult and critical decision, especially if the product is a durable good—one that has a relatively long useful life. The difficulty of pricing the new product arises from the fact that demand may not be known with confidence. If the price is initially set too low, some potential customers will be able to buy the product at a price below what they are willing to pay. These lost profits will be gone forever. This problem is accentuated when the firm initially has limited production capacity for the new product. In contrast, if the firm sets a high price and maintains this price over a long time period, new competition will be encouraged.

Under these circumstances, many firms have adopted a strategy of **skimming**, or pricing down along the demand curve. The initial price is set at a high level, even though the firm fully intends to make later price reductions. When the product is first introduced, there will be a group of fashion-conscious or technology-conscious early adopters who are willing to pay the high price established by the firm. Once this source of demand has been exhausted, the price is reduced and a new group of customers is attracted. This strategy is readily apparent in mainframe computers and explains the prevalence of capital leasing in that industry. As we discuss in Web Chapter 16, manufacturers who engage in a predictable pattern of price skimming need credibility mechanisms to assure early full-price customers that later discounting will be limited.

Skimming
A new-product pricing strategy that results in a high initial product price. This price is reduced over time as demand at the higher price is satisfied.

EXAMPLE

APPLE IMAC COMPUTER

Since its initial introduction, several price reductions have been made on the iMac personal computer. This pricing strategy can be illustrated using Figure 9.8. Panel (a) shows the estimated demand curve DD and the marginal revenue curve MR for the iMac computer, as well as the marginal

cost curve MC. As a monopolist for the iMac, Apple would set price P_1 and produce output Q_1.

Suppose, however, that Apple chooses to follow the skimming strategy for its personal computer. It could initially set a price higher than P_1, such as P'. At that price,

FIGURE 9.8

Example of Demand Skimming: iMac Personal Computer

Panel (a) shows the profit-maximizing price P_1 and output Q_1 if the iMac will be produced and sold in only one period. However, if the computer will be produced and sold in more than one period, Apple may well choose to set a higher price P' and lower output Q'. Panel (b) shows demand curves for successive periods, as the quantity sold in the previous period is subtracted to obtain the demand curve in each new period.

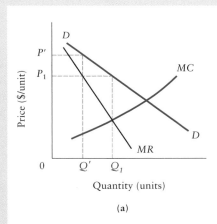
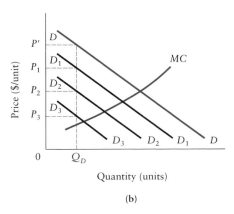

(a)

(b)

only Q' units would be demanded and sold. By setting the initial price at P', all consumers who are willing to pay that price or more will buy the product. Once this has occurred, Apple can then lower the price to capture the demand from the next segment of customers.

Panel (b) shows new demand curves, such as D_1D_1. The new demand curve is less than the initial demand curve DD—it is shifted to the left—by an amount equal to the Q' units that have already been purchased at price P'. A new lower price is now established, such as P_1, and Q_D units are sold at this price. The new price P_1 may be set in such a manner that it approximately matches the firm's production capacity. When demand has been exhausted at this price, the price is lowered again, to a level such as P_2. The new demand curve D_2D_2 is lower and to the left of D_1D_1 by an amount

equal to the Q_D units that were sold at the previous price. (Although panel (b) shows quantity demanded to be the same amount for each price level, this is not necessary. The figure is merely drawn that way for ease of presentation.)

This strategy can be continued many times to capitalize on the unique product characteristics and availability until competition forces the firm to a "permanently" more competitive price level. The rate at which reductions are made may depend on production capacity, the speed of competitive product introductions, and the tradeoff between receiving profits now and deferring them into the future by use of the skimming strategy. In the case of Apple and the original IBM machines, price reductions were strongly resisted until true IBM "clone" PCs became available from competitor firms such as Dell.

Prestige Pricing

Prestige Pricing
The practice of charging a high price for a product to enhance its perceived value.

Some products are priced to increase their perceived value to potential consumers. **Prestige pricing** is the practice of charging a high price so as to limit potential buyers and create the impression that the product is of higher quality than similar mass market products. For example, in the automotive market, the sporty European sedans, such as the Mercedes, Audi, and BMW, are priced in the $35,000 to $125,000 range. These cars have been highly successful in attracting a loyal, prestige-oriented clientele. At the same time, a car such as the Honda Accord has received wide acclaim from such impartial panels as the Consumers Union when it was compared with these more expensive vehicles. Its price is considerably less than the European alternatives, because it has not attracted the loyal following of prestige-oriented consumers that the European sedans have.

Cartier's, in conjunction with the De Beers diamond cartel, which controls at least 80 percent of the world's uncut diamond market, effectively sets prices for diamonds by greatly restricting their availability. For example, in the early 1980s, it appeared that the South African cartel might collapse. A sharp decline in demand, coupled with the withdrawal of Zaire (the world's largest producer of diamonds) from the cartel and huge new discoveries in Australia threatened to undercut the cartel. But by holding nearly $1 billion in diamonds off the market, De Beers was able to avoid a price decline and bring Zaire and Australia back into the cartel. This pricing strategy assured potential diamond buyers of the ongoing value of their investment, and it has prevented diamonds from becoming too commonplace.

Pricing on the Internet[9]

Several problems are unique to Web-based transactions. First is the anonymity of buyers and sellers, who often are identified by only a Web address. Offers to buy (and sell) may

---

[9] An excellent survey of pricing strategy for Internet products is provided in John Figueriredo, "Finding Sustainable Profitability in Electronic Commerce," *Sloan Management Review,* Summer 2000, pp. 41–52. See also "The Click Here Economy," *BusinessWeek,* June 22, 1998, pp. 122–126.

be reneged, receivables may never arrive, and items delivered may not be what buyers thought they bought. The incidence of all these events is much greater in the virtual sales environment. As a result, offers are higher, and bids are lower. From another perspective, the bid–ask spread in an Internet transaction rises to cover the cost of fraud insurance.

A second problem that the Internet accentuates is the inability to confirm variable product quality with hands-on examination. Internet pricing of commodity products like crude oil, newsprint, and sheet metal, on the left-hand side of Table 9.3, often pursues a low-cost strategy. The availability of quick resale at predictable commodity prices reassures buyers and sellers, and here Internet pricing at very tight bid–ask spreads proves to be quite efficient. However, as one moves to the right in Table 9.3, product quality becomes harder and harder to detect at the point of sale. Firms like Amazon seek to substitute brand equity for the inability of customers to examine the product. Amazon and Priceline have spent tens of millions of dollars establishing their brand equity.

In toys, suits, homes, and new autos, consumers search for that look and feel for which they're willing to pay. Brands again play an important role in certifying quality but, in this case, it is product branding (Game Boy, Harry Rosen, Harris tweed) that matters, not website brands. Customers rely on the hostage associated with the sunk cost investment in the product brand names to establish credibility in a relationship with the original equipment manufacturer, not the website reseller. Finally, with highly variable quality in tires, PCs, produce, and lumber, only strong warranties, escrow accounts, and replacement guarantees or deep discounts can replace the reputation effects that help sell these experience goods in nonvirtual settings.

Internet sellers can add value and reduce some transaction costs in these markets by customizing and selling direct to the customer like Dell, which provides order fulfillment and manufactures almost nothing. Perhaps this is why services have grown so quickly on the Net. The travel industry itself accounted for 35 percent of all online sales in 2002. Table 9.4 shows that the growth rate of services far surpassed growth in consumer products online.

In other words, the Web allows a firm to profitably enter market niches that are simply unprofitable for a bricks-and-mortar store. For example, Apple's iTunes online music store has virtually unlimited storage capacity because it stores music tracks electronically. Since customers buy and then directly download these tracks, Apple can profitably sell even obscure tracks that are not in the top 10,000 (i.e., marketing in the "long tail" of the probability distribution of music popularity).[10]

Visit the Amazon and Priceline websites at **www.amazon.ca** and **www.priceline.ca**.

Table 9.3	Pricing Strategy for Various Internet Products		
Commodity Products	**Quasi-Commodity Products**	**Look-and-Feel Search Goods**	**Experience-Goods Variable Quality**
Crude oil	Books	Suits	PCs
Newsprint	CDs	Homes	Produce
Sheet metal	Videos	New autos	Tires
Paper clips		Toys	Lumber
Low-cost, low-price strategy	Differentiate with reliable delivery and extra services	Employ differential pricing based on brands and time of adoption in fashion cycle	Customize and build-to-order with low- and high-price tiers

[10] Based on "Profiting from Obscurity," retrieved May 7, 2005, from *The Economist* (www.economist.com/finance/displayStory.cfm?story_id=3936129), and Chris Anderson "The Long Tail," retrieved May 7, 2005, from *Wired* (www.wired.com/wired/archive/12.10/tail.html).

Table 9.4	Growth in Online Sales		
	1997	**2001**	**Compound Annual Growth Rate (%)**
Consumer Services			
Travel	$654 million	$7.4 billion	83
Event ticket	79 million	2 billion	124
Financial services	1.2 billion	5 billion	43
Consumer Products			
Apparel	$92 million	$514 billion	53
Books/CDs	156 million	1.1 billion	63
PCs	863 million	3.8 billion	45
B2B	$8 billion	$183 billion	119

Source: Websites of *BusinessWeek* (www.businessweek.com) and Forrester Research (www.forrester.com).

Contrast this with a chain of retail music stores located in shopping malls. Each store has a limited capacity to display CDs. Thus, the chain maximizes its profits by stocking each store with only the most popular titles and deliberately avoids the "long tail."

In business-to-business (B2B) transactions, pricing is more complex than in the above business-to-consumer transactions. In B2B, multiple attributes come into play in the price negotiation. B2B customers haggle over date of shipment, delivery costs, warranty service times and locations, delivery reliability, and replacement guarantees. These additional considerations typically mean pricing is a part of a two- or three-step process. First, customers match their nonnegotiable requirements to the suppliers with those attributes, and those firms become the order-qualified suppliers. Then, the remaining attributes may be negotiated away against demands for a lower price point. B2B Internet sales grew twentyfold from $8 billion in 1997 to $183 billion by the beginning of 2002.

Dynamic Pricing
A price that varies over time based on the balance of demand and supply, often associated with Internet auctions.

Internet pricing in these B2B settings requires a matching process to qualify for an order and then a **dynamic pricing** algorithm to trade off the remaining attributes. Information technology complexity in these B2B transactions arises because customers are heterogeneous, and the attributes that qualify a firm to supply one group of customers may not match the requirements of other customers. In addition, as we shall see in Web Appendix 9A, delivery reliability—i.e., the probability of stockout and backorder—is a continuous variable that should be optimized with a revenue management solution, not a simple on-again/off-again attribute to promise or refuse a potential customer in exchange for a somewhat larger or smaller markup. Internet auctions may eventually allow the development of dynamic pricing tools to quote real-time opportunity costs for delivery reliability and change order responsiveness.

Transfer Pricing

Associated with the tremendous growth in the size of corporations has been a trend toward decentralized decision making and control within these organizations. Because of the exceedingly complex coordination and communication problems within large multiproduct national or multinational firms, such firms typically are broken up into a group of semiautonomous operating divisions. Each division constitutes a profit centre with the responsibility and authority for making operating decisions and an appropriate set of rewards and incentives to motivate profit-maximizing decisions.

Transfer Price
The price at which an intermediate good or service is transferred from the selling to the buying division within the same firm.

With decentralization, firm profit-maximizing **transfer prices** must be set, say at General Motors, between upstream divisions such as Delco (batteries, spark plugs) and Fisher Body (auto bodies) for downstream divisions such as Chevrolet and Cadillac that produce final outputs (autos).

The price at which each intermediate good or service is transferred from the selling to the buying division affects the revenues of the selling division and the costs of the buying division. Consequently, the price–output decisions and profitability of each division will be affected by the transfer price. This section considers the situation where the intermediate products have only internal markets. Web Appendix 9B considers the situation where the intermediate products can be sold in perfectly or imperfectly competitive external markets as well as internally.

In the following analysis, assume that a decentralized firm consists of two separate divisions that form a two-stage process to manufacture and market a single product. The production division manufactures an intermediate product, which is sold internally to the marketing division at the transfer price. The marketing division converts the intermediate product into a final product, which it then sells in an imperfectly competitive (that is, monopolistic) external market.

With no external market for the intermediate product, the production division would be unable to dispose of any excess units over and above the amount desired by the marketing division. Likewise, if demand for the final product should exceed the capacity of the production division, the marketing division would be unable to obtain additional units of the intermediate product externally. Therefore, the quantity of the intermediate product manufactured by the production division must necessarily be equal to the amount sold by the marketing division.[11]

The determination of the profit-maximizing price–output combination and the resulting transfer price are shown in Figure 9.9. The marginal cost per unit to the firm,

FIGURE 9.9

Determination of the Transfer Price with No External Market for Intermediate Product

When there is no external market for the intermediate good, the transfer price P_t for this good should be set equal to the marginal cost of producing this good at the profit-maximizing output level for the firm.

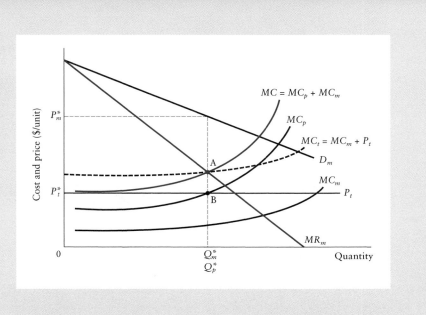

[11] This analysis assumes that all units produced during the period must be sold during the period. That is, no inventories of the intermediate product can be carried over into the next period.

MC, of any level of output is the sum of the marginal costs per unit of production, MC_p, and marketing, MC_m. By equating marginal cost MC to external marginal revenue MR_m (point A), one obtains the firm's profit-maximizing decisions—P_m^* as the optimal price and Q_m^* as the optimal quantity of the final product to be sold by the marketing division in the external market. Therefore, the optimal transfer price P_t^* is set equal to the marginal production cost per unit MC_p at the optimum output level Q_p^* (point B). This will cause each division, when seeking to maximize its own division profit, to maximize the overall profit of the firm. This result can be demonstrated in the following manner.

Once the transfer price is established, the production division will face a *horizontal* demand curve (and corresponding marginal revenue curve) at the given transfer price for the intermediate product. The profits of the production division will be maximized at the point where its divisional marginal cost equals divisional marginal revenue—in this case where the P_t line intersects the MC_p curve. This condition yields Q_p^* as the optimum quantity of the intermediate product, which is identical to the optimum quantity of the final product Q_m^* determined previously. Similarly, once the transfer price is established, the marketing division is faced with a marginal cost curve MC_t, which is the sum of the marginal marketing cost per unit MC_m and the given transfer price P_t. The profits of the marketing division will be maximized at the point where its divisional cost is equal to its divisional marginal revenue—in this case, where the MC_t and MR_m curves intersect. This condition yields the same optimal price and output decision (that is, P_m^* and Q_m^*) as was obtained previously in maximizing the overall profits of the firm.

Table 9.5 summarizes the optimal transfer price under the various situations that may arise when upstream and downstream units of a firm have external market opportunities as well as simply internal opportunities for transferring output.

Table 9.5   Optimal Transfer Pricing*

External Market	Market Structure	Optimal Transfer Price
No	Not applicable	$MC_p = P_t$
Yes: $Q_p > Q_m$	Perfectly competitive	$MC_p = P_t = P_{ext}$
Yes: $Q_p < Q_m$	Perfectly competitive	$MC_p = P_t = P_{ext}$
Yes: $Q_p > Q_m$	Imperfectly competitive	$MC_p = P_t < P_{ext}$
Yes: $Q_p < Q_m$	Imperfectly competitive	$MC_p = P_t > P_{ext}$

* For more information on situations not discussed in this chapter, see the "Transfer Pricing" section of Web Appendix 9B.

EXAMPLE

DETERMINING THE OPTIMAL TRANSFER PRICE: AB ELECTRONICS

The production division (*p*) of the AB Electronics Company manufactures a component that it sells internally to the mar-keting division (*m*), which promotes and distributes the product through its own domestic retail outlets. Assume that there is no external market for this component (i.e., the production division cannot sell any excess production of the component to outside buyers and the marketing division cannot obtain additional components from outside suppliers). The marketing division's demand function for the component is

$$(9.15) \qquad P_m = 100 - 0.001 Q_m$$

where P_m is the selling price (in dollars per unit) and Q_m is the quantity sold (in units). The marketing division's total cost function in dollars (excluding the cost of the component) is

$$(9.16) \qquad C_m = 300{,}000 + 10 Q_m$$

The production division's total cost function (in dollars) is

$$(9.17) \qquad C_p = 500{,}000 + 15 Q_p + 0.0005 Q_p^2$$

where Q_p is the quantity produced and sold.

We are interested in determining the profit-maximizing outputs for the production and marketing divisions and the optimal transfer price for intracompany sales. The marginal cost per unit to the firm, MC, is equal to the sum of the marginal costs of production, MC_p, and marketing, MC_m:

$$(9.18) \qquad MC = MC_p + MC_m$$

The marginal cost of the production division is equal to the first derivative of C_p (Equation 9.17):

$$(9.19) \qquad MC_p = \frac{dC_p}{dQ_p}$$
$$= 15 + 0.001 Q_p$$

The marginal cost of the marketing division is equal to the first derivative of C_m (Equation 9.16):

$$(9.20) \qquad MC_m = \frac{dC_m}{dQ}$$
$$= 10$$

Substituting Equations 9.19 and 9.20 into Equation 9.18 and recognizing that

$$Q_m = Q_p$$

we obtain

$$(9.21) \qquad MC = 15 + 0.001 Q_m + 10$$
$$= 25 + 0.001 Q_m$$

The marketing division's total revenue function is equal to

$$(9.22) \qquad TR_m = P_m Q_m$$
$$= (100 - 0.001 Q_m) Q_m$$
$$= 100 Q_m - 0.001 Q_m^2$$

Taking the first derivative of TR_m (Equation 9.22) gives

$$(9.23) \qquad MR_m = \frac{d(TR_m)}{dQ_m}$$
$$= 100 - 0.002 Q_m$$

Setting Equation 9.21 equal to Equation 9.23 gives the optimal output for the marketing division:

$$MC = MR_m$$
$$25 + 0.001 Q_m = 100 - 0.002 Q_m$$
$$Q_m^* = 25{,}000 \text{ units}$$

Because $Q_p = Q_m$, the optimal output for the production division is

$$Q_p^* = 25{,}000 \text{ units}$$

Therefore the optimal transfer price for intracompany sales of the component is equal to the marginal production cost per unit at the optimal output level of $Q_p^* = 25{,}000$ units, or

$$P_t^* = MC_p$$
$$= 15 + 0.001(25{,}000)$$
$$= \$40 \text{ per unit}$$

Thus, to maximize profits, AB's production division should produce and sell 25,000 units of the component to the marketing division. The marketing division should distribute 25,000 units of the component through its retail outlets. The optimal transfer price for intracompany sales is $40—the production division's marginal cost per unit at an output of 25,000 units.

Transfer Pricing, Taxes, and Ethics*

Many articles and papers are available on transfer pricing and multinational firms at the Organisation for Economic Co-operation and Development (OECD) website at **www.oecd.org**.

Multinational corporations have a great deal of flexibility in setting transfer prices, because there are often no external market standards for setting these intrafirm prices. In the absence of differential tax rates between the various countries in which a firm does business, the establishment of appropriate transfer prices involves application of microeconomic decision rules and cost accounting principles. However, because large multinational firms operate in several different countries, each with its own system of taxation and its own unique corporate income tax rates and policies, the use of transfer pricing to aggressively manage and reduce tax liabilities is common and profitable.

For example, in 2004, the Australian government charged Toyota with systematically overcharging its Australian subsidiary for most of the vehicles and parts sold in Australia. The effect of these actions was to transfer profits that would have been booked (and taxed at high rates) in Australia to Japan, where tax rates are much lower. Toyota denied any wrongdoing.

The issue of setting proper transfer prices is extremely complex. Many differences between company policies and government regulations arise because of the complexity of the issue. Managers of multinational firms will have to give this issue greater attention in coming years, if they expect to achieve the goal of maximizing shareholder wealth within the bounds of legal and ethical standards of business practice.

* Based on L. Martz, "The Corporate Shell Game," *Newsweek,* April 15, 1991, pp. 48–49.

Managerial Challenge Revisited

Pricing of Apple Computers: Market Share vs. Current Profitability

Apple is still selling most of its computers at premium prices. Some of its new products are also sold at premium prices. However, during 2004–2005, some lower-priced products such as the iPod mini, the iPod flash, the iPod shuffle, and the Mac mini were introduced, as well as a new version of the Final Cut digital video software.

Summary

- All pricing decisions should be *proactive, systematic, and value-based*—for example, related to careful detailed assessment of customer value.

- *Price discrimination* is the act of selling the same good or service produced by a given firm at different prices to different customers. Two conditions are required for effective price discrimination:
  1. One must be able to segment the market and prevent the transfer of the product (or service) from one segment to another.
  2. There must be differences in the elasticity of demand at a given price between the market segments.

- To maximize profits using price discrimination, the firm must allocate output in such a way that marginal revenue is equal in the different market segments.

- Price discrimination is often implemented through two-part pricing. Optimal *two-part prices* entail a lump sum access fee and a user charge that exceeds marginal cost and varies per unit consumed.

- *Bundling* is another way to price-discriminate while charging the same prices to different customers.

- For firms selling multiple products with interdependent demands, decisions to add or delete products in existing product lines may have (positive or negative) impacts on the sales of the firm's current outputs. In the analysis of such decisions, it is necessary to include the costs of these impacts in the marginal cost calculations.

- Pricing strategy varies throughout the product or service life cycle. A frequent pattern is target pricing, followed by penetration pricing, value-based pricing, limit pricing, and finally niche pricing.

- Many actual business pricing practices, such as *full-cost pricing* and *target pricing,* can be consistent with the marginal pricing rules of economic theory. *Incrementalism* is a widely applicable method of economic analysis that may help management to achieve a more efficient and profitable level of operation.

- When new products are introduced, firms may use the *skimming* strategy to price the product and increase total profits. *Prestige pricing* is often used in segmenting markets. Web-based pricing for products sold over the Internet requires different pricing strategies, depending on the type of product: commodity product, quasi-commodity product, search good, or experience good.

- A firm is often faced with the problem of pricing items that are produced and used internally in the firm. This is the emphasis of *transfer pricing* analysis. The appropriate profit-maximizing transfer price is a function of the marginal costs and revenues of the respective divisions in the firm.

Self-Test Exercises

1. The price elasticity of demand for air travel differs radically from first class (-3) to unrestricted coach (-4) to restricted discount coach (-9). What can one say about optimal prices (fares) on a cross-country trip with incremental variable costs (marginal costs) equal to $240?

2. Phillips Industries makes a certain product that can be sold directly to retail outlets or to the Superior Company for further processing and eventual sale by them as a completely different product. The demand function for each of these markets is

$$\text{Retail Outlets: } P_1 = 60 - 2Q_1$$
$$\text{Superior Company: } P_2 = 40 - Q_2$$

where P_1 and P_2 are the prices charged and Q_1 and Q_2 are the quantities sold in the respective markets. Phillips's total cost function for the manufacture of this product is

$$TC = 10 + 8(Q_1 + Q_2)$$

a. Determine Phillips' total profit function.
b. What are the profit-maximizing price and output levels for the product in the two markets?
c. At these levels of output, calculate the marginal revenue in each market.
d. What are Phillips' total profits if the firm is effectively able to charge different prices in the two markets?
e. Calculate the profit-maximizing level of price and output if Phillips is required to charge the same price per unit in each market. What are Phillips' profits under this condition?

3. General Medical makes disposable syringes that it sells to hospitals and medical supply companies. The company uses cost-plus pricing and currently charges 150 percent of average variable costs. General Medical has learned of an opportunity to sell 300,000 syringes to CIDA if they can be delivered within three months at a price not in excess of $1 each. General Medical normally sells its syringes for $1.20 each.

If General Medical accepts the CIDA order, it will have to forego sales of 100,000 syringes to its regular customers over this time period, although this loss of sales is not expected to affect future sales.

a. Should General Medical accept the CIDA order?
b. If sales for the balance of the year are expected to be 50,000 units less because of some lost customers who do not return, should the order be accepted (ignore any effects beyond one year)?

Exercises

1. Why does the phone company offer different pricing structures for business and personal phone lines? Compare this with the reasons why a bank has a different pricing structure for business and personal chequing accounts.

2. DVDs and DVD players are no longer a niche product. Sony sells both DVD players and DVDs. What should be Sony's approach to pricing? What difference will it make to Sony's pricing if customers have now become dissimilar?

3. The price elasticity of demand for a textbook sold in North America is estimated to be -2.0, whereas the price elasticity of demand for books sold overseas is -3.0. The North American market requires hardcover books with a marginal cost of $50; the overseas market is normally served with softcover texts, having a marginal cost of only $30. Calculate the profit-maximizing price in each market.

$$\textit{Hint: Remember that } MR = P\left(1 + \frac{1}{E_D}\right)$$

4. North American Export–Import Company operates a general cargo carrier service between both Montreal and New York and several Western European ports. It hauls two major categories of freight: manufactured items and semimanufactured raw materials. The demand functions for these two classes of goods are

$$P_1 = 100 - 2Q_1$$
$$P_2 = 80 - Q_2$$

where Q_i = tonnes of freight moved. The total cost function for the firm is

$$TC = 20 + 4(Q_1 + Q_2)$$

    a. Determine the firm's total profit function.

    b. What are the profit-maximizing levels of price and output for the two freight categories?

    c. At these levels of output, calculate the marginal revenue in each market.

    d. What are the firm's total profits if it is effectively able to charge different prices in the two markets?

    e. If the firm is required by law to charge the same per-tonne rate to all users, calculate the new profit-maximizing level of price and output. What are the profits in this situation?

    f. Explain the difference in profit levels between the discriminating and nondiscriminating cases. To do this, one should calculate the point price elasticity of demand under the nondiscriminating price–output solution.

5. a. Many university bookstores offer to professors price discounts that are generally not available to students. What conditions make this sort of price discrimination feasible and profitable for the bookstores?

    b. Similarly, students are often given discounts to attend cultural and athletic events, whereas professors do not receive these discounts. What conditions make this sort of price discrimination possible and desirable?

6. In the face of stable (or declining) enrollments and increasing costs, many universities have found themselves in progressively tighter financial dilemmas. This has led to a basic reexamination of the pricing schemes used by institutions of higher learning. One proposal advocated by the Committee for Economic Development (CED) and others has been for the use of more nearly full-cost pricing of higher education, combined with the government's provision of sufficient loan funds to students who would otherwise not have access to reasonable loan terms in private markets. Advocates of such proposals argue that the private rate of return to student investors is sufficiently high to stimulate socially optimal levels of demand for education, even with the higher tuition rates. Others have argued against the existence of significant external benefits to undergraduate education to warrant the current high levels of public support.

    As with current university pricing schemes, proponents of full-cost pricing generally argue for a standard fee (albeit higher than at present) for all students. Standard-fee proposals ignore relative cost and demand differences among activities in the university.

    a. Discuss several possible rationales for charging different prices for different courses of study.

    b. What are the income-distribution effects of a pricing scheme that charges the same fee to all students?

    c. If universities adopted a system of full-cost (or marginal cost) pricing for various courses, what would you expect the impact to be on the efficiency of resource allocations within the university?

    d. Would you complain less about large lecture sections taught by graduate students if these were priced significantly lower than small seminars taught by outstanding scholars?

    e. What problems could you see arising from a university that adopted such a pricing scheme?

7. Culinary Products, Inc. (CPI) performs a target return pricing calculation as part of its analysis of any proposed new products. CPI's research and development department has provided the following information concerning a new food processor it has designed:

- Labour costs (per unit): $22
- Material costs (per unit): $11
- Marketing costs (per unit): $2
- Fixed overhead costs (per year): $1,500,000
- Gross investment (operating assets): $6,000,000
- Required rate of return on investment (per year): 25%

Determine the target price based on projected sales per year of

a. 80,000 units

b. 100,000 units

c. 60,000 units

8. The Pear Computer Company has just developed a totally revolutionary new personal computer. It estimates that it will take competitors at least two years to produce equivalent products. The demand function for the computer has been estimated to be

$$P = 2,500 - 0.0005Q$$

The marginal (and average variable) cost of producing the computer is $900.

a. Compute the profit-maximizing price and output levels assuming that Pear acts as a monopolist for its product.

b. Determine the total contribution to profits and fixed costs from the solution generated in part (a).

Pear Computer is considering an alternative pricing strategy of sliding down the demand curve. It plans to set the following schedule of prices over the coming two years:

Time Period	Price	Quantity Sold	Time Period	Price	Quantity Sold
1	$2,400	200,000	6	1,600	200,000
2	2,200	200,000	7	1,500	200,000
3	2,000	200,000	8	1,400	200,000
4	1,800	200,000	9	1,300	200,000
5	1,700	200,000	10	1,200	200,000

Are there alternative solutions to the congestion problem? Read the abstract *Congestion Pricing for Congestion Avoidance* on the Microsoft Research site at **http://research.microsoft. com/research/pubs/view. aspx?pubid=637**.

c. Calculate the contribution to profit and overhead for each of the 10 time periods and prices.

d. Compare your results in part (c) with your answers in part (b).

e. Explain the major advantages and disadvantages of "sliding down the demand curve" as a pricing strategy.

9. During times of peak usage of network resources such as highways, mainframe computers, and power transmission lines, providing access to an additional user can have negative impacts on all other users. Congestion or peak-load pricing systems at least partially internalize the external costs of congestion. But while congestion pricing may make economic sense, how can charging commuters higher prices be made politically viable?

DeSoto: Transfer Pricing (Part A)

(Part B of this Case Exercise is in Web Appendix 9B)

DeSoto Engine, a division of International Motors, produces auto engines. It sells these engines to the auto assembly division within the firm. A dispute has arisen between the managers of the DeSoto division and the assembly division concerning the appropriate transfer price for intracompany sales of engines. The current transfer price of $385 per unit was arrived at by taking the standard cost of the engine ($350) and adding a 10 percent profit margin ($35), based on an estimated volume of 450,000 engines per year. The manager of the DeSoto division argues that the transfer price should be raised because the division's average profit margin on other products is 18 percent. The manager of the assembly division claims that the transfer price should be lowered because an assembly division manager at a competing company indicated that engines cost his division only $325 per unit. The corporation's chief economist has been asked to solve this intracompany pricing problem.

The economist collected the following demand and cost information. Demand for autos is given by the following function:

$$P_m = 10,000 - 0.01Q_m$$

where P_m is the selling price (in dollars) per auto and Q_m is the number of vehicles sold. (Assume for simplicity that price is the only variable that affects demand.) The total cost function for the assembly division (*excluding* the cost of the engines) is

$$C_m = 1,150,000,000 + 2500Q_m$$

where C_m is the cost (in dollars). The DeSoto division's total cost function is

$$C_p = 30,000,000 + 275Q_p + 0.000125Q_p^2$$

where Q_p is the number of engines produced and C_p is the cost (in dollars).

Questions

Assume that no external market exists for these engines (that is, the DeSoto division cannot sell any excess engines to outside buyers and the assembly division cannot obtain additional engines from outside suppliers).

1. Determine the profit-maximizing output (vehicles) for the assembly division.
2. Determine the profit-maximizing output (engines) for the DeSoto division.
3. Determine the optimal transfer price for intracompany sales of engines.
4. Calculate (a) total revenue, (b) total cost, and (c) total profits for each division at the optimal solution found in Questions 1, 2, and 3.

Part 4 addresses the special topics of the new organizational architecture, government regulation, and international managerial economics. Building on the game-theory concepts introduced in Chapters 6 and 8, Chapter 10 discusses the theory of business contracting, the principal–agent problem and corporate governance, vertical integration, and, more generally, the choice of organizational form.

Chapter 11 then expands on the regulatory concepts introduced in Chapter 7 to address the economic regulation of business, including externalities, market failure, competition regulation, patenting, and licensing, as well as regulatory quotas and approvals.

Chapter 12 introduces the major topics of international managerial economics, including international supply chains, and the relationship between exchange rates and import/export sales, as well as the reasons for and patterns of trade in the world's economy, with special attention to regional trading blocs such as NAFTA.

CHAPTER 10

Organizational Architecture

Chapter Preview

This chapter explores the coordination and control problems faced by every organization and the mechanisms to solve these problems in a least-cost manner. The most important organizational decision is the determination of the boundary of the organization—i.e., the breadth of the span of hierarchical control. In dealing with external suppliers, outsource partners, internal divisions, authorized distributors, franchisees, and licensees, every firm must decide where the internal organization stops and where market transactions take over. Contracts provide an *ex ante* framework defining these relationships, but all contracts are purposefully incomplete. Consequently, every firm must address the potential for postcontractual opportunistic behaviour by partners and then design governance mechanisms to reduce these contractual hazards.

Should Dell make or buy subassembly components for its PCs? Should Kodak license its digital camera technology for Internet distribution by AOL, or should it invest in a strategic partnership with AOL? Instead, should Kodak vertically integrate by buying an Internet service provider as Microsoft did in buying WebTV?

We address these questions initially from the perspective of contracting within the moral hazard framework of purposefully incomplete contracts. The principal–agent problem is explained and then resolved with incentive contracting and governance mechanisms. Thereafter, we develop the choice of organizational form between contracting and vertical integration. Then we illustrate the coordination game between manufacturers developing or licensing products using the game-theoretic techniques introduced in Chapters 6 and 8.

Web Chapter 16 continues the discussion of organizational architecture with a focus on optimal mechanism design. Web chapters and appendixes can be accessed on the Nelson website for this book at www.mcguigan.nelson.com.

Learning Objectives

After studying this chapter, you should be able to:

1. Understand that firms make choices about organizational form that define the span of hierarchical control.

2. Understand that all external and internal business relationships require a solution to the problems of coordination and control.

3. Explain the issues surrounding *incomplete information,* incomplete contracting, and postcontractual opportunism.

4. List the various governance mechanisms and explain why they are necessary.

5. Explain the various ways that managerial labour can be hired and how pure profit-sharing results in moonlighting.

6. Explain the managerial issues related to the *principal–agent problem.*

7. Explain how the form of organization—contracting or vertical integration—depends on the contractual hazards that need to be solved.

8. Understand that vertical integration is an optimal organizational form when the assets are one-way dependent on complementary assets and are largely nonredeployable.

9. Understand that whether to develop and license or wait and imitate is an organizational form decision.

Controlling the Vertical: Ultimate TV*

Enormous business opportunities loom on the horizon for companies operating at the intersection of Web-based Internet services and TV. Personal computers have penetrated into 70 percent of North American households, but televisions are present in literally every household, with penetration now reaching 98 percent. Over the next five to ten years, 220 million analog television sets may be replaced by $150 billion worth of television-enabled PCs and digital televisions. The lure for customers will be Internet-based interactive services and much higher digital picture quality.

Microsoft has invested heavily in digital entertainment programming for these "smart televisions" and television-enabled PCs. Its know-how and trade secret investments are largely nonredeployable and include the operating system and user interface backbone for everything from interactive museum tours to distance-learning virtual courses to Web page construction.

However, all these investments may be focused on the wrong distribution channel. WebTV Networks Inc. (now MSN TV) has a system that allows consumers to surf the Internet through their low-end TVs. The core of this system is a patented signal compression chip that crams the capabilities of a TV tuner, cable modem, and high-speed video modem into one $50 unit. This technology frees content providers of the bandwidth limitations that prevent the Net from transmitting high-speed Web images and video. It may also free consumers of the need to upgrade to digital TV. Most households are able to connect the device to their analog TV set and begin surfing the Internet within 15 minutes.

If twenty-first-century households will be able to cruise the Net and download video with inexpensive network PCs or old televisions, Microsoft's huge investment in digital entertainment will decline exponentially in value. Digital TV manufacturers quickly established partnerships with WebTV to assess the danger and perhaps take an equity stake. Consequently, in late 1997, Microsoft decided to vertically integrate and bought WebTV for $425 million. Microsoft intended to combine its one-way dependent and reliant digital entertainment assets with WebTV's technology to produce digital consumer products for cellphones, pagers, and hand-held PCs. In addition, because cable companies appear most likely to trigger the adoption of "Ultimate TVs" through their leasing of set-top control boxes to residential customers, Microsoft sought to become a cable TV industry standard by investing over $10 billion in several North American and European cable firms. The ensuing equity transfers of ownership upstream to the set-top software provider were the inception of Microsoft's vertical integration into interactive TV.

---

* Based on "Why Microsoft Is Glued to the Tube," *BusinessWeek,* September 22, 1997, p. 96; "Microsoft to Buy WebTV for $425 Million," *The Wall Street Journal,* May 7, 1997, p. A8; and "Smart TV Gets Even Smarter," *BusinessWeek,* April 16, 2001, pp. 132–133.

Organizational Form and Institutional Arrangements

Organizational form and institutional arrangements play an extensive role in eliciting efficient behaviour. Incentive contracts can motivate manager–agents to pursue the interests of owner–principals. Incentive-compatible revelation mechanisms can elicit true cost information to increase the market value of joint ventures between partners like IBM, Siemens, and Toshiba. On another front, allowing the freewheeling of electricity from one public utility to another or privatizing British Telecom, Japan Air Lines, Teléfonos de México, and Société Générale can improve the incentives to maximize capitalized value in these formerly bloated public monopolies. However, the role of institutions in motivating efficient behaviour goes far beyond the design of incentive contracts and recent deregulation and privatization initiatives.

Institutional choices also involve the form of organization that companies adopt. For example, some firms like IBM and Goodyear Tires develop franchise dealerships rather than attempt to contract over selling procedures and warranty service with the independent retailers preferred by manufacturers like Apple and Michelin. Other firms adopt stand-alone subsidiaries as independent divisions but centralize the production of common components. Perhaps the most important application of these concepts occurs in deciding the boundary of the firm—i.e., whether it should vertically integrate throughout the supply chain like Petro-Canada or outsource like Dell.

The Function of Commercial Contracts

Contracts

Third-party enforceable agreements designed to facilitate deferred exchange.

Contracts are binding, third-party enforceable agreements often designed to facilitate deferred exchanges. A *promisee* undertakes some costly action (perhaps paying a consideration) in exchange for and relying on the *promisor's* pledge of a subsequent performance. A contract provides a hostage beyond the mere reputational asset that prospective distributors might offer. In exchange for an agreed consideration, the promisee receives a credible promise. The promisor's commitment to perform is credible because the legal rules of contract interpretation and enforcement (in the courts) provide assurance that any expectations that the parties clearly spell out (i.e., stipulate) will be met. Although courts seldom order recalcitrant contractors to perform specifically as was promised, they are quick to award **expectation damages** that leave the parties no worse off than was anticipated under the contract. Standard contract remedies therefore provide incentives for efficient precaution by the promisor and for no more than efficient reliance on the promise by the promisee.

Expectation Damages

A remedy for breach of contract designed to elicit efficient precaution and efficient reliance on promises.

This stipulation procedure works exceptionally well for fully anticipated events. Moreover, contract law reduces the transaction costs of renegotiation and settlement when unanticipated events do occur. For example, suppose the market price of a truck collapses because a competitor's new and improved substitute product is introduced. If the truck manufacturer and distributor agreed to a fixed-price contract six months earlier, the manufacturer will get the agreed-upon revenue because the distributor took that risk.

On the other hand, what if these two parties entered into a forward sales contract for diesel fuel to be used as a promotion to enhance the distributor's selling effort, and subsequently the price of diesel fuel doubled? The default rule for forward sales contracts is nonexcusal. If the manufacturer sold the distributor 1,000,000 litres of diesel at $0.50 per litre in June for delivery in December, and the December price is $1, the manufacturer took *that* risk. A pleading by the manufacturer that it would be ruinous financially to deliver as promised will have no effect. The manufacturer must either deliver the 1,000,000 litres in December or face a swift and certain court judgment of $($1 - 0.50) \times 1,000,000 = $500,000$ awarded to the distributor. Every commercial contract must therefore stipulate the allocation of such risks or operate under these

CRANKSHAFT DELIVERY DELAY CAUSES PLANT CLOSING

The role of contract remedies as incentives is well illustrated by the famous case of *Hadley v. Baxendale, Court of Exchequer 1854, 9 Exch. 341.* A mill owner ordered a replacement for a broken crankshaft from a machine shop that agreed to a standard repair and return of the mill owner's equipment. When return delivery was delayed because of poor road conditions, the mill owner sued for lost profits resulting from an extended plant closing. The court rejected this argument because the machine shop had taken the customary shipping precautions and would have been expected to do more (perhaps by arranging for an expedited delivery by express coach) only if the mill owner had stipulated the extraordinary damages that would arise from further delay. In other words, the machine shop was entitled to expect that the mill owner would not rely excessively on the promise of a three-day repair unless informed to the contrary. If the mill owner had time-sensitive business scheduled immediately thereafter and no temporary substitute crankshaft available, it was his responsibility to disclose those potentially destructive private facts, thereby eliciting a different level of precaution. Otherwise, the mill owner's reliance was excessive and inefficient, not deserving of the reinforcement that would have resulted from a court award of lost profit.

default rules that are intended to increase predictability and thereby reduce the transaction costs of business contracting.[1]

In some cases, contract promises are excused altogether. These excusals fall into two categories: exceedingly rare *formation excusals* and more frequent *performance excusals.* One formation excuse is that of mutual mistake. If Sam agrees to sell Harry what both parties think is an antique Mercedes-Benz, but the car turns out to be a Buick, the court will set aside the agreement to purchase. Similarly, if I sell you a damaged Learjet without disclosing the damage, you, the buyer, can ask to be excused. On the other hand, an astute buyer of a damaged jet who recognizes the potential for enhancing the value through inexpensive repair can profit from personal asymmetric information without concern about whether the courts might later set aside the sales contract and restore the plane to its original owner. Requiring the disclosure of destructive facts without abating the incentive to develop asymmetric information that would enhance value (constructive facts) is a delicate balance that these contract rules of formation excusal seek to achieve.

In a typical performance excuse, contingent events may frustrate the purpose of a contract. If the city of Montreal hires retired policemen to provide additional security for a visiting French presidential visit to Old Montreal, and if the president cancels the visit so that the added security personnel are never needed, the city will be excused from its obligation to pay. In this case, the allocation of cancellation risk might have been stipulated by the parties but if not, the default rule of frustration of purpose will set aside the contract. Both parties understand this in advance and plan accordingly, while saving the expense of negotiating the contingent outcomes.

---

[1] An excellent discussion of the role of contract remedies as incentives for efficient reliance and efficient precaution against nonperformance appears in R. Cooter and T. Ulen, *Law and Economics,* 2nd ed. (Reading, MA: Addison-Wesley, 1997), pp. 214–232.

ENFORCEMENT AND EXCUSAL OF CONTRACT PROMISES: THE EXTRAORDINARY CASE OF 9/11*

Perhaps most extraordinary are contracts that are excused because an act of God or of war prevents performance. For example, on the morning of September 11, 2001, the bond trading house Cantor Fitzgerald on the 101st floor of the North Tower of the World Trade Center had contract promises to make markets in (i.e., set the price and execute trades in) U.S. Treasury, DuPont, and Eurodollar bonds. Over the next several hours, 658 of the firm's 960 employees died in the terrorist attack on the World Trade Center. Prices were not negotiated, some orders were lost, and some trades went unexecuted. Sellers lost money when the value of their assets plunged in the aftermath of the tragedy. Yet, few wondered whether the courts would hold Cantor Fitzgerald responsible for the expectation damages.

In a related example, Bank of New York was obligated to clear and provide cash settlements for about 84,000 government security transactions on 9/11. Client firms like Merrill Lynch & Co., Salomon Smith Barney, and JPMorgan Chase & Co. had invested large sums in real-time, hard-wired data feeds and sophisticated telecommunications connections to Bank of New York. Yet, three of the bank's buildings in lower Manhattan were either damaged or forced to close because of the terrorist attack. At one point, Bank of New York owed Citigroup and JPMorgan Chase & Co. $30 million each on settlements the bank could not authorize for final clearance. Under other circumstances, each day the settlement was delayed could have resulted in a claim against Bank of New York for expectation damages of approximately $(1/365) \times 2\% \times \$30$ million $= \$2,000$ per contract per day. With razor-slim margins on these clearing and settlement operations, such damages would have exhausted all profit. Yet, again, under these circumstances, an act of war had prevented performance of the contract, and Bank of New York was entitled to a performance excuse.

These rules of contract law evolve out of the complex interplay between sophisticated disputants in the courts. They are what Ludwig von Mises called "a result of human action rather than an act of human design." Whether or not contracts are enforced (and on what terms) determines the rate of economic growth across nations and the likelihood of foreign direct investment in developing and less developed countries.[†] In a social contract sense, the common law of contract provides a pivotal feature of the competition between nations and represents a crucial part of Western democracy's efficient institutional arrangements.

---

* Based in part on "Little Changes at Bank of New York," *The Wall Street Journal*, March 8, 2002, p. C11.
[†] Douglas Cecil North, *The Rise of the Western World: A New Economic History* (Cambridge: Cambridge University Press, 1999).

Incomplete Information, Incomplete Contracting, and Postcontractual Opportunism

Practically all such exchanges, whether for products, financial claims, or labour services, are conducted under conditions of incomplete information. On the one hand, decision makers often face uncertainty (incomplete information) as to the effect of random disturbances on the outcome of their actions. This uncertainty typically leads to insurance markets. On the other hand, decision makers are sometimes uncertain as to the payoffs or even types of choices they face. This type of incomplete information typically leads to intentionally incomplete contracting. Let's see why.

Potential losses from repetitive risks such as workplace injuries and weather hazards are often insured for a small periodic cash flow. Risk spreading is the primary purpose of insurance markets, which pool such casualty risks and thereby reduce the loss exposure to any individual business or household. Randomly occurring injuries at a consumer electronics assembly plant seldom coincide with injuries in a firm's delivery trucks or severe weather disruptions at a firm's mill. As a result, modest insurance premiums can cover the cost of the anticipated claims involving such diversifiable risk events. In this sense, uncertainty and incomplete information are routine business problems handled in routine ways by insurance contracting. Even oil pipelines, nuclear power plants, and skyscrapers on earthquake faults typically can get insurance.

However, incomplete information as to remote risks—i.e., what possible outcomes might occur—may prevent the parties at risk from writing insurance contracts that apportion the gains and losses under any and all contingencies. Consider the **full contingent claims contract** you and your surgeon would need to write before an organ transplant operation. Or alternatively, consider the full contingent claims contract two pharmaceutical companies would need before one licensed the rights to produce a pregnancy-related drug to the other. To develop all of the accurate information required for a full contingent claims contract involving multigenerational cumulative health hazards is simply prohibitively expensive. Consequently, few transplant patients and few business partners attempt to negotiate full contingent claims contracts. The fact that information costs can be prohibitively large leads to the important insight that contracts are often incomplete by design.

One immediate consequence of incomplete contracts is that, after signing, one can expect to observe **postcontractual opportunistic behaviour** not specifically prohibited by the restrictive covenants contained in the incomplete contract. Surgical patients may go fishing in swampy bacteria-infested water before their incisions fully heal. Employees who receive on-the-job training (OJT) may moonlight with their newly honed skills. Managers may reconfigure assets following a labour contract concession in ways their employees did not anticipate. Baseball players may attempt a holdout at the time of contract renewals just before a World Series. Knowing this, surgeons must defend against more injury suits, companies provide less OJT, workers agree to fewer wage concessions, and owners develop more farm team players than they otherwise would.

The incompleteness of contracts results in inefficient behaviour that is the inescapable consequence of costly and therefore incomplete information. To reduce these inefficiencies, companies adopt **governance mechanisms** to help resolve postcontractual disputes. Examples of corporate governance mechanisms include monitoring by independent directors, rank-order tournaments for promotion, and mandatory arbitration agreements. In the next two sections, we explore the complementary roles of governance mechanisms and pay-for-performance incentive systems for managers.

Corporate Governance and the Problem of Moral Hazard

Whether manufacturers and distributors will decide to employ contracts or vertical integration depends on the relative transaction costs of coordination and control. In professing this transactions cost approach, Oliver Williamson has emphasized that contracts pose the *ex ante* framework but that **governance structures** provide the *ex post* implementation required to maximize value:

> Transaction cost economics works out of an economizing perspective in which organization is featured and farsighted but incomplete contracting is projected.

Full Contingent Claims Contract
An agreement about all possible future events.

Postcontractual Opportunistic Behaviour
Actions that take advantage of another party's vulnerabilities.

Governance Mechanisms
Processes to detect, resolve, and reduce postcontractual opportunism.

Governance Structure
A mechanism that poses an alternative to incentives or direct monitoring for eliciting contractually expected behaviour.

The parties to commercial contracts are thus held to be perceptive about the nature of the contractual relations of which they are a part, including an awareness of potential contractual hazards. However, because complex contracts are unavoidably incomplete—it being impossible or prohibitively costly to make provision for all possible contingencies *ex ante*—much of the relevant contractual action is borne by the *ex post* structures of governance.[2]

A franchise contract between a manufacturer and distributor will need to resolve coordination and control issues. For example, advertising may have enhanced effectiveness if the distributor shares its superior on-the-spot information about current trends in the marketplace. The information-sharing objective can be achieved through cooperative advertising allowances rebated back to the distributor out of the franchise fees.

Unobservable effort in fulfilling contract promises is a more difficult but standard business contracting problem—i.e., a "moral hazard" in all contractual agreements. After securing terms to their liking, contract partners must be wary of the potential for postcontractual opportunistic behaviour—i.e., shirking on the agreement in inconspicuous and hard-to-detect but potentially ruinous ways. For example, the selling effort of the distributor may be inherently unobservable. This contractual issue is sometimes referred to as the problem of hidden action (or inaction) to distinguish it from the adverse selection (lemons market) problem of hidden asymmetric information. Nobel Prize winner Ronald Coase has emphasized that introducing creative and ingenious incentives into contracts can help resolve these moral hazard problems and induce self-enforcement of promises.[3] For example, as discussed in the next section, the problem of providing incentives for unobservable managerial work effort can be at least partially solved with performance-based profit-sharing bonuses. Nevertheless, governance mechanisms continue to play an important role.

Consider a lender's incentive contracting and **moral hazard problem** with eliciting unobservable borrower effort in selecting safe working capital projects. A known reliable borrower may approach a lender with a randomly occurring liquidity crisis that necessitates an extension of its bank line of credit.[4] The lender then offers terms for the loan renewal—i.e., an interest rate, principal amount, collateral requirements, and loan term. If the borrower decides to accept, a line of credit extension is granted. Then a random process intervenes, presenting one of several uncertain business opportunities to the borrower. The possible business opportunities are a spectrum from the relatively safe investments in inventory during periods of backorders and stockouts to an extension of the firm's receivables policy allowing customers to pay within 90 days rather than pay cash at the point of purchase. Because product sales may be very sensitive to credit terms such as "90 days same as cash," the latter use of working capital has a higher expected return but is very risky, in that uncollected customer accounts may skyrocket.

The moral hazard problem for the lender is then motivated. The bank wants the borrower to exercise great care, high effort, and good judgment in selecting projects on which to expend its newly granted working capital from the line of credit extension. However, banks must move carefully in setting the loan terms to elicit this largely hidden

To read about moral hazard issues in the news, go to **http://radio.weblogs. com/0113343/ categories/ moralHazard**.

Moral Hazard Problem
A problem of postcontractual opportunism that arises from unverifiable or unobservable contract performance.

---

[2] Oliver Williamson, "Economics and Organization: A Primer," *California Management Review,* Winter 1996, p. 136. See also Williamson's *The Mechanisms of Governance* (New York: Oxford University Press, 1996).
[3] R. Coase, "The Problem of Social Cost," *The Journal of Law and Economics,* 2 (October 1960), pp. 1–44.
[4] In other circumstances, lenders may face an adverse selection problem of detecting whether unknown borrowers are from a fraudulent or reliable subpopulation of loan applicants, and the offered terms of the loan will then affect the acceptance and refusals that determine the proportion of the loan portfolio from each group. Moderate interest rates and high collateral are intended in that situation to allow borrowers to signal their reliable intent to repay. In the situation examined here, we abstract from the hidden information problem of adverse selection (by assuming that the borrowers are known customers of the lending institution) to focus attention on the hidden action problem of moral hazard in commercial lending.

action. Remember, the bank does not know in advance what business opportunity the borrower will be facing. This is not a case of project financing, where the commercial banker can take part in assessing the company's capital budgeting proposals and directly monitor its return on investment (ROI). Instead, the bank makes the funds available and must then elicit subsequent borrower effort in appropriately screening projects that are randomly presented for possible investment.

What loan terms should the lender offer? Large loans with long repayment terms are most desired by the borrower to gain the most financial flexibility in the face of its current liquidity crisis. Having more funds and more time to straighten out a business plan that has gone awry is preferable from the point of view of the borrower. But do these terms elicit more or less effort in screening projects so as to prevent or contain a loss? Clearly, a high interest rate forces reliable borrowers to seek out the riskier working capital projects in order to secure higher expected returns and therefore be in a position to repay the loan. Moderate rates with extensive collateral pledges of security would seem to move the reliable borrower in the direction of more effort to find safer projects.

However, the most important aspect of the lender–borrower relationship may not involve these terms in the loan contract at all. The most effective way to manage the risks of default and nonpayment may be for the borrower to establish a frequent reassessment and renewal governance mechanism, whereby the borrower must submit financial ratios on a regular basis to secure ongoing access to the extended line of credit. The more frequent, more convenient, and more audited these financial reports, the better the governance mechanism will work. In essence, a real-time governance mechanism, whereby the bank becomes almost a project financing partner for every major use of its funds, is the ideal way to elicit the desired care, effort, and judgment from the borrower. In the end, a project-by-project financing approval process is excluded by the definition of the problem, but the closer a governance mechanism can come to this result, the less likely a default will be.

The Need for Governance Mechanisms to Prevent Holdup

The hiring of managerial talent involves the three standard problems of all business contracts: (1) the allocation of residual risk problem because all contracts are purposefully incomplete, (2) the moral hazard problem because some actions with a bearing on contract performance (call it "effort") are always inherently unobservable, and (3) the holdup problem of postcontractual opportunism.

There is the moral hazard problem of unobservable effort (possible shirking and devotion of one's creative ingenuity to entrepreneurial endeavours unrelated to one's job). There is the postcontractual opportunism problem of holdup (extracting large sums from the compensation subcommittee of the board of directors when managers have acquired unique skills and knowledge and the company has made specific investments not redeployable to others). And of course, finally, company performance whether measured by cash flows, earnings, or even sales is subject to random disturbances. Since it proves prohibitively expensive to contract in advance what the pay will be for every possible remote occurrence, one seldom if ever gets full contingent claims contracts. Instead, managerial contracts are purposefully incomplete. We misblame managers at times for poor performance and fail to acknowledge managerial merit at times for good performance.

"Incentive contracting" with a minimum salary guarantee and a performance-based bonus (like a stock option) is an efficient solution to the moral hazard and residual risk problems. But incentive contracting alone is insufficient because of postcontractual opportunism that may be small (e.g., numerous inconspicuous, but potentially ruinous, violations of duty) or large (e.g., postcontractual holdup and outright fraud). Governance mechanisms are the key to resolving this remaining problem of postcontractual

MORAL HAZARD AND HOLDUP AT ENRON AND WORLDCOM*

Misaccounting for short-term business expenses as long-term capital investments required a $3.8 billion restatement of lower operating profits at WorldCom in fiscal year 2000. Enron executives depleted pension reserve accounts while heralding the attractiveness of employee stock option plans for retirement planning. Business news in 2002 made it abundantly clear that governance mechanisms are needed, but still the question remains, "Why, exactly?" Why don't debt contracts of bondholders, personal loan contracts that senior executives use to relocate their often lavish households, and performance-based incentive contracts aligning owner and managerial interests prevent these abuses? Is it just that too many gratuitous payments have been extracted from compensation committees, too many executive loans have been forgiven, and too many deferred stock options have been reset to lower strike prices when share prices fell? That is, are the incentives in all this incentive contracting just misaligned? The answer is decisively "No." There is a more basic, more fundamental problem: Incomplete contracts invite opportunistic behaviour, requiring vigorous governing mechanisms.

* Based on "Taken for a Ride," *The Economist*, July 13, 2002, p. 64, and "WorldCom Aide Conceded Flaws," *The Wall Street Journal*, June 16, 2002, p. A3.

opportunistic behaviour. Table 10.1 provides a list of these interdependent implementation mechanisms of corporate governance.

Table 10.1 Implementation Mechanisms of Corporate Governance

- Internal monitoring by independent board of director subcommittees
- Internal/external monitoring by large creditors
- Internal/external monitoring by owners of large blocks of stock
- Auditing and variance analysis
- Internal benchmarking
- Corporate culture of ethical duties
- High employee morale supportive of whistle-blowers

The Principal–Agent Model

Many types of owner–principals hire manager–agents to stand in and conduct their business affairs in exchange for a claim on some of the residual income. Parent companies set up principal–agent relationships with subsidiaries. Manufacturer principals employ retail distributor and advertising agents. And most importantly, equity owners hire executives with managerial incentive contracts. The owners' objective in such principal–agent relationships is to preserve value-maximizing incentives while compensating risk-averse managers for a risky income stream and foregone alternative employment opportunities.

The Efficiency of Alternative Hiring Arrangements

Managerial hiring contracts may take on several pure or hybrid forms, including straight salary, wage rate, or profit sharing. In straight salary contracts, the manager and firm agree on a total compensation package and specific conditions of employment.

In other contexts, such as consulting, the managerial consultant may receive an hourly wage rate equal to the best alternative employment opportunity in the competitive labour market for that type of consulting services. In Figure 10.1, the managerial consultant is hired for, say, 50 hours per week at wage rate W_a. D_l is the firm's input demand, which is the marginal revenue product of these labour services—namely, the marginal output of additional hours times the marginal revenue from selling the resulting additional output. Because each firm is atomistic in the labour market for these management consulting services, S_l is the perfectly elastic supply facing any given employer at the going market wage. Beyond 50 hours, the declining D_l no longer exceeds the incremental input cost along S_l.

Managers also may secure employment under a pure profit-sharing contract. Like pure commission-based salespeople or manufacturer's trade representatives, the manager may accept a percentage (say, 40 percent) of the receipts directly attributable to personal efforts in lieu of wage or salary income. Think of the percentage finder's fee sometimes offered for cost-saving suggestions in big corporations. Again in Figure 10.1, we can represent this third alternative hiring arrangement as the ray AB, wherein the manager receives 40 percent of the owner's willingness to pay for each hour of management services. Initially, this profit share will exceed the wage rate alternative. For example, during the first 22 hours of work, the profit-sharing contract will overcompensate by area ADJ (shaded area **O**). Thereafter the profit share falls below the manager's market wage rate per hour.

If 40 percent proves to be an equilibrium profit share, the overcompensation (shaded area **O**) will just equal the undercompensation for the last 28 hours of work (shaded area DCF labelled **U**). This leaves both the owner and the manager indifferent

FIGURE 10.1

Alternative Managerial Labour Contracts

This figure compares three alternative compensation plans. The rectangle OJCG represents the compensation for 50 hours at the market-determined hourly wage rate W_a. The triangle OAB represents compensation for a profit share of 40 percent. The triangle OIB represents compensation for a profit share of 35 percent. Compensations are equal for the hourly and 40 percent profit-sharing plans.

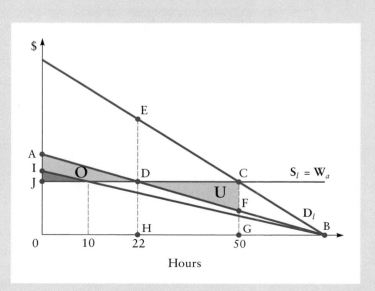

between this hiring arrangement and the alternative 50-hour-per-week wage rate contract at W_a. If the profit share were reduced to, say, 35 percent (represented by the ray IB), the dark-shaded amount of overcompensation for the first 10 hours would fail to offset the massive undercompensation for hours 10 to 50. The manager would then reject the profit-sharing contract in favour of the wage rate offer. By raising the profit share back to 40 percent, the firm appears able to restore the attractiveness of each contract, at least for certain types of workers. In reality, as we shall now see, the situation in hiring managerial talent is often rather different.

Work Effort, Creative Ingenuity, and the Moral Hazard Problem in Managerial Contracting

Pure profit-sharing contracts contain the seeds of their own destruction. Suppose several individuals are involved in generating pharmaceutical sales, and the input that the profit sharer contributes to team production is largely unobservable. No time card can successfully monitor the input, perhaps because a measure of work effort rather than work hours is really what is required. This is an instance of truly "hidden actions" by an employee. The rational employee then considers alternatives. As long as the profit-sharing compensation exceeds the alternative wage rate, the employee dedicates unobservable work effort to this job. Beyond 22 hours of work effort, however, the employee can earn more by working for someone else at the alternative wage rate W_a. Therefore, the disloyal (but rational) trade representative underworks the territory. The rep moonlights. This predictable response is another aspect of the *moral hazard problem*. Only a *moral* sense of duty to one's employer prevents this problem from becoming a real *hazard* to the business.

Predicting such behaviour, the employer may decide to withdraw the offer of a pure profit-sharing contract. Let's see why. If the territory is underworked by 28 hours, the employer saves profit-sharing payments equal to area DFGH in Figure 10.1, but loses output valued at ECGH and therefore is out the net value (ECGH − DFGH − the overpayment ADJ = EDC) relative to a wage contract that just paid piece rates for 50 hours of work at an implicit wage rate of W_a per hour. The fact that work effort is largely unobservable makes the pure profit-sharing contract unattractive to the employer relative to a piece-rate contract. This is not always so. For example, in hiring attendants for parking garages, the time clock and customer complaints (e.g., horn blowing and broken parking gate barriers) monitor the required input quite well. A dismissal policy in the employment contract making time-on-task a condition of employment elicits the required input. Similar time-on-task constraints and output quotas are employed in hiring sharecroppers and retail salesclerks. In these instances, the firms and their employees have evolved ways to resolve the moral hazard problem. Again, Ronald Coase has emphasized that private voluntary bargaining between principals and agents will often find ways to contract around such problems.[5]

The debilitating problem of moral hazard arises then only when an action such as work effort is unobservable except at a prohibitive cost. Consider again the pharmaceutical sales representative for whom appointment logbooks and random follow-up monitoring simply cannot detect the persuasive effort necessary to secure orders from physician customers. One could trail around after the sales representative and interview each physician after the sales calls were completed to try to detect the ingenuity and perseverance the sales rep displayed, but quite obviously, this monitoring practice would be prohibitively expensive. Instead, in the face of truly "hidden actions," the pharmaceutical

---

[5] This implication of the Coase Theorem is addressed at length in Chapter 11. See also J. Farrell, "Information and the Coase Theorem," *Journal of Economic Perspectives* (Fall 1987), pp. 113–129.

Benchmarking
A comparison of performance in similar jobs, firms, plants, divisions, etc.

company is more likely to jettison the pure profit-sharing contract in favour of some other performance-based incentive contract involving benchmarking. During a period of **benchmarking**, the employer reassigns previously low productivity sales territories to above-average trade representatives to see whether their efforts can alter the success rate per sales call. If so, the employer concludes that lack of effort by prior sales representatives was responsible for the low sales. After several such benchmarkings, the employer is able to identify those sales representatives to be kept and those to be dismissed. Importantly, the "keepers" are then allowed to retain all of the productive accounts they have developed.

For managerial jobs, however, the moral hazard problem is significantly harder to resolve. The input senior management contributes to team production is not time on task at the desk, but rather what we might call "creative ingenuity"—i.e., creative ingenuity in formulating and solving problems that may not even have arisen as yet. Managers are paid to think, and think hard, about proactive problem solving, not to shuffle papers. The difficulty is that it is hard to detect when creative ingenuity is being applied to the employer's business, rather than another business for which the manager may mentally be moonlighting. Of course, eventually the difference will show up in performance, but over how long a period and how big a difference? These are tough questions to answer satisfactorily to shareholders after a senior manager has shirked duties and has finally been let go.

More problematically, the shirking manager may never be let go, and the hardworking manager may never be rewarded. If random disturbances affect the company's performance, it is difficult even after the fact to separate unobservable shirking from negative random disturbances. How, then, are owners to know when to blame senior managers for downturns in company performance and when to give them credit for upturns? One mechanism often employed to analyze these variances is the **company audit**. Managers are required to report on the sources and uses of funds in accordance with generally accepted accounting principles (GAAP). Independent auditors can then attempt to verify the managers' explanations for the period-to-period variances by sampling company records.[6] Despite dedicated efforts and substantial auditing fees, separating the effects of management decisions from random disturbances in company performance remains an elusive goal. That is, the moral hazard problem is much harder to solve when combined with the performance uncertainty most firms face.

Company Audit
A governance mechanism for separating random disturbances from variation in unobservable effort.

The Principal–Agent Problem

In isolation, neither hidden effort (unobservability) nor performance uncertainty pose any special difficulty for owner–principals hiring manager–agents. The moral hazard resulting from the unobservability of a manager's input is, by itself, resolvable by assigning the manager lagged residual income claims (e.g., deferred stock options or restricted stock). Settling up *ex post* with a manager, after all the effects of personal effort and ingenuity have had time to influence performance, creates just the performance-based incentives that are required.

Similarly, performance uncertainty taken alone creates a risk-allocation problem that may be easily resolved with insurance. Managers are somewhat less able to diversify than owners because of the specific human capital the former often invest in a long-term relationship with the employer. This usually results in risk-averse owners and risk-averse managers structuring some sort of risk-sharing agreement to accomplish internally the manager's desire for at least partial insurance. A guaranteed baseline salary combined with a performance-based bonus is just such a risk-sharing agreement.

---

[6] This audit mechanism is explored in greater length in the Case Exercise at the end of this chapter.

INDEXED STOCK OPTIONS AT ADOBE SYSTEMS*

To align managerial incentives with equity owner interests, most companies regularly award deferred stock options to their managers. These performance-based bonuses entitle the holder to purchase company shares at a slight discount to their current value. If the firm's performance subsequently improves, capitalized value rises and both shareholders and the managers stand to gain. To exercise their options, managers often must wait three to five years, but they sometimes realize gains of 50 to 80 percent or more.

To acquire the shares for these deferred compensation programs, some companies dilute equity by issuing new shares, while other firms repurchase shares on the open market. To reduce the cost of these "buybacks," especially in a rising market, some companies like Adobe Systems index the exercise price for their deferred options to the average share price of their industry. When all the related companies do well, the value of the option rises, but so does the exercise price. As a result, the managers do not exercise their options at that juncture and instead are motivated to outperform their peers in related companies in both good times and bad.

Another advantage of indexed options is that managers are not penalized for the unavoidable economic malaise that follows a disaster like 9/11. Some companies reset strike prices of executive options to lower levels in a period of stock market downturns. Because of the enormous power wielded by CEOs and the resulting potential for opportunistic holdups of the compensation committees of corporations, it is far better simply to index the executives' stock options.

* Based on "Stock Options That Don't Reward Laggards," *The Wall Street Journal,* March 30, 1999, p. A26; "Corporate America Faces Declining Value of Options," *The Wall Street Journal,* October 16, 2000, p. A1; and "The Gravy Train Just Got Derailed," *BusinessWeek,* November 19, 2001, p. 118.

P&G PAYS AD EXECUTIVES BASED ON PERFORMANCE

Procter & Gamble places over $3 billion per year in advertising through ad agencies. Traditionally, the ad agencies earned flat-rate fees assessed as 15 percent of the ad dollars expended for the client. In the 1990s, P&G broke out of this flat-rate system and began paying a baseline fixed fee plus a performance bonus. Now, account executives at the agencies earn a fixed salary if their creative communica-tions are less than compelling and P&G sales stay flat. On the other hand, a hugely successful ad campaign can earn multimillion-dollar bonuses if P&G's sales growth can be attributed to the advertising. Both the clients, the ad agency owners, and the account execs now share in the risks of consumer whimsy, but a base salary provides a safety net should random misfortune occur.

Principal–Agent Problem
An incentives conflict in delegating decision-making authority.

The real difficulty for principal–agent contracting arises when both input unobservability and performance uncertainty are present simultaneously. The coexistence of these problems constitutes the so-called **principal–agent problem** most firms face. Settling up *ex post facto* with management teams then no longer creates the desired incentives. Some managers get unlucky and receive blame they do not deserve, and others get lucky and receive credit they did not earn. Many companies often attempt to address the problem of managerial moonlighting by benchmarking one manager against another (say, in comparable plants or geographic divisions). They hope that the effects of business cycle factors and random time-series disturbances will be highly correlated across plants and divisions, and that the manager's effort and creative ingenuity will therefore correspond with the plant or division's differential performance. Unfortunately, they are usually wrong. As a result, Japanese companies rely on intense loyalty-building exercises, peer pressure, and lifetime employment contracts to reduce mental moonlighting and other forms of shirking.

Incentive Compatibility Constraint
An assurance of incentive alignment.

Participation Constraint
An assurance of ongoing involvement.

The principal–agent problem can be formalized as an optimization problem subject to dual constraints. The principal chooses a profit-sharing rate and a manager's salary guarantee to maximize the expected utility of the risk-averse owner–principals' profit where profit depends on the manager–agent's effort, on the cost of the managerial incentives contract, and on random disturbances. An **incentive compatibility constraint** then aligns the effort chosen by the manager in response to the share and salary offer with that effort that maximizes the expected utility of the owner–principals. That is, an incentive-compatible profit share and salary elicit the managerial effort and creative ingenuity required to maximize the owner's value. Third and finally, the **participation constraint** ensures that the manager will reject the next best offer of alternative employment (e.g., at a known certain wage rate). However, do not be misled. An optimal managerial incentives contract is easier to describe than to attain.[7] See the Case Exercise at the end of this chapter.

Contract Renewals and the Holdup Problem

Shareholders face one final problem (a holdup problem) in their principal–agent relationships. Senior corporate officers often have specific company knowledge and experience that makes their institutional memory at least somewhat irreplaceable. Consequently, when it comes time to renew their contracts, senior managers often engage in postcontractual opportunism. Evidence of such holdups is rampant: Massive executive "loans" are often forgiven, golden parachutes that will insure the manager's security even if removed in a hostile takeover are often negotiated, and option strike prices are often reset to lower levels in down markets. All of these events suggest again that strong corporate governance is needed. Considerable effort to retain experienced senior managers is clearly value-maximizing, but the compensation subcommittee of the board must be an independent body that monitors these contract renewals.

Choice of Efficient Organizational Form

Ultimately, the choice of organizational form—contracting or vertical integration—depends on what best suits the governance needs of the assets involved. Assets can be specific investments with little or no value in second-best use, like remote plants, or

---

[7] See Jean Tirole, *The Theory of Industrial Organization* (Cambridge, MA: MIT Press, 1988), pp. 35–54, and David Kreps, *A Course in Microeconomic Theory* (Princeton, NJ: Princeton University Press, 1990), Chapter 16.

WHY HAVE RESTRICTED STOCK GRANTS REPLACED EXECUTIVE STOCK OPTIONS AT MICROSOFT?*

In July 2003, Microsoft announced that it would join numerous other firms in granting restricted stock rather than stock options as a performance-based bonus to over 10,000 of its 30,000 employees. Why make this change in the Microsoft incentive contracts?

There seem to be several reasons. First, restricted stock cannot be sold if an executive leaves the company. Once stock options vest, in contrast, they are typically sold, and in the heyday of the booming information economy in the late 1990s, Microsoft's options created literally thousands of multimillionaires among Microsoft's senior ranks. Too many of these valuable human resources simply choose to retire early and move on to other pursuits. One former executive took up professional bowling. So, restricted stock is expected to enhance the retention of pivotal employees relative to granting options.

A second reason for preferring restricted stock is that boards of directors find it difficult to keep senior managers from extracting from compensation subcommittees option features that work against optimal incentive contracting. For example, few option exercise prices are indexed relative to the industry group or strategic competitors. So option value rewards mediocrity when all share prices in an industry rise together. In addition, most senior executive options are "reloaded." As soon as the option contracts vest (in two to five years) and are exercised, senior managers negotiate that new options be issued with new exercise prices but the old expiration date (typically of 10 years). This allows executives to profit from induced volatility in their share prices. Why not take out a corked bat and swing for the fences with a high-risk project? Finally, few stock option contracts restrict in any way the executive's ability to "unwind" personal risk exposure by hedging the risks the options create. None of these practices is consistent with the objective of aligning managerial incentives with shareholder interests.

* "Microsoft Ushers Out Era of Options," *The Wall Street Journal,* July 9, 2003, p. A1; Lucian Bebchuk et al., "Managerial Power and Rent Extraction in the Design of Executive Compensation," 69 *University of Chicago Law Review,* 751, Summer 2002; and B. Hall and K. Murphy, "The Trouble with Stock Options," *Journal of Economic Perspectives,* Summer 2003.

Nonspecific Investment
A fully redeployable asset.

nonspecific investments that are fully redeployable, like corporate jet aircraft. In addition, some assets are dependent on unique complementary investments (e.g., specially designed computer hardware and closed-architecture software), while others are not dependent (e.g., a coal- or gas-fired power plant). One classic example of these asset-characteristic dichotomies is the hot-rolled steelmaking process, which requires a blast furnace, converter, reduction furnace, and rolling mill. Because achieving the high temperatures of the molten steel intermediate products requires substantial energy, thermal economies of scope require locating these plants beside one another to avoid the reheating expense. However, the organization form question is not whether the operations will be physically integrated and in adjacent locations, but rather whether they will be jointly or separately owned and managed.

At one end of the spectrum, spot market recontracting is efficient for fully redeployable durable assets not dependent on other complementary assets. Rental cars provide a good illustration of such assets that may be allocated through spot markets with no loss of efficiency, as shown in the top left-hand corner of Table 10.2. The limiting feature of this organizational form, however, is the potential for holdup inherent in the frequent renewal of spot market contracts. Should one party have nonredeployable assets (e.g., a steel mill's blast furnace or a major league sports franchise and stadium), spot market recontracting provides too many opportunities for metallurgical engineers or players with mobile skills and marketable talent to appropriate the surplus value in any business relationship. Should all parties have nonredeployable assets as in the hot-rolled steelmaking process, they all want to avoid this holdup hazard.

Reliant assets are nonredeployable durable assets sold in thin markets for less than their value in first-best use. These assets are highly specific to their current use because of substantial unrecoverable sunk cost investments either in acquisition, distribution, or promotion. Specialized equipment in remote locations is the most common reliant asset. Where reliant assets are dependent on unique complements in order to achieve any substantial value added, one has the maximum potential for holdup in spot market recontracting. These dependency relations may be either one way or bilateral. Manufacturers with independent distributors are a good example of a bilateral dependent relationship involving reliant assets. For example, each party in a truck manufacturer/distributor relationship is equally dependent on the other. In such cases, independent dealers often gravitate toward contracts with a fixed profit share, as shown in the bottom right-hand corner of Table 10.2.

When assets are dependent on unique complements but not reliant because of their substantial redeployability, the parties often adopt long-term performance-based **relational contracts.** Redeployable corporate jets and pilots provide a good illustration. Pilots need not own the planes nor secure fixed profit-share contracts to operate the planes. Instead, as indicated in Table 10.2, the organizational form of a jet charter company is normally one of long-term relational contracts with standby pilots who report on short notice for piecemeal assignments. This alliance works well, and both the pilots and plane owners understand that the longevity and reliability of the relationship enhances value relative to spot market recontracting. To take a related example, Genentech's biotechnology is fully redeployable but one-way dependent on marketing behemoth partners like Pfizer or GlaxoSmithKline. As a result, in 1996, Genentech entered into 10 marketing partnerships, 20 licensing agreements, and numerous research alliances with larger drug makers.

Reliant Assets
At least partially nonredeployable durable assets.

Relational Contracts
Promissory agreements of coordinated performance among owners of highly interdependent assets.

Find more on organizational architecture at **www.ctiarch.com**.

Table 10.2	**Alternative Organizational Forms Based on Asset Characteristics**	
	Fully Redeployable Durable Assets	**Nonredeployable Reliant Assets**
Not Dependent on Unique Complements	Spot market recontracting	Long-term supply contracts + *risk management*
One-Way Dependent Assets	Relational contracts (alliances)	Vertical integration
Bilateral Dependent Assets	Relational contracts (joint ventures)	Fixed profit-sharing contracts

YAHOO! AND ROGERS LAUNCH ALLIANCE FOR INTERNET ONLINE SERVICE

When Yahoo! built a widely used Internet search engine, it clearly required an Internet service provider (ISP) to complement the website in providing online search services. However, just as clearly, Yahoo! was redeployable to more than one ISP. Consequently, although Yahoo! was dependent on ISP complements, there was little contractual hazard of *ex post* holdup. Since Yahoo! was one-way dependent but not reliant on Rogers, and Rogers was neither dependent nor reliant on Yahoo!, a relational contract to establish an alliance between Yahoo! and Rogers was the efficient organizational form.

Another example of a relational contract between one-way dependent but not reliant assets is provided by the Kodak–AOL alliance to distribute digital photography online. AOL is fully redeployable to many other uses than providing online delivery of digital prints from film submitted to one of Kodak's 30,000 retail developing locations. Kodak believes, however, that it will soon be one-way dependent on an online partner as customers increasingly view, store, and share photos—and order reprints—over the Internet.

In contrast, consider the relational contract between a PC assembler and a chip supplier. This illustrates a bilateral dependency, since without specially designed Motorola computer chips, Apple PCs have little value, and without Apple PCs, these Motorola chips have little value. Yet, each manufacturer makes reliant investments that are specific to the other partner's design decisions. Hence, as indicated in Table 10.2, a joint venture is the efficient organizational form.[8] Web Chapter 17 addresses incentive-compatible revelation mechanisms for joint ventures.

Finally, when reliant assets are one-way dependent on unique complementary resources, the most efficient organizational form is vertical integration. Remote aluminum plants are one-way dependent on nearby bauxite mines. In contrast, because the bauxite can be shipped anywhere, the mine owners are not dependent on the local aluminum plant. Both assets entail substantial sunk cost investment, but only the remote aluminum plant is a nonredeployable durable asset—i.e., one with little value to other companies should the nearby bauxite source disappear. This is the situation in which upstream vertical integration by the manufacturer is required in order to prevent opportunistic holdup. Sometimes capitalized value is dependent on a downstream firm. eBay's huge success in attracting sellers of one-of-a-kind items to its network of auction buyers necessitated an electronic payments platform. PayPal captured that market, so in July 2002, eBay paid $1.4 billion to acquire PayPal and thereby vertically integrate downstream. PayPal had become a unique complement to nonredeployable eBay assets.

---

[8] The term *joint ventures* is often reserved for bilateral relationships that establish a separate corporate identity.

Economies of Scale and International Joint Ventures in Chip Making*

Approximately one dozen large electronics companies in the United States, Europe, and Japan were once involved in producing memory chips. Upfront costs for each item were staggering. For example, the cost of developing the 64-megabit memory chip design and production technology was estimated to range from $600 million to $1 billion. Once developed, memory chips then required investment of an additional $600 million to $750 million in a plant that produced up to 10 million chips a month.

Because of the massive scale economies that are available, many of the semiconductor companies involved in these research and development efforts formed international joint ventures to share the huge fixed costs and risks involved. These joint ventures took various forms. For example, Texas Instruments and Hitachi agreed to develop a common design and manufacturing process and then do low-volume production together, with mass production and marketing to be done separately by each company. Motorola and Toshiba entered into a partnership to co-manufacture memory (and logic) chips. In the end, massive scale economies from production rates of millions per plant per month led to a consolidation of production in the Hitachi and Toshiba plants in Japan.

* Based on "The Costly Race Chipmakers Cannot Afford to Lose," *BusinessWeek,* December 10, 1990, pp. 185–187, and "Two Makers of Microchips Broaden Ties," *The Wall Street Journal,* November 21, 1991, p. 84.

Vertical Integration

Search, bargaining, and holdup costs are all reduced when internal transfers and the monitoring and incentive systems within the firm replace the spot market contracting and recontracting necessitated by operating at arm's length with outside suppliers and independent distributors. As we have seen, Nobel laureate Ronald Coase and Oliver Williamson argue that these factors explain why the firm emerged as an organizational form despite the diseconomies of ever-wider spans of managerial control.[9] Another motive for a manufacturer to vertically integrate upstream to suppliers or downstream to retail distributors involves the inefficiency of successive monopolization (i.e., the presence of market power over price at more than one stage of production). For example, the transfer of WebTV's downstream equity to Microsoft (the upstream digital entertainment content provider in this interactive TV business model) is a method of precommitment by Microsoft to exercise upstream price restraint and not spoil the downstream market. We now illustrate these ideas further with a detailed study of vertical integration in the hosiery industry.

Consider, first, an upstream yarn supplier who operates in a perfectly competitive intermediate product market and a downstream hosiery manufacturer who enjoys the market power to mark up the wholesale price for pantyhose above its marginal cost. Figure 10.2 on page 318 illustrates the situation each firm faces when the yarn inputs are combined in fixed proportions with manufacturing labour and machinery to yield

[9] For more extensive discussion of this topic, see S. Hamilton and K. Stiegert, "Vertical Coordination," *The Journal of Law and Economics,* April 2000.

CABLE ALLIES REFUSE TO ADOPT MICROSOFT'S WEBTV AS AN INDUSTRY STANDARD*

Demand for interactive television with Internet surfing, Web shopping, interactive sports, and e-mail has grown quickly in hotel and airport lounges but very slowly elsewhere. Cable companies appear most likely to trigger the adoption of these smart TVs in households through their leasing of set-top control boxes to residential customers. After acquiring WebTV (renamed MSN TV) for $425 million in 1997, Microsoft shifted to an alliance strategy to secure the adoption of its complex software by the cable TV operators. Microsoft's interactive WebTV product known as UltimateTV was fully redeployable across competing cable service companies, and the cable companies sought to remain fully redeployable across interactive TV software providers. Since Microsoft/WebTV was one-way dependent on cable providers, but cable had numerous other ways to generate value without Microsoft, an alliance was the efficient organizational form for these asset characteristics.

Microsoft's product offering required the cumbersome software architecture of Windows CE. Standard set-top control boxes don't have enough memory or fast enough microprocessors to support Microsoft's operating system. Consequently, during 1991–2000, Microsoft invested over $10 billion in co-designing digital entertainment networks and new set-top control boxes with seven cable companies worldwide, including Rogers in Canada. One cable company, TCI, promised forward sales contracts for a total of 10 million set-top control boxes employing Microsoft CE software in a Motorola-built unit, the DCT5000. Today, the first 250,000 DCT5000s sit idly stacked in a Seattle warehouse. Microsoft's software was simply too complex, too costly, and too late.

After Microsoft insisted on the exclusion of the simpler Sun Microsystems' OS, the full installation costs for the DCT5000 cable networks skyrocketed to $500 per control box. Yet marketing research showed that cable subscribers would willingly add only $5 per month to their cable bills in order to secure these enhanced services. Ongoing delays induced Europe's largest cable company, United Pan-Europe Communications (UPC), to order set-top digital entertainment software from Liberate, a Microsoft rival. By March 2002, even AT&T announced that it had no plans at present to deploy interactive WebTV software and that Microsoft would build only the replacement for the scrolling online TV guide. Microsoft's eHome Division has now refocused on delivering TV services, music, and digital photography through the PC rather than the other way around.

Had the cable companies allowed Microsoft/WebTV to become an industry standard, full-scale vertical integration would have been warranted. Microsoft's digital entertainment assets would then have been one-way dependent on cable service providers, whose assets would have no longer been redeployable. This is the classic case for vertical integration, shown in the middle of the right-hand column of Table 10.2. At one point in 1997, while Bill Gates was presenting UltimateTV as a possible industry standard, a cable company president half-jokingly suggested that Microsoft buy the entire cable industry.

---

* Based on "Microsoft's Blank Screen," *The Economist,* September 16, 2000, p. 74, and "Set-Top Setback: Microsoft Miscues," *The Wall Street Journal,* June 14, 2002, p. A1.

FIGURE 10.2

Hosiery Integration Analysis with Upstream Competitor

When an upstream supplier sells its good in a perfectly competitive market, the downstream manufacturer has no profit motive for backwards integration into the yarn supplier's business.

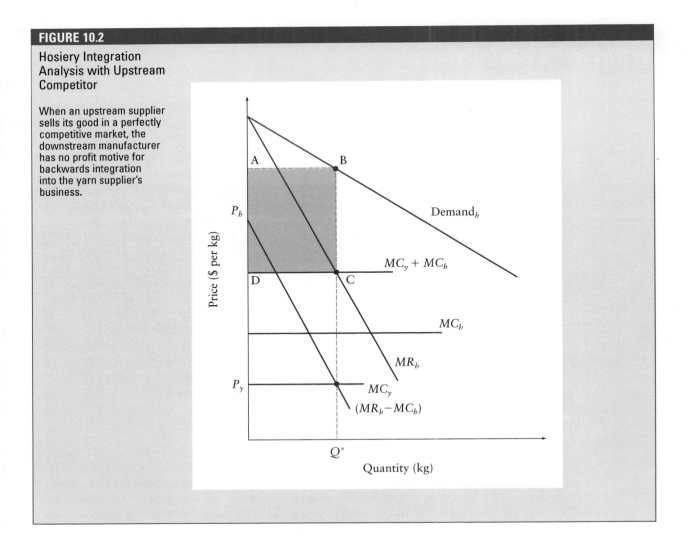

hosiery output. The outside demand curve and its marginal revenue capture the hosiery manufacturer's revenue opportunities in the wholesale pantyhose product market. Given the marginal cost of hosiery production (MC_h) and the competitive price of yarn ($P_y = MC_y$), the manufacturer sets summed marginal cost of hosiery production and yarn inputs ($MC_h + MC_y$) equal to hosiery marginal revenue (MR_h) at output Q^*. This proves to be a joint profit-maximizing output decision because the output that maximizes hosiery profits also sets the marginal cost of yarn equal to the net marginal revenue product of the yarn supplier. That is, subtracting the downstream marginal cost (MC_h) from the downstream marginal revenues (MR_h) leaves the *net* revenue opportunity available to the upstream yarn supplier—i.e., ($MR_h - MC_h$). Setting this derived demand for yarn inputs equal to upstream marginal costs (MC_y) identifies Q^* as the yarn supplier's preferred throughput rate as well as the hosiery manufacturer's preferred output rate. Thus, the upstream supplier who prices yarn so as to just recover marginal cost imposes no throughput constraint on downstream hosiery operations.

Since the hosiery manufacturer in Figure 10.2 would change neither the yarn input prices, nor the wholesale output prices, nor the throughput quantity if the manufacturer were to vertically integrate upstream and operate the yarn supplier, vertical integration can only result in disadvantages associated with a wider span of managerial control. For profits ABCD to remain unchanged, these disadvantages would need to be offset by some other factor, like reduced transaction costs. In general, in the absence of other factors, we would conclude that in Figure 10.2, the hosiery manufacturer has no profit motive for backwards integration into the competitive yarn supplier's business.

In contrast, however, consider the case in which the yarn supplier has a proprietary process that is unique and adds substantial value to the hosiery manufacturing process. In Figure 10.3, the derived demand for the yarn input is again $(MR_h - MC_h)$ and everything else about the hosiery operations remains the same as in Figure 10.2, except that now the upstream firm has the market power to mark up its own marginal cost (MC_y). Taking then a double marginalization of the revenue,[10] subtracting off the hosiery

---

Hosiery Integration Analysis with Upstream Market Power

When the upstream supplier has market power, the downstream manufacturer's net marginal revenue function $(MR_h - MC_h)$ becomes the upstream supplier's demand function. Compared to the perfectly competitive supplier, this results in a double marginalization process. This in turn leads to a reduction of quantity supplied from Q^* to Q' and an increase in price from P^* to P'. The downstream manufacturer now has an incentive to form a joint venture or to vertically integrate.

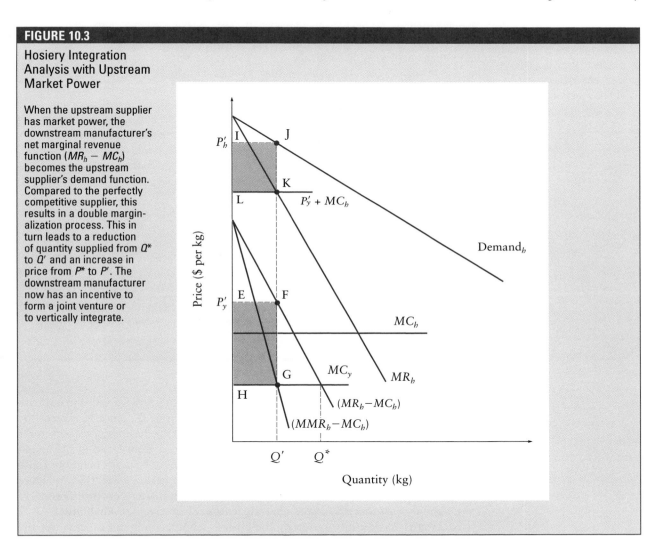

---

[10] The demand function for hosiery depicted in Figure 10.3 is linear and downward sloping. Thus, it can be represented as $P = a - bQ$, where a and b are positive constants. The marginal cost of producing hosiery excluding the cost of yarn in Figure 10.3 can be represented by $MC_h = c$, where c is a positive constant with $a > c$. The derived demand function for yarn is $MR_h - MC_h = (a - 2bQ) - c$. The marginal revenue function for yarn is $MMR_h - MC_h = (a - 4bQ) - c$. This is what is meant by the double marginalization of the revenue for hosiery. Strictly speaking, double marginalization of the cost of producing hosiery excluding yarn also occurs. For example, if the total cost of production excluding yarn was of the form $cQ + dQ^2$, with d also being a positive constant, then the marginal revenue function for yarn is $MMR_h - MMC_h = (a - 4bQ) - (c + 4dQ)$. However, since $d = 0$ in this example, $MMC_h = MC_h = c$.

Chapter 10 Organizational Architecture **319**

DELL REPLACES VERTICAL INTEGRATION WITH VIRTUAL INTEGRATION*

See what Dell's chairman of the board, Michael Dell, had to say about virtual integration at **www.dell.com**.

New developments in information technology, such as the enterprise resource planning system SAP, have widened the efficient span of hierarchical control. But rather than enabling larger vertically integrated companies, SAP enables virtual integration. Dell Computer Corp. owns almost no PC component manufacturing operations. Instead, the company outsources its requirements to several hundred supplier-partners who are tied together in a real-time monitoring, adaptation, and control system using the Internet. Dell's patented build-to-order business model must handle effectively an extraordinarily complex set of just-in-time component flows to support a final product assembly that ships 10,000 possible product configurations direct to a customer. Information technology clearly plays a key role in the governance mechanisms for this type of virtually integrated supply chain management. When this business model is successful, plant and equipment decline, inventories decline, and operating leverage rises substantially.

With less fixed capital investment than a vertically integrated competitor, the return on invested capital climbs accordingly. Dell was the fifth most quickly appreciating stock of the 1990s, increasing in value 297-fold between October 1990 and October 2000. By late 2000, Dell became the leading PC manufacturer, with market shares distributed as follows: Dell, 20 percent; Compaq, 16 percent; Hewlett-Packard, 11 percent; Gateway, 9 percent; and IBM, 6 percent.

* Based on "Identity Crisis," *The Wall Street Journal,* October 10, 2000, p. C1; "Direct Hit," *The Economist,* January 9, 1999, pp. 55–58; and J. Margretta, "The Power of Virtual Integration," *Harvard Business Review,* March/April 1998, pp. 72–85.

---

production cost, and setting $(MMR_h - MC_h) = MC_y$, the yarn supplier maximizes upstream profits EFGH by choosing a price P'_y at throughput Q'. Since P'_y exceeds the upstream marginal cost MC_y, the summed marginal cost facing the hosiery manufacturer is now higher and, consequently, the desired output declines from Q^* to Q'. Although hosiery prices rise to P'_h, the higher costs and smaller output of hosiery operations cause the profits of the downstream firm (the manufacturer) to decline—i.e., IJKL in Figure 10.3 < ABCD in Figure 10.2. That is, the presence of profit margins upstream results in a throughput constraint that unambiguously reduces downstream profitability.[11]

Backwards vertical integration by the hosiery manufacturer can squeeze out the margins upstream by simply setting an internal transfer price for yarn $P_y = MC_y$. This was precisely the transfer pricing strategy recommended in Chapter 9 for the vertically integrated firm with no external market for the intermediate product. This change will return the optimal throughput to Q^*, the profit-maximizing level for the consolidated yarn and hosiery operations. That is, even after paying the upstream profits EFGH to

---

[11] This implication holds without qualification here because of fixed proportions production, i.e., the efficient input mix remains unchanged despite the reduction in output. Under variable proportions, vertical integration may be motivated or not, depending on the input substitutability and possible cost savings.

secure the control rights from the yarn company, the downstream hosiery manufacturer has higher net profits (ABCD − EFGH) than its profit from independent operations IJKL. Consequently, we would expect these two firms to coordinate their operations either as a joint venture or as a vertically integrated firm. Joint ventures are further discussed in Web Chapter 17.

Licensing, Patents, and Trade Secrets

Another choice of organizational form involves the decision as to whether to license patents and trade secrets to competitors. (Licensing, patents, and trade secrets are further discussed in Chapter 11 in the context of government regulation.) Think of Microsoft's machine code, Pfizer's drug discovery technology, and Disney's films and characters. Fifty years ago, about 75 percent of the assets of North American nonfinancial corporations were tangible assets (real estate, inventories, and plant and equipment). Today that figure is just about 50 percent. Intangible assets such as patents, copyrights, and goodwill have grown to nearly dominate the account books. In addition, as the information economy comes centre stage, intellectual property has become an all-important source of competitive advantage.

By 1999, Microsoft held over 600 patents and Sun Microsystems held 1,223, topping Thomas Edison's record of 1,093. IBM Corporation was seeking patent protection at the astounding rate of 10 patent applications per working day.[12] Some of this activity is strategic patenting of technology portfolios, where companies do not wish to make a new device immediately, but they can plausibly describe how they would make it, what the device is used for, and the novelty of the idea. These are the evidentiary requirements for obtaining a patent. Not just electronic devices, genetic engineering, and computer software, but also business process methods are "hot" current areas of patenting activity. Dell received a patent on the direct-to-the-consumer business model, and Walker Digital (parent of Priceline.ca) received a patent on the Internet-based reverse auction, in which buyers post prices that sellers can then "hit" to execute a sale. Patent attorneys believe the ATM machine, frequent flyer programs, and even credit cards could be patented as business processes if they were invented today.

Table 10.3 shows that the financial markets definitely capitalize this "knowledge capital" into the equity market value of companies with patents, trade secrets, and proprietary know-how. Almost half of the $22-billion market value of Dow Chemical and more than a third of the $140-billion market value of Merck is discounted cash flow from intangible assets, mostly intellectual property. Much of Amazon.com's $11-billion market value arises from licensing fees on its business methods patents. Between 1994 and 1999, IBM boosted its annual revenues from licensing its intellectual property by over 200 percent, from $500 million to $1.6 billion. In consumer products, too, Reebok recently paid $250 million in royalties to obtain a 10-year exclusive licence to market National Football League-branded uniforms, hats, and equipment and to have its trademark on the players' apparel of all NFL teams. So, the revenue available from licensing is very substantial, but of course there are dangers from enlivening one's competitors.

Much debate rages about the role of patent and trade secret protection in providing incentives for first-mover companies to innovate while stifling technological research by fast-second companies. Imitators often substantially advance some aspect of any new technology but must license the original patents or run the risk of defending

---

[12] "The Knowledge Monopolies," *The Economist*, April 8, 2000, pp. 75–78; "Business Methods Patents," *The Wall Street Journal*, October 3, 2000, p. B14; and "Mind Over Matter," *The Wall Street Journal*, April 4, 2002, p. A1.

Table 10.3 Knowledge Capital, 1998 ($ billions)

	Sales	Book Value	Total Market Value	Market Value of Intangibles*
Merck	23.6	12.6	139.9	48.0
Bristol-Myers Squibb	16.7	7.2	107.0	30.5
Johnson & Johnson	22.6	12.4	92.9	29.7
DuPont	39.9	11.3	87.0	26.4
Dow Chemical	20.1	7.7	21.8	10.2
Monsanto	7.5	4.1	33.2	6.0

Business Method Patents

Patent Number	Date Issued	Device/Process	Inventors	Affiliate
5,797,127	8/18/98	Reverse auctions	Jay Walker et al.	Priceline.com
5,960,411	9/28/99	One-click buying	Jeff Bezos et al.	Amazon.com

*Estimated market value attributable to intangible, nonfinancial assets.

Source: Baruch Lev, *CFO*, February 1999, and *The Economist*, June 12, 1999, p. 62.

WHAT WENT RIGHT
WHAT WENT WRONG

TECHNOLOGY LICENCES COST PALM ITS LEAD IN PDAS*

In 1996, Palm single-handedly created the personal digital assistant (PDA) craze. Like Apple, Palm builds its own software and hardware. Worldwide, Palm operating systems run three-quarters of all hand-held devices that are capable of surfing the Internet. Unlike Apple, Palm decided to license its OS technology to competing manufacturers Handspring and Sony. Within two short years, Handspring surpassed Palm in manufacturing sales of PDAs by offering expansion slots and peripheral equipment like phones and music players.

Licensing always entails such risks, but Palm really had little choice in the matter. Cellphone giant Nokia had licensed its Series 60 mobile phone software to Siemens and Matsushita. The three firms together control 47 percent of the global cellphone market. Series 60 technology enables a cellphone to send and receive digital camera pictures, e-mail, and, most importantly, to browse a stripped-down version of the Net. If either Nokia or Palm succeeds in getting its OS adopted as an industry standard for hand-held Web surfing, it will set in motion a virtuous circle of increasing returns. In 2003, Palm and Handspring merged into palmOne to achieve a larger installed base.

* "Matsushita to Use Nokia's Cellphone Software," *The Wall Street Journal,* December 20, 2000, p. B10, and "One Palm Flapping," *The Economist,* June 2, 2001, p. 65.

COMPETING BUSINESS PLANS AT CELERA GENOMICS AND HUMAN GENOME SCIENCES

Genomics has revolutionized drug discovery and development. Celera Genomics, the firm that co-announced completion of the reading of the human genome sequence in 2000, expects to sell information, in effect to license its genome database, for as much as $90 million a year. It is hoped that comparing which genes are expressed and which remain recessive in various diseases will lead drug scientists to new blockbuster therapies and early detection of harmful side effects. However, an in-depth understanding of the biology of therapeutic mechanisms at the molecular level will also be key. Human Genome Sciences, Inc. (HGS) has decided therefore to position itself as a drug maker, attempting to patent drug processes, not simply license genetic information to traditional drug companies. HGS's first product, a wound healer, is in clinical trials.

themselves against patent infringement lawsuits. Jeff Bezos of Amazon.com has proposed that 20-year patent protection for computer software and business methods be reduced to only 3 to 5 years. Global patent protection is already diminished. In Europe, patent applications invite legal challenge, and a majority of initial patents have been overturned. The EU has also decided not to issue patents for either computer software or business methods. In this environment, trade secrets, proprietary know-how, and internal business practices take on added importance. Whether to "bury" the trade secrets or to acknowledge openly their existence and license them to competitors is a significant strategic decision about the firm's contracting and governance mechanisms. No less important is the decision as to whether, on the one hand, to attempt to develop know-how in-house or, on the other, to license proprietary know-how from competitors.

In Table 10.4, Motorola, Inc., and Lucent Technologies are trying to decide whether to develop in-house or license proprietary trade secrets in telecommunications engineering and software. Because of Lucent's long-term experience in this arena, if Motorola develops and patents the process and devices, Lucent expects to be very successful as an imitator earning $9 billion. Should licensing of some proprietary

Table 10.4 To License or Develop Expertise In-House? ($ billions)

		Motorola	
		Develop/Patent	Imitate/License
Lucent	Develop/Patent	$5 billion / $1 billion	$4 billion / $3 billion
	Imitate/License	$9 billion / −$1 billion	0 / 0

know-how prove necessary, Lucent believes an inexpensive limited licence will be sufficient. Consequently, Motorola will be unable (in that circumstance) to recover its fully allocated research and development costs and will therefore lose money (i.e., the −\$1 billion payoff in the southeast cell).

In contrast, if Lucent undertakes to develop and patent the needed process, its first-mover advantage would yield substantial licence fees from Motorola, whose solo attempts at imitation would render it unable to proceed without the proprietary knowledge gained through the trade secret licence. Hence, the payoffs describing this situation are \$4 billion/\$3 billion in the northeast cell. To complete the description of the payoff matrix, if neither firm develops the process, no profits accrue to either party. And if they compete head to head in a patent race, we assume the development costs will rise such that total profits fall from \$7 billion to \$6 billion, divided \$5 to \$1 between the technology leader Lucent and follower Motorola. What should Lucent do?

If Lucent could be sure Motorola was proceeding, Lucent would most prefer to wait and play "fast second." \$9 billion in the southwest cell is certainly attractive relative to \$5 billion in the northwest cell. However, Motorola can be expected to avoid the development expense and attempt to wait, imitate, and license as required to fill in the gaps in its own trade secrets and proprietary know-how. Indeed, Motorola has a dominant strategy to wait, imitate, and license. Consequently, Lucent anticipates that the payoff (\$4 billion/\$3 billion) in the northeast cell will emerge as an iterated dominant equilibrium. Recall from Chapter 8 that an iterated dominant equilibrium strategy is a self-interest maximizing action, in this case by Lucent, that is consistent with the dominant strategy responses of Motorola.

Although the numbers in Table 10.4 are only illustrative, thinking through the game-theoretic analysis can often prove very insightful in predicting rival reaction to company moves and countermoves. In this case, an analysis like Table 10.4 could well have helped, because it clearly indicates the desirability of the licensing alternative rather than the in-house development Motorola actually pursued.

Whether or not to license depends in part on the availability of increasing returns and the enormous competitive advantage such cost reductions offer. In Europe, where few industry standards have emerged for information technology products and where patents are often successfully challenged, first-mover firms have licensed to competitors rather than simply watch their trade secrets and proprietary know-how be steadily eroded by imitators. The result has been markedly increased competition, lower prices for consumers, and a faster rate of technological adoption. For example, prices for some digital TV components (e.g., digital video broadcasting chips) keep dropping, and the digital technology is quickly being incorporated into related products like cellphones, pagers, and secure video business networks for corporate meetings.

Red Hat uses a general public licence to penetrate as quickly as possible into the operating systems market with its Linux-based software that is intended to compete with Windows. Red Hat allows its suppliers and customers to copy, modify, and redistribute Red Hat software at no charge, as long as they do so without charge. This open-source software strategy is an attempt to achieve the inflection point for increasing returns that other Microsoft competitors like Apple never reached.

A final tactical advantage of licensing comes from the analysis of recontracting hazards, which is further discussed in Web Chapter 16. In purchasing high-end Alpha chips from Digital Equipment Corporation, a division of Hewlett-Packard, many workstation manufacturers worry about the postcontractual opportunism to which they are vulnerable. At contract renewal, once their designs are optimized for the Alpha technology, the manufacturers worry that the price for these sole-source-supplied chips may rise steeply. Digital can credibly commit to more stable prices and thereby increase the

MOTOROLA: WHAT THEY DIDN'T KNOW HURT THEM*

Motorola, Inc., was a pioneer in communications engineering with many of the early analog devices in radio, television, and military signal processing to its credit. More recently, Motorola developed and successfully launched the first hand-held cellphones and also took the lead in satellite-based wireless communications with Iridium, a global cellular network project. Ambitious future projects include a satellite-based, high-speed, high-security videoconferencing network for corporate customers and a satellite-based transcontinental and transoceanic connection for land-based cellphone companies.

Network reliability problems began to arise, however, when Motorola insisted on slowly developing its own digital wireless proprietary know-how rather than licensing the needed trade secrets and patents from Lucent or QUALCOMM Incorporated. Motorola had little expertise in digital switches, computing equipment, and communications software. Yet, proprietary knowledge in these areas proved critical in attempting to integrate Motorola's satellite system with land-based cellphone networks. At one point, Motorola launched a cellphone system whose software essentially blocked any other user from simultaneously connecting through the same cell tower and receiving station. In effect, this device crashed the local cell network anytime it was in use. Consequently, during a period in 1998 when QUALCOMM cellphones sold by the hundreds of thousands, Motorola was late to market with a competing product launch and even then announced a series of further delays. The operations problems were exacerbated by Motorola's lack of a common platform for its product configurations. Rather than mixing and matching standard components like Dell's operations strategy for assembling PCs, Motorola assembles cellphones from 10 different platforms with few interchangeable components.

Perhaps it is not surprising that QUALCOMM and Lucent experienced less trouble adding know-how in wireless technology to their long-standing expertise in wire-based telecommunications networks than Motorola experienced trying to add know-how in digital switches and communications software to their long-standing expertise in analog wireless hardware. Motorola should have licensed the proprietary know-how rather than attempt to develop it in-house.

---

* Based on "Unsold State: Motorola Struggles to Regain Its Footing," *The Wall Street Journal,* April 22, 1998, p. A1, and "How Motorola Roamed Astray," *The Wall Street Journal,* October 26, 2000, p. B12.

rate of adoption for its product by licensing to AMD or Intel. Allowing customers to dual source the Alpha chip technology credibly commits Digital to renew its supply contracts without price gouging. Thus, Digital can discourage the development of the licensees' substitute products. Intel employed this licensing strategy itself while trying to establish the Pentium series of chips as an industry standard in PCs. Apple Computers pursued the opposite nonlicensing strategy, thereby effectively slowing the rate of adoption of Macs.

Controlling the Vertical: Ultimate TV

For more information, visit the MSN TV website at **http://join.msn.com**.

Microsoft is still working hard to develop appropriate software and hardware for its intended move into the cable TV market. So far, however, they have not succeeded. However, MSN TV, the new version of WebTV was announced in late 2004. Microsoft is forming strategic alliances with MTV and Fuji Film, among others, to develop premium content for MSN TV.

Summary

- Businesses make choices about organizational form that define the span of hierarchical control from the vertically integrated oil company at one extreme to the virtual manufacturer Dell, which outsources all manufacturing and most assembly to supplier-partners.

- All external and internal business relationships require a solution to the twin problems of coordination and control.

- Long-term contracts provide an *ex ante* framework for resolving coordination and control problems between manufacturers, suppliers, and distributors.

- *Incomplete information* refers to the uncertainty that is pervasive in practically all transactions and motivates insurance markets.

- Contracts are seldom complete because full *contingent claims contracting* is often prohibitively expensive. Intentionally incomplete contracting allows *postcontractual opportunistic behaviour* that requires governance mechanisms to reduce several types of contractual hazards. The *moral hazard problem* arises because of the unobservability of effort in assuring contract performance. The *postcontractual opportunistic behaviour* called "holdup" presents another commonly occurring contractual hazard.

- Governance mechanisms include internal monitoring by director subcommittees and large creditors, internal/external monitoring by large block shareholders, auditing and variance analysis, benchmarking, an ethically dutiful corporate culture, and whistle-blowing.

- Managerial labour can be hired in several ways—for example, straight salary, wage rate, or profit sharing. Pure profit sharing results in moonlighting, however, because the manager's inputs—namely, effort and creative ingenuity—are largely unobservable. Unobservable effort leads to the *moral hazard problem,* which can be resolved by settling up *ex post facto* (e.g., with deferred stock options).

- In combination, random disturbances in firm performance and unobservable managerial effort present a more difficult *principal–agent problem* to resolve. Owner–principals do not know when to blame manager–agents for weak performance or give credit for strong performance. An incentive-compatible profit share and salary can, in principle, resolve the principal–agent problem.

- What form of organization to adopt—contracting or vertical integration—depends on the contractual hazards that need to be avoided. What contractual hazards arise in business relationships depends on the asset characteristics, on the redeployability or specificity of the fixed assets, and on the relative dependence of those fixed assets on unique complementary assets.

- Vertical integration is an optimal organizational form when the assets are one-way dependent on complementary assets and are largely nonredeployable.

- Whether to develop and license or wait and imitate is an organizational form decision about the protection afforded by patents, the relative importance of proprietary know-how, the availability of industry standards, technological lock-in, value-enhancing complements, and other sources of increasing returns.

Self-Test Exercises

1. If contract promises were not excused because of acts of God (like earthquakes in Vancouver) or acts of war (like the terrorist attack on the World Trade Center), what precautions would banks have to take to assure contract performance? How could one decide whether such precautions were deficient or excessive?

2. If coal mine output can be shipped elsewhere cheaply, but an adjacent coal-fired power plant is not redeployable to other uses, what organizational form would be adopted by the power plant owners? Why?

Exercises

1. Would warehouse operators insist on owning their own trucking companies? Why or why not? What coordination and control problems and contractual hazards would these companies encounter?

2. In benchmarking sales representatives against one another, what problems arise from continuing to reassign the above-average trade representatives to previously unproductive sales territories?

3. If the decision to develop and license or wait and imitate in Table 10.4 is a simultaneous-play repeated game between Lucent and Motorola for each new generation of technology, what happens if the Motorola payoff in the southeast cell is positive $2 billion? How should Motorola "play" in this modified licensing game? How should Lucent play?

DESIGNING A MANAGERIAL INCENTIVE CONTRACT*

Specific Electric Co. asks you to implement a pay-for-performance incentive contract for its new CEO. The CEO can either work hard with a personal cost of $200,000 or reduce her effort, thereby avoiding the personal cost. The CEO faces three possible outcomes: Her company experiences good luck with probability 0.3, medium luck with probability 0.4, or bad luck with probability 0.3. Although the management team can distinguish the three "states" of luck as the quarter unfolds, the Compensation Committee of the board of directors (and the shareholders) cannot do so. Sometime thereafter, the CEO decides to expend high or low work effort, and one of the observable shareholder values then results.

	Shareholder Value		
	Good Luck (30%)	Medium Luck (40%)	Bad Luck (30%)
High CEO effort	$1,000,000,000	$800,000,000	$500,000,000
Low CEO effort	$ 800,000,000	$500,000,000	$300,000,000

Assume 10 million shares and a $65 initial share price, implying a $650,000,000 initial shareholder value. Since the CEO's effort and the company's luck are unobservable to the owners and company directors, it is not possible on observing a reduction to $50 share prices and $500,000,000 value to distinguish whether the company experienced low CEO effort and medium luck, or high CEO effort and bad luck.

Answer the following questions from the perspective of a member of the Compensation Committee of the board of directors who is aligned with shareholder interests and is deciding on bonus plans for the CEO.

Questions

1. What is the maximum amount it would be worth to shareholders to elicit high CEO effort all the time rather than low CEO effort all the time?

2. If you decide to pay 1 percent of this amount (in Question 1) as a cash bonus, what performance level (what share price or shareholder value) in the table should trigger the bonus? Suppose you decide to elicit high CEO effort when and if medium luck occurs by paying the bonus for $800,000,000 outcomes. What criticism can you see of this incentive contract plan?

3. Suppose you decide to elicit high CEO effort when and if good luck occurs by paying the bonus for $1,000,000,000 outcomes only. What criticism can you see of this incentive contract plan?

4. Suppose you decide to elicit high CEO effort when and if bad luck occurs by paying the bonus for $500,000,000 outcomes. What criticism can you see of this incentive contract plan?

---

* An earlier version of this exercise was suggested by B. Ramy Elitzur of Tel Aviv University.

VERTICAL INTEGRATION AT GM–FISHER BODY

Read the three papers by R. H. Coase, R. Freeland, and B. Klein in the April 2000 issue of *The Journal of Law and Economics,* and then explain the competing arguments as to why General Motors vertically integrated upstream to buy out Fisher Body Co.

CHAPTER 11

Externalities, Market Failure, and Government Regulation

Chapter Preview

This chapter further develops the discussion of government regulation that was introduced in Chapter 7. As managers make decisions designed to lead to the maximization of shareholder wealth, they are faced with many constraints. Some of these constraints are external social pressures that constitute the moral social responsibilities of business. Other constraints have been codified into legal obligations of all firms in a similar industry or class (e.g., to avoid anticompetitive trade practices).

These statutory constraints are supplemented by a wide array of government regulations designed to ensure the smooth, efficient, and competitive functioning of the economy. To make wealth-maximizing price–output decisions, managers must fully understand the regulatory aspects of their environment. This chapter explores several types of regulatory issues: externalities and market failure, competition, licensing, patents, trademarks, and copyrights, as well as quotas.

Learning Objectives

After studying this chapter, you should be able to:

1. Explain the importance of *externalities*, how they may cause market failures, and how pecuniary externalities result in no inefficiencies.

2. Explain the importance of the *Coase Theorem*.

3. List the impediments to *private voluntary bargaining*.

4. Identify the various solutions to problems of externalities.

5. Describe *market performance, market conduct,* and *market structure*.

6. Understand the theory of *contestable markets*.

7. Define the various measures of market concentration including the *market concentration ratio* and the *Herfindahl–Hirschman Index* (HHI).

8. Understand why *competition laws* exist.

9. Describe various regulatory policies that restrict competition.

Deregulation and the Coase Theorem

D. FALCONER/PHOTOLINK/PHOTODISC

The 1991 Nobel Prize in economics was awarded to Professor Ronald Coase of the University of Chicago Law School. Professor Coase is best known for his work on the relationships among property rights, transaction costs, and the role of government. Coase challenged the prevailing view that economic externalities, such as water, air, and noise pollution, were "problems" in need of government action. It had been argued that firms will not consider these "external" costs when making choices regarding output levels and technology choices.

Coase argued that externalities should not be viewed as one party inflicting harm on another party. Rather, he viewed externalities as a problem of allocating a scarce resource. For example, a factory might use the surrounding buildings to absorb noise from its production process. The owners of a nearby amusement park might desire less noise so that they could attract more tourists. Coase claimed that this externality problem would be resolved without government intervention if the transaction costs of arriving at the solution were kept low. *The issue is one of arriving at the appropriate specification and assignment of property rights.*

In the broadly defined arena of government regulation of business, there has been a resurgence of interest in allowing market forces to operate, rather than relying on government regulators. Deregulation of most aspects of the transportation industries is complete. Natural gas pipelines and telephone companies have been greatly deregulated. Furthermore, there is substantial movement toward deregulation of the electric utility industry. *The trend toward greater deregulation will open new opportunities for future managers and confront them with new challenges.*

www

Read an autobiography of Ronald Coase at the Nobel Foundation Internet site at **http://nobelprize.org/ economics/laureates/ 1991/coase-autobio. html**.

Externalities and Bargaining

In the normal course of business, every firm faces decisions influenced by externalities. This section analyzes the potential for resource misallocation (market failure) with externalities, emphasizing Ronald Coase's mechanism design for handling reciprocal externality problems. Other possible solutions are then considered, including regulatory directives, effluent or emission taxes (and subsidies), mergers, and the sale of pollution rights. Both managers and the public have a keen interest in least-cost implementation of the kinds of remedies that society mandates for controlling externalities.

Externalities

Externality
A spillover of benefits or costs from one production or utility function to another.

Externalities exist when a third party receives benefits or bears costs arising from an economic transaction in which this party is not a direct participant. This occurs when producers or consumers provide benefits to third parties or impose costs on third parties for which the market system does not enable them to receive full payment in return. This *market failure* leads to misallocation of resources.

A commuter, for example, may decide to drive rather than use public transportation to get to work in the morning. This results in additional road congestion and costs (in terms of the opportunity cost of lost time as well as greater operating expenses) to all those who had already entered the road. This commuter, however, looks only at personal operating costs and personal commuting time in deciding whether to drive or use public transportation. Another typical externality exists with pollution byproducts of trucking deliveries that combine with certain atmospheric conditions to cause smog. In places like Toronto, this problem may impose significant costs on asthmatic residents and sightseeing businesses. In short, externalities arise with any interdependency of household utility or firm production functions that is not reflected in market prices.

Pecuniary Externalities

Pecuniary Externality
A spillover that is reflected in prices and therefore results in no inefficiency.

Only externalities that are not conveyed through the price system result in any inefficiency. Thus, when mad cow disease causes preference for meat to shift from beef to chicken, the price of beef will fall and that of chicken will rise, making beef producers and chicken consumers worse off, and chicken producers and beef consumers better off, because of the price change. But all of these interdependencies have operated through the market price system, and they are therefore identified as **pecuniary externalities** that pose no inefficiency.

The legal doctrine of "coming to the nuisance" illustrates the principle that pecuniary externalities result in no inefficiency. If the land you purchase for an eventual subdivision development is located next to a cattle feedlot, the price you pay per acre will reflect the stench. The reduced price of the land will internalize the spillover effects. Later, if residents of the subdivision complain about the stench and the feedlot is declared a pubic nuisance, you, the developer, may have to pay to relocate the cattle feeding business. Again, when external effects *are* reflected in prices, all affected parties directly participate in the transaction, and there is no inefficiency.

Externalities and Market Failure Due to Resource Misallocation

Market Failure
The price system fails to provide the correct signals to firms making output and resource-allocation decisions.

When nonpecuniary externalities are present, resources are likely to be misallocated by producers or consumers, whether the externality is beneficial or harmful to its recipients. If producers or consumers make a contribution to society's well-being for which they are not compensated, they are less likely to engage in the action generating the external benefit than if they are fully reimbursed for all benefits generated. Similarly, in the case of negative externalities, a producer or consumer will likely overallocate resources to some production or consumption activity if part of the cost of engaging in this activity is shifted to others. The reason for this likely misallocation of resources is that when nonpecuniary externalities exist, the price system fails to provide the correct signals to firms making output and resource-allocation decisions. This is **market failure.**

The general principle of how much of society's resources should be allocated to solving the externality problem is clear. An external cost, for example, should be reduced up to the point where the marginal spillover costs saved by any further reduction just equal the marginal lost profits from the externality-generating activity. Similarly, an action that generates external benefits should be expanded to the point where the marginal benefits to all of society from such an expansion just equal the societal marginal costs.

Coasian Bargaining for Reciprocal Externalities

In many cases, externalities arise because of incompatible uses of air, land, or water resources. For example, late-night takeoffs and landings by FedEx jets may disturb sleep in houses around the airport. Feeding of thousands of animals in a small, enclosed feedlot may create offensive odours in adjacent subdivisions. Agricultural land runoff of nutrient-rich water may adversely affect downstream intake by a bottled water plant. No adverse consequences would occur if either party were absent.

Reciprocal Externality
A spillover that results from competing incompatible uses.

Nobel Prize winner Ronald Coase has argued that an efficient solution to such **reciprocal externalities** can generally be achieved if the generator and the recipient of the externality get together and reach an agreement through bargaining. Among the numerous examples in Coase's famous article "The Problem of Social Cost," perhaps the most discussed is a reciprocal externality between a spark-throwing railroad and a farmer with adjacent flammable fields. Coase's ingenious and intriguing claim was that under certain conditions involving full information and low transaction costs, an answer to the question "Who is liable and therefore who should pay damages?" had no effect on the resource-allocation decisions of these parties. In particular, if the railroad had the property right to throw sparks along its right-of-way, the trains scheduled down this track and the land area planted along it would be exactly the same as if the railroad had the liability for all spark-induced damages along its tracks.

EXAMPLE

COASE'S RAILROAD

To see how this remarkable result arises through Coasian bargaining, consider the payoffs in Table 11.1. If the railroad has the property right (i.e., Table 11.1, panel [a]), the farmer incurs $600 worth of crop destruction per train per 10 hectares planted along the tracks. Initially, the railroad ignores these external spillover costs and chooses an activity level of trains that maximizes its own profits (i.e., two trains in the bottom row of Table 11.1, panel [a]). The farmer would plant 10 rather than 20 hectares along the tracks in order to earn $300 and avoid losing $800 (in the extreme southeast cell). If there were substantial impediments to bargaining, no further action would take place in an unregulated laissez-faire market environment. Otherwise, a

Table 11.1 Coasian Bargaining

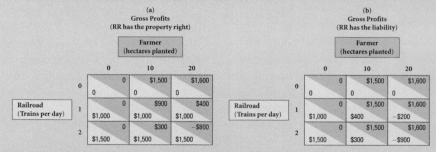

Source: Adapted from R. Coase, "The Problem of Social Cost," *The Journal of Law and Economics*, 2 (October 1960), pp. 1–44.

mutually beneficial private voluntary bargaining opportunity would exist.

In particular, if the railroad were to cut back to one train, the farmer's profit would rise from $300 to $900, while the railroad's profit would decline by $500 (from $1,500 to $1,000). Accordingly, $501 is a minimally sufficient incentive payment (bribe) to elicit the lower train-activity level, and $600 is the savings in fewer crops burned. Thus, Coase predicted that if the parties have few impediments to bargaining, the farmer would offer a side payment sufficient to abate the incremental (second) train and its spark hazard, because the second train is worth less (to the railroad) than the incremental agricultural losses cost the farmer. Just how much the farmer will pay and how little the railroad will accept is not addressed, but one thing is clear: Potential gains from trade do motivate a bargain to reduce railroad activity from two trains to one and area planted from 20 to 10 hectares.

Now, consider the case in which the railroad has the liability for spark-induced crop damages. Initially, the farmer prepares to plant 20 hectares along the tracks, as this activity level maximizes the farmer's profit (at $1,600). However, no trains are profitable with this much area in production since $600 in damages per train per 10 hectares (i.e., $1,200 altogether) is owed when the railroad has $1,000 gross profit with one train, and $2,400 in damages is owed when the railroad has $1,500 gross profit with two trains.

Table 11.1, panel (b), displays the net profits after crop damages have been compensated. Directing your attention to the middle row of Table 11.1, panel (b), the railroad offers the farmer an incentive payment in excess of $100—perhaps, $101—to scale back the area planted from 20 hectares, where farmer profit is $1,600, to 10 hectares, where farmer profit is $1,500. This reallocation of activities is worth $600 in damage savings to the railroad. Again, Coasian bargaining leads the parties to agree on one train and 10 hectares.

Coase Theorem
A prediction about the emergence of private voluntary bargaining in reciprocal externalities with low transaction costs.

The **Coase Theorem** states that reciprocal externality generators and recipients will choose efficient activity levels whatever the initial liability assignment. It makes no claim about the distributional consequences of reversing the direction of a liability assignment. Quite obviously, making the railroad liable in one instance and asking the farmer to cover personal crop losses from burned fields in the other result in quite different net profit outcomes. However, what the Coase Theorem does assert is that in reciprocal externality settings, resource allocation as to the externality-generating and externality-receiving activity levels will be unchanged independent of the initial liability assignment. One train will be scheduled, and 10 hectares will be planted.

Qualifications of the Coase Theorem

Some powerful qualifications are in order, many of which Coase himself recognized. First, technical transaction costs of searching for and identifying the responsible owners and affected parties, of detecting violations of one's property rights, and of internally negotiating the side payments (say, within a group of claimants) must all remain low and be unaffected by the reversal of the liability assignment. Second, neither party can operate in a purely competitive market, because then the profits required for incentive or side payments would be nonexistent. And, third, and perhaps most important, one party quickly makes an offer the other is willing to accept only when the information regarding the payoffs in Table 11.1 (a) or Table 11.1 (b) is complete, certain, and known to both parties. When information is incomplete and impacted, private voluntary bargaining need not lead to resource allocation that is invariant to the direction of liability assignment. And this asymmetric information

Chapter 11 Externalities, Market Failure, and Government Regulation

qualification to the Coase Theorem holds even if property rights are fully specified, completely assigned, and enforced at no cost.

The problem presented by asymmetric information is present in all incompatible use situations where *reported* damages and the precautionary actions of the plaintiff and the defendant have some bearing on the assignment of liability. For example, the parties in Coase's railroad example would avoid liability in part by employing spark arresters or land setbacks, as long as the benefit in crop-loss savings exceeded the cost. However, the problem posed by asymmetric information is that some aspects of precaution are inherently unobservable or unverifiable (e.g., attentiveness to subtle signals of impending hazard) while others are observable but affect accident avoidance in a nondeterministic way (e.g., good brakes may lock up on rain-slickened roads when less effective brakes would not).

Uncertainty and unobservability together result in the problem of moral hazard, which we discussed in Chapter 10. There is no incentive-compatible mechanism that can both preserve the voluntary nature of the Coasian bargaining and also elicit true revelation of the unobservable damages. Therefore, contrary to the traditional understanding of the Coase Theorem, disputants in reciprocal externality conflicts might be expected not to engage in private voluntary bargaining alone, but rather to delegate the question of damage assessment and recovery to third-party court systems. Civil procedural rules in an impartial court system can be seen as credible commitment mechanisms by which potential disputants bind themselves to liability assignments and wealth transfer remedies that motivate efficient accident avoidance despite frequently asymmetric information. So, the implication of the Coase Theorem is sustained. Externality disputants will contract their way to an efficient allocation of resources unless prohibitive transaction costs prevent the required bargaining.[1]

Impediments to Bargaining Several impediments to private voluntary bargaining as a mechanism for resolving externalities are well recognized in the legal system. Prohibitive notification and search costs (to identify absentee owners and notify all the affected parties) are the justification for certifying **class action suits.** Class actions prove critical to reducing these transaction costs in the case of oil spills and other large-scale externalities affecting many claimants. Voluntary private bargaining about incompatible uses also may be impeded by the need for continuous monitoring of an unverifiable deal like the maximum rate of harvest of a deep-sea fishery. However, unquestionably the most significant impediment to bargaining in large-numbers externality cases is the strategic holdout or strategic free-rider problem.

When a court grants an injunction against a polluter's operation, relief from the injunction may necessitate the polluter securing a unanimous waiver from the affected parties. If many claimants are certified as possessing such a right of waiver, each claimant has an incentive to hold out for more compensation than would be required to cover personal damages. The predictable presence of **strategic holdouts** in large-numbers externalities short-circuits the private voluntary bargaining hypothesized by the Coase Theorem to resolve the externality. In such cases, the courts therefore adopt other mechanisms involving liability rules and the payment of permanent damages.

Other Solutions to the Externality Problem

Solution by Prohibition

One simplistic approach to solving externality problems is merely to prohibit the action that generates the external effects. A little reflection, however, should indicate that in most cases this is at least suboptimal and frequently impractical. Auto emissions could

---

[1] See F. Harris, "Economic Negligence, Moral Hazard, and the Coase Theorem," *Southern Economic Journal,* 56 (3), January 1990, pp. 698–704.

Class Action Suit
A legal procedure for reducing the search and notification costs of filing a complaint.

Strategic Holdout
A negotiator who makes unreasonable demands at the end of a unanimous consent process.

be cut to zero if autos were banned, but the effects of such a move, at least in the short run, would be disastrous. Pollution in the St. Clair River could practically be abolished if industries dumping waste products were prohibited from doing so. But employment would also grind to a halt if such a step were taken. Furthermore, an optimal solution does not require that externalities be completely eliminated, but rather that the *right amount* of them be eliminated. A strict zero-pollution policy often entails excessive pollution abatement costs.

Solution by Regulatory Directive

The problem of controlling externalities is to eliminate an externality up to the point where the marginal costs of further reductions are just equal to the marginal benefits derived therefrom. We have seen that outright prohibition will often be suboptimal, so another possibility that has been suggested is to let the government decide just how much of the externality may be produced (e.g., of air pollution emissions). Cancer-causing lead additives in gasoline and ozone shield-depleting chlorofluorocarbon (CFC) refrigeration gases have been massively reduced by regulatory directives.

One problem with this approach to setting an overall emissions standard arises when multiple sources of pollution are present, as in the acidification of rain by coal-fired power plants. Each of the polluting entities (each point source) must be directed as to how it should act. A simple proportionate distribution of "pollution rights" to each plant would overlook the dramatic difference in the cost of abatement from one plant to another. Instead, optimality requires that the marginal effectiveness of the last dollar spent on pollution abatement by each polluter be equated. So, a low-cost point source's regulatory permit should require more abatement than a permit for a high-cost point source. Yet, this sort of detailed point-source regulation is seldom achieved.

Solution by Taxes and Subsidies

Another potentially efficient solution to externality problems is to provide subsidies (either in the form of cash or tax relief) to those whose activities generate significant external benefits and to tax those whose activities create external costs. Such a tax and subsidy scheme, however, requires a tremendous amount of information if it is to be administered in an optimal fashion.

Consider the analysis required for a per-unit pollution tax T^* in Figure 11.1. Demand per truck is the private willingness to pay (WTP) for trucking deliveries throughout the Toronto area. Setting marginal private cost (MPC) equal to private WTP, the trucking company will put 50,000 kilometres a year on its typical delivery truck. Still more delivery kilometres are avoided by the managers because the price that additional customers are willing to pay for deliveries is less than the MPC of operating the truck. The problem is that trucking kilometrage generates the byproduct nitrous oxide (NO_2), which causes smog. Through careful environmental science, sightseeing businesses and asthmatic citizens estimate that the air pollution causes damages from lost tourist business as well as eyes, nose, and throat irritants of area BCD. Consequently, although marginal benefit (P_o) equals MPC at the private market equilibrium point A, additional costs attributable to the NO_2 externality—namely, CB at 50,000 kilometres—suggest that full costs are substantially higher: namely, at point E, MPC (AB) + MExC (CB) > P_o. With summed private plus external costs exceeding marginal benefits to the delivery truck's customers at 50,000 kilometres, the joint product trucking kilometrage/NO_2 is produced in excess of its optimal level. Fifty thousand kilometres per year is too much trucking. However, the question, as always, comes down to *how much less* trucking and associated pollution abatement is optimal.

In Figure 11.1, the reduced kilometrage at which marginal social cost (MSC)—the sum of MPC + (MExC)—just equals marginal willingness to pay for trucking is

FIGURE 11.1

Optimal Per-Unit Pollution Tax

When there are negative externalities, the market determined price is lower and the output is higher than the social optimum. An optimal per-unit pollution tax can correct for this market failure.

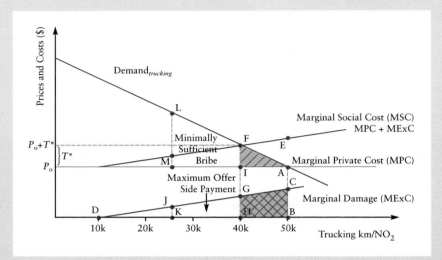

40,000 kilometres at point F. Clearly, the smog victims have damages (area GHBC) great enough to compensate the trucking company for its lost profits (area FIA) associated with a 10,000-kilometre reduction in kilometrage. The maximum side payment smog victims would offer for the next 10,000-kilometre reduction from 40K to 30K—namely, area JKHG—is smaller than the minimally sufficient bribe (area LMIF) that the trucking company would accept. But zeroing in on 40,000 kilometres as the optimal kilometrage (not 35K, 38K, 42K, or 45K) is very difficult because accurate marginal external cost information is so hard to come by. An optimal per-unit tax of T^* levied on delivery truck kilometrage reduces the kilometrage chosen from 50,000 to 40,000 through user charges in the amount $P_o + T^*$ that reflect the marginal social cost of the (trucking/NO_2) joint product. But again, T^* assumes heroically that the regulators know that 40,000 constitutes the optimal kilometrage.

In practice, a tax or emission charge would be placed on a firm's pollutants, such as kilograms of particulate matter emitted from a delivery truck or power plant smokestack. A firm could continue to pollute if it pays the per-unit tax, or it could find that it is cheaper to buy pollution control equipment. If, after a reasonable period of time, a community still believes that the level of particulate matter in the air is too high, the tax per kilogram of pollutant would be increased in a step-wise fashion until the community was satisfied with the result. The per-unit tax solution avoids the rigidity of all-or-nothing regulatory prohibitions or directives. And it induces firms to consider continuously the least-cost method of abating pollution.

An emissions tax approach has a number of problems of its own, however. First, only certain types of pollution can be measured easily with metering devices. Yet, an inexpensive method of accurately measuring pollutants is essential to such an emission-charge scheme. Second, although the tax scheme provides the possibility of building incentives for firms to move from densely to sparsely populated areas, this result is not likely to be greeted with universal acclaim by those living in the sparsely populated, relatively pollution-free areas. Third, the exact amount of an optimal effluent tax or emission tax is extremely difficult to estimate.

Solution by Sale of Pollution Rights

Another increasingly popular approach to the problem of pollution is the sale of pollution rights. Licences could be sold that give the licence holder a right to pollute up to some specific limit during a particular period of time. A government agency sets a maximum level of some pollutant that may be safely emitted in an area. The agency then sells, at auction, licences to individual firms, giving them the right to pollute up to a specified amount. The licences could be freely traded in an organized market, permitting their price to fluctuate with market demands and abatement technology discoveries. The advantage of this approach is that it is essentially market-oriented, forcing pollution costs to be internally recognized in all of the price and production decisions of individual firms. This is the approach adopted in the United States. However, Canadians living on the other side of the St. Clair River are also affected by U.S. pollution. Canadian pollutants also affect U.S. residents. NAFTA has not, so far, remedied this cross-border problem.

Solution by Merger

When the entities generating and absorbing the externalities are firms, merger is a very attractive way of internalizing externalities. If a paper mill is polluting a stream so that a chemical firm downstream must make large expenditures on water purification before using the water in its processes, the problem may be eliminated by a merger of the two firms. After the merger, it is in the best interest of the new consolidated firm to consider the chemical plant's water purification costs in determining what quality of effluent should be emitted from the paper mill. A similar example involving adjacent urban landowners is discussed below.

Externalities and Urban Renewal

The theory of externalities can explain why blighted areas develop and persist in our cities and why urban renewal mechanisms can help if properly designed. Profit-maximizing landowners don't always find it in their best interest to keep their properties in good repair because the value of any particular property in a neighbourhood is dependent not only on its size, design, and state of repair, but also on similar characteristics of the surrounding property. In short, real estate property value depends on three things: location, state of repair, and what the neighbours choose as their state of repair. Real estate maintenance therefore exhibits strong externalities.

The nature of this urban real estate interdependence may be illustrated with the Prisoner's Dilemma game. Let us assume that two adjacent property owners, Mr. Smythe and Ms. Jones, have made an initial investment in their properties and are currently reaping a competitive return. Both are now faced with the decision to make additional redevelopment investments. The return that each receives will be affected not only by one's own investment decision but by the decision of the other landowner as well. This may be illustrated in Table 11.2, which is read as follows: The entry below the diagonal in each cell represents the rate of return to Smythe from his action (Invest or Not invest) while the entry above the diagonal represents Jones's return from her action (Invest or Not invest). Beyond their initial investment, both Smythe and Jones have an additional amount available to invest in the properties. This additional sum is currently invested in corporate bonds yielding 10 percent. If neither Smythe nor Jones invests additional funds in real estate, they will continue to earn the 10 percent return, as is indicated in the "Not invest–Not invest" southeast cell. Alternatively, if both decide to invest and upgrade their properties, they will each earn a return of 15 percent, as indicated in the Invest–Invest northwest cell.

When Smythe invests and Jones does not, or vice versa, the one who redevelops earns only 8 percent because the new building is still in a predominantly old

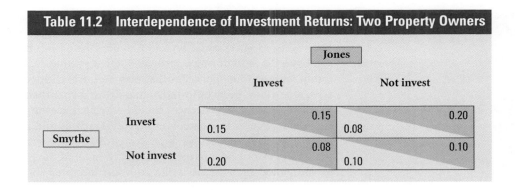

Table 11.2 Interdependence of Investment Returns: Two Property Owners

		Jones			
		Invest		**Not invest**	
Smythe	**Invest**	0.15	0.15	0.08	0.20
	Not invest	0.20	0.08	0.10	0.10

neighbourhood, whereas the one who does not invest gets the benefits from the improvement in the neighbouring property with no additional required outlay of funds. Let us see why this might occur. If Jones demolishes her old building and builds a new one, complete with off-street parking and other attractions, this would mean that Smythe's tenants would, for example, have a better chance to find on-street parking spaces. In addition, Smythe's tenants might value living next door to some higher income people and having their children mix with each other. As a result, Smythe may be able to raise his rents somewhat. Jones, however, is not so lucky, because potential renters would have to evaluate the neighbourhood (including Smythe's old building). Consequently, Jones cannot charge the rents she would like. Thus, Jones's return is only 8 percent, whereas Smythe gets a 20 percent return.

Being aware of the possible outcomes indicated in Table 11.2, both Smythe and Jones could well decide not to invest. Let us examine the payoff matrix from Smythe's point of view. If Jones invests, Smythe can get a return of 15 percent if he also invests, but a 20 percent return by not investing. If Jones does not invest, the best Smythe can hope for is a 10 percent return by also not investing. Thus, no matter what Jones does, Smythe is better off not investing. Similar logic follows for Jones. Each player, acting in one's own self-interest in the absence of cooperation, will decide *not to invest* and will thus receive only a 10 percent return. But this solution is not optimal, because they could both receive a 15 percent payoff by getting together and agreeing to redevelop their properties. In the simple two-person case illustrated here, voluntary cooperation is likely, especially if the same two landowners replay the game again and again in each maintenance cycle (see the discussion entitled "Escape from Prisoner's Dilemma" in Web Chapter 16). However, as the number of property owners increases, the chances of getting such voluntary cooperation diminish rapidly.

Perhaps the most obvious solution is for one landowner to buy out the other (i.e., to merge). Another possibility is that some third party might step in, purchase both properties (thereby internalizing the externalities), and receive the 15 percent return on each. This does in fact happen quite often. But without the public right of eminent domain, there is always the chance that some of the property owners will refuse to sell in order to reap the externalities of development themselves, or they may hold out for such a high price that it appropriates all the expected profits from the developer. In such cases, urban renewal including the use of public condemnation orders and eminent domain seizure (with market-based compensation) is required to effect the optimal solution of mutual maintenance of all properties.

In this section we have examined several approaches for solving externality problems. It should be apparent that no one best solution exists for all cases. Because of the great diversity of externality problems, appropriate policies must be tailored to meet the specific problem while comparing the costs and benefits of alternative solutions. Policymakers may then be guided in their decision making to choose that abatement mechanism where net benefits are likely to be maximized and the social costs are effectively internalized, forcing firms to treat social costs as a part of their relevant costs for decision-making purposes.

Market Structure, Conduct, and Performance

Competition (anticombines or antitrust) regulation is designed to increase the incidence of competition by eliminating attempts to monopolize an industry, as well as by attacking certain patterns of market conduct that are believed to have harmful effects on a workably competitive market structure.

Market Performance

Ultimately what society would like from the producers of goods and services is a multidimensional performance concept that includes these elements:

1. Resources should be allocated in an *efficient* manner, sometimes labelled "static efficiency."

2. Producers should be *technologically progressive.* That is, they should attempt to develop and quickly adopt new techniques that will result in lower costs, improved quality, or a greater diversity of new and better products. This concept is sometimes labelled "dynamic efficiency." Smaller drug firms, like AstraZeneca, for example, are often more innovative than the pharmaceutical industry giants like Schering-Plough, Bristol-Myers Squibb, and Pfizer.

3. Producers should operate in a manner that encourages *full employment* of productive resources, including human capital.

Unfortunately, these elements of good market performance are not always completely compatible with one another or agreed on by everyone. This prevents the development of an unambiguous index that might be used to assess the performance characteristics of a firm or an industry. Consequently, research on market performance has tended to focus on certain specific, measurable aspects of market performance such as profit rates, price–cost margins, actual costs versus technologically possible costs, selling cost in relation to price or total costs, relative price flexibility, stability of employment throughout the business cycle, and improvements in the productivity of labour.

Market Conduct

With good performance as the ultimate objective, it is important to develop a conceptual model that will help explain the causes of good or bad performance. Joe Bain's structure–conduct performance model of the factors influencing market performance is illustrated in Figure 11.2.

Performance is viewed as dependent on the market conduct of firms in an industry. In general, market conduct includes the following patterns of behaviour:

1. *Pricing behaviour of the firm or group of firms:* This includes a consideration of whether prices charged tend to maximize individual profits, whether collusive practices in use tend to result in maximum group profits, or whether price discrimination is followed.

2. *Product policy of the firm or group of firms:* For example, is product design frequently changed (as with auto style changes)? Is product quality consistent or variable? What variety of products is made available?

3. *Sales promotion and advertising policy of the firm or group:* How important are sales promotions and advertising in the firm's or industry's market plans? How is the volume of this activity determined?

For more information on the research and development that AstraZeneca does in Montreal, visit **www.astrazeneca.ca**.

FIGURE 11.2

A Conceptual Market Structure–Conduct Performance Model

Fundamental market and environmental conditions affect both market structure and market conduct. These in turn affect market performance.

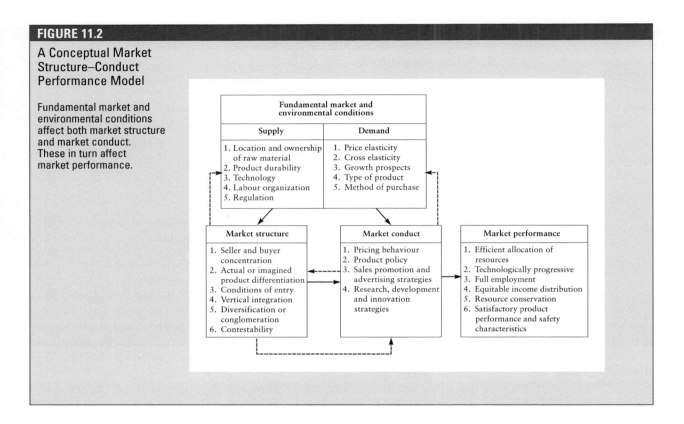

4. *Research, development, and innovation strategies employed by the firm or group:* How substantial are expenditures for these purposes? To what extent is new technology available to smaller firms? How quickly do leading firms adopt new technology?

Although the distinction between conduct and performance may sometimes be blurred, it is important to remember that performance refers to the *end results* of the policies or processes of adjustment pursued by a firm, whereas market conduct encompasses the *processes* whereby the end results are reached.

Market Structure

Market performance and market conduct are both dependent on the structure of a particular market. The concept of market structure refers to three main characteristics of buyers and sellers in a particular market:

1. The degree of *seller and buyer concentration* in the market, as well as the size distribution of these sellers or buyers: On the seller side, this determines whether an industry is classified as monopoly, oligopoly, pure competition, or some variant thereof. It is also important to know if there is a significant "fringe" of potential competitors confronting the larger firms in a concentrated industry. Buyer concentration is also important because the bargaining power of buyers determines in part the gross margin sellers can earn.

2. The degree of actual or imagined *differentiation* between the products or services of competing producers: When buyers perceive the product of one firm to be different from that of another, these buyer preferences will impart a degree of market power to the seller that ultimately affects that seller's market conduct and performance.

3. The *conditions surrounding entry* into the market and later exit therefrom: This refers to the relative ease with which new sellers may enter a market. When significant barriers to entry exist, competition may cease to become a disciplining force on existing firms, and we are likely to see performance that departs from the competitive ideal. Exit barriers diminish the competitive discipline imposed by potential (as opposed to actual) competitors.

Other related aspects of market structure include the extent to which firms are vertically integrated back to their sources of supply or forward to the final markets, because that is also likely to impact market power and lead to unsatisfactory conduct and performance.

Threat of Entry

The threat of entry is a measure of the height of the barriers that exist against new competitors and that protect existing firms from potential competition. The height of the barriers to entry in an industry may be measured conceptually as "the largest percentage by which established sellers can persistently elevate their prices above the minimized or competitive average costs of production and distribution without inducing new sellers to enter the industry."[2] The importance of entry barriers may be seen in a patent entry barrier example. Consider the case of a monopolist who knows that raising prices above a level that just yields a normal rate of return on the investment will result in a large influx of new competitors in the industry. The monopolist may choose no competitors and normal profits in the short run to preserve a long-run position. Alternatively, when substantial barriers to entry exist or when entry is completely blocked, as in the case of the possession of patent rights, the monopolist may be expected to charge the highest price consistent with short-run profit maximization over the useful life of the patent. We can see that the relative ease or difficulty of entry for new firms in an industry can have a significant impact on industry performance.

When firms are able to raise their prices somewhat above those that would prevail under competition without inducing the entry of new firms, some barriers to new entry must exist. These may be classified into three types. These general types of entry barriers and how they arise are summarized on the left-hand side of Table 11.3. The consequences of the entry barriers on new competitors are enumerated on the right.

Contestable Markets and the Structure–Performance Relationship

William Baumol, J. C. Panzar, and R. D. Willig[3] have developed a theory of *contestable markets* that provides additional useful insights into the structure, conduct, and performance relationship. The theory of contestable markets yields the same results as the theory of perfect competition but requires substantially fewer assumptions. It explains the emergence of competitive performance in a market characterized by multiproduct economies and few firms.

A perfectly contestable market is one that is easily accessible to potential entrants and easy to escape because capital investments are redeployable (trucks, planes, information). The potential competitors use the incumbent firms' preentry price as the basis for evaluating the profitability of entry. With freedom of entry and exit, potential competitors need not fear the pricing reactions of incumbents. If profit potential disappears after initial entry, the new entrants can simply leave the industry. The possibility of hit-and-run profits by potential entrants will cause even a dominant incumbent firm to set prices equal to average cost, because at any higher price there will be an opportunity for profitable entry.

---

[2] Joe Bain, *Industrial Organization* (New York: John Wiley & Sons, 1968), p. 237.
[3] William J. Baumol, J. C. Panzar, and R. D. Willig, *Contestable Markets and the Theory of Industry Structure* (New York: Harcourt Brace Jovanovich, 1982).

Chapter 11   Externalities, Market Failure, and Government Regulation

Table 11.3   Type and Consequences of Barriers to Entry

Type	*Consequences for New Entrants*

A. Product differentiation barriers arise from
  1. Buyer preferences, conditioned by advertising, for established brand names
  2. Patent control of superior product designs by existing firms
  3. Ownership or control of favoured distribution systems (for example, exclusive auto dealerships)
	A. 1. New entrants cannot sell their products for as high a price as existing firms can.
	  2. Sales promotion costs for new entrants may be prohibitive.
	  3. New entrants may be unable to raise sufficient capital to establish a competitive distribution system.

B. Absolute cost advantages of established firm's production and distribution arise from
  1. Control of superior production techniques by patent or secrecy
  2. Exclusive ownership of superior natural resource deposits
  3. Inability of new firms to acquire necessary factors of production (management, labour, equipment)
  4. Superior access to financial resources at lower costs
	B. Costs of new entrants are higher than for existing firms. Hence, while existing firms may charge a price that results in above-normal profits, new entrants may be unable to make even a normal profit at that price.

C. Economies of large-scale production and distribution (or sales promotion) arise from
  1. Capital-intensive nature of industry production processes
  2. High initial start-up costs
	C. 1. The entry of a new firm at a sufficient scale will result in an industry price reduction and a disappearance of the profits anticipated by the new entrants.
	  2. New firms may be unable to acquire a sufficient market share to sustain efficient operations.

D. Limited access to distribution channel	**D.** Closed shelf-space or Internet portals will necessitate massive slot-in investments and may prohibit certain business models.

Source: Joe Bain, *Industrial Organization* (New York: John Wiley & Sons, 1968), pp. 237–265.

The theory of contestable markets has shifted the focus of attention in market structure, conduct, and performance relationships to the conditions of exit. The lower the barriers to entry *and exit,* the more nearly a market structure fits the perfectly contestable market model, and consequently, the more likely it is that the resulting set of prices and outputs will meet the perfectly competitive market norm of price equal to average unit cost.

EXAMPLE

ARE CITY-PAIR AIRLINES A CONTESTABLE MARKET?

Airplanes, of course, are the classic redeployable asset. However, there are several features of the airline business that do not meet the conditions of contestable markets. First, hub investments are sunk costs often not redeployable into other airline route structures. Second, costs of switching from one airline to another are often raised by frequent flyer programs, flight schedules, and ticket promotions that restrict interline transfers. Finally, airline incumbents change prices two or three times a day, adjusting to competitive threats much more quickly than hit-and-run entrants can move in and out of city pairs. So city-pair airlines are *not* a contestable market. Think of trucking or Internet search engines instead.

Market and Environmental Conditions

Market structure, conduct, and ultimately performance are also influenced by certain *fundamental market and environmental conditions.* These may be divided into factors primarily influencing the *supply* or *input side* of the production equation and those whose primary impact is on the *demand side.* The supply side includes the location and ownership distribution of essential raw materials, the durability of the product, the available technology and production techniques commonly used, the degree to which labour inputs are readily available and organized (unionized), and the extent to which the firm's activities are regulated by government. On the demand side, such factors as the price elasticity of demand, the number of close substitutes that are available (measured by the cross elasticity of demand), the growth prospects of the industry, the type of good or service being produced (intermediate, consumer, specialty, convenience, and so on), and the method of purchase by buyers (list price acceptance, negotiation or haggling, sealed bid) must be included in an analysis of fundamental conditions influencing market structure, conduct, and performance.

The solid arrows in Figure 11.2 indicate flows that are primarily causal in the model, resulting ultimately in some observable market performance. As the dashed arrows indicate, however, some secondary and feedback flows are also involved. The major concern of studies in the field of market structure, conduct, and performance is to develop the capability to predict market performance, based either on observations of the fundamental market and environmental conditions, market structure, and market conduct, or on some contemplated and controllable changes in these factors.

We wish to emphasize one final point about the usefulness of this model in providing guidance for developing regulatory policies: There is no one place in the causal chain, from fundamental conditions to market performance, at which regulation (or deregulation) will always work best. In some cases, direct control of market structure may be effective. In other cases, direct control over certain business practices (that is, over market conduct) will be more effective.

Market Concentration

The purpose of measuring market concentration is to indicate the extent to which market exchanges take place in a competitive market structure. When industry sales, assets, or contributions to value added are concentrated in a few hands, market conduct and performance are less likely to be competitive in nature.

This is not always so. Occasionally, very concentrated industries are highly competitive. For example, Intel and AMD together control over 90 percent of the chip production for microprocessors in desktop PCs, yet margins are slim except for top-of-the-line processors. However, in general, consolidation mergers rationalize excess capacity in an industry but accomplish little more. Risk-adjusted cumulative returns to acquiring-firm shareholders are consistently negative, offsetting many sizable premiums paid to target-firm shareholders.[4] Hence, efficiency gains from further consolidation in already concentrated industries are very few.

Market Concentration Ratio
The percentage of total industry output produced by the 4, 8, 20, or 50 largest firms.

One widely used index of market concentration is the **market** (or *industry*) **concentration ratio.** It may be defined as the percentage of total industry output (measured, for instance, in terms of sales, employment, value added, or value of shipments) attributable to the 4, 8, 20, or 50 largest companies. Data on market concentration ratios are regularly made available by government agencies such as Statistics Canada and the U.S. Census Bureau. Industries are defined in terms of the NAICS (North American Industry Classification System) codes that were developed by NAFTA members Canada, Mexico, and the United States to replace the earlier SIC (Standard Industrial Classification system) categories. Under the NAICS, an industry is defined as a group of

---

[4] See Robert Bruner, "Does M&A Pay?" *Journal of Applied Finance,* Spring/Summer 2002, pp. 45–68.

Chapter 11   Externalities, Market Failure, and Government Regulation

For more information, go to **www.statcan.ca/ english/Subjects/ Standard/naics/2002/ naics02-index.htm**.

establishments producing a single product or a more or less closely related set of products. The NAICS consists of up to a seven-digit category code, indicating increasing specificity of industry and product as the number of digits increases. All manufacturing, for example, is specified by the first digit, food and kindred products by a two-digit category, candy and other confectionary products by a four-digit category, and sugar- or chocolate-coated nuts by a five-digit category.

It is necessary to use care in interpreting concentration ratios. In some cases, the four-digit NCAIS industry designation will be too broad, including many products that do not serve the same function and hence are not substitutable. In other cases, they are too narrow, failing to include ready substitutes. For example, metal, glass, and paper containers are classified as separate industries. Another problem with the concentration ratios is that in some instances they understate the true level of concentration for bulky, low-value commodities that cannot be economically transported far from their places of production. This occurs in such industries as cement, milk supply, and concrete block and brick. Some industries have become highly concentrated, such as breakfast cereals, turbine generators, light bulbs, and silverware. Some industries, such as hosiery and sporting goods, are very fragmented at the national level.

Another important measure of market concentration is the **Herfindahl–Hirschman Index,** or HHI:

$$HHI = \sum_{i=1}^{N} S_i^2$$

Herfindahl–Hirschman Index
A measure of market concentration equal to the sum of the squares of the market shares of the firms in a given industry.

where S_i is the market share of the ith firm and N is the number of firms in the industry. For example, in a relevant market consisting of just three firms, such as baby food (where Gerber has 70 percent, Beech-Nut has 16 percent, and Heinz has 14 percent market share), the HHI is $70^2 + 16^2 + 14^2$, which is equal to 5,352. HHI has a maximum value of 10,000 and decreases as the number of firms (N) increases. The HHI is generally highly correlated with other measures of market concentration, such as the four-firm sales concentration ratio, but accentuates the potential influence of leading firms with asymmetrically large market shares.

Competition (Antitrust) Regulation

Most capitalistic countries have passed legislation with the intent of maintaining competition and preventing monopoly (**competition [antitrust] regulation**). The ultimate objective of these laws is to protect the public from the abuses and inefficiencies that are thought to flow from the possession of monopoly power. Regulation of prices for natural monopolies was previously discussed in Chapter 7. The focus here is preventing monopoly in the absence of natural monopoly conditions.

Competition (Antitrust) Regulation
Laws that limit monopoly power and maintain competition.

Government regulatory agencies can use various methods to enforce the laws. They may negotiate with companies that are thought to be engaged in anticompetitive activities or they may institute court cases against such firms. The Competition Bureau of Canada (as well as the similar agency in the EU) prefers to use the courts as a last resort. In contrast, the U.S. agency seems to be much more eager to bring court cases. Court cases take many years and have high costs, so the moral suasion and negotiation approach may be more effective and in Canada leads to *alternative case resolutions* (ACR).

Many court cases are settled with *registered consent agreements* negotiated between the company and enforcement officials. Under a registered consent agreement (called a "consent decree" in the United States), a company agrees to take certain actions (or not engage in other actions) in return for the government agreeing not to seek additional penalties in the courts. In other cases, the courts may issue an *injunction* requiring (or prohibiting) certain actions by the firm. The courts may also impose *fines* and, in certain instances, *prison sentences* if the defendants are found guilty of violating the competition laws. In cases involving charges of monopolization, the courts may require *divestiture* of certain assets by the company.

Canada's Competition Bureau has not always been specific about how it makes decisions and there are not very many Canadian court cases to serve as precedents. Hence, Canadian firms frequently rely on U.S. decisions as guides to behaviour because of the NAFTA harmonization agreement. Thus, if a Canadian firm is onside with the U.S. regulations, it is likely to be acceptable to both Canada and Mexico as well. As more decisions are made by the Competition Bureau and the other similar agencies around the world, the regulatory environment will become clearer to managers. Another enlightening example is the insistence by the EU antitrust commission that British Airways divest itself of 353 landing slots at London's Heathrow Airport if British Airways and American Airlines wished to merge. Rather than lose this many of its prized assets, British Airways decided to continue competing with American Airlines.

Prohibition of Selected Business Decisions

Collusion

Explicit agreements among competitors to fix prices, along with other overt forms of collusion such as market-sharing agreements, are usually illegal, regardless of whether they cause injury to competitors. The legality of other less explicit forms of collusion is not as clear-cut. Other implicit forms of collusion, such as the price leadership practised in some industries, normally are not prosecuted. In a few cases, such as in the worldwide sugar industry, producers have been legislatively exempted from the competition laws and are legally permitted to jointly set prices and allocate output (quotas).

Mergers That Substantially Lessen Competition

A number of difficult legal and economic issues are encountered in attempting to determine whether a proposed merger will be challenged by government regulatory agencies. First is the issue of what is meant by the term *substantially lessening competition*. Every horizontal merger reduces competition by eliminating at least one competitor, by definition. For example, the United States uses merger guidelines based on the Herfindahl–Hirschman Index (HHI) in deciding whether to challenge a proposed merger:

1. For markets with an HHI above 1,800, the government is likely to challenge a merger that increases the index by 50 to 100 points or more.

2. For markets with an HHI between 1,000 and 1,800, a merger challenge by the government is unlikely unless the index increases by 100 or more points.

3. For markets with an HHI below 1,000, the government is unlikely to challenge a merger.

A merger increases the HHI by two times the product of the market shares of the candidate firms. So when Beech-Nut and Heinz's baby food division wanted to merge, the merger was challenged because the 5,352-point HHI changed as follows:

$$\text{HHI before} = S_{\text{Gerber}}^2 + S_{\text{Beech-Nut}}^2 + S_{\text{Heinz}}^2 = 5,352$$
$$\text{HHI after} = S_{\text{Gerber}}^2 + (S_{\text{Beech-Nut}} + S_{\text{Heinz}})^2$$
$$= S_{\text{Gerber}}^2 + (S_{\text{Beech-Nut}}^2 + S_{\text{Heinz}}^2 + 2S_{\text{Beech-Nut}}S_{\text{Heinz}})$$
$$= 70^2 + (16^2 + 14^2 + 2 \cdot 16 \cdot 14)$$
$$= 5,352 + \Delta\text{HHI}$$
$$= 5,352 + 448 = 5,800$$

The merger guidelines also list other factors that are considered in the analysis, including the ease with which competitors can enter the industry, likely failure of the to-be-acquired firm without the merger, and possible gains in efficiency for the (combined) firm.

A second important issue is the relevant product market to be used in computing statistics of market control, such as the HHI. Rather than measuring the cross price elasticity of demand, the United States, for example, uses a 5 percent price increase test—namely, what products, if not present in the market, would allow a monopolist to raise prices on a nontransitory basis by at least 5 percent? All such products should be included in the relevant market definition.

In addition to defining the relevant product market, the geographical market is also important in determining market control or power. Is the market local, regional, national, or international? Generally, a narrower definition of the market will heighten the measure of potential monopoly power and raise the probability of a merger substantially lessening competition.

Monopolization

As we saw earlier, firms engaged in overt forms of collusion with other companies can be successfully prosecuted. Companies acting alone also can be charged under the *Competition Act* with illegally attempting to monopolize a market or engaging in monopolistic practices. However, proving such alleged violations of the laws often is quite difficult.

EXAMPLE

POTENTIALLY ANTICOMPETITIVE PRACTICES: MICROSOFT'S TYING ARRANGEMENTS*

It was alleged that dominant software maker Microsoft used its leading position in the market for computer operating systems to gain an unfair advantage in the market for applications software. Netscape had complained that Microsoft illegally tied its Internet access software (Internet Explorer) to sales of Windows 95, which provided the operating system for 92 percent of the personal computers in the United States. Microsoft distributed Explorer free with every sale of Windows 95 to Compaq and Dell computers, priced Windows 95 without Explorer much higher, and threatened to remove the Windows 95 licence if any Web browser other than Internet Explorer was preinstalled on the PCs Compaq shipped. Over four quarters in late 1996 and 1997, Microsoft's share of the Web browser market grew from 20 percent to 39 percent. By 1999, Netscape's share had fallen to 47 percent, and Microsoft's anticompetitive practices had resulted in a 53 percent share. Was this evidence of "substantial harm to competition" or just substantial harm to a particular competitor?

Tying arrangements that extend the monopoly power of a dominant firm in one market to another distinct product and relevant market are illegal per se. In May 1998, the U.S. Department of Justice and 20 state attorney generals filed suit, alleging illegal tying arrangements and other anticompetitive practices. Microsoft vigorously defended itself for almost two years but in April 2000 was found guilty of the alleged violations. Microsoft was required to unbundle the two products and change its pricing practices.

* Based on "Browse This," *U.S. News & World Report,* December 5, 1997, p. 59; "U.S. Sues Microsoft Over PC Browser," *The Wall Street Journal,* October 21, 1997, p. A3; "Knowing the ABCs of the Antitrust Case Against Microsoft," *The Wall Street Journal,* October 30, 1997, p. B1; "Microsoft's Browser: A Bundle of Trouble," *The Economist,* October 25, 1997, p. 74; and "Microsoft on Trial," *The Wall Street Journal,* April 4, 2000, p. A16.

Wholesale Price Discrimination

A large company that operates as a manufacturer or distributor in two (or more) different geographic (or product) markets and cuts wholesale prices in one market and not in the other market can be accused of engaging in illegal price discrimination. Differential pricing directly to final product customers is allowed (and often based on "what the market will bear") but not so in pricing to intermediate product resellers (wholesalers, distributors, etc.).

Differentiating between the normal operation of a competitive market and illegal price-cutting with the intent of eliminating current or potential competitors is a complex issue. Proving that a company has engaged in illegal price discrimination can be quite difficult because activity-based cost accounting is quite intricate.

Refusals to Deal

In general, a manufacturer can refuse to deal with any retail distributor who fails to follow company policies that are based on legitimate business justifications. However, there are three limitations on this authority. First, the orders of a renegade discounter can be refused if and only if the manufacturer acts independently of compliant dealers whose sales at higher price points are suffering because of the increased competition. Second, an explicit well-justified policy must be in place in advance. The manufacturer cannot pressure individual dealers, threaten suspension of shipments of new "hot" products, or offer to reinstate if the offending discounters agree to raise their prices. Finally, manufacturers cannot lock in buyers of durable products by refusing to supply parts to independent service organizations (ISOs), especially if the ISO prices are far below the manufacturer's service prices. Customers should be able to select independent service and nonwarranty repair well after the sale.

Command and Control Regulatory Constraints

Many governments are involved in the regulation of business enterprises. Regulatory constraints can be imposed on individual firms, entire industries, or on all businesses. For example, the European Union prohibits direct-to-consumer advertising of prescription drugs. These constraints can affect a firm's operating costs (both fixed and variable), capital costs, and revenues.

The Deregulation Movement

Beginning in the late 1970s and continuing through the 1980s and 1990s, sentiment has increased for relying less on government regulation and more on the marketplace to achieve desired economic objectives. This sentiment for increased deregulation has been felt in new legislation that gives affected industries greater pricing flexibility.

Government Protection of Business

Besides regulating business enterprises, numerous government programs and policies protect businesses by restricting the entry of competitors.

Restricting Competition

Many public policies pursued by the government have the effect, if not always the intent, of restricting competition. These policies take numerous forms, including the issuance of licences, patents, trademarks and copyrights, and the restrictions on price competition. Such import controls as tariffs and quotas have the same impact.

Licensing When the government requires and issues a licence permitting someone to practise a particular business, profession, or trade, it is by definition restricting the entry of some potential new competitors into that practice. Licensing is generally used to protect the public from fraud or incompetence in those cases where the potential for harm is quite large. Thus, doctors are required to meet certain educational standards of professional competence. Restaurants need to meet public health standards. Real estate agents must meet certain standards of professional knowledge. Financial trustees must be bonded to ensure the public against fraud. Cab drivers are licensed with the intent of protecting the public from problem drinkers and accident-prone drivers. Nevertheless, the restricting of output by government licensure has tangible costs.

Patent

A legal government grant of monopoly power that prevents others from manufacturing or selling a patented article.

Patents **Patents** are by definition a legal government grant of monopoly power. The holder of a patent may prevent others from manufacturing or selling a patented product or from using some patented process. The patent holder may grant a licence permitting others to make limited use of the patent in exchange for some sort of royalty payment. The monopoly granted by a patent is not, however, an absolute one. First, it is limited to a maximum of 20 years in Canada, 17 years in the United States, and 15 years in Mexico, and few renewals are permitted. Second, competing firms are not prohibited from engineering around an existing patent and bringing out a closely competing, alternative design. Third, many patents are successfully challenged by competitors, especially in the European Union, where patent applications are not kept secret. Even an unsuccessful legal challenge of a patent, particularly a challenge by a large firm on patents held by a smaller firm, may be successful in forcing the challenged firm to license its patent to pay for lengthy legal battles.

Society pays two definite costs when it grants monopoly power to an individual or firm. First, once an invention is made, it may cost very little for others to reverse-engineer and duplicate it, except for the necessary production costs. Yet the monopoly grant entitles the inventor to receive a premium above the cost of production, either in the form of higher-than-competitive-level prices or royalty payments from licences for a period of validity of the patent. It is possible that a shorter patent monopoly period would provide sufficient incentives to encourage a high level of inventive activity. Serious proposals suggest shortening the patent period to just four years for computer software, for example.

Second, it has been observed that critical patents frequently help create strong monopoly positions that remain long after the original patent expires, because of other barriers to entry that are built up in the interim. This has been the case in such industries as aluminum, shoe manufacturing, braking systems, rayon, cigarettes, metal containers, photographic equipment and supplies, and gypsum products.

Offsetting these monopoly costs is the increase in inventive activity that the patent monopoly is alleged to encourage. Unfortunately, it is impossible to assess this impact in any meaningful, quantitative manner. Although doubtlessly some reduction in inventive activity would occur if the patent right were abolished, firms may protect the profits from inventions in other ways, including the following:

1. By keeping the technical aspects of the invention secret (trade secrets).
2. By taking full advantage of the lead time over competitors that a new invention provides (first-mover advantages).

Patents are used quite extensively by some industries, such as the electronics, drug, and chemical industries, whereas auto manufacturers, paper, machinery, and rubber processors use them very little, preferring first-mover advantage and trade secrets. (Licensing, patents, and trade secrets were discussed in Chapter 10 in the context of the choice of organizational form.)

Import Quotas

Another major policy that has protected domestic businesses by restricting competition is the use of import quotas. Faced with tough competition from producers abroad, many industries have sought restrictions on imports of products from abroad. Most vocal among these industries have been the textile, sugar, steel, and automobile industries. These industries have argued that without restrictions on foreign competition, thousands of workers would lose their jobs and critical domestic industries could be faced with extinction.

Import quotas inevitably lead to higher prices being paid for goods subject to the import restrictions. For example, in the automobile industry, the Japanese auto import restrictions had the effect in the early 1980s of increasing the average price for a Japanese car by $1,300, or about 20 percent. Under the import restrictions, the supply of Japanese-made cars fell short of the demand and many dealers were able to charge as much as $1,000 more than the official sticker price for some of the most popular models. In addition, because of the higher prices being charged for Japanese-made vehicles, North American manufacturers were able to charge higher prices for their products. Import quotas are further discussed in Chapter 12. Tariffs are another form of import control that protects domestic firms, and are also discussed in Chapter 12.

Trademarks and Copyrights Trademarks and copyrights also provide protection similar to a patent monopoly. A firm uses trademarks, which may be words, symbols, or designs to identify itself and its products. The purpose of trademark protection is to prevent a disreputable firm from duping customers by using the trademark (or something very similar) of a reputable firm.

A copyright protects literary, dramatic, musical, or artistic works for a period of 50 years in Canada. Like a patent, the intent is to provide a financial incentive to create.

Managerial Challenge Revisited

Deregulation and the Coase Theorem

In the broadly defined arena of government regulation of business, there is still considerable worldwide support for allowing market forces to operate, rather than relying on governmental regulators. The consensus in Canada seems to be that the CRTC should not regulate voice over Internet telephone service nor should it prevent the Italian TV channel from being aired within Canada as desired by the large Italian Canadian population. The trend toward greater deregulation continues and will open new opportunities for future managers and confront them with new challenges as well.

Summary

- *Externalities* exist when a third party receives benefits or bears costs arising from an economic transaction in which this party is not a direct participant. The impact of externalities is felt outside of (external to) the normal market pricing and resource-allocation mechanism and causes market failure.

- *Pecuniary externalities,* in which spillover effects are reflected in the market pricing mechanism, result in no inefficiencies.

- Ronald Coase has shown that an efficient allocation of resources can generally be achieved in the case of small-numbers externalities by contractual bargaining between the creator and recipient of the externality.

- Impediments to private voluntary bargaining include prohibitive search and notification costs, internal negotiation costs among large numbers of affected parties, prohibitive monitoring costs, and an absence of the surpluses required for making side payments.

- Many possible solutions to problems of externalities exist. These include solution by voluntary side payment, government prohibition, regulatory directive, imposition of pollution taxes or subsidies, a sale of rights to create the externality, and merger.

- *Market performance* refers to the efficiency of resource allocation within and among firms, the technological progressiveness of firms, and the tendency of firms to fully employ resources.

- *Market conduct* refers to the pricing behaviour; the product policy; the sales promotion and advertising policy; and the research, development, and innovation strategies.

- *Market structure* refers to the degree of seller and buyer concentration in a market, the degree of actual or imagined product differentiation between products or services of competing producers, and the conditions surrounding entry into the market.

- *Contestable markets* are assumed to have freedom of entry and exit for potential competitors and low switching costs for consumers. In a perfectly contestable market, the resulting set of prices and outputs approaches those expected under perfect competition.

- Measures of market concentration include:

  1. The *market concentration ratio,* defined as the percentage of total industry output attributable to the 4, 8, 20, or 50 largest companies.

  2. The *Herfindahl–Hirschman Index* (HHI), which is equal to the sum of the squares of the market shares of all firms in an industry

- *Competition laws* have been passed to prevent monopoly and to encourage competition.

- Many governments impose regulations on business enterprises. *Regulatory constraints* can affect a firm's operating costs (both fixed and variable), capital costs, and revenues.

- The current political and economic environment favours a significant reduction in the amount of government regulation and interference in the operation of the private sector of the economy.

- A number of regulatory policies are designed to restrict competition. These include licensing; issuing patents, trademarks, and copyrights; and using import controls, such as tariffs and quotas.

Self-Test Exercises

1. Branding Iron Products, a specialty steel fabricator, operates a plant in West Star, Saskatchewan. The town has grown rapidly because of recent discoveries of oil and gas in the area. Many of the new residents have expressed concern at the amount of pollution (primarily particulate matter in the air and wastewater in the town's river) emitted by the firm. Three proposals have been made to remedy the problem:

   a. Impose a tax on the amount of particulate matter and the amount of waste-water emitted by the firm.

   b. Prohibit pollution by the firm.

   c. Offer tax incentives to the firm to clean up its production processes.

   Evaluate each of these alternatives from the perspectives of economic efficiency, equity, and the likely long-term impact on the firm.

2. The demand for specialty glue is given as follows:

$$P = 1,200 - 6Q$$

   where P is the price per 100 kilograms of specialty glue produced and Q is the amount produced and sold in hundreds of kilograms.

   The marginal cost of producing glue for the entire glue industry is as follows:

$$MPC = 700 + 2Q$$

   a. What will industry output and price be in the absence of regulation?

   b. The production of specialty glue results in the following marginal pollution costs:

$$MC = 200 + Q$$

   What is the marginal *social* cost for the production of specialty glue?

   c. If the firms in the industry attempt to achieve a *socially* optimal level of output, what price should be charged, and what should be the level of output?

3. An industry is composed of Firm 1, which controls 70 percent of the market, Firm 2 with 15 percent of the market, and Firm 3 with 5 percent of the market. About 20 firms of approximately equal size divide the remaining 10 percent of the market. Calculate the Herfindahl–Hirschman Index before and after the merger of Firm 2 and Firm 3 (assume that the combined market share after the merger is 20 percent). Would you view a merger of Firm 2 with Firm 3 as procompetitive or anticompetitive? Explain.

4. How can you justify the existence of government-granted monopolies for such public utilities as local telephone service, natural gas distribution, and electricity in the light of the traditional economic argument that the more competition there is, the more likely it is that an efficient allocation of resources will occur?

5. An industry produces its product, Scruffs, at a constant marginal cost of $50. The market demand for Scruffs is equal to

$$Q = 75,000 - 600P$$

   a. What is the value to a monopolist who is able to develop a patented process for producing Scruffs at a cost of only $45?

   b. If the industry producing Scruffs is purely competitive, what is the maximum benefit that an inventor of a process that will reduce the cost of producing Scruffs by $5 per unit can expect to receive by licensing the invention to firms in the industry?

6. The demand curve in a competitive industry has been estimated to be

$$P = 1,500 - 9Q$$

The industry's short-run supply curve is

$$P = 80 + 3Q$$

A single firm emerges as the dominant firm in the industry and gradually acquires all of the other firms in the industry. The marginal cost curve for the monopolist becomes

$$MC = 50 + 3Q$$

as a result of effecting a number of operating economies.

a. Calculate the competitive market's price and output levels.
b. Calculate the price and output levels for the industry once the monopolist assumes control, assuming that industry demand remains unchanged.
c. If this monopolist is regulated so that the maximum price the monopolist is allowed to charge is $450, what is the benefit to consumers and the cost to the monopolist?

Exercises

1. Discuss the problems of aircraft noise around an airport from an externality perspective and propose a possible solution if (a) housing existed in the airport area before the airport was built and (b) housing was built adjacent to the airport after the airport was built.

2. A sheep rancher has leased the mineral rights beneath her grazing land to an oil company. She fears that discharges from the oil wells will pollute her underground water resources. Consequently, the contract for the sale of mineral rights requires that the rancher and the oil company reach a mutually agreeable solution to the water contamination problem, should it occur. If this bargaining fails to reach a conclusion acceptable to both sides, the mineral rights lease will be terminated automatically, and the rancher will be required to return a portion of the lease proceeds to the oil company. The portion that must be returned to the oil company is to be determined through a process of binding arbitration. Discuss likely outcomes should this problem arise.

3. Lead Weight Refining Ltd. operates an ore smelter in Smelterville, NWT. The firm produces lead ingots that are later used to manufacture batteries for heavy-duty equipment. In the lead-refining process, a substantial amount of air pollution is generated. A local mothers' organization is concerned about the health hazards posed by the emissions of the firm. After consulting with local officials, the mothers convince the city to impose a pollution tax on the discharge of the firm.

Each unit of output, Q, is composed of one unit of lead, Q_L, and one unit of air pollution (particulates), Q_A. The total cost function of the firm is

$$TC = 25,000 + 8Q + 4Q^2$$

The demand for lead is

$$P_L = 4,522 - 4Q_L$$

The demand function for the firm's particulate pollution is derived from the use of these pollutants as an input in the battery production process. The demand function for these discharges is as follows:

$$P_A = 400 - Q_A$$

a. In the absence of any pollution tax, what price, quantity, and profit levels will prevail for the firm?

b. Compute the marginal revenue for lead output and for pollution output at this price and output level.

c. What is the minimum tax that must be charged to completely eliminate pollution by the firm?

d. Discuss the reasons why it is necessary to be able to measure the damage from pollution so the affected parties may reach an optimal solution through bargaining.

e. Is this same information also necessary to elicit the optimal amount of pollution abatement with a per-unit emissions tax? Why or why not?

4. Under what circumstances would you defend pure competition as the most efficient market structure? What arguments can you make to the contrary?

5. Discuss the proposition that corporate "raiders" are a valuable element in the efficient operation of the economy and that such takeover threats result in long-run benefits to shareholders and more efficient management.

6. What are the major factors to be considered, for competition regulation purposes, in determining the relevant market in which a firm operates?

7. Suppose an industry is composed of eight firms with the following market shares:

A	30%	E	8%
B	25	F	5
C	15	G	4
D	10	H	3

Would the government likely challenge a proposed merger between

a. Firms C and D (assume the combined market share is 25 percent)?

b. Firms F and G (assume the combined market share is 9 percent)?

Explain your answer.

8. Evaluate the importance of the concept of price elasticity of demand when attempting to identify the ultimate incidence of the impact of government regulations on business that (a) increase fixed costs and (b) increase variable costs.

9. Discuss the pros and cons of the regulation of oil and natural gas prices.

10. What economic arguments can be made in favour of mandatory seat belt usage laws in automobiles and mandatory helmet laws for motorcycles?

11. What are the incentives to innovate for a monopoly firm as compared with a firm in a competitive market if patent protection is not available? Does your answer change if patent protection is available?

12. Would you consider the airline industry to be a contestable market? Explain.

13. Specific Motors Corporation (SMC) is one of the Big Three auto manufacturers in Transylvania. SMC's share of the domestic auto market is 55 percent. The next two closest competitors control 25 percent and 15 percent of the market, respectively, and the rest may be accounted for by two small, specialized firms. SMC has been under pressure from Transylvania's government for monopolistic practices. To discourage any attempts to break up SMC, management has decided to maintain its market share below 55 percent of the total domestic automobile sales revenues.

SMC estimates that to stay within its constraint of 55 percent of the market, its total sales should not exceed $2.8 billion.

The firm faces the following demand and cost functions:

$$P = 16,000 - 0.02Q$$

$$TC = 850,000,000 + 4,000Q$$

a. Calculate the unconstrained profit-maximizing level of price and output for SMC.

b. At this level, what will total sales revenues be? Total profits?

c. If the firm constrains its sales revenue to $2.8 billion, calculate price, output, and profit levels under the constraint. (*Hint:* Remember the quadratic formula: $x = \dfrac{-b \pm \sqrt{b^2 - 4ac}}{2a}$ based on the equation $ax^2 + bx + c = 0$.)

d. What is the cost to the firm of this market-share constraint?

14. The industry demand function for bulk plastics is represented by the following equation:

$$P = 800 - 20Q$$

where Q represents millions of kilograms of plastic.

The total cost function for the industry, exclusive of a required return on invested capital, is

$$TC = 300 + 500Q + 10Q^2$$

where Q represents millions of kilograms of plastic.

a. If this industry acts like a monopolist in the determination of price and output, compute the profit-maximizing level of price and output.

b. What are total profits at this price and output level?

c. Assume that this industry is composed of many (500) small firms, such that the demand function facing any individual firm is

$$P = \$620$$

Compute the profit-maximizing level of price and output under these conditions (the industry's total cost function remains unchanged).

d. What are total profits, given your answer to part (c)?

e. Because of the risk of this industry, investors require a 15 percent rate of return on investment. Total industry investment amounts to $2 billion. If the monopoly solution prevails (parts [a] and [b]), how would you describe the profits of the industry?

f. If the competitive solution most accurately describes the industry, is the industry operating under equilibrium conditions? Why or why not? What would you expect to happen?

g. The Clean Water Coalition has proposed pollution control standards for the industry that would change the industry cost curve to the following:

$$TC = 400 + 560Q + 10Q^2$$

What is the impact of this change on price, output, and total profits under the monopoly solution?

15. A product you produce has the following annual demand function:

$$P = 90 - 0.003Q$$

The marginal cost of producing the product is $30. If the firm pays a fee of $50,000 to an independent testing lab, it can have its product's effectiveness certified. The demand function for a certified product is expected to be

$$P = 100 - 0.003Q$$

a. Calculate the price, output, and profit contribution if the product is not certified.

b. Calculate the price, output, and profit contribution if the product is certified.

c. Should the firm undergo the certification process?

16. Assume an industry produces a relatively homogeneous product, such that all sales must be made at approximately the same price. Assume also that the industry is dominated by one large firm, but a fringe of smaller, competitive firms exists. Fringe competitors and potential new entrants are so small in size that they have no perceptible influence on price.

   Discuss graphically or verbally the pricing strategies available to the dominant firm:

   a. If the profit-maximizing price charged by the dominant firm is below the lowest attainable average total cost (including normal profits) for the smaller existing competitive firms and potential entrants.

   b. If the profit-maximizing price charged by the dominant firm exceeds the competitive fringe firms' lowest attainable average costs, including a normal profit. Would you expect a different strategy to be followed if the dominant firm sought to maximize short-run rather than long-run profits?

   c. If the dominant firm is relatively unsure of the industry's future or perceives a rapidly changing technology in the industry such that an optimal scale of operation can be achieved with an increasingly small plant size. What strategy would you expect the dominant firm to follow?

   d. If the dominant firm adopts a long-run strategy to deter new entry. Explain how the use of full-cost pricing rules can lead to nearly maximum long-run profits.

17. If OPEC agrees to raise the price of oil by $3 per barrel and if all other world oil prices increase by a similar amount, is the additional economic cost to consumers equal to $3 per barrel, something more, or something less?

CASE EXERCISE

MICROSOFT TYING ARRANGEMENTS

1. Which of the following is a violation of the competition laws and why? (a) Microsoft monopolizes the market in PC operating systems with a 92 percent market share; (b) Microsoft attempts to monopolize the market in Internet portals with a pattern of anticompetitive tactics (tying arrangements, refusals to deal, etc.); (c) Microsoft sells Windows plus Microsoft Internet Explorer for less than Windows without Internet Explorer installed as the default browser; (d) Microsoft gives Internet Explorer away free to individual adopters with variable cost estimated at $0.0067; (e) Microsoft threatens to de-license Dell, which would then be unable to preinstall Windows on PCs it ships unless Dell excludes Netscape's Internet browser from the user interface.

2. What difference does it make to the tying arrangement issues if Internet Explorer is a functionally integrated component of Windows? What if it's more like a radio in an automobile than a steering post interlock device?

CHAPTER 12

Introduction to International Managerial Economics

Chapter Preview

Today, business plans involve supply chain management, production operations, and targeted marketing on several continents. Most large companies, including some Canadian firms, engage in foreign direct investment and manufacture abroad. Some companies outsource manufacturing to low-wage partners, affiliates, or operating divisions in places like China, Mexico, Portugal, Indonesia, and the Caribbean. Others buy parts and supplies or assembled components from foreign firms. Almost all manufacturers produce an export product to sell abroad. Indeed, export markets are increasingly the primary source of sales growth for many firms. Careful analysis and accurate forecasting of these international purchases and international sales provide pivotal information for capacity planning, for production scheduling, and for pricing, promotion, and distribution plans in many companies.

In this chapter, we investigate the relationship between exchange rates and import/export sales. International trade plus capital flows determine long-term trends in exchange rates, which we analyze with standard demand and supply tools in the market for Canadian and U.S. dollars as foreign exchange (FX). Purchasing power parity conditions provide a way to assess these FX trends and incorporate export sales into business planning.

We then explore the reasons for and patterns of trade in the world's economy with special attention to regional trading blocs, like the European Union and NAFTA. Our attention throughout is focused on the special challenges for individual firms that arise out of global competition and the growing importance of the import/export sector in the modern economy.

Learning Objectives

After studying this chapter, you should be able to:

1. Understand that export sales are very sensitive to changes in exchange rates.

2. Understand that major currencies are traded in the foreign exchange markets.

3. Explain the determinants of *long-term trends in exchange rates.*

4. Explain the determinants of *transaction demand for currencies.*

5. Explain why companies often demand payment and offer their best fixed-price quotes in their domestic currency.

6. Explain how firms can manage *foreign exchange risk.*

7. Define the *law of one price.*

8. Define *purchasing power parity.*

9. Define *strategic trade policy.*

10. Define *comparative advantage.*

11. Explain how free trade increases the economic growth of both industrialized and developing nations.

12. Explain the roles of the *European Union* and *NAFTA.*

Export Market Pricing at Toyota*

In January 1994, the Canadian dollar exchanged for about ¥84.75 (yen). A 1994 Toyota Celica ST Coupe made in Japan and shipped to Canadian dealers sold for $22,750—i.e., each sale realized revenue approximately equal to ¥2 million (i.e., ¥1,928,063). Just 16 months later in April 1995, the Canadian dollar was worth only about ¥58.4. This 31 percent decline in the value of the dollar made Japanese exports to Canada potentially much more expensive. To recover costs and maintain its 1994 profit margin, Toyota was presented with the prospect of pricing that same Toyota Celica ST Coupe at $33,015—i.e., ¥1,928,063 ÷ (¥58.4/$). Since domestic North American producers of comparable small sporty cars had raised prices only 5 to 10 percent over the intervening period, Toyota faced a tough decision: Increase the car's price well ahead of the competition and try to limit the erosion of market share by emphasizing manufacturing quality and service or, alternatively, reduce margins and protect current market share.

As we will see in this chapter, different firms react in different ways to the challenges presented by such severe currency fluctuations. GM and Ford tend to maintain margins. In contrast, Toyota chose to increase the 1995 Celica ST Coupe price by only 2 percent, to $23,889, despite the consequential 28 percent decline in realized yen per-unit sale. Because of these pricing and related decisions, between 1994 and 1997, Toyota's share of the Canadian passenger car market increased, while the Big Three's share of the Canadian passenger car market fell.

* Based on G. Gardner, "The Fading Big Three Car Market," *Ward's Automotive World,* September 1997, pp. 41–46, and Jack Gillis, *The Car Book* (Washington, DC: Center for Auto Safety, 1997).

Industry Canada provides information on international trade and export opportunities for Canadian firms at **http://strategis.gc.ca**.

Globalization

Around the globe, the reduction of trade barriers and the opening of markets to foreign imports have increased the competitive pressure on manufacturers who once dominated their domestic industries. Tennis shoes and dress footwear once produced in large factories in Britain and the United States now come from Korea, China, and Italy. Automobiles, once dominated by the Big Three of Ford, GM, and Chrysler, now come in large numbers from Japan and Korea. Boeing and Microsoft are now the largest U.S. exporters. Bombardier is Canada's leading exporter. In retailing, McDonald's operates in over 100 countries, and both GM and Coca-Cola's international sales will soon exceed their U.S. sales. Exports have become the key to growth for many leading manufacturing firms, service companies, and franchise retailers.

Similarly, outsourcing parts, components, and supplies to foreign companies has become standard "supply chain management" practice for North American manufacturers. For a minivan, DaimlerChrysler may decide to cast engine blocks in Mexico, acquire electronics from Taiwan, tool ball bearings in Germany, and do the final assembly in Canada. The world of business has truly become a matter of managing in the global economy.

Import/Export Sales and Exchange Rates

An excellent source of exchange rate information is the University of British Columbia's Sauder School of Business website at **http://fx.sauder.ubc.ca**.

Export and import sales are very sensitive to changes in exchange rates. A Dodge minivan manufactured in Windsor that retails in Toronto for $30,000 can be transported to Munich for about €300 (euros). In 1999, when the Canadian dollar exchanged for 0.57 euros, the Dodge dealer in Munich had to charge $30,000 × €0.57/$ = €17,100 to replace the dollar revenue from a foregone sale in Canada. Including the transportation cost, a Dodge minivan in Munich would therefore retail for €17,400. Now suppose the exchange rate changes and the value of the euro trends downward for an extended period. If 0.79 euros exchange for a Canadian dollar by late 2000, a Munich Dodge dealer will need to raise the retail price to €24,000 (0.79 × $30,000 = €23,700 + €300) in order to match the revenue available from a domestic sale in Toronto. If competition for minivans is stiff, this €6,600 price increase may substantially diminish sales. Alternatively, a rollback of the price increase would substantially reduce margins.

No feature of the car has changed. No service offering has changed. No warranty has changed. The exports by Dodge to Germany became €6,600 more expensive simply because the domestic currency of the foreign buyers in Germany became weaker. Price increases of this magnitude in export markets caused by changes in long-term trend exchange rates are common. Over the 1970s, 1980s, and 1990s, exchange rates were four times more volatile than interest rates and ten times more volatile than inflation rates. Analyzing and forecasting the cash flow effects of such changes provide key information for the marketing, operations, and merger plans of companies like Bombardier, Microsoft, and DaimlerChrysler.

Such operating risk exposures necessitate substantial risk management initiatives and are distinguished from two other less significant types of foreign exchange risk exposure: translation risk exposure and transaction risk exposure. **Foreign exchange translation risk exposure** occurs when a firm's foreign assets (or liabilities) are affected by exchange rate movements. Accordingly, the accounting books in the home country must translate these balance sheet adjustments back into home country currency. During a financial crisis, when firms worry about violating their bond covenants against excessive balance sheet debt, translation risk exposure receives more attention. This was especially true during the "Asian crisis" in 1998–2000.

Foreign exchange transaction risk exposure is a much more generally significant problem in managing exports. Transaction risk exposure occurs when a purchase agreement or sales contract (a specific "transaction") commits the company to make future payables or accept future receivables in a foreign currency. Over the time period between executing the contract and actually making or receiving the payments, the firm has foreign exchange transaction risk exposure. Many financial derivatives like foreign exchange (FX) forward contracts, FX swap contracts, and FX options contracts have emerged to assist corporate treasurers in laying off this transaction risk exposure for a modest risk premium known and fixed in advance. A later section discusses the use of these derivative instruments to construct covered hedges that lay off the transaction risk exposure.

Finally, exchange rate fluctuations that result in substantial changes in the operating cash flow of foreign subsidiaries, like those befalling Toyota in the Managerial Challenge

Foreign Exchange Translation Risk Exposure
An accounting adjustment in the home currency value of foreign assets or liabilities.

Foreign Exchange Transaction Risk Exposure
A change in cash flows resulting from contractual commitments to pay in or receive foreign currency.

**Foreign Exchange
Operating Risk Exposure**
A change in cash flows from
foreign or domestic sales
resulting from currency
fluctuations.

and Dodge maker DaimlerChrysler, are examples of **foreign exchange operating risk exposure.** Operating risk exposures are more difficult to forecast than transaction risk exposures and more difficult to lay off than translation risk exposures. As a result, operating risk exposures necessitate still more managerial attention and careful analysis. For one thing, the deterioration of export revenues from sales in foreign subsidiaries is just one side of the problem that a rising domestic currency poses. In addition, depending on the viability of global competition, operating risk exposures may entail a substantial deterioration of domestic sales as well, because competing import products become cheaper in the home market.

The Market for Canadian Dollars as Foreign Exchange

Canadian manufacturers incur many of their expenses at domestic manufacturing sites in Canadian dollars. Ideally, these manufacturers would prefer to require that export purchase orders be payable in Canadian dollars. However, this is not always possible, especially if exporting to a country like the United States that has a much larger economy.[1]

To simplify the discussion here, we will focus on firms that do bill foreigners in Canadian dollars. A foreign purchaser in this case must deal with two markets: the market for the good or service being acquired and the foreign exchange market. For example, a German firm will supply euros and demand dollars to secure the currency required for the dollar-denominated purchase order and payment draft awaited by the Canadian firm. This additional demand for the dollar and the concurrent additional supply of euros drive the price of the dollar higher than it otherwise would have been. Thus, the equilibrium exchange rate in euros per dollar rises (i.e., the price of the dollar as foreign exchange rises). In general, any such unanticipated increase in export sales results in an appreciation of the domestic currency.

Similarly, any unanticipated decrease in export sales results in a depreciation of the domestic currency. This automatic self-correcting adjustment of flexible exchange rates in response to trade flow imbalances is one of the primary arguments for adopting a freely fluctuating exchange rate policy.

Import/Export Flows and the Transaction Demand for a Currency

To examine these effects more closely, let's turn the argument around and trace the currency flows when Canadians increase their demand for imported goods. Suppose an unexpectedly large number of baby boomers wish to recapture their youth by purchasing sporty BMW convertibles. The BMW dealers would have some inventory stock on hand. But, in anticipation of some custom orders, the dealers' banks would have a carefully selected amount of foreign currency on hand to support the necessary purchase order transactions with BMW headquarters in Munich. Our interest lies in tracing the consequences of an unanticipated upswing in Canadian demand for these imported convertibles. What exactly happens in the currency markets in that case?

First, BMW wants to be paid in euros. Therefore, BMW purchase orders must be accompanied by euro cash payments. The local BMW dealer in Charlottetown therefore requests a wire transfer from its banker, Scotiabank. Scotiabank debits the dollar account of the dealer, then authorizes payment from its euro cash balances and presents a wire transfer for an equivalent sum (minus fees) to the Munich branch of Deutsche Bank for deposit in the BMW account. Both import buyer and foreign seller have done

---

[1] About 23 percent of Canadian firms quote prices to foreigners in Canadian dollars, according to J. Murray, J. Powell and L.-R. Lafleur, "Dollarization in Canada: An Update," *Bank of Canada Review,* Summer 2003, p. 31.

business in their home currencies and exchanged a handsome new car. And the merchandise trade account of the Canadian balance of payments would show one additional import transaction valued at the BMW convertible's purchase price.

If Scotiabank anticipated fewer such import transactions and euro requests than actually occurred, the bank's foreign currency portfolio would now be out of balance. Euro balances must be restored to support future import transactions. The bank would therefore go (electronically) into the interbank foreign currency markets and demand euros. Therefore, unanticipated demand by Canadians for German imports both raises the demand for euros and (as the flip side of that same transaction) increases the supply of Canadian dollars in the foreign exchange markets. Hence, more Canadian dollars are now required to purchase euros.

Foreign Exchange Risk Management

Internal Hedge
A balance sheet offset to foreign currency cash flows.

To reduce the potentially wide swings in net assets and cash flows from currency fluctuations, companies use internal hedges and financial hedges.[2] **Internal hedges** may be either operating hedges (such as matching anticipated foreign sales receipts with foreign expenses in that same currency) or balance sheet hedges (such as buying foreign plants). Operating hedges address operating risk exposure. Balance sheet hedges address primarily translation risk exposure by matching assets and liabilities in various countries and their respective currencies. *Financial hedges* address primarily transaction risk exposure by setting up positions in financial derivative contracts to offset cash flow losses from currency fluctuations. Such hedging isn't cheap. It costs approximately 5 percent of the value at risk.

Internal Hedges

The FX transactions required to purchase a BMW would have been unnecessary if BMW had set up an internal hedge in the form of offsetting payables in Canadian dollars. For example, the North American subsidiary of BMW might have simply accepted purchase orders with payment in Canadian dollars and then used those same dollars to cover BMW marketing expenses owed in Canada. Alternatively, BMW might have used the Canadian dollar receivables to buy Canadian parts and supplies or fixed assets. Such offsetting positions in payables and receivables are a way of balancing BMW assets and liabilities in Canadian dollars.

Covered Hedges: Forwards, Options, and Swaps

In addition to internal hedges, any company can reduce the transaction risk exposure of exchange rate fluctuations by establishing a short position in the foreign currency forward or option market to hedge the domestic cash flow from its export sales receipts. For example, suppose Cascades Inc. is exporting paper products to Germany and runs the risk that the euro declines relative to the Canadian dollar. So, to lay off this exchange rate risk, Cascades sells a euro forward contract in the foreign exchange derivative markets to establish a hedge. This transaction is described as a "covered hedge" because Cascades anticipates euro receivables equal to the amount of its short forward position. That is, its contract sales receipts "cover" its obligation to deliver as a seller of euro forward contracts.

Besides setting up internal hedges or short forward positions, Cascades could enter into a currency-swap contract with a German company like Siemens. Siemens would

---

[2] K. A. Froot et al., "A Framework for Risk Management," *Journal of Applied Corporate Finance,* 3, Fall 1994, pp. 22–31, and A. P. Marshall, "Foreign Exchange Risk Management in Multinational Companies," *Journal of Multinational Financial Management,* 10, 2000, pp. 185–211.

swap a prespecified amount of its anticipated dollar receipts from sales in Canada for a prespecified amount of Cascades' anticipated euro sales receipts in Germany.[3] However; these swap contract alternatives to demanding payment in the domestic (home) currency impose some costs on Siemens and Cascades. Therefore, Siemens generally will offer its best fixed price on an export transaction to a Canadian or other foreign buyer on a purchase order payable in euros. For the same reason, the best fixed price from Cascades generally will be available on a purchase order payable only in Canadian dollars.

Of course, the problem facing the managers of Siemens and Cascades is more serious than a mere transaction risk exposure on constant receivables in their respective foreign subsidiaries. In addition, a steeply rising home currency also means a likely decline in both foreign and domestic *unit* sales. As we will see, some companies react to this *operating risk exposure* from domestic currency appreciation by slashing margins to maintain market share abroad, whereas others sacrifice foreign market share to maintain margins. Understanding the magnitude, the timing, and the forces that set in motion these exchange rate-induced swings in sales and profits is crucial for effectively managing export businesses in pursuit of the maximization of capitalized value.

Determinants of Long-Run Trends in Exchange Rates

Short-term movements in FX rates are caused by speculative demand. Sometimes, the current events set speculators off in support of a currency (a long position) and sometimes, the reverse (a short position). Behaviourally, each speculator tries to guess what the other will do, and much herd-like stampeding occurs.

Long-run trends in FX rate are different. Quarter-to-quarter or year-to-year trends depend on three factors: real growth rates, real interest rates, and anticipated inflation rates. We now discuss each of these determinants.

The Role of Real Growth Rates

As we have seen, a primary determinant of the year-to-year exchange rate fluctuations is the net direction of trade flows. Unanticipated increases in imports lower a local currency's value, whereas unanticipated increases in exports raise a local currency's value. The stimulus underlying such trade flow imbalances may be business cycles, productivity increases, or the introduction of protectionist trade barriers. In a business cycle or productivity-based expansion, consumption (including import consumption) increases. In a contraction, import consumption decreases.

The Role of Real Interest Rates

The second factor determining long-run trends in exchange rates is comparable interest rates adjusted for inflation. The higher the real rate of interest in an economy, the greater the demand for the financial assets offered by that economy. If a Japanese, German, or Swiss investor or financial institution can earn higher real returns (for equivalent risk) from Canadian bonds than from German or Japanese bonds, foreign owners of capital will move quickly toward Canadian financial markets as foreign portfolios are rebalanced to incorporate more Canadian assets. The foreign investor who desires Canadian financial assets must first acquire Canadian dollars to complete the

---

[3] At each future settlement date in a swap contract, the difference between the spot market exchange rate and the forward rates prespecified at the start of the swap contract actually determines who pays whom. For complete explanations of the use of forwards, options, and swap contracts in managing foreign exchange risk, see J. Madura, *International Financial Management,* 7th. ed. (Mason, OH: Thomson South-Western, 2003).

Learn about options at the Montreal Exchange website at **www.me.org**.

transactions. So, a higher real interest rate in Canada (relative to German, Japanese, and Swiss rates) implies international capital inflow into Canada and an increased demand for and appreciation of Canadian dollars.

The Role of Expected Inflation

Inflationary expectations provide an important third determinant of long-term trends in exchange rates. Cost inflation is usually compared across economies by examining an index of producer prices or wholesale prices.

The relative purchasing power parity (PPP) hypothesis says that the exchange rate between two currencies adjusts sufficiently to reflect entirely the inflation differential. That is, between Canada and Germany, a 3.5 percent differential in the producer price index favouring Canada should, according to PPP, raise the value of the dollar 3.5 percent against the euro. We discuss purchasing power parity in the next section.

Purchasing Power Parity

When there are no significant costs or other barriers associated with moving goods or services between markets, then the price of each product should be the same in each market. This conclusion is known as the *law of one price*. When the different markets represent different countries, the law of one price says that prices will be the same in each country after making the appropriate conversion from one currency to another. Alternatively, one can say that exchange rates between two currencies will equal the ratio of the price indexes between the countries. In international finance and trade, this relationship is known as the absolute version of purchasing power parity.

Relative Purchasing Power Parity
A relationship between differential inflation rates and long-term trends in exchange rates.

A less restrictive form of the law of one price is known as **relative purchasing power parity**. The relative PPP principle states that in comparison to a period when exchange rates between two countries are in equilibrium, changes in the differential rates of inflation between two countries will be offset by equal, but opposite, changes in the future spot exchange rate. For example, if prices in Canada rise by 4 percent per year and prices in Europe rise by 6 percent per year, then relative PPP asserts that the euro will weaken relative to the Canadian dollar by approximately 2 percent.

The exact relative purchasing power parity relationship is

(12.1) $\quad\quad\quad$ Relative PPP: $\quad \left(\dfrac{S_1}{S_0}\right) = \left(\dfrac{1 + \pi_h}{1 + \pi_f}\right)$

where S_1 is the expected future spot rate for the home currency per unit of the foreign currency at time period 1, S_0 is the current spot rate, π_h is the expected home country (Canada) inflation rate, and π_f is the expected foreign country inflation rate. Using the previous example, if Canadian prices are expected to rise by 4 percent over the coming year, prices in Europe are expected to rise by 6 percent during the same time, and the current spot exchange rate (S_0) is \$1.60/€, then the expected spot rate in one year (S_1) will be

$$S_1/\$1.60 = (1 + 0.04)/(1 + 0.06)$$
$$S_1 = \$1.57$$

The higher European inflation rate can be expected to result in a decline in the future spot value of the euro relative to the dollar by 1.875 percent.[4]

---

[4] Several other parity conditions in international finance are discussed in Chapter 18 of Don Cyr et al., *Contemporary Financial Management,* 1st Canadian ed. (Toronto: Thomson Nelson Canada, 2004).

Qualifications of PPP

Purchasing power parity calculations can be very sensitive to the starting point for the analysis. Purchasing power parity has several other qualifications as well. For the full PPP adjustments to take place in exchange rates as domestic prices inflate, the traded goods must be nearly identical in quality and use in the two economies. Cross-cultural differences (e.g., the Islamic aversion to Western clothing for women) can short-circuit these adjustments. In addition, both economies must have similar trade policies. If Europe has much higher agricultural subsidies and trade barriers than Canada, that policy may prevent the trade flows and subsequent exchange rate adjustments hypothesized by PPP. Similar qualifications apply to differences in value-added taxes and other sales taxes across economies. Finally, the markups and profit margins arising from the degree of competition in an economy must be comparable for purchasing power parity to hold. Despite these caveats, purchasing power parity has proved to be a useful benchmark for assessing trends in currency values.

No one would ever execute a currency **arbitrage** trade (buying a currency cheap and selling it elsewhere for an immediate profit) based on the predictions of the purchasing power parity hypothesis. Currency arbitrage is triggered by unanticipated events that generate very temporary profit opportunities lasting only several hours or a few days. The trade flows predicted by PPP in response to inflation differentials, on the other hand, are a much longer term process requiring several quarters or even years. Companies with a substantial proportion of their sales abroad must identify these longer term trends in exchange rates, and purchasing power parity proves useful for just that purpose.

Being attuned to the international business environment does not allow fine-tuning, but it does allow better medium-term planning of production volume, proactive pricing, targeted marketing, and segmented distribution channels, all of which may offer profit advantages. Some companies make these considerations a focus of their business plans and prosper in international markets. Others are less successful.

The Appropriate Use of PPP: An Overview

What, then, is the appropriate role of purchasing power parity in managing international business? First, one should be aware that PPP is a very long-run proposition that depends on cross-national arbitrage in goods and services. Arbitrage activities are motivated whenever the price of auto tires or canned green beans in one economy departs markedly from the price of similar goods in another economy, not far distant. In such circumstances, entrepreneurs emerge to buy cheaply in one location and sell dearly in the other, but goods arbitrage takes time. Goods arbitrage requires logistical infrastructure like freight terminals, distribution networks or reliable relationships, and effective transnational marketing campaigns. Until all of these matters can be resolved, international markets remain somewhat segmented, thereby preventing the complete convergence of prices of identical products between Canada and Japan, between Canada and the United Kingdom, and even between Canada and the United States. Unlike arbitrage in financial markets, the goods arbitrage underlying PPP may take months, years, or even decades. As a result, the variance of prices for like goods across countries is larger (often 10 times larger) than the variance of prices through time within an economy.[5]

In the short run, therefore, when the prices of traded goods in Canada diverge from those in the United Kingdom, nominal exchange rates may not respond to fully offset the price differentials, as predicted by PPP. Instead, price stickiness in traded goods

Arbitrage
Buying cheap and selling elsewhere for an immediate profit.

---

[5] C. Engel and J. H. Rogers, "How Wide Is the Border?" *American Economic Review,* 86 (1996), pp. 1112–1125, and "Goods Prices and Exchange Rates," *Journal of Economic Literature,* 35 N (1997), pp. 1243–1272.

combined with the lemming-like behaviour of herds of foreign exchange speculators leads to more volatile nominal exchange rates than would characterize a fully adjusting price regime. In particular, nominal exchange rates may overshoot or undershoot their equilibrium levels in adjusting to demand or monetary shocks. To avoid the problem of comparing prices across countries at these contemporaneous exchange rates that may bias the assessment, many analysts perform cross-border comparisons of price levels or trade statistics using purchasing power parity estimates for at least the prior 10- to 15-year period.

For example, if one observes that 10 metres of 0.019-gauge gutter pipe sells in do-it-yourself stores in Canada for $3.36 and that in 2000 the value of the British pound was $2.70/£ (i.e., £0.37/$), it might be very misleading to calculate that identically priced gutter pipe should sell for £1.24 in the United Kingdom. (i.e., $3.36 × £0.37/$). Even if the British are paying £1.79, the apparent arbitrage profit of (£1.79 − £1.24) × $2.70/£ = $1.52 per 10 metres may not be available. Consequently, rushing out to organize the distribution and export of gutter pipe for sale in Great Britain every time the exchange rate overshoots does not make sense.

International Trade: A Managerial Perspective

Regional Trading Blocs

Most nations continue to protect with tariffs and other trade barriers some infant or politically sensitive industries. France, for example, remains a largely agricultural polity and therefore lowers its agricultural trade barriers only after great hand-wringing and extended periods of tough negotiations with its European neighbours. In the 1980s, both Canada and the United States imposed import restraints on Japanese automobiles. Fortunately, regional trading blocs like the European Union (EU) and the North American Free Trade Agreement (NAFTA) were highly successful in the 1990s at removing trade barriers, negotiating multilateral reductions in tariffs, and promoting free trade as a mechanism of peaceful competition between nations. This is extremely important to a country like Canada whose exports were 43 percent of GDP in 2002.

Across the world economy, five major regional trading blocs have emerged (see Figure 12.1). In South America, Argentina, Brazil, Paraguay, Uruguay, Bolivia, and Chile have formed one trading block (MERCOSUR). It attempts to mirror the NAFTA free trade agreements of Canada, Mexico and the United States. Seven Southeast Asian (ASEAN) and 16 trans-Pacific economies including Japan and Mexico (APEC) have also formed trading blocs. Trade *within* these trading blocs has swelled as a percentage of the member states' total trade, especially in NAFTA and MERCOSUR. For example, Canada–U.S.–Mexico trade grew from 37 percent to 47 percent between 1990 and 2000.[6] In addition, with fully 88 percent of Mexican trade now involving its two NAFTA partners, 34 nations in Central and South America, Canada, Mexico, and the United States have agreed in principle to form a Free Trade Area of the Americas (FTAA) with 800 million people and combined output equal to US$12 trillion.

- ASEAN website:
  www.aseansec.org
- APEC website:
  www.apecsec.org.sg
- FTAA website:
  www.ftaa-alca.org

Comparative Advantage and Free Trade

Within a regional trading bloc like EU, NAFTA, MERCOSUR, or APEC, each member can improve its economic growth by specializing in accordance with comparative advantage and then engaging in free trade. Intuitively, low-wage countries like Spain, Mexico, China, and Thailand enjoy a cost advantage in the manufacture of labour-intensive goods such as garment sewing and the provision of labour-intensive services like coupon or insurance claims processing. Suppose one of these economies also enjoys a cost advantage in more capital-intensive manufacturing, such as auto assembly. One of the powerful insights of international microeconomics is that in such circumstances,

---

[6] "Trade in the Americas," *The Economist*, April 21, 2001, pp. 20–24.

FIGURE 12.1

Regional Trading Zones (Percentage of World Trade)

This figure shows the member states in the world's five major trading zones.

Source: WTO website, 2000.

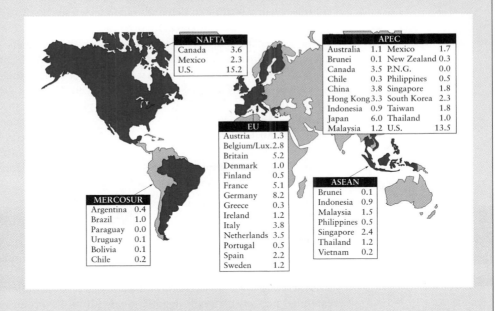

NAFTA	
Canada	3.6
Mexico	2.3
U.S.	15.2

APEC			
Australia	1.1	Mexico	1.7
Brunei	0.1	New Zealand	0.3
Canada	3.5	P.N.G.	0.0
Chile	0.3	Philippines	0.5
China	3.8	Singapore	1.8
Hong Kong	3.3	South Korea	2.3
Indonesia	0.9	Taiwan	1.8
Japan	6.0	Thailand	1.0
Malaysia	1.2	U.S.	13.5

EU	
Austria	1.3
Belgium/Lux.	2.8
Britain	5.2
Denmark	1.0
Finland	0.5
France	5.1
Germany	8.2
Greece	0.3
Ireland	1.2
Italy	3.8
Netherlands	3.5
Portugal	0.5
Spain	2.2
Sweden	1.2

MERCOSUR	
Argentina	0.4
Brazil	1.0
Paraguay	0.0
Uruguay	0.1
Bolivia	0.1
Chile	0.2

ASEAN	
Brunei	0.1
Indonesia	0.9
Malaysia	1.5
Philippines	0.5
Singapore	2.4
Thailand	1.2
Vietnam	0.2

EXAMPLE

MERCOSUR AVERTS A TRADE WAR

MERCOSUR website:
www.mercosur.com.ar

MERCOSUR was formed as a free trade area to secure the free flow of goods and services in the cone at the base of South America. The dominant trading partners Brazil and Argentina joined with Uruguay and Paraguay and pledged under the Treaty of Asunción in 1991 to avoid punitive tariffs and import quotas (later extended to the associate members Chile and Bolivia). These commitments were sorely tested during a recession in 1998–1999. GDP growth plummeted from 7.1 percent to −3 percent in Brazil, while Argentina slowed from 8.6 percent to 1.8 percent but continued to grow.

To jump-start its economy, Brazil devalued its currency, the real (which immediately raised the cost of imports by 40 percent), and adopted an industrial policy of offering tax breaks, free land, and other subsidies to any Argentine automobile parts suppliers, shoe manufacturers, and corporate farms that would move to Brazil. Argentina retaliated by threatening to place tariffs on Brazilian textile exports, claiming that said exports were so heavily subsidized that their prices fell below replacement cost. The World Trade Organization (WTO) allows any member to impose antidumping duties on export products sold below cost. However, under MERCOSUR's procedures, Brazil and Argentina agreed instead to negotiate a reduction in the subsidies and a removal of the threat of punitive tariffs while attempting to harmonize their fiscal policies and inflation targets, much like the European Union experience with the Maastricht Treaty. A nasty trade war was narrowly averted.

the low-cost economy should not produce both goods, but rather it should specialize in that production for which it has the lower relative cost, while buying the other product from its higher cost trading partner. Let's see how this **law of comparative advantage** in bilateral trade reaches such an apparently odd conclusion.

Consider the bilateral trade between Canada and Japan in automobile carburetors and computer memory chips. Suppose the cost of production of carburetors in Japan is ¥10,000 compared to $120 in Canada. At an exchange rate of, say, 100 yen to the dollar, the Japanese dollar price of $100 is lower than the Canadian price of $120. Suppose, in addition, that memory chips cost ¥8,000 in Japan compared to $300 in Canada. Again, the dollar price of the Japanese product (i.e., $80) is lower than the price of the Canadian product. Japan is said to enjoy an absolute cost advantage in the manufacture of both products. However, Japan is 83 percent (i.e., $100/$120) as expensive in producing carburetors as Canada while being only 27 percent (i.e., $80/$300) as expensive in producing memory chips. Japan is said to have a comparative advantage in memory chips and should specialize in the manufacture of that product.

The gains from specialization in accordance with comparative advantage and subsequent trade are best demonstrated using the real terms of trade. **Real terms of trade** identify what amounts of labour effort, material, and other resources are required to produce a product in one economy relative to another. In Japan, the manufacture of memory chips requires the sacrifice of resources capable of manufacturing 0.8 carburetors (see Table 12.1), whereas in Canada the manufacture of a memory chip requires the sacrifice of 2.5 carburetors. That is, Japan's relative cost of memory chips (in terms of carburetor production that must be foregone) is less than a third as great as the relative cost of memory chips in Canada. On the other hand, Canadian carburetor production requires the resources associated with only 0.4 Canadian memory chips, while Japanese carburetor production requires the sacrifice of 1.25 Japanese memory chips. The Canadian relative cost of carburetors is much lower than that of the Japanese. Said another way, the Japanese are particularly productive in using resources to manufacture memory chips, and Canada is particularly productive in using similar resources to produce carburetors. Each country has a comparative advantage: the Japanese in producing memory chips and Canadians in producing carburetors.

Table 12.1 Real Terms of Trade and Comparative Advantage

	Absolute Cost, Canada	Absolute Cost, Japan
Automobile carburetors	$120	¥10,000
Computer memory chips	$300	¥8,000
	Relative Cost, Canada	**Relative Cost, Japan**
Automobile carburetors	$120/$300 = 0.4 Chips	¥10K/¥8K = 1.25 Chips
Computer memory chips	$300/$120 = 2.5 Carbs	¥8K/¥10K = 0.8 Carbs
	Gains from Trade, Canada	**Gains from Trade, Japan**
Initial Goods	1.0 Carb + 1.0 Chip	1.0 Carb + 1.0 Chip
After specialization:		
Carburetors produced	(1.0 + 2.5) Carbs	0
Memory chips produced	0	(1.0 + 1.25) Chips
Trade	+1.0 Chip	+1.5 Carbs
	−1.5 Carbs	−1.0 Chip
Net goods	2.0 Carbs + 1.0 Chip	1.5 Carbs + 1.25 Chips

Source: International Monetary Fund, *The Direction of Trade Statistics*.

Assess what happens to the total goods produced if each economy specializes in production in accordance with comparative advantage and then trades to diversify its consumption. Assume that Canada and Japan produced one unit of each product initially, that labour is immobile, that no scale economies are present, and that the quality of both carburetors and both memory chips is identical. If the Japanese cease production of carburetors and specialize in the production of memory chips, they increase memory chip production to 2.25 chips (see Table 12.1). Similarly, if Canada ceases production of memory chips and specializes in the production of carburetors, it increases carburetor production to 3.5 carburetors. In these circumstances, Canada could offer Japan 1.5 carburetors for a memory chip, and both parties would end up unambiguously better off. Canada would enjoy a residual domestic production after trade of 2.0 carburetors plus the import of one memory chip. And the Japanese would enjoy a residual domestic production after trade of 1.25 memory chips plus the import of 1.5 carburetors. As demonstrated in Table 12.1, each economy would have replaced all the products they initially produced, plus each would enjoy additional amounts of goods—i.e., unambiguous gains from trade.

Import Controls and Protective Tariffs

In the Mercantilist period from 1500 to 1750, many nations rejected free trade policies and instead attempted to restrain the purchase of foreign imports in order to expand the production of their domestic industries (as Brazil attempted in 1999). To bar imports, some nations adopted "beggar thy neighbour" policies such as protective tariffs that raised the domestic prices of foreign goods. Others tried direct import controls like a maximum allowable quota of a specific type of foreign import. England, for example, banned the export of Cotswold wool to French cloth manufacturers in Flanders in hopes of retaining the cloth weaving, finishing, and dyeing industries in Britain. When expensive unsold British cloth accumulated, Flanders cloth imports were restricted. Between 1500 and 1603, the unintended consequence of these import–export quotas was a 500 percent inflation in cloth prices in Britain.

A few of these ill-advised import control ideas even survive to the present day—e.g., the North American voluntary import restraint agreement with Japanese automobile manufacturers in the mid-1980s. Again, the net results of import controls were not as expected. Toyota and Honda simply built assembly plants all over North America, and still more GM, Ford, and Chrysler workers were laid off. In general, national income and employment in the country barring imports eventually falls relative to the potential income available under freer trade policies. Even mercantilist Brazil agreed and reversed its 1999 mercantilist trade policy.

The reason why hinges on an understanding of exchange rates and trade balances. Import controls lead inevitably to a reduction in the supply of a nation's currency in the foreign exchange market. For example, when some Canadian households are prohibited from completing import purchases of Toyotas and Hondas they would otherwise have bought, those households fail to request the yen they would have needed to accomplish the import purchases. Accordingly, they also fail to supply the dollars that would have been exchanged for the requisite foreign currency. A reduction in the supply of dollars, all other things being the same, implies that the dollar must appreciate. Therefore, reduced imports imply a rise in value of the domestic currency. However, this exchange rate adjustment raises the price of Canadian exports, since the number of yen or euros a foreign buyer must pay to acquire dollar-denominated goods and services inevitably rises, and Canadian exports then decline. These consequences normally unfold even if the domestic producers attempt to offset their currency's appreciation with reduced profit margins. Ultimately, therefore, the attempt to improve domestic output and raise national income by imposing import controls often results in a collapse of the export sector sufficient to worsen the trade balance (exports minus imports) and actually decreases national income.

NETWORK EXTERNALITIES AT MICROSOFT: A ROLE FOR PROTECTIVE TARIFFS?

The information economy has a higher incidence than the industrial economy of these increasing returns phenomena. Frequently, in the information economy context, cost reductions at larger market share are associated with externalities in the installation of a network or the adoption of a technical standard. As the installed base of Windows software expands, Microsoft finds it increasingly less difficult to convince new customers to adopt their product. Computer users find it much easier to exchange documents and explain new applications, for example, if their PCs employ the same operating system. As a result, the marketing cost to secure the next adoption from a marginal buyer actually declines the larger the market share that Windows attains.

Should strategic trade policy in any country try to protect a company with the possibility of achieving increasing returns? Microsoft poses a good case in point. *Without* import controls and protective tariffs, Microsoft successfully achieved a larger dollar volume of export trade than any other American company.

Is it an appropriate role of the government to pursue such cost advantages for one domestic company or an alliance of domestic companies? Or should government pursue the consumer interest of lowest prices wherever that product is produced? These are the questions hotly debated in strategic trade policy today.

Free trade and open markets offer the prospect of higher national income. Developing countries with open economies grew by 4.5 percent per year in the 1970s and 1980s, whereas those with import controls and protective tariffs grew by only 0.7 percent per year. Rich country comparisons also favoured free trade: 2.3 percent to, again, 0.7 percent. In the 1990s, this gap widened still further. Those developing countries whose import plus export trade as a percentage of GDP ranked in the top 50th percentiles of developing countries had GDP growth per person of 5 percent. Those in the bottom 50th percentiles saw GDP growth per person actually shrink by 1 percent.[7] Clearly, globalization and trade enhance prosperity, even in the lesser developed countries.

The Case for Strategic Trade Policy

Although the logic of free trade has dominated academic debate since 1750, and the 20th century saw the repeal of many import controls and tariffs, a few exceptions are worth noting. The WTO has very effectively spearheaded the negotiation of *mutual* trade liberalization policies. However, *unilateral* reduction of tariffs when trading partners stubbornly refuse to relax import controls or open their domestic markets seldom makes sense. Instead, negotiated mutual reduction of trade barriers illustrates the concept of strategic trade policy.

---

[7] "Globalization, Growth and Poverty," World Bank report, December 2001.

Increasing Returns

Another motivation for strategic trade policy arises in markets where domestic producers encounter increasing returns. Suppose Bombardier finds that learning curve effects in airframe manufacturing offer a 1 percent reduction in *variable* cost for every market share point above 30 percent. A firm with a 40 percent market share of the world output for a 50-passenger aircraft will experience variable costs only 90 percent as great as smaller competitors. A firm with a 50 percent market share will experience variable costs only 80 percent as great as smaller competitors, and so forth. These circumstances are very rare indeed in the industrial sector of the economy, since they imply that diminishing returns in production are more than offset by economies of scope or learning curve advantages at higher output. However, where such circumstances exist, some nations attempt to jump-start the preemptive development of new aircraft models with public subsidies to research and development (a so-called industrial policy). Others impose import controls or protective tariffs to assure the attainment of the 30 percent market share baseline volume required to trigger the emergence of learning curve advantages. This, too, entails strategic trade policy.

Free Trade Areas: The European Union and NAFTA

The Role of the European Union

Free trade and specialization in accordance with comparative advantage leaves economies vulnerable to trade interruptions and punitive tariffs on essential inputs. Nevertheless, the European Union provides an example of what can be accomplished. Starting with the Treaty of Rome in 1957, 12 original European Community members established the groundwork for a **free trade area,** which they subsequently consolidated in the Single European Act of 1986. Between 1986 and 1992, 12 very dissimilar European economies realized 5 percent additional cumulative growth of GDP attributable to the increased intra-European trade.

Increased specialization in accordance with comparative advantage has the relatively low-wage Spaniards and Portuguese assembling high value-added German components for BMWs and Blaupunkt radios. Reduced trade barriers at borders have cut transportation time. The English Channel ferry now unloads in 15 minutes rather than the previous 1½ hours, and yogurt from Nestlé's subsidiary in Birmingham, England, now speeds across Europe to target customers in Milan in 11 hours rather than the previous 38. Reduced intra-European tariffs on foodstuffs, beer, wine, and autos have markedly reduced the cost of living. Although corporate tax rates still differ from 45 percent in Italy and Germany to 30 percent in Ireland, wide differences in value-added taxes have been reconciled at uniform 17 percent rates in most cases.

The Role of NAFTA

Canada, not Japan, is by far the largest trading partner of the United States, with almost twice the share (23.6 percent) of American goods exported to Canada than anywhere else in the world's economy. U.S. exports to Canada include everything from merchandise, like Microsoft's software and DaimlerChrysler's automobile components for assembly at an automated minivan plant in Ontario, to professional services like strategic management consulting by McKinsey & Company. Canada is also the largest source of U.S. imports (18 percent), with natural resources and finished goods manufacturing heading the list.

Mexico consumes and assembles a 14.3 percent share of U.S. exports (up 50 percent since 1996) and provides 11.5 percent of U.S. imports. Mexico supplies large quantities of auto parts, steel, and oil to the United States. From 1993–2003, following the passage of NAFTA, Mexican tariffs declined from 40 percent to 16 percent, and exports to the United States increased from 67 percent to 89 percent of total Mexican exports.

Free Trade Area
A group of nations that has agreed to reduce tariffs and other trade barriers.

European Union website:
http://europa.eu.int.

NAFTA website: **www. nafta-sec-alena.org**.

A Comparison of the EU and NAFTA

Between the EU and NAFTA regional trading blocs, NAFTA has the larger share of world population (6.2 percent compared to 5.0 percent in 2002) and the larger share of world output (24.5 percent compared to 15.7 percent in 2002), but the EU has the larger share of world trade (31.2 percent compared to 17.2 percent in 2002). However, much of the EU trade is with other members inside the regional *trading bloc* (see Table 12.2).

This countertrade pattern within the trading bloc does characterize Canada and Mexico but it does not characterize the United States. Table 12.3 shows that although

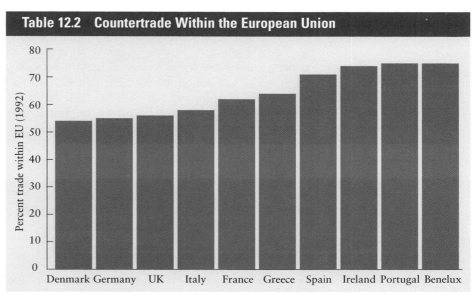

Table 12.2   Countertrade Within the European Union

Source: *International Monetary Fund Yearbook,* various editions.

Table 12.3   Destination of U.S. Goods Exports

Country	1970–1975 Share (%)	Country	1998–2003 Share (%)
Canada	21.4	Canada	24.0
Japan	10.2	Mexico	13.5
Germany	5.4	Japan	9.4
United Kingdom	4.9	United Kingdom	5.2
Mexico	4.4	Germany	3.9
Netherlands	3.9	Korea	3.8
France	3.1	Taiwan	3.2
Italy	2.9	Netherlands	2.9
Brazil	2.7	France	2.8
Belgium-Luxembourg	2.3	China	2.4

Source: *Federal Reserve Bank of St. Louis Review,* March/April 1999, p. 35 (http://research.stlouisfed.org/publications/review).

Mexico's share of U.S. exports tripled from 4.4 percent before NAFTA to 13.5 percent after NAFTA, the majority of U.S. export trade (100% − 24.0% to Canada − 13.5% to Mexico = 62.5%) goes elsewhere in the world economy.

Another important perspective can be obtained by considering competitiveness in the world economy. EU unit labour costs and intermediate costs declined between 1987 and 1994 in motor vehicles and electrical equipment. These are Germany's two largest export categories to Britain and the United States. However, Japanese and U.S. costs in these industries declined even further. In other cases, like aerospace equipment, basic chemicals, and office machinery, EU competitiveness suffered still more. Between 1990 and 2002, the U.S. share of world exports rose from 11.7 percent to 13.9 percent and Japan's share shrank slightly from 8.5 percent to 7.8 percent. In that same period, the German, French, Italian, and British shares all declined. For example, the Western European share of world exports plummeted from 28.6 percent to 22.3 percent.

The EU allocates "structural funds" to upgrade roads, bridges, and port infrastructure in less developed regions of Europe. Between 2000 and 2006, €42 billion will go to Spain, €28 billion to southern Italy, €27 billion to former East Germany, and €20 billion to Greece and Portugal. But these redistributive efforts, restrictive labour laws, and social programs in Europe impose a heavy burden on manufacturing competitiveness.

EXAMPLE

HOUSEHOLD IRON MANUFACTURER IN MEXICO BECOMES MAJOR ENGINE BLOCK SUPPLIER: CIFUNSA SA*

Since its passage in 1994, the NAFTA has made Mexico into a leading outsourcing location for the worldwide auto parts industry. Duty-free access to Canada and the United States for auto subassemblies like transmissions and wiring harnesses, plus a growing sector of skilled nonunionized workers, induced GM, Ford, DaimlerChrysler, and Volkswagen, as well as Mexican firms like San Luis Corporación and Grupo Industrial Saltillo, SA, to invest US$18 billion in auto plants and equipment between 1994–2000.

Cifunsa SA is a Grupo subsidiary that, immediately after WWII, specialized in the manufacture of metal castings for household appliances, especially hand irons. Today, Cifunsa has converted its aluminum and steel casting expertise to the production of engine blocks. Indeed, Cifunsa has the dominant position as a supplier of engine monoblocks to North American car companies. Other Mexican metal casters play a major role in supplying heavy axles and coil springs for trucks and SUVs.

Many windshields installed in cars and trucks assembled in North America also come from Mexico. Although some of this import–export trade is motivated by lower wage rates at Mexican parts suppliers than at comparable Canadian and U.S. establishments, another factor is the desire of the American and European car companies to decrease their dependence on unionized plants. A 1998 strike at GM's Delphi subsidiary lasted almost eight weeks. Even the Saturn assembly plant in Spring Hill, Tennessee, suffered its first strike in 1998.

* Based on "Mexico Is Becoming Auto-Making Hot Spot," *The Wall Street Journal,* June 23, 1998, and "Mexico Becomes a Leader in Car Parts," *The Wall Street Journal,* March 30, 1999, p. A21.

Grey Markets, Knockoffs, and Parallel Importing[8]

The prices charged for identical goods varied widely across Europe both before and after the formation of the Common Market. In 1998, a Ford Mondeo cost 50 percent more in Germany than in Spain. To lower overall consumer prices and to improve competitiveness throughout the EU, the European Commission (EC) has often adopted policies that encourage price competition. Goods arbitragers who want to buy Black & Decker power tools in Spain and sell them in Germany or buy Kawasaki motorcycles in Holland and sell them in Britain are encouraged to do so. Volkswagen was fined €15 million for refusing to supply Northern Italian VW dealers that sold cars to large numbers of Munich weekenders who had travelled across the Alps for the Verona Opera (and the inexpensive German car prices in Italy). The EC also has eliminated any contractual link between product sales and after-market service. Any government-certified repair shop can purchase parts to perform VW, Nikon, or IBM maintenance and service. The problem, of course, is that such grey markets may lead to counterfeit sales and substandard service passed off as branded sales and authorized service.

The price impact of a policy prohibiting parallel imports can be enormous. Australians carefully protect intellectual property by aggressively prosecuting grey-market sellers of music CDs. Cheap imitations and counterfeit substitutes are rare indeed, but popular music CDs sell for $8.50 more in Australia than in other Far Eastern economies. The United Kingdom and China, therefore, choose the opposite policy for selected products. The British obtain almost 10 percent of their pharmaceuticals and over 30 percent of their wine, liquor, and beer through parallel importing. China permits the copying of patented medicines. Eli Lilly's Prozac, an antidepressant, sells for $2.50 per capsule, but a chemically identical "knockoff" from Shanghai Zhong-Xi Pharmaceutical and Jiangsu Changzhou Pharmaceutical sells for about $1.35 per capsule under the brand name You Ke.

Managerial Challenge Revisited

Export Market Pricing at Toyota

During the years 1971–1973, the Canadian dollar was approximately at par with the U.S. dollar. In 1974, the Canadian dollar was even worth US$1.0225. However, in 1975 it dropped to only US$0.9829. The Canadian dollar then continued to drop in value relative to the U.S. dollar until 2002, when it reached US$0.6367. This long-term drop in the relative value of the Canadian dollar made it easier for Canadian firms to export.

In 2003, however, the Canadian dollar continued to increase in value, averaging US$0.7135 for the year. In 2004, the Canadian dollar again jumped, to finish the year at US$0.8319. Many Canadian firms complained that the rising value

---

[8] Based on "Set-Back for Parallel Imports," *BBC World Service,* July 16, 1998; "Parallel Imports," *Financial Times,* May 20, 1996; "Music Market Indicators," *The Economist,* May 15, 1999; D. Wilkinson, "Breaking the Chain: Parallel Imports and the Missing Link," *European Intellectual Property Review,* 1997; and "Prozac's Maker Confronts China Over Knockoffs," *The Wall Street Journal,* March 25, 1998, p. B9.

of the Canadian dollar was hurting their profitability as well as their capacity to export. Cascades, for example, exports most of its output and found that every one-cent increase in the value of the Canadian dollar cuts the firm's operating profit by $5 million, or almost five percent.*

Many Canadian firms have invested in new capital equipment to increase their productivity, but they still complain about the rapid increase in the value of the Canadian dollar. (You might want to investigate what has happened to the value of the Canadian dollar relative to the value of the U.S. dollar since this book was published.)

---

* Based on data retrieved from the Bank of Canada website at www.bankofcanada.ca, and Greg Quinn and Alexandre Deslongchamps, "David Dodge's Dilemma," *Ottawa Citizen,* December 7, 2004, p. F3.

Summary

- Export sales are very sensitive to changes in *exchange rates*. Domestic exports become more expensive (cheaper) in the foreign currencies of other countries when the domestic currency of the manufacturer strengthens (weakens).

- Major currencies are traded in the *foreign exchange markets*. There are markets for Canadian dollars as foreign exchange, British pounds as foreign exchange, euros as foreign exchange, etc. Demand and supply in these markets reflect the speculative and transactions demands of investors, import–export dealers, corporations, financial institutions, the International Monetary Fund (IMF), central bankers, and governments throughout the global economy.

- Companies often demand payment and offer their best fixed-price quotes in their domestic currency because of *transaction risk exposure* and *operating risk exposure* to exchange rate fluctuations. Alternatively, such firms can manage the risk of exchange rate fluctuations themselves by setting up internal or financial hedges involving forward, option, or currency swap contracts.

- *Internal hedges* may be either balance sheet hedges addressing translation risk or *operating hedges* matching anticipated foreign sales receipts with anticipated expenses in that same foreign currency. *Financial hedges* often address transaction risk exposure by setting up positions in financial derivative contracts to offset cash flow losses from currency fluctuations. Such hedging costs about 5 percent of the value at risk.

- Foreign buyers (or their financial intermediaries) usually must acquire euros to execute a purchase from Mercedes-Benz or yen to execute a purchase from Toyota. Each buyer in these international sales transactions usually supplies domestic currency. Additional imports by Canadians of Japanese automobiles would normally therefore result in an increased demand for the yen and an increased supply of dollars in the foreign currency markets (i.e., dollar depreciation).

- Long-term trends in exchange rates are determined by transaction demand, government transfer payments, and central bank or IMF interventions.

- Three transaction demand factors are *expected cost inflation, real (inflation-adjusted) growth rates*, and *real (inflation-adjusted) interest rates*. The lower the expected cost inflation, the lower the real growth rate, and the higher the real rate of interest in one economy relative to another, the higher the exports, the lower the import demand, and the higher the demand for financial instruments from that economy. All three determinants imply an increased demand or decreased supply of the domestic currency (i.e., a currency appreciation).

■ *Consumer price inflation* serves as a good predictor of the combined effect of all three transactions demand factors on post-redemption returns to foreign asset holders. Projected changes in consumer inflation therefore directly affect international capital flows, which can easily overwhelm the effect of trade flows on exchange rates.

■ *Free trade* increases the economic growth of both industrialized and developing nations. Tariffs, duties, and import quotas sometimes play a role in strategic trade policy to force multilateral reduction of tariffs, open markets, or secure increasing returns.

■ *Speculative demand* especially influences short-term changes in exchange rates. Since the total dollar volume of foreign currency trading worldwide is US$1.5 trillion *per day,* these short-term fluctuations can be quite volatile.

■ International capital flows and the flow of tradable goods across nations respond to *arbitrage opportunities*. Arbitrage trading ceases when parity conditions are met. One such condition is relative purchasing power parity.

■ *Relative purchasing power parity* (PPP) hypothesizes that exchange rates are related to differential rates of inflation across economies. PPP serves a useful benchmark role in assessing long-term trends in exchange rates.

■ The European Union (EU) and the North American Free Trade Agreement (NAFTA) are two of several large trading blocs that have organized to open markets to free trade.

■ The United States is both the largest single-nation exporter and the largest importer in the world economy. The largest trading partner of the United States is Canada.

Self-Test Exercises

1. If the Canadian dollar depreciates 20 percent, how does this affect the export and domestic sales of a Canadian manufacturer? Explain.

2. Unit labour costs in Spain and Portugal rose 3.5 percent from a low base in 1999–2001, while producer price indices also rose 2.6 percent and 6.0 percent, respectively. In contrast, unit labour costs in Japan declined 1.5 percent and producer prices were unchanged. What effect should these factors, by themselves, have on export trade, and why?

Exercises

1. If the Canadian dollar were to appreciate substantially, what steps could a domestic manufacturer take in advance to reduce the effect of the exchange rate fluctuation on company profitability?

2. After an unanticipated dollar appreciation has occurred, what would you recommend a company do with its strong domestic currency?

3. Would increased cost inflation in Canada relative to its major trading partners likely increase or decrease the value of the Canadian dollar? Why?

4. If the domestic prices for traded goods rose 50 percent over 10 years in Japan and 100 percent over that same 10 years in Canada, what would happen to the yen/dollar exchange rate? Why?

5. If Bombardier's dollar aircraft prices increase 20 percent and the yen/dollar exchange rate declines 15 percent, what effective price increase is facing a Japanese commuter airline for the purchase of a Bombardier 50-passenger plane? Would Bombardier's margin likely rise or fall if the yen then depreciated and competitor prices were unchanged? Why?

6. How would a reduced flow of international capital into Canadian stock and bond markets affect the dollar's exchange rate, and why? Would expectations of continuing withdrawals from Canadian markets have any additional effect on exchange rates, and why?

 Part Five

Estimating and Forecasting

 Part Six

Game-Theory Extensions

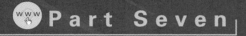 Part Seven

Long-Term Investment Decisions and Risk Management

PART FIVE addresses the topics of estimating demand and cost, as well
as forecasting. Web Chapter 13 discusses the estimation of demand functions, and Web Appendix 13A discusses how to apply the linear regression
model as well as its extensions. Web Appendix 13B contains statistical
tables of the normal distribution, the *t*-distribution, the *F*-distribution,
and the Durbin–Watson statistic. Web Chapter 14 discusses the estimation of cost functions. Web Appendix 14A discusses mass customization
and the learning curve. Web Chapter 15 discusses the major topics of
forecasting business and economic data.

PART SIX addresses some advanced topics of game theory. Web Chapter 16 discusses the best practices of game-theoretic rivalry. When there are few rivals, effective tactics are needed. Effective tactics require methods for anticipating rival initiatives, responses, and counter-responses. Web Chapter 17 discusses the optimum mechanism design for auctions and other institutional procedures, such as queuing and profit sharing.

PART SEVEN looks at the capital investment decision of a firm. Investments in new, long-term assets have a major impact on a firm's future stream of cash flows and the risk of those cash flows. As such, the long-term investment decision has a significant impact on the value of the firm. Capital investment decisions can be viewed as the link between the short-run price and output decisions made by managers of a firm and the long-run decisions made by those managers. A capital investment involves a change in the production technology used by the firm and/or a change in the scale of operations of the firm. In Web Chapter 18, we re-introduce the concept of a project's net present value. The net present value of a project can be viewed as the increment to shareholder wealth that is expected to accrue as a result of undertaking a capital investment project. The same tools that are relevant to capital investment analysis by private sector managers also can be used, with minor modifications, by managers in public and not-for-profit enterprises. Web Appendix 18A provides more information about the time value of money, a concept that is of central importance in capital investment decisions. Web Appendix 18B includes the time value of money tables that can be used in making time value of money calculations. Web Chapter 19 examines decision making under risk and reviews the techniques for managing risk.

A

Activity-Based Costing (ABC) A method of allocating direct fixed cost to time on task or other activities closely related to actual production events.

Adverse Selection A limited choice of lower quality alternatives attributable to asymmetric information.

Agency Costs Costs associated with resolving conflicts of interest among shareholders, managers, and lenders. Agency costs include the cost of monitoring and bonding performance, the cost of constructing contracts designed to minimize agency conflicts, and the loss in efficiency resulting from unresolved agent–principal conflicts.

Agency Relationship A basis for delegating decision-making authority from principals to agents.

Allocative Efficiency A measure of how closely production achieves the least-cost input mix or process, given the desired level of output.

Appraisal An estimate of value by an independent expert.

Arbitrage Buying cheap and selling elsewhere for an immediate profit.

Asset Specificity The difference in value between first-best and second-best use.

Asymmetric Information Unequal, dissimilar knowledge.

Authorization Level Capacity authorized for sale in lower margin segments.

Autocorrelation An econometric problem characterized by the existence of a significant pattern in the successive values of the error terms in a linear regression model.

Average Product The ratio of total output to the amount of the variable input used in producing the output.

B

Backwards Induction Reasoning in reverse time sequence from later consequences back to earlier decisions.

Benchmarking A comparison of performance in similar jobs, firms, plants, divisions, etc.

Benefit–Cost Analysis A resource-allocation model that can be used by public sector and not-for-profit organizations to evaluate programs or investments on the basis of the magnitude of the discounted costs and benefits.

Benefit–Cost Ratio The ratio of the present value of the benefits from a project or program (discounted at the social discount rate) to the present value of the costs (similarly discounted).

Brand Loyalty A customer sorting rule favourable to incumbents.

Break-Even Analysis A technique used to examine the relationship among a firm's sales, costs, and operating profits at various levels of output.

Budget Lines These limit the choices available for consumption based on the prices of various goods and the consumer's income.

Business Risk The inherent variability or uncertainty of a firm's operating earnings (earnings before interest and taxes).

C

Capital Asset A durable input that depreciates with use, time, and obsolescence.

Capital Asset Pricing Model (CAPM) A theory that formally describes the nature of the risk-required return tradeoff. It provides one method of estimating a firm's cost of equity capital.

Capital Budgeting The process of planning for and evaluating capital expenditures.

Capital Expenditure A cash outlay designed to generate a flow of future cash benefits over a period of time extending beyond one year.

Capital-Intensive A characteristic of costs associated with a high proportion of fixed to variable inputs, usually due to extensive investment in plant and equipment.

Cartel A formal or informal agreement among firms in an oligopolistic industry. Cartel members may agree on such issues as prices, total industry output, market shares, and the division of profits.

ceteris paribus Latin for "all other things remaining unchanged."

Chain Store Paradox A prediction of always-accommodative behaviour by incumbents facing entry threats.

Class Action Suit A legal procedure for reducing the search and notification costs of filing a complaint.

Coase Theorem A prediction about the emergence of private voluntary bargaining in reciprocal externalities with low transaction costs.

Cobb–Douglas Production Function A particular type of mathematical model, known as a "multiplicative exponential function," which is used to represent the relationship between inputs and output.

Coefficient of Determination A measure of the proportion of total variation in the dependent variable that is explained by the independent variable(s).

Coefficient of Variation The ratio of the standard deviation to the expected value. A relative measure of risk.

Common-Value Auction Auction where bidders have identical valuations when information is complete.

Company Audit A governance mechanism for separating random disturbances from variation in unobservable effort.

Competition (Antitrust) Regulation Laws that limit monopoly power and maintain competition.

Complementary Goods Two goods are complementary if the quantity demanded of one *decreases* (increases) when the price of the other *increases* (decreases), assuming all other factors affecting demand remain unchanged.

Congestion Pricing Charging a fee that reflects the true marginal cost imposed by demand in excess of capacity.

Conspicuous Focal Point An outcome that attracts mutual cooperation.

Contestable Market An industry with exceptionally open entry and easy exit, where incumbents are slow to react.

Contingent Payments A fee schedule conditional on the outcome of uncertain future events.

Contracts Third-party enforceable agreements designed to facilitate deferred exchange.

Contribution Analysis A comparison of the additional operating profits to the direct fixed costs attributable to a decision.

Contribution Margin The difference between price and variable cost per unit.

Contribution Margin Percentage The difference between the profit-maximizing price and marginal cost, often expressed as a percentage of the price. When more than one unit sale is involved, contribution margin is the difference between revenue and incremental variable cost.

Cooperative Games Game structures that allow coalition formation, side payments, and binding third-party enforceable agreements.

Cost-Effectiveness Analysis An analytical tool designed to assist public decision makers in their resource-allocation decisions when benefits cannot be easily measured in dollar terms, but costs can be monetarily quantified.

Cost Function A mathematical model, schedule (table), or graph that shows the cost (such as total, average, or marginal cost) of producing various quantities of output.

Cost of Capital The cost of funds that are supplied to a firm. The cost of capital is the minimum rate of return that must be earned on new investments undertaken by a firm.

Credible Threat A conditional strategy that the threat-maker is worse off ignoring than implementing.

Credible Commitment A promise that the promise-giver is worse off violating than fulfilling.

Cross Price Elasticity The ratio of the percentage change in the quantity demanded of product A to the percentage change in the price of product B, assuming that all other factors influencing demand remain unchanged.

Cross-Sectional Data Series of observations taken on different observation units (for example, households) at the same point in time.

Cyclical Variations Major expansions and contractions in an economic series that usually are longer than a year in duration.

D

Degree of Operating Leverage (DOL) The percentage change in a firm's earnings before interest and taxes (EBIT) resulting from a given percentage change in sales or output.

Demand Amount of a good or service that consumers are willing and able to buy at every possible price.

Demand Function The relationship that exists during some period of time between the number of units of a good or service that consumers are willing to buy and a given set of conditions that influence the willingness to purchase, such as price, income level, and advertising.

Derivative A measure of the marginal effect of a change in one variable on the value of a function. Graphically, it represents the slope of the function at a given point.

Diseconomies of Scale Rising long-run average costs as the level of output is increased.

Diversification The act of investing in a set of securities or assets having different risk-return characteristics.

Dividend Valuation Model A model (or formula) stating that the value of a firm (i.e., shareholder wealth) is equal to the present value of the firm's future dividend payments, discounted at the shareholders'

required rate of return. It provides one method of estimating a firm's cost of equity capital.

Dominant Strategy An action rule that maximizes the decision maker's welfare independent of the actions of other players.

Dutch Auction A descending-price auction.

Durable Good A good that yields benefits to the owner over a number of future time periods.

Dynamic Pricing A price that varies over time based on the balance of demand and supply, often associated with Internet auctions.

E

Economic Profit The difference between total revenue and total economic cost. Economic cost includes a "normal" rate of return on the capital contributions of the firm's owners.

Economies of scope Economies that exist whenever the cost of producing two (or more) products jointly by one plant or firm is less than the cost of producing these products separately by different plants or firms.

Efficient Rationing A customer sorting rule in which high-willingness-to-pay customers absorb the capacity of low-price entrants.

Elasticity of Production A measure of proportionality between changes in the variable input(s) and the resulting change in output.

Endgame Reasoning An analysis of the final decision in a sequential game.

Engineering Cost Technique A method of estimating cost functions by deriving the least-cost combination of labour, capital equipment, and raw materials required to produce various levels of output, using only industrial engineering information.

English Auction An ascending-price auction.

Expansion Path The input combinations that minimize cost for each level of output.

Expectation Damages A remedy for breach of contract designed to elicit efficient precaution and efficient reliance on promises.

Expected Utility The product of the utility of each outcome times its respective probability of occurrence, summed over all possible outcomes.

Expected Value The weighted average of the possible outcomes, where the weights are the probabilities of the respective outcomes.

Experience Goods Products and services whose quality is undetectable when purchased.

External Diseconomy of Scale An increase in unit costs reflecting higher input prices.

External Economy of Scale Volume discounts in purchasing inputs.

Externality A spillover of benefits or costs from one production or utility function to another.

F

Fair Division Games Procedures for dividing assets by consensual agreement.

First-Order Condition A test to locate one or more maximum or minimum points of an algebraic function.

Fixed Costs The costs of inputs to the production process that are constant over the short run.

Focal Outcomes of Interest Payoffs involved in an analysis of equilibrium strategy.

Focus Group A market research technique employing close observation of discussion among target consumers.

Folk Theorem A conclusion about cooperation in repeated Prisoner's Dilemma games.

Foreign Exchange Operating Risk Exposure A change in cash flows from foreign or domestic sales resulting from currency fluctuations.

Foreign Exchange Transaction Risk Exposure A change in cash flows resulting from contractual commitments to pay in or receive foreign currency.

Foreign Exchange Translation Risk Exposure An accounting adjustment in the home currency value of foreign assets or liabilities.

Free Trade Area A group of nations that has agreed to reduce tariffs and other trade barriers.

Full Contingent Claims Contract An agreement about all possible future events.

Full-Cost (or Cost-Plus) Pricing A method of determining prices in which a charge to cover overhead, plus a percentage markup or margin, is added to variable production and marketing costs to arrive at a selling price.

G

Game Theory A mathematical theory of decision making by the participants in a conflict-of-interest situation.

Game Tree A schematic diagram of a sequential game.

Governance Mechanisms Processes to detect, resolve, and reduce postcontractual opportunism.

Governance Structure A mechanism that poses an alternative to incentives or direct monitoring for eliciting contractually expected behaviour.

Grim Trigger Strategy A strategy involving infinitely long punishment schemes.

Gross Profit Margin Revenue minus the sum of variable cost plus direct fixed cost, also known as "direct costs of goods sold" in manufacturing.

H

Hedge A risk-reducing strategy of taking offsetting positions in the ownership of a derivative security and an underlying asset.

Herfindahl–Hirschman Index A measure of market concentration equal to the sum of the squares of the market shares of the firms in a given industry.

Heteroscedasticity An econometric problem characterized by the lack of a uniform variance of the error terms about the regression line.

Hostage Mechanism A mechanism for establishing the credibility of a threat or commitment.

Hostage or Bonding Mechanism A procedure for establishing trust by assigning valuable property contingent on nonperformance of an agreement.

I

Identification Problem A difficulty encountered in empirically estimating a demand function by regression analysis. This problem arises from the simultaneous relationship between two functions, such as supply and demand.

Incentive-Compatible Revelation Mechanism A procedure for aligning incentives with revelation of true value.

Incentive Compatibility Constraint An assurance of incentive alignment.

Income Effect Movement from one indifference curve to another due to the change in "real" income caused by a price change.

Income Elasticity The ratio of the percentage change in quantity demanded to the percentage change in income, assuming that all other factors influencing demand remain unchanged.

Incomplete Information Uncertain knowledge of payoffs, choices, etc.

Indifference Curves These curves reveal the consumer's preferences for various combinations of goods.

Infinitely Repeated Game A game that lasts forever.

Input A resource or factor of production (such as a raw material, labour skill, or piece of equipment) employed in a production process.

Incremental Analysis The real-world counterpart to marginal analysis. Incremental analysis requires that an estimate be made of the changes in total cost and revenue that will result from a price change or from a decision to add or delete a product, accept or reject a new order, or undertake a new investment.

Internal Economies of Scale Declining long-run average costs as the rate of output for a product, plant, or firm is increased.

Internal Hedge A balance sheet offset to foreign currency cash flows.

Internal Rate of Return (IRR) The discount rate that equates the present value of the stream of net cash flows from a project with the project's net investment.

Inverse Intensity Rationing A customer sorting rule that assures that low-willingness-to-pay customers absorb the capacity of low-price entrants.

Iterated Dominant Strategy An action rule that maximizes self-interest in light of the predictable dominant-strategy behaviour of other players.

J

Joint Products Products that are interdependent in the production process, such as gasoline and fuel oil in an oil refinery. A change in the production of one produces a change in the cost or availability of the other.

L

Law of Comparative Advantage A principle defending free trade and specialization in accordance with lower relative cost.

Law of Demand Quantity demanded of a good or service increases (decreases) as its price decreases (increases).

Law of Supply Quantity supplied of a good or service increases (decreases) as it price increases (decreases).

Learning Curve Effect Declining unit cost attributable to greater cumulative volume.

Lemons Market Asymmetric information exchange leads to the low-quality products and services driving out the higher quality products and services.

Life Cycle Pricing Pricing that varies throughout the product life cycle.

Limit Pricing Setting a low price to deter entry.

Long Run The period of time in which *all* of the resources employed in a production process can be varied.

M

Marginal Analysis A basis for making various economic decisions that analyzes the additional (marginal) benefits derived from a particular decision and compares them with the additional (marginal) costs incurred.

Marginal Cost The incremental increase in total cost that results from a one-unit increase in output.

Marginal Factor Cost (MFC) The amount that an additional unit of the variable input adds to total cost.

Marginal Product The incremental change in total output that can be obtained from the use of one more unit of an input in the production process (while holding constant all other inputs).

Marginal Rate of Technical Substitution (MRTS) The *rate* at which one input may be substituted for another input in producing a given quantity of output.

Marginal Resource (or Factor) Cost The price of buying another unit of input plus any increase in price for each of the existing units the firm wishes to buy.

Marginal Revenue The change in total revenue that results from a one-unit change in quantity demanded.

Marginal Revenue Product (MRP) The amount that an additional unit of the variable production input adds to total revenue. Also known as "marginal value added."

Market A place where buyers and sellers transact.

Market Concentration Ratio The percentage of total industry output produced by the 4, 8, 20, or 50 largest firms.

Market Equilibrium Price at which quantity demanded equals quantity supplied.

Market Failure The price system fails to provide the correct signals to firms making output and resource-allocation decisions.

Minimum Efficient Scale (MES) The smallest scale at which minimum costs per unit are attained.

Mixed Bundling Selling multiple products both separately and together for less than the sum of the separate prices.

Monopolistic Competition A market structure very much like pure competition, with the major distinction being the existence of a differentiated product.

Monopoly A market structure characterized by one firm producing a highly differentiated product in a market with significant barriers to entry.

Monopsonist The sole buyer in a market.

Moral Hazard Problem A problem of postcontractual opportunism that arises from unverifiable or unobservable contract performance.

Multicollinearity An econometric problem characterized by a high degree of intercorrelation among some or all of the explanatory variables in a regression equation.

N

Natural Monopoly An industry in which maximum economic efficiency is obtained when the firm produces, distributes, and transmits all of the commodity or service produced in that industry. The production of natural monopolists is typically characterized by increasing returns to scale throughout the range of output demanded by the market.

Net Present Value (NPV) The present value of expected future cash flows minus the initial outlay.

Network Effect A source of unit cost reduction based on network value rather than scale of operations or volume purchase discounts.

Niche Pricing Setting a high price to stay in a market niche.

Noncooperative Games Game structures that prohibit collusion, side payments, and binding agreements enforced by third parties.

Nonredeployable Assets Assets whose value in second-best use is near zero.

Nonredeployable Reputational Asset A reputation whose value is lost if sold or licensed.

Nonspecific Investment A fully redeployable asset.

Normal Form of the Game A representation of payoffs in a simultaneous-play game.

O

Oligopoly A market structure in which the number of firms is so small that the actions of any one firm are likely to have noticeable impacts on the performance of other firms in the industry.

Operating Leverage The use of assets having fixed costs (e.g., depreciation) in an effort to increase expected returns.

Opportunity Costs The value of a resource in its next best alternative use. Opportunity cost represents the return or compensation that must be foregone as a result of the decision to employ the resource in a given economic activity.

Optimal Incentives Contract An agreement about payoffs and penalties that creates appropriate incentives.

Optimal Output for a Given Plant Size Output rate that results in lowest average total cost for a given plant size.

Optimal Overbooking A marginal analysis technique for balancing the cost of idle capacity (spoilage) against the opportunity cost of unserved demand (spill).

Optimal Plant Size for a Given Output Rate Plant size that results in lowest average total cost for a given output.

Optimal Plant Size Plant size that achieves minimum long-run average total cost.

Overall Production Efficiency The product of allocative, technical, and scale efficiency.

P

Partial Derivative A measure of the marginal effect of a change in one variable on the value of a multivariate function, while holding constant all other variables.

Participation Constraint An assurance of ongoing involvement.

Patent A legal government grant of monopoly power that prevents others from manufacturing or selling a patented article.

Peak-Load Pricing The process of charging a higher price during those periods of time when demand is heaviest and lower prices when demand is light.

Pecuniary Externality A spillover that is reflected in prices and therefore results in no inefficiency.

Penetration Pricing Setting entry price below target price to gain market share.

Postcontractual Opportunistic Behaviour Actions that take advantage of another party's vulnerabilities.

Present Value The value today of a future amount of money or a series of future payments evaluated at the appropriate discount rate.

Prestige Pricing The practice of charging a high price for a product to enhance its perceived value.

Price Discrimination Selling the same good or service, produced by a single firm, at different prices to different buyers, during the same time period.

Price Elasticity The ratio of the percentage change in quantity demanded to the percentage change in price, assuming that all other factors influencing demand remain unchanged. Also called "own price elasticity."

Price Leadership A pricing strategy followed in many oligopolistic industries. One firm normally announces all new price changes. Either by an explicit or an implicit agreement, other firms in the industry regularly follow the pricing moves of the industry leader.

Principal–Agent Problem An incentives conflict in delegating decision-making authority.

Private-Value Auction Auction where the bidders have different valuations when information is complete.

Probability The percentage chance that a particular outcome will occur.

Producer's Good A good that is not produced for direct consumption, but rather is the raw material or capital equipment that is used to produce a consumer good (or some other producer's good).

Production Function A mathematical model, schedule (table), or graph that relates the maximum feasible quantity of output that can be produced from given amounts of various inputs.

Production Isoquant An algebraic function or a geometric curve representing all the various combinations of two inputs that can be used in producing a given level of output.

Production Process A fixed-proportions production relationship.

Protection Level Capacity reserved for sale in higher margin segments.

Public Goods Goods that may be consumed by more than one person at the same time with little or no extra cost, and for which it is expensive or impossible to exclude those who do not pay.

Public Utilities A group of firms, mostly in the electric power, natural gas, and communications industries, that are closely regulated by one or more government agencies. The agencies control entry into the business, set prices, establish product quality standards, and influence the total profits that may be earned by the firms.

Pure Competition A market structure characterized by a large number of buyers and sellers of a homogeneous (nondifferentiated) product. Entry and exit from the industry is costless, or nearly so. Information is freely available to all market participants, and there is no collusion among firms in the industry.

R

Random Rationing A customer sorting rule reflecting randomized buyer behaviour.

Real Terms of Trade Comparison of relative costs of production across economies.

Reciprocal Externality A spillover that results from competing incompatible uses.

Relational Contracts Promissory agreements of coordinated performance among owners of highly interdependent assets.

Relative Purchasing Power Parity A relationship between differential inflation rates and long-term trends in exchange rates.

Relevant Market A group of firms that interact with each other in a buyer–seller relationship.

Reliance Relationship Long-term, mutually beneficial agreements, often informal.

Reliant Assets At least partially nonredeployable durable assets.

Reservation Price The maximum price a customer will pay to reserve a product or service.

Returns to Scale The proportionate increase in output that results from a given proportionate increase in *all* of the inputs employed in the production process.

Risk A decision-making situation in which there is variability in the possible outcomes, and the probabilities of these outcomes can be specified by the decision maker.

Risk-Adjusted Discount Rate A discount rate that reflects the risk associated with a particular investment project.

S

Scale Efficiency A measure of how close the potential average cost of production is to the lowest possible minimum average cost.

Search Goods Products and services whose quality can be detected through market search.

Seasonal Effects Variations in a time series during a year that tend to appear regularly from year to year.

Second-Order Condition A test to determine whether a point that has been determined from the first-order condition is either a maximum point or a minimum point of the algebraic function.

Secular Trends Long-run changes (growth or decline) in an economic time-series variable.

Self-Enforcing Reliance Relationship A noncontractual, mutually beneficial agreement.

Sequential Game A game with an explicit order of play.

Shareholder Wealth A measure of the value of a firm. Shareholder wealth is equal to the value of a firm's common shares. This, in turn, is equal to the present value of all future cash returns expected to be generated by the firm for the benefit of its owners.

Short Run The period of time in which one (or more) of the resources employed in a production process is fixed or incapable of being varied.

Simultaneous Game A game in which players must choose their actions simultaneously.

Simulation A decision-making tool that models some event, such as cash flows from an investment project.

Skimming A new-product pricing strategy that results in a high initial product price. This price is reduced over time as demand at the higher price is satisfied.

Social Discount Rate The discount rate to be used when evaluating benefits and costs from public sector investments.

Standard Deviation A statistical measure of the dispersion or variability of possible outcomes.

Standard Error of the Estimate The standard deviation of the error term in a linear regression model.

Strategic Holdout A negotiator who makes unreasonable demands at the end of a unanimous consent process.

Strategy Game A decision-making situation with consciously interdependent behaviour between two or more of the participants.

Stratified Lottery A randomized mechanism for allocating scarce capacity across demand segments.

Substitute Goods Two goods are substitutes if the quantity demanded of one *increases* (decreases) when the price of the other *increases* (decreases), assuming all other factors affecting demand remain unchanged.

Substitution Effect Movement along an indifference curve due to a price change while holding "real" income constant.

Sunk Cost A cost incurred regardless of the alternative action chosen in a decision-making problem.

Supply Amount of a good or service that producers are willing and able to offer for sale at every possible price.

Survivor Technique A method of estimating cost functions from the shares of industry output coming from each size class over time. Size classes whose shares of industry output are increasing (decreasing) over time are presumed to be relatively efficient (inefficient) and have lower (higher) average costs.

T

Target Return-on-Investment Pricing A method of pricing in which a target profit, defined as the desired profit rate on investment times total gross operating assets, is allocated to each unit of output to arrive at a selling price.

Technical Efficiency A measure of how closely production achieves maximum potential output given the input mix or process.

Threshold Sales Curve A level of advance sales that triggers reallocation of capacity.

Time-Series Data A series of observations taken on an economic variable at various past points in time.

Transfer Price The price at which an intermediate good or service is transferred from the selling to the buying division within the same firm.

Trembling Hand Trigger Strategy A punishment mechanism that forgives random mistakes and miscommunications.

Two-Person Zero-Sum Games Game in which net gains for one player necessarily imply equal net losses for the other player.

U

Uncertainty A decision-making situation in which the decision maker is either unable or unwilling to specify the probabilities of occurrence of the possible outcomes of the decision.

Unravelling Problem A failure of cooperation in games of finite length.

V

Value-Based Pricing Adding value to maintain price.

Variable Costs The costs of the variable inputs to the production process.

Vickery Auction An incentive-compatible revelation mechanism for eliciting sealed bids equal to private value.

Y

Yield Management (YM) A cross-functional order acceptance and refusal process.

Solutions to Self-Test Exercises

CHAPTER 1

MTV operates in a highly concentrated, near-monopoly market where fixed costs are low and hence intensity of rivalry is reduced. MTV also faces little supplier power from numerous nonunique musical groups. The networks, in contrast, face much greater supplier power. MTV has few substitutes, whereas the networks now face 150 or more channels of substitutes for each type of programming.

CHAPTER 2

1. Because the price distribution is normal, the expected price is halfway between the most optimistic price and the most pessimistic price, or $1.5 million.

2. From Table 13B.1 of Web Appendix 13B, the z value corresponding to leaving 10 percent in the lower tail of a normal distribution is approximately -1.28. Therefore, -1.28 standard deviations correspond with a distance of $500,000 below the mean ($1 million minus $1.5 million). Hence, one standard deviation is equal to

$$-1.28\sigma = -\$500,000$$
$$\sigma = \$390,625$$

3. $z = (\$1.2 \text{ million} - \$1.5 \text{ million})/\$390,625 = -0.77$.
   From Table 13B.1, the $p(z < -0.77) = 22.06\%$.

CHAPTER 3

1. Forecasted demand =

   11 million [1 + income elasticity $\times$ %Δ in DPI + price elasticity $\times$ %Δ in price]

Chow	11 M [1 + 3.0(0.04) − 1.2(0.06)] = 11.528 M
Alkinson	11 M [1 + 2.5(0.04) − 1.4(0.06)] = 11.176 M
Roos	11 M [1 + 2.5(0.04) − 1.5(0.06)] = 11.11 M
Suits	11 M [1 + 3.9(0.04) − 1.2(0.06)] = 11.924 M

2. Week 1–2: Price elasticity

   $E_D = [(95 - 100)/(95 + 100)]/[(5.20 - 5.00)/(5.20 + 5.00)] = -1.31$

   Week 2–3: Income elasticity

   $E_Y = [(100 - 95)/(100 + 95)]/[(550 - 500)/(550 + 500)] = 0.538$

   Week 3–4: Cross elasticity

   $E_X = [(105 - 100)/(105 + 100)]/[(0.95 - 0.90)/(0.95 + 0.90)] = 0.902$

   Week 4–5: Price elasticity

   $E_D = -2.32$

   Week 5–6: Cross elasticity

   $E_X = 1.68$

   Week 6–7: Income elasticity

   $E_Y = 0.512$

   Week 7–8: Price elasticity

   $E_D = -1.81$

   Week 8–9: Cross elasticity

   $E_X = 1.90$

   Week 9–10: Income elasticity

   $E_Y = 0.900$

3. If the price of DVD players declines by 20% and the total revenue rises, this indicates that the demand for DVD players is price elastic. We cannot determine the impact of this price reduction on the firm's profits without also knowing the firm's cost function.

Chapter 4

1. a.

Crew Size	$TP_X = Q$	$AP_X = Q/X$	$MP_X = \Delta Q / \Delta X$
0	0	—	—
2	3	1.50	1.5
3	6	2.00	3.0
4	11	2.75	5.0
5	19	3.80	8.0
6	24	4.00	5.0
7	28	4.00	4.0
8	31	3.88	3.0
9	33	3.67	2.0
10	34	3.40	1.0
11	34	3.09	0.0
12	33	2.75	−1.0

(i)   Increasing returns: $0 - 5$ (MP_X increasing)
(ii) Constant returns: None (MP_X constant)
(iii) Decreasing returns: $5^+ - 11$ (MP_X decreasing)
(iv) Negative returns: $11^+ - 12$ (MP_X negative)

b. Max $Q = 34$. This corresponds to a crew size of 10 or 11. Assuming a positive cost for additional crew members, a crew size of 10 should be used to minimize the cost of obtaining this output.

c. Max $AP_X = 4.00$. This corresponds to a crew size of 6 or 7. Again, for any positive cost for additional crew members, a crew size of 6 is preferred to achieve this objective.

2.

Crew Size	Output (×100 kg)	Marginal Product	Total Revenue	Marginal Revenue	Marginal Revenue Product	Marginal Factor Cost
0	0	—	0	—	—	—
2	3	1.5	225	75	112.5	150
3	6	3.0	450	75	225	150
4	11	5.0	825	75	375	150
5	19	8.0	1425	75	600	150
6	24	5.0	1800	75	375	150
7	28	4.0	2100	75	300	150
8	31	3.0	2325	75	225	150
9	33	2.0	2475	75	**150**	**150**
10	34	1.0	2550	75	75	150
11	34	0.0	2550	75	0	150
12	33	−1.0	2475	75	−75	150

The optimal crew size occurs where $MRP_X = MFC_X$. From the table above it can be seen that this condition occurs at a crew size of 9 (value = 150).

3. a. $Q = 10X - 0.5X^2$

   $MP_X = 10 - 1.0X$

   $MR_Q = 10$

   $MRP_X = (10 - 1.0X)10 = 100 - 10X$

   b. $MFC_X = 20$

   c. The optimal level of the variable input occurs where:

   $MRP_X = MFC_X$

   $100 - 10X = 20$

   $X^* = 8$

4. a. (i) $E_L = \beta_1 = 0.45$

      (ii) $E_F = \beta_2 = 0.20$

      (iii) $E_K = \beta_3 = 0.30$

   b. $E_L = \%\Delta Q / \%\Delta L$

   $E_L = 0.45$

   $\%\Delta L = 0.02$

   $\%\Delta Q = 0.45(0.02) = 0.009$, or 0.9%

   c. $E_K = \%\Delta Q / \%\Delta K$

   $E_K = 0.30$

   $\%\Delta K = -0.03$

   $\%\Delta Q = 0.30(-0.03) = -0.009$ or -0.9%

   d. $\beta_1 + \beta_2 + \beta_3 = 0.45 + 0.20 + 0.30 = 0.95$

   Since the sum of the elasticities is less than one, the bus transportation system exhibits decreasing returns to scale.

5. a. $Q = 1.5X^{0.70}Y^{0.30}$

   $Q' = 1.5[X(\lambda)]^{0.70}[Y(\lambda)]^{0.30}$

   $Q' = \lambda^{1.00}[1.5X^{0.70}Y^{0.30}]$

   $Q' = \lambda Q$

   Output increased by exactly λ; therefore, the function exhibits constant returns to scale.

   b. $Q = 0.4X + 0.5Y$

   $Q' = 0.4[X(\lambda)] + 0.5[Y(\lambda)]$

   $Q' = \lambda[0.4X + 0.5Y]$

   $Q' = \lambda Q$

   Output increases by exactly λ; therefore, the function exhibits constant returns to scale.

   c. $Q = 2.0XY$

   $Q' = 2.0[X(\lambda)][Y(\lambda)]$

   $Q' = \lambda^2[2.0XY]$

   $Q' = \lambda^2 Q$

   Output increases by more than λ (i.e., λ^2); therefore, the function exhibits increasing returns to scale.

   d. $Q = 1.0X^{0.60}Y^{0.50}$

   $Q' = 1.0[X(\lambda)]^{0.60}[Y(\lambda)]^{0.50}$

   $Q' = \lambda^{1.10}[1.0X^{0.60}Y^{0.50}]$

   $Q' = \lambda^{1.10}Q$

   Output increases by more than λ, therefore the function exhibits increasing returns to scale.

CHAPTER 5

1. a. **Accounting profits:**

Revenues	$5,000,000
Less: Variable operating costs	4,500,000
Less: Depreciation	40,000
Less: Wages	50,000
Equals: Operating income	$410,000
Less: Interest expense	400,000
Accounting income before tax	$10,000

b. **Economic profits:**

Revenues	$5,000,000
Less: Variable operating costs	4,500,000
Less: Opportunity value of Bowen's income potential	30,000
Less: Economic depreciation	60,000
Equals: Economic profit before financial costs	$410,000
Less: Interest expense	400,000
Less: Opportunity cost of $1 million equity investment	100,000
Equals: Economic profit	($90,000)

If these calculations are representative of Bowen's regular performance, he would be better off financially by selling the farm and working for someone else. Of course, this analysis ignores many intangible factors that may affect Bowen's decision.

2. a. $VC = 150Q - 10Q^2 + 0.5Q^3$

$AVC = 150 - 10Q + 0.5Q^2$

$d(AVC)/dQ = -10 + 1.0Q = 0$

$Q^* = 10$

$d^2(AVC)/dQ^2 = +1$, thus $Q^* = 10$ represents a minimum.

b. $VC = 150(10) - 10(10)^2 + 0.5(10)^3$

$VC = \$1,000$

$AVC = \$1,000/10 = \$100$

c. $MC = 150 - 20Q + 1.5Q^2$

$d(MC)/dQ = -20 + 3.0Q = 0$

$Q^* = 6.67$

$d^2(MC)/dQ^2 = 3.0$, thus $Q^* = 6.67$ represents a minimum.

d. $VC = 150(6.67) - 10(6.67)^2 + 0.5(6.67)^3$

$VC = \$704$

$MC = 150 - 20(6.67) + 1.5(6.67)^2$

$MC = \$83.33$

3. a. 1 plant: $TC = \$900,000 + (6,000 + 4,500 + 3,000)\$250 = \$4,275,000$

3 plants: $TC = (\$475,000 + \$425,000 + \$400,000) + (6,000 + 4,500 + 3,000)\$225 = \$4,337,500$

One plant should be built.

b. 1 plant: $TC = \$900,000 + (18,000)\$250 = \$5,400,000$

3 plants: $TC = (\$475,000 + \$425,000 + \$400,000) + (8,000 + 6,000 + 4,000)\$225 = \$5,350,000$

Three plants should be built.

c. A forecast of the future demand for subassemblies.

CHAPTER 6

1. a. $Q_D = 12,000 - 4,000P$
   $TC = 4,000 + 0.5Q$

   b. $MC = d(TC)/dQ = 0.5$

   c. $P = 3 - Q/4,000$
   $TR = 3Q - Q^2/4,000$

   d. $MR = 3 - Q/2,000$

   e. $\pi = TR - TC$
   $\pi = 3Q - Q^2/4,000 - 4,000 - 0.5Q$
   $\pi = 2.5Q - Q^2/4,000 - 4,000$
   $d\pi/dQ = 2.5 - Q/2,000 = 0$
   $Q^* = 5,000$
   $P^* = (12,000 - 5,000)/4,000 = \$1.75$
   $\pi^* = 1.75(5,000) - 4,000 - 0.5(5,000) = \$2,250$

   f. $0.5 = 3 - Q/2,000$
   $Q^* = 5,000$

   g. Monopoly or monopolistic competition

2. a.

Output	VC/Unit	TVC	FC	TC	MC/Unit	ATC
0	0	0	100	100	—	—
50	5.00	250	100	350	5.00	7.00
100	4.50	450	100	550	4.00	5.50
150	4.00	600	100	700	3.00	4.67
200	3.50	700	100	800	2.00	4.00
250	3.00	750	100	850	1.00	3.40
300	2.75	825	100	925	1.50	3.08
350	3.00	1050	100	1150	4.50	3.29
400	3.50	1400	100	1500	7.00	3.75

   b. $P = MR = \$4.50$
   $MC = MR = \$4.50$ (profit-maximizing output)
   $Q^* = 350$ units

   c. $\pi = TR - TC$
   $\pi = 4.5(350) - 1,150 = \$425$
   $\pi/Q = 425/350 = \$1.21$

   d. No, since $P = MR = MC > ATC$.

3. a. $E_D = \%\Delta Q_D/\%\Delta P$
   $-2.0 = 15\%/\%\Delta P$
   $\%\Delta P = -7.5\%$
   $-0.075 = (P_2 - 15.00)/[(P_2 + 15)/2]$
   $P_2 = \$13.92$
   $\Delta P = \$13.92 - \$15 = -\$1.08$
   $0.15 = (Q_2 - 30,000)/[(Q_2 + 30,000)/2]$
   $Q_2 = 34,865$

   b. (i) Before: $TR_1 = 15(30,000) = \$450,000$
   After: $TR_2 = 13.92(34,865) = \$485,321$
   $\Delta TR = +\$35,321$

(ii) Before: $FC_1 = \$90{,}000$

$VC/\text{unit} = \$180{,}000/30{,}000 = \$6.00$

$VC_1 = 6(30{,}000) = 180{,}000$

$TC_1 = 90{,}000 + 180{,}000 = \$270{,}000$

After: $FC_2 = \$90{,}000$

$VC/\text{unit} = \$6.00 - 0.60 = \$5.40$

$VC_2 = \$5.40 \times 34{,}865 = \$188{,}271$

$TC_2 = 90{,}000 + 188{,}271 = \$278{,}271$

$\Delta TC = \$8{,}271$

(iii) Before:

$\pi_1 = \$450{,}000 - \$270{,}000 = \$180{,}000$

After:

$\pi_2 = \$485{,}321 - \$278{,}271 = \$207{,}050$

$\Delta\pi = +\$27{,}050$

CHAPTER 7

1. a. The most important factor that needs to be considered is the price elasticity of demand. Given opportunities to conserve in both the long run and the short run, it is possible that achieving a 16% rate of return is not feasible.

   b. If individuals are prohibited from drilling their own wells, the demand function would become relatively more inelastic.

   c. Because of the high fixed costs that must be covered, the loss of even a small number of customers can compound the problem for the utility and force it to seek additional rate increases in order to cover all of its fixed costs.

2. a. $Q = 45 - 5P$

   $P = -0.2Q + 9$

   $TR = -0.2Q^2 + 9Q$

   $MR = -0.4Q + 9 = 5 = MC$

   $Q^* = 10$

   $P^* = -0.2(10) + 9 = \$7$

   $\pi^* = 7(10) - 12 - 5(10) = \$8$

   b. Price and output will remain the same. Profits will decline by $10 to $-\$2$.

   c. New $VC = \$5.50$ per unit

   $MR = MC$

   $-0.4Q + 9 = 5.5$

   $Q = 8.75$

   $P^* = -0.2(8.75) + 9 = \$7.25$

   $\pi = 7.25(8.75) - 5.5(8.75) - 12$

   $\pi^* = \$3.31$

   d. $P = 6$

   $Q = 45 - 5(6) = 15$

   $\pi = 6(15) - 5(15) - 12 = \$3$

CHAPTER 8

1. a. $\pi_C = PQ_C - TC_C$

   $= (600 - Q_C - Q_D)Q_C - (25{,}000 + 100Q_C)$

   $= -25{,}000 + 500Q_C - Q_C^2 - Q_CQ_D$

$$\pi_D = (600 - Q_C - Q_D)Q_D - (20{,}000 + 125Q_D)$$
$$= -20{,}000 + 475Q_D - Q_D^2 - Q_CQ_D$$
$$\partial\pi_C/\partial Q_C = 500 - 2Q_C - Q_D$$
$$\partial\pi_D/\partial Q_D = 475 - 2Q_D - Q_C$$

Conditions for an optimum require that both partials be set equal to zero and the resulting equations be solved simultaneously for optimal values of Q_C and Q_D:

$$Q_D^* = 150 \text{ units}$$
$$Q_C^* = 175 \text{ units}$$
$$P^* = \$275$$

b. $\pi_C^* = -25{,}000 + 500(175) - (175)^2 - 175(150)$
   $= \$5{,}625$
   $\pi_D^* = -20{,}000 + 475(150) - (150)^2 - 175(150)$
   $= \$2{,}500$

2. a. The profit-maximizing condition for Firm C is the same as before.
   $$\partial\pi_C/\partial Q_C = 500 - 2Q_C - Q_D = 0$$
   Firm D solves the above equation for Q_C in terms of Q_D to incorporate in its profit function Firm C's reaction to quantity changes made by Firm D.
   $$Q_C = 250 - 0.5Q_D$$
   $$\pi_D = [600 - (250 - 0.5Q_D) - Q_D]\,Q_D - [20{,}000 + 125Q_D]$$
   $$d\pi_D/dQ_D = 600 - 250 + Q_D - 2Q_D - 125 = 0$$
   $$Q_D = 225$$
   $$Q_C = 250 - (0.5)(225) = 137.5$$
   $$P = \$600 - \$137.50 - \$225 = \$237.50$$

b. $\pi_C = (\$237.50)(137.50) - [\$25{,}000 + (\$100)(137.50)]$
   $\pi_C = \$32{,}656.25 - \$25{,}000 - \$13{,}750 = -\$6{,}093.75$
   $\pi_D = (\$237.50)(225) - [\$20{,}000 + (\$125)(225)]$
   $\pi_D = \$53{,}437.50 - \$20{,}000 - \$28{,}125 = \$5{,}312.50$

   Note that if Firm C accepts Firm D's Stackelberg leadership, Firm C will eventually go out of business!

3. a.

		Toshiba Strategies	
		Limited Advertising Campaign	Extensive Advertising Campaign
Hitachi Strategies	Limited Advertising Campaign	$7.5*; $7.5	$4.0; $9.0
	Extensive Advertising Campaign	$9.0; $4.0	$5.0; $5.0

* Payoffs are in millions of dollars

b. The dominant advertising strategy for Hitachi is an extensive advertising campaign. It yields a guaranteed minimum profit (i.e., security level) of $5.0 million, regardless of which strategy Toshiba chooses.

c. The dominant advertising strategy for Toshiba is likewise an extensive advertising campaign. This strategy yields a guaranteed minimum profit of $5.0 million, regardless of which strategy Hitachi chooses.

d. The firms may decide to engage in limited cooperation, such as a "tit-for-tat" strategy, when the game is repeated over multiple decision-making periods. By selecting such a strategy it may be possible for the firms to earn profits above the guaranteed minimum payoff.

CHAPTER 9

1. Optimal price discrimination would equate the derived MR in each market equal to the $240 marginal cost of the latest seat sold. From the given elasticities and from Equation 9.2, MR in each market in terms of its price and elasticity appears on the right-hand side of the following equations:

$$\$240 = P_1 (1 - 1/3)$$
$$\$240 = P_2 (1 - 1/4)$$
$$\$240 = P_3 (1 - 1/9)$$

Solving these equations for the respective prices yields

$$P_1 = \$360$$
$$P_2 = \$320$$
$$P_3 = \$270$$

2. a. $\pi = TR - TC$
$$= -10 + 52Q_1 - 2Q_1^2 + 32Q_2 - Q_2^2$$

   b. $\partial\pi/\partial Q_1 = 52 - 4Q_1 = 0$
   $Q_1^* = 13$ units
   $P_1^* = 60 - 2(13) = \$34$/unit

   $\partial\pi/\partial Q_2 = 32 - 2Q_2 = 0$
   $Q_2^* = 16$ units
   $P_2^* = 40 - 16 = \$24$/unit

   c. $TR_1 = 60Q_1 - 2Q_1^2$
   $MR_1 = 60 - 4Q_1$
   $\quad\quad = 60 - 4(13) = \$8$/unit

   $TR_2 = 40Q_2 - Q_2^2$
   $MR_2 = 40 - 2Q_2$
   $\quad\quad = 40 - 2(16) = \$8$/unit

   d. $\pi^* = -10 + 52(13) - 2(13)^2 + 32(16) - (16)^2$
   $\quad = \$584$

   e. $P_1 = P_2$
   $60 - 2Q_1 = 40 - Q_2$
   $Q_2 = 2Q_1 - 20$
   $\pi = -1,050 + 196Q_1 - 6Q_1^2$
   $\partial\pi/\partial Q_1 = 0$
   $\quad = 196 - 12Q_1 = 0$
   $Q_1 = 16.333$ units
   $Q_2 = 2(16.333) - 20 = 12.667$ units
   $Q^* = 16.333 + 12.667 = 29$ units
   $P^* = 60 - 2(16.333) = \$27.33$/unit
   $\pi^* = -1,050 + 196(16.333) - 6(16.333)^2 = \$550.67$

3. a. Contribution for CIDA order:

$AVC = 1.20/1.5 = 80$ cents

$\pi = 300,000(20$ cents contribution$)$

less lost contribution from lost regular sales $(100,000)(40$ cents$)$

$= \$60,000 - \$40,000 = \$20,000$

b. The additional lost sales have a cost of $50,000(40$ cents$) = \$20,000$. Under these conditions, the firm will be indifferent.

CHAPTER 10

1. Yes, bank customers would make no backup plans to buy and sell securities and clear their trades through other financial intermediaries, even in the event of acts of God or acts of war disabling the financial centres. Efficient reliance would constitute customers' undertaking risk exposures that might occur due to an event like 9/11. Excessive reliance would then be a much narrower concept (since contract promises would be excused in fewer circumstances) exemplified by unanticipated risk exposures that customers undertake without informing their bankers.

2. Vertical integration if power plant is dependent on this type of coal. Otherwise, long-term supply contracts.

CHAPTER 11

1. a. The tax alternative is desirable in that it internalizes costs to the firm, causing it to adjust price, output, and production technology in order to maximize profits, while considering the cost of the externalities it generates. The most difficult aspect of this alternative is specifying the high pollution tax rate so that the firm will reduce its pollution to a "satisfactory" level.

b. It is probably not desirable to absolutely prohibit pollution by the firm, since it is likely that the cost of eliminating the last few percentage points of pollution will be very high.

c. Tax incentives may motivate a profitable firm to reduce pollution but are difficult for governments to enforce so that "satisfactory" results are actually achieved.

2. a. $P = 1,200 - 6Q$

$MC = 700 + 2Q$

$MR = MC$

$1,200 - 12Q = 700 + 2Q$

$Q^* = 35.71$

$P^* = 1,200 - 6(35.71) = \$985.74$

b. Marginal social cost (MSC) equals marginal production cost + marginal pollution costs.

$MSC = 700 + 2Q + 200 + Q = 900 + 3Q$

c. $1,200 - 12Q = 900 + 3Q$

$Q^* = 20$

$P^* = 1,200 - 6(20) = \$1,080$

3. Before: $HHI = (70)^2 + (15)^2 + (5)^2 + 20(0.5)^2 = 5,155$

After: $HHI = (70)^2 + (20)^2 + 20(0.5)^2 = 5,305$

A merger of firms number two and three might well be considered as procompetitive, since the resulting firm would be in a stronger position to challenge the market dominance of the leading firm. Whether this is desirable or not depends on the economies of scale that exist in the industry, the amount of research and development that is required by a firm, and other barriers to entry in the industry.

4. Justification should focus on the economies of scale in public utilities, the inherent waste of duplicating facilities, and the essential nature of these services, as well as the public value of providing them to as many people as possible at reasonable rates. There is a growing body of evidence that argues that these traditional rationales for public utility regulation are not sufficient to justify divergence from a competitive model. For an excellent discussion of some of this literature, see Robert W. Poole, Jr., ed., *Unnatural Monopolies: The Case for Deregulating Public Utilities* (Lexington, MA: Lexington Books, 1985).

5. a. $Q = 75{,}000 - 600P$

$P = 125 - Q/600$

$TR = 125Q - Q^2/600$

$MR = 125 - Q/300 = 50 = MC$

$Q^* = 22{,}500$

$P^* = \$87.50$

$\pi(\text{contribution}) = \$87.50(22{,}500) - \$50(22{,}500)$

$= \$843{,}750$ profit before patent

$125 - Q/300 = 45$

$Q^* = 24{,}000$

$P^* = \$85$

$\pi(\text{contribution}) = \$85(24{,}000) - \$45(24{,}000) = \$960{,}000$ profit after patent

Patent benefit to monopolist $= \$116{,}250$ per year

b. $P = 125 - Q/600 = 50 = MC$

$Q = 45{,}000$

$P = \$50$

$\pi(\text{contribution}) = 0$

The inventor can charge the difference between the original price, $50, and the new cost, $45, or $5. With savings of $5 per unit on the product selling 45,000 units per year, the inventor's gain will be $225,000 per year. When the patent expires, the market price will decline to $45 and the consumers will then receive benefits from the patent.

6. a. $1{,}500 - 9Q = 80 + 3Q$

$Q = 118.33$

$P = 1{,}500 - 9(118.33) = \$435.00$

b. MR for monopolist $= 1{,}500 - 18Q$

$1{,}500 - 18Q = 50 + 3Q$

$Q^* = 69.05$

$P^* = 1{,}500 - 9(69.05) = \$878.55$

Output is greatly restricted by the monopolist and price is increased from $435.00 to $878.55.

c. $450 = 1{,}500 - 9Q$

$Q = 116.66$

$P = \$450$

Profit contribution under monopoly:

$\pi = TR - TVC$

$= 878.55(69.05) - 50(69.05) - 3(69.05)^2$

$= \$42{,}907.67$

Profit contribution under regulation:

$\pi = 450(116.67) - 50(116.67) - 3(116.67)^2$

$= \$5,832.33$

The profit contribution to the monopolist declines by \$37,075.34. Consumers pay a lower price and receive more output.

CHAPTER 12

1. Export sales increase since the euro, yen, and pound price of Canadian goods will decline, assuming constant markups. In addition, domestic sales increase because the dollar price of foreign imports rises, again assuming constant markups.

2. Lower unit labour cost and producer prices in Japan imply an increase in Japanese exports to Spain and Portugal and a decline in Spanish and Portuguese exports to Japan.

Check Answers to Selected Exercises

CHAPTER 2

1. Budget = $875 million
2. c. $v = 0.067$
4. a. 0.0062

CHAPTER 3

1. Revenue declines by 8.50% as sales fall to $Q_{A2} = 1,830$.
3. 44%
5. a. $E_D = -0.3/\{(\$1.00 - \$0.50)/ [(\$1.00 + \$0.50)/2]\}$
   $= -0.45$
8. $P = \$90$
10. a. $E_D = -0.59$
17. -3%
20. a. $E_X = 1.34$; the products are close substitutes.
22. $Q_{2003} = 5,169$
23. c. $Q_2 = 505$

CHAPTER 4

4. b. $AP_L = 6L - 0.4L^2$
5. b. $Q^* = 44$
9. a. 4.88%
10. a. (i) $E_L = \beta_L = 0.70$

CHAPTER 5

2. No, sell the land and build elsewhere.

CHAPTER 6

4. a. $P = \$8$
6. c. (iii) $15
9. b. $P^* = \$1,220$
10. d. $\pi = \$9,000$
12. b. $900,000

CHAPTER 7

3. c. $Q^* = 125$
5. e. $\pi^* = \$263,625$
6. b. $P^* = \$60$
9. a. ROI = 12.98%

CHAPTER 8

1. a. $P^* = \$145$; $Q_A^* = 30$
6. a. $P^* = \$9,666.67$
7. c. $P^* = \$125$
9. b. Not abide.

CHAPTER 9

3. $P_{NA} = \$100$
4. a. $\pi = -20 + 96Q_1 + 76Q_2 - 2Q_1^2 - Q_2^2$
7. a. $P = \$72.50$

3. a. $170,000
7. a. $TC = 150 + 200Q - 9Q^2 + 0.25Q^3$
7. c. $Q^* = 18$

CHAPTER 10

2. If employers choose to penalize high-performance sales reps by continuously reassigning them to previously unproductive sales territories, the reps in question will eventually reduce their effort and the profitability of the firm will decline. Disincentives to effort and creative ingenuity also affect behaviour.
3. Take turns imitating and licensing the first and, thereafter, every other generation of products.

CHAPTER 11

3. c. $1,314
7. a. HHI before = 1,964
13. a. $P^* = \$10,000$
14. b. $\pi^* = \$450$ (million)

CHAPTER 12

2. Outsource abroad and buy foreign assets.
4. Decline 25% due to relative purchasing power parity.

---

*Numbers in italics refer to chapters or appendixes on the www.mcguigan.nelson.com website. References to Web chapters are preceded by a *W*; references to appendixes contain either an *A* or a *B* (e.g., *W14*-4–5 refers to pages 4–5 in Chapter 14; *18B*-3 refers to page 3 in Appendix 18B). Page references followed by an "n" (e.g., 201n) refer to a footnote on that page.